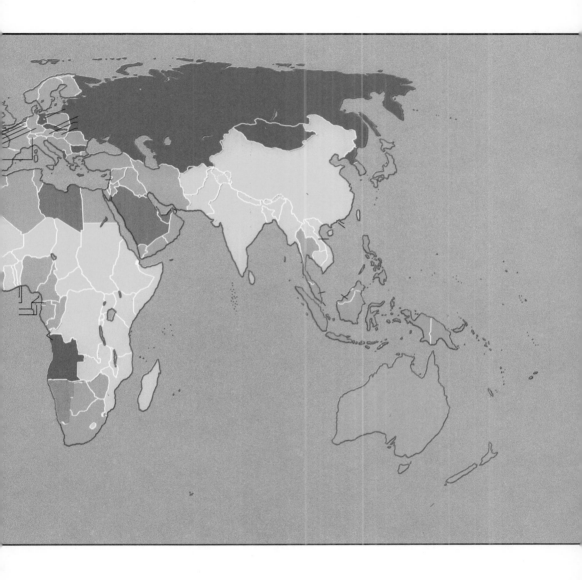

International Business and Multinational Enterprises

**The Irwin Series in Management
and The Behavioral Sciences**

L. L. Cummings and E. Kirby Warren Consulting Editors

International Business and Multinational Enterprises

Stefan H. Robock
R. D. Calkins Professor Emeritus of International Business
Graduate School of Business
Columbia University

Kenneth Simmonds
Professor of Marketing and International Business
London Business School

1989 Fourth Edition

Homewood, IL 60430
Boston, MA 02116

Sponsoring editor: William R. Bayer
Developmental editor: Sheila Smith
Project editor: Ethel Shiell
Production manager: Bette Ittersagen
Compositor: Arcata Graphics/Kingsport
Typeface: 10/12 Times Roman
Printer: The Maple-Vail Book Manufacturing Group

Library of Congress Cataloging-in-Publication Data

Robock, Stefan H.
    International business and multinational enterprises.

    Includes index.
    1. International business enterprises—Management.
2. International business enterprises—Case studies.
I. Simmonds, Kenneth.   II. Title.
HD62.4.R63   1989   338.8′8   88–9304
ISBN 0-256-03634-9
ISBN 0-256-07346-5 (Int'l Ed.)

Printed in the United States of America

1 2 3 4 5 6 7 8 9 0 MP 5 4 3 2 1 0 9 8

Preface

One of the most dramatic and significant events of recent years has been the internationalization of the world economy. A major force underlying this world trend has been the rapid, sustained growth of international business. In its traditional form of international trade as well as its newer form of multinational business operations, international business has become massive in scale and has come to exercise a major influence over political, economic, and social development throughout the world.

This growth in business activity across national boundaries has brought with it many changes. The rise of the multinational enterprise has confronted nation-states with local business units that are closely linked with operations lying outside the nations' local jurisdiction. As a result nation-states have had to grapple with a wide range of new policy issues that are not satisfactorily covered by the traditional conceptual framework for thinking about the protection of national interests—a framework primarily focused on controlling transfers of goods and money as they cross national borders.

The business enterprise operating internationally has been confronted with new management problems. Methods have had to be developed for operating simultaneously in many different and differently changing environments, for dealing with new elements of risk and conflict, and for assessing the impact of the firm on social and economic change. The management task has expanded and changed considerably from that faced within purely domestic operations, although the domestic manager has also had to make many adjustments to meet growing foreign competition in the home market.

It was not until the early 1960s that awareness of the problems that arise when business operations extend across national boundaries began to have any significant impact on business education. By this time there was a growing realization that existing theories, generalizations, and techniques of business management that had been built up largely from business experience within the United States were neither general nor universal. More explicit attention to the international dimension of business began to appear in business curricula, particularly as extended horizons to conventional functional courses such as finance and marketing.

There are international management skills, however, that extend across all aspects of international business operations; and after several decades of experimentation and research international business has evolved into a field of study and research with its own identity. Its central focus is the set of management problems stemming from the movement of goods, human resources, technology, finance, or ownership across national boundaries. As befits a course for business managers, the field has a managerial orientation; and assessment of national issues is placed in this perspective. Furthermore, the field of international business has moved well beyond an applied international economics orientation to draw heavily upon other related fields such as politics, sociology, anthropology, and law, where materials from these disciplines are relevant to the tasks of the international manager. It is now widely accepted that international business courses can provide a basic frame of reference and develop the international dimension of business teaching in a way that other subject areas, with their own focuses and conceptual approaches, are unlikely to achieve.

This book grew out of the authors' experience of teaching international business courses in graduate business schools and executive programs around the world since the early 1960s. It is a general introductory text designed for relatively advanced students, with a direct focus on the development of management skills in handling the problems of multinational business. Extensive footnotes have been included as an aid to more advanced study of areas in which students may have a special interest. While the book is designed primarily for readers with a business orientation, it has also proved useful for government decision makers who must take into account the present and future behavior patterns of international firms in designing national policies, and for students of political science.

The text is divided into six parts. Part One introduces the new field of international business and examines the forces underlying its expansion and the patterns that are emerging from this growth. Part Two presents the monetary, trade, and regulatory frameworks within which international business transactions take place. Part Three examines the construction of global strategies, including the assessment of demand. It also presents and analyzes the alternative organizational structures available to firms for building and implementing global strategies. Part Four is concerned with the goals of nation-states regarding international business and the controls nations adopt to achieve their goals. It also examines risks in the environment within which the international firm operates. Part Five covers the operational management of the multinational firm, paying particular attention to the issues that are specific to international activity. Part Six looks ahead to the future of international business.

Experience in teaching has shown that a course covering topics in the order in which they are presented in this text produces a clear, interesting progression. It begins with an introduction to the concepts and terminology of international transactions, proceeds to the wider issues of the firm's strategy and relationship with different national interests, and then moves on to the operational decisions of individual multinationals. Whatever course design is adopted, however, students clearly appreciate a continual examination of the relevance of the material to the management task. Discussion exercises and questions designed with this in mind have been included at the end of each chapter. Also available at the end of the text is a series of problems and cases that can be drawn upon to support the course design adopted by the instructor. All of these materials are aimed at strengthening practical analysis and decision-making skills within international business situations.

Many professional colleagues and practitioners have given the authors invaluable assistance in the ongoing task of preparing the editions of the book. Particularly helpful in the preparation of this Fourth Edition have been Geza Grosschmid, Paul R. Johnson, Heidi Vernon-Wortzel, and Philip K. Y. Young.

In previous editions we acknowledged the support of the postal services on both sides of the Atlantic and wondered why they both made losses. Perhaps this time we should add a word of acknowledgment to the airlines and international telecommunications that have made it possible for us to operate internationally, as international business professors should.

Stefan H. Robock
Kenneth Simmonds

Contents

PART TWO
The Framework for International Transactions   *63*

Limitations.   International Negotiations: *Changing Host Country Benefits.   The Negotiation Process.   Bargaining Power.   Negotiating Skills.*

14   Doing Business with the Centrally Planned Economies   *337*

An Economic Overview: *Population.   Economic Size.   International Business Activity.*   A Brief Treatise on Economic Systems.   The Soviet Model and Foreign Trade: *Planning Foreign Trade.   Foreign Trade Organizations.   Trade Problems.   Compensation Agreements. COMECON—The Eastern Trading Bloc.*   The Chinese Model: From Central Planning to Market Socialism: *Some History.   What Is Market Socialism?   Trading with China.*   Foreign Investment and Industrial Cooperation Agreements: *Industrial Cooperation Agreements.   Joint Ventures.   Foreign Investment in China.   The Political Overlay.*   Some Business Guidelines: *Assymetry in Objectives. Negotiation Styles.*

15   Using the Countervailing Power of International Business   *360*

Defensive Adjustments to Business Operations: *Changing the Business Activity.   Changing Location and Dispersal of Operations.   Retaining Control of Intangible Assets.   Retaining Control of Markets.   Changing Sourcing and Movement of Funds and Profits.*   Actions to Involve and Gain Support from Others: *Enlisting Home-Country Support.   Stimulating Local Enterprise.   Developing Local Allies.   Sharing Ownership with Nationals.   Selective Ownership Divestment.   Introducing Multiple Foreign Ownership.   Bringing in Third Countries.   Forming Business Coalitions.*   Direct Countervailing Actions: *Lobbying. Negotiating.   Renegotiating.   Resorting to Legal Defenses. Boycotting.   Changing Nationality.   Refusing to Participate.* Deciding the Corporate Response.

16   Assessing Political Risk and National Controls   *376*

Political-Risk Assessment: *Some General Observations.   Defining Political Risk.   Sources of Political Risk.   Political-Risk Effects. Political-Risk Perceptions and Realities.   Forecasting Political Risk.* National-Control Forecasting: *International Business as a Game. Objectives and Decision Rules of the Representative Firm.   Objectives and Decision Rules of Representative Countries.   General Features of Country Strategies.   Country Strategies over Time.*   Risk Forecasting Procedures: *Projecting into the Future.   How One Company Forecasts.   Minimizing Political and Control Risk.*

Unit.   Parent Company Executives Everywhere.   Mixed Policies.
Multinational Management Recruitment.   Management Development and
Training.   Cross-National Transfers: *Adapting at Work.   Social
Adaptation.   Selection for Transfer.   Repatriation.*   International
Compensation Policies: *Executive Compensation.   Components of
Expatriate Compensation.   International Wage and Benefit Policies.*
Labor Relations and the Multinational Firm: *Centralized versus
Decentralized Policies.   The Union View of the Multinationals' Power.
Multinational Union Organization.   Codes of Conduct and Industrial
Relations.   Prospects for Multinational Bargaining.   Codetermination and
the Multinationals.*   Treatment of Disadvantaged Groups.

PART ONE

The Nature and Scope of International Business

CHAPTER 1

The Field of International Business

A DEFINITION OF INTERNATIONAL BUSINESS
    International Business, Foreign Operations, and Comparative
    Business
THE SCOPE OF INTERNATIONAL BUSINESS ACTIVITIES
    The Multinational Corporation
    What Is Different about International Business?
INTERNATIONAL BUSINESS TRAINING
EXERCISES AND DISCUSSION QUESTIONS

A DEFINITION OF INTERNATIONAL BUSINESS

International business as a field of management training deals with the special features of *business activities that cross national boundaries.* These activities may be movements of goods, services, capital, or personnel; transfers of technology, information, or data; or even the supervision of employees. International business has emerged as a separate branch of management training, because the growing scale and complexity of business transactions across national boundaries gives rise to new and unique problems of management and governmental policy that have received inadequate attention in traditional areas of business and economics.

Business transactions that extend between different sovereign political units are not new phenomena on the world economic scene. Some business firms have had foreign direct investments and foreign operations for many years, predominantly in (but not limited to) the fields of mining, petroleum, and agriculture.[1] Foreign trade, moreover, has a venerable history dating back to the emergence

---

[1] Mira Wilkins. *The Emergence of Multinational Enterprise: American Business Abroad from the Colonial Era to 1914* (Cambridge, Mass.: Harvard University Press, 1970). This study shows that U.S. direct foreign investment prior to 1914 was not limited to extractive industries and utilities but also included "a surprising number of . . . U.S. headquartered multinational manufacturing companies" (p. ix).

3

of the nation-state. But since the end of World War II a dramatic change has occurred in the patterns of international business activities. Thousands of business firms in many nations have developed into multinational enterprises with ownership control or other links that cross national boundaries. These firms take a global view of all aspects of business—from markets to resources—and they integrate markets and production on a world scale. Traditional international trade in the form of transactions between independent firms in different nations has continued to grow. But the *relative* importance of trade in the total picture has declined as other forms of cross-border business transactions have expanded more rapidly.

The international business field is concerned with the issues facing international companies and governments in dealing with all types of cross-border business transactions. The field encompasses international transactions in commodities, international transfers of intangibles such as technology and data, and the performance of international services such as banking and transportation. It gives special attention to the multinational enterprise—an enterprise based in one country and operating in one or more other countries—and the full range of methods open to such enterprises for doing business internationally.[2]

International Business, Foreign Operations, and Comparative Business

To clarify the scope of the authors' approach to international business, we should differentiate between international business, foreign business, and comparative business. The last two concepts are sometimes used as synonyms for international business. Foreign business refers to domestic operations within a foreign country. Comparative business focuses on similarities and differences among countries and business systems. The great merit of comparative studies in business, as well as in other fields such as politics, sociology, and economics, is the new perspective and better understanding of home institutions and environments that is frequently secured.[3]

The three concepts—international business, foreign business, and comparative business—are interrelated and have large overlaps. The international manager may benefit greatly from many types of comparative business studies and from a knowledge of many aspects of foreign business operations. At the same time, foreign business operations and comparative business as fields of inquiry do not have as their major point of interest the special problems that arise when business activities cross national boundaries. For example, the vital question of potential conflicts between the nation-state and the multinational firm, which receives major

---

[2] David E. Lilienthal, "The Multinational Corporation," in *Management and Corporations 1985*, ed. M. H. Anshen and G. L. Bach (New York: McGraw-Hill, 1960). The term *multinational firm* was probably first used by David E. Lilienthal in a paper delivered at Carnegie Institute of Technology in April 1960.

[3] For example, see Simcha Ronen, *Comparative and International Management* (New York: John Wiley & Sons, Inc., 1986).

attention in international business studies, is not likely to be central or even peripheral in foreign operations and comparative business studies.

An example from the field of accounting will illustrate the principal boundaries and focus of international business. A manager engaged in foreign business needs to know only the accounting practices in the host country. A comparative approach to accounting examines the systems and practices in many countries with the main objective of identifying similarities and differences among countries as well as universal patterns, if they exist. International business concentrates on the accounting needs for managing a multinational firm doing business across national boundaries. The accounting problems and techniques for international business operations are related to differences in national accounting systems. In some important respects, the accounting activities of the multinational firm will be influenced by tax and legal considerations of the specific countries in which the firm is operating. Within these constraints, however, accounting in international business is primarily concerned with fulfilling the needs of multinational operations through an effective and uniform accounting system that cuts across national boundaries.

THE SCOPE OF INTERNATIONAL BUSINESS ACTIVITIES

The scope of international business covers a wide range of significant business sectors. International transactions in physical goods involve products from mining, petroleum, agriculture, and manufacturing activities. Transactions in services are extensive in the construction, hotel, tourism, business consulting, and retailing and wholesaling sectors; in financial areas such as commercial and investment banking, securities, and insurance; in air and ocean transportation; and in communications media such as radio, television, telegraph, telephone, magazines, books, newspapers, news services, and movies. Transactions in intangibles occur in fields such as technology, trademarks, and cross-border data transmission.

International business activities also include an extensive range of optional methods available to firms for doing business internationally that involve different degrees of foreign direct investment commitments. Even where it assumes an ownership position in foreign facilities, the firm has options ranging from the construction of sales offices, warehouses, and packaging and assembly operations to full-scale production facilities.

Foreign direct investments are defined as investments that give the investor effective control and are accompanied by managerial participation. In contrast, *portfolio investments* are undertaken for the sake of obtaining investment income or capital gains rather than entrepreneurial income. The dividing line between direct and portfolio investments is often difficult to determine.

Direct investment may be financed in a number of ways other than through capital movements abroad. Foreign investments may be financed by borrowing locally, by reinvesting foreign earnings, by the sale to the foreign affiliate of nonfinancial assets such as technology, or through funds generated by licensing fees and payments for management services to the parent company. More accurately, direct foreign investment is not so much international capital movement as capital formation abroad.

Without making foreign direct investment commitments, firms can engage in international business through exporting and importing, licensing of nonaffiliated foreign firms, sale of technology, foreign management contracts, and selling turnkey projects. In a turnkey project, the seller plans, constructs, and places in operation a foreign facility that is then transferred to a local owner. The seller receives a fee for its services but usually retains no ownership interest.

In addition to options as to scale and type of foreign operations, the direct investment approach offers a range of possibilities as to ownership patterns. Foreign facilities may be wholly owned or may be a *joint venture* with one or more partners. The partners may be private firms or governments in the host country, or they may be other international firms of different nationalities.

The Multinational Corporation

The multinational corporation has become well recognized as a key feature of the changing international business pattern. But general agreement on the definition of a multinational corporation does not yet exist, and the United Nations prefers to use the label "transnational corporation."[4] Some definitions emphasize structural criteria such as the number of countries in which a firm is doing business, or ownership by persons from many nations, or the multinational composition of top management. Other definitions stress performance characteristics such as the absolute amount—or relative share—of earnings, sales, assets, or employees derived from or committed to foreign operations. Still other definitions are based on behavioral characteristics of top management such as "thinking globally."

The definitional debate is not simply a matter of semantics. It reflects the reality that there are many types of so-called multinational enterprises. It is also a reminder that operational definitions will vary with the purposes at hand. Consequently, in dealing with the subject of multinational corporations, one must be alert to the specific definition being used.

In this book, the labels of *multinational, transnational,* and *international corporations* will be used interchangeably. They refer to a cluster of corporations controlled by one headquarters but with operations spread over many countries. Also, multinational corporations can be of private, government, or mixed ownership.

With the growing international involvement of business firms, more and more companies—U.S., Canadian, European, Japanese, and others—are finding that a large share of their assets are deployed around the world; that many of their employees are foreign citizens; that a large amount of their earnings are in

---

[4] Yair Aharoni, "On the Definition of a Multinational Corporation," *Quarterly Review of Economics and Business.* Autumn 1971, pp. 27–37; see also "The Issue of Defining Transnational Corporations," in *Transnational Corporations in World Development: A Re-Examination* (New York: United Nations, 1978), pp. 158–61.

foreign currencies; and that they are operating to an important extent outside the legal jurisdiction of the country in which the parent company is incorporated. In these circumstances, the companies have become multinational corporations; and the nature of their operations has been significantly transformed. They come to be managed as world enterprises, with international considerations dominating their decisions. The world becomes the company's market and sphere of operation, and the home country becomes but one part.

The multinational enterprise is not uniquely a U.S. invention. In fact, if one were looking several decades ago for examples of multinational firms, the names of European rather than U.S.-based corporations would have come to mind: the British-Dutch companies—Unilever and the Royal Dutch Shell Group, Switzerland's Nestlé, Britain's Imperial Chemical Industries, the Netherland's Philips Lamps, and Sweden's Ericsson Telephone.

Not all international business is conducted by multinational enterprise. Export and import activities, for example, do not require that a company establish and operate overseas branches, affiliates, or other units of the home corporation. The licensing of patents and technology in foreign countries can be accomplished without a predominantly domestic company becoming multinational.

The dividing line to mark the stage at which a company becomes multinational is difficult to determine. Many domestic companies go through a gradual evolution toward making direct investments, first establishing marketing, procurement offices, or warehouses in foreign countries. Even when a business firm crosses the imaginary and imprecise boundary between domestic and multinational, its degree of international commitment and internationalization may range over a wide spectrum.

In one sense, the emergence of the multinational corporation reflects a differential pace in the evolution of political institutions relative to business organizations. While business activities have become more and more internationalized, the development of international governmental organizations has not accompanied business and economic trends. As one example, no international agency has been created with the authority to grant international incorporation. Consequently, business corporations still must be created and exist under the jurisdiction of a specific nation state. Yet multinational firms may have different patterns of ownership and control. In most cases, in the present stage of evolution, both ownership and control of the multinational corporation reside in the base country. In other significant cases, ownership and control may be divided between two or more countries, even though the enterprise is the legal creation of a single nation state.

Multinational operations raise managerial problems because of the need to deal with a wide range of environmental factors in several different countries. Multinational operations also raise new internal issues in organization and management. From the standpoint of world-development aspirations, the multinational corporation offers a nongovernmental vehicle for transferring technology, financial resources, management techniques, and marketing experience among nations at various stages of development.

What Is Different about International Business?

One can recognize the growing international involvement of business firms and the rapid trend toward multinational enterprises, yet question the need for international business as a separate field of study. The argument can be made that management principles are universal and that concepts being taught in the functional fields of marketing, finance, production, and control are as relevant to business management in one country as they are in another. The manager in the world economy, the argument goes, may need only supplementary training in the traditional fields of international economics and international trade.

Despite these arguments, a trend has emerged to give explicit attention to the international dimension of business and to recognize international business as a separate field in the business area. The trend is supported by the view that earlier theories, generalizations, principles, methods, and techniques, developed in response to norms in the United States where management training has had its greatest flowering, were neither general nor universal. In contrast to purely domestic operations, business activities across national boundaries require considerable familiarity with international means of payments and involve new elements of risk, conflict, environmental adjustment, and influence over social and economic change. At best, only some of these elements are covered in traditional international economics and trade courses and have been treated only briefly in traditional management courses.

There are four aspects of international business activity around which new types of thinking have emerged. These four aspects overlap to some degree and do not exhaust the potential for new approaches that may evolve. Each stems from unique problems that develop when business crosses national boundaries, and each gives rise to a new area of study and body of concepts.

International Risk.   The special risk elements confronted in international business activity include financial, political, regulatory, and tax risks. They arise from causes such as the existence of different currencies, monetary standards, and national goals; but they are all measurable through their effect on profitability or ownership.

The financial risk elements involve balance-of-payments considerations, varying exchange rates, differential inflation trends among countries, and divergent interest rates. In the political area, the risk of expropriation or lesser harrassment directed toward the foreign firm must be considered for many years ahead when heavy capital investments are being contemplated. The regulatory risks arise from different legal systems, overlapping jurisdictions, and dissimilar policies that influence such conditions as the regulation of restrictive business practices and the application of antitrust laws. In the tax field, unforeseen changes in fiscal policies can affect significantly the profitability of the multinational corporation. Furthermore, uncertainty as to application of tax laws frequently creates a risk of double taxation.

The need has become recognized for a continuing business intelligence activity of considerable complexity to identify and predict international risks. Ideally, international risks should be analyzed for underlying causal forces, and projections into the future should be formulated in terms of probabilities and quantified in terms of potential costs.

Multinational Conflicts. Of major concern to international business are the conflicts that arise because of different national identities of owners, employees, customers, and suppliers and because of divergence between the interests of sovereign national states and the business goals of multinational corporations. Some of the conflicts occur within the international firm, and others involve the firm's relationship to the external environment. One study of five major multinationals identified 650 conflict situations encountered by these firms over a recent 10-year period.[5]

An extremely troublesome area of external conflict concerns profit-motivated decisions that result in the transfer of funds, production, and employment from one country to another. The results of these decisions may at times run contrary to the national economic policies of one or all of the countries involved. For example, extension of credit to foreign subsidiaries at times when the foreign nation is attempting to dampen purchasing power through monetary restrictions and exchange controls can undermine national objectives as well as place local firms at a competitive disadvantage. The list of areas in which conflicts occur also includes such matters as contribution to local exports or reduction of imports, national interests in strengthening local research and management, or the country's international competitive position.

Within the international corporation, the mixture of national allegiances raises further issues. Home-country nationals tend to dominate top-management echelons of multinational firms, and there is a tendency to retain research and administration functions in the developed countries. Disparities in wage and salary rates have also led to widely practiced discrimination on the basis of nationality. A number of nations have already placed restrictions on the numbers of foreign expatriates they will allow in local operations.

The conflict aspect of international business requires thinking that will relate a multiplicity of interests, each with different objectives and different criteria for evaluating potential outcomes. No other business field covers this successfully. The international manager trained to identify each conflicting interest and to think through the possible actions and reactions from each viewpoint will be better prepared to plot the best strategy in a complex situation. One function of international business study should be to erase any tendency to make blindly nationalistic decisions or revert to pure economic arguments.

Multiple Environments. The most pervasive distinction between international and domestic business lies in the environmental framework. Aside from

---

[5] Thomas N. Gladwin and Ingo Walter, *Multinationals Under Fire: Lessons in Conflict Management* (New York: John Wiley & Sons, Inc., 1980).

its relationship to the elements of risk and conflict discussed above, the multiplicity of environments in international business creates a wide range of operational problems that require new concepts, analytical methods, and information. The wider the scope of the firm's international activities, the greater become the environmental diversities; and the more crucial becomes the task of identifying, evaluating, and predicting environmental variables. The environmental framework must be enlarged to include forces operating at a supranational level—such as the European Community—and forces involving relations between pairs of countries as well as variables associated with different national settings.

An important environmental variable relates to business activity open to the international business firm and to the form of business organization that must be used. Public utilities, including electric power, communications, and transportation, are not open to private enterprise in most countries. Business activity in natural resources such as petroleum and mining is restricted by many nations to domestic private or public enterprises. In some situations, the options open to international business firms require joint ventures with majority local ownership or joint ventures with government.

A second major category of environmental variables involves the diversity of institutional settings. Labor unions, for example, are organized on different philosophical foundations and play different roles from country to country. Patterns of national, regional, and local economic planning vary greatly in scope and in their influence over business activity. Capital markets and financial institutions are in different stages of development and, in some cases, are evolving along different paths.

Another broad environmental variable involves cultural differences that affect business management. International managers need to know how cultural differences influence the behavior of customers, suppliers, and employees, and how these influences on behavior will change. This aspect of international business encompasses the full range of communication problems arising out of different languages, customs, and values.

International business has begun to develop its own body of cultural analysis following the functional division of business, with marketing questions receiving most attention. Considerable management literature has focused on the cultural adjustment of expatriate management and on differences in foreign management and work force that might require adjustment of organizational structures or procedures. While concern for specific problems initially channeled cultural analysis along these functional lines, the common need throughout many business functions to understand cultural factors is for a more unified approach, which might be titled "Cultural Analysis for Business Decisions."

International Business and Development.   International business is frequently a major change agent, a means of transferring technology, and a key force in the economic and social development of a nation. This is especially true for the less developed countries. Thus, international business requires new concepts that provide an understanding of what can and what cannot be achieved by the change agent and the potential contributions that international business can make to development.

The primary concern of the developing countries is the contribution that a proposed international business activity can make to their economic, social, and political development. They recognize that the attractiveness of a project to the foreign firm in terms of business profits may diverge greatly from the attractiveness of the project to the country in terms of its development goals. It is a near certainty, therefore, that international firms will be required to justify their proposed activities in terms of costs and benefits to the country. To meet this requirement, international firms need considerable specialized knowledge on economic development.

To illustrate, consider the development issue of the positive and negative impact of international business on indigeneous entrepreneurship. On the positive side, the international firm may create new entrepreneurial opportunities external to the firm for local suppliers and merchants. On the negative side, by attracting and employing much of the entrepreneurial potential in a country, the international firm may inhibit the possibilities for development of national enterprises.

The role of international business in development raises moral and ideological issues. It is frequently true that short-term profit motivation will keep a firm away from the less developed markets. Yet the opportunity for the greatest long-term good from the viewpoint of both the corporation's home country and the developing nations may strongly favor entering the developing country.[6]

Once a corporation has entered a developing country, a whole range of new issues arise. One such issue is the degree to which the firm should become involved in the community and undertake expenditures normally the function of the public sector.[7] As a number of studies have demonstrated, the paternalistic firm, which provides much of the normal functions of the public sector, can foster animosity among the local population.

INTERNATIONAL BUSINESS TRAINING

Some students will study international business as a field of concentration, intending to follow a career working in foreign countries or in the headquarters of a multinational firm that uses nationals for operating foreign subsidiaries. Others will study international business as a supplement to their concentration in the functional fields of accounting, marketing, finance, and so on. Still others will be interested in international business as a preparation for working in government positions on the development and implementation of policies and programs for assisting and controlling business activities across national boundaries. For

---

[6] Nathaniel Leff, "Multinational Corporate Pricing Strategy in the Developing Countries," *Journal of International Business Studies*, Fall 1975, pp. 57–74.

[7] Clifton R. Wharton, "Aiding the Community: A New Philosophy for Foreign Operations," *Harvard Business Review*, March–April 1954, pp. 64–72.

all these kinds of clientele, a minimum preparation for dealing effectively with the international dimension of business should include two goals: to develop familiarity with the body of knowledge on international business and to develop in the person special sensitivities, attitudes, flexibility, and tolerance.

The need for personal and emotional training to deal with international business matters deserves particular emphasis in this introduction because such training requires more than textbook reading. Ethnocentrism and personal parochialism can be diluted in a number of ways, some of which can be included within a broad framework of international business training. Student exchange programs can stimulate personal reconditioning through the experience of living and working in a foreign environment. When students from various countries and cultures are studying together, the students can be exposed to other cultures and values through class discussions and through team projects, if the teams are composed of different nationalities.

International managers need training experience that develops in them a special kind of personal and emotional radar to alert them to situations where specific values and ways of action that they take for granted in their own environment are different in other cultures and nations. Successful international managers need enough flexibility to understand what underlies these differences and enough tolerance to recognize that types of behavior and sets of values different from their own may be valid for other people. In an operational sense, they must recognize that what are constants for domestic business may be variables in international business.

EXERCISES AND DISCUSSION QUESTIONS

1. "To deny that international business is a valid field for academic effort is to suggest by analogy that such subjects as international politics, international economics, and international law are equally not academically respectable. It is true that international business borrows very heavily from all three, as they borrow from each other, but the core problem in international business is quite different." Discuss.
2. Of the top 50 foreign companies in *Fortune's* list of "500 Largest Industrial Corporations Outside the U.S.," which would you consider to be not multinational? Why?
3. There is no separate field of "international" chemistry or "international" physics. Why should there be a separate field of international business?

CHAPTER 2

Patterns of International Business

The patterns of international business keep changing—and textbooks have to be revised. As long ago as 2800 B.C., international business in the form of trade existed between Egypt and the Phoenician city of Byblos, as revealed by recent excavations in Greece.[1] Over time, trade led to direct investment, primarily as a means of securing sources of supply for raw materials and natural resources. The Dutch East India Company, founded in 1602 and not dissolved until almost

---

[1] See George Rawlinson, *Phoenicia*, (New York: G. P. Putnam & Sons, 1898) (repr. 1973) and Sabatino Moscati, *The World of Phoenicians* (trans.) (London: Weidenfeld & Nicholson, 1968).

13

three centuries later in 1874, was one of the world's first international corporations and an example of the direct investment, resource-seeking phase. The multinational enterprise as we know it today dates back to the mid-1800s, when the Singer Company expanded internationally and began operating with a global horizon.[2]

Over the centuries, international business expanded both in absolute size and relative to the growth of nations. Current patterns are an extension of the quantum leap and radical change in the form of international business operations dating from the end of World War II. Although statistical data are not easily available on many dimensions of international business, the broad patterns and major changes in international business activity can be described with reasonable accuracy.

This chapter will present the available data on the size of international business, the industries and commodities that are highly internationalized, the nationalities of the participants, and the geographical patterns.

THE UNDERDEVELOPED DATA BASE

A reasonably complete statistical picture of international business patterns should have several components. It should show the types of inter-nation transactions and their values—that is, transfers of goods, services, technology, foreign production, information and data, and so on. It should show the geographical patterns—that is, the nations involved in the cross-border movements. It should show the trends over time. It should show the relative importance of the international business sector within the total economic activity for specific nations and globally.

Unfortunately, the data base for presenting such a picture is underdeveloped. No international agency exists that has legal authority to collect such information from business enterprises or from national governments. Thus the principal sources of data are the independent statistical programs of the individual nations, and these programs have adjusted only slowly to the changing structure of international business. All nations collect detailed data on merchandise trade. But national programs to collect relevant data on international business activities other than trade are still limited. And even where relevant data are collected, the information is difficult to combine because of statistical inconsistencies among the national programs such as differences in coverage, definitions, methodology, disaggregation, and time periods.[3]

With the rise of global firms, companies can serve foreign markets or secure foreign products in many ways other than traditional importing and exporting. International firms can establish foreign production facilities that produce for local or third-country markets and thus substitute for home-country exports. Firms can license foreign producers to manufacture goods that the licensing firm might

---

[2] Mira Wilkins, *The Emergence of Multinational Enterprise: American Business Abroad from the Colonial Era to 1914* (Cambridge, Mass.: Harvard University Press, 1970), pp. 37–47.

[3] See William H. Witherell, "OECD Improves Direct Investment Statistics," *The CTC Reporter,* Spring 1984, p. 40.

otherwise export from its home country. These and other newer dimensions of international business activity are poorly covered by the existing data base (see Box 2–1). Although the data base has been improving, much more progress is needed to depict with greater precision what is really happening in international business.

How much difference will it make if better information on international business is available? International agencies need such data in order to adjust the monetary system to the changed structure of the international economy. Nations need to know a great deal about the operations of multinational business firms to develop policies such as those relating to exports and foreign exchange earnings. The business firm interested in allocating its efforts over global markets also requires extensive information on international transactions and international business patterns.

THE BIG PICTURE

Let's start with the big picture, based on available data, and then examine the subsectors. The big picture has to be put together from different data sources, and the most recent year for which considerable data are available is 1984.

The size of the world economy, as measured by gross national product (GNP), was estimated at $12,500 billion for 1984. GNP, the value of total output,

---

BOX 2–1
Mickey Mouse Goes to France

Paris—Mickey Mouse is taking up residence in France. Walt Disney Productions ended more than a year of speculation by announcing a preliminary agreement to build a $1 billion EuroDisneyland theme park and resort complex about 20 miles east of Paris in Marne-la-Vallee.

The theme park will open in late 1990 or early 1991, employ about 10,000 people, and attract 10 million visitors in the first year. Along with the Magic Kingdom theme park, the site will have hotels, campgrounds, shopping centers, golf courses, water attractions, and convention facilities.

A definitive agreement is expected to be reached within three months between Disney and the French government for creation of a French-owned company to develop the site. Disney will receive fees for operating the park and royalties on admissions, rides, food, and other operations. The French company will control development of the entire project.

In 1983, a Japanese company opened the Disneyland park near Tokyo under an extensive licensing and development agreement with Disney. Disney doesn't have an equity stake in the Japanese park, which has proved hugely popular.

SOURCE: Adapted from *The Wall Street Journal*, December 19, 1985. © Dow Jones & Company, Inc., 1985. Used with permission. All rights reserved.

is the usual measure of the size of a country's economy. In the same year, international business activity had an estimated total volume of at least $3,700 billion, or the equivalent of about 30 percent of world economic activity. The expression *equivalent* is used because GNP is estimated on a value-added basis and cannot be compared directly with the total revenues from international business activity. This picture, of course, is only a snapshot at one point in time and needs to be supplemented with data on trends.

The estimate of $3,700 billion for international business activity includes both international trade and foreign production, with an overlap adjustment to eliminate double counting. The overlap adjustment is necessary because a large share of so-called international trade consists of transfers between units of the same enterprise located in different countries. Many foreign automobile assembly plants, for example, rely largely on imported components. A number of foreign pharmaceutical plants during an early state of development may receive bulk shipments from the home country and perform merely a repackaging and distribution function. The intrafirm transfers are recorded as international trade because they cross national boundaries. Double-counting occurs because these intrafirm transfers are also included in the value of production by the foreign affiliates.

In 1984, total world exports were at a level of $1,900 billion. Foreign production in the same year is estimated to have reached $2,100 billion. The estimated overlap for exports also included in the value of foreign production is $300 billion. Thus, the global picture as of 1984 was an international business sector that measured a minimum of $3,700 billion ($1,900 billion plus $2,100 billion minus $300 billion). The size of the overlap is important because it indicates that a large share of so-called international trade consists of transfers among units of international enterprises.

Foreign production, as defined here, is the value of goods and services produced in a given country by a foreign enterprise. It normally involves moving management, personnel, technology, and capital, rather than final products, across national boundaries. The concept of foreign production has not yet been adopted by national statistical gathering agencies. But foreign production can be estimated from available foreign direct investment data.

Foreign direct investment statistics are "stock" data. They present a static picture as of a given moment in time of the value of the accumulated investment flows over the years. Trade statistics are "flow" data. They measure movements during a given period, usually a year. Consequently, to show total international business activity, the flow of goods and services from facilities established in foreign countries by international firms (foreign production) must be estimated and combined with trade flow data.

Foreign production as estimated from direct investment data, is, however, necessarily incomplete because of data limitations. For example, the investment in aircraft used for international operations is not classified as foreign investment because airplanes are mobile pieces of equipment. Also, data are not available on the increased amount of cross-border arrangements not linked to foreign equity investments. Such activities include the licensing of trademarks and technology, franchising, management contracts, and the leasing of films and television reruns. Yet, in the absence of better alternative methods of measurement, the foreign direct investment method must serve.

MERCHANDISE TRADE

The merchandise trade component of international business is the easiest to examine in detail because most governments collect comprehensive data on merchandise exports and imports. The value of world exports, as previously noted, was $1,922 billion in 1985 measured in current dollars.[4] Trends in the value of world trade, of course, reflect both changes in prices and in physical volume.

Global Trends. In terms of physical volume, world trade has grown faster than world production of commodities. From 1960 to 1969, world commodity output increased at an annual rate of 6 percent, but world exports increased by 8.5 percent annually, as shown in Table 2–1. From 1970 to 1979, both commodity output and trade volume expanded at slower rates. But the growth in trade volume continued to exceed that of commodity output—5.5 percent and 4 percent, respectively.

Manufactured goods have had the most rapid growth rates in both output and trade volume. The output and trade volume of agricultural products also continued to expand but at a lesser rate than manufactured goods. The minerals category, including petroleum, had no increase in output over the 1980–85 period; and trade volume actually declined. In value terms, however, petroleum exports gained greatly after 1973 because of price increases.

TABLE 2–1   Growth of World Merchandise Trade and Production, 1960–85
(average annual percentage change in volume)

	1960–69	1970–79	1980–83	1984	1985
Exports:					
All merchandise	8½	5½	½	9½	3
Agriculture	4	3	1½	4	−1
Mining	6½	2½	−5½	2	−2½
Manufacturing	10½	7½	2	12	6
Production:					
All merchandise	6	4	0	5½	3
Agriculture	2½	2½	2	5	2
Mining	5	3½	−3½	0	−2
Manufacturing	7½	4½	1	7	4

SOURCE: General Agreement on Tariffs and Trade, *International Trade 1985/86* (Geneva, 1986), p. 13.

---

[4] General Agreement on Tariffs and Trade, *International Trade 1985/86* (Geneva, 1986), p. 139.

Commodity Patterns.   The commodity composition of world trade has been changing significantly. In terms of value, agricultural products and minerals, other than fuels, have been the slowest growth areas. Agricultural products as a share of the total value of world exports dropped sharply from 29 percent in 1963 to 15 percent in 1984. The biggest gainer in value terms was petroleum, whose share of the total doubled to 20 percent after 1973. Manufactures have long been the largest component of world trade, maintaining their relative share of about 60 percent, more through increases in volume than in prices.

What are the leading products in world trade, and how have patterns been changing? As of 1983, when petroleum prices were still at record levels, the leading product in trade among the market economies (i.e., excluding the centrally planned countries) was crude petroleum and petroleum products (see Table 2–2). The next important group was passenger motor cars, parts, and accessories for motor vehicles and trucks (lorries). Other leading products in the manufactures category were textiles, clothing, office machines, iron and steel, and chemicals. The important agricultural products were cereals, fruits and vegetables, vegetable oils, and coffee and tea. As compared to 1973, the largest declines in relative shares were recorded by steel and textiles. In relative terms, the largest increase occurred in data processing equipment and electronic components.

An important category in international trade that frequently goes unmentioned in economic studies is arms and military goods. The international arms trade was estimated to total more than $40 billion in 1982.[5] The major exporters of arms in order of importance were the United States, the Soviet Union, France, the United Kingdom, Germany, and, more recently, Brazil. For 1984, total U.S. arms sales to foreigners were estimated at about $15 billion, almost 7 percent of total U.S. merchandise exports.[6] Another interesting comparison is that U.S. arms exports in 1984 exceeded the $10 billion in civilian aircraft exports and was comparable to $14.3 billion in exports of electronic computers and parts.

Among the several major commodity categories, trade in agricultural products comes closest to the traditional trade patterns of transfers between independent importers and exporters in different countries. Although foreign private investment in such agricultural projects as tea, rubber, and banana plantations was characteristic of 19th century patterns, it has moved almost entirely out of agricultural production in recent decades. In contrast, a large share of the trade in petroleum and manufacturing has been dominated by multinational enterprises and consists of transfers between units of the same enterprise located in different countries.

The Trade Network.   The large bulk of world exports and imports has been flowing between the industrialized countries. As of 1985, the developed countries accounted for 66.5 percent of world exports and 68.5 percent of world imports, as shown in Table 2–3. The share of the developing countries in the value of world exports peaked in 1980 at 28 percent but receded to 23 percent

---

[5] *New York Times*, March 18, 1984, p. F4.

[6] *New York Times*, September 29, 1985, p. E5.

TABLE 2–2   Leading products in World Merchandise Trade of Market Economies in 1983[*]

Rank		Product Categories	Percentage Shares in Value of World Trade		Percentage Shares in Value of World Trade Excluding Fuels	
1983	1973		1983	1973	1983	1973
1	1	Crude petroleum	12.4	7.6	—	—
2	7	Petroleum products	4.9	2.4	—	—
3	4	Passenger motorcars	3.8	3.8	4.7	4.2
4	2	Iron and steel	2.8	4.6	3.5	5.1
5	3	Textile yarn, fabrics, made-up articles	2.6	4.1	3.2	4.6
6	9	Clothing	2.2	2.2	2.8	2.5
7	20	Office machines, data processing equipment, parts	2.2	1.4	2.8	1.5
8	8	Parts and accessories of motor vehicles	2.0	2.2	2.5	2.5
9	45	Gas, natural manufactured	2.0	0.3	—	—
10	15	Artificial resins, plastic materials, articles of plastic	2.0	1.9	2.4	2.1
11	18	Organic chemicals	1.9	1.6	2.4	1.8
12	6	Wood manufactures, paper	1.9	2.4	2.3	2.7
13	5	Cereals and preparations	1.8	2.7	2.2	3.0
14	10	Fruits and vegetables	1.5	2.2	1.9	2.4
15	11	Oilseeds, vegetable oils, oil cakes	1.5	2.2	1.8	2.4
16	24	Aircraft	1.2	0.9	1.5	1.0
17	17	Telecommunication equipment, parts, accessories	1.2	1.6	1.5	1.7
18	37	Transistors, etc. (electronic components)	1.2	0.7	1.5	0.8
19	27	Coffee, tea, cocoa, spices	1.1	0.9	1.4	1.0
20	26	Lorries, special vehicles	1.1	0.9	1.4	1.0
		Total of above	51.3	46.6	—	—
		World trade (market economies)	100.0	100.0	—	—

[*] Trade data are based on import statistics.

SOURCE: General Agreement on Tariffs and Trade, *International Trade 1984/85* (Geneva, 1985), p. 17.

TABLE 2–3   Regional Composition of World Merchandise Trade, 1963–85
(percentage shares in the value of world exports and imports)

		Total Trade			Trade Excluding Fuels		
		1963	1973	1985	1963	1973	1985
Developed countries	Exports	67½	71	66½	72	77	75
	Imports	67½	72	68½	66½	71	68
Developing areas	Exports	20½	19	23	16	13	15½
	Imports	21	18	20½	21½	18½	21
Eastern trading area	Exports	12	10	10½	12	10	9½
	Imports	11½	10	11	12	10½	11

SOURCE: General Agreement on Tariffs and Trade, *International Trade 1985/86,* (Geneva, 1986) p. 15.

in 1985. This fluctuation largely reflects the rise and subsequent fall of the share of fuels in the value of world trade. If fuels are excluded from world trade, the share of the developing countries' exports in 1985 was about the same as in 1963 and significantly above the share in 1973. The 1973–85 gain in market share was largely based on the export expansion of a small number of developing countries.

The 20 leading exporting and importing countries as of 1985 are shown in Table 2–4. Several observations can be made from these data. First, the United States was still the leading exporting country but its share of world exports declined significantly over the 1973–85 period. At the same time, the U.S. role as an importer increased to the point that the United States had become the market for more than one sixth of total world trade. Second, three of the four economies that joined the 1985 list of leading exporters are the so-called newly industrializing countries (NICs) of Asia; namely Taiwan, the Republic of Korea, and Hong Kong. The fact that Korea and Hong Kong joined the list of importers as well as exporters underlines the point that dynamic suppliers are also dynamic customers. Third, the export gains of the NICs that joined the list have been mainly a result of increasingly diversified manufacturing sectors, thus blurring the distinction between developed and developing countries as exporters of manufactures. By 1985, for example, all of the Asian NICs had moved up the list ahead of, or even with, such traditional exporters of manufactures as Switzerland and Sweden.

WHY TRADE PATTERNS ARE CHANGING

An understanding of the forces underlying changes in trade patterns can be helpful to the business enterprise interested in supplying world markets. Four principal factors have been the so-called Engel's Law, price trends, technological developments, and the expansion of multinational enterprises.

Engel's Law, named after the 19th-century German economist Ernst Engel, explains changes in consumer demands as incomes rise. The law states that as personal incomes rise, consumer expenditures for food grow at a lesser rate. In statistical jargon, the demand for food has an income elasticity of less than one. Engel's Law has been extended to predict that as incomes rise consumers will spend increasing *shares* of their income on luxury goods—generally manufactures—and decreasing *shares* on necessities, including food. The logic of the law is that the capacity of individuals to enlarge their consumption of necessities is more limited than their capacity to enlarge their consumption of luxury goods.

Engel's Law has two related implications for trade patterns. One relates to consumer goods, the other to producer goods. After the end of World War II, the world experienced an unprecedented period of sustained economic growth. This growth trend was accompanied by changes in consumer demand and therefore in trade patterns. As might be expected from Engel's Law, trade in agricultural products expanded but at significantly lower rates than trade in manufactured goods.

The opposite side of the coin is that the development strategies of most

TABLE 2–4 The Leading Exporters and Importers in World Merchandise Trade in 1985: Ranks 1 to 20 (percentages)

Exports

Rank 1985	Rank 1973	Area	Share in World Exports 1985	Share in World Exports 1973
1	1	United States	10.7%	12.5%
2	2	Germany, Fed. Rep.	9.6	11.8
3	3	Japan	9.1	6.4
4	5	United Kingdom	5.3	5.2
5	4	France	5.1	6.3
6	10	USSR	4.5	3.7
7	6	Canada	4.5	4.4
8	9	Italy	4.1	3.9
9	7	Netherlands	3.6	4.2
10	8	Belgium-Luxembourg	2.8	3.9
11	27	Taiwan	1.6	0.8
12	11	Sweden	1.6	2.1
13	24	Hong Kong	1.6	0.9
14	39	Korea, Rep. of	1.6	0.6
15	20	China	1.4	1.0
16	12	Switzerland	1.4	1.7
17	14	Saudi Arabia	1.4	1.6
18	17	Brazil	1.3	1.1
19	16	German Dem. Rep.	1.3	1.3
20	23	Spain	1.3	0.9
		Total	73.8%	74.3%

Imports

Rank 1985	Rank 1973	Area	Share in World Imports 1985	Share in World Imports 1973
1	1	United States	17.3%	12.4%
2	2	Germany, Fed. Rep.	7.9	9.1
3	4	Japan	6.4	6.4
4	3	United Kingdom	5.5	6.4
5	5	France	5.4	6.2
6	6	Italy	4.5	4.7
7	10	USSR	4.1	3.5
8	8	Canada	3.8	3.9
9	7	Netherlands	3.3	4.0
10	9	Belgium-Luxembourg	2.8	3.7
11	23	China	2.1	0.9
12	28	Korea, Rep. of	1.6	0.7
13	11	Switzerland	1.5	1.9
14	14	Spain	1.5	1.6
15	22	Hong Kong	1.5	0.9
16	12	Sweden	1.4	1.8
17	24	Singapore	1.3	0.9
18	48	Saudi Arabia	1.3	0.3
19	20	German Dem. Rep.	1.2	1.3
20	19	Australia	1.2	1.1
		Total	75.6%	71.7%

SOURCE: General Agreement on Tariffs and Trade, *International Trade 1985/86* (Geneva, 1986), p. 23.

nations have given priority to industrialization as the "fast track" for rapid economic growth. This has meant rapid rates of growth for international trade in manufactured producer goods to support industrialization programs.

The effect of price changes on trade patterns is illustrated by the case of petroleum. Since 1973, petroleum prices have risen, but the physical volume of petroleum trade has not. The higher prices discouraged petroleum consumption by encouraging fuel conservation and a shift to alternative cheaper sources of energy such as coal.

The third factor—technology—has affected world trade in a number of primary products through developing synthetic substitutes for natural raw materials. In the food category, synthetic products have substituted for oils, fats, and sugar. Synthetic fibers have substituted for natural fibers, synthetic rubber for natural rubber, and plastics for metals. Synthetic substitutes can frequently be produced domestically with the result that international trade in many natural raw materials has expanded only slowly.

A fourth factor explaining changes in trade patterns is the substitution by multinational enterprises of foreign production for exports. Many firms began their internationalization by developing demand in foreign markets through exports. As demand grows sufficiently to support an economic-size production facility, the firm may substitute foreign production for exports. In some cases, the shift from exports to foreign production may be encouraged by a threat of protectionist measures against imports.

An example of the latter situation is the case of Japanese television manufacturers such as Sony and Matsushita and automobile companies such as Toyota and Honda. These firms secured large market shares in the United States through exports and subsequently established manufacturing facilities in the States. Thus, even though Japanese exports may decline, Japanese firms can still maintain their share of a foreign market.

FOREIGN DIRECT INVESTMENT

Foreign direct investment data are the most widely used indicators of multinational enterprise activity. In concept, direct investment relates to financial flows accompanied by managerial involvement and effective control. As defined by the International Monetary Fund (IMF), foreign direct investment is "investment that is made to acquire a lasting interest in an enterprise operating in an economy other than that of the investor, the investor's purpose being to have an effective voice in the management of the enterprise."[7]

As "effective" control is difficult to determine, the various countries have adopted quantitative criteria from which control is inferred. The United States defines direct investment as an ownership interest in foreign enterprises of at

---

[7] International Monetary Fund, *Balance of Payments Manual* (Washington, D.C.: 1977), para. 408.

least 10 percent. Individual country practices diverge, however, with the minimum percentage of ownership criterion ranging from 5 percent to 50 percent.[8] In order to make direct investment statistics more comparable, the Organization for Economic Cooperation and Development (OECD) has recently recommended that all countries adopt the 10 percent minimum of ordinary shares or voting stock as the criterion for "control."[9]

On a global basis, the estimated book value of foreign direct investment was a minimum of US$610 billion at the end of 1984. Book value estimates, however, substantially understate current values. They are cumulative totals of historical cost at the time the investment was made. They have not been adjusted for the effects of appreciation in values and inflation since the investment was made.

The global estimate does not include the direct investments of the socialist countries of Eastern Europe, China (see Box 2–2), and the USSR.[10] But the

---

BOX 2–2
China Goes Multinational

China International Trust & Investment Corp. (Citic), the country's main vehicle for attracting foreign investment and technology, said it plans to conclude half a dozen joint-venture contracts for industrial projects overseas in the next two years, establishing a base for the company to become China's first multinational, Citic officials said.

The Peking-based state agency wants to invest in a pulp-making concern in Canada, several mines in Brazil and Chile, and an opal-extraction project and a woolen company in Australia. Negotiations on all these are under way, Citic officials said.

On August 6, the agency formally took a 10 percent stake in an Australian aluminium plant following 12 months of negotiations. Citic spent $100 million on this investment, its biggest ever at home or abroad. In 1984, Citic invested in several U.S. forestry companies through a Seattle-based subsidiary, Citifor Ltd.

While many Chinese companies have invested overseas since 1978—mainly in trading and services, such as running restaurants—involvement in industrial projects has been rare.

SOURCE: *The Wall Street Journal*, August 18, 1986. © Dow Jones & Company, Inc., 1986. Reprinted by permission. All rights reserved.

---

[8] For a discussion of the definitional and statistical problems of using foreign direct investment data, see *Private Direct Foreign Investment in Developing Countries*, World Bank Staff Working Paper No. 348 (Washington, D.C.,: World Bank, July 1979), p. 47.

[9] Organization for Economic Cooperation and Development, *Detailed Benchmark Definition of Foreign Direct Investment* (Paris, 1983).

[10] See Chapter 14.

estimates do include the foreign investments of the emerging Third World multinationals. Firms in Argentina, Brazil, Hong Kong, India, Mexico, the Philippines, and South Korea are among those that have gone multinational, investing mainly in other developing countries.[11]

The leading home-base country for the multinationals in 1984 was still the United States, with 35 percent of total foreign direct investment, as shown in Table 2–5. The United Kingdom was next with about 14 percent. Other important home countries are West Germany, Japan, Switzerland, the Netherlands, Canada, the Benelux countries, and Sweden.

How fast has multinational foreign investment been increasing? The expansion rate has varied over different time periods but has consistently exceeded the growth rate of the global economy. During the decade of the 1960s, foreign direct investment expanded at an annual average rate of about 10 percent. During the 1970s, the rate increased to about 12 percent annually but slowed markedly to less than 5 percent annually during the first half of the 1980s. Factors contributing to the slow growth rate in the 1980s were the world debt situation and a world economic environment characterized by slow growth.

The nationality pattern of direct investment flows has been changing, as will be discussed below. From 1960 to 1980, the direct investment position

TABLE 2–5   World Stock of Direct Investment Abroad by Country of Ownership: 1984 (dollars in US$ billions)

Countries	Foreign Direct Investment	
	Amount	Percent
United States	$213	35.0%
United Kingdom	85	13.9
West Germany	54	8.9
Japan	50	8.2
Switzerland	41	6.7
Netherlands	39	6.4
Canada	35	5.7
France	30	4.9
Italy	11	1.8
Other	52	8.5
Total	$610	100.0%

SOURCES: U.S. Department of Commerce, *International Direct Investment* (Washington, D.C.: August 1984), p. 45; United Nations, *Recent Developments Related to Transnational Corporations and International Economic Relations,* January 20, 1986 (E/C.10/1986/2), p. 11; Japan External Trade Organization, *1986 JETRO White Paper on World and Japanese Overseas Direct Investment (Summary),* (Tokyo, March 1986), p. 7.

---

[11] See Louis T. Wells, Jr., *Third World Multinationals: The Rise of Foreign Investment from Developing Countries* (Cambridge, Mass.: MIT Press, 1983); Sanjaya Lall et al., *The New Multinationals: The Spread of Third World Enterprise* (Chichester, U.K.: John Wiley & Sons, Ltd., 1984).

abroad of U.S. firms expanded at an average annual rate of 10 percent,[12] including adjustments for divestments.[13] But after 1980, U.S. investment outflows declined sharply, as did those of the principal investor countries of Europe. The major exception was Japan, whose foreign investment greatly accelerated. In 1984, for example, Japan increased its overseas investments by more than $10 billion,[14] not including reinvested earnings, as compared with the U.S. increase of less than $4 billion in the same year.

FOREIGN PRODUCTION

What is the value of the goods and services produced abroad by the multinationals? In many respects, foreign production data are more meaningful than measures of the stock of direct investment. Although country data on foreign production are not generally available, the United States provides good statistical coverage on this aspect of international business, and these data can be used to make a rough estimate of total foreign production by all multinationals.

The U.S. 1982 Benchmark Survey shows a total of $198 billion in U.S. direct investment and $938 billion in sales by "nonbank foreign affiliates of nonbank U.S. parents" in 1982.[15] By using a factor similar to what the economists call a capital-output ratio, specific ratios for each of the major industrial sectors were applied to available data on the composition of direct investment for the major investing countries to secure a global estimate of foreign production. On this basis, foreign production in 1984 was conservatively estimated at a level of $2,100 billion.

The foreign production estimate includes some activities other than the production of physical goods. It includes foreign operations in retail and wholesale trade, finance, insurance, construction, transportation, communications, and services that are based on foreign direct investment. In this sense, the picture it presents of international business activity gets away from the myopic concentration on commodities as the main substance of international business activity.

The major omission is the international transfer to nonaffiliated foreigners of technology and industrial property rights, such as trademarks, that are not accompanied by direct investment. Such international trade in intangibles has become a significant component of international business activity. For example,

[12] Obie G. Wichard, "Trends in the U.S. Direct Investment Position Abroad, 1950–79," *Survey of Current Business*, February 1981, p. 40.

[13] See Brent D. Wilson, *Disinvestment of Foreign Subsidiaries* (Ann Arbor: University of Michigan Press, 1980).

[14] Japan External Trade Organization, *1986 JETRO White Paper on World and Japanese Overseas Direct Investment (Summary)* (Tokyo, 1986), p. 4.

[15] U.S. Department of Commerce, *U.S. Direct Investment Abroad: 1982 Benchmark Survey Data* (Washington, D.C.: U.S. Government Printing Office, 1985), pp. 120, 162. The sales to investment ratios varied from 1.5 for mining to 13.8 for construction.

the U.S. firms covered by the 1977 census of U.S. investment abroad reported trademark agreements with 11,000 unaffiliated foreigners.[16] In 1982, payments to U.S. firms from unaffiliated foreigners for the use of rights of intangible property (copyrights, trademarks, patents, techniques, processes, formula, designs, franchises, manufacturing rights, etc.) exceeded $5 billion.[17]

INVESTOR COUNTRY TRENDS

On a global basis, the expansion of foreign direct investment occurred in three rather distinct phases after World War II. The first phase began in 1946 and extended until the late 1950s. It was characterized by a dominance of business firms from the United States and the United Kingdom, with investments heavily concentrated in foreign petroleum and other raw materials projects. A second phase, beginning about 1958 and extending to about 1971, saw a resumption of activity by other Western European countries and Japan with a steady loss in dominance by the United States and the United Kingdom. Direct investments shifted from resource-seeking projects to manufacturing and trade activities and were heavily directed toward the European Common Market and European Free Trade Association countries. A third phase beginning about 1971 was characterized by accelerated activity by non-U.S. firms, considerable disinvestment in petroleum and mining projects, and a dramatic increase in the attraction of the United States as a host country for foreign investment.

Phase 1, 1946–1960: Dominance by U.S. Multinationals

It is not surprising that the countries that had not been devastated by World War II emerged as the dominant investor countries during the immediate postwar period. In Western Europe and Japan, most business firms were concentrating on domestic reconstruction.[18] Furthermore, these countries had serious shortages of foreign exchange and were restricting the outflow of capital through rigid controls. In addition, German and Japanese firms had lost their investments abroad through war-related expropriations and felt that the risks involved in foreign direct investment were high.

In contrast, U.S. companies were in an especially advantageous position for expanding internationally. They had accumulated financial resources and had developed new technologies during the war period. They were not constrained by government controls over dollar outflows. Furthermore, the official policy of

---

[16] U.S. Department of Commerce, *U.S. Direct Investment Abroad: 1977 (Washington:* U.S. Government Printing Office, 1981), p. 191.

[17] U.S. Department of Commerce, *1982 Benchmark Survey,* p. 159.

[18] See Vassilis Droucopolous, "Expanding the Frontiers of Capital: Evidence from West Germany," in *Recent Research on the Internationalization of Business,* ed. L. D. Mattsson and F. Wiedersheim-Paul (Stockholm: Almqvist & Wiksell International, 1979), pp. 148–59; Sueo Sekiguchi, *Japanese Direct Foreign Investment* (Montclair, N.J.: Allenheld, Osmun, 1979).

the United States was to encourage foreign direct investment as an aid to European and Japanese reconstruction and as a form of assistance for the developing countries. In fact, it was common during this period to view the multinationalization of business through direct investment as an exclusively U.S. phenomenon.

At the end of the 1950s, foreign direct investment from all investor countries probably totaled slightly less than $60 billion in current dollars. The United States accounted for an estimated 55 percent and the United Kingdom for another 20 percent of the total. The remaining 25 percent was accounted for mainly by the Netherlands, Switzerland, Canada, and France.

Phase 2, 1960–1970: Emergence of Non-U.S. Multinationals

The dominant event marking the second phase was the creation of the European Common Market in 1958 and the European Free Trade Association in 1960.[19] These major economic integration movements enlarged greatly the markets available to plants located in these areas and attracted large flows of direct investment for manufacturing projects. Western European and Japanese firms began to invest overseas as government restraints on capital outflow were eased. The West German ban on direct investment abroad was completely revoked in 1961, and the Japanese restrictions began to be liberalized in 1969. Also, the "next door" location opportunities for European investors undoubtedly seemed to present low levels of political risk.

During the 1960s, the United States and the United Kingdom continued to be the dominant foreign investor countries. But their share of the total declined as direct investment by other countries accelerated. By 1970 the U.S. share declined to about 50 percent of the total and the U.K. share to about 16 percent. The investment patterns by industrial sectors of non-U.S. investors are not available for this period. In the case of the United States, the share of the total foreign direct investment going into manufacturing rose from 32 percent in 1957 to 47 percent in 1974. The share accounted for by mining and petroleum declined from 45 to 24 percent of the total over the same period.[20]

Phase 3, 1970 and Beyond: The United States Becomes the Major Host Country

The third phase began in the early 1970s and continued into the 1980s. Direct investment by non-U.S. investor countries accelerated, and a large share of the increased investment flowed into the United States. During the 1960–70

---

[19] The economic integration movements are discussed in Chapter 7. See also U.N. Centre on Transnational Corporations, *Trends and Issues in Foreign Direct Investment and related Flows* (New York: United Nations, 1985), p. 16.

[20] Stefan H. Robock, "The Rise and Decline of U.S. International Business: 1950–1980," in *The Multinational Enterprise in Transition,* 2nd edition, ed. Philip D. Grub, Fariborz Ghadar, and Dara Khambata (Princeton, N.J.: The Darwin Press, 1984), p. 44.

decade, Japanese and European enterprises had achieved phenomenal growth in size, managerial capability, and access to resources—all of which supported international expansion. Also, the technology balance had shifted with the success of European and Japanese firms in closing the well-publicized post-World War II "technology gap." Still another factor was the devaluation of the dollar in the early 1970s, which for many industries made foreign direct investment a more economic way than exports for serving the U.S. market. The rise in the international value of European and Japanese currencies relative to the U.S. dollar also made the acquisition of U.S. firms "cheaper" in the revalued currencies, especially in periods when the U.S. stock market was depressed.

Many parts of the world other than the United States experienced large investment inflows. But foreign direct investments in petroleum and mining declined in importance. Many countries with petroleum and mineral resources had developed an indigenous capability to handle production domestically and were not receptive to further foreign investment in these industries.

By the end of 1984, the U.S. share of global direct investment had declined to about 35 percent of the total as compared with 48 percent in 1973. Whereas the stock of U.S. overseas investment had doubled from 1973 to 1984, over the same period the stock of direct investment by Japanese, West German, and Canadian firms had increased by almost fivefold. Increases by Switzerland, the Netherlands, the United Kingdom, and Sweden[21] were also at faster rates than those for the United States.

Most of the principal investor countries had about half of their overseas investments in manufacturing projects, with about 20 percent in extractive industries and the remainder in finance, trade, and service activities. West German firms, however, had three fourths of their investments in manufacturing and very little in extractive industries. Japan's early overseas investments were mainly in natural resource projects and labor-intensive manufacturing in developing countries. But by the 1980s, the Japanese emphasis was on technology-intensive manufacturing industries in the industrialized countries. In the extractive industries, the United States, the United Kingdom, and the Netherlands were mainly in petroleum. Japanese resources industries investments included mining, forestry, fisheries, and agriculture as well as petroleum.

THE HOST COUNTRIES: WHERE DOES FOREIGN DIRECT INVESTMENT GO?

Which areas are the principal recipients of foreign direct investment? Globally speaking, the bulk of the investment flows have been "North-North," a shorthand expression for movements from one industrialized country to another. Of the total stock of overseas investment, three fourths has been placed in the economically advanced countries. The other one fourth, located in the less developed countries,

[21] See Sune Carlson, *Swedish Industry Goes Abroad* (Lund, Sweden: Studentlitteratur, 1979).

is referred to as "North-South" flows. The "East-West" expansion of multinational business activity—to the socialist countries from the Western nations—is significant and has been expanding. But because special kinds of non-equity arrangements, described in Chapter 14, have been used in dealing with the socialist countries, this sector of international business activity is not reflected in the direct investment data.

The Leading Host Countries

Until recently, Canada was host to the largest amount of foreign direct investment. Furthermore, because of its relatively small economy, Canada had the largest share of its total domestic output accounted for by foreign enterprises (see Box 2–3). The stock of foreign direct investment in Canada totaled C$73 billion in 1983, the latest year for which data are available. Thus, with slightly less than 3 percent of total world GNP, Canada was host to about 12 percent of global foreign direct investment. Beginning in the 1970s, however, the Canadian government initiated a vigorous program of screening acquisitions by foreigners and shifting petroleum investments to national ownership, all directed toward reducing the foreign dominance in the Canadian economy. By 1984, foreigners controlled only 45 percent of the capital employed in the oil and gas industry, down from 75 percent in the mid-70s.

More recently, the United States has become the largest host as well as

---

BOX 2–3
Who Owns Canada?

Among the industrial countries, Canada is the most dependent on foreign capital. Outsiders control about 10,000 businesses in Canada, and more than one third of these are wholly owned subsidiaries of foreign-owned firms. Seven of the country's biggest companies are owned and operated from outside Canada, including the biggest of all—General Motors' Canadian subsidiary.

Foreign investors own more than 90 percent of the country's motor and rubber industries as well as a large share of Canada's oil and gas, pharmaceuticals, chemicals, office equipment, and mining industries. The few industries where foreigners do not own much are often those that are tightly regulated by government (e.g., railways, other utility companies, publishing, and broadcasting).

Of the C$72.5 billion of fixed assets owned by foreigners by the end of 1983, C$56.5 billion (or 78 percent) came from the United States; C$6.6 billion (or 9 percent) from Britain; and C$2 billion from West Germany. Japan has moved up from sixth to fourth place in the past four years, thanks mainly to the purchase by Japanese companies of stakes in coal mines in British Columbia and other natural resources.

SOURCE: Adapted from *The Economist*, November 3, 1984, pp. 88–89.

home country for foreign direct investment. In the late 1970s, inbound investment expanded at a rapid rate and reached a cumulative $183 billion in 1985. This represented about 28 percent of the world stock of foreign direct investment. In 1970, U.S. firms had almost six times as much invested abroad as foreign firms had in the United States. By 1985, U.S. investment abroad was only 1.3 times inbound investment.

The United Kingdom and the Western European nations are the other important host countries for foreign direct investment. Among the industrialized countries, Japan has the smallest share of inbound investment. Until recently, Japan's policy was to encourage the licensing of Japanese firms, and entry into Japan via direct investment was severely limited.

Neighborly Trends

Two clear geographical patterns have evolved in direct investment. One is geographical proximity. The other is a continuance of relationships between former colonial powers and their colonies. The proximity pattern is illustrated by the large two-way flow of direct investment between Canada and the United States. Likewise, a large share of the investments by European firms is in other European countries; and much of Japan's overseas investments is in nearby Asian countries.

The former colonial ties are illustrated by Britain and France. British overseas investments are heavily concentrated in Commonwealth countries that were former British colonies. If the United States is included as a former British colony, old colonial ties would be the overwhelming characteristic of U.K. overseas investment. French trade and investment relations are largely with former colonies, particularly in Africa, now referred to as the "franc area."

The Developing Countries

The developing or Third World countries, as noted earlier, have been the host to about one quarter of the overseas direct investment. But this overall picture obscures several important sectoral and regional trends. The investments are heavily concentrated in a few countries, and the concentration of the investment inflows increased during the early 1980s. The 20 largest developing country recipients of foreign direct investment during the early 1980s accounted for almost 90 percent of all flows to developing countries, as compared with 70 percent in the early 1970s.[22] This leaves only a small amount of direct investment distributed among the remaining 100 or so third world countries.

These funds go to very specific groups of countries. Foreign investment is associated with the development of oil resources (Algeria, Cameroon, Egypt,

---

[22] U.N. Centre on Transnational Corporations, *Trends and Issues,* p. 28; See also International Monetary Fund, *Foreign Private Investment in Developing Countries* (Washington, D.C.: January 1985).

Nigeria, and Tunisia in Africa; Trinidad and Tobago in the western hemisphere; and Indonesia, Malaysia, and Oman in Asia) or other minerals (Chile). It is made to take advantage of relatively large domestic markets (Argentina, Brazil, Colombia, Mexico, Philippines, Thailand, and Venezuela). It is oriented to the export of manufactures (predominantly in Singapore, but also in Malaysia and the Philippines). Countries that possess neither exploitable raw materials, nor large domestic markets, nor a disciplined but low-wage labor force have not been able to attract significant foreign investment flows, even when their governments have been favorably disposed to it and have offered generous and varied forms of incentives.

The Centrally Planned Economies

Multinational corporations have been active in the centrally planned or socialist countries but generally in forms other than conventional foreign direct investment.[23] A variety of institutional arrangements have evolved as alternatives to foreign direct investment because foreign-owned subsidiaries as a rule have been prohibited in socialist countries. In the late 1960s, however, several Eastern European countries began to enact legislation permitting foreign capital to participate in equity joint ventures. Comprehensive statistics on the volume of foreign direct investment and related flows to the centrally planned economies are not available, but qualitative and descriptive information is discussed in Chapter 14, "Doing Business with the Centrally Planned Economies."

SUMMARY

International business activity is large and growing rapidly. The premier role in international business still belongs to the United States, even though the growth rate of U.S. activity has been lagging behind that of most other industrialized countries. Its dominance, however, has been in foreign direct investment and foreign production rather than in exports. The member countries of the European Community play a leading role in both trade and direct investment; Switzerland, Sweden, and Japan are other major players in the international business field.

The relative importance of specific countries has been changing, with international business activity becoming more equally distributed among the advanced countries. The socialist countries have become active both as investor countries and as host countries to multinational business arrangements. In recent years, even the less developed countries have become the home country for multinationals.

The data and the estimates presented in this chapter provide a reasonably accurate overview of international business patterns. They are rough estimates in many cases, however, and do not have the precision to answer many specific

[23] U.N. Centre on Transnational Corporations, *Trends and Issues in Foreign Direct Investment and Related Flows* (New York: United Nations 1985), pp. 41–45.

policy questions of international agencies, national governments, or international business firms themselves. A determined effort to collect data that depict what is really happening in the world today is urgently needed. A prerequisite for this effort would be a wider realization that today's world no longer fits the theoretically assumed image of how imports and exports occur. The need for a new theoretical framework is the subject of the next chapter.

EXERCISES AND DISCUSSION QUESTIONS

1. Write a report for government officials of a specified country suggesting a program for statistical collection with a view to monitoring and controlling multinational business operations as they affect the country. Explain the concepts you think are relevant and indicate the data requirements as precisely as you can.
2. For a selected minor country, assess the size and roles of multinational business within its economy. Indicate the sources of your information and how you have arrived at your particular estimates.
3. How would you explain the much greater concern about inbound foreign direct investment in Canada than in the United States?
4. How do you reconcile patterns of entering into joint ventures with Western capitalist firms by some socialist countries and the ideology of these countries that proscribes private ownership of property?
5. Why has international trade in agricultural products been expanding at a slower rate than exports of manufactured goods?
6. How would you explain the fact that in 1982 the exports to third countries from the majority-owned foreign affiliates of U.S. firms ($176 billion) were almost equal to total merchandise exports from the United States ($211 billion)?

International Business Theories

What general concepts explain international business patterns? For many centuries, the dominant form of inter-nation transactions was international trade between independent buyers and sellers in different countries. In such a world it was logical to look to international trade theory as a framework for understanding and predicting international business patterns. With the emergence of supranational business enterprises that conduct inter-nation transactions in many new forms other than traditional importing and exporting, trade theory has proved to be too limited for explaining the current realities of international business.

In response to the changing patterns, a growing number of theoretical contributions have been advanced. Each has added to our understanding, and some of the contributions have been approaching a comprehensive explanation of recent patterns. This chapter examines trade theory and the various new theories of international business. It will emphasize both the explanatory power and limitations of the various contributions. It will also introduce a geobusiness model as a comprehensive theoretical framework.

INTERNATIONAL TRADE THEORY

With its long history and high refinement, the pure theory of international trade continues to shape much business thinking and, even more so, the actions of government. Thus, the international manager who is familiar with trade theory will be better able to understand, analyze, predict, and influence government policies in the international business field. Governments are constantly reshaping the environment within which the enterprise operates through changes in tariffs, import quotas, and nontariff barriers. Traditional trade theory is usually the underlying rationale for such policy changes.

The main questions on which classical and neoclassical theories focus are:

Why do countries import and export the sorts of products they do, and at what relative prices or terms of trade?

How are these trade flows related to the characteristics of a country, and how do they affect domestic factor prices?

What are the effects of trade intervention such as tariffs?

What are the gains from trade, and how are they divided among trading countries?

Within trade theory, the foundation stone for explaining patterns and gains from trade is the *doctrine of comparative advantage.* The doctrine demonstrates that if a country specializes in the products in which it has the greatest *comparative advantage* relative to other nations and trades those products for goods in which it has the greatest *comparative disadvantage,* the country's total availability of goods secured from a given amount of resources will be enlarged. In other words, by emphasizing *comparative* rather than *absolute* advantages, the doctrine shows that every country has a basis for trade and that specialization and trade are more efficient than policies of national self-sufficiency.

The Basis for Trade

Absolute Advantage.   The easiest explanation for trade is the concept of absolute advantage. Mexico exports petroleum to Japan. Honduras exports bananas to the United States. The United States exports airplanes to Sweden. The examples illustrate the principle called *absolute advantage* wherein the exporting country holds a superiority in the availability and cost of certain goods.

Absolute advantage may come about because of such factors as climate, quality of land, and natural resource endowments or because of differences in labor, capital, technology, and entrepreneurship. Some nations have petroleum, and most do not. This is a case of absolute advantage because of physical availability. A tropical country can produce bananas efficiently because of climate. The United States can import bananas at much less cost than if the United States tried to produce bananas in hothouses. The acquired advantages, as in the case of airplanes, can be the result of specialization and large-scale production.

The concept of absolute advantage can be illustrated by a simplified example of two countries and two products. Let us take Australia and Belgium as the countries and wheat and cloth as the products. To simplify the example even further, we will use units of resource input (land, labor, and capital) for comparison rather than introduce money and exchange rates at this stage. The following hypothetical example compares the production resulting from the use of 10 units of resources.

Production from 10 Units of Resources

	Bushels of Wheat	Yards of Cloth
Australia	100	40
Belgium	20	100

Clearly, Australia has an absolute advantage in the production of wheat. It produces 10 bushels of wheat per resource input as compared to 2 in Belgium. Belgium's absolute advantage is in the production of cloth at the rate of 10 to 4 over Australia. It appears sensible for each country to specialize in the product in which it has an absolute advantage and secure its needs of the product in which it has a disadvantage through trade.

The extent of the benefit from specialization and trade will depend, of course, on the prices at which trading takes place. Here we will introduce the concept of *opportunity cost,* meaning what a country will have to give up of one good in order to secure another. The opportunity cost for cloth in Australia is 1 unit of cloth for 2.5 units of wheat, because one resource unit can produce *either* 4 yards of cloth *or* 10 bushels of wheat. If Australia can buy 1 yard of cloth from Belgium for less than its opportunity cost—say, 1 bushel of wheat—it will either save resources to be used for other purposes or end up with more cloth than by trying to be self-sufficient. Belgium will gain even more by trading cloth for wheat at the rate of 1 yard of cloth for 1 bushel of wheat, because Belgium would have to give up 5 yards of cloth to produce 1 bushel of wheat with its own resources.

Comparative Advantage. Trade based on absolute advantage is easy to understand. But what happens when one country can produce *all* products with an absolute advantage? Would trade occur? Should it occur? Can trade still be mutually advantageous to the trading partners?

Here we encounter the *doctrine of comparative advantage* first introduced by David Ricardo early in the 19th century. The doctrine emphasizes *relative* rather than *absolute* cost differences. As noted above, the doctrine demonstrates that mutually advantageous trade can occur even when one trading partner has an absolute advantage in producing *all* the products being traded. Although basically a simple concept, the doctrine of comparative advantage is sometimes elusive and is frequently misunderstood.

The details of the doctrine have been modified and further developed by other theorists since Ricardo, but the concept of comparative advantage is still widely accepted. The original Ricardo version assumed that costs are determined only by the amount of labor time required in production. The modern version takes all factors of production into account on the cost side and defines costs in terms of opportunity costs.

If international trade is based on differences in comparative costs, what explains these cost differences? The question is answered by the Heckscher-Ohlin theorem, which attributes differences in comparative costs to differences among countries in factor endowments.[1] Countries have a comparative disadvantage in and tend to import those goods whose production requires the factors in relative scarcest supply in the country.

Country A with large and fertile land resources and few people may produce wheat *relatively* cheaply compared to Country B with little land and an educated urban population. Country B in turn may produce manufactured goods *relatively* cheaply. Country A would then export wheat and import manufactured goods, while Country B would export manufactured goods and import foods.

In the simplest application of the doctrine of comparative advantage, factor endowments (or resources) would be classified as land, labor, or capital. For more advanced analysis, distinctions are drawn among different types of labor or management skills; the specific production and distribution facilities built up in the past; and the specific natural resources—minerals, rainfall, or agricultural land—that are abundant.

A simple arithmetic example can illustrate how the principle of comparative advantage can lead to mutually beneficial trade *even where one of the trading parties has an absolute advantage in all of the products being traded.* Let us return to Australia and Belgium as the two countries and wheat and cloth as the two products. Assume that each country has a total of 100 productive units that can be used in the production of either wheat or cloth. The output of each product

---

[1] For a more detailed examination of trade theory, see Peter H. Lindert, *International Economics,* 8th ed. (Homewood, Ill.: Richard D. Irwin, 1986), pp. 15–66.

will vary with the number of productive units devoted to it. The production alternatives and outputs are shown in Table 3–1.

If all the productive units in Australia were devoted to the production of wheat, the output would be 100 million bushels. If, instead, these same resources were directed to cloth production, the output would be 80 million yards. For combinations of the two products, Australia would have to forego 1.25 bushels of wheat for every yard of cloth produced. Thus, if Australia could not trade with the rest of the world and wanted 20 million yards of cloth, it would cost the Australians the alternative of 25 million bushels of wheat. This would be the *opportunity cost,* or price, for obtaining the cloth.

For Belgium, the extreme production alternatives are 40 million bushels of wheat or 60 million yards of cloth. In this case, only 0.67 bushels of wheat would be given up for each yard of cloth; and if the population wished to have 30 million yards of cloth, it would cost them the alternative of 20 million bushels of wheat.

So long as the two countries remain isolated without trade, cloth will be exchanged internally for wheat at the rate of one yard for 1.25 bushels in Australia and one yard for 0.67 bushels in Belgium. These ratios are easily derived from Table 3–1, which is so constructed that the ratios remain constant for all production combinations of wheat and cloth. Thus prices in Australia and Belgium will differ, given our simplifying assumptions, and there will be opportunity and incentive for trade.

In this hypothetical example, Australia has an absolute advantage over Belgium in the production of both products. In the case of wheat, Australia can produce 100 million bushels as compared with 40 million for Belgium with the 100 productive units. In the case of cloth, Australia can produce 80 million yards of cloth as compared with 60 million for Belgium, if all of the productive units are used. Thus, Australia's absolute advantage in wheat is 10 to 4 and in cloth it is 8 to 6. On a relative basis, Australia's comparative advantage is greatest in wheat (2.5 to 1 versus 1.33 to 1 for cloth) and Belgium's comparative disadvantage is least in cloth (1 to 1.33 versus 1 to 2.5 for wheat).

TABLE 3–1   Production Alternatives for Australia and Belgium

Productive Units Devoted to		Production			
		Australia		Belgium	
Wheat	Cloth	Wheat (million bushels)	Cloth (million yards)	Wheat (million bushels)	Cloth (million yards)
100	0	100	0	40	0
75	25	75	20	30	15
50	50	50	40	20	30
25	75	25	60	10	45
0	100	0	80	0	60

Trade under Constant Opportunity Costs.   Continuing our example, what happens when trade takes place? Australia would specialize in wheat, which it then trades for cloth. Conversely, Belgium would specialize in cloth and trade the cloth for the wheat it needs. The opportunity for trade creates a single market for the two countries. If we overlook transport costs, a single price for cloth and wheat will emerge.

The new price will lie somewhere between the internal price ratios—that is, the national prices under isolated conditions. The exchange price for a yard of cloth would have to be less than 1.25 bushels of wheat, the opportunity cost for Australia, and higher than 0.67 bushels of wheat, the opportunity cost for Belgium. Otherwise, there would be no incentive for the countries to forego domestic production in favor of trade. With trade at a price between these limits, each country will end up with a larger supply of goods than if it tried to be self-sufficient.

The gains that result from trade can be seen by continuing the example. Let us suppose that Australians and Belgians each demand 30 million yards of cloth for consumption and that the trade price between Australia and Belgium is set at one bushel of wheat for one yard of cloth. This exchange rate benefits Australia, because with domestic production Australia would have to give up 1.25 bushels of wheat to produce one yard of cloth. The rate benefits Belgium because through domestic production Belgium would produce only 0.67 bushels of wheat by giving up 1 yard of cloth. Through reallocating resources in both countries, the introduction of trade enables total wheat production to increase from 82 to 100 while still maintaining the cloth requirements, as shown in Table 3–2. Through trade, Belgium would concentrate on cloth and Australia on wheat, and they would exchange 30 wheat for 30 cloth. Both end up with a larger supply of wheat than before.

Each country does not have to limit itself to only one product. Had the total demand for cloth been 50 million yards and not 60 million, then Belgium would have produced some wheat as well. Nor does it necessarily follow that

TABLE 3–2   Gains from Trade

	Australia		Belgium		Total	
	Wheat (million bushels)	Cloth (million yards)	Wheat (million bushels)	Cloth (million yards)	Wheat (million bushels)	Cloth (million yards)
Without trade:						
Production and consumption	62	30	20	30	82	60
With trade:						
Production	100	—	—	60	100	60
Exports (−)	−30	—	—	−30	−30	−30
Imports (+)	—	30	30	—	30	30
Consumption	70	30	30	30	100	60

the gains from trade are shared equally by both countries. For example, the trade price of one bushel of wheat for one yard of cloth gives the largest share of the gains from trade to Belgium. Belgium gets 30 million bushels of wheat through specializing in cloth and trading, whereas it could produce only 20 million bushels of wheat by using the same resources to produce wheat domestically. This 50 percent gain for Belgium compares to a 25 percent gain for Australia. Through trade, Australia gives up 30 million bushels of wheat to get 30 million yards of cloth, whereas it would have had to forego the equivalent of 37.5 million bushels of wheat to produce the same amount of cloth domestically.

Trade with Monetary Costs. Up to this point the examples have used barter prices, measured by the opportunity cost of the alternative output possibilities. The example becomes more realistic if production is measured in monetary cost and exchange rates are introduced. Let us assume that each productive unit equals 1 million labor hours, that wage rates are A$4 per hour in Australia and 100 francs per hour in Belgium, and that the rate of exchange is 25 Belgian francs for 1 Australian dollar.

Before trade, the costs and prices locally and in foreign exchange equivalents are as follows:

	Australian Prices		Belgian Prices	
	($)	(Fr.)	(Fr.)	($)
Wheat (cost per bushel)	4	100	250	10.00
Cloth (cost per yard)	5	125	167	6.67

Australia's absolute advantage shows clearly in that its costs, and therefore its prices, in Australian dollars or francs, are below the Belgian prices for both wheat and cloth.

Let us again assume that the international price settles so that a bushel of wheat sells for the same price as a yard of cloth—say, a price of A$5 (or 125 francs). It would then pay Australia to switch resources from cloth to wheat. In Australia, as shown in Table 3–1, one resource unit will produce either 0.8 yard of cloth or one bushel of wheat. The export of wheat will earn A$5 as compared to the A$4 worth of cloth given up by shifting resources. It would also pay Belgian firms to switch to cloth. In Belgium, the resources needed to produce one yard of cloth would produce only two thirds of a bushel of wheat. Belgium gains $5 for the cloth export and gives up the $3.35 that could be earned by using the same resources for producing wheat domestically.

Thus far we have been dealing with the case of constant opportunity costs at different levels of production. In the real world, situations of increasing or decreasing costs are more likely to be the rule. If Australia expands wheat production, less fertile land may have to be used, and unit costs will increase. In capital-intensive manufacturing, increased output may reduce unit costs because of economies of scale. More elaborate versions of trade theory have been developed to deal with the cases of increasing and decreasing costs. They demonstrate that in the world of decreasing and increasing cost industries there are still gains from trade, and countries will still find it profitable to follow their comparative advantage.[2]

The Limitations of Trade Theory

It may be a disappointment for the international manager, after mastering the logic and examples of trade theory, to learn that international trade theory is in flux. Recent empirical tests have failed to support the theory convincingly, and, as one writer notes, these empirical challenges "might be met either by extending the theory or replacing it. Economists are still debating which route is more promising."[3]

The limitations of trade theory flow in part from the simplifying assumptions of the model. Some key assumptions are that the factors of production (land, labor, and capital) are immobile between countries; that perfect information exists as to international trade opportunities; and that trading firms in different countries are independent entities. Also, the model assumes perfect competition and does not allow for oligopoly or monopoly. Nor does it explicitly recognize technology, know-how, or management and marketing skills as significant factors of production which can be the basis for comparative advantage.[4]

Probably the most important limitation of trade theory is that it sees the business enterprise simply as a black box "converting inputs into outputs and fully described by its production function."[5] As a result it did not anticipate nor does it attempt to explain international business activity in forms other than the movement of goods. A direct reflection of this is the way that trade theory poses the key question it tries to answer. Trade theory asks the question, "Why do countries trade?" This is the wrong question.

The question should be, "Why are goods and services transferred between countries?" Then it becomes apparent that the decision-making unit is the business enterprise and not the country. To be sure, the enterprise may be state-owned as well as private; and government actions and programs may heavily influence

[2] Lindert, *International Economics*, pp. 28–29, 40–42.

[3] Lindert, Ibid., p. 43.

[4] See Raymond Vernon, "The Location of Economic Activity," in *Economic Analysis and the Multinational Enterprise*, ed. John H. Dunning (New York: Praeger Publishers, 1974), p. 90.

[5] Peter J. Buckley, "New Theories of International Business: Some Unresolved Issues," in *The Growth of International Business*, ed. Mark Casson (London: George Allen & Unwin, 1983), p. 35.

business decisions. Nevertheless, the initial focal point for explaining most international business transactions is the enterprise.

When the enterprise is envisaged as more than a black box, a whole range of wider issues is opened. We recognize the reality that the business firm has numerous ways besides traditional importing and exporting for supplying foreign markets or securing foreign goods. It can supply foreign demand through licensing or foreign production. It can secure foreign goods through direct-investment projects. Trade theory rules out these options through its limiting assumptions. It also misses the rational behind the 20th-century development of marketing by assuming that commodities sold in the international marketplace are standard, basic, and transferable—wheat, cotton, and wine, for example. Today's firms, however, are continually adjusting many dimensions of their products against their assessments of customers' wants—against the market. There is no simple standard commodity.

The implications of the multinational enterprise for international trade theory have begun to receive serious attention by economic theorists, and considerable reconstruction is under way, particularly to allow for some internationally mobile factors.[6] But the emphasis of the reconstruction efforts is more on ways to make traditional theory relevant than on developing a theoretical framework for explaining the multinational enterprise phenomenon.

FOREIGN DIRECT INVESTMENT THEORIES

While trade theorists have been working to extend trade theory to include foreign direct investment, other theorists have been making important contributions under the rubric of theories of foreign direct investment or theories of the multinational enterprise.[7] Most of the new theoretical work, however, has been done outside the general equilibrium framework of international trade and investment theory. The various theories have added greatly to our understanding of modern international business patterns, but the process of developing a comprehensive theoretical framework is still under way.

As might be expected, the various theoretical contributions give special emphasis to the professional field of specialization of the contributors. Specialists in

---

[6] See Asim Erdilak, "Can The Multinational Corporation Be Incorporated Into the General Equilibrium Theory of Trade and Investment?", *Social and Economic Studies,* September 1976, pp. 280–90; H. P. Gray, "Towards a Unified Theory of International Trade, International Production and Direct Foreign Investment," in *International Capital Movements,* ed. J. Black and J. H. Dunning (London: Macmillan, 1982), pp. 58–83; Paul Krugman, "New Theories of Trade Among Industrial Countries," *American Economic Review,* May 1983, pp. 343–47.

[7] See Neil Hood and Stephen Young, *The Economics of Multinational Enterprise* (New York: Longman Group, 1979); A. L. Calvet, "A Synthesis of Foreign Direct Investment Theories and Theories of the Multinational Firm," *Journal of International Business Studies,* Spring/Summer 1981, pp. 43–59; Peter J. Buckley and Mark Casson, *The Economic Theory of the Multinational Enterprise* (New York: St. Martin's Press, 1985).

industrial organization have explained direct investment in terms of product differentiation, oligopoly, and imperfect product and factor markets. Specialists in international finance have focused on capital market imperfections. Management and decision theory experts have focused on the internal decision-making process of the firm.

The Global Horizons Approach

An early contribution comes from the work of Aharoni on the forces that change the geographical horizon of the firm and stimulate it to "go international."[8] In classical economic theory, the issue of geographical horizons for the business enterprise does not arise. The firm is assumed to have perfect and costless knowledge of and be prepared to take advantage of attractive opportunities wherever they exist. The reality is that the business firm is usually born with a geographical horizon limited to a locality, a region, or a home country. Brilliant foreign opportunities may exist beyond the firm's geographical horizon of which the enterprise is not aware. But the horizon of the firm is not necessarily static or immutable.

As part of the firm's growth process, geographical horizons change. The change may be a result of internal forces or exogenous stimuli stemming from the firm's environment. The internal forces may be the influence of a high executive, the development of new technology or products, dependence on foreign sources for raw materials, the desire to find a use for old machinery, the observed need for a larger market, and so on. External forces may be the influence of customers, the initiative of foreign governments, the foreign expansion of a competitor, or a dramatic event such as the formation of the European Community. The role of horizon-widening factors, as part of the growth process of the firm, provides a necessary but incomplete explanation of modern international business patterns. These factors explain the awareness of opportunities. Other factors are needed to explain how the firm responds to the perceived opportunities.[9]

The Market Imperfections Approach

Another major advance toward understanding international business patterns comes from the market imperfections approach. The core of this approach is a deceptively simple proposition. Assuming that the enterprise has a global horizon,

---

[8] Yair Aharoni, *The Foreign Investment Decision Process* (Boston: Harvard Business School, 1966).

[9] For related studies that emphasize the growth and evolution of the firm into multiproduct, multifunction, and eventually multinational stages, see L. Fouraker and J. Stopford, "Organizational Structure and the Multinational Strategy," *Administrative Science Quarterly*, June 1968, pp. 47–64; and Mira Wilkins, *The Maturing of Multinational Enterprises* (Cambridge, Mass.: Harvard University Press, 1974), p. 414.

its foreign investment decision is explained as a move to take advantage of certain capabilities not shared by local competitors.[10]

The foreign firm entering a specific country faces a number of additional costs or disadvantages as compared to a local firm. The local firm would have an intimate knowledge of the economic, social, legal, and governmental environment. The foreign firm can only acquire this knowledge at a cost. Furthermore, the foreign firm incurs foreign exchange risks, risks of possible errors and misunderstandings from cross-cultural operations, and additional costs of operating at a distance.

To operate successfully in foreign areas, therefore, the firm must have compensating advantages that more than offset the innate advantages of local firms. These advantages must be transferable within the enterprise and across distances. These advantages are referred to as *firm-specific* or *ownership-specific* factors.

The competitive advantage of firms is explained by imperfections in markets for goods or factors of production. In the theoretical world of perfect competition, firms produce homogeneous products and have equal access to all productive factors. In the more realistic world of imperfect competition, as explained by industrial organization theory, firms acquire competitive advantages through product differentiation, brand names, special marketing skills, and restrictions to entry. Other sources of competitive advantage may be patented technology, internal or external economies of scale, or even differences in access to capital markets.

Technology advantages in a broad sense relate to special marketing skills, superior organization know-how and management techniques, as well as products and industrial processes. Basically, technology advantages are the possession of knowledge, and knowledge has been characterized as a "public good" to the firm—that is, the know-how, once developed, can be made available to foreign subsidiaries without any additional cost to the parent firm. In contrast, competitors would incur costs in obtaining the knowledge or skills.

A knowledge advantage, however, must be more easily transferable within the firm than between different firms. When the knowledge market is imperfect, the firm may be able to earn a higher return by using the knowledge within the firm than by selling it to a potential buyer.[11]

The market imperfections approach can explain both horizontal and vertical investments. Horizontal investments are to produce in foreign locations the same goods manufactured in the home market. Vertical investments are supply oriented, intended to produce abroad raw materials or other production inputs, which are

---

[10] This theory was originally propounded in a thesis at the Massachusetts Institute of Technology by Stephen H. Hymer in 1960. The thesis was eventually published in 1976. See Stephen H. Hymer, *The International Operations of National Firms: A Study of Direct Investment* (Cambridge, Mass.: MIT Press, 1976).

[11] Richard E. Caves, "International Corporations: The Industrial Economics of Foreign Investment," *Economica* 38 (February 1971), pp. 5–6.

then supplied to the firm at home or to other subsidiaries. The foreign firm may have privileged access to raw materials or minerals because of firm-specific advantages such as an established marketing system, managerial capacity, control over transportation, or access to capital. The petroleum industry, with a small number of international firms that dominated the world scene for a number of years, is an example of supply-oriented direct investments. This industry is also an example of how the competitive advantage of firms can change and erode over time.

The oligopoly structure of certain industrial markets has been identified as a source of competitive advantage and a motivation for a "follow-the-leader" behavior in such industries.[12] An oligopolistic market is characterized by restricted entry and a small number of firms. Restricted entry may result from such factors as patented technology, unpatented secret know-how, large capital requirements, and economies of large-scale production. The market may be international rather than national, as in the case of aluminum and petroleum.

In the oligopoly model, each of the small number of firms is motivated to follow its competitors into foreign markets as a defensive strategy. By being in all markets occupied by its competitors, each firm has the potential of responding to price cuts or other competitive actions. Because of this response potential, competition is reduced, and the market situation becomes "stabilized." This pattern is also referred to as an "exchange of threat" motivation.[13]

The market imperfections model helps to identify the industries in which firms are likely to expand their direct operations either domestically or internationally. The model needs to be supplemented by the global horizon contributions, however, because it assumes that the firm is constantly aware of foreign opportunities. The model also leaves many important questions unanswered. Given the special advantage that permits the firm to invest abroad (i.e., the necessary condition), the model stops short of explaining why foreign production is the preferred means of exploiting the advantage (i.e., the sufficient condition). The firm's advantage can also be exploited through exporting or licensing. Furthermore, the theory needs a time dimension in the sense that the advantage may erode and require disinvestment.

Several other theoretical contributions that emphasize the financial aspects of international operations should be mentioned in a summary of market imperfections theories. One writer explains international business expansion as a response to imperfections in foreign exchange and capital markets.[14] Another contribution

---

[12] F. T. Knickerbocker, *Oligopolistic Reaction and Multinational Enterprise* (Boston: Harvard Business School, 1973).

[13] Edward M. Graham, "Transatlantic Investment by Multinational Firms: A Rivalistic Phenomenon?", *Journal of Post-Keynesian Economics,* Fall 1978, pp. 82–99.

[14] Robert Z. Aliber, "Money, Multinationals, and Sovereigns" in *The Multinationals in the 1980s,* ed. Charles P. Kindleberger and D. B. Audretsch (Cambridge, Mass.: MIT Press, 1983), pp. 245–59.

extends portfolio theory to explain international expansion as a means of diversifying risk and stabilizing earnings by being in a "basket of markets."[15]

The Internalization Approach

The internalization explanation extends the market imperfections approach by focusing on imperfections in intermediate-product markets rather than on final-product markets.[16] It assumes that the firm has a global horizon and it recognizes that the enterprise needs a competitive advantage or a unique asset to expand. But the emphasis of the internalization concept is on the motivations of the firm to extend its own direct operations rather than use external markets.

Many intermediate-product markets, particularly for types of knowledge and expertise embodied in patents and human capital, are difficult to organize and costly to use. In such cases, the firm has an incentive to create internal markets whenever transactions can be carried out more efficiently within the firm than through external markets. This internalization involves extending the direct operations of the firm and bringing under common ownership and control the activities linked by the market (see Box 3–1).

The creation of an internal market permits the firm to transform an intangible piece of research into a valuable property specific to the firm. The firm can exploit its advantage in all available markets and still keep the use of the information internal to the firm in order to recoup its initial expenditures on research and knowledge generation. In this respect, the internalization theory is similar to the "appropriability" approach. The appropriability approach emphasizes potential returns from technology creation and the ability of the multinational firm to ensure full appropriability of the returns.[17]

The internalization approach goes a long way toward synthesizing the various explanations of the motives for foreign direct investment.[18] The explanatory value

[15] Alan Rugman, *International Diversification and the Multinational Enterprise* (Lexington, Mass.: Lexington Books, 1979); see also Raj Aggarwall, "Investment Performance of U.S. Based Multinational Companies: Comments and a Perspective on International Diversification of Real Assets," *Journal of International Business Studies,* Spring/Summer 1980, pp. 98–104; V. R. Errunza and L. W. Senbet, "The Effects of International Operations on the Market Value of the Firm: Theory and Practice," *Journal of Finance,* May 1981, pp. 401–17.

[16] Peter J. Buckley and Mark Casson, *The Future of the Multinational Enterprise* (New York: Holmes & Meier, 1976), p. 33; See also Jean-Francois Hennart, *A Theory of Multinational Enterprises* (Ann Arbor: University of Michigan Press, 1982).

[17] Stephen P. Magee, "Information and the Multinational Corporation: An Appropriability Theory of Direct Foreign Investment," in *International Financial Management,* ed. D. R. Lessard (Boston: Warren, Gorham, & Lamont, 1979), p. 57.

[18] Alan M. Rugman, "Internalization is Still a General Theory of Foreign Direct Investment: A Re-Appraisal of the Literature," *Weltwirtschaftliches Archiv* (Review of World Economics), September 1985, pp. 570–75.

BOX 3–1
Internalization in the Cocaine Business

The cocaine trade is, in a sense, just another multibillion-dollar industry—Latin America's "only successful multinational," as a Peruvian President has put it. And although it is largely hidden from public view, interviews with scores of traffickers and industry observers suggest that it can be analyzed in business terms.

Ten years ago, the cocaine trade was a haphazard cottage industry. Since then it has moved away from its entrepreneurial origins through a brutal shakeout to a relatively stable and mature industry dominated by a few well-entrenched giants. Conservatively reckoned, the industry's U.S. wholesale revenue in 1984 was at least $15 billion.

By 1978, Colombian producers had grabbed an estimated 70 percent of the U.S. marijuana market by supplying Cuban-American and other middlemen and wholesalers in Miami. And when buyers began asking for cocaine, they began shipping that as well to many Miami-based middlemen. But by 1979, as the U.S. demand for cocaine grew at a frenzied rate, the Colombians decided to move from being suppliers to being competitors in cocaine. This "internalization" move resulted in a two-year period of confusion and violence in South Florida—dubbed the "cocaine wars"—with Miami drug murders peaking in 1981 at 101.

Everyone who fought in or witnessed the war seems to have a different explanation for its cause. What is clear is that certain Colombian organizations emerged from the war in command of the wholesale level. As a federal prosecutor puts it, the Colombians moved in when they realized that "the real jackpot" was in Miami, not Colombia. In business school terms, those Colombian organizations, by installing their own middlemen in Miami, "forward integrated" to capture an additional level of profit.

By moving into Miami, the Colombians also reduced their risks. "One of the things they learned was that with Cubans, there were a lot of informants," says a Miami private investigator. That didn't happen with their own nationals, he says. "When they brought in their own people, they'd make sure they had some family back in Colombia. If they messed up, their family would be killed."

SOURCE: Adapted from "Inside Dope," by Thomas E. Ricks, in *The Wall Street Journal*, June 30, 1986. © Dow Jones & Company, Inc., 1986. Used with permission. All rights reserved.

of the internalization concept rests on an analysis of why firms, in some specific cases, are more efficient than markets.[19]

Internalization, however, is a general theory that explains the expansion of multiplant firms *both domestically and internationally*. The expansion of the multi-

---

[19] David J. Teece, "Transaction Cost Economics and the Multinational Enterprise," *Berkeley Business School International Business Working Paper Series* No. IB-3 (Berkeley, California: University of California, January 1985).

national enterprise is a special case of the general theory in which internalization of markets occurs across national boundaries. The theory focuses on the motives and decision process within the firm but gives only limited attention to the potential of national control policies and other external factors as they can affect the benefits and costs of internalization.

The Product Cycle Model

The product cycle model relates trade and direct investment as sequential stages that follow the life cycle of a product. The model suggests that firms innovate new products at home and in relation to the home market. In this *new product stage,* the product is manufactured in the home country and introduced into foreign markets through exports. In the *mature product stage,* the product has become sufficiently standardized that price competition becomes important. As cost factors begin to dictate that foreign markets be serviced by local production, foreign manufacturing facilities are established, generally in other high-income countries.

In the third stage, the *standardized product stage,* price competitiveness becomes even more important; and production may shift to low-cost locations in low-income countries, from which goods may be exported back to the home country or other markets. Or, only the labor-intensive phases of production may be separated and carried out in countries where labor is cheapest.[20]

The product cycle model provided a useful framework for explaining the early post-World War II expansion of U.S. manufacturing investment in other advanced countries. But its explanatory power has waned with changes in the international environment.[21] Many multinational enterprises have expanded their product development horizons beyond their home markets and are innovating products in response to opportunities or threats in any of the markets to which they are exposed. Also, initial production does not necessarily occur in the market area that inspired the innovation. Production will be located wherever costs are advantageous and possibly at an appropriate facility already existing in the system. The model does not address the strategy issue of why multinational firms undertake investment abroad instead of, say, licensing. Nor does it seem to explain supply-oriented raw materials foreign direct investments.

International Production

The various foreign direct investment theories help to explain which firms tend to go international (those with a competitive advantage) and the motivation

[20] Raymond Vernon, "International Investment and International Trade in the Product Cycle," *Quarterly Journal of Economics,* May 1966, pp. 190–207; R. W. Moxon, "Offshore Production in the Less Developed Countries," *The Bulletin* (Institute of Finance, New York University, July 1974), pp. 98–99.

[21] Raymond Vernon, "The Product Cycle Hypothesis in a New International Environment," *Oxford Bulletin of Economics and Statistics,* November 1979, pp. 255–67.

for engaging in foreign production (internalization). They do not explore to any extent the "where," or the pattern of location, for exploiting these advantages. The theory of international production addresses the issue of where foreign production takes place by integrating location theory into the theories of the multinational enterprise.

The "eclectic theory of international production"[22] enlarges the theoretical framework by including both home-country and host-country characteristics as additional explanatory factors. It argues that the extent, form, and pattern of international production are determined by the configuration of three sets of advantages as perceived by enterprises. First, as a necessary condition, there must be the *ownership* (O) advantage. Second, the host country must offer a *locational* (L) advantage as a production base. Finally, there must be an *internalization* (I) advantage in order for the firm to transfer its O advantages across national boundaries within its own organization rather than sell them or their rights to foreign firms. Thus the level and distribution of international production will be determined by the relative strength of these three sets of factors—OLI for short.

One limitation of the eclectic theory is that it does not take into account variations in the strategies of specific firms. It presupposes that different firms have broadly similar objectives and respond to economic signals both consistently and in the same direction. The model also has limitations for analyzing public policy issues. It does not separate the largely policy-determined characteristics of the country environments from those locational characteristics less amenable to change by policy choices.[23] Still another limitation is the omission of internation variables, such as the role of foreign exchange rates, to be discussed below.

The Marxist Imperialism Model

The Marxist imperialism model for explaining and predicting international business patterns has not attracted a wide following in business circles. But many political groups accept this explanation as a rationale for opposing multinational business, even though their philosophic position has been undermined by the pragmatic activities of the socialist countries. The USSR, other Eastern European countries, and the People's Republic of China have their own "multinationals" operating in nonsocialist countries. In the reverse direction, many special arrangements have been negotiated for permitting multinationals from the capitalist coun-

---

[22] John H. Dunning, *International Production and the Multinational Enterprise* (London: George Allen & Unwin, 1981), pp. 72–108; John H. Dunning, "The Eclectic Paradigm of International Production: A Restatement and Some Possible Extensions," *Journal of International Business Studies,* Spring 1988, pp. 1–31.

[23] Rachel McCulloch, "U.S. Direct Foreign Investment and Trade: Theories Trends, and Public Policy Issues," in *Multinationals as Mutual Invaders: Intra-Industry Direct Foreign Investment,* ed. Asim Erdilek (New York: St. Martin's Press, 1985), pp. 129–51.

BOX 3–2
Marxism versus Pragmatism

Calcutta—The Marxist-led coalition government in the state of West Bengal said it is willing to put aside ideological differences and welcome foreign investment.

Chief Minister Jyoti Basu said West Bengal has slipped from its position as India's premier industrial state and needs the technology and jobs brought by multinational corporations. He added, "We want the latest in technology, whatever the company and whatever its complexion."

Mr. Basu made his remarks while inaugurating a $27.5 million investment by Hindustan Lever Ltd., the Indian subsidiary of the Anglo-Dutch Unilever group.

SOURCE: *The Wall Street Journal,* October 15, 1979. © Dow Jones & Company, Inc., 1979. Reprinted by permission. All rights reserved.

---

tries to operate in Eastern Europe. Even more significant has been the policy reversal of the People's Republic of China in the late 1970s, which resulted in an open invitation for foreign direct investment.

The Marxist view explains the international expansion of business and the multinational enterprise as a logical stage in the evolution of capitalist enterprise, "a stage during which innate tendencies of the capitalist firm come into full power."[24] The nature of capitalist enterprises impose on the individual firm the necessity to expand continuously. This expansion results in the accumulation of capital and a growing concentration of capital in fewer and fewer hands. These two factors—investment expansion and concentration of corporate power—along with the growth of world markets create a set of conditions that are uniquely fulfilled by the multinational corporation.

The Marxist view of multinational enterprises as a part of a historical process does not differ greatly from many of the non-Marxist explanations for the internationalization of business. The main difference relates to the social value of the international business phenomenon. The Marxist view is as follows:

> The multinational firm may indeed be a more efficient organism, but the issue is: efficient for what? Its superiority is in the realm of profit-making of oligopolistic organizations designed to exploit to the hilt the existing hierarchy of nations, in other words the imperialist world order.
>
> The global corporations . . . have been built to obtain the maximum-profit advantage out of the artificial interdependence imposed by the long history of colonialism and imperialism.[25]

---

[24] Harry Magdoff, "The Multinational Corporation and Development—a Contradiction?", in *The Multinational Corporation and Social Change,* ed. David E. Apter and Louis W. Goodman (New York: Praeger Publishers, 1976), p. 200.

[25] Ibid., pp. 211–12.

LIMITS OF INTERNATIONAL BUSINESS THEORIES

As a framework for explaining *overall* international business patterns, recent theoretical contributions have several limitations.[26] Most explanations are partial in that they focus on only one method by which international business patterns change. They may throw light on either trade movements or direct investment but not on both as interrelated activities. Also, they generally have a limited view of the international strategies that may be adopted by the firm.

Some deal with the case of the market seeker but do not encompass the extensive activity of resource seekers. Another limitation is that existing theories are one way. They are not reversible. They offer explanations of investment and not of disinvestment.[27]

These limitations are noted not as a criticism of the theories but as a recognition that the theorists had limited objectives. In general, their objective was to explain only certain aspects of the international business phenomenon. They touch the phenomenon at different points and provide partial explanations of it from different perspectives. In a nondisparaging sense, the situation can be likened to the fable of the blind men and the elephant.

> Four blind men feel an elephant's leg,
> tail, ear and body respectively, and
> conclude it is like a log, a rope, a fan,
> and something without beginning and end.[28]

For the wider objective of explaining *overall* international business patterns, the underlying model or framework must of necessity be appropriately broadened. As a guide for the business enterprise, the model should recognize the full range of internal and external variables that influence the firm's international operations. As a guide to governments interested in influencing international business patterns, the model should identify the ways in which country and inter-nation variables can shape international business patterns. Above all, governments should be aware that measures intended to control one form of business transaction may cause the foreign enterprise to shift to another method.

THE GEOBUSINESS MODEL

The geobusiness model attempts to provide a comprehensive framework for explaining and predicting overall international business patterns. The label

---

[26] Mark Casson, *General Theories of Multinational Enterprise A Critical Examination*, University of Reading Discussion Paper No. 77, January 1984; Peter J. Buckley, "A Critical View of Theories of the Multinational Enterprise" in Buckley & Casson, *The Economic Theory . . . ,* pp. 1–19.

[27] Jean J. Boddewyn, "Foreign and Domestic Divestment and Investment Decisions: Like or Unlike," *Journal of International Business Studies,* Winter 1983, pp. 23–35.

[28] Archer Taylor, *English Riddles from Oral Tradition* (Berkeley: University of California Press, 1951).

geobusiness refers to the relationship between geography and international business in the same sense that *geopolitics* describes the relationship between geography and international politics.

The model encompasses the international business actions of *all* firms and not just those classified as multinationals. It incorporates a large number of key variables whose *interaction* changes the geographical source and destination of inter-nation business activity. It recognizes that the individual enterprise is the motive force and that international business patterns are shaped by the adjustments of specific enterprises, operating competitively over a range of national environments to survive and grow. The variables of the model can be grouped under three headings: (1) conditioning variables; (2) motivation variables; and (3) control variables, as illustrated in Figure 3–1.

The Basic Variables

The conditioning variables, or what the economist calls "necessary but not sufficient conditions," indicate whether an opportunity exists for business activity to cross national boundaries. They include characteristics of the product or service, characteristics of the home and host country, and inter-nation variables. The interaction of these three sets of variables creates an incentive for business to cross national boundaries. They also determine the extent to which it is possible

FIGURE 3–1 Basic Variables of a Geobusiness Model

Conditioning Variables:

Product-specific	Product and factor requirements, technology, and production characteristics.
Country-specific	*a.* National market demands. *b.* Disparities in natural and human resource endowments. *c.* Disparities in technological, cultural, institutional, economic, and political environments.
Inter-nation	International financial, trade, transportation, and communication systems and agreements that affect the spatial movement of information, money, goods, people, etc.

Motivation Variables:

Firm-specific	Geographical perception and resource availability.
Competitive	The relative competitive position of individual enterprises and competitor moves and threats.
Strategy	Internalization advantages and disadvantages.

Control Variables:

Country-specific	Administrative actions, laws, and policies of home-country and host-country governments that directly or indirectly influence international business through positive incentives and/or negative controls.
Inter-nation	International agreements, treaties, and codes of conduct directly affecting the pattern of international business.

to carry the product or the services across national boundaries without the costs outweighing the gains.

The motivation variables indicate whether the enterprise perceives and has a motive to realize any such net gains. These variables include firm-specific factors such as the firm's geographical horizon and its access to necessary resources for crossing national boundaries. A firm's competitive position, as affected by moves and threats of direct and indirect competitors, will also motivate it to change its international business pattern in a specific direction. A rational firm is unlikely to make a move into competitive disadvantage—it must perceive some advantage to be gained. Also, the firm's motivation will depend on its strategy goals and the action alternatives for implementing them.

Control variables indicate restricting or encouraging actions on the part of home and host countries to influence international business patterns. Even if the necessary conditions exist and specific firms are motivated to make a particular change in patterns, the change may be negated or redirected by the actions of an individual country or countries working in cooperation.

Conditioning Variables

Product-Specific.   The need for foreign firms to have a competitive advantage over local producers has been fully elaborated by existing theories. The types of competitive advantage are numerous. They can be in product development; product differentiation; production processes; managerial skills; marketing know-how; heavy capital requirements; economies of large-scale production; and other characteristics of the product, the firm, or the industry. These product and industry characteristics may operate as barriers to entry and result in oligopolistic markets.

Product-specific competitive advantages, of course, are not static. In mining and petroleum production, for example, access to technology, capital, and marketing networks has often been the basis for the competitive advantage of foreign firms. But in many cases, these advantages have eroded over time and disinvestment has occurred. Conversely, industries specializing in energy-conserving technologies and products, such as fuel-efficient automobiles, gained competitive advantages for foreign operations from "old" technologies as world scarcities in energy and natural resources developed in the late 1970s and fuel and raw materials prices escalated.

Country-Specific.   Specific home-country characteristics frequently generate and sustain the competitive advantages of enterprises.[29] The economic size and income levels of the home country, for example, both stimulated and inhibited U.S. firms in going international. For some firms, the large size of the U.S. market provided production advantages from large-scale operations, extensive experience in managing geographically dispersed multiplant companies, and valu-

---

[29] See Dunning, *International Production and the Multinational Enterprise,* pp. 81–98.

able marketing skills that have been built on as competitive advantages for international expansion. Other U.S. firms have been inhibited from developing international operations because the U.S. domestic market is sufficiently large for them to achieve scale economies and expansion aspirations. In contrast, a small home market has spurred enterprises in countries such as Switzerland to develop international horizons.

Home-country resource scarcities and resource availabilities can affect the motivations and capabilities of firms for expanding internationally. Japan's resource-poor situation, for example, has stimulated Japanese firms to engage heavily in foreign trade and direct investment to secure resources for their nation. The extensive international activity of U.S. firms in petroleum may result from the fact that the modern petroleum industry began in the United States in 1859, when commercial quantities of oil were discovered in Pennsylvania. This and subsequent oil discoveries enabled U.S. firms to develop petroleum industry skills that gave them a competitive advantage for going overseas.

Home-country environments can be a source of technology advantage where governments make heavy expenditures for research and large public investments in education and technical training. Home-country political systems have operated as both a pull and a push for international business. A number of European firms, for example, were motivated to diversify their operations internationally because of concern for periodic antibusiness political forces in their home country. A home-country infrastructure such as developed capital markets can provide a firm with an advantage in access to financial resources. Home-country social and cultural patterns can also play a role. Social mobility and a status hierarchy that gives prominence to business leaders are closely associated with the development of entrepreneurship and a dynamic business sector.

Host-country characteristics will condition whether an opportunity exists for business to cross national boundaries. Natural resource availability in the host country can be the attraction for a foreign resource-seeking enterprise. The size, growth trends, and income levels of the host-country market can be the attraction for market seekers. An underdeveloped capital market in the host country may be a source of competitive advantage for the foreign firm. Human resource availability may be important for production efficiency projects or research and development facilities. Cultural characteristics can condition local business opportunities as they affect consumer demands and the behavior patterns of potential employees. The host-country political environment may appear risky and act as a deterrent, or it may appear reasonably stable and act as an attraction.

Inter-Nation Variables.   The inter-nation variables have generally been neglected in the new theories. They include the operations of the international financial system, the international trade framework, international patent and trademark agreements, tax treaties, and so on. As they will be discussed in detail in the next chapters, only a few examples will be cited here to illustrate their conditioning role.

The international financial system adopted at the end of World War II supported three decades of unprecedented international business expansion by reducing financial risks and achieving relative stability in the values of national currencies. Some have argued that the system overvalued the U.S. dollar for this long period and created unusually favorable conditions for the expansion of U.S. firms by direct investment, rather than by exporting. With the realignment of major world currencies during the middle 1970s, however, the reverse seemed to happen. The undervaluation of the U.S. dollar against other major currencies stimulated a wave of foreign direct investment in the United States.

In the trade area, many inter-nation agreements have affected international business activity. The creation of the European Community; international commodity agreements; the emergence of the producers' association in oil (OPEC—Organization of Petroleum Exporting Countries); and agreements to reduce tariff and nontariff barriers have been some of the more important influences.

Motivation Variables

Whenever conditioning variables favor a change in business patterns across national boundaries, only a proportion of firms will take action. The geobusiness model thus requires provision for variables that identify these firms and their motivations. Motivation variables are divided into those that are specific to the firm, those based on its competitive relationship to other firms, and those based on the strategy options of internalization versus the use of external markets.

Firms differ in their geographical horizons—and these horizons change over time. The firms motivated to expand internationally are those that have developed a geographical perception capability to become aware of foreign opportunities.

The geographical horizon of a specific firm at a point in time has both a spatial and a functional dimension. In a spatial sense, it will fall along a continuum from myopic to global. At a partial stage of horizon widening, for example, the U.S. firm may be alert to opportunities in Canada but not to those in Latin America or Asia. In a functional sense, the geographical horizon may be global for exporting but not for direct investment. In Japan, for example, until the late 1960s a combination of historical, cultural, and public policy reasons limited the horizon for most Japanese firms to exporting.

The firm may have developed its radar so that potential foreign opportunities or threats are brought into view, but a companion capability is required to translate the data on the radar screen into effective business action. Unlike decision making for domestic expansion, the firm must be able to evaluate opportunities and threats that involve such variables as different currencies, foreign exchange risk, political risk, and so on. The firm must have access to sufficient expertise to give the international variables reasonably accurate values. Numerous examples exist of internationally inexperienced firms losing out on favorable opportunities because they were not capable of properly evaluating political or foreign exchange risk.

To take advantage of an identified foreign opportunity, the firm must have access to the necessary financial and managerial resources. Thus the German chemical industry was long aware of many foreign opportunities but did not have access to the capital needed to exploit these opportunities. During the 1970s, however, the industry was able to undertake major international investments because rapid domestic expansion had by then generated the large amounts of capital needed.[30] Access to personnel that could operate cross-culturally has limited the international expansion of many Japanese companies. In a number of cases, however, the unique Japanese general trading companies have been able to supply this scarce resource.

The second group of motivation variables covers the firm's competitive position and the moves made by competitors. The requirement that the firm have a competitive advantage *specific to the target area of operations* has previously been noted. This requirement, however, is unnecessarily restrictive. The firm may act to remove a competitive disadvantage or to prevent the building of a competitor's advantage. The necessary conditions, perhaps, are that the firm will not expand into disadvantage and that it must perceive some ultimate gain from its action. Moreover, *this gain may be perceived in accounting terms as benefits captured in the enterprise system elsewhere than in the local project.*

A third category of motivation variables are the advantages and disadvantages of the various action alternatives available for implementing the firm's international strategy. The choices can range along a continuum, with exporting or importing at one extreme and complete internalization at the other. The action alternatives for the firm, of course, may have a positive (expansion) or a negative (contraction) side. Emphasizing the positive side, most actions by the enterprise will be taken pursuant to one or more of the following strategies:

1. Market seeker.
2. Resource seeker.
3. Production-efficiency seeker.
4. Technology seeker.
5. Risk avoidance.
6. Defensive or "exchange of threat."

The market-seeker and the resource-seeker motivations are the basis for horizontal and vertical integration, respectively. The production-efficiency seeker changes the international pattern of its operations to take advantage of lower labor costs.

The technology seeker may take several types of international action. The enterprise may acquire foreign companies to secure access to some technology that the foreign firm controls. It may establish research or production facilities in a foreign area to take advantage of available trained personnel (see Box 3–3). It may undertake operations in an advanced product market to acquire product development and marketing experience used elsewhere in the multinational system.

The risk avoidance and diversification motives attempt to minimize the possi-

---

[30] *German-American Trade News,* July–August 1980, p. 19.

BOX 3–3
The Technology Seekers—Learn from Thy Neighbors

Santa Clara, Calif.—The Japanese come to Silicon Valley to shop for U.S. know-how; the Russians to steal it, if they can. But the Koreans are here to learn it the hard way—by starting their own companies in this hotbed of high technology.

In recent months three South Korean concerns have set up operations in Silicon Valley, a concentration of high-technology companies south of San Francisco. The Samsung Group will turn out silicon wafers, from which semiconductors are made, in a Sunnyvale plant. The Hyundai Group has set up a U.S. venture to design electronic circuitry and components for its Korean-made ships and cars. A third Korean conglomerate, the Lucky-Gold Star Group, will simply coordinate work with a number of U.S. partners from its Sunnyvale premises.

The Korean companies are trying to bring their technology up to U.S. levels by working in proximity to the top electronic producers here, with access to some of the best technicians. They also hope to gain respectability in the global electronics trade by establishing a presence in Silicon Valley.

Samsung and Hyundai are following the strategy already common among U.S. high-tech producers: using Silicon Valley—where the costs of factory space, housing, and skills are rapidly escalating—only for the incubation of state-of-the-art technology, then moving operations elsewhere.

And Korean companies aren't flying in planeloads of their own engineers. As it happens, there is enough Korean talent already in the country, holding doctoral degrees from nearby Stanford University and the University of California at Berkeley and possessing years of experience in U.S. high-tech companies.

SOURCE: Adapted from *The Wall Street Journal,* October 3, 1983. © Dow Jones & Company, Inc., 1983. Used with permission. All rights reserved.

---

bilities of production interruption, to achieve more stable demand through operating in a "basket of markets," or to reduce total political risk to the system. The exchange-of-threat strategy, as previously noted, occurs in oligopolistic industries.

Control Variables

The potential match between a foreign enterprise and a local business opportunity may be present. One or more firms may be motivated to exploit this potential. Yet the potential may not be realized because of national control policies in either or both the home and host countries. National control variables consist of laws and administrative actions of both home and host governments intended to achieve national welfare goals. These control factors can act as incentives or constraints; they keep changing over time as national goals keep changing. The specific types of incentive and controls are myriad, and many of them represent great imagination and ingenuity. They are examined in detail in Part IV of this text.

In the case of domestic expansions, firms may encounter both incentive and control factors. Many communities, states, and regions offer special tax and financial incentives to attract new business, whereas some domestic governments try to limit industrial expansion through constraints such as rezoning laws. But control/incentive factors are much more important in movements across national boundaries. The "foreignness" of firms raises many national policy issues that are not raised by domestic business expansion.

As a home country, the United States has export control laws restricting the export of goods and technology by U.S. firms that might "prove detrimental to the national security of the United States." For many years after World War II, Japan and most Western European countries adopted controls on capital outflows to improve a weak balance-of-payments situation. The effect of these controls was to allow national firms to use only the export option for engaging in international business. Home governments have also developed incentive programs to encourage international business expansion, such as providing political risk insurance, offering loans, and allowing tax credit for tax payments to foreign governments.

Host-country control/incentive programs are more numerous and varied than home-country policies. They may proscribe certain business areas for foreign investors, restrict foreign exchange remittances, control technology transfer agreements, require sharing of ownership with locals, and so on. They may even effectively ban foreign direct investment. Thus, until recently Japan maintained controls over inbound investment that left open only the licensing option for foreign firms in most business areas.

International controls are less extensive. The OECD (Organization for Economic Cooperation and Development), of which the industrialized countries are members, has adopted a voluntary code of conduct for multinationals. A related code is being developed by the United Nations.

A GEOBUSINESS THEORY OF INTERNATIONAL ADJUSTMENT OF THE FIRM

Against this specification of the underlying geobusiness model, it is possible to advance many theories of international business adjustment. A highly simplified general theory might be that business transactions will cross national boundaries when such activity is profitable to the parties. This can be a valid explanation but of limited usefulness. A balance has to be struck between simplicity and explanatory depth.

The theory advanced here is one based on the relatively simple rational global planning model for the firm. Its objective is to explain business actions by firms that have developed their geographical perception into a global scanning capability and have access to the resources necessary for international operations.

The Rational Global Planning Model

On the basis of a world reconnaissance of opportunities and threats, the firm selects the markets it wants to be in. Working back from its market objectives and following location economics criteria, the firm will develop logistic models on a world scale that represent rational patterns for supplying the selected markets. The logistic models will include sources of raw materials; production sites; service and marketing facilities; research activities; and even sources of labor, management, and capital. By incorporating the marketing and logistic options into a general programming model, the firm develops its optimal business operations strategy.

The global planning approach is basically the same for either domestic or international expansion, except that a new range of variables and risks resulting from crossing national boundaries must be included in the decision-making process. Thus the geobusiness theory recognizes that many explanations for international business are not uniquely international. Necessary conditions such as a competitive advantage are also necessary conditions for domestic expansion by a firm beyond its local area. Some of the common factors differ only in degree. Other factors such as currency risks are differences in kind rather than in degree, in the sense that they are constants for domestic expansion and variables for going international. This is particularly true for inter-nation and national control variables. Also, new variables such as tariffs, local content requirements, etc., must be added to traditional location economics criteria in international decision making.

What methods of adjustment to the international pattern of a firm's operations will the global planning approach lead to? The polar choices are traditional trade, at one extreme, and complete internalization, at the other. In between the poles are a range of methods involving varying degrees of participation by the enterprise in foreign direct operations. These include licensing; loan-purchase agreements for resource seekers; establishing foreign procurement or subcontracting offices; or making direct investments in foreign marketing and warehousing facilities, in assembly and repackaging operations, or in full-scale foreign production. In the case of direct investment, expansion through acquisition may be an alternative to initiating a completely new operation.

Where internalization advantages are not present, because intermediate product and factor markets are efficient, the firm will supply foreign markets through exports and secure inputs through imports. Where internalization produces net benefits because of imperfections in intermediate-product or factor markets, location factors will determine the location of production for either horizontal or vertical integration. The location factors are generally modified by government intervention. Internalization, however, can be an evolutionary process that begins with exporting at an early stage and later leads to foreign production.

Empirical Testing

Empirical testing is needed to determine the validity and explanatory power of any theory. International business research has only recently become accepted as a significant area of investigation, however, and the amount of research presently available is still modest. Moreover, major data limitations exist. Most governments still do not collect data in a form that permits analysis of the interrelationships of various alternatives for transacting international business. There is also a vast data deficiency on the internal operations of international enterprises, such as motivations and decision-making criteria.

Broadly speaking, most of the relevant research available falls into three categories. A large amount of research has focused on trade patterns and determinants of trade. Unfortunately, few of these studies recognize and explore the interaction between trade and investment. A second group of studies focus exclusively on foreign direct investment and the internal operations of multinational enterprises. The direct investment studies attempt to explain the determinants of direct investment by examining the industrial composition of flows to specific host countries. The internal operations studies have been characterized as "neither comprehensive nor particularly satisfactory" and often "not designed to test the theory."[31]

A third category includes studies on the economic and political impact of the multinational enterprise on both host and home countries and the related issue of the incidence and effectiveness of national controls on multinational business operations. Most host-country impact studies relate to the less developed countries. The control studies are generally inconclusive as to how far individual countries have succeeded in improving their share of the benefits.

Among the more comprehensive studies available are studies of the international business patterns of Japanese firms[32] and a major study of foreign investment in the United States.[33] Both research programs went beyond statistical analysis to include field investigations and interviews. The results of these studies are broadly consistent with most aspects of the geobusiness model. They demonstrate that explanations and predictions of international business patterns hold good only for specified types of business activity flows between specific pairs of countries. Both research programs overlap to the extent that Japanese investment in the United States is examined from both the home- and host-country perspectives.

Japanese international business patterns reflect a dominant role played by home-country conditioning variables. Japan has extremely limited supplies of natural resources and depends heavily on foreign countries for almost all important raw materials and energy. To secure a stable supply of natural resources, a large share of Japanese overseas investment has been in agriculture, fishery, mining, and forest resource projects. Early investments in the resources area, particularly mining, were of the loan-purchase type, whereby the foreign capital supplied by Japanese firms was repaid by a share of the output from the project. At that time, Japanese firms preferred this strategy because of a shortage of experienced personnel for participating in the management of these projects. Over time, the necessary managerial resources were developed, and the strategy shifted to equity investments with managerial participation.

---

[31] Hood and Young, *Economics of Multinational Enterprise,* pp. 175–76.

[32] See Yoshi Tsurumi, *The Japanese Are Coming* (Cambridge, Mass.: Ballinger Publishing, 1976). The Ministry of International Trade and Industry (MITI) annually conducts a survey of the overseas activities of Japanese firms. A summary of the survey results are published in the ministry's yearly *Overseas Activities of Japanese Firms.*

[33] U.S. Department of Commerce, *Foreign Direct Investment in the United States,* vols. 1–9 (Washington, D.C., 1976).

Home-country labor market characteristics played a major role in another large category of overseas investments in labor-intensive industries. As wage levels in Japan continued to increase rapidly throughout the 1970s, the developing countries became increasingly attractive to Japanese manufacturers in such labor-intensive industries as textiles and home electronics. Inter-nation variables were also extremely important as a motivation for overseas production-efficiency seekers. Labor costs increased even more sharply as measured in foreign currencies because the Japanese yen had appreciated from ¥358 to US$1 in 1970 to ¥210 to the US$1 in 1978 to about ¥145 in 1987.

It is interesting to note that many Japanese firms had developed strong competitive advantages in a number of product areas such as steel, shipbuilding, home electronics, motorcycles, and automobiles that did not lead to overseas manufacturing investments. To a large extent, the firm-specific competitive advantage in these cases was dependent on home-country variables that dictated home-country production. The location pattern began to change in the 1980s as overseas production was initiated in several of these industries as a hedge against growing protectionism in many major market areas. Also, pollution controls and scarcity of land in Japan forced some steel expansion to occur offshore, but in locations that fulfilled the input requirements rather than in the market areas.

Japanese firms have been active as technology seekers. They have acquired or made large investments in U.S. computer, computer software, and biotechnology firms in order to gain access to new technology. Thus the Japanese patterns include resource seekers, production-efficiency seekers, technology seekers, market seekers, and defensive investments against the threat of protectionism.

Control variables have been of great importance in shaping Japanese patterns. Home-country controls that limited foreign investment in Japan gave Japanese firms a large and protected home market in which to develop technological competence and economies of large-scale production. The Japanese government also assisted Japanese firms in many other ways, such as through financial incentives and long-range planning to develop product-specific advantages for competing in foreign markets. Host-country control variables, as previously noted, have stimulated many Japanese firms to substitute foreign production for exports in response to growing protectionist sentiments in those market areas.

Another comprehensive research study is the study of foreign direct investment in the United States published in 1976. This project combined a complete statistical census of inbound foreign direct investment with extensive field investigation of the motives and behavior patterns of foreign firms. All of the enterprise strategies—except the production-efficiency strategy, which has been the basis for sourcing investments in low-wage countries—were identified as motivations for inbound U.S. investment.

Much of the recent foreign direct investment in the United States was by market seekers with a competitive advantage in the U.S. market. Some firms had extended their horizons through exporting to the United States and were substituting foreign production for exports because of the realignment of national currencies. The economic size, high income levels, and growth trends of the U.S. market were important attractions.

Other investments were by resource seekers, such as Japanese firms in the coal, forestry, and aluminum industries, representing an evolution from an importing strategy to direct investment and managerial participation. Foreign investors entered the United States as technology seekers by acquiring some U.S. firms with new technologies and by establishing research and development facilities in the United States.

Defensive investments were made in several oligopolistic industries (such as petroleum and aluminum) so that foreign firms could be in all of their competitors' major markets. The attraction of a politically safe U.S. environment produced another strategy for some firms with concern for political risk in their home country.

The U.S. study illustrates the dynamic nature of international business patterns as they relate to technology advantage. The technology gap that developed during World War II and that supported much international expansion by U.S. firms during the postwar period has been closing. With the revival of research and development in Western Europe and the emergence of dramatic technological progress in Japan, business enterprises in these countries had developed competitive advantages by the late 1960s and early 1970s that became a basis for extending their operations to the United States.

The recent U.S. experience as a host country for foreign investment also reflects the influence of home- and host-country control variables. As previously mentioned, the home-country controls that existed in most European countries and Japan after World War II had been removed by the 1970s. Thus the strategy options of European and Japanese firms had expanded, and foreign direct investment had become a concrete possibility. On the side of host-country controls, the principal actions by the United States influencing the patterns were potential trade barriers that encouraged foreign firms to substitute local production in the United States for exports. The risk of possible restraints on imports was an important factor influencing a number of Japanese electronic firms—such as Sony and Matsushita—to establish production facilities in the United States.

SUMMARY

Practice has clearly run ahead of theory in the international business field. The new patterns of business transactions across national boundaries have become extremely complex. Traditional trade theory did not anticipate nor does it explain the internationalization of business in forms other than the international movement of goods.

A series of new approaches, evoked by the international business reality, are beginning to provide a theoretical framework for explaining and predicting international business patterns. Among these are growth theories of the firm and the emergence of the multinational enterprise as a mechanism for exploiting oligopolistic advantages in foreign areas.

The geobusiness model is presented as a comprehensive framework against which a range of theories about international business changes can be advanced. It recognizes the enterprise as the active force in changing international business patterns. But the motivations and capabilities of the enterprise for changing international business patterns are not related exclusively to the characteristics of the firm. They also depend heavily on home and host country environmental factors, inter-nation variables, and national and international controls.

EXERCISES AND DISCUSSION QUESTIONS

1. Explain the difference between comparative advantage and absolute advantage.
2. What are the principal limitations of trade theory in explaining current international business patterns?
3. As an executive of a predominantly domestic firm that seems unaware of foreign opportunities, what would you do to expand the geographical perception of the firm and "go international"?
4. Why has the U.S. pharmaceutical industry been internationally minded while the iron and steel industry has not?
5. As an international manager, how could you use the geobusiness model to guide the international business activities of your firm?
6. As a government official, how could you use the geobusiness model to reduce (or increase) foreign direct investment in your country?

PART TWO

The Framework for International Transactions

A natural starting point for studying international business is to examine the inter-nation framework that has grown up over the centuries for dealing with business transactions across national boundaries. This overall framework is made up of three different though interrelated components:

1. The *international financial framework* deals with the means (foreign exchange), the recording (balance of payments), and the facilitating of international transfers of monetary claims (the international monetary system).

2. The *international trade framework* deals with the means, the recording, and the control of international transfers of goods and services.

3. The *international legal environment* deals with the nature, contents, and limits of arrangements nations have entered into for determining how to treat business rights, obligations, and opportunities that extend across national frontiers.

These three frameworks provide the basic vocabulary for international transactions and, as such, introduce many of the terms and concepts necessary for describing international business. They also influence the language of government controls imposed on international transactions. These controls are determined largely by the information collection and reasoning that stem from the conventions of these frameworks. Knowledge of the traditional frameworks is thus important for understanding and predicting the environment within which international business operates.

None of these three frameworks, however, is focused uniquely on international business. Each has been molded by the heritage of arms-length trading between independent buyers and sellers residing in different countries—quite different from the international transactions of large multinational businesses. This heritage has produced a body of knowledge, theories, and controls that concentrates on aggregate flows of goods and finance across a country's boundaries and pays attention only incidentally to the objectives and decisions of the business enterprises that arrange the transactions. Thus, the frameworks have limitations, given the reality of today's world of multinational firms.

A basic similarity in the three frameworks is the absence of a world authority that can override the jurisdiction of national governments. Each framework is, in effect, a system for relating a particular segment of the economic activities and regulations of different sovereign states. The financial framework is concerned with the way in which the currencies of individual countries are exchanged. With no legal international currency, international transactions must be measured, accounted for, and paid for by converting one national currency into another. The trade framework is concerned with the relationship of the productive output of one country to that of another. What one country produces for another's markets is subject to a variety of natural and imposed conditions. Finally, the regulatory framework begins to provide a system whereby governments agree on how they will align their legal constraints and privileges for activities that carry into more than one jurisdiction.

CHAPTER 4

Foreign Exchange and International Money Markets

In a world of many national currencies, participants in international business need a mechanism for exchanging one national currency for another. The institutional setting for this process, usually referred to as *currency conversion,* is the foreign exchange market, which also serves as a mechanism for reducing exposure to the risks of fluctuating exchange rates.

This chapter describes the foreign exchange market, the ways in which foreign exchange rates are quoted, the principal types of foreign exchange transactions,

65

the participants in the market, and the relationship between foreign exchange and other financial markets. Foreign exchange rates fluctuate over time, reflecting a country's economic conditions and external relations with other nations.

THE FUNCTIONS OF THE FOREIGN EXCHANGE MARKET

Foreign exchange is defined as the currency of another nation. To a Japanese firm the U.S. dollar is foreign exchange. To an American company the Japanese yen is foreign exchange. *Foreign exchange rates* are the rates at which currency conversion takes place. On July 6, 1988, for example, the exchange rate was 133.60 Japanese yen to 1 U.S. dollar.

The two main functions of the foreign exchange market—currency conversion and reduction of foreign exchange risk—can be illustrated by the case of a Japanese exporter selling steel products to Brazil. The Japanese seller might invoice the Brazil buyer in Japanese yen, Brazilian cruzados, or U.S. dollars, depending upon which currency has been previously agreed to by the parties. Whichever currency is used, one or both parties will need to transfer to or from its national currency. If cruzados are used, the Japanese seller will have to convert them into yen. If yen are used, the Brazilian buyer will have to transfer cruzados into yen. If dollars are used, the Brazilian buyer will have to change cruzados into U.S. dollars, and the Japanese seller will need to convert the U.S. dollar into Japanese yen. The foreign exchange market provides the mechanism for these currency transactions.

When time elapses between a transaction and payment, a risk exists that the exchange values of the national currencies may fluctuate. This risk is normally referred to as a *transactions exposure*. If the parties had agreed upon payment in U.S. dollars, both the Japanese seller and the Brazilian buyer are "exposed" in the sense that they are not certain how much local currency will be paid or received on the payment date. Exposure may, of course, result in either gains or losses to the party exposed.

Let us assume that payment is to be made in U.S. dollars and that the Japanese seller prefers to make its normal profit on the sale rather than to speculate on eventually receiving a greater or lesser profit as a result of changes in exchange-rate values. Through forward and future contracts or foreign currency options, the foreign exchange market provides a means of removing the foreign exchange risk. The Japanese seller may contract to sell U.S. dollars for future delivery at a fixed rate and thus be sure of the amount of Japanese yen that will be received when payment is made.

THE NATURE OF THE FOREIGN EXCHANGE MARKET

The foreign exchange market is a network of banks, brokers, and foreign exchange dealers in many locations connected by rapid means of communications. The more important exchange markets are in London, New York, Zurich, Frankfurt, Tokyo, Singapore, Hong Kong, and Paris. These markets are so closely integrated that together they constitute a single world market, despite the distances and the time differentials involved. This closeness exists even though the banks, brokers, and traders are not formally linked and do not share common facilities in the various cities.

The foreign exchange markets are governed by an unwritten code of conduct for all participants. Most market transactions are handled informally—by telephone, telex, or computer linkages—rather than in written legal form. The apparently casual nature of the market transactions belies the strictness of the unwritten code and the swift punishment of anyone who reneges.

The major participants in the foreign exchange market are large commercial banks that operate at two levels—retail and interbank. At the retail level, they deal with bank customers who want to buy or sell foreign exchange. At the interbank level, they trade in foreign exchange with other domestic and foreign banks. Interbank transactions are both direct and through foreign exchange brokers who receive a small commission for their services. Many banks prefer to pay fees to brokers rather than incur the expense of supporting a full-time, professional trading staff.[1]

Almost all foreign exchange trading takes place among a small number of currencies, the most important of which is the U.S. dollar (US$). The nondollar segment of the market is dominated by the West German mark (DM-deutsche mark), Japanese yen (¥), British pound sterling (£), and Swiss franc (Fr). Relatively few nations permit free convertibility of their currencies, and currencies with restricted convertibility play virtually no role in the foreign exchange markets.[2] Full *convertibility* of a currency means that national governments permit both residents and nonresidents to purchase or sell unlimited amounts of that nation's currency. An example of a nonconvertible currency is the Russian ruble, the import or export of which the USSR prohibits by law.

The size of the foreign exchange market is enormous, and trading volume has grown phenomenally in recent years. The volume of foreign exchange trading in the world's three leading markets totaled $188 billion *daily* in March 1986. London was the most important trading center, with a *daily* turnover of $90 billion, followed by New York with $50 billion *daily,* and Tokyo, with $48 billion *daily* in foreign exchange transactions.[3]

Until rather recently, foreign exchange trading took place mainly in Europe and, to a lesser extent, in New York. The New York market opened later in the day; and when it closed daily operations, there was virtually no trading until Europe opened the next morning. Since the 1970s, however, markets in the Far East have emerged; Tokyo, Hong Kong, and Singapore have become important

---

[1] Michael D. Andrews, "Recent Trends in the U.S. Foreign Exchange Market," *Federal Reserve Bank of New York Quarterly Review,* Summer 1984, p. 42.

[2] The standard reference for foreign restrictions prevailing in specific countries is the *Annual Report on Exchange Arrangements and Exchange Restrictions,* published by the International Monetary Fund (Washington, D.C.).

[3] *The Wall Street Journal,* August 20, 1986.

foreign exchange trading centers. As a result, there is almost no time during the day when foreign exchange trading is *not* taking place (see Figure 4–1).

The trading day normally begins in Tokyo and ends with the close of the New York market. The most active period in New York is from 7:00 to 9:00 in the morning, when the business day is near closing in Europe. From the point of view of active dealing, there is a brief gap between the New York close and the beginning of daily trading in the Far East. Otherwise, there is continuous trading as the markets overlap each other and the center of trading shifts from country to country following the sun.[4]

Foreign Currency Futures and Options

Recent additions to the foreign exchange market have been foreign currency futures contracts and foreign currency options. Trading in futures contracts of a standard amount of a specific currency, similar to commodities futures, were initiated in 1972 by the International Monetary Market (IMM) of Chicago. Subsequently, other exchanges in the United States and in foreign centers also began trading in currency futures. Trading in foreign currency options was started by the Philadelphia stock exchange in late 1982 and quickly attracted other markets and commercial banks.

Futures trading takes place on organized exchanges that are physical locations and employ standardized contracts. Futures contracts are traded for only a limited number of currencies and for a given delivery date. However, actual delivery is rare with futures contracts. Instead, most buyers of futures will close out the position before the contract matures by making an offsetting sale or purchase.

A currency option is the right but not the obligation to buy (called a *call*) or sell (called a *put*) a set amount of currency at a specified price by some future date. The option buyer pays a premium for the option and can either take advantage of the agreed-on exchange rate or not, depending on what happens to the value of the currency during the time period of the option.[5]

THE LANGUAGE OF FOREIGN EXCHANGE

Transactions in the foreign exchange market may be either *spot* or *forward.* In the spot market, currencies are traded for immediate delivery (although in practice delivery and payment are completed within two working days). In the forward market, trades are made for future dates, usually less than one year away. The exchange rate is agreed upon when the contract is made, but payment

---

[4] See David E. Bodner, "The Major Foreign Exchange Markets," in *The International Banking Handbook,* ed. William H. Baughn and Donald R. Mandich (Homewood, Ill.: Dow Jones-Irwin, 1983), pp. 339–47, for a description of operations in each of the major markets.

[5] See Robert A. Feldman, "Foreign Currency Options," *Finance & Development,* December 1985, pp. 38–41.

FIGURE 4-1 The Market that Never Stops

The map shows the world's key foreign exchange trading centers and lists the major financial markets in each. Trading hours are shown in New York time. Since the market is unregulated, the times listed are customary, not official. Trading can begin earlier or extend later if a broker or trader answers the phone.

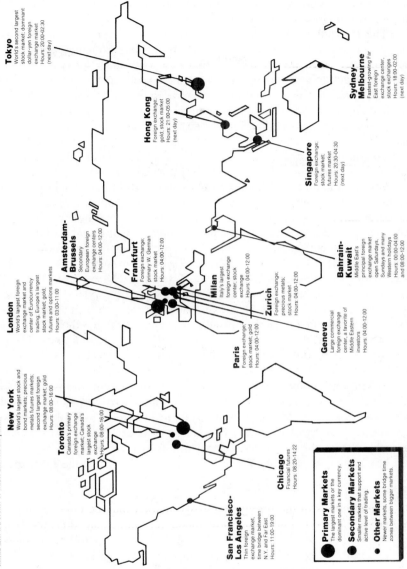

New York
World's largest stock and bond markets; precious metals futures markets; second largest foreign exchange market; gold
Hours 08:00–16:00

San Francisco-Los Angeles
Thin foreign exchange market, time bridge between N.Y. and Far East
Hours 11:00–19:00

Toronto
Canada's primary foreign exchange market; Canada's largest stock exchange
Hours 08:00–16:00

Chicago
Financial futures
Hours 08:20–14:22

London
World's largest foreign exchange market and center of Eurocurrency trading; Europe's largest stock market; gold; futures and options markets
Hours 03:00–11:00

Paris
Foreign exchange; stock market; gold
Hours 04:00–12:00

Amsterdam-Brussels
Secondary European foreign exchange centers
Hours 04:00–12:00

Frankfurt
Foreign exchange; primary W. German stock market
Hours 04:00–12:00

Milan
Italy's largest foreign exchange center; stock exchange
Hours 04:00–12:00

Zurich
Foreign exchange; precious metals; stock market
Hours 04:00–12:00

Geneva
Large commercial foreign exchange center, a favorite of Middle Eastern investors
Hours 04:00–12:00

Bahrain-Kuwait
Middle East's principal foreign exchange market open Saturdays, Sundays and many Western holidays
Hours 00:00–04:00 and 08:00–12:00

Tokyo
World's second largest stock market; dominant dollar-yen foreign exchange market
Hours 20:00–02:30 (next day)

Hong Kong
Foreign exchange; gold; stock market
Hours 21:00–05:00 (next day)

Singapore
Foreign exchange; stock market; futures market
Hours 20:30–04:30 (next day)

Sydney-Melbourne
Fastest-growing Far East foreign exchange center; stock exchanges
Hours 18:00–02:00 (next day)

● **Primary Markets**
The largest markets or the dominant one in a key currency.

● **Secondary Markets**
Smaller markets that support and active level of trading.

● **Other Markets**
Newer markets; some bridge time zones between bigger markets.

SOURCE: *The New York Times*, May 4, 1986, p. F10. Copyright © 1986 by the New York Times Company. Reprinted by permission.

and delivery are not required until maturity. Forward markets, however, exist only for the major currencies.

The forward market and the futures market perform similar functions, but with a difference. In the forward market, foreign exchange dealers can enter into a contract to buy or sell any amount of a currency for delivery at any date in the future. Thus customers can tailor their needs as to amount and timing. In contrast, the IMM deals in futures contracts of a standard size (for example, £25,000 or DM125,000), and the contract will be for a given month (March, June, September, or December), with the third Wednesday of the month as delivery date.

Forward exchange contracts are drawn up between banks and their clients, frequently other banks. The market is informal and does not have a physical being. It is similar to the spot market, with an informal structure of telephone, teletype, and computer linkages. Currency futures do not involve commercial banks; they are agreements between futures dealers and their customers.

Foreign exchange rates are usually quoted in different national markets in terms of the local currency required to purchase a foreign monetary unit. As shown in Table 4–1, the New York selling rate on Wednesday, November 18, 1987, for spot transactions was $1.7735 for £1. The reciprocal exchange rate shown in the third column was £0.5639 required to buy $1.00. The actual quotes would be on a buy and sell (or bid and offer) basis with a small margin—usually less than 1 percent for large transactions—as a profit for the trader. Table 4–1 uses the "middle rate" between the actual bid and offer quotations. The exchange rate for the U.S. dollar and virtually all foreign currencies is shown in Table 4–2.

Where foreign exchange quotes are available only in terms of one currency, such as the US$, *cross rates* between any other two currencies quoted can be calculated easily by relating them to a third currency—US$. The cross rates between the £ (British) and the DM on November 18, 1987, for example, can be derived from their relationship to US$. As shown in Table 4–1, U.S. $1.00 = £0.5639 = 1.6850 DM. The price of the £ in terms of the DM, therefore, is

$$\frac{DM}{£} = \frac{1.6850}{0.5639} = 2.9881 \text{ DM}$$

Likewise, the value of the DM in terms of the £ is

$$\frac{£}{DM} = \frac{0.5639}{1.6850} = £0.3347$$

Some sources, such as the *Financial Times,* will publish cross rates for the principal trading currencies. Cross rates are important because for many pairs of currencies there are no direct markets. They must be traded through a third currency.

Spot rates are always "flat"—that is, the exchange rate is written out with the proper number of decimal places. Forward rates are generally given either

TABLE 4–1

FOREIGN EXCHANGE

Wednesday, November 18, 1987
The New York foreign exchange selling rates below apply to trading among banks in amounts of $1 million and more, as quoted at 3 p.m. Eastern time by Bankers Trust Co. Retail transactions provide fewer units of foreign currency per dollar.

Country	U.S. $ equiv. Wed.	U.S. $ equiv. Tues.	Currency per U.S. $ Wed.	Currency per U.S. $ Tues.
Argentina (Austral) ...	.2857	.2857	3.50	3.50
Australia (Dollar)	.6950	.6970	1.4388	1.4347
Austria (Schilling)	.08460	.08389	11.82	11.92
Belgium (Franc)				
Commercial rate ...	.02831	.02822	35.32	35.44
Financial rate	.02821	.02811	35.45	35.58
Brazil (Cruzado)	.01677	.01695	59.64	59.00
Britain (Pound)	1.7735	1.7665	.5639	.5661
30-Day Forward	1.7709	1.7636	.5647	.5670
90-Day Forward	1.7675	1.7606	.5658	.5680
180-Day Forward	1.7622	1.7552	.5675	.5697
Canada (Dollar)	.7617	.7593	1.3128	1.3170
30-Day Forward	.7609	.7585	1.3143	1.3184
90-Day Forward	.7593	.7570	1.3170	1.3210
180-Day Forward	.7567	.7544	1.3215	1.3255
Chile (Official rate) ...	.004356	.004356	229.55	229.55
China (Yuan)	.2687	.2687	3.722	3.722
Colombia (Peso)	.003877	.003877	257.91	257.91
Denmark (Krone)	.1545	.1533	6.4725	6.5240
Ecuador (Sucre)				
Official rate	.003697	.003697	270.50	270.50
Floating rate	.004843	.004843	206.50	206.50
Finland (Markka)	.2427	.2413	4.1200	4.1435
France (Franc)	.1750	.1748	5.7140	5.7200
30-Day Forward	.1747	.1745	5.7230	5.7292
90-Day Forward	.1743	.1741	5.7380	5.7435
180-Day Forward	.1737	.1735	5.7570	5.7630
Greece (Drachma) ...	.007555	.007524	132.37	132.90
Hong Kong (Dollar) ...	.1282	.1282	7.7960	7.8015
India (Rupee)	.07663	.07675	13.05	13.03
Indonesia (Rupiah) ...	.0006083	.0006083	1644.00	1644.00
Ireland (Punt)	1.5830	1.5710	.6317	.6365
Israel (Shekel)	.6410	.6410	1.5600	1.5600
Italy (Lira)	.0008065	.0008045	1240.00	1243.00
Japan (Yen)	.007386	.007381	135.40	135.48
30-Day Forward	.007406	.007402	135.03	135.09
90-Day Forward	.007448	.007445	134.26	134.32
180-Day Forward	.007506	.007506	133.22	133.23
Jordan (Dinar)	2.8902	2.8902	.346	.346
Kuwait (Dinar)	3.6284	3.6284	.2756	.2756
Lebanon (Pound)	.001980	.001980	505.00	505.00
Malaysia (Ringgit)	.3994	.3994	2.5040	2.5035
Malta (Lira)	3.0912	3.0912	.3235	.3235
Mexico (Peso)				
Floating rate	.0005889	.0005914	1698.00	1691.00
Netherland(Guilder) .	.5273	.5259	1.8965	1.9015
New Zealand (Dollar)	.6205	.6220	1.6116	1.6077
Norway (Krone)	.1560	.1555	6.4110	6.4320
Pakistan (Rupee)	.05701	.05701	17.54	17.54
Peru (Inti)	.05	.05	20.00	20.00
Philippines (Peso)	.04740	.04739	21.10	21.10
Portugal (Escudo)	.007348	.007353	136.10	136.00
Saudi Arabia (Riyal) ..	.2666	.2666	3.751	3.751
Singapore (Dollar)	.4892	.4889	2.0440	2.0455
South Africa (Rand)	♦			
Commercial rate ...	.5010	.5025	1.9960	1.9900
Financial rate	.3088	.3063	3.2383	3.2647
South Korea (Won) ...	.001252	.001251	798.50	798.50
Spain (Peseta)	.008830	.008760	113.25	114.15
Sweden (Krona)	.1649	.1641	6.0650	6.0930
Switzerland (Franc) ..	.7233	.7225	1.3825	1.3840
30-Day Forward	.7258	.7251	1.3777	1.3792
90-Day Forward	.7299	.7291	1.3699	1.3716
180-Day Forward	.7363	.7359	1.3582	1.3589
Taiwan (Dollar)	.03367	.03366	29.70	29.71
Thailand (Baht)	.0393	.0393	25.445	25.445
Turkey (Lira)	.001059	.001059	944.36	944.36
United Arab(Dirham) .	.2723	.2723	3.673	3.673
Uruguay (New Peso)				
Financial	.003820	.003820	261.75	261.75
Venezuela (Bolivar)				
Official rate	.1333	.1333	7.50	7.50
Floating rate	.03198	.03198	31.27	31.27
W. Germany (Mark) .	.5935	.5922	1.6850	1.6885
30-Day Forward	.5952	.5940	1.6801	1.6834
90-Day Forward	.5989	.5978	1.6697	1.6729
180-Day Forward	.6029	.6027	1.6586	1.6592
SDR	1.34305	1.34272	0.744574	0.744759
ECU	1.21488	1.21810		

Special Drawing Rights are based on exchange rates for the U.S., West German, British, French and Japanese currencies. Source: International Monetary Fund.
ECU is based on a basket of community currencies. Source: European Community Commission.
z-Not quoted.

TABLE 4–2

World Value of the Dollar

The table below, compiled by Bank of America, gives the rates of exchange for the U.S. dollar against various currencies as of Wednesday November 18, 1987. Unless otherwise noted, all rates listed are middle rates of interbank bid and asked quotes, and are expressed in foreign currency units per one U.S. dollar. The rates are indicative and aren't based on, nor intended to be used as a basis for, particular transactions.

BankAmerica International doesn't trade in all the listed foreign currencies.

Country (Currency)	Value 11/18	Value 11/11
Afghanistan (Afghani-o)	50.60	50.60
Albania (Lek)	5.737	5.6504
Algeria (Dinar)	4.67	4.67
Andorra (Fr. Franc)	5.7415	5.6565
(Sp. Pesata)	114.26	112.045
Angola (Kwanza)	29.918	29.918
Antigua		
(E. Caribbean $)	2.70	2.70
Argentine (Austral)	3.50	3.50
Aruba (Florin)	1.79	1.79
Australia (Dollar)	1.4457	1.4652
Austria (Schilling)	11.922	11.71
Azores		
(Port. Escudo)	137.00	135.60
Bahamas (Dollar)	1.00	1.00
Bahrain (Dinar)	0.3769	0.3769
Balearic Islands		
(Sp. Pesata)	114.26	112.045
Bangladesh (Taka)	30.93	32.975
Barbados (Dollar)	2.0113	2.0113
Belgium (franc-c)	35.45	34.83
(franc-f)	35.605	34.945
Belize (Dollar)	2.00	2.00
Benin (CFA Franc)	287.075	282.825
Bermuda (Dollar)	1.00	1.00
Bhutan (Ngultrum)	13.03	12.93
Bolivia		
(Boliviano-o)	2.13	2.13
(Boliviano-f)	2.15	2.15
Botswana (Pula)	1.6407	1.601
Brazil (Cruzado-o)	59.157	57.531
Brunei (Dollar)	2.042	2.0445
Bulgaria (Lev)	0.8478	0.8645
Burkina Faso		
(CFA Franc)	287.075	282.825
Burma (Kyat)	6.3954	6.3314
Burundi (Franc)	119.82	118.623
Cameroun Rp		
(CFA Franc)	287.075	282.825
Canada (Dollar)	1.3163	1.3178
Canary Islands		
(Sp. Pesata)	114.26	112.045
Cape Verde Isl		
(Escudo)	72.185	72.185
Cayman Isl (Dollar)	0.835	0.835
Central Africa Rep		
(CFA Franc)	287.075	282.825
Chad (CFA Franc)	287.075	282.825
Chile (Peso-o)	230.08	229.55
China		
(Renminbi Yuan)	3.722	3.722
Colombia (Peso-o)	257.91	257.91
Comoros		
(CFA Franc)	287.075	282.825
Congo, Ppls Rep of		
(CFA Franc)	287.075	282.825
Costa Rica (Colon)	66.75	66.75
Cote d'Ivoire		
(CFA Franc)	287.075	282.825
Cuba (Peso)	0.7333	0.7333
Cyprus (Pound*)	2.1584	2.1887
Czechoslovakia		
(Koruna-o)	5.40	5.40
Denmark (Krone)	6.5223	6.4178
Djibouti, Rp of		
(Franc)	176.83	176.83
Dominica		
(E. Caribbean $)	2.70	2.70
Domin. Rp (Peso)	3.505	3.505
Ecuador (Sucre-d)	290.50	270.50
(Sucre-f)	211.50	206.50
Egypt		
(Pound-o)	0.70	0.70
(Pound-d)	2.2028	2.1927
El Salvador		
(Colon-o)	5.00	5.00
(Colon-f)	5.00	5.00
Eq'tl Guinea		
(CFA Franc)	287.075	282.825
Ethiopia (Birr-o)	2.07	2.07
Faeroe Isl		
(Danish Krone)	6.5223	6.4178
Falkland Islands		
(Pound*)	1.7605	1.7875
Fiji (Dollar)	1.4959	1.497
Finland (Markka)	4.1435	4.0995
France (Franc)	5.7415	5.6565
Fr. C'ty in Af		
(CFA Franc)	287.075	282.825
Fr. Guiana (Franc)	5.7415	5.6565
Fr. Pacific Isl		
(CFP Franc)	104.391	102.845
Gabon (CFA Franc)	287.075	282.825
Gambia (Dalasi)	7.44	7.44
Germany, East		
(Ostmark-o)	1.6948	1.6641
Germany, West		
(Mark)	1.6948	1.6641
Ghana (Cedi)	173.00	173.00
Gibraltar (Pound*)	1.7605	1.7875
Greece (Drachma)	132.88	131.105
Greenland		
(Danish Krone)	6.5223	6.4178
Grenada		
(E. Caribbean $)	2.70	2.70
Guadeloupe (Franc)	5.7415	5.6565
Guam (US $)	1.00	1.00
Guatemala		
(Quetzal-o)	1.00	1.00
(Quetzal-h,i)	2.59	2.585
Guinea Bissau		
(Peso)	650.00	650.00
Guinea Rep (Franc)	340.00	340.00
(Franc-i)	300.00	300.00
Guyana (Dollar)	10.00	10.00
(Dollar-a)	20.00	20.00
Haiti (Gourde)	5.00	5.00
Honduras Rep		
(Lempira-o)	2.00	2.00
Hong Kong (Dollar)	7.797	7.807
Hungary (Forint) (2)	48.352	47.458
Iceland (Krona)	37.26	36.91
India (Rupee)	13.03	12.93
Indonesia (Rupiah)	1650.00	1644.00
Iran (Rial-o)	68.6921	68.0057
Iraq (Dinar)	0.3109	0.3109
Irish Rep (Punt*)	1.5701	1.5598
Israel (New Shekel)	1.57	1.56
Italy (Lira)	1244.65	1227.00
Jamaica (Dollar-o)	5.47	5.47
Japan (Yen)	135.85	134.35
Jordan (Dinar)	0.346	0.346
Kampuchea (Riel) (1)	100.00	100.00
Kenya (Shilling)	16.8626	16.6941
Kiribati		
(Aust Dollar)	1.4457	1.4652
Korea, North (Won)	0.94	0.94
Korea, South (Won)	798.40	798.50
Kuwait (Dinar)	0.2791	0.2756
Laos, Ppls D. Rep		
(Kip)	35.00	35.00
Lebanon (Pound)	495.00	505.00
Lesotho (Maloti)	1.9944	1.9612
Liberia (Dollar)	1.00	1.00
Libya (Dinar)	0.2857	0.2829
Liechtenst'n		
(Sw. Franc)	1.388	1.3636
Luxembourg		
(Lux Franc)	35.45	34.83
Macao (Pataca)	8.0309	8.0412
Madagascar D.R.		
(Franc)	1283.93	1264.92
Maderia		
(Port. Escudo)	137.00	135.60
Malawi (Kwacha)	2.1272	2.1664
Malaysia (Ringgit)	2.5045	2.495
Maldive (Rufiyaa)	10.10	10.10
Mali Rep		
(CFA Franc)	287.075	282.825
Malta (Lira*)	3.0534	3.0912
Martinique (Franc)	5.7415	5.6565
Mauritania		
(Ouguiya)	74.80	74.80
Mauritius (Rupee)	12.5701	12.748
Mexico (Peso-d)	1704.50	1676.50
(Peso-a)	1699.90	1672.30
Miquelon		
(Fr. Franc)	5.7415	5.6565
Monaco (Fr Franc)	5.7415	5.6565
Mongolia (Tugrik-o)	3.3555	3.3555
Montserrat		
(E. Caribbean $)	2.70	2.70
Morocco (Dirham)	7.96	7.88
Mozambique		
(Metical)	404.00	404.00
Namibia (S.A. Rand)	1.9944	1.9612
Nauru Isl		
(Aust Dollar)	1.4457	1.4652
Nepal (Rupee)	21.00	21.00
Netherlands		
(Guilder)	1.9079	1.8725
Neth Ant'les		
(Guilder)	1.79	1.79
New Zealand		
(Dollar)	1.6134	1.6069
Nicaragua		
(Cordoba)	900.00	900.00
(Cordoba-o)	70.00	70.00
(Cordoba-d)	2190.00	2190.00
Niger Rep		
(CFA Franc)	287.075	282.825
Nigeria (Naira-d)	4.3432	4.2989
Norway (Krone)	6.4285	6.3625
Oman, Sultanate of		
(Rial)	0.385	0.385
Pakistan		
(Rupee)	17.5438	17.5438
Panama (Balboa)	1.00	1.00
Papau N.G. (Kina)	0.8933	0.8965
Paraguay		
(Guarani-o)	320.00	320.00
(Guarini-p)	550.00	550.00
(Guarini-d)	877.50	950.00
Peru		
(Inti-o.n)	20.00	20.00
(Inti-f)	41.20	41.62
Philippines (peso)	21.10	21.10
Pitcairn Isl		
(N.Z. Dollar)	1.6134	1.6069
Poland (Zloty-o)	304.00	304.00
Portugal (Escudo)	137.00	135.60
Puerto Rico (US $)	1.00	1.00
Qatar (Riyal)	3.641	3.641
Reunion, Ile de la		
(Fr Franc)	5.7415	5.6565
Romania (Leu-c)	8.73	8.73
Rwanda (Franc)	76.4395	75.6757
St. Christopher		
(E. Caribbean $)	2.70	2.70
St. Helena (Pound*)	1.7605	1.7875
St. Lucia		
(E. Caribbean $)	2.70	2.70
St. Pierre		
(Fr. Franc)	5.7415	5.6565
St. Vincent		
(E. Caribbean $)	2.70	2.70
Samoa, Western		
(Tala)	2.0542	2.0542
Samoa, Am (US $)	1.00	1.00
San Marino (It. Lira)	1244.65	1227.00
Sao Tome & Principe		
(Dobra)	33.6762	33.3397
Saudi Arabia (Riyal)	3.751	3.751
Senegal		
(CFA Franc)	287.075	282.825
Seychelles (Rupeé)	5.3841	5.3303
Sierra Leone		
(Leone)	22.00	22.00
Singapore (Dollar)	2.042	2.0445
Solomon Isl (Dollar)	1.9861	1.996
Somali Rep		
(Shilling-o)	100.00	100.00
South Africa		
(Rand-f)	3.2363	3.3333
(Rand-c)	1.9944	1.9612
Spain (Peseta)	114.26	112.045
Span Ports in N. Afr		
(Sp. Pesata)	114.26	112.045
Sri Lanka (Rupee)	30.493	30.494
Sudan Rep (Pound-o)	4.50	4.50
(Pound-k)	2.93	2.93
(Pound-f)	4.00	4.00
Surinam (Guilder)	1.785	1.785
Swaziland		
(Lilangeni)	1.9944	1.9612
Sweden (Krona)	6.096	6.028
Switzerland		
(Franc)	1.388	1.3636
Syria (Pound-o)	3.925	3.925
Taiwan (Dollar-o)	29.75	29.81
Tanzania (Shilling)	74.2168	74.001
Thailand (Baht)	25.49	25.445
Togo, Rep		
(CFA Franc)	287.075	282.825
Tonga Is/Pa'anga)	1.4457	1.4652
Trinidad & Tobago		
(Dollar)	3.60	3.60
Tunisia (Dinar)	0.797	0.79
Turkey (Lira)	962.30	944.36
Turks & Caicos		
(US $)	1.00	1.00
Tuvalu		
(Aust Dollar)	1.4457	1.4652
Uganda		
(Shilling-l)	59.542	60.488
Utd Arab Emir		
(Dirham)	3.673	3.673
Utd Kingdom		
(Pound Sterling*)	1.7605	1.7875
Uruguay (Peso-m)	260.80	261.75
USSR (Rouble)	0.6115	0.6035
Vanuatu (Vatu)	105.68	104.624
Vatican (Lira)	1244.65	1227.00
Venezuela		
(Bolivar-o)	14.50	14.50
(Bolivar-n)	7.50	7.50
(Bolivar-d)	30.75	31.275
Vietnam (Dong-o)	80.00	80.00
Virgin Is, Br (US$)	1.00	1.00
Virgin Is, US (US$)	1.00	1.00
Yemen (Rial)	10.00	10.00
Yemen PDR (Dinar)	0.343	0.343
Yugoslavia		
(Dinar) (3)	1295.24	1016.84
Zaire Rep		
(Zaire)	126.972	126.458
Zambia (Kwacha)	7.8989	8.1699
Zimbabwe (Dollar)	1.6829	1.6595

U.S. dollars per National Currency unit. (a) Freemarket central bank rate. (b) Floating rate. (c) Commercial rate. (d) Free market rate. (e) Controlled. (f) Financial rate. (g) Preferential rate. (h) Nonessential imports. (i) Floating tourist rate. (j) Public transaction rate. (k) Agricultural products. (l) Priority rate. (m) Market rate. (n) Essential imports. (o) Official rate. (p) Exports. (na) Not available.

(1) Kampuchea, Oct 87: Riel Devalued by approx. 70%. (2) Hungary, 11 Nov 87: Forint devalued by an average 5%. (3) Yugoslavia. 17 Nov 87: Dinar devalued by approx. 24.6%.

Further information available at BankAmerica International.   *Source: Bank of America Global Trading, London.*

flat (also termed *outright*) or in points *premium* or *discount,* which must be added to or subtracted from the spot rate. Outright rates are given to retail customers. The quotes in terms of points of discount or premium are used by traders in the interbank market.

Both spot and forward foreign exchange rates are published daily in financial papers such as *The Wall Street Journal* in the United States and the *Financial Times* in London. The published rates, however, are not offers to trade. They are only indicative rates. The bank's FX traders need to be contacted directly to obtain a firm quote.

The spot and forward rates on November 18, 1987, for the British pound and the Swiss franc published in *The Wall Street Journal* were as follows:

	U.S. $ Equivalent	
	British (pound)	*Swiss (franc)*
Spot	1.7735	.7233
30-day forward	1.7709	.7258
90-day forward	1.7675	.7299
180-day forward	1.7622	.7363

The 90-day forward rate for the pound is quoted at a discount of 60 points (1.7735 − 1.7675). The Swiss franc 90-day forward rate is quoted at a premium of 66 points (.7233 − .7299).

A foreign currency is at a forward discount when the forward price is lower than the spot price. The opposite is true in the case of a forward premium. The forward discount of the British pound reflects the judgment of the market that the spot rate in 90 days will be lower. The Swiss franc premium reflects the market judgment that the spot rate will increase in 90 days.

Forward discounts and premiums are quoted in terms of percentage per annum (p. a.) as well as in points. The 90-day forward rate for the British pound is at a discount of 1.35 percent per annum. The formula for calculating discount or premium is as follows:

$$\frac{\text{Forward rate} - \text{Spot rate}}{\text{Spot rate}} \times \frac{12}{\text{Number of months forward}} = \begin{array}{l}\text{Premium or}\\\text{discount as}\\\text{percent p. a.}\end{array}$$

Applying the formula to the 90-day quote for British pounds in Table 4–1:

$$\frac{1.7675 - 1.7735}{1.7735} \times \frac{12}{3} = -.0135 = 1.35\% \text{ p. a. discount}$$

FOREIGN EXCHANGE TRANSACTIONS

Transactions for immediate delivery are relatively simple. Travelers going abroad will exchange their national currency at a bank or foreign exchange dealer for the currency of the country they intend to visit at the spot rate on the date of the transaction. In a typical spot business transaction, a U.S. firm arranging for an immediate payment of £100,000 to another firm in London would pay its U.S. bank about $177,350 (as of November 18, 1987) and the U.S. bank would notify its correspondent bank in London to credit the equivalent amount (£100,000) to the account of the London firm. However, many (if not most) international business transactions have a time dimension that may dictate the use of the forward markets.

Hedging

Hedging involves entering into a contract at the present time to buy or sell foreign exchange at a specified price on a given future date. Goods and services are usually paid for in the currency of the seller, but a different currency of payment can be agreed upon by the buyer and seller. If a U.S. importing firm (the buyer) knows that it must take delivery on goods valued at 200,000 DM from West Germany in six months, the U.S. firm is certain that it will have to deliver 200,000 DM on that date. What the firm does not know is the "price" of DMs—that is, the exchange rate that will prevail at that future data and how many U.S. dollars will be required to make payment.

The U.S. importer can be sure of the cost by entering into a forward contract with a bank for delivery of those DMs in 180 days. As shown in Table 4–1, the 180-day forward rate for West German marks was $0.6029, so the dollar price for DM 200,000 would be $120,580. There should be no transaction costs because the bank makes its profit through the margin between buying and selling rates. The importer has now *hedged* or *covered* its foreign exchange exposure. Whether the spot rate is higher or lower in six months, the importer knows what the U.S. price of the goods will be.

The commercial bank that agrees to supply the foreign exchange in the future will simultaneously make arrangements for an offsetting future purchase of foreign exchange from an exporter. By matching forward purchases with foreign sales, the bank eliminates its risk and avoids "taking a position" in foreign exchange. If the bank does not match its forward sales and purchase commitments of a specific currency, it is taking an uncovered position and speculating on the future of the currency.

An alternative hedge involves the use of foreign exchange futures contracts available on the International Monetary Market or even a foreign exchange futures option. However, these are available only for a small number of currencies.

The importer has several alternatives other than a forward market hedge. The firm can buy DMs immediately at the spot rate and hold them for six months until payment is due. At the spot rate of US$0.5935 the DM 200,000 will cost $118,700, thus saving $1,880 compared to the six-month forward rate. This gain of about 3.2 percent on an annual basis, however, must be balanced against the opportunity cost, or what might have been earned with the dollars, during the six-month period. Of course, the importer can deposit the DMs in Germany to earn interest during the six-month period (i.e., use a money market hedge).

But as will be discussed below, interest rate differentials are generally the reverse of the discounts or premiums on foreign exchange forward rates; and the importer is likely to earn about 3.2 percent less on DMs deposited in Germany than on U.S. dollars deposited in the United States. In other words, the results of the forward market and money market hedges are likely to be the same.

Another possibility is to do nothing at this time and wait six months to buy the DMs at whatever spot rate prevails at that time. This option makes the firm a speculator in foreign exchange and may result in a gain or a loss against using a forward contract. Using a forward contract means that the cost of the goods to the importer will be $1,880 more than today's price, but the cost is certain and can be passed along when the goods are distributed in the United States.

Unfortunately, managers cannot always arrange a hedge. Forward markets do not exist for many currencies, and even where they exist the supply of forward contracts may be inadequate, or contracts may be unavailable for the precise period of time for which the cover is needed. Where hedging opportunities exist, the hedging mechanism to reduce the risk resulting from exchange rate fluctuations may be applied to a variety of international business purposes, such as protecting the value of foreign direct investments and portfolio investments. Other uses will be discussed in greater detail in the chapter on multinational financial management. In fact, virtually anyone who deals in or with foreign currencies may have a need for the hedging mechanism.

Covered Interest Arbitrage

Arbitrage is the simultaneous purchase and sale of an item in different markets to profit from unwarranted differences in prices. Arbitrage occurs in foreign exchange markets as well as in domestic securities and commodities markets. In a free market, a good such as money should have the same price wherever traded. Thus, interest rates should be the same around the world. Yet, as shown in Table 4–3, interest rates for loans or securities of similar risk and maturity vary among nations.

According to the theory of interest rate parity, the differences in interest rates should be equal but opposite in sign to the forward exchange rate premium or discount between currencies. Where an imparity exists between the various interest rates and forward rate structures, interest rate arbitragers will be attracted to these situations, and the process of arbitrage will bring these markets into parity. The arbitrager who seeks out the highest rates will always hedge in the forward market. Such capital flows are therefore "covered" or hedged arbitrage, rather than pure speculation.

As an example of covered interest arbitrage, let us assume that U.K. Treasury bills with three-month maturity are selling to yield investors 10 percent per annum, whereas comparable U.S. Treasury bills yield 6.8 percent. Under the interest parity theory and in normal markets, the forward discount rate of the pound would be 3.2 percent per annum. Thus an imparity exists because the 90-day

TABLE 4–3 Commercial Bank Lending Rates to Prime Borrowers (at or near end of month)

	1984 December	1985 December	1986 December	1987 July
United States	10.75	9.50	7.50	8.25
Canada	11.25	10.00	9.75	9.50
Austria	9.25	9.00	9.00	8.50
Belgium	14.00	11.50	9.75	8.75
Denmark	10.50	8.50	8.00	9.50
Finland	10.68	10.37	8.81	8.93
France	12.00	10.60	9.45	9.45
Germany	7.75	7.25	6.75	6.25
Ireland	15.75	12.50	15.75	12.75
Italy	18.00	15.88	13.00	12.50
Netherlands	6.25	6.25	7.12	5.62
Norway	13.00	12.40	n.a.	n.a.
Portugal	29.00	22.50	17.50	19.50
Spain	15.84	14.75	14.22	16.62
Sweden	14.50	15.05	11.50	11.50
Switzerland	6.00	6.00	5.75	5.00
United Kingdom	9.50	11.50	11.00	9.00
Australia	14.00	21.00	18.50	15.75
Japan	5.50	5.50	3.75	3.37
New Zealand	14.00	21.00	18.50	21.00
South Africa	24.00	16.50	12.00	12.50
Argentina*	32.05	7.30	11.30	13.20
Brazil†	31.00	19.00	250.00	n.a.
Chile	60.82	33.34	29.13	27.11
Hong Kong	11.00	7.00	6.50	7.50
Indonesia	23.50	18.75	19.75	26.00
Korea	10.00	10.00	10.00	10.00
Malaysia	12.00	10.50	10.00	7.25
Mexico	47.54	65.66	95.33	92.91
Philippines	44.00	15.00	10.50	n.a.
Singapore	9.40	7.20	6.10	6.10
Taiwan	10.00	9.50	9.00	9.00
Thailand	16.50	15.50	12.00	n.a.
Venezuela	16.00	13.00	13.00	13.00

* Percent per month.

† Spread above monetary correction until February 1986; nominal rate of interest until January 1987; spread above LBC thereafter.

SOURCE: Morgan Guaranty Trust Company, *World Financial Markets*, September–October 1987, p. 23.

discount rate for the pound, as calculated above, is 1.35 percent instead of 3.2 percent per annum. An opportunity exists, therefore, for taking advantage of the higher U.K. interest rates without risk of losing the higher interest through foreign exchange fluctuations.

The arbitrager in New York would buy British pounds for U.S. dollars at the spot rate and simultaneously cover the exchange exposure by entering into a three-month forward contract to sell pounds in the amount of principal and interest. Then the arbitrager would purchase U.K. treasury bills in England, wait 90 days for maturity, collect principal and interest, and deliver the pounds for dollars in fulfillment of the forward contract. On an annual basis, these funds earned a return of 8.6 percent as compared to the 6.8 percent that could have been earned on U.S. treasury bills.

The price discrepancies that create arbitrage opportunities are generally small and disappear quickly.[6] Consequently, only active participants in the markets are in a position to recognize and exploit the fleeting opportunities.

Swapping Currencies

Swap transactions represent a major part of the forward foreign exchange markets. A *swap transaction* in the interbank market is a combination of a spot deal with a reverse deal at some future date. Both transactions are usually between the same two banks. A common type of swap is "spot against forward."[7] Bank A buys a currency in the spot market and simultaneously sells the same amount in the forward market to the same bank. The difference between the spot and the forward rates, called the *swap rate,* is known and fixed.

Swaps are popular with banks because it is difficult to avoid risk when trading in many specific future dates and in many currencies. On some days, for example, a bank will be "long" in British pounds because it has purchased more than it has agreed to sell or already holds more than it wants. The bank can seek out another bank with a reverse position and make a swap. Bank A will sell pounds spot and buy pounds forward. Bank B will do the opposite. Thus both banks can balance their spot versus their forward positions while economizing on the number of transactions to achieve this.

Currency swaps between multinational companies, rather than banks, are frequently used both as a hedge and as a means of securing overseas financing. The swaps may be bilateral or multilateral. They may be simple or spectacularly complex (see Box 4–1). As a relatively simple example, a French company may have a Brazilian subsidiary that needs more local currency for expansion. Through an investment bank or a broker, the French company locates a British firm whose Brazilian subsidiary has surplus domestic currency. The French company makes the swap by buying the the Brazilian cruzados from the British company and simultaneously entering into an agreement to reverse the sale at some future date. Nominal interest rates are agreed upon at the outset.

The swap is a hedge in the sense that a foreign currency liability is matched by a similar foreign currency asset. Furthermore, neither loan requires the approval of any government agency; and the cost of funds can be cheaper than funds

---

[6] John L. Hilley, Carl R. Beidleman, and James A. Greenleaf, "Does Covered Interest Arbitrage Dominate in Foreign Exchange Markets?" *Columbia Journal of World Business,* Winter 1979, pp. 99–107.

[7] For a discussion of the many kinds and uses of swaps see Carl R. Beidleman, *Financial Swaps: New Strategies in Currency & Coupon Risk Management* (Homewood, Ill.: Dow Jones-Irwin, 1985.)

BOX 4–1
The New Game of Swaps

A major Fortune 500 corporation recently sought ideas on providing some $80 million of funding for subsidiaries in four European countries. Morgan's international funding experts, including swap teams in New York and London, quickly structured an innovative cost-effective package involving a bond issue plus 13 swaps.

Arranging the Deal

First we identified the least expensive dollar source of funding for the company—a dollar-yen dual-currency issue. This involved a then relatively new bond structure with interest paid in yen and principal in dollars.

Then we tapped our knowledge of worldwide markets to swap the dual currency-bond cash flows into variable rate financing, and finally we executed swap contracts to generate the Deutschemarks, French francs, Belgian francs, and Dutch guilders that the subsidiaries needed. The transaction involved seven currencies and nine counterparties in five countries and was completed in less than three weeks.

The result: an estimated savings to the client of about ⅜ percent per year and tighter control over its long-term risk.

SOURCE: Adapted from an advertisement by The Morgan Bank in *The New York Times*, Wednesday, April 2, 1986.

---

from alternative sources. Also, the swap may be one of the few sources open to nonresident companies for securing the use of foreign exchange over a period of time at a fixed rate.

Credit Swaps.   *Credit swaps* have become widely used, particularly where local credit is not available and where there is no forward exchange market. A credit swap is an exchange of currencies between a company and a bank (frequently a central bank) of a foreign country which is to be reversed by agreement at a later date. Such credit swaps have been common in Brazil. A U.S. firm may deposit U.S. dollars with the Central Bank of Brazil and receive cruzados at the prevailing official rate. Although the cruzado may fall in value in relation to the U.S. dollar, the U.S. firm is obligated to repay only the cruzado amount it originally received. After payment, the original deposit in U.S. dollars will be returned.

Why should the two parties engage in such a transaction? The motive of the Central Bank is that it has use of the U.S. dollars interest-free. The U.S. firm has the advantage that it recovers the original dollar principal regardless of what happens to the value of the cruzado during the period of the arrangement. The basic attraction of the credit swap is the ability to minimize the risk and the cost of financing operations in a weak-currency country.

Outright Speculation

Foreign exchange transactions by business firms are generally motivated by the desire to reduce risk. If risk is deliberately undertaken, the participant is a speculator, and foreign exchange markets—as is also true of commodity, interest futures, and other markets—provide a mechanism for outright speculation. Firms or individuals that have an established relationship with a commercial bank may be able to execute speculative transactions through the bank's foreign exchange department. Other speculators generally use the futures markets such as the IMM or the currency options markets. The futures markets allow participants to operate on margin—that is, without depositing the full value of the transaction. The currency options market requires the payment of a fee that may vary from 1 to 5 percent of the value of the contract.

Whichever market is used, if the foreign currency is expected to appreciate against the local currency (say, U.S. dollars), the speculator will want to buy the foreign currency or a *call* (i.e., go long). Conversely, if the expectation is that the foreign currency will depreciate, the speculator will want to sell the foreign currency or a *put* (i.e., go short).

THE ACTORS

Most of the principal actors or participants in the foreign exchange markets have already been mentioned. The importer or exporter uses the markets to convert currencies and to reduce the risk of foreign exchange fluctuations as they affect accounts receivable or payable. Firms engaged in multinational operations use the markets for trade-related transactions, for meeting foreign exchange needs related to takeovers and acquisitions of foreign entities, to hedge money flows such as expected repatriation of foreign currency profits, and to reduce the risk of devaluation affecting assets held in foreign currencies. Business firms also engage in covered interest arbitrage to increase earnings on liquid funds. Nonbank financial institutions—such as securities firms—use the markets to provide foreign exchange services related to securities transactions such as international portfolio diversification.[8] Still another set of actors are the foreign exchange arbitragers and speculators.

Commercial banks actually make the foreign exchange market by trading on behalf of commercial business clients and nonbank financial institutions. Over recent years, a growing number of U.S. banks have also become active participants in the market on their own account to take advantage of the profit opportunities perceived in fluctuating exchange rates. After the failure of the German Herstatt

---

[8] See Cheol S. Eun and Bruce G. Resnick, "Currently Factors in International Portfolio Diversification," *Columbia Journal of World Business,* Summer 1985, pp. 45–53; Michael Adler and Bernard Dumas, "International Portfolio Choice and Corporation Finance: A Synthesis," *Journal of Finance,* June 1983, pp. 925–84.

bank in 1974, attributed to foreign exchange speculation,[9] many European countries imposed restrictions on foreign exchange transactions by banks. But U.S. authorities resisted the imposition of official controls despite a similar failure in 1974 of a large U.S. bank. Most U.S. banks, however, have internal controls that involve close daily and even hourly supervision of the traders to minimize losses (see Box 4–2).

The other major participants are the central banks of countries. These government institutions frequently intervene in the foreign exchange markets to smooth fluctuations and for reasons of government policy. The banks may want to keep the discount or premium on their currency within a certain range and may sell or buy currencies to achieve this goal. They may intervene independently or in cooperation with one other. For example, in the three months ended April 30, 1980, the world's central banks intervened in foreign exchange markets to support the international value of the dollar with a near-record of purchases and sales totaling $37 billion. By 1985, the reverse problem had become acute; and the central banks of the major industrial countries made a coordinated effort to reduce the value of the dollar, which had appreciated steadily since 1980 by some 65 percent against other major currencies. A first effort in early 1985 with a combined intervention of substantially more than $5 billion had little effect; but another concerted intervention later in the year, accompanied by an agreement for greater consistency in economic policies, resulted in a significant depreciation in the international value of the dollar.

Central banks on occasion offer large swap facilities to each other on a

---

BOX 4–2
Fuji Bank—Too Far Forward

Tokyo—In little more than two years, Japan's two biggest banks have both blushingly had to admit that foreign exchange dealers in their foreign branches have lost them billions of yen from unauthorized dealings. On November 7, Fuji Bank revealed that its New York foreign-exchange dealer lost ¥11.5 billion ($47.9 million) this summer when he bet that the dollar would crash against the yen. After keeping his losses secret for three months, he was fired. Fuji's board of directors all have taken a 20 percent pay cut for the next six months to demonstrate their shame.

In September 1982, Dai-Ichi Kangyo Bank, the country's biggest, revealed that a dealer in its Singapore branch had lost the bank ¥9.7 billion between 1978 and 1982 through unauthorized speculation against the dollar. He was dismissed and the bank's deputy president publicly apologized for the bank's shortcomings.

SOURCE: Adapted from *The Economist*, November 10, 1984, pp. 93–94.

---

[9] Robert Z. Aliber, "International Banking: Growth and Regulation," *Columbia Journal of World Business*, Winter 1975, pp. 9–16.

formal or ad hoc basis; that is, banks agree to lend their currencies to each other with the understanding that the original transactions will later be reversed. In this fashion, one central bank obtains large amounts of another country's currency.

FORECASTING FOREIGN EXCHANGE RATES

Are changes in exchange rates predictable on a relatively consistent basis? With fluctuating exchange rates a major cause of uncertainty in international business (see Figure 4–2), this question is extremely important for international business participants.

It is an important issue, also, for government officials who have decision responsibility for intervening in foreign exchange markets and for many trade and monetary policies related to expected future exchange rates. It is not surprising, therefore, that foreign exchange rate analysis has become a major growth industry

FIGURE 4–2   Effective Exchange Rates of Selected Currencies, 1980–87 (monthly averages, June 1980 = 100)

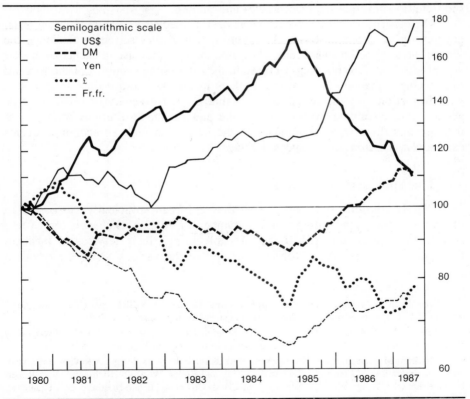

SOURCE: Bank for International Settlements, *Fifty-Seventh Annual Report,* June 15, 1987, p. 158.

in recent years. While a completely satisfactory and workable model of exchange rate dynamics has yet to be developed, the various theoretical and empirical studies have yielded greater understanding of the forces that influence exchange rate movements.[10]

The Efficient Market View

Easily accessible forecasts of future foreign exchange rates are the forward rates quoted in the foreign exchange markets. Such forecasts, however, are generally available only for the major currencies and for future periods of one year or less. The efficient market view argues that these forward rates are "unbiased" predictors of future spot rates and that exchange rate forecasting cannot consistently beat the market forecasts.

An efficient market is defined as one where prices fully reflect all available information. If competition exists and transaction costs are low, prices tend to respond rapidly to new information, and speculation opportunities are quickly bid away. *Unbiased* does not mean that the predictions are accurate in any specific situation but that the predictions are not *consistently* above or below the future spot rate; in sum, that the inaccuracies are random.

The efficient market hypothesis has been subjected to many empirical tests, but with inconclusive results.[11] The more recent studies seriously challenge the view of an unbiased forward rate. They also show an increase in exchange market volatility and a corresponding decrease in the forecasting accuracy of the forward rate.[12] One explanation is that the markets in the short run do not fully reflect *all* information. Another explanation is that a great diversity of opinion exists about future economic events; and public and private institutions often act to increase this diversity of opinion, with the result that realized economic events can be very far from their expected values.

The Forecasting Services

Clearly, the efficient market view has not been sufficiently persuasive to discourage forecasting efforts; and a number of foreign exchange forecasting services have been established that are able to sell their services to business firms and investors. The performance record of the various services has varied

---

[10] See Sven W. Arndt, Richard J. Sweeney, and Thomas D. Willett, eds., *Exchange Rates and the U.S. Economy* (Cambridge, Mass.: Ballinger Publishing Company, 1985).

[11] Steven W. Kohlhagen, *The Behavior of Foreign Exchange Markets: A Critical Review of the Empirical Literature* (New York: N.Y.U. Series in Finance and Economics, 1978).

[12] Richard M. Levich, "The Efficiency of Markets for Foreign Exchange: A Review and Extension," in *International Finance,* ed. Gerald D. Gay and Robert W. Kolb (Richmond, Va.: Robert F. Dane, Inc., 1983), pp. 397–428. See also Jean-Claude Cosset and Bruno Doutraixux de la Rianderie, "Political Risk and Foreign Exchange Rates: An Efficient-Markets Approach," *Journal of International Business Studies,* Fall 1985, pp. 21–55.

in accuracy over time and by specific currencies. An analysis of the forecasts of 12 major forecasting services over the five-year period 1978–82 concluded that the forecasters in general had not displayed expertise.[13]

The forecasting services use two types of forecasting techniques: judgmental and econometric models. The judgmental forecasters make projections based on a detailed analysis of the economies of individual countries. They analyze economic indicators such as trade data and gross national product; political factors such as a forthcoming national election; technical factors such as potential intervention by the central bank, and psychological factors that might be called "a feel for the market."

The econometric modelers use equation-based forecasts with some judgment overlay. Specific models have been developed for individual countries that attempt to incorporate the fundamental forces on which exchange rates depend: inflation, industrial production, trade flows, and capital flows. The method is equation based, with judgment coming in when the results of the equation appear to be unreasonable.

Economic Theories of Exchange-Rate Determination

In considering the issue of foreign exchange forecasting, the international manager will find useful a familiarity with the basic economic theories that relate to exchange-rate determination. These include the purchasing power parity, the monetary model, interest rate parity, and the portfolio balance approach.

The theory of purchasing power parity (PPP) focuses on differences in inflation rates between countries as a principal explanation of exchange rate movements. Broadly stated, PPP implies that differences between two countries in rates of inflation tend to be offset by opposite changes in the spot rate. In other words, the currency of the country with the higher rate of inflation will tend to depreciate to compensate for the loss in purchasing power. Thus, if the United Kingdom is experiencing a higher rate of inflation than the United States, the PPP theory predicts that the pound sterling will decrease in value relative to the U.S. dollar to keep purchasing power equal in the two currencies. On this premise all that is needed to forecast exchange rate changes is a forecast of comparative inflation rates.

As in the case of the efficient market hypothesis, many empirical attempts have been made to test the PPP theory. Probably the most widely accepted view emerging from these studies is that prices and exchange rates are eventually, but not immediately, offsetting.[14] Other dynamic forces in the market (such as political developments) can cause extensive variations from PPP projections. Also,

---

[13] Richard M. Levich, "Currency Forecasters Lose Their Way," *Euromoney*, August 1983, p. 140. *Euromoney* usually has one article each year in its August issue reviewing and evaluating the foreign exchange forecasting services.

[14] Charles Pigott and Richard J. Sweeney, "Purchasing Power Parity and Exchange Rate Dynamics," in Arndt et al, *Exchange Rates*, p. 73.

access to the appropriate price indexes—those of internationally traded goods and services—are not always available. Thus, while PPP is useful for understanding long term movements in spot rates, it has definite limitations over the short term.[15] (See Box 4–3.)

The theory of interest-rate parity states that except for transaction costs a difference in national interest rates for securities of similar risk and maturity should be equal but opposite in sign to the forward exchange-rate discount or premium for the foreign currency. The rationale of this theory is that covered interest arbitrage will eliminate interest-rate differentials between equivalent interest-bearing securities denominated in different currencies.

The monetary approach argues that the exchange rate between two currencies is determined on the whole by the relative money supplies, money velocities—the frequency with which the currencies change hands over a certain period—and levels of real income in the countries involved.[16] The expectation is that the exchange rate will move against the country with the higher rate of money supply expansion. In the country with the greater increase in money supply relative to demand, inflationary expectations will increase and be reflected in higher interest rates. The higher inflationary expectations will cause the currency to depreciate because people become less willing to hold domestic currencies. This result runs directly counter to the interest-rate parity theory where interest rate increases are mirrored by currency appreciation.

Both the monetary and interest-parity approaches have been tested in empirical studies, but there does not appear to be a strong simple relationship of either sign between interest rate and foreign exchange changes. The reason for this may be that interest rate changes may result from different factors. If the change in the nominal rate of interest reflects a change in the *real* (the nominal minus the expected rate of inflation) rate of interest, as a result of a tightening of monetary policy, we would expect the currency to appreciate. If the rise in the nominal rate of interest reflects an increase in the expected rate of inflation, we would expect higher interest rates to be accompanied by a falling currency.[17]

Still another approach is the portfolio balance model.[18] This view argues that a country's exchange rate is determined by the relative supply and demand for financial assets denominated in different currencies. It assumes that domestic and foreign securities identical in maturity, taxability, and default risk have different degrees of foreign exchange risk because of their currency composition. Currencies

---

[15] See Michael Melvin, *International Money and Finance* (New York: Harper and Row, 1985), pp. 74–90: Allan M. Loosigian, *Foreign Exchange Futures* (Homewood, Ill.: Dow Jones-Irwin, 1981), pp. 118–40.

[16] See John F. O. Bilson, "The Monetary Approach to the Exchange Rate: Some Empirical Evidence," *IMF Staff Papers,* March 1978, pp. 47–75.

[17] See Waseem Kahn and Thomas D. Willet, "The Monetary Approach to Exchange Rates: A Review of Recent Empirical Studies," *Kredit and Kapital,* January 1984, pp. 199–200.

[18] Michael P. Dooley and Peter Isard, "The Portfolio-Balance Model of Exchange Rates and Some Structural Estimates of the Risk Premium," *Staff Papers* 30, (December 1983), pp. 1161–76.

BOX 4–3
Hamburger Parity

Remember the McDonald's hamburger standard which *The Economist* launched last year? We offered it as a rough and ready guide to whether currencies are at their "correct" exchange rates. It is based on the idea that exchange rates should produce purchasing-power parity (PPP)—i.e., they should equate the prices of similar goods (in this case, a Big Mac) bought in different countries.

Following the EMS realignment. Big-Mac watchers want to know the Mac-PPP cross-rates for the D-mark against other member currencies. In Cologne, for instance, a Big Mac costs DM4.10; in Paris, FFr17.40. Dividing the franc price by the D-mark price gives a Mac-PPP of FFr4.24. This week, the D-mark was trading at FFr3.34. Conclusion: on Mac-PPP grounds, the D-mark is 21% under-valued against the French franc.

The D-mark appears to be undervalued against the Belgium franc, the Danish krone and the Italian lira (see table). It looks about right against the Dutch guilder, but it is 28% overvalued against the Irish Punt. The table also shows the Mac-PPPS for the D-mark against the dollar and sterling. Evidently, both have been heavily oversold: the D-mark rate is 36% overvalued against the dollar and 29% against the pound. Britain should join the EMS at once—and go in at a super-competitive rate.

Big MacCurrencies
Hamburger prices

Country	Price* in local currency	Implied† purchasing power parity of the D-mark	Latest exchange rate	% over (+) or under (-) valuation of the D-mark
Britain	£ 1·13	0·28	0·36	+29
United States	$ 1·60	0·39	0·53	+36
Belgium	BFr 90	21·95	20·74	-6
Denmark	DKr 21·50	5·24	3·81	-27
France	FFr 17·40	4·24	3·34	-21
Holland	Fl 4·50	1·10	1·13	+3
Ireland	IR£ 1·18	0·29	0·37	+28
Italy	Lire 3,300	805	711	-12
West Germany	DM 4·10	-	-	-

* Prices may vary slightly between branches.
† Foreign price divided by D-mark price.
SOURCE: McDonald's.

SOURCE: *The Economist,* January 17, 1987.

that are seen to have a higher risk must pay a higher return in interest rates. A wide variety of factors—such as government policies—can change the risk expectations and investor preferences, causing exchange rates to change.

The virtue of the portfolio approach is that it relates the complex interactions among financial markets to the foreign markets. At the same time, it does not provide a clear identification of which factors will or will not change investor expectations and thereby affect exchange rates.

While there is much merit in the various economic theories, any simple formula is doomed to failure in an imperfect and changing world. No single theory will determine the movement of a currency. This does not mean that PPP, for example, is not a useful long-term equilibrium model or that a more complex model cannot be a useful forecasting tool. But the forecaster in international business cannot avoid the multiplicity of noneconomic as well as economic factors that might determine exchange-rate changes (see Box 4–4).

While economic analysis can suggest what an exchange rate should be at any point in time, few governments allow their exchange rates to fluctuate freely. In most cases the decision to let exchange rates fluctuate without intervention will be influenced by a variety of local political, bureaucratic, and social pressures. Consequently, for short-term forecasting, the analyst must also become familiar with the views and behavior patterns of government decision makers. Forecasting involves timing of changes as well as amounts. And timing is extremely important because the cost of hedging against foreign exchange risk is high and increases with the time for which the cover is sought.

BOX 4–4
The Secret to Foreign Exchange Forecasting?

"So there is a wide range of trading theories from which to choose, both fundamental and technical. Of course, we want to know how we find the best method. If I knew for certain I wouldn't bother to write this book. I would have retired on the proceeds."

SOURCE: Julian Walmsley, *The Foreign Exchange Handbook* (New York: John Wiley & Sons, 1983), p. 194.

"A dynamic model of price and exchange rate dynamics in which the nominal exchange rate is a freely flexible variable whose value at each instant of time must be consistent with money market equilibrium, interest rate parity, and rationality of expectations concerning the future change of the exchange rate, and in which the domestic price level is a slowly adjusting variable that responds gradually to the extent of disequilibrium as measured by the existing deviation from purchasing power parity, as well as the expected rate of change of its own equilibrium value."

SOURCE: Michael L. Mussa, "Official Intervention and Exchange Rate Dynamics," in *Exchange Rate Management Under Uncertainty,* ed. Jagdeep S. Bhandari (Cambridge, Mass.: MIT Press, 1985), p. 1.

THE INTERNATIONAL MONEY MARKET

A firm may avoid foreign exchange risk by insisting that all of its transactions be denominated in its home-country currency. In this way, the firm can be sure that its money inflows and outflows will not fluctuate with changes in foreign rates. When a firm's home-country currency is one of the major convertible currencies, parties dealing with the firm can secure the currency through the international money markets.

The international money market parallels the foreign exchange market. It is located in the same centers as its foreign exchange counterpart. The market operates only in those currencies for which forward exchange markets exist and that are easily convertible and available in sufficient quantity. In the relatively few currencies in which it is operative, the international money market channels money in and out of domestic markets. Regulations permitting, it also acts as a provider and user of funds for many parties that normally might not be involved in foreign exchange. These include governments and corporations looking for long-term financing, and individual investors whose opportunities are severely constrained in the local national market.

Eurocurrency Markets

The principal international money market is the Eurocurrency market. Eurocurrencies are monies traded outside the country of their origin. Eurodollars are U.S. dollar deposits at either non-U.S. banks or branches of U.S. banks located outside the United States. Eurosterlings are sterling deposits outside the United Kingdom. Other Eurocurrencies are West German marks, Swiss francs, Dutch guilders, Japanese yen, and French francs. They all share the Eurodollar's main characteristic. They are national currencies deposited outside their own borders.

The Eurodollar was the first of the Eurocurrencies and is still much the largest, accounting for almost 70 percent of international banking in Eurocurrencies and more than 40 percent of recent Eurobond issues.[19] As its name implies, the Eurodollar was originally U.S. dollar held in Europe; the *Euro* prefix has been subsequently attached to other currencies, even though the Euromarket no longer is exclusively in Europe. In addition to Europe, financial institutions in the Bahamas, Bahrain, Canada, Cayman Islands, Hong Kong, Japan, Netherland Antilles, Panama, Singapore, and the international banking facilities (IBFs) of U.S. banks (referred to as *offshore banking*) deal in Eurocurrencies.

There are three basic parts to the Euromarkets: the Eurocurrency market, the Eurobond market, and the Euro-commercial paper market. The Eurocurrency market deals with bank deposits and bank credits of generally short-term or medium-term maturities. Eurobonds are long-term debt instruments—normally 10 or 20 year maturities—that are issued and sold outside the country of the currency in

---

[19] Morgan Guaranty Trust Company, *World Financial Markets,* September–October 1987, pp. 17–18.

which they are denominated. Euro-commercial paper likewise is issued outside the country whose currency is used to denominate the issue.

The Eurocurrency market is the oldest and most important element of the Euromarkets. Over the 1970–80 decade, the estimated size of the Eurocurrency market expanded more than thirteenfold and since 1980 doubled to an estimated $2,000 billion in 1987. The Eurobond market, measured by the value of new issues, expanded from $3 billion to $24 billion annually over the 1970–80 decade, and accelerated by the mid-1980s to an annual value of $226 billion in new issues during 1986. The Euro-commercial paper market, for which statistics are not available, is less significant than the Eurocurrency and Eurobond market.

In the Eurocurrency market, bank credits usually carry a rate of interest tied by convention to LIBOR (the London interbank offer rate). The actual rate is often a margin over LIBOR, the amount of the spread reflecting the credit rating of the borrower. The market is partly an interbank market and partly a market for loans to corporations and to governments.[20] Many developing countries have borrowed in the Eurocurrency market rather than from the International Monetary Fund because, as discussed in the next chapter, the IMF generally imposes stringent economic conditions to be fulfilled by borrowers.

The Eurobond market provides an alternative source of funds for the borrower who wishes to avoid the regulation and expenses of floating the bonds in a domestic market. It can also assist in foreign exchange risk management by arranging for liabilities to be denominated in any of the major currencies (see Box 4–1 in the section on swaps). Eurobonds require no registration. They are usually bearer bonds—that is, not registered in anyone's name—which may have advantages in avoiding taxes. In general, the same currencies dominate in the Eurobond market as in the Eurocurrency market.

Why do these markets exist? The simple answer is government regulations. Euromarkets are almost totally free of control by national governments, international agencies, or even a self-policing association of participants. In contrast, national governments have imposed a host of restrictions on domestic banking, including interest rate ceilings, reserve requirements, taxes, and the like. These restrictions involve a cost in time and money and have caused both lenders and borrowers to seek out more attractive terms in the offshore markets.

Paradoxically, the Soviet Union gets credit for accidently starting what is now characterized as the biggest and most efficient form of capitalist finance. At the height of the Cold War in the mid- and late 1950s, the Soviet Union wanted to maintain international reserves in dollars, but not in U.S. banks, for fear that their dollars would be frozen by the U.S. government. The Soviets persuaded European banks to accept the dollar balances, and the Europeans began lending dollars to other banks and to borrowers.

These events demonstrated the feasibility of avoiding national controls by keeping a currency in a bank outside of its country of origin, and the market

---

[20] See Christopher M. Korth, "The Eurocurrency Market," in Baughn and Mandich, eds., *Handbook,* pp. 16–34.

expanded rapidly after 1963 as other parties gradually discovered this method of securing higher yields and less restricted borrowing. In a relatively short time, the Eurocurrency market became a form of financial intermediation that has attracted depositors and borrowers away from purely domestic financial institutions.

The concept of an unregulated interbank deposit market in an international financial center is not new. What is historically unique is the extent to which the Euromarkets have become a critical structural element for hundreds of banks throughout the world, most of whom did no business outside their borders until the late 1960s. The reason is that the modern Eurocurrency market represents a highly efficient response by international banks both to investors seeking high-yielding, safe, and liquid investments and to business firms and governments looking for low-cost funds with a high degree of assured availability.

The rapid growth of the Eurocurrency market has made it the focus of controversy as to the wisdom of imposing some sort of controls. Its mammoth size, its rate of growth, and its freedom from national regulation have caused concern by several nations as to the influence of the market on worldwide inflation and exchange rate instability. As of the early 1980s, several plans for control were proposed and were being debated. But the efficiency with which the Euromarkets have been operating appears to have quieted these concerns.

The Internationalization of Financial Intermediaries

The last three decades have witnessed a dramatic internationalization of banks—both commercial and investment—and of securities firms. International banking has a history dating back for many centuries, with various European centers and different merchant bankers rising and declining in importance.[21] But by the early 1930s, with the advent of the Great Depression and the collapse of international finance and world trade, international banking activities were completely abandoned. After three decades of hibernation, however, international banking again came alive in its modern form during the 1960s, as a result of new environmental forces unique to the post-World War II period.[22] The commercial banks were the first to respond to these new forces. They were later followed by investment banks and securities firms.

To a large extent, the financial institutions were dragged into international operations by external events. These events included the growth of multinational enterprises, the emergence of the Euromarkets, and changes in national banking regulations, particularly in the United States. As a result, international banking became a "growth industry" from the early 1960s to the early 1980s.

---

[21] See Charles P. Kindleberger, *Multinational Excursions* (Cambridge, Mass.: The MIT Press, 1984), pp. 153–70.

[22] See Yoon S. Park and Jack Zwick, *International Banking in Theory and Practice* (Reading, Mass.: Addison-Wesley Publishing Co., 1985), pp. 1–5; Ian Giddy, "Theory and Industrial Organization of International Banking," in *Research in International Business and Finance,* Vol. 3, ed. Robert G. Hawkins et al. (Greenwich, Conn.: JAI Press Inc., 1983), pp. 195–243.

Because U.S. business firms were the most active in expanding internationally after World War II, U.S. commercial banks led the international banking movement. They followed their domestic customers overseas to service better their clients' international operations. They soon discovered the Euromarkets; and when the U.S. imposed capital controls in the mid-1960s, the banks expanded their activities by developing foreign sources of funds for their multinational customers and for domestic lending in the United States.[23] After establishing many foreign branches, the banks also began to service foreign customers, including foreign governments.

In 1960, 8 U.S. banks had 131 branches abroad. By 1975, 125 U.S. banks had gone international with 732 overseas branches. Foreign banks started their international expansion about a decade after the U.S. banks but quickly made up for lost time. As of 1981, 175 foreign banks from 39 countries were operating 441 offices in the United States.

The 1970s were an euphoric and spectacularly profitable decade for international banking. Multinational enterprises kept expanding rapidly, as did their banking needs. The Euromarkets continued to grow in size and in flexibility. The energy crisis, brought about by the sharp increase in oil prices, created a great need for "recycling" surplus revenues of the Organization of Petroleum Exporting Countries (OPEC) back to deficit-plagued, oil-importing countries— mainly the less developed countries. In fact, loans to the less developed countries were the fastest growing category of loans by international banks during the 1970s.

But the euphoric 1970s were followed by the international debt crisis of the early 1980s, discussed in the next chapter, which marked a turning point in the internationalization of financial markets. Commercial banking activities slowed dramatically while investment banks and other financial institutions expanded. Lending by commercial banks to many of the less developed countries came to a virtual halt. The debt crisis coincided with the disappearance of OPEC surplus funds and the emergence of large financial surpluses in Europe and Japan. While OPEC investors had displayed a preference for bank deposits, investors in Europe and Japan were more interested in marketable securities. Also, as a result of a spate of domestic loan problems, particularly by some U.S. banks, bank deposits lost some of their status as being completely safe.[24]

The movement away from traditional bank deposits and loans toward a greater reliance on securities—and the resulting international expansion of nonbank financial institutions—was also encouraged by the deregulation and liberalization of financial markets in many countries. This has blurred the boundaries between bank credit and bond markets and between the types of activities in which the different categories of financial institutions could engage.[25] Also, the increased

---

[23] Arvind Mahajan and Peter S. Rose, "Banking in North America: Regulation and Innovation," *Columbia Journal of World Business,* Winter 1984, p. 72.

[24] Bank for International Settlements, *Fifty-Fifth Annual Report,* (Basle: 1985), pp. 125–27.

[25] International Monetary Fund, *International Capital Markets: Developments and Prospects, 1985, Occasional Paper 43,* (Washington, D.C.: 1986), p. 24.

volatility of interest rates and exchange rates has favored the use of highly complex bonds that give implicit options to borrowers and investors as to which risks they wish to cover and to bear. And although commercial banks participated to a large extent in the move toward securitization, they gradually lost their central place as the world's financial intermediaries.

Both business firms and investors have become more sophisticated and have extended their financial horizons globally. More savings are channelled through institutions than before, and these institutions have been diversifying their portfolios into international investments. They generally have access to electronic screens that give instant information on stock and bond markets around the world. This growth in international portfolios of big investors means that investment banks and securities firms have had to extend their geographic reach to have a presence in foreign markets for buying and selling and to keep a finger on the pulse in these markets.[26]

What does this mean for international enterprises? It means a tremendous expansion in the sources of capital, kinds of currencies, and financial instruments available for international business operations. It also means that international finance has become a major international business activity in its own right. At the same time, international financial management has grown gigantically in complexity, with the result that many business firms operating internationally have created large corporate finance departments that are expected to be constantly familiar with the changing global financial environment.

SUMMARY

The foreign exchange market is a worldwide network of traders—mainly working for commercial banks—linked by rapid means of communications. The market provides the mechanism for converting the currency of one country into the currency of another. It also provides a means of reducing foreign exchange risk. There is almost continuous trading as the various country markets overlap each other and trading shifts from country to country following the sun.

International business firms are among the major users of foreign exchange markets. Other major participants are nonbank financial institutions such as securities firms; central banks, which frequently intervene in the markets for reasons of government policy; and speculators.

Because exchange rates fluctuate, strong interest has developed in the feasibility of and techniques for forecasting them. Underlying this effort to forecast are various economic theories of exchange-rate determination.

The boundaries between national money markets have been crumbling as governments have relaxed their controls. Within fewer than three decades, world financial institutions have become truly internationalized and financial markets have become integrated: domestic and Euromarkets, credit and capital markets, and markets for different currencies. Commercial banks led the internationalization and have been followed by other financial institutions such as investment banks

---

[26] *The Economist,* March 16, 1985, p. 23.

and securities firms. For borrowers and investors, the world has become their "oyster."

EXERCISES AND DISCUSSION QUESTIONS

1. Currency recognition: Write the number of the country next to the name of the currency. (Note: Some currency names are used in more than one country.)

won	1. Argentina
ringgit	2. Australia
naira	3. Austria
krona	4. Brazil
pesta	5. Chile
rand	6. China, People's Republic of
cruzado	7. Finland
renminbi (yuan)	8. India
markka	9. Guatemala
quetzal	10. Hong Kong
dinar	11. Italy
shekel	12. Kuwait
peso	13. Korea, South
krone	14. Israel
escudo	15. Malaysia
baht	16. Mexico
schilling	17. Nigeria
dollar	18. Norway
rupee	19. Portugal
lira	20. Singapore
austral	21. South Africa
	22. Spain
	23. Sweden
	24. Thailand
	25. Yugoslavia

Check your results against Table 4–2.

2. If the Swiss franc is quoted at US$0.7233 spot and US$0.7363 for a 180-day forward contract, how much is the forward premium in percent per annum?

3. Your Canadian subsidiary must make a payment of US$25 million to New York headquarters in three months. The subsidiary already has the U.S. dollars and must decide to invest them for three months. The three-month Treasury bill rate is 7 percent in the United States and 10 percent for Canadian treasury bills. The spot rate for the Canadian dollar is US$0.762 and the 90-day forward rate is US$0.759.
   a. Where should you invest for maximum yield with no risk?
   b. Given the stated interest rates, what forward quotation would create equilibrium with no advantage or disadvantage associated with investing in one country or the other? Ignore transaction costs.
   c. Given the spot and forward exchange rates and the U.S. interest rate, what is the equilibrium or break-even Canadian interest rate?

4. Using the forward market in foreign exchange is the most common hedging technique. More adventurous corporate treasurers have begun to use currency options or futures contracts. What are the advantages and disadvantages of these alternative forms of hedging?

5. "The foreign exchange market is no different from any other financial market in its susceptibility to being profitably predicted. Those who have inside information about events that will affect the value of a currency or of a security should benefit handsomely. Those who do not have this access will have to trust either to luck or to the existence of a market imperfection such as government intervention to assure them of above average risk-adjusted profits. The trick is to predict government actions." Comment.

6. How has the internationalization of national money markets affected the ability of a multinational enterprise to manage better its foreign exchange risk?

7. Given the data in the section on covered interest arbitrage, how must profit in U.S. dollars could you make by a covered investment in £100,000 for 90 days?

CHAPTER 5

The International Monetary System

The International monetary system provides the institutional setting, the instruments, and the rules and procedures within which the foreign exchange markets operate. An ideal international system might be a world central bank and an international currency, but nations have not been willing to transfer to an international agency their sovereign right to issue currency and to control their monetary system. They do, however, recognize the mutual need for maintaining a workable system of international payments and have entered into various cooperative arrangements. These arrangements are continually changing. At the present stage of evolution, the international monetary system is described as a managed float system. This chapter explains how the current system works. It also provides some historical background and identifies some major issues for the future.

94

SOME HISTORY

The Gold Standard

In the days when foreign trade was limited to a few luxury goods imported from abroad, payments were settled one by one in gold and silver, according to the market price of these precious metals at the time the settlement took place. But as international transactions expanded dramatically in the 19th century, a better means of international payments had to be found. The solution, however, could not infringe on the jealously guarded sovereign right of each nation to issue currency. The monetary arrangement that emerged in response to this demand came to be called the *gold standard*. It was an arrangement that evolved naturally rather than a system established by formal agreements among nations.

Under the gold standard, national currencies were linked to gold at a fixed parity; that is, each nation defined its currency unit as equal to the value of a certain weight of pure gold. From the common gold denominator, the value of any currency in units of any other was easily determined. The U.S. dollar, for example, was defined as containing 23.22 grains of fine gold. As there are 480 grains in a troy ounce, the implied price of an ounce of gold was $20.67 (480 ÷ 23.22), at which price the U.S. government freely bought and sold gold. The British pound was defined as containing approximately 113 grains of fine gold. The exchange rate for pounds to dollars, therefore, was £ 1 = $4.8665 (113 ÷ 23.22). This dollar amount was termed the *par value* of the pound.

Rates of exchange were not supposed to undergo major variations. Governments were expected to maintain the value of their currency equivalent to the declared gold content by standing ready to buy and sell gold in unlimited quantities. In this way, deficits or surpluses in a nation's external accounts gave rise to gold movements that in turn were supposed to trigger an *automatic* adjustment process. A continuing surplus in one country would increase that country's gold stock (hence its money supply), thus provoking a general price rise. The price rise would result in falling exports and rising imports until the surplus disappeared. In the case of a persistent deficit, the money supply would diminish, causing the reverse phenomenon.

The gold standard worked acceptably for a period of more than 40 years up to World War I. The success of the system is explained in large part by the general economic tranquility of the period. The world economy was not subjected to shocks as severe as World Wars I and II, the Great Depression of the 1930s, and the OPEC oil price escalation of 1973–74. Moreover, virtually all of today's developing countries were then colonies, and no one paid much attention to the balance of payments between a colony and its metropolitan power. The gold standard applied almost exclusively to the major European powers and the United States. The period is remembered with great nostalgia by many people, and some influential economists and politicians continue to recommend that it be reinstated.

The economic disruptions of World War I ended the stability of exchange rates for currencies of major industrial nations and the gold standard was temporarily abandoned. Most currencies were allowed to fluctuate freely as the war ended. All attempts to restore the gold standard in the early 1920s were short-lived. By the end of the decade the severest recession in modern history was beginning and great financial turmoil prevailed throughout the Great Depression of the 1930s. The outbreak of World War II in late 1939 deferred any new efforts to reestablish a more orderly international monetary system. Not surprisingly, during World War II most of the major trading currencies except the U.S. dollar lost their convertibility.[1]

After World War II the United States stood virtually alone as a holder of wealth and producer of goods. Recognizing the need to restructure the international monetary system, free-world representatives met at Bretton Woods, New Hampshire, in 1944 and agreed to establish a new monetary order centered around the International Monetary Fund (IMF, also called *the Fund*) and the International Bank for Reconstruction and Development (World Bank).

Gold Exchange Standard 1944–1973

The Bretton Woods agreement adopted a fixed exchange-rate system called the *gold exchange standard*. Member governments agreed to fix the value of their currencies in terms of gold but were not required to exchange their currencies for gold. The U.S. dollar was the exception. It remained convertible into gold at the fixed rate of $35 an ounce.

All participating countries agreed to try to maintain the value of their currencies within 1 percent above or below the official parity by selling foreign exchange or gold as necessary. If the currency became too weak to defend, the country could devalue up to 10 percent without formal approval by the IMF. Any larger devaluation required prior IMF approval.

Currency devaluation was envisaged as a last resort, to be approved by the IMF only in the case of fundamental equilibrium and to be avoided if possible by the use of IMF credits. Adjustments in parities were not excluded, but stability through the fixed relationships to gold was the prime objective of the system. Because parities could be adjusted, the system was also called the "adjustable peg" system.

The IMF was established as a permanent institution for consultation and collaboration on international monetary problems. Its broad goals were:

1. To facilitate the balanced growth of international trade.
2. To promote exchange stability and orderly exchange arrangements and to discourage competitive currency depreciation.
3. To seek the elimination of exchange restrictions that hinder the growth of world trade.

---

[1] See Mordecai E. Kreinen, *International Economics,* 4th ed. (New York: Harcourt Brace Jovanovich, 1983), pp. 171–82.

4. To make financial resources available to members, on a temporary basis and with adequate safeguards, to permit them to correct payments imbalances without resorting to measures destructive to national and international prosperity.

It is important to note that the emphasis in the original IMF articles of agreement was on facilitating world trade. The phenomenal expansion of foreign direct investment and multinational enterprises, which later came to place severe strains on the IMF system, was not foreseen.

When the fund opened its doors in March 1946, 40 countries were members. By 1987, IMF membership had grown to 151 nations. The only Eastern European countries that are IMF members are Yugoslavia (a founding member), Romania (joined in 1972), Hungary (joined in 1982), and Poland (joined in 1986). The USSR and the socialist countries of Czechoslovakia, Poland, and Yugoslavia participated in the Bretton Woods conference. The USSR chose not to join. Czechoslovakia and Poland joined but shortly withdrew. The reasons advanced for the abstention of the Eastern European countries relate to the system of weighted voting that gave the United States a veto power in respect to important decisions, the requirement that members report their gold and foreign exchange holdings and keep part of them in the United States where the IMF is located, and the terms on which members are allowed access to IMF resources.[2]

The IMF was funded by quota contributions from its members. The quotas, which have been frequently revised, are determined by a formula that takes into consideration various factors that reflect each member's relative economic standing. Each member is required to pay in an amount equal to its quota; 25 percent must be paid in U.S. dollars, special drawing rights (SDRs) to be described below, or other reserve assets; the remainder is to be paid in the member's own currency. The size of the quota determines the member's voting power and the amount of funds the member is entitled to borrow under various credit arrangements the Fund provides.

The special status of the U.S. dollar at the end of World War II gave the United States a unique position within the system. The U.S. dollar was universally accepted as an international reserve currency, and it was freely convertible into gold upon request from foreign official agencies. As the standard of value for other currencies, the dollar could be revalued or devalued under IMF rules only by changes in its parity with gold. In effect this meant changing the price of gold for the entire system, but the relationship of the U.S. dollar to other currencies would remain the same. The responsibility of member nations to maintain the value of their currency within 1 percent above or below official parity did not apply to the United States, for it was formally required to meet all offers from foreign central banks to buy or sell gold for dollars at the official price of $35 per ounce. The resulting fixed exchange-rate system of foreign currencies pegged

---

[2] "Background Notes on the International Monetary Fund," *Development Dialogue* 2 (1980), p. 96.

to the dollar and the dollar pegged to gold worked unusually well for more than 20 years.

Breakdown of the Fixed Exchange-Rate System

The formal demise of the fixed exchange-rate system occurred in 1973, but the breakdown of the system began much earlier.[3] An inherent structural problem of the system was the lack of a satisfactory mechanism for controlling international liquidity. A growing world economy needed an increased supply of international reserves, yet the IMF had no power to meet international needs. The main reserve assets were gold and foreign exchange, and additions to the stock of reserves were haphazard and not determined by the needs of the system. The supply of gold reserves depended on discoveries, mining costs, and competing commercial demands. An increase in the supply of reserve currencies required that the providers of reserves—mainly the United States but also Great Britain—run balance-of-payments deficits so that other countries could accumulate dollar and pound reserves. The system thus had a built-in paradox. The more the reserve countries ran deficits, the less confidence the holders of dollars and pounds had in the ability of the Federal Reserve and the Bank of England to convert these reserve currencies into gold at the agreed price.[4]

Many proposals were advanced for controlling the growth of reserve assets. The eventual result was a decision to give the Fund authority to create a new reserve asset called special drawing rights (SDRs) that the Fund could allocate periodically to members as the need arose. But even as the SDR was being created, concern about the liquidity crisis was being replaced by fear of a dollar surplus.

During the 1950s, the United States was supplying international liquidity through a steady net outflow of dollars for economic aid, military expenditures, and private foreign direct investment. At the time, the increased supply of dollars was welcomed by Western Europe for replenishing their depleted international reserves. But by the end of the 1960s, the U.S. balance of payments deficits had grown to massive proportions; and the U.S. dollar was losing status as a safe asset.

The dramatic economic revival of Western Europe and Japan had greatly reduced the competitive position of the United States in the world economy. The dollar had become overvalued in relation to other major currencies; and under the system where the dollar was the reserve currency, there was no way to secure a realignment. While the U.S. was running persistent and growing payments deficits, other countries such as Germany and Japan were recording growing payments surpluses. But because surplus nations did not need IMF resources, the IMF had no way to induce such countries to resolve surplus imbalances

---

[3] See Franklin R. Root, *International Trade and Investment*, 5th ed. (Cincinnati, Ohio: South Western Publishing Co., 1984), pp. 164–81.

[4] Maurice Levi, *International Finance* (New York: McGraw-Hill, 1983), p. 141.

by revaluing their currencies. This limitation in the adjustment role of the IMF also contributed to the erosion of the fixed exchange-rate system.

Among the more skeptical holders of dollars was France, which began in 1962 to exchange dollars for gold. The French had doubts about the future value of the dollar. They also objected to the dominant role of the U.S. dollar in the Bretton Woods system. As the French continued to convert their dollar holdings into gold, other nations became concerned about whether sufficient gold would remain for them after the French had finished selling dollars. Other holders of large dollar reserves began switching to gold and the U.S. gold stock dropped from U.S. \$24 billion in 1948 to U.S. \$15 billion in 1964 and U.S. \$11 billion in 1971. Under the fixed exchange-rate system, the United States was forced to bear large adjustment costs by losing its gold reserves or change the rules. The United States opted to change the rules.

The beginning step toward the managed float system occurred in 1968 when the United States suspended the sale of gold except to official parties; and on August 15, 1971, the United States closed the gold window completely. A series of additional measures forced the other industrialized countries to revalue their currencies against the U.S. dollar. By March 1973 the system of fixed rates was abandoned, and virtually every major currency was floating without much formal discipline remaining.

The result of the move from fixed exchange rates to the managed float on the international value of the major currencies in relation to the U.S. dollar is shown in Figure 5–1. By 1980, the U.S. dollar had declined by 20 percent from its 1970 level, whereas the West German deutsche mark (DM) and the Japanese yen had appreciated by more than 60 percent.

A short-lived effort to secure greater exchange-rate stability was attempted in 1972 by six members of the European Community—plus the United Kingdom and Denmark, which were about to join the Community—through the creation of the European Monetary Union (EMU). Member countries agreed to limit fluctuations among their currencies within a small band, but the group as a whole could fluctuate against other currencies. The EMU had limited success; but the continued desire for monetary stability among the European currencies eventually resulted in formation of the European Monetary System (EMS) in 1979.

Special Drawing Rights

Special drawing rights, sometimes called *paper gold,* continue to be a part of the system. Actually, SDRs are merely accounting entries. They have become reserve assets because Fund members are committed to accept them for a wide range of transactions and because they are recognized by the Fund as part of the holder's international reserves, along with gold and foreign exchange.

The SDR is the unit of account for all purposes of the Fund. Outside the Fund, it is widely used as a unit of account in private contracts such as SDR-denominated deposits with commercial banks. A number of the Fund's member countries peg their currency to the SDR.

FIGURE 5–1   Effective Exchange Rates (index 1970 = 100)

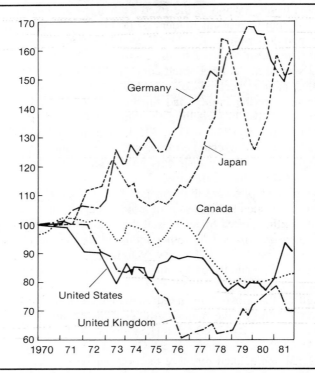

source: *IMF SURVEY*, February 8, 1982, p. 38.

When first created, the SDR was linked to gold. But since 1974 its value is based on the daily market exchange rates of a basket of currencies. The basket in 1986 consisted of the currencies of the five members with the largest share in world exports—the U.S. dollar, DM, pound sterling, French franc, and Japanese yen. The cumulative total allocations as of January 2, 1987, reached SDR 21.4 billion, or US$26.3 billions based on the rate of SDR 1 = US$1.231 as of that date. Although it is the declared intention of member countries that the SDR should eventually become the principal reserve asset in the international monetary system, the SDRs in existence still accounted for only 6–7 percent of total international reserves, excluding gold holdings.

THE MANAGED FLOAT SYSTEM

In April 1976, the IMF board of governors amended the IMF Articles of Agreement to legitimize the changes that had occurred, and the international monetary system formally moved into the present managed float system.

Fixed versus Flexible Exchange Rates

The relative merits of fixed exchange rates, flexible or floating exchange rates, or a compromise between them has long been a matter of policy debate in the international arena. Although a compromise solution evolved from the crisis of the early 1970s, the policy debate continues.[5]

The most important argument in favor of flexible rates is that they provide a much smoother adjustment mechanism than do fixed rates. An incipient deficit with flexible rates will merely cause a decline in the foreign exchange value of the currency rather than require politically difficult domestic policy changes to reduce income or prices, as would fixed exchange rates. Other arguments for flexible rates include better confidence because large persistent deficits are prevented, better liquidity because reserves are not needed, greater independence in national policies and less need for tariffs and other restrictions.[6]

The case against flexible rates includes the arguments that they cause uncertainty and inhibit trade and investment, and that they encourage destabilizing speculation. The uncertainty argument has not been supported by the empirical evidence of continued expansion in both trade and investment since the demise of the fixed-rate system.[7] An answer to the speculation issue is that destabilizing speculation has also occurred with fixed rates.

For the international enterprise, two key issues are the greater uncertainty and risk attributed to the flexible rate system and the relative ease or difficulty of managing international operations with flexible rates. The forward exchange markets that have developed along with the flexible rates system can be used to avoid foreign exchange risk. The managerial problem with flexible rather than fixed rates is different but not more difficult. Under both systems, changes in exchange values occurred. But under the fixed system, changes were generally abrupt and large. The fixed system often gave business firms a false sense of security and caused them to neglect exchange-rate surveillance and forecasting. Under the flexible system, business firms have become more alert to the existence of foreign exchange risk and better prepared to anticipate and adjust to changes in foreign exchange rates.

The Managed Float Compromise

The compromise international monetary regime that emerged in the late 1970s was a mixture of fixed and floating rates called a *managed float*. In theory, floating means that the price of Currency A in terms of Currency B is determined by the daily market forces of supply and demand, not fixed by government fiat.

---

[5] Peter H. Lindert, *International Economics*, 8th ed. (Homewood, Ill: Richard D. Irwin, 1986), pp. 506–22.

[6] Levi, *International Finance*, pp. 131–38.

[7] International Monetary Fund, *Exchange Rate Volatility and World Trade*, Occasional Paper No. 28 (Washington, D.C.: IMF, July 1984).

In practice, however, most of the currencies of the smaller economies are fixed in the sense that they are tied to another currency, often that of their major trading partner. The currencies of the bigger economies are floating against each other, and most of the trade and investment flows are conducted across floating exchanges. Even among the smaller nations whose currencies are pegged, most of their transactions are with countries whose currencies are floating.

Among the pegged currencies, the largest number of small countries are tied to the U.S. dollar (see Table 5–1). Another large group tie their currencies to the SDR, and much of French West Africa remains linked to the French franc.[8] Some countries, mainly in Latin America, tie their currency to the U.S. dollar but adjust the exchange rate frequently according to a set of indicators. Brazil, for example, has a mini-devaluation policy of frequent small adjustments that are intended to compensate for the difference between Brazilian and U.S. inflation rates.

Even among the so-called floaters, currency ties exist. Eight members of the European Community formed the EMS in 1979 and fix their currency values in relation to each other, although they float en bloc against the rest of the world. This left, as of 1987, the U.S. dollar, Japanese yen, British pound, Swiss franc, and Canadian dollar as the principal untied currencies. But none of the floating rates are freely determined by supply and demand conditions in foreign exchange markets. As discussed in Chapter 4, central banks frequently intervene unilaterally to prevent their currency from moving up or down to a degree considered excessive or undesirable. They also intervene in cooperation with each other to smooth fluctuations in foreign exchange markets. At times the interventions can be massive, but there is no longer an official commitment to keep the fluctuations within fixed limits.

TABLE 5–1   Exchange Arrangements of Member Countries (June 30, 1987)

Type of Arrangement	Number of Countries
Currency pegged to	
U.S. dollar	34
French franc	14
Other currency	5
SDR	10
Other currency composite	27
Exchange rate adjusted to set of indicators	5
Cooperative exchange arrangements	8
Other arrangements	48
Total	151

SOURCE: International Monetary Fund, *Annual Report 1987*, p. 77.

---

[8] The exchange-rate regime to which a specific country adheres is regularly reported by the IMF in the monthly *IMF Survey* and in its *Annual Report*.

The *compromise-managed float* differs from a *free float* system in two significant respects. First, under a free float the exchange rate of a specific currency is
presumed to settle at or around its equilibrium value—that is, a value that reflects
underlying economic factors and that would bring about a balance in that country's
external accounts. In a managed float, no such presumption can be made. Intervention may have driven the exchange rate away from rather than to the equilibrium
rate. Second, under a free float, a nation does not accumulate nor need international
reserves because the exchange rate will always clear the market. By contrast, a
country that is managing its currency needs reserves to sell for its own currency
when moderating a decline in the exchange rate; and it accumulates reserves
when selling its own currency to moderate an increase in the currency's value.

The currencies of the centrally planned or socialist countries remain inconvertible and outside the managed float system. International business transactions
with these countries generally require barter arrangements for which money payments are not needed, or *triangular deals*. Under a triangular arrangement, the
party scheduled to receive payment in a nonconvertible currency sells this asset,
usually at a discount, to another party that needs the currency to buy goods or
services from the particular country. In fact, a substantial banking business has
developed in Vienna, Austria, for working out such triangular or multilateral
deals.

Role of the IMF

In the managed float system, IMF members are free to choose their exchange
arrangements, but they are required to notify the IMF of their choice and of any
change made in these arrangements. The IMF is charged with surveillance of
the floating system; but in practice, this surveillance of the major currencies has
been weak. Members are supposed to refrain from "dirty floating," which means
manipulating exchange rates to gain an unfair competitive advantage over other
members. A country floats "dirtily" if it attempts to hold down a strong currency
in order to keep its exports competitive, when all objective analysis would suggest
that the currency is undervalued.

The IMF still lacks sanctions to apply against strong economies. It has
continued and greatly expanded its role as a temporary supplier of resources to
weak countries, and when a weak country ends up on its doorstep, the IMF has
considerable influence in getting the country to make policy changes. But strong
countries do not need help from the IMF. Thus the IMF is stuck with the asymmetry
of obligation that confirms the old rule of one law for the rich and another for
the poor. In particular, the Fund has little control over its largest member. The
United States needs foreign currency only to support the dollar but not to finance
its deficits because dollars are still a reserve asset.

The Fund's loanable resources come mostly from the quota contributions
of its members. The quotas are increased periodically to boost the Fund's resources.
The latest increase, implemented in 1984, brought the total to SDR 89.3 billion,
or US$110 billion at the exchange rate of SDR 1 = US$1.231 as of January 2,

1987. In addition, the Fund may supplement its resources through borrowing up to a limit of between 50 and 60 percent of the total of Fund quotas. The resources of the Fund are still relatively small when compared to the $100 billion debt problem in 1986 of just one Fund member—Mexico—or the 1986 balance of trade deficit of the U.S., totaling about $170 billion.

A country making use of the Fund's resources is generally required to carry out an economic policy program aimed at achieving a viable balance-of-payments position over an appropriate time period. This requirement is known as *conditionality*, and it reflects the principle that balance of payments financing and adjustment must go hand-in-hand.

The Fund makes "loans" to members by selling them SDRs or currencies of other countries (typically dollars or other readily usable currencies) for their own currency. The Fund's resources are available for limited periods, and members who "purchase" foreign currencies from the Fund must subsequently "buy" their currency back, that is, repay the loan. The several facilities under which a member can borrow from the Fund are shown in Figure 5–2. These facilities differ mainly in the type of balance of payments need they address and the degree of conditionality they involve.

Usually, repurchases are required to be made within three to five years from the date of purchase; but under the Extended Fund facility, the period for

FIGURE 5–2   Financial Facilities of the Fund and Their Conditionality

---

Tranche policies: Repurchases in 3–5 years
  First credit tranche
  Program representing reasonable efforts to overcome balance of payments difficulties; performance criteria and installments not used.

  Higher credit tranches
  Transactions requiring that member give substantial justification of its efforts to overcome balance of payments difficulties; resources normally provided in the form of stand-by arrangements that include performance criteria and drawings in installments.

Extended Fund facility
  Medium-term program for up to three years to overcome structural balance of payments maladjustments; detailed statement of policies and measures for first and subsequent 12-month periods; resources provided in the form of extended arrangements that include performance criteria and drawings in installments; repurchases in 4½–10 years.

Enlarged access policy
  For use in support of programs under stand-by arrangements reaching into the upper credit tranches or beyond, or under extended arrangements, subject to relevant policies on conditionality, phasing, and performance criteria; repurchases in 3½–7 years; charges based on borrowing costs.

Compensatory financing facility
  Existence of either a temporary export shortfall for reasons largely beyond the member's control or a temporary excess in the cost of cereal imports; member cooperates with Fund in an effort to find appropriate solutions for any balance of payments difficulties; repurchases in 3–5 years.

Buffer stock financing facility
  Contribution to an international buffer stock accepted as suitable by Fund; member expected to cooperate with Fund as in the case of compensatory financing; repurchases in 3–5 years.

SOURCE: *IMF Survey*, September 1985, p. 8.

repurchases is within 4½–10 years, and under the supplementary financing and the enlarged access policy, within 3½–7 years. An exception to the conditionality and repayment requirements is the *reserve tranche*. Borrowing under this facility represents the "right" to obtain a "refund" of the reserve assets paid to the Fund at the time of its quota subscription (i.e., 25 percent of the quota). Purchases in the reserve tranche do not require Fund approval, and there is no repayment requirement.

The amount of assistance available to members from Fund resources is determined by guidelines adopted by the Fund and changed from time to time. The limits are normally expressed as a percent of the member's quota. In 1986, the maximum available by using all Fund facilities was 600 percent of the member's quota. In exceptional circumstances, the Fund can provide amounts in excess of these limits.

But the role of the Fund has gone beyond that of direct financial assistance to its members. As will be discussed below, with the emergence of an international debt crisis beginning in 1982, the Fund became a catalyst for generating additional credit and capital for its members from commercial banks and other non-Fund sources.

The European Monetary System

Europe's second scheme to lock intracontinental exchange rates came into existence early in 1979. The EMS is the European Community's device for linking the currencies of West Germany, France, Italy, Ireland, Denmark, Belgium, Luxembourg, and the Netherlands within agreed limits in a joint float against the U.S. dollar and other major currencies. Britain, however, kept its currency out of the EMS; and the other EC members—Greece, Portugal, and Spain—do not participate.

Each member has a fixed "central rate" against a new international currency, the European Currency Unit (ECU). The ECU is a basket of the members' currencies weighted by the economic importance of each country. After a slow start, the use of the ECU as a unit of account in international financial transactions has increased rapidly. International contracts, bank accounts, and even travelers' checks are being denominated in ECUs. The ECU has become the fourth most popular currency for international borrowing and lending operations after the U.S. dollar, Japanese yen and West German DM.[9]

The system has intervention limits around the central rate that must be observed by both weak and strong currency countries. The system assumes that EMS members will work toward integrating their economies and harmonizing their economic policies. As a future step, EMS members are committed to establish a European Monetary Cooperation Fund, which would account for 20 percent of each country's official reserves of gold and foreign currencies. This step had

---

[9] Bank for International Settlements, *Fifty-Seventh Annual Report*, Basle, 15th June 1987, p. 106.

not been achieved by the late 1980s because of difficulties in coordinating national monetary policies and a reluctance to cede national sovereignty over basic economic policies to a supranational authority.

THE INTERNATIONAL DEBT CRISIS

The role of the IMF was greatly enlarged in the early 1980s in response to an unprecedented international debt crisis. During the 1970s, flush with huge deposits being made by the oil producing countries, the commercial banks aggressively increased their lending to the developing countries. This "recycling of petrodollars" was encouraged at the time by the generally favorable economic performance of the borrowing nations. By the early 1980s, however—as the overall debt of the developing countries began to surpass $700 billion—the economic situation of the debtor countries began to deteriorate dramatically. Their ability to service foreign debts was eroded by several crucial events.[10] Another major increase in oil prices occurred in 1979–80. Their export earnings declined because of a severe recession in the industrial nations. And world interest rates soared as a result of the anti-inflation monetary measures adopted by the industrialized countries. As the current account deficits of the debtor nations widened, many banks became frightened and closed their windows to new loans and tried to reduce their existing exposure.

When voluntary private lending to the developing countries came to a halt in mid-1982, many of the indebted countries turned to the Fund for assistance. Between mid-1982 and the end of 1984, the Fund itself lent SDR 22 billion in support of adjustment programs to 70 member countries. But whatever direct financial assistance the Fund could provide was clearly inadequate to meet the debt crisis, and the IMF responded to the crisis by undertaking other crucial steps to quell the near panic among international banks. Through these initiatives, it has been estimated that each dollar of Fund lending unlocked four to seven dollars of new loans and refinancing from commercial banks and governments. To keep banks lending to key debtors, the Fund requested that the commercial banks make financial commitments for "new" money before the Fund approved adjustment programs and provided financing from its own resources.[11]

Between January 1984 and April 1985, 21 Fund members concluded restructuring agreements with international banks. Amounts thus restructured totalled $150 billion, or the equivalent of 20 percent of the bank debt of the developing countries. The willingness of the commercial banks to agree to lower spreads and to longer repayment and grace periods was encouraged in large measure by the strength of the adjustment efforts undertaken by Fund members supported by the Fund resources during this period.

---

[10] See the special issue of the *Columbia Journal of World Business,* Fall 1986, on "The Debt Crisis of the Third World."

[11] International Monetary Fund, *Recent Developments in External Debt Restructuring,* Occasional Paper No. 40, 1985.

Despite the progress achieved by dealing with the debt crisis on a case-by-case method, the problems encountered by a number of debtor countries, heavily concentrated in Latin America and Africa, had not found a lasting solution as of the late 1980s. Further progress depended on domestic reforms in the countries concerned and a continuing favorable international environment.

Various new proposals have been made to ease the payments burden of the debtors.[12] One group of alternatives would have the governments of the creditor countries take over the foreign bank debts of the developing countries, write off part, and distribute the loss between the lender banks and taxpayers. A second set of proposals has been to cap annual debt servicing by suspending amortization and limiting interest payments to some maximum percentage of the debtor country's export earnings, the unpaid interest being capitalized in new bank loans. A third alternative would be a combination of interest capping and the mobilization of foreign assets of the residents of the debtor countries, mainly so-called flight capital. A fourth proposal is to convert the sovereign debt into local currency equity investments in local private or government enterprises in the debtor country.[13] Of course, the debtor countries can default on their external obligations; but the resulting penalty appears to be a forceful disincentive for choosing this alternative.

As far as the international financial system is concerned, the international debt crisis of the 1980s has demonstrated institutional weaknesses and pragmatic resourcefulness. There is no permanent institutional structure such as a world central bank to serve as a lender of last resort. Yet forceful initiatives by the IMF and several other official bodies—including the U.S. government—have occurred as needed to work out partial solutions. The question still remains as to whether ad hoc initiatives can provide the needed confidence in the international financial framework (see Box 5–1).

SOME REFORM ISSUES FOR THE FUTURE

Although disagreement persists as to the merits and demerits of the managed float system, a return to the old fixed-rate system is unlikely. Proposals to return to the gold standard recur from time to time; but such proposals have not attracted significant support, especially from monetary officials. There is general recognition, nevertheless, that the present system has weaknesses and the principal reform issues focus on measures to improve rather than to change the basic system.

The main areas of dissatisfaction relate to the wide fluctuations that have been occurring in exchange rates, the limited effectiveness of the Fund's surveillance responsibility, and the adequacy of international liquidity. In addition, repre-

---

[12] David Felix, "How to Resolve Latin America's Debt Crisis," *Challenge,* November–December 1985, pp. 44–51.

[13] See Richard J. Bentley, "Debt Concession in Latin America," *Columbia Journal of World Business,* Fall 1986, pp. 37–40.

BOX 5–1
The Debtors Get Tough

Mexican President Miguel de la Madrid Hurtado said his country intends to limit its debt payments to its "capacity to pay."

Foreign creditors, he said, will have to make "sacrifices."

In a speech Friday before 250 Mexican leaders, Mr. de la Madrid sketched a negotiating strategy that is likely to prove the most bitterly contested yet in the three and one-half years that banks have been dealing with financially troubled nations. One point the president made clear is that Mexico doesn't want to go on taking new loans to service its old ones, a policy that has kept the nation solvent for the past three and one-half years but which has heaped up its debt without attacking root economic problems.

Mexico's new policy differs only in spirit from one the Peruvian President Alan Garcia unilaterally announced last July limiting the country's debt-service payments to 10 percent of its export revenue. Nigeria, too, has taken a similar step.

But Mexico's creditor banks are preparing to go to the mat on this one. If they give in to Mexico's demands for interest concessions, they undoubtedly will face demands for similar treatment from other Latin American debtors. If they give in to everyone, their earnings will fall precipitously.

"What he's saying clearly is going to hurt us," said one U.S. banker, who was relieved the president didn't announce he was stopping payments altogether.

SOURCE: Adapted from *The Wall Street Journal*, February 24, 1986. © Dow Jones & Company, Inc., 1986. Used with permission. All rights reserved.

---

sentatives of the developing countries would like to increase their share in the total votes in the Fund from 38 percent to 50 percent.

The main recommendations for achieving greater exchange rate stability have to do with the need for close and continuing cooperation among countries, especially more coordination in the conduct of national policies by the industrial countries. The underlying issue is the extent to which member countries will make exchange rate stability an important objective of national policy rather than a residual of domestically oriented policy actions. The freedom in domestic policy making that the present system permits is both a strength and a weakness of the system. The system allows nations to insulate their domestic price levels from inflation abroad and facilitates the pursuit of sound monetary policies geared more directly to domestic conditions. At the same time, considerable volatility in exchange rates can result when major nations adopt fiscal and monetary policies independently, without serious consideration of the impact of these national policies on the world economy.

The surveillance responsibility of the Fund is supposed to be a partial answer to greater exchange rate stability. But both the industrial and the developing countries believe that surveillance has not been sufficiently effective in influencing national policies and promoting exchange rate stability. As previously noted, the Fund cannot apply direct pressures on members unless the members are asking for Fund assistance. The proposals for strengthening the surveillance function are weak and emphasize dialogue, persuasion through peer pressure, and greater publicity for policy conclusions arrived at through surveillance reviews.[14]

On the issue of international liquidity, the industrial and the developing countries have taken opposing positions. The developing countries have urged that the allocation of SDRs be increased on an annual basis with a view to ensuring that their proportion in reserves rises progressively. The industrial countries emphasize that liberalization and integration of national capital markets have permitted a significant increase in international capital flows and enhanced the ability of creditworthy countries to meet their financing needs. Furthermore, some industrial countries have argued that the new SDR allocations could delay needed adjustments that problem countries should make.

The debate on reform issues continues to fall short of serious suggestions for a central-bank type of international agency. The willingness of nations to give up national control over economic and monetary policies has not increased significantly, even during the debt crisis years of the mid-1980s. Some progress seems to be underway for more frequent consultation and coordination by the major industrial countries through the Organization for Economic Cooperation and Development (OECD) and ad hoc meetings.

THE WORLD BANK GROUP

The 1944 Bretton Woods Conference had two objectives: (1) to restructure the international monetary system, and (2) to provide financial assistance for postwar reconstruction and development. The IMF was created in response to the former. The World Bank was established to achieve the latter. The World Bank, whose official name is the International Bank for Reconstruction and Development (IBRD), now has two affiliates—the International Finance Corporation (IFC) and the International Development Association (IDA). The three organizations, which form the World Bank Group, have become the major *public* international source of financing.

The World Bank proper is owned by the governments of member countries (151 in 1987). The Bank finances its lending operations primarily from borrowing in the world's capital markets and deals mainly in long-term loans to member countries for specific reconstruction or development projects. When governments endorse and guarantee loans, the Bank can also lend for private projects. From the standpoint of international business enterprises, however, the World Bank is more important as a general force for stimulating economic development than as a direct source for financing.

---

[14] See the "Group of 10 Deputies Report," *IMF Survey Supplement,* July 1985, for the views of the industrial countries and the "Group of 24 Deputies' Report," *IMF Survey Supplement,* September 1985, for the recommendations of the developing countries.

After World War II, much of the lending was to European countries for reconstruction. More recently, lending has been exclusively to the developing countries. Traditionally, the Bank concentrated on financing capital infrastructure such as roads and railways, telecommunications, and ports and power facilities. Loans for energy and transportation projects continue to be important, but increasingly, loans have been directed toward assisting the poorest segments of society in developing countries through projects for agricultural and rural development, urban water and sewage facilities, low-cost housing, and small industries projects.

With the emergence of the international debt crisis in the early 1980s, the Bank initiated a new program of structural-adjustment lending aimed at helping developing countries carry out the difficult process of policy and institutional reform in an unfavorable international economic environment. This new initiative required the Bank to increase its collaboration with the Fund to ensure complementarity between the structural-adjustment lending and the balance-of-payments adjustment programs supported by the IMF.

The IFC was established in 1956. Its function is to assist the economic development of less developed countries by promoting growth in the private sector of their economies and by helping to mobilize domestic and foreign capital for the business sector. The IFC can make equity investments and provide loans without government guarantees. Thus the IFC, which had 128 member countries in 1986, is a source for financing international enterprises. Its portfolio as of June 30, 1986, contained loan and equity investments in 377 companies located in 72 developing countries with a total value of $2.4 billion.

The IDA was created in 1960 for making soft loans—that is, loans with long maturity, low interest rates, and easy repayment terms—to the poorest of the developing countries. The terms of IDA credits, which are made to governments only, are a 10-year grace period, 50-year maturities, and no interest. An annual service fee of 0.75 percent is charged on the disbursed portion of each credit. IDA loans are made exclusively for development purposes and are concentrated in some 50 countries with an annual per capita gross national product of less than $791 (in 1983 dollars). As is true of the World Bank, the IDA's importance to international business is as a general force for stimulating development.

SUMMARY

Prior to World War II, the international monetary system was based on the gold standard. For 25 years following World War II, the free-world economies for the most part adhered to the tenets of the Bretton Woods agreement—namely, a system of fixed exchange rates under which individual countries were expected to make adjustments to imbalances in their external accounts without resorting to exchange-rate depreciations or currency controls. On occasion, individual countries were unable to comply with the terms of the agreement. Yet the system remained intact until the late 1960s when the United States, the most important country for the viability of the international financial structure, concluded that the arbitrary discipline of the system was no longer tenable. With the subsequent devaluations of the U.S. dollar and unhinging of the dollar from gold, the free-world economies entered into an era of floating exchange rates. An arrangement has emerged (perhaps it too could be called a system) in which individual countries decide whether to permit their respective currencies to float or to remain pegged to the currency values of some other country. While the arrangement has shown many weaknesses and may be modified, a return to the old, fixed-rate system is unlikely.

If the only criterion were its impact on international business, the managed float system would have to be judged reasonably satisfactory. Both trade and other forms of international business activity have continued to expand. Futures markets have developed that permit business firms to reduce the risk of fluctuating exchange rates, and financial officers have become more active and more skilled in managing foreign exchange risk.

The international debt crisis of the 1980s placed an extraordinary amount of pressure on the system and accelerated efforts to improve its functioning. Reform issues remain on the agenda, such as means of reducing exchange rate volatility, better management of international liquidity, and an increased role for the developing countries. It is hoped that the system will evolve smoothly and become even better adapted to the complex and often conflicting needs of an increasingly interdependent world economy.

EXERCISES AND DISCUSSION QUESTIONS

1. Which of the following opposing views would you accept and why?

   "An exchange rate is nothing but a price. Just as we do not fix the prices of manufactured products, so there is no need to fix the price of currencies in terms of each other."

   "Exchange rates are not like any other price, for they involve monetary values. Just as it is essential to have a fixed ratio between the New York dollar and the California dollar, so it is useful to have fixed ratios between national currencies. Otherwise, commodity traders and investors cannot make advance estimates of costs and prices."

2. What are SDRs and what purpose do they serve?

3. Why was the Bretton Woods system able to last for 25 years?

4. What would be the advantages and disadvantages of a world central bank and an international currency?

5. What are the most likely next steps in the evolution of the international monetary system? Will there be a return to the gold standard as a way to reduce global inflationary trends?

6. List some reasons why you believe that it is important for an international business executive to understand how the international monetary system works. How could such an understanding help in forecasting?

7. Is tomorrow's exchange rate more or less predictable in a system of flexible rates than in a system of fixed rates? Why?

8. It has been argued that one of the factors contributing to the international debt crisis of the 1980s was excessive lending by commercial banks and that part of the solution should be for the banks to write off some of the debt. Comment.

The Balance of Payments

In assessing a country's currency prospects, international firms must take numerous factors into account. Ranking high among these factors is the nation's economic relations with other countries. A principal source of information on these external relations is the country's balance of payments. Just as the balance-of-payments accounts indicate the strength or weakness of a country's currency to its government officials, these accounts also assist the international firm in anticipating changes in the foreign exchange value of a currency. And together with the data on a country's international investment position, they serve as a valuable framework for analyzing and interpreting a wide range of problems dealing with a country's economic and business life.

This chapter describes the balance-of-payments accounting system and illustrates the methodology for interpreting the accounts. It also discusses the measures countries can adopt for adjusting their balance-of-payments situation. Fortunately for students who are not versed in business accounting, a business accounting background is not necessary for understanding and analyzing the balance-of-payments accounts.

THE BALANCE-OF-PAYMENTS ACCOUNTS

Each nation periodically publishes a set of statistics that summarizes for a given period all economic transactions between its residents[1] and the outside world. This statistical statement is referred to as the *balance-of-payments accounts*. The accounts show how a nation has financed its international activities during the reporting period. They also show what *changes* have taken place in the nation's financial claims and obligations vis-a-vis the rest of the world. A focal point of the balance of payments is the nation's *external liquidity*—that is, the country's ability to meet claims and acquire goods and services from the outside world.

The Standard Presentation

The broad categories used for grouping international transactions are current account, capital account, and reserves. *Current account* items are concerned with the country's trading activities in real goods and services, including payments and receipts for the use of factors of production such as capital and technology, as well as unrequited or unilateral transfers. *Unrequited transfers* are items such as gifts, donations, and aid in the form of goods or money without expectation of payment. *Capital account* items are concerned with the country's transactions in monetary and ownership claims other than the transactions of the monetary authorities. The monetary authority items are separated into the *reserve account*. Finally, an entry usually appears for *errors and omissions* or *statistical discrepancies,* which will be explained below.

The classifications, definitions, and statistical accuracy of items vary considerably from country to country. The IMF, however, has worked with significant success to standardize the system and the form of presentation.[2] An abbreviated version of the IMF's Standard Presentation is shown in Table 6–1. The official U.S. presentation differs somewhat from the IMF format, as we shall see. Neverthe-

---

[1] *Residents* are defined by the IMF as all persons and institutions who reside or have their "center of interest" in the country. Citizenship is not relevant except for government and military personnel stationed abroad who are treated as residents of their home country.

[2] See *Balance of Payments Manual,* 4th ed. (International Monetary Fund, 1977).

TABLE 6-1 Balance of Payments: IMF Standard Presentation

	Debits	Credits
I. Current account A. Goods, services, and income: 1. Merchandise Trade balance	Imports from foreign sources (acquisition of goods)	Exports to foreign destinations (provision of goods)
2. Shipment and other transportation	Payments to foreigners for freight and insurance on international shipments; for ship repair, stores, and supplies; and international passenger fares.	Receipts by residents from foreigners for services provided.
3. Travel	Expenditures by residents (including internal transportation) when traveling in a foreign country.	Receipts by residents for goods and services (including internal transportation) sold to foreign travelers in reporting country.
4. Investment income	Profits of foreign direct investments in reporting country, including reinvested earnings; income paid to foreigners as interest, dividends, etc.	Profits of direct investments by residents in foreign countries, including reinvested earnings; income received by residents from abroad as interest, dividends, etc.
5. Other official	Foreign purchases by government not included elsewhere; personal expenditures of government civilian and military personnel stationed in foreign countries.	Expenditures of foreign governments for goods and services, not included elsewhere; personal expenditures of foreign civilian and military personnel stationed in reporting country.
6. Other private	Payments to foreigners for management fees, royalties, film rentals, construction, etc.	Receipts from foreigners for management fees, royalties, film rentals, construction, etc.
Goods, services, and income balance		
B. Unrequited transfers 1. Private	Payments in cash and kind by residents to foreigners without a quid pro quo such as charitable gifts and gifts by migrants to their families.	Receipts in cash and kind by residents from foreign individuals or governments without a quid pro quo.
2. Official	Transfers by government of reporting country for pensions, reparations, and grants for economic and military aid.	Transfers received by governments from foreigners in the form of goods, services, or cash as gifts or grants. Also tax receipts from nonresidents.
Current account balance		

II. Capital account

C. Capital, excluding reserves:

1. Direct investment
- a. Increased investment in foreign enterprises controlled by residents including reinvestment of earnings.
- b. Decreases in investment in domestic enterprises controlled by foreigners.
- a. Decreased investment in foreign enterprises controlled by residents.
- b. Increases in investment in domestic enterprises by foreigners.

2. Portfolio investment
- a. Increases in investment by residents in foreign securities.
- b. Decreases in investment by foreigners in domestic securities such as bonds and corporate equities.
- a. Decreases in investments by residents in foreign securities.
- b. Increases in investment by foreigners in domestic securities.

3. Other long term, official
- a. Loans to foreigners.
- b. Redemption or purchase from foreigners of government securities.
- a. Foreign loan reductions.
- b. Sales to foreigners of government securities.

4. Other long term, private
- a. Long-term loans to foreigners by resident banks and private parties.
- b. Loan repayments by residents to foreign banks or private parties.
- a. Long-term loans by foreigners to resident banks or private parties.
- b. Loan repayments by foreigners to residents.

5. Other short term, official
- a. S-T loans to foreigners by central government.
- b. Purchase from foreigners of government securities, decrease in liabilities constituting reserves of foreign authorities.
- a. S-T loans to resident central government by foreigners.
- b. Foreign sales of S-T resident government securities, increases in liabilities constituting reserves of foreign authorities.

6. Other short term, private
- a. Increases in S-T foreign assets held by residents.
- b. Decreases in domestic assets held by foreigners, such as bank deposits, currencies, debts to banks, and commercial claims.
- a. Decreases in S-T foreign assets held by residents, increase in foreign liabilities of residents.
- b. Increase in domestic S-T assets held by foreigners or decrease in S-T domestic liabilities to foreigners.

III. Reserves

D. Reserves:
1. Monetary gold
2. Special drawing rights
3. IMF reserve position
4. Foreign exchange assets

{ Increases in holdings of gold, SDRs, foreign convertible currencies by monetary authorities; decrease in liabilities to IMF or increase in IMF assets position.

Decreases in holdings of gold, SDRs, or convertible currencies by monetary authorities; increase in liabilities to IMF or decrease in IMF assets position.

E. Net errors and omissions:

Net understatement of recorded debts or overstatement of recorded credits.

Net understatement of recorded credits or overstatement of recorded debits.

Balances: Balance on merchandise trade   A-1 credits minus A-1 debits
Balance on goods, services, and income   A-1 through A-6 credits minus A-1 through A-6 debits
Balance on current account   A and B credits minus A and B debits

115

less, it is important for U.S. managers to be familiar with the IMF form of presentation because it is so widely followed.[3]

Double-Entry System

The balance of payments is a double-entry system. Every transaction is recorded as if it consisted of an exchange of something for something else— that is, both as a debit and a credit. In the case of merchandise imports, for example, goods are normally acquired for money or debt. Imports are recorded as a debit and payment as a credit. Likewise, exports are recorded as a credit and payment as a debit. Where items are given rather than exchanged, special types of counterpart entries are made in order to furnish the required offsets.

The words *debits* and *credits* have no value-laden meaning—either good or bad. They are merely rules or conventions: they are not economic truths. Under the conventions of double-entry bookkeeping, an increase in the assets of an entity is always recorded as a debit and an increase in liabilities as a credit. Thus a debit records (1) the import of goods and services, (2) increase in assets, or (3) reductions in liabilities. A credit records (1) the export of goods and services, (2) a decrease in assets, or (3) increases in liabilities.

For the reader who is unfamiliar with debit and credit concepts of double-entry accounting, it is probably easier to view the debit and credit classifications in terms of the net effect of transactions on a country's *external liquidity*—that is, its ability to meet foreign claims against it. Exports and capital inflows *(credits)* increase external liquidity. As shown on the *debit* side under the double-entry system, they result in increases in holdings of foreign assets or decreases in foreign liabilities. Imports and capital outflows *(debits)* decrease external liquidity. This is reflected in the counterpart *credit* entries as decreases in foreign assets or increases in foreign liabilities. For those who are familiar with accounting, a comparison of corporate accounts and balance-of-payments accounts is presented in the appendix to this chapter.

Referring to Table 6–1, we can begin analyzing the various transactions and identifying their debit and credit components.

The Current Account

The current account items are analogous to the revenues and expenses of a business. When combined, they provide important insights into a country's international economic performance, just as a company's profit-and-loss statement conveys important information concerning its performance.

---

[3] The annual *Balance of Payments Yearbook* of the IMF is a valuable source for comparing various countries because a comparable format is used for the balance-of-payments statistics of each nation.

Merchandise Trade.   For most countries, merchandise exports and imports are the largest single component of total international transactions. The sale of goods to foreigners (exports) is a source of funds and, as previously noted, is recorded as a credit. As payment for the exports, the exporting country acquires a claim against foreigners. This claim is recorded as a debit. Conversely, purchases of goods from foreigners (imports) are a use of funds and recorded as a debit. To pay for the imports, the importing country either reduces its claims on foreigners or increases its foreign liabilities. Either payment method is recorded as a credit.

A specific example, using Table 6–1, can illustrate the effects of a transaction on the U.S. balance of payments. Let us assume that Volkswagen in Germany sells $100,000 of engine parts to the Ford Motor Company in the United States. The imports would be recorded as a debit to the current account (A-1). If Ford pays for the imports by drawing on its dollar account with a New York bank, a credit is recorded to the "other short term" capital account (C-6*b*). The domestic bank deposits held by foreigners has increased. If Ford pays for the imports by drawing on its account with a German bank, a credit is recorded to the C-6*a* "other short-term" capital account. The short-term foreign assets held by U.S. residents have been reduced because VW now owns the offshore deposits previously owned by Ford.

The transaction is recorded as follows:

		Debit	Credit
A-1	Merchandise imports	$100,000	
C-6*b*	Increase in domestic S-T assets held by foreigners		$100,000
	or		or
C-6*a*	Decrease in S-T foreign assets held by residents		$100,000

In terms of U.S. external liquidity, what has been the effect of this transaction? Simply, the United States has reduced its external liquidity by either increasing its foreign liabilities or decreasing its foreign assets. The transfer of foreign currency deposits to foreigners reduced the ability of U.S. residents to meet claims against the United States.

Services.   The service category, sometimes called *invisibles,* includes freight and insurance on international shipments (A-2); travel and related tourist expenditures (A-3); personal expenditures of government, civilian, and military personnel stationed in foreign countries (A-5); and payments for management fees, royalties, film rentals, and construction services (A-6). Purchases of services from foreigners are comparable to imports and recorded as debits. Conversely, sales of services to foreigners are similar to exports and recorded as credits.

As an illustration, continuing with the preceding example, Volkswagen's terms of sale are FOB (free on board). Thus, Ford must pay international freight and insurance from a German seaport. Ford uses a German freighter at a cost of $1,000 and pays with a check drawn on its dollar account in its New York bank. The transaction is recorded as follows:

		Debit	Credit
A-2	Shipment	$1,000	
C-6*b*	Other short term		$1,000

Ford has in effect purchased a German shipping service—a debit to the current account. It has paid for this service by increasing the domestic short-term assets held by foreigners—a credit in the capital account.

Transactions for international services between residents of the same country do not enter into the balance of payments. Examples of such transactions might be a resident of France using a French airline for international travel or a French exporter insuring its international shipments with a French insurance company. Although such transactions save foreign exchange for France compared to buying such services from a foreign firm, they are considered domestic transactions.

The investment income item (A-4) includes all interest payments; dividend remittances; and profits earned on investment in foreign enterprises effectively controlled by residents (direct investment). *These financial transfers are included in the current account because they are considered as factor income—that is, payments for the use of capital. In contrast, factor movements such as capital flows are included in the capital accounts.*

It is general practice to include all foreign earnings on direct investment in the balance-of-payments accounts even though some or all of the profits have not been transferred as dividend remittances. The rationale for including undistributed or reinvested earnings as a financial flow is that such earnings become the property of the foreign parent whether or not they are remitted. In order to follow the double-entry convention, therefore, profits accrued but not transferred that are included as investment income (a credit) must have an offsetting entry—reinvested earnings—in the capital accounts (a debit).

Assume that Volkswagen in the United States earned a profit of $1 million in a given year but remitted only $500,000 to Volkswagen in Germany by drawing on Volkswagen-U.S.'s New York bank account. The transaction is recorded as follows in the U.S. balance of payments:

		Debit	Credit
A-4	Investment income	$1,000,000	
C-1	Direct investment (reinvested earnings)		$500,000
C-6*b*	Other short-term		$500,000

Unrequited Transfers.   Unrequited transfers are noncommercial international transactions without a quid pro quo made by either private parties or governments. An important type of private transfer for many countries is remittances from workers abroad to their families. Other private transfers may be philanthropic activities and relief organization shipments. Government transfers consist of money, goods, and services given as grants to other nations or foreign residents. Thus, the United States provides military pensions to many residents of the Philippines who served in the U.S. Armed Forces during World War II when that country was still a U.S. colony.

If the transfer is in the form of goods, the value of the goods is recorded as an export credit, and a corresponding debit is recorded in the transfer account. If the transfer is in the form of money, the disbursing country will show a credit in the short-term capital account and an offsetting debit in the unrequited transfer account.

The American Red Cross, for example, sends $100,000 of food to Africa as part of a drought-relief program. The gift appears in the U.S. accounts as follows:

		Debit	Credit
B-1	Unrequited transfers, private	$100,000	
A-1	Merchandise exports		$100,000

The Capital Account

Capital account items are transactions in ownership claims. Financial assets and liabilities with a maturity of one year or less are considered short term. Those with longer maturities or no maturity (equity capital) are treated as long term.

Direct investment (C-1) in a general sense involves managerial participation in a foreign enterprise and is also described as effective control. In a statistical sense, however, it has proved difficult to find an objective definition of direct investment. Consequently, the statistical criteria vary among countries. The United

States classifies investments that give the investor more than 10 percent ownership as direct investments. *Portfolio investment* (C-2) is defined by the IMF as "undertaken for the sake of obtaining investment income or capital gains," as contrasted to entrepreneurial income.[4]

If, for instance, IBM invests an additional $10 million in one of its foreign subsidiaries by supplying it with equipment, the balance-of-payments entries are as follows:

		Debit	*Credit*
C-1	Direct investment	$10 million	
A-1	Exports		$10 million

If the investment is made by drawing on IBM's bank account in the United States, the credit entry would be:

C-6   Other short term $10 million credit

The "other long-term" capital account differentiates between government (C-3) and private transactions (C-4) of the reporting country. The transactions may be either in the form of loans or securities with an original maturity of more than one year. They may involve foreign private parties or foreign governments, except for transactions exclusively between monetary authorities. A government loan to a private party might be a loan by the U.S. Export-Import Bank to a foreign airline to finance the sale of U.S. airplanes. A private loan to a foreign government could be a Chase Manhattan Bank loan to the government of Brazil.

The "other short-term" capital accounts also separate government (C-5) and private (C-6) transactions. The principal government items are short-term loans and transactions in short-term securities of the reporting government. Private short-term items cover mainly short-term commercial obligations and deposits in or debts to banks. Commercial obligations and claims include trade bill acceptances and other short-term claims arising from the financing of trade. Open-book accounts and utilized lines of credit, except for intercompany accounts, are also included. Intercompany accounts are included as direct investment even though they may be short-term transfers.

As several of the examples illustrate, changes in the short-term capital accounts may be *compensatory* or *financing* shifts, in the sense that they result from current account transactions, transfers, or long-term investments. They can also be *autonomous* transactions undertaken for their own sake, such as movements by short-term investors to take advantage of interest differentials among countries.

---

[4] John Alves, *The Balance of Payments: A Glossary of Terms* (Washington, D.C.: International Monetary Fund, 1979), p. 5.

Reserves

Reserve assets (D-1 through 4) are the actual (spot) holdings of SDRs, gold, and foreign convertible currencies, together with the country's IMF position. These are the assets available to the monetary authorities to meet balance-of-payments deficits. They are closely analogous to the cash and near-cash assets of a private company. Only purchases and sales by official monetary authorities such as the Federal Reserve System of the United States, the Bank of England, and the Bank of France are entered in this account. A country's own currency is not foreign exchange and, therefore, by definition is not included as reserve assets. On the other hand, because the U.S. dollar is a convertible currency, dollar holdings of the Bank of England and the Bank of France are reserve assets for Britain and France.

The Bank of France decides that it has accumulated too many dollar deposits and buys U.S. $2 million in gold from the Federal Reserve Bank of New York, paying with a check on that bank. The U.S. balance-of-payments entries would be:

		Debit	Credit
C-5b	Other short-term capital, official	$2 million	
D-1	Monetary gold		$2 million

The debit and credit treatment of reserve items may appear puzzling. How can a decrease in monetary gold stocks, for example, be a credit item? The reason is that, in the example noted above, the United States has reduced its liabilities to foreigners (dollar deposits owned by foreigners) in exchange for monetary gold. In a sense, the sale of gold is like an export of merchandise and thus a credit.

Net Errors and Omissions or Statistical Discrepancies

In theory, the balance of payments should balance because all debits are offset by credits and vice versa. In practice, they never balance. The sources on which the entries are based may be incomplete or inaccurate. Also, different sources that may not be consistent with one another are generally used for the credit and debit flows of the same transaction. The net errors and omissions is a balancing item that compensates for any excess of recorded credits over recorded debits or vice versa. The total can be large if the reporting system is weak or if clandestine transactions are important.

INTERPRETING THE ACCOUNTS

How does the international firm make use of the balance-of-payments statistics? The balance-of-payments data are a principal source for assessing a country's currency prospects. Furthermore, these currency prospects are a major consideration in shaping national control policies over international transfers of merchandise and funds. Another important reason for understanding the balance-of-payments accounts is that the international firm is frequently required to analyze the impact of its own operations on the balance of payments of both home and host countries. This aspect will be discussed in Chapter 13 on measuring benefits to the nation-state.

Measures of Deficits and Surpluses

If the balance of payments always balances, in the sense that debits are equal to credits, why then do we hear of balance-of-payments *surpluses* or *deficits?* The reason for this apparent anomaly has to do with the methods used to interpret balance-of-payments results. A balance-of-payments *deficit* may be defined as a negative balance *of certain transactions* within the balance of payments as a whole. A *surplus* is a positive balance of the same types of transactions. Thus when reference is made to a deficit or a surplus, it is necessary to identify the transactions being referred to.

In order to analyze a firm's financial situation, various ratios are calculated from its balance sheet and income statement. Such items as the debt equity ratio and "number of times interest earned" provide clues as to a company's liquidity and ability to service debt. Similarly, analytical measures are derived from a country's balance of payments that focus on certain aspects of the country's financial situation.

The conventional measures used to interpret a country's position are the merchandise trade balance, the current account balance, and the basic balance. Figure 6–1 shows the components of each and their interrelationships.

Each of these measures attempts to detect future trends in external liquidity. And each measure pays particular attention to so-called autonomous transactions

FIGURE 6–1   Measures of a Country's Balance-of-Payments Position

```
          Exports minus imports
     =    Merchandise trade balance
                ⎧ Freight, net
                ⎪ Military, net
          ±     ⎨ Investment income, net
                ⎪ Other income, net
                ⎪ Other services, net
                ⎩ Transfers, net
     =    Current account balance
     ±    Long-term net capital
          flows
     =    Basic balance
```

that have their own economic justification for taking place, independent of other entries in the balance-of-payments accounts. Autonomous transactions usually respond to business conditions at home and abroad. The financing or compensating transactions that balance the accounts, such as foreign exchange received in payment for commodity exports, are then disregarded. The sum of the autonomous transactions—also called *above the line* items—is a measure of the balance-of-payments surplus or deficit. If autonomous payments exceed autonomous receipts, the resulting deficit indicates that a country's international purchasing power has decreased.

A country's deficit or surplus will change according to the definition of autonomous transactions. The merchandise trade balance designates only exports and imports as autonomous items. By this measure the surplus or deficit results exclusively from the country's performance as an international trader. The current account balance is wider. It includes invisibles and transfers—as well as merchandise trade—as autonomous items. This performance measure for a country is analogous to the net profit calculation for a business concern.

The basic balance considers long-term capital transactions together with current account items as autonomous. It is intended to measure long-term tendencies in the balance of payments that are not distorted by fluctuating, easily reversible, or speculative short-term financial flows. A developing country may be expected (indeed encouraged) to incur current account deficits so long as long-term capital inflows offset the operating shortfalls. Under such circumstances, the basic balance may be the best indicator of overall country performance.

Of the various payments accounts balances, the simplest is the *change in official reserves* held by the government. Reserves are needed if the country wishes to intervene in the foreign exchange market or meet balance-of-payments deficits. But here, again, the significance of the measure varies from country to country. A small and shrinking reserve base may be dangerous for a purely trading country but simply efficient banking for a country whose currency serves as a medium for international trade and investment.

It should now be apparent that the determination of a surplus or deficit as a guidepost for policy action cannot be based on a single figure. Instead, an assessment of the external liquidity situation of a country requires an analysis of the balance of payments as a whole in the context of economic development at home and abroad. In recognition of this fact, the IMF publishes so-called analytic presentations that show several balances.

The United States has its own unique balance-of-payments characteristics— in particular, the reserve currency role of the dollar. To fit its own special needs, the United States presently uses the modified form of presentation shown in Table 6–2. This presentation shows several types of balance (lines 66–69) but does not include the basic balance measure. The reason given for dropping the basic balance is that in many cases it is not possible to distinguish between short-term and long-term capital movements. For example, direct investment flows are classified as long-term capital movements. Yet this category includes short-term and easily reversible intercompany flows between parents and foreign affiliates.[5]

An Analytic Approach

Keeping in mind the different definitions of surpluses and deficits, the analyst can examine recent changes and trends in a country's external relations for valuable clues about the future. If the analyst determines that a serious balance-of-payments problem exists, some of the principal questions to be asked are the following:

1. What correction measures are most applicable to the country, given its present difficulties?

2. Is the payments deficit temporary or does it reflect more permanent, structural difficulties?

   A firm's loss for the year may either result from an extraordinary loss or be a trend. Likewise, a country's deficit may reflect an "extraordinary loss"— temporary rise/fall in imports/exports, natural disaster, labor disruption, and so on—or, alternatively, be evidence of a permanent condition.

3. Is the country heavily dependent on external debt and/or large capital inflows?

   If so, short-term liquidity questions are important even if the country has good medium-term or long-term prospects. A crucial issue becomes the country's capacity to continue meeting its current obligations.

4. What are the composition and outlook for the nation's exports?

   Are exports diversified as to composition? As to markets? How "elastic" is the foreign demand for exports—that is, are foreign sales highly sensitive to changes in price and income?

5. Can imports be reduced without adverse consequences?

   Imports will be difficult to reduce if they are essential for producing export items, or if domestic demand is insensitive to price increases.

6. What are the country's medium and long-term prospects?

   Trading firms are most concerned with short-term prospects. Investors and creditors will be more affected by medium and long-term prospects. The relevant issue for creditors is repayment prospects in the future. A key issue for investors is whether they will be able to repatriate profits or liquidate investments in the future.

7. Are the country's reserves sufficient?

8. What are the country's prospects for additional foreign borrowing from private, official, and international sources?

---

[5] Jack J. Bame, "Analyzing U.S. International Transactions," *Columbia Journal of World Business,* Fall 1976, pp. 74–76.

9. Can the country depend upon inflows from private foreign investors and/or transfers of official aid?

10. What is the government's commitment to remedying the deficits?

There are no ironclad rules to use in obtaining definitive answers to such questions. It is essential, therefore, to determine the most probable courses of action by government officials to remedy the imbalances. The strategy, or combinations of strategies, of governments will have different impacts on the domestic economy and on the foreign exchange markets. Any number of steps might be taken to remedy a trade deficit. Restrictions can be imposed on imports. Preferential exchange rates may be established to encourage certain categories of exports or discourage certain imports. Special tax incentives may be made available to promote exports or new industries with good potential for either export expansion or import substitution. Or the currency can be devalued.

The strategy mix of governments to remedy payments imbalances will also have varying impacts on different types of international business operations. An international firm that uses domestic inputs for a manufacturing facility in the country may be indifferent to, or even benefited by, new restrictions on imports. Another firm that relies heavily on imported equipment or materials might find such an action to be disastrous. Hence we see the need to conduct balance-of-payments intelligence in devising a company's strategy for responding to environmental changes.

THE U.S. BALANCE OF PAYMENTS

It would be simpler to illustrate the methodology for analyzing a country's balance-of-payments situation by using the case of a relatively simple economy like Malawi in Africa, as is done in one of the IMF publications.[6] In contrast, the U.S. balance-of-payments accounts are highly complex. Yet, because the United States plays such a dominant role in the world economy, international managers generally find it essential to be informed on the U.S. situation.

The U.S. balance-of-payments situation over the period from 1980 to 1985 was both traumatic and dramatic. By the end of the period, as shown in Table 6–2, the U.S. deficit on current account (line 69) had reached an unprecedented level of $118 billion, mainly as a result of a massive trade deficit (line 66) of $124 billion. The current account deficit was "financed" by large inflows of private funds from foreigners to purchase U.S. private and government securities (lines 60–61), by a huge increase in U.S. liabilities to foreigners (line 63), and by a substantial positive statistical discrepancy (line 65), probably as a result of unrecorded capital inflows. The end result, as shown in Table 6–3, is that the United States became in 1985 the largest debtor nation in the world, with the

---

[6] See Poul Høst-Madsen, *Macroeconomic Accounts: An Overview* (Washington, D.C.: International Monetary Fund, 1979), pp. 45–47.

TABLE 6–2 U.S. International Transactions ($ millions)

Line	(Credits +; debits −)[1]	1971	1976	1980	1981	1982	1983	1984	1985	Line
1	**Exports of goods and services[2]**	**68,838**	**171,630**	**342,485**	**375,759**	**348,665**	**333,257**	**360,111**	**358,498**	1
2	Merchandise, adjusted, excluding military[3]	43,319	114,745	224,269	237,085	211,198	201,820	219,900	214,424	2
3	Transfers under U.S. military agency sales contracts	1,926	5,454	8,274	10,041	11,986	12,221	10,103	9,001	3
4	Travel	2,534	5,742	10,588	12,913	12,393	11,408	11,353	11,663	4
5	Passenger fares	615	1,229	2,591	3,111	3,174	3,037	3,028	2,989	5
6	Other transportation	3,299	6,747	11,618	12,560	12,317	12,590	13,812	13,972	6
7	Royalties and license fees from affiliated foreigners[4]	1,927	3,531	5,780	5,794	3,507	3,597	3,923	4,123	7
8	Royalties and license fees from unaffiliated foreigners	618	822	1,305	1,490	1,669	1,625	1,619	1,700	8
9	Other private services from affiliated foreigners					1,816	2,532	2,437	2,526	9
10	Other private services from unaffiliated foreigners	1,546	3,584	5,158	5,856	6,522	6,547	7,086	7,235	10
11	U.S. Government miscellaneous services	347	489	398	499	533	630	629	874	11
	Receipts of income on U.S. assets abroad:									
12	Direct investment	9,160	18,999	37,146	32,549	21,381	20,499	21,509	34,320	12
13	Other private receipts	2,641	8,955	32,798	50,182	58,050	51,920	59,483	50,180	13
14	U.S. Government receipts	906	1,332	2,562	3,680	4,118	4,832	5,229	5,491	14
15	**Transfers of goods and services under U.S. military grant programs, net**	**3,546**	**373**	**756**	**679**	**585**	**194**	**190**	**64**	15
16	**Imports of goods and services**	**−66,414**	**−162,109**	**−333,020**	**−361,995**	**−348,879**	**−370,380**	**−454,420**	**−461,191**	16
17	Merchandise, adjusted, excluding military[3]	−45,579	−124,228	−249,749	−265,063	−247,642	−268,900	−332,422	−338,863	17
18	Direct defense expenditures	−4,819	−4,895	−10,511	−11,224	−12,260	−12,590	−11,930	−11,918	18
19	Travel	−4,373	−6,856	−10,397	−11,479	−12,394	−13,556	−15,449	−16,502	19
20	Passenger fares	−1,290	−2,568	−3,607	−4,487	−4,772	−5,484	−6,502	−7,322	20
21	Other transportation	−3,130	−6,852	−11,790	−12,474	−11,710	−12,222	−14,835	−15,928	21
22	Royalties and license fees to affiliated foreigners[4]	−118	−293	−428	−362	−326	−405	−597	−467	22
23	Royalties and license fees to unaffiliated foreigners	−123	−189	−297	−289	−292	−315	−362	−380	23
24	Other private services to affiliated foreigners					403	471	478	694	24
25	Other private services to unaffiliated foreigners	−956	−2,006	−2,909	−3,002	−3,543	−3,404	−3,801	−3,965	25
26	U.S. Government miscellaneous services	−592	−911	−1,214	−1,287	−1,460	−1,567	−1,531	−1,737	26
	Payments of income on foreign assets in the United States:									
27	Direct investment	−1,164	−3,110	−8,635	−6,898	−3,155	−5,598	−9,229	−8,068	27
28	Other private payments	−2,428	−5,681	−20,893	−28,553	−33,443	−28,987	−38,471	−35,429	28
29	U.S. Government payments	−1,844	−4,520	−12,592	−16,878	−18,285	−17,825	−19,769	−21,306	29
30	**U.S. military grants of goods and services, net**	**−3,546**	**−373**	**−756**	**−679**	**−585**	**−194**	**−190**	**−64**	30
31	**Unilateral transfers (excluding military grants of goods and services), net**	**−3,856**	**−5,314**	**−7,593**	**−7,425**	**−8,917**	**−9,481**	**−12,157**	**−14,983**	31
32	U.S. Government grants (excluding military grants of goods and services)	−2,043	−3,146	−4,731	−4,466	−5,501	−6,286	−8,536	−11,196	32
33	U.S. Government pensions and other transfers	−696	−1,250	−1,818	−2,041	−2,251	−2,207	−2,194	−2,171	33
34	Private remittances and other transfers	−1,117	−917	−1,044	−918	−1,165	−987	−1,427	−1,616	34

Line	Item								
35	**U.S. assets abroad, net (increase/capital outflow (−))**	−12,475	−51,269	−86,118	−111,031	−121,273	−50,022	−23,639	−32,436
36	U.S. official reserve assets, net[5]	2,349	−2,558	−8,155	−5,175	−4,965	−1,196	−3,131	−3,858
37	Gold	866	.....	.....	(*)	.....	.....	.....	.....
38	Special drawing rights	−249	−78	−16	−1,824	−1,371	−66	−979	−897
39	Reserve position in the International Monetary Fund	1,350	−2,212	−1,667	−2,491	−2,552	−4,434	−995	908
40	Foreign currencies	382	−268	−6,472	−861	−1,041	−3,304	−1,156	−3,869
41	U.S. Government assets, other than official reserve assets, net	−1,884	−4,214	−5,162	−5,097	−6,131	−5,005	−5,523	−2,824
42	U.S. credits and other long-term assets	−4,181	−6,943	−9,860	−9,674	−10,063	−9,966	−9,640	−7,579
43	Repayments on U.S. credits and other long-term assets[6]	2,115	2,596	4,456	4,413	4,292	5,012	4,499	4,644
44	U.S. foreign currency holdings and U.S. short-term assets, net	182	133	242	164	−360	−51	−382	111
45	U.S. private assets, net	−12,940	−44,498	−72,802	−100,758	−110,177	−43,821	−14,986	−25,754
46	Direct investment	−7,618	−11,949	−19,222	−9,624	−2,369	−373	−3,858	−18,752
47	Foreign securities	−1,113	−8,885	−3,568	−5,778	−8,102	−7,007	−5,082	−7,977
48	U.S. claims on unaffiliated foreigners reported by U.S. nonbanking concerns	−1,229	−2,296	−3,174	−1,181	6,626	−6,513	5,081	1,665
49	U.S. claims reported by U.S. banks, not included elsewhere	−2,980	−21,368	−46,838	−84,175	−111,070	−29,928	−11,127	−691
50	**Foreign assets in the United States, net (increase/capital inflow (+))**	22,970	36,518	58,112	83,322	94,078	85,496	102,767	127,106
51	Foreign official assets in the United States, net	26,879	17,693	15,497	4,960	3,593	5,968	3,037	−1,324
52	U.S. Government securities	26,570	9,892	11,895	6,322	5,085	6,496	4,703	−841
53	U.S. Treasury securities[7]	26,578	9,319	9,708	5,019	5,779	6,972	4,690	−546
54	Other[8]	−8	573	2,187	1,303	−694	−476	13	−295
55	Other U.S. Government liabilities[9]	−510	4,627	615	−338	605	725	436	483
56	U.S. liabilities reported by U.S. banks, not included elsewhere	819	969	−159	−3,670	−1,747	545	555	522
57	Other foreign official assets[10]		2,205	3,145	2,646	−350	−1,798	−2,657	−1,488
58	Other foreign assets in the United States, net	−3,909	18,826	42,615	78,362	90,486	79,527	99,730	128,430
59	Direct investment	367	4,347	16,918	25,195	13,792	11,946	25,359	17,856
60	U.S. Treasury securities	−24	2,783	[14]2,645	[14]2,946	[14]7,052	[14]8,721	23,059	20,500
61	U.S. securities other than U.S. Treasury securities	2,289	1,284	5,457	7,176	6,392	8,636	12,759	50,859
62	U.S. liabilities to unaffiliated foreigners reported by U.S. nonbanking concerns	369	−578	6,852	917	−2,383	−118	4,704	−1,172
63	U.S. liabilities reported by U.S. banks, not included elsewhere	−6,911	10,990	10,743	42,128	65,633	50,342	33,849	40,387
64	**Allocations of special drawing rights**	717	.....	1,152	1,093	.....	.....	.....	.....
65	**Statistical discrepancy (sum of above items with sign reversed)**	−9,779	10,544	24,982	20,276	36,325	11,130	27,338	23,004
	Memoranda:								
66	Balance on merchandise trade (lines 2 and 17)[11]	−2,260	−9,483	−25,480	−27,978	−36,444	−67,080	−112,522	−124,439
67	Balance on goods and services (lines 1 and 16)[11]	2,423	9,521	9,466	13,764	−214	−37,123	−94,308	−102,694
68	Balance on goods, services, and remittances (lines 67, 33, and 34)	610	7,354	6,604	10,805	−3,630	−40,317	−97,929	−106,481
69	Balance on current account (lines 67 and 31)[11]	−1,433	4,207	1,873	6,339	−9,131	−46,604	−106,466	−117,677
	Transactions in U.S. official reserve assets and in foreign official assets in the United States:								
70	Increase (−) in U.S. official reserve assets, net (line 36)	2,349	−2,558	−8,155	−5,175	−4,965	−1,196	−3,131	−3,858
71	Increase (+) in foreign official assets in the United States (line 51 less line 55)	27,389	13,066	14,881	5,298	2,988	5,243	2,601	−1,807

127

Footnotes to Table 6–2

General notes: *ᴾ* Preliminary.   * Less than $500,000 (±)   n.a. Not available.

1. Credits, +: Exports of goods and services; unilateral transfers to United States; capital inflows (increase in foreign assets (U.S. liabilities) or decrease in U.S. assets); decrease in U.S. official reserve assets; increase in foreign official assets in the United States.
   Debits, −: Imports of goods and services, unilateral transfers to foreigners; capital outflows (decrease in foreign assets (U.S. liabilities) or increase in U.S. assets); increase in U.S. official reserve assets; decrease in foreign official assets in the United States.
2. Excludes transfers of goods and services under U.S. military grant programs (see line 14).
3. Excludes exports of goods under U.S. military agency sales contracts identified in Census export documents, excludes imports of goods under direct defense expenditures identified in Census import documents, and reflects various other adjustments (for valuation, coverage, and timing) of Census statistics to balance of payments basis.
4. Beginning in 1982, line 7 and line 22 are redefined to include only net receipts and payments for the use or sale of intangible property rights, including patents, industrial processes, trademarks, copyrights, franchises, designs, know-how, formulas, techniques, and manufacturing rights. Other direct investment services, net, which include fees for management, professional, and technical services, charges for the use of tangible property, film and television tape rentals, and all other charges and fees are shown in line 9 and line 24. Data on the redefined basis are not separately available prior to 1982.
5. For all areas, amounts outstanding March 31, 1985, were as follows in millions of dollars: Line 36, 44,918; line 37, 11,090; line 38, 7,839; line 39, 12,025; line 40, 13,965.
6. Includes sales of foreign obligations to foreigners.
7. Consists of bills, certificates, marketable bonds and notes, and nonmarketable convertible and nonconvertible bonds and notes.
8. Consists of U.S. Treasury and Export-Import Bank obligations, not included elsewhere, and of debt securities of U.S. Government corporations and agencies.
9. Includes, primarily, U.S. Government liabilities associated with military agency sales contracts and other transactions arranged with or through foreign official agencies.
10. Consists of investments in U.S. corporate stocks and in debt securities of private corporations and State and local governments.
11. Conceptually, the sum of lines 67 and 62 is equal to "net foreign investment" in the national income and product accounts (NIPA's). However, the foreign transactions account in the NIPA's (a) includes adjustments to the international transactions accounts for the different treatment of gold, (b) excludes capital gains and losses of foreign affiliates of U.S. parent companies from the NIPA's measure of income receipts from direct investment abroad, and from the corresponding income payments on direct investment in the United States, and (c) includes an adjustment for the different geographical treatment of transactions with U.S. territories and Puerto Rico, and (d) includes an adjustment for services furnished without payment by financial intermediaries, except life insurance carriers. In addition, for NIPA purposes, U.S. Government interest payments to foreigners are excluded from "net exports of goods and services" but included with transfers in "net foreign investment." A reconciliation table of the international accounts and the NIPA foreign transactions account appears in the "Reconciliation and Other Special Tables" section in this issue of the *Survey of Current Business.*
12. Includes return import into the United States, at a depreciated value of $21 million in 1972-IV and $22 million in 1973-II, of aircraft originally reported in 1970-III in line 3 as a long-term lease to Australia.
13. Includes extraordinary U.S. government transactions with India. See "Special U.S. Government Transactions," June 1974 *Survey,* p. 27.
14. Includes foreign currency denominated notes sold to private residents abroad.

SOURCE: *Survey of Current Business,* June 1986, pp. 42–43.

foreign holdings of assets in the United States exceeding U.S. assets abroad by more than $100 billion.

The Trade Deficit

Throughout the 20th century until 1971, the United States always had a favorable balance of trade, with exports exceeding imports. But during the 1970s, except for 1973 and 1975, the U.S. trade deficits persisted and grew to a level of $25 billion by 1980. The trade picture continued to deteriorate rapidly during the 1980s, with the deficit reaching the unprecedented total of $124 billion in 1985.

By comparing merchandise exports (line 2) with merchandise imports (line 17), we see that the expanding deficit from 1980 to 1985 reflects a massive increase in U.S. imports while U.S. exports stagnated and even declined. In absolute terms, imports increased by almost $90 billion while exports decreased $10 billion over the 1980–85 period.

An examination of the product composition of trade sheds additional light on the U.S. trade situation.[7] The decline in export earnings resulted mainly from a sharp drop in the export of agricultural products. The principal increases in imports occurred in three product categories: automotive vehicles, capital goods (mainly machinery), and consumer goods other than automotive. A major factor contributing to the loss of competitiveness of U.S. products in both foreign and domestic markets was the large increase in the international value of the U.S. dollar, as shown in Figure 4–2 in Chapter 4.

Services

During most of the 1970s, the U.S. net surpluses on service transactions more than offset the merchandise trade deficits. In this respect, the 1980 data illustrate this past pattern. In 1980, a positive balance on service transactions of $35 billion more than offset the trade deficit and resulted in a surplus of $9.5 billion in the balance on goods and services (line 67). The United States had net outflows for military expenditures (lines 3 and 18) and for travel and transportation (lines 4–6 and 19–21). The main surplus was receipts of income on U.S. assets abroad of $72.5 billion (lines 12–14) as against payments of income on foreign assets in the U.S. (lines 27–29) of only $42.1 billion. More than half of the income on U.S. assets abroad were profits from foreign direct investment. The United States also had surpluses from royalties and license fees as well as from the sale of services such as banking, accounting, and consulting.

This pattern changed dramatically in 1982. The U.S. continued to earn a surplus on services, even though the strong dollar encouraged many Americans to travel abroad and caused a deficit in that category. Yet the trade deficits continued to grow so large that the positive balances on services became only a small offset, and the United States experienced a steady and growing deficit in the current account (line 69).

Unilateral Transfers

Unlike the situation in a number of countries, where unrequited transfers have been positive as a result of large inflows from residents working abroad and from foreign grants, the United States has consistently had a net deficit on

---

[7] *Survey of Current Business,* June 1986, Table 3, p. 52.

unilateral transfers. The major factor in this category has been grants from the U.S. government, such as foreign aid (line 32).

The Capital Accounts—Balancing the Current Account Deficits

How can this 1980–85 phenomenon be explained—namely, a growing current account deficit concurrent with a rising foreign exchange value of the U.S. dollar? Under a floating exchange rate system, according to the textbooks, current account deficits would increase the foreign supply of U.S. dollars and dollar claims, leading to a devaluation of the dollar. This in turn should bring the accounts back into balance by discouraging imports and encouraging exports. By the end of 1985, the downward adjustment of the U.S. dollar did begin to occur. Yet the U.S. patterns during the 1980–85 period clearly demonstrate, as discussed in Chapter 4, that a complex set of factors, going beyond payments deficits, are involved in foreign exchange movements.

In a statistical sense, the balance-of-payments accounts show that foreigners were willing to finance the deficit by buying U.S. government securities, by investing in the U.S. stock and bond markets, and by being willing to increase their holdings of U.S. liabilities. In 1985, for example, foreigners purchased more than $70 billion of U.S. treasury and private securities (lines 60–61), while U.S. residents purchased only $8 billion in foreign securities (line 47). Foreigners increased their holdings of U.S. liabilities by $39 billion (lines 62–63) while U.S. claims on foreigners increased by only $2.4 billion (lines 48–49). In addition to these net inflows, there was a statistical discrepancy (unrecorded inflows) of $23 billion. In total, during 1985 foreigners were willing to finance a U.S. deficit of $118 billion.

The motivations of foreigners were mixed and generally influenced by available alternatives. High interest rates in the U.S. relative to those in other countries were an attraction for some foreigners. The revival of the U.S. economy while domestic growth rates were low in most of the other industrialized countries was another factor attracting profit-seeking direct and portfolio investments. Other foreign investors were motivated mainly by safety considerations rather than profitability and looked upon the United States as a "safe haven" for a share of their assets.

By the mid-1980s, the United States had become greatly concerned about the continuing trade deficits and its deteriorating international investment position. There was a general consensus that the deficits could not continue indefinitely and that a loss of confidence in the U.S. dollar could have serious consequences. As a result, the central banks of the major industrialized countries, as noted in Chapter 4, began cooperating to reduce the strength of the dollar and (they hoped) to reduce the U.S. trade deficit.

THE INTERNATIONAL INVESTMENT POSITION

The balance of payments accounts records only *flows* during the reporting period. A separate statement referred to as the International Investment Position presents a *static picture* at a given point in time of a country's balance of indebtedness. The statement takes into account valuation adjustments for changes in prices and exchange rates, that are not included in the balance of payments, as well as capital flows. A nation's net position is the difference between that country's assets abroad and its liabilities to nonresidents. Although priority attention is generally given to the balance of payments accounts, the two statements should be analyzed together.

Not all deficits have the same effect on a country's international financial strength. A deficit caused by increased imports of consumer goods may permanently

---

BOX 6–1
Let U.S. Be a Debtor but Not a Deadbeat

If recent predictions of the United States sliding back into debtor-nation status come true, one can only hope that we play the role better this time than we did during our first fling at being an international debtor—when the Poet Laureate of England and a host of angry foreign creditors tried to make the terms "American" and "con artist" synonymous.

The time was the late 1830s, when the foreign-financed binge of railroad-building and canal-building on which several U.S. states had embarked was interrupted by the cold, gray dawn of the Panic of 1837. State after state was shocked into sobriety—and default.

William Wordsworth was not particularly concerned about most of the states that went under, but Pennsylvania's default in 1842 touched close to home: the poet's brother and several other relations and friends were heavily invested in bonds issued by the Keystone state and several Philadelphia-based companies that threatened to collapse.

For several years, Wordsworth's correspondence with American friends was dominated by descriptions of the sorry plight of his relatives and friends. As the years of default dragged on, the exasperated poet finally damned the recalcitrant debtors in the sonnet "To the Pennsylvanians." It is not one of his greatest works, but it certainly attracted more immediate attention on its publication on the American side of the Atlantic than any of his other poems. After a description of how the Quaker colony's sober reputation and natural endowment had "won confidence, now ruthlessly betrayed" the poem concludes:

> All who revere the memory of Penn
> Grieve for the land on whose wild woods his name
> Was fondly grafted with a virtuous aim.
> Renounced, abandoned by degenerate Men
> For state-dishonour black as ever came
> To upper air from Mammon's loathsome den.

Of course, it was all sorted out eventually: The depression finally dissipated, and most of the states resumed payment on their debts.

SOURCE: Adapted from an article by W. H. Earle in *The Wall Street Journal*, February 27, 1984. © Dow Jones & Company, Inc., 1984. Used with permission. All rights reserved.

TABLE 6–3 International Investment Position of the United States at Year-end, 1970–85 (U.S. $ millions)

Line	Type of investment	1980r	1981r	1982r	1983r	1984r	1985p
1	**Net international investment position of the United States (line 2 less line 20)**	**106,037**	**140,704**	**136,200**	**88,494**	**4,384**	**−107,440**
2	**U.S. assets abroad**	**606,867**	**719,687**	**824,875**	**874,053**	**898,187**	**952,367**
3	U.S. official reserve assets[1]	26,756	30,075	33,957	33,748	34,933	43,185
4	Gold[1]	11,160	11,151	11,148	11,121	11,096	11,090
5	Special drawing rights[1]	2,610	4,096	5,250	5,025	5,641	7,293
6	Reserve position in the International Monetary Fund[1]	2,852	5,054	7,348	11,312	11,541	11,947
7	Foreign currencies[1]	10,134	9,774	10,212	6,289	6,656	12,856
8	U.S. Government assets, other than official reserve assets	63,545	68,451	74,333	79,250	84,636	87,418
9	U.S. loans and other long-term assets[2]	61,821	66,995	72,651	77,553	82,657	85,587
10	Repayable in dollars	59,597	64,722	70,675	75,692	80,847	83,811
11	Other[3]	2,224	2,273	1,976	1,861	1,810	1,776
12	U.S. foreign currency holdings and U.S. Short-term assets	1,724	1,456	1,682	1,697	1,979	1,831
13	U.S. private assets	516,566	621,161	716,585	761,055	778,618	821,764
14	Direct investment abroad[4]	215,375	228,348	207,752	207,203	212,994	232,667
15	Foreign securities	62,653	63,452	75,672	84,270	89,997	114,147
16	Bonds	43,487	45,791	56,698	57,719	62,071	73,425
17	Corporate stocks	19,166	17,661	18,974	26,551	27,926	40,722
18	U.S. claims on unaffiliated foreigners reported by U.S. nonbanking concerns[5]	34,672	35,853	28,583	35,077	29,996	28,220
19	U.S. claims reported by U.S. banks, not included elsewhere[6]	203,866	293,508	404,578	434,505	445,631	446,730
20	**Foreign assets in the United States**	**500,830**	**578,983**	**688,675**	**785,559**	**893,803**	**1,059,807**
21	Foreign official assets in the United States	176,062	180,425	189,109	194,599	199,127	202,308
22	U.S. Government securities	118,189	125,130	132,587	136,987	143,014	143,736
23	U.S. Treasury securities[7]	111,336	117,004	124,929	129,716	135,510	136,036
24	Other[7]	6,853	8,126	7,658	7,271	7,504	7,700
25	Other U.S. Government liabilities[8]	13,367	13,029	13,639	14,362	14,798	15,280
26	U.S. liabilities reported by U.S. banks, not included elsewhere.	30,381	26,737	24,989	25,534	26,090	26,611
27	Other foreign official assets[7]	14,125	15,529	17,894	17,716	15,225	16,681

28	Other foreign assets in the United States	324,768	398,558	499,566	590,960	694,676	857,499
29	Direct investment in the United States[9]	83,046	108,714	124,677	137,061	164,583	182,951
30	U.S. Treasury securities[7]	16,113	18,524	25,802	33,922	58,330	83,832
31	U.S. securities other than U.S. Treasury securities[7]	74,114	75,353	93,567	114,710	128,560	207,770
32	Corporate and other bonds[7]	9,545	10,727	16,805	17,454	32,724	81,831
33	Corporate stocks[7]	64,569	64,626	76,762	97,256	95,836	125,939
34	U.S. liabilities to unaffiliated foreigners reported by U.S. nonbanking concerns[5]	30,426	30,606	27,532	26,937	31,024	29,102
35	U.S. liabilities reported by U.S. banks, not included elsewhere[6]	121,069	165,361	227,988	278,330	312,179	353,844

Notes

[r] Revised.

[p] Preliminary.

1. Total reserve assets include increases from changes in the par value of the dollar: on May 8, 1972, the increase totaled $1,016 million, consisting of $828 million gold stock, $155 million special drawing rights (SDR), and $33 million U.S. reserve position in the International Monetary Fund (IMF); on October 18, 1973, the increase totaled $1,436 million, consisting of $1,165 million gold stock, $217 million SDR, and $54 million reserve position in the IMF. The gold stock is valued at $35 per fine troy ounce through May 7, 1972; thereafter, at $38 per fine troy ounce through October 17, 1973, pursuant to the Par Value Modification Act (P.L. 92-268); and, thereafter, at $42⅖ per fine troy ounce pursuant to an amendment (in P.L. 93-110) to the Par Value Modification Act. Beginning in 1974, the value of the SDR, in which the U.S. holdings of SDR and the reserve position in the IMF are denominated, fluctuates based on the weighted average of exchange rates for the currencies of principal IMF members. Foreign currency reserves are valued at exchange rates at time of purchase through 1973 and at current exchange rates thereafter.

2. Also includes paid-in capital subscriptions to international financial institutions and outstanding amounts of miscellaneous claims that have been settled through international agreements to be payable to the U.S. Government over periods in excess of one year. Excludes World War I debts that are not being serviced.

3. Includes indebtedness that the borrower may contractually, or at its option, repay with its currency, with a third country's currency, or by delivery of materials or transfer of services.

4. Estimates are linked, for 1982 forward, to the U.S. Department of Commerce 1982 benchmark survey and, for 1977–1981 and 1966–76, to the Commerce 1977 and 1966 benchmark surveys, respectively.

5. Breaks in the series reflect: in 1971, 1972, and 1978, expanded reporting coverage; in 1982, an increase in reporters' exemption levels.

6. Breaks in the series reflect: in 1971 and 1972, expanded reporting coverage; in 1978, expanded coverage of bank holding companies and of brokers' and security dealers' reporting of liabilities; in 1981, expanded coverage of brokers' and security dealers' reporting of claims; and in 1977 and 1982, an increase in reporters' exemption levels.

7. Estimates include results of 1974 and 1978 portfolio benchmark surveys conducted by the U.S. Department of the Treasury. Beginning with the 1978 benchmark, marketable Treasury bonds are valued at market price; previously, they were valued at acquisition price.

8. Primarily includes U.S. Government liabilities associated with military sales contracts and other transactions arranged with or through foreign official agencies.

9. Estimates are linked, for 1980 forward, to the U.S. Department of Commerce 1980 benchmark survey; for 1973–79, to the Commerce 1974 benchmark survey; and through 1972 to the Commerce 1959 benchmark survey.

SOURCE: Survey of Current Business, June 1986, p. 28.

reduce a country's international liquidity. A deficit caused by the import of capital goods may reduce liquidity over the short run but build up productive capacity that can increase the long-term strength of the country by expanding exports or substituting for imports. Likewise, a deficit caused by capital outflow for foreign direct investment will reduce liquidity but increase a country's long-term strength by generating return flows of investment income.

The shift in the U.S. international investment position from a net surplus to a net deficit is shown in Table 6–3. The table reveals that foreign governments have helped finance the U.S. deficit by holding more than $200 billion of official assets in the United States (line 21). Another significant item has been the comparative trends in foreign direct investment. From 1980 to 1985, U.S. direct investment abroad (line 14) increased by only $17 billion; whereas direct investment in the United States (line 29) expanded by $100 billion. Still another major factor was the increase of $100 billion in the holding of U.S. securities by foreigners as compared to a gain of $50 billion in the value of foreign securities held by U.S. residents (line 15).

The effect of valuation adjustments, although not shown in Table 6–3 was significant. Between 1984 and 1985, the value of foreign holdings of corporate stocks (line 33) increased by $30 billion. Only $5 billion resulted from capital inflows, whereas $25 billion resulted from gains in the value of the total portfolio held by foreigners during the stock market boom of the 1980s.[8]

Anticipating the U.S. slide into debtor-nation status, a writer in 1984 dipped into past history and urged: "Let U.S. be a debtor but not a deadbeat" (see Box 6–1).

ADJUSTMENT MEASURES FOR PAYMENTS IMBALANCES

With the advent of floating exchange rates, the significance of balance-of-payments deficits or surpluses has changed. Theoretically, if foreign exchange rates are freely floating, the market will automatically adjust for deficits through lower foreign exchange values and for surpluses through higher values. According to the theory, foreign exchange values will continue to change until equilibrium is restored. Under the floating rate regime, therefore, official reserves become unimportant or play no major role.

With the floating system in fact becoming a managed float for the major currencies and with most other countries still following a fixed exchange system, the issue of what governmental measures can be taken for payments imbalances still remains an important subject. As discussed in Chapter 4, nations are still not ready to allow the value of their currencies to be freely determined by market forces because of numerous domestic and national policy considerations.

If deficits are temporary and recognized as such outside of a country, a country can use government reserves or borrowing from the IMF to meet the deficits. For more serious or persisting deficits, governments have the choice of

---

[8] See *Survey of Current Business,* June 1986, p. 27.

several lines of action. If they require substantial IMF assistance, the IMF will require that certain of these actions be undertaken as a condition for such assistance. Adjustments can be attempted through changes in the exchange rate, through internal measures, through controls, or through a combination of these actions.

With the devaluation approach, as previously noted, exports are stimulated because the price of a nation's goods in foreign currencies has been reduced. Imports are retarded because the domestic cost of imported goods has risen. The strength of these effects will depend upon the size of the devaluation and the price elasticities of demand. If consumers continue to purchase the same quantity of goods even if the price is measurably reduced or raised, demand is said to be *highly price inelastic*. But if buyers vary their purchases greatly with higher or lower prices, demand is considered to be *highly price elastic*. For imports or exports that are price elastic, devaluation can both increase foreign exchange export earnings and reduce foreign exchange expenditures on imports. A revaluation will have the reverse effect and contribute to equilibrium by reducing surpluses.

The capital accounts can also be influenced by a devaluation or revaluation. In the case of a *devaluation*, imports are likely to lose competitiveness in the domestic market and foreign firms will tend to make direct investments in the country to establish local production facilities. The opposite tendency is encouraged by *revaluations*, namely, a reduction in direct investment flows.

Adjustment measures through new or modified domestic policies often accompany a devaluation but may be difficult to accomplish.[9] Domestic inflation, for example, may be responsible for increasing the prices of a nation's goods in foreign markets and reducing export earnings. But solutions to the domestic inflation problem are frequently not easy to find. Furthermore, the traditional anti-inflation approach of controlling inflation by reduced government expenditures, economic slowdowns, and increased unemployment rarely wins domestic political support.

The imposition of exchange controls and import restrictions and/or export incentives may well be an easier political path than internal deflation for a country to take. The wide range of available control measures and the implications of protectionist policies are discussed at length in Chapter 12. Controls generally do not tackle the basic causes of the payments imbalance. At best, controls may provide some respite from further deterioration of a situation while other more basic remedies are being implemented. Yet in many cases, restrictions and controls have remained as permanent fixtures.

SUMMARY

The balance-of-payments accounts reflect a country's economic and financial relations with the rest of the world. Using a double-entry bookkeeping system,

---

[9] See Karim Nashashibi, ''Devaluation in Developing Countries: The Difficult Choice,'' *Finance and Development,* March 1983, pp. 14–17; Wanda Tseng, ''The Effects of Adjustment,'' *Finance and Development,* December 1984, pp. 2–5.

various transactions involving a country's residents and their counterparts in other countries are collected and disseminated on a regular basis. To interpret the meaning of these data, one must make some judgments regarding which transactions are important—that is, induced by underlying economic and financial forces. Analysis of these transactions, in turn, permits one to assess whether a given country has balance-of-payments problems. If there is a problem, the country in question must find a solution. By considering various options open to the country, the analyst can develop extremely useful insights into the likely strategies that the country will pursue. Foreknowledge of likely developments can be extremely crucial to the international business enterprise, for the firm can often take steps to reduce its vulnerability in advance of a full-blown crisis.

Appendix: Corporate Accounts and Balance-of-Payments Accounts

For the reader familiar with accounting, a short review of accounting concepts as applied to balance-of-payments accounting should clear up any difficulties in comprehending the classification of balance-of-payments items as debits or credits.

Under the conventions of double-entry accounting, the assets of an entity are always recorded as debits and the liabilities as credits. There are two sorts of liability, however—those to outside parties and those to owners of the entity. The liability to owners represents the basic net worth of the entity according to the rules adopted in keeping the accounts and may be expressed as the excess of assets over outside liabilities. Thus the fundamental equation in double-entry accounting is:

$$\text{Assets (debit)} = \text{Liabilities (credit)} + \text{Net worth (credit)}$$

It is a simple step from this equation to work out the debit and credit entries for any change in assets, liabilities, or net worth. For example, whenever an asset is added (debit), there must be an increase in liabilities (credit), an increase in net worth (credit), or a decrease in another asset (credit). Conversely, when an asset is reduced (credit), there must be a reduction in a liability (debit), a reduction in net worth (debit), or an increase in another asset (debit). For activities aimed at building net worth, the accounts classification is extended to introduce accounts for costs and revenue. Revenue represents an increase in net worth and hence is recorded as a credit, while costs, in effect, decrease net worth and are recorded as debits. Hence:

$$\text{Revenues (credit)} - \text{Costs (debit)} = \text{Net worth (credit)}$$

When costs are incurred (debit), there must be an offsetting credit—either an increased liability or a decreased asset. Likewise, when a revenue earning sale is made, revenue is credited and an asset or a liability account debited. The entry in an asset account might record the cash received or the customer debt for the sale. If the entry is in a liability account, it might record a reduction in the amount owing to a creditor.

Applying these double-entry concepts to balance-of-payments accounting, a country's international net worth can be viewed as the difference between the country's external claims against the rest of the world (debit) and the rest of the world's claims against the country's own wealth (credit). This net worth is not a measure of the country's entire wealth, only that portion of it that its residents have channeled through international transactions. When a country exports goods, international net worth is increased by the value of goods channeled into exports (credit), and there is an increase in claims against foreigners to whom the exports are made (debit). Or if a resident pays a foreign account with foreign currency obtained from the resident's bank, the effect is to reduce the country's foreign liabilities by the amount paid (debit) and to reduce the country's foreign assets by the same amount (credit)—that is, foreign currency held by the bank is reduced.

Corporate accounts and balance-of-payments accounts are compared in Table 6A–1.

TABLE 6A–1 Corporate Accounts and Balance-of-Payment Accounts Compared

Corporate Accounts		Balance-of-Payment Accounts		
Debits	*Credits*	*Debits*	*Credits*	*Relation to Table 6–1*
Profit and loss items			*Current items*	
	Sales		Exports	A1 (cr)
	Other income		Other current account income	A2 − A6; B1 − B2 (dr)
Cost of goods sold		Imports		A1 (dr)
Other costs (except depreciation), taxes, and dividends		Other current account expenditures		A2 − A6; B1 − B2 (dr)
	Net retained profit before depreciation		Current account balance	A + B credits minus A + B debits
Balance sheet items			*Capital and reserve items*	
	Increase in current liabilities		Net increase in foreigners' short-term claims	C2b, C5b, C6b credits minus debits
	Increase in long-term liabilities and equity		Net increase in foreigners' long-term claims	C1b, and C3b credits minus debits
Increase in current assets except cash		Increase in private short-term foreign assets		C2a, C5a, C6a debits minus credits
Increase in fixed assets		Increase in long-term foreign assets		C1a, C3a, C4a debits minus credits
Increase in cash		Increase in official holdings of gold and foreign exchange		D debits minus D credits

EXERCISE AND DISCUSSION QUESTIONS

1. What is meant by a balance-of-payment surplus or deficit?
2. How can a country have balance-of-payments deficits and still be strengthening its international economic position?
3. West Germany has revalued its DM several times. Why should a country revalue its currency?
4. Explain how the move to manage floating rates has changed the way the United States attempts to manage its balance-of-payments accounts.
5. As the manager of a U.S. manufacturing affiliate in Freelandia how would you measure the effects of your operations in Freelandia on the Freelandia balance of payments?
6. Show in double-entry format the entries that would be made in the U.S. balance-of-payments accounts. Use the account numbers of the U.S. presentation format shown in Table 6–2, as illustrated in *(a)*.
   a. A Japanese company sells electronic equipment to GE in the United States for $2 million. Freight ($3,000) and insurance ($2,000) are arranged in the United States and paid for by GE. Payment to the Japanese company is made by check drawn on the Bank of America in New York.

	Account No.	Debit	Credit
17.	Merchandise imports	$2 million	
63.	U.S. liabilities reported by U.S. banks		$2 million

   b. A U.S. company decides to establish a new plant in Hong Kong to take advantage of cheap labor. The cost of setting up a plant during the year totaled $8.6 million. Half of this was paid out of an account held in Hong Kong, the rest from a U.S. account.
   c. A U.S. company exports $400,000 worth of agricultural equipment to New Zealand and accepts $200,000 worth of shares in the local distributor as part payment. The rest is paid in New Zealand dollars.
   d. Charles L. Hangover went on a trip to the Pacific islands. He paid his airfare of $2,000 in the United States, but half the travel was done on Quantas (Australian) and the rest on United Airlines (U.S.). The fare was divided between airlines accordingly. He spent a further U.S. $1,500 in the islands.
   e. The U.S. government extends a loan to Israel to purchase military equipment. The loan is for $500 million. It is all spent on fighter aircraft bought from U.S. firms.
   f. An investment trust in the United States buys 30,000 Unilever, Ltd. shares in London Unilever for $40 each and pays for them from its U.S. account.
   g. Unilever directors declare a dividend of £1 and this is paid into the trust's U.S. account. The exchange rate is £1 = U.S. $2.
   h. The United States spends $1.5 million on military exercises in the Pacific. Of this, $.9 million is paid to foreign countries for the use of docking and airport facilities.
   i. Pedro Lopez migrated from Mexico to the United States and found satisfactory employment. After working for three months, he sent his mother in Mexico a check for $500 drawn on his new checking account with the Bank of America.

CHAPTER 7

The International Trade Framework

"No state shall, without the consent of the Congress, lay imposts or duties on imports or exports, ..."

Section 10, Article 2, Constitution of the United States,
signed September 17, 1787

139

For more than two centuries, trade within the United States has been free of trade barriers, in accordance with the free trade principle adopted in the U.S. Constitution. In contrast, trade among nation-states has always been subject to trade barriers. During some eras of history, the barriers have been stringent and detailed. But since the end of World War II, many national barriers have been greatly reduced through international cooperation. Furthermore, an international trade framework of permanent international and regional organizations has been established for negotiation and implementation of trade agreements.

This chapter will examine the motivations of nation-states for controlling international trade, the types of controls, and the international trade framework within which international business operates.

A BRIEF HISTORY OF COMMERCIAL POLICIES

A country's commercial policies are those designed to influence its trade relations with the rest of the world. Over many centuries, until David Ricardo published his theory of comparative advantage in 1817, mercantilist views shaped the trade policies of most nations. The mercantilists believed that the economic power of the state was enhanced by the accumulation of precious metals in the national treasuries. National policies, therefore, were directed toward achieving as large a trade surplus as possible by encouraging exports and restraining imports. The surplus of exports over imports was to be settled by payments in gold or other precious metals. Clearly, extensive government controls over trade and exchange were required to achieve the mercantilist goals.

As the theory of comparative advantage gained acceptance, mercantilism steadily gave way to a more liberal conception of international trade and economic relations. By the end of the 19th century, trade liberalization had become the dominant philosophy; and nations were imposing relatively few restrictions on trade. This trend toward liberalization was interrupted in the 1930s, however, when nations responded to the Great Depression by reverting to severe protectionist policies.

In the United States, the height of protection was reached in 1930 with the passage of the Smoot-Hawley tariff. Other nations retaliated with new higher tariffs. Beggar-thy-neighbor policies spread everywhere, and rival economic blocs emerged. Between 1929 and 1933, world trade fell by almost two thirds. In fact, the signing of the Smoot-Hawley tariff has been characterized as the "most disastrous mistake any American President has ever made in international relations" because it helped convert what would have been otherwise a normal economic downturn into a major world depression, which in turn sowed the seeds of World War II by undermining the position of political moderates in Japan and Germany.[1]

The return to the trade liberalization path was led by the United States

---

[1] Richard N. Cooper, "Trade Policy and Foreign Policy," *University of Michigan Conference on U.S. Trade Policies in a Changing World Economy,* March 28–29, 1985, p. 2.

with the passage of the Reciprocal Trade Agreements Act in 1934. Under this initiative, trade restrictions were significantly reduced through bilateral negotiations and agreements. But the liberalization move was again interrupted by World War II. It was resumed after the war, with the United States once more providing leadership. The remarkable feature of the post-World War II period was the introduction of the multilateral negotiation principle and the creation of an international trade framework.

Until the postwar period, each nation fashioned its own trade policies unilaterally or through bilateral negotiations. Since World War II, international cooperation in the field of trade has become the general rule, and permanent international and regional organizations have been established for sponsoring multilateral negotiations and for overseeing the implementation of trade agreements.

The international trade framework that has evolved consists of a series of trading agreements under various international organizations. These trading arrangements can be grouped into the following broad categories:

1. Global arrangements directed toward multilateral trade expansion on a nondiscriminatory basis.
2. Global arrangements directed toward international income redistribution through restructuring the "International Economic Order."
3. Regional arrangements that focus on the economic relations of a particular geographic or political area.
4. Commodity-product arrangements that focus on the international terms of trade of a specific product or commodity.
5. Bilateral trading arrangements that normally do not involve international agencies.

TRADE CONTROLS

National governments use many types of trade controls to change or modify the prices, product composition, volume, and direction of imports and exports. In the case of imports, trade controls are almost always restrictive and may be in the form of tariff and/or nontariff barriers (NTBs). In the case of exports, nations use both promotional and restrictive devices. The national motivations for adopting trade controls are discussed in the next section.

Tariffs

A *tariff* is the most common form of trade restriction. A tariff is a tax or duty levied on a commodity when it crosses the boundary of a customs area. A customs area usually coincides with national political boundaries, although sometimes it includes colonies or territories of the country.

Tariffs may be levied on commodities leaving an area *(export duties)* or on merchandise entering an area *(import duties)*. Import duties are more common than export duties because most nations are anxious to expand exports and increase their foreign exchange earnings. Import duties may be either specific, ad valorem, or a combination of the two—compound duties. *Specific duties* are levied on the basis of some physical unit such as dollars per bushel, per kilo, or per meter. *Ad valorem duties* are calculated as a percent of the value of the goods. The term *drawback* refers to duties paid on imported goods that are refunded if the imported components are reexported.

A country's *tariff schedule* is a listing of all its import duties. The schedule may have one or more columns. In a single-column schedule, the tariff is the same for a specific good regardless of the country of origin. A multicolumn schedule discriminates among exporting countries, with lower rates applying to countries with which tariff treaties have been negotiated. The advantage of the multicolumn tariff is its flexibility for tariff bargaining.

Tariffs have the advantage that they can be selectively levied in terms of products and with differential rates. Thus a nation may achieve rather precise objectives with tariffs while at the same time increasing government revenues. The negative aspect of tariffs is that they increase the cost of imports to the customer. Also, they are difficult to reduce or eliminate because of political pressures from domestic groups benefited by the tariff. Such political pressures can limit a country's flexibility in bargaining with other nations, particularly when tariffs are established by law and a change of law is necessary to change a tariff.

An important feature of tariff agreements is the most favored nation (MFN) principle. A nation entering into a tariff treaty that includes the MFN principle is required to extend to all signatories any tariff concessions granted to any participating country. The purpose of such a treaty provision is to simplify tariff bargaining and increase the likelihood of tariff reductions. All members of GATT, to be described below, are entitled to MFN treatment. As an illustration of the importance ascribed to the principle, a key issue in trade negotiations during the 1980s between the United States and the USSR (not a member of GATT) was whether the United States was willing to grant MFN status to the USSR.

Nontariff Barriers

Nontariff barriers (NTBs) are less visible than tariffs, but they are extremely effective restraints on trade. The principal categories of NTBs are as follows:

1. Government participation in trade.

   Discrimination in government procurement, state trading, subsidies, countervailing duties, etc.

2. Customs and entry procedures.

   Regulations covering valuation methods, classification, documentation, health, and safety.

3. Standards.

   Standards for products, packaging, labeling, marking, etc.

4. Specific limitations.

Quotas, import restraints, licensing, foreign exchange controls, etc.

5. Import charges.

Prior import deposits, credit restrictions for imports, special duties, variable levies, and so on.

Quotas or quantitative restrictions are the most common form of nontariff barrier. A quota limits the imports (or exports) of a specific commodity during a given time period. The limits may be in physical or value terms. Quotas may be on a country basis or global, without reference to countries of origin. They may be imposed unilaterally, as in the case of sugar imports into the United States. They can also be negotiated on a so-called voluntary basis, as in the case of Japanese automobile imports into the United States during the 1980s. Obviously, exporting countries do not readily agree to limit their sales. Thus, the "voluntary" label usually means that the importing country threatened to impose even worse restrictions if voluntary cooperation was not forthcoming.

Quotas are more certain and precise as trade restraints than tariffs. An import duty that is not prohibitive will reduce imports, but it does not impose an absolute limit on imported goods. A quota system limits with certainty the extent of foreign competition in the domestic market. Quotas also provide greater flexibility in bargaining and administration. The greatest disadvantage of quotas is that they insulate domestic producers from pressures to become more competitive with foreign producers.

In the importing country, quotas usually require a licensing system and an agency to distribute the quota shares to domestic importers. Where the total quota is small relative to the total domestic market, domestic prices are likely to be higher than the price of imports. Quota recipients, therefore, will gain windfall profits. Governments could capture the windfall profits by auctioning off the licenses to the higher bidder. The more general practice, however, is for the profits to go to private parties. Thus inequities and corruption may occur in the allocation of quotas.

If the quota is allocated within the exporting country, rather than the importing country, a similar system is required for allocating the export quota to individual exporting firms. Such allocations are frequently based on each firm's foreign market share before the quota limits go into effect. If a firm anticipates the future imposition of quotas, its strategy will be to gain as much market share as possible regardless of profitability. After the exporter is granted a sizable share of the quota, importers from the foreign country become dependent on these specific exporters as a source of supply. The exporting firm has then gained sufficient bargaining power to raise prices and more than compensate for lost profits. In the case of some exporting countries, quota holders may earn their greatest profits by selling or renting their quotas to other local firms rather than by using the quotas for exports (see Box 7–1).

Many NTBs other than those specifically mentioned are used to restrict

BOX 7–1
The Quota Brokers

Hong Kong, unlike Taiwan and South Korea, allows unused bits of its textile-export quotas to be traded. The original recipients of the quotas, negotiated under international agreements such as the Multi-Fibre Arrangement, can sell all or part of their quotas to fellow manufacturers who have export orders but no export licences. In this nifty way, Hong Kong has ensured the profitable use of 95–100 percent of its hard-won quotas.

In the past, when yet another category of textiles was subjected to quotas, the Hong Kong government awarded the negotiated allocation evenly (and free) to the exporters who had built up the market for that particular item. Some of Hong Kong's oldest and largest textile firms retain quotas based on exports dating from the 1960s.

Critics say that this system amounts to nothing more than subsidising well-established companies. Trade officials complain that manufacturers can often earn more from selling the quotas than from making the goods. And, they argue piously, in the end consumers have to pay in higher-priced clothing.

SOURCE: Adapted from *The Economist*, February 15, 1986.

trade, and ingenious new barriers are constantly being developed. Some are legitimate regulatory functions, such as antipollution regulations that require automobiles to meet certain exhaust emission standards. Others may ostensibly be introduced for reasons of health, safety, or national security but are actually intended to restrict trade.

Export Restrictions

While restrictions on imports have traditionally been the main type of trade controls, many nations also have a variety of restrictions on exports. Export controls may be in the form of bans or embargos, quantitative restrictions or quotas, licensing, export taxes, minimum export prices, and the reservation of exports to designated trading entities. The International Monetary Fund publishes an annual report describing the current policies and practices of each member country that is a valuable reference source for international managers.[2]

Malaysia has a ban on the export of timber logs, presumably to encourage further processing within the country. India bans border trade between India and the Tibet region of the People's Republic of China and all exports to South Africa. The United States has an embargo on trade with Cuba, Libya, and Nicara-

---

[2] International Monetary Fund, *Annual Report on Exchange Arrangements and Exchange Restrictions* (Washington, D.C.).

gua. The United States also imposed an embargo on grain sales to the Soviet Union (discontinued in April 1981) after the Soviet invasion of Afghanistan.

Quotas and quantitative restrictions are used to implement international commodity and producer agreements to be discussed below. Export licensing is used by the United States to restrict exports to the Soviet Bloc nations of advanced-technology products, technological and scientific information, and manufacturing skills that are considered detrimental to the national security of the United States. As a complement to the U.S. export licensing program, the Western nations have a Coordinating Committee for Export Controls (COCOM) that cooperates on a voluntary basis to agree on technologies that should be kept out of the hands of the Eastern Bloc. Some of the difficulties in drawing the line between commercial and military products and in policing the export control program are shown in Box 7–2.

Minimum export prices are enforced by Brazil on coffee exports; by Japan on exports of videotape recorders to the European Community; and by India on

---

BOX 7–2
Policing High-Tech Exports

The Blurred Line between Commercial and Military Products

The same basic semiconductors and integrated circuits that go into video games also go into missile-guidance systems. The same small computer that can be used by an American moving company to make sure a vanload of household goods gets from Cleveland to Boston can be used by a Russian commander to make sure a division of soldiers gets from Odessa to Prague. Military planners envision the day when the laser technology that now is able to fuse detached retinas will also be capable of disabling enemy communications satellites.

SOURCE: John Zonderman, "Policing High-Tech Exports," *New York Times Magazine,* November 27, 1983, p. 125.

Technology Smuggling

A federal judge closed out a sensitive technology smuggling case by imposing a $3,120,000 fine on a Swedish telecommunications equipment company. The company allegedly broke the terms of its U.S. export license and supplied U.S.-made parts to the Soviet Union for an air-traffic control system, thus giving the network the capability of tracking military aircraft with the use of sophisticated U.S. equipment.

Federal investigators said that the Swedish executives hand-carried circuit boards in several trips to Moscow after assuring the U.S. Commerce Department that such vital parts wouldn't be included in the Soviet installation.

SOURCE: Adapted from *The Wall Street Journal,* April 30, 1984, p. 6. © Dow Jones & Company, Inc., 1984. Used with permission. All rights reserved.

exports of sheep meat, goat meat, and buffalo meat. India also follows a practice of reserving the export of certain commodities for state-trading enterprises.

Export Promotion

Nations adopt programs for promoting exports as well as for restricting imports. The less developed countries in particular feel a great need to earn foreign exchange through expanding exports. And the United States itself, with persistent balance-of-trade deficits since 1970, has established programs for export promotion.

Governmental action to promote exports may even include assuming responsibility for normal business functions, such as sponsoring market research on foreign sales opportunities, arranging trade fairs, and establishing trade promotion offices in foreign countries. At the more traditional level, governments offer tax incentives such as exemption from certain domestic taxes if goods are exported, direct bonus payments or subsidies through administration of exchange controls, special credit for exporters, and insurance programs under which the government assumes varying degrees of political and commercial risk.

The United States has its Export-Import Bank, which promotes U.S. exports by providing medium-term and long-term financing to foreign buyers. The bank is also a partner in the private Foreign Credit Insurance Association that makes export credit insurance available to U.S. exporters. As incentives for expanding exports, the association offers low-cost blanket insurance policies covering both commercial and political risks in selling abroad on credit. Most big exporting countries have a similar institution to provide exporters with cover against risk. Britain, for example, has its Export Credit Guarantee Department, which performs this function.

Another export promotion device sponsored by the United States is the Foreign Sales Corporation (FSC), which provides tax-saving incentives for U.S. persons or corporations having export activities. The FSC was introduced in 1984 to replace the Domestic International Sales Corporation (DISC), which had been created in 1971 as a means of promoting U.S. exports through tax deferral incentives. The FSC replaced the DISC because of foreign complaints that the DISC violated GATT rules by providing illegal export subsidies.[3]

The Export Trading Act of 1982 is still another U.S. initiative to expand exports. It encourages business firms, particularly small companies, to join together and form export trading companies. The law provides antitrust protection for joint exporting and permits banks to provide equity capital by taking an ownership interest in these exporting ventures. Prior to this law, U.S. banks were prohibited by the Glass-Steagall Act of 1933, inspired by the banking crisis of the Great Depression, from making venture-type investments.

---

[3] See B. E. Lee and Donald R. Bloom, "Deficit Reduction Act of 1984: Changes in Export Incentives," *Columbia Journal of World Business,* Summer 1985, pp. 63–67.

NATIONAL MOTIVATIONS FOR CONTROLLING INTERNATIONAL TRADE

In view of the widely espoused benefits of free trade, why do nations attempt to control international transfers? What national goals are they trying to achieve through particular controls?

Revenue Goals.   Some nations rely on international transfers as a major source of government revenue. Many tariffs were originally imposed primarily to raise revenue. Tariffs are among the easiest taxes to collect because the import and export of goods are usually concentrated in a relatively small number of locations, such as ports. A tariff imposed entirely for revenue purposes, however, would be applied to different products and be at a lower rate than a protective tariff. A tariff level considered too high might keep goods from entering or leaving a country or might encourage smuggling and evasion and yield no revenue.

Job Protection.   Strong domestic pressures for protection arise when foreign competition threatens established economic activities. Protection controls are notable in the textile field in both the United States and the United Kingdom. The industry employs a large number of workers and is a major contributor to national output. As imports have threatened local industries in their home markets, both employers and labor unions have pressed for tariff increases and quota restrictions to protect domestic industry against "low wage" foreign producers. The desire to protect domestic workers from foreign competition can also be a reason for restrictive immigration policies. The rationale is that the welfare of domestic workers will be undercut by influxes of foreign workers who might be willing to work for less money.

Development Goals and Industrial Policies.   Tariffs, quotas, and other nontariff barriers may be adopted to implement economic development goals and to encourage the establishment of new economic activities. Here we have the venerable "infant industry" argument that is directed toward changing the structure of a nation's economy and accelerating economic growth. The argument is that latecomer countries must provide a period of protection to infant industries for the time-consuming learning processes and for expanding to an efficient scale of production. It assumes that new industries have a potential for becoming economically viable without protection after the learning period and after reaching a feasible scale of operations. To encourage such infant industries, nations ban or restrict imports through tariffs, foreign exchange controls, import quotas, and similar measures. It is interesting to note that in his Report on Manufacturers submitted in 1791 to the U.S. House of Representatives, Alexander Hamilton elaborated most persuasively the infant industry argument as the central justification for U.S. policies to encourage manufacturing.[4]

---

[4] See Alexander Hamilton, *Papers on Public Credit, Commerce and Finance,* ed. Samuel McKee, Jr. (New York: Columbia University Press, 1934), p. 204.

Development goals may be the justification for creating special tax or foreign exchange incentives to encourage exports and foreign direct investment. In other situations, development goals may also be the reason for removing tariffs and moving toward free-trade policies that are expected to stimulate greater efficiency and higher levels of output from domestic industry.

Balance-of-Payments Goals.   Nations are constantly under pressure to achieve equilibrium in their international transactions and to maintain relatively stable exchange rates. Controls over financial flows and international trade in goods and services are frequently adopted on a temporary or indefinite basis to assist in the resolution of balance-of-payments problem, as discussed in Chapter 6.

Health and Safety Protection.   Nations frequently restrict the import of certain commodities—generally agricultural or animal products—to protect the health of their citizens. Such restrictions, which attempt to keep out agricultural pests and diseases, may be temporary or permanent and generally are applied to commodities from specific infected areas. In other less usual cases, exports may be restricted for health reasons, such as a U.S. law that barred pharmaceutical companies from exporting drugs before they were approved by the Food and Drug Administration for use in the U.S.

International Political Goals.   Trade controls have long been used by nations to reward political friends and to oppose political enemies. The Arab countries have imposed boycotts on trading with foreign firms that do business with Israel. The United States created special trading preferences for the Philippines after that country emerged from 50 years of colonial status to become an independent nation. France maintains special trade relationships with its former colonies. The United States imposes controls over East-West trade—that is, trade with the Soviet-bloc countries. Trade has been completely forbidden with countries such as Cuba, with whom the United States has not enjoyed friendly relations, on the grounds that trade helps potential enemies to be stronger and eventually works to the political disadvantage of the United States. More recently, U.S. trade with Libya has been banned because of Libya's support of terrorist activities.

National Security Goals.   The more traditional manifestations of national security goals have been in protecting high-cost domestic industries, such as the U.S. steel industry, so that supplies of critical materials are more likely to be domestically available in the case of war. National and international policies have also emerged for controlling international transfers of nuclear raw materials and technology.

Special interest groups in a country have used national-security arguments as an excuse to limit competition rather than to achieve sound national-security goals (see Box 7–3). Often there is no general agreement in a country as to what are valid national-security considerations, and at times bitter controversies

BOX 7–3
"Shoe Gap" Threatens U.S. Defense

Defense experts, long preoccupied with debates over cruise missiles and space-based weapons, are beginning to hear about a new weakness in the nation's defenses: shoes.

The shoe industry hopes to persuade Congress to enact import quotas by using the national security argument.

"In the event of war or other national emergency, it is highly unlikely that the domestic footware industry would provide sufficient footwear for the military and civilian population," says a letter to Congress from the president of the Footwear Industries of America. "In the event of mass mobilization, the United States will not have time to train new workers to be tanners or cutters or heelers. Nor will we be able to wait for ships to deliver shoes from Taiwan, Korea, Brazil, and Eastern Europe."

That shortage could cripple our battle plans in Europe, the group says, where NATO is deemphasizing tanks and armored divisions. "This strategy will fail if the foot soldier is without shoes."

A Defense Department spokesman says he knows of no plan to investigate the prospects of a war-time shoe crisis. What's more, federal law already requires the military to buy footwear exclusively from U.S. companies.

SOURCE: Adapted from *The Wall Street Journal*, August 24, 1984. © Dow Jones & Company, Inc., 1984. Used with permission. All rights reserved.

arise between domestic interest groups as to what kind of protection is justified on national-security grounds and the best way of achieving national security.

Opponents of trade controls argue that the national-security policies on which these controls are based assume an obsolete type of warfare. In a nuclear war, they say, victories or defeats will be decided quickly; and the availability of materials after the initiation of such warfare will no longer be of critical importance. Furthermore, by allowing more imports, domestic resources will be conserved for national defense emergencies rather than rapidly consumed.

THE GENERAL AGREEMENT ON TARIFFS AND TRADE (GATT)

The General Agreement on Tariffs and Trade, known as GATT, is the principal global arrangement for trade liberalization. Although originally designed as a temporary arrangement, GATT evolved into a permanent and important institution. It became effective in 1948 with 19 countries as members. Its membership has since expanded to include almost all of the important noncommunist nations and several socialist countries of Eastern Europe.

GATT's Accomplishments

The broad goal of GATT has been to reduce trade restrictions erected by individual nations in pursuit of their narrow national interests. The goal is to be achieved through multilateral negotiations, through rules of conduct for GATT members, and through providing a forum for the settlement of trade disputes. Mutual tariff concessions are negotiated among the so-called contracting parties, and the parties commit themselves not to raise import tariffs above the negotiated rates. Nondiscrimination, a key rule of conduct, is achieved by generalizing the negotiated rates to all contracting parties through the most-favored nation principle.

While aiming at "developing the full use of the resources of the world and expanding the production and exchange of goods,"[5] GATT does not envision full liberalization of all trade barriers. GATT permits exceptions to its general rules that require the eventual elimination of all import restrictions. But the exceptions are subject to safeguards intended to protect the legitimate interests of other trading nations.

The GATT exceptions have recognized the special protection given to agriculture by most nations and allowed many import restraints to protect domestic farmers. The GATT rules make exceptions for countries that are in balance-of-payments difficulties and allow developing countries to protect their infant industries. GATT also permits members to form customs unions, provided there is no overall increase in barriers to outsiders.

From 1947 to 1967, GATT sponsored six rounds of multilateral trade negotiations. By the end of the so-called Kennedy Round in 1967, the weighted average tariff for the major trading nations had been reduced to 2 percent on raw materials and 7.7 percent on all industrial products.[6]

GATT's role in the settlement of trade disputes has also helped to stimulate trade liberalization. Before GATT, there was no way to resolve trade disagreements between two countries. With GATT, a group of experts is convened when a complaint is received. The group establishes the facts, makes a judgment as to the merits of the complaint in light of the GATT rules, and recommends a solution to the dispute.

Thus, in spite of the remaining trade barriers, the situation after the Kennedy Round could be characterized as a liberal world trading system with a substantially free exchange of nonagricultural goods. This postwar movement toward trade liberalism engendered a general sense of international responsibilities and, complemented by a stable monetary system, fostered an unprecedented sixfold rise in the volume of international trade between 1948 and 1973.

The 1970s were a more difficult period for continued trade liberalization. Major changes were occurring in the world economy. The fixed-exchange rate

---

[5] GATT, *Basic Instruments and Selected Documents,* vol. 4, Text of the General Agreement (Geneva: March 1969), p. 1 (Preamble).

[6] Bahram Nowzad, *The Rise of Protectionism* (Washington, D.C.: International Monetary Fund, 1978), p. 1.

financial system was moving toward an untried managed float system. International oil prices had quadrupled in 1973, and a sharp worldwide economic recession followed in 1974–75. A number of developing countries had diversified their export base and were challenging the industrialized countries in new sectors such as steel, shipbuilding, and electronics. All of these factors, particularly the economic slowdown, were contributing to an environment of rising protectionism.

By the spring of 1979, after more than five years of negotiation, the seventh and so-called Tokyo Round of multilateral negotiations was concluded. Tariffs were lowered by 27 percent to an average level of less than 5 percent. Even more significant was the adoption of several nontariff barrier agreements or codes. The steady decline in tariffs over the years had shifted the liberalization focus to nontariff barriers as the remaining restraints on trade.

Nontariff codes established new discipline or liberalization in such areas as subsidies, standards, government procurement, customs valuation, licensing, and antidumping. They also established dispute settlement procedures and review committees to examine new issues that might arise. The nondiscrimination rules of GATT requiring equal treatment of imports do not apply to the new codes. Only signatory countries to each code enjoy the benefits of the code. By mid-1985, six years after the round of negotiations ended, there still had not been a stampede to sign the codes. The standards code had 33 signatories, the government procurement code 21, and the subsidies code only 19. Nevertheless, the Tokyo Round is generally considered to have made net contributions to an open trading system.

The Uncertain Future of GATT

GATT continues as the symbol of a broad international commitment to trade liberalization. But commitment to the ideal has weakened and the appropriateness of the GATT framework to the changing world economy has been questioned. Spurred on by domestic protectionist pressures, many industrialized countries have forsaken the open market commitment of GATT and entered into bilateral and multilateral arrangements outside of GATT, called *market-sharing agreements,* that cover a good part of the world's trade in steel, cars, consumer electronics, and textiles. In the words of the GATT "Wisemen's" group assembled in 1985 to study the trading system, "Today the world market is not opening up, it is being choked by a growing accumulation of restrictive measures. Demands for protection are heard in every country, and from one industry after another."[7]

An eighth round of trade negotiations under the auspices of GATT was formally launched in September 1986. The talks, to be known as the Uruguay Round, are expected to extend into the early 1990s. They will seek to draft trading rules to cover four major sectors not previously regulated—agriculture,

---

[7] See GATT, *Trade Politics for a Better Future: Proposals for Action,* March 1985—referred to as the GATT Wisemen's Report.

services, investment, and intellectual property rights (patents, trademarks, copy-rights, etc.). The negotiators also will push to strengthen GATT as an institution for settling trade disputes. As of 1986, GATT had a professional staff of fewer than 200 people, compared with about 1,700 IMF employees and more than 6,000 World Bank employees.[8]

The main problem for GATT is that it has been undermined in recent years by a shift in the techniques of protectionism. The emphasis has moved from tariffs, from which GATT draws its name, to subsidies and market-sharing agreements. And it is not clear that the major trading nations want to avoid managed trade.

THE UNITED NATIONS CONFERENCE ON TRADE AND DEVELOPMENT (UNCTAD)

The developing countries constitute a majority of the GATT membership, but most of them reject the free-trade approach and make extensive use of trade barriers. They may agree in principle that free trade maximizes world output *with a given international economic structure*. Their priority objective, however, is to change the international structure in order to accelerate their growth and narrow the economic gap between them and the industrialized nations. In their view, the path for achieving these goals is not through free trade. They are convinced that in the present world environment the terms of trade have been systematically turning against them.

Terms of Trade

The terms of trade concept needs further elaboration. There are several terms of trade concepts, but the most commonly used is the *commodity terms of trade*. This measure is an index number showing how the price of exports has changed relative to the price of imports at some reference time. The commodity terms of trade, T_{nb}, is defined as

$$T_{nb} = \frac{P_{xt}/P_{xo}}{P_{mt}/P_{mo}},$$

where P represents an index of the prices of exports (x) or imports (m) and the subscripts t and o refer to the present and base-period times, respectively.[9]

---

[8] See C. Michael Aho and Jonathan David Aronson, *Trade Talks* (New York: Council on Foreign Relations, 1985), p. 33; S. J. Anjaria, "A New Round of Global Trade Negotiations," *Finance & Development*, June 1986, pp. 1–6.

[9] See H. Peter Gray, *International Trade, Investment and Payments* (Boston: Houghton Mifflin, 1979), pp. 27–30.

The developing countries claim that the prices they receive for their exports, mainly primary commodities, are not rising as fast as the prices they pay for imports, mainly manufactured goods. The logical support for this belief is Engel's Law, discussed in Chapter 2, which suggests that the income elasticity for raw material exports is less than for manufactured imports. The developing countries also contend that the world markets for their exports are highly competitive, whereas the markets for their imports involve administered prices and oligopolistic structures. These views led the developing nations to press for global trade arrangements that would work for structural changes and international redistribution of income.

The Birth of UNCTAD

When GATT was initiated in 1948, its principal concern was to liberalize trade among the industrialized countries. The postwar decolonization movement was only beginning, and the strong development aspirations of the Third World were yet to emerge. It is not surprising, therefore, that after observing the first decade and a half of GATT's operations, the developing countries became convinced that GATT was not the institution to adequately represent their trade interests.

In response to this sentiment, the United Nations Conference on Trade and Development (UNCTAD) was convened in 1964 and attended by representatives of 119 nations. The result of the conference was to establish UNCTAD as a permanent United Nations agency. Given its origin and structure, UNCTAD came to represent the trade interests of the developing countries, and its prime objective has been the international redistribution of income through trade. UNCTAD has no executive powers, and its main activity is to sponsor a meeting every four years that has become a principal intergovernmental forum for examining North-South issues in trade, finance, and development.

As the dominant force in UNCTAD, the developing countries have used the seven UNCTAD conferences held from 1964 to 1987 to make demands on the industrialized countries. At UNCTAD I, the developing countries asked for freer access to the markets of the industrialized countries for exports of manufactured goods. They wanted unilateral tariff reductions—without having to make reciprocal concessions—and aid in shifting their export base from primary commodities to manufactured goods.

After about a decade of continued pressure, the advanced countries agreed to this demand by establishing what is called a *generalized system of preferences* (GSP). Under GSP, the industrialized countries have reduced tariffs for fixed amounts of specific manufactured imports from the developing countries. GSP results have not been substantial, however. The quotas have been restrictive as to products and amounts. Furthermore, only a small number of countries have been able to take advantage of the concessions, and these countries have not been the poorest of the developing countries.

The New International Economic Order

The developing countries escalated their demands in the early 1970s through having the United Nations endorse the need for a New International Economic Order (NIEO). The general thrust of NIEO is for a major restructuring of the international economy. Under the "old order," the developing countries feel that they bear an inequitable burden in times of economic recession and do not participate equitably in periods of world prosperity.

As of the 1980s, the details of the NIEO were still being spelled out.[10] Some specifics of the NIEO emerged at the UNCTAD IV meetings in Nairobi in 1976. The developing countries pressed for an "integrated" program of commodity agreements with a common fund for buffer stock financing, a code governing international technology transfers, long-term financial assistance from the IMF, and measures for alleviating the debt problems of the developing countries. These issues were again on the conference agenda of UNCTAD V (Manila, 1979); UNCTAD VI (Belgrade, 1983); and UNCTAD VII (Geneva, 1987). The Belgrade meetings, with 3,000 delegates from 164 nations participating, were characterized by a climate of confrontation. Many resolutions were processed—but without arousing specific pledges of support from industrialized nations. In contrast, the Geneva meetings reflected a more constructive effort to identify common interest and to negotiate broad policy directions in a spirit of cooperation.

REGIONAL TRADE ARRANGEMENTS

Regional trade arrangements form another part of the international trade framework. The GATT agreement allowed for regional groupings with the proviso that such groupings should not result in increased discrimination against nonmembers. As subsequent events demonstrated, neighboring countries had strong desires to pool their political and economic strength despite the existence of global trade agreements. And the establishment of regional common markets and free trade areas—referred to as *regional economic integration*—began to occur.

There are various forms and degrees of regional economic integration. The loosest and least intensive form is the *free-trade area*. In a free-trade area all artificial restrictions on the movement of goods and services among the participating countries are removed; but each country may retain its own tariffs, quotas, or other restrictions on trade with nonparticipating countries. The *customs union* is one degree further along the scale. In addition to the complete elimination of tariffs and quotas on internal trade, a common external tariff is established on goods entering the union from outside. A *common market* represents the next higher degree of economic integration. Besides eliminating internal trade barriers and establishing a common external tariff, a common market also removes national restrictions on the movement of labor and capital among participating countries and on the right of establishment for business firms.

[10] See Paul Streeten, "Approaches to a New International Economic Order," in *The Contemporary International Economy, Second Edition*, ed. John Adams (New York: St. Martin's Press, 1985), pp. 495–524.

The economic gains from the formation of a common market can be dramatic. With the elimination of internal tariffs, the market area can be greatly enlarged and no longer bounded by the borders of the individual countries. Gains from increased economic efficiency can arise from the reallocation of production within the area on the basis of national endowments and comparative advantage. These gains can be reinforced by economies of scale that individual firms may be able to achieve and by increased competition within the expanded market area. Even more important can be the impetus to economic growth induced by the reduction of internal barriers to trade.

The extent to which these gains are shared with or achieved at the expense of outside countries depends in large part on the balance between trade creation and trade diversion effects. *Trade creation* exists when the elimination of internal trade barriers increases the volume of trade by making lower cost goods and services available. *Trade diversion* occurs when less efficient producers inside the market area replace more efficient external producers because the outsider still faces external tariffs. The degree to which trade diversion occurs will depend, of course, on the height of the external tariffs.

The European Community (EC)

The most successful case of economic integration has been the European Economic Community. It was established January 1, 1958, based on the Treaty of Rome, by Belgium, France, West Germany, Luxembourg, Italy, and the Netherlands. It was preceded by a Coal and Steel Community set up in 1952. Together with the European Atomic Community (Euratom), also founded in 1958, the three groups are jointly referred to as the European Community (EC).

The original six nations were joined in 1973 by the United Kingdom, Denmark, and Ireland; in 1981 by Greece; and in 1986 by Spain and Portugal. The 12 members of the Community had a total population in 1987 of 323 million, as compared with 243 million for the United States. The total gross national product in 1987 of the EC was estimated to be US$4,300 billion as compared with US$4,488 billion for the United States. Although average per capita income in Germany and Denmark was comparable to the U.S. level of $18,500 in 1987, the average for the entire EC was somewhat lower, at about $13,200.[11] As a trading group, the EC has become the world's biggest exporter, accounting in 1984 for 22 percent of world imports and 21 percent of world exports, excluding intra-Community trade.[12]

The European Community evolved out of a series of post-World War II moves toward economic and political union in Western Europe. The economic community was expected to reduce costly political and economic rivalries and

---

[11] *Survey of Current Business,* March 1988, p. 4. for U.S. data. *The New York Times,* May 22, 1988, p. F4 for EC data.

[12] Commission of the European Communities, *EUR 12: Diagrams of the Enlarged Community* (Brussels: March 1986), p. 12.

evolve into a United States of Europe. The economic accomplishments have been phenomenal, but the political results have been less impressive. After 20 years, a European Parliament was established in 1979, but the new institution has limited authority.

Under the customs union agreed to in the Rome Treaty, all customs duties and restrictions on intra-Community trade were abolished by July 1, 1968. A common external tariff became fully operational at the same time. Through participation in the GATT multinational negotiations, the external tariffs of the Community have been gradually reduced while retaining the principle of a common external tariff.

In the agricultural sector, the Community developed a protective common agricultural policy. The system adopted was one of domestic support prices for separate commodities and sliding tariffs. When domestic prices are low because of bountiful crops, the tariff protection is high—and vice versa. In the agricultural area, therefore, trade diversion is the result, with more efficient external producers being excluded.

The Rome Treaty has numerous provisions that could eventually lead to a full economic union. Some provisions—such as those concerned with a common antitrust policy, a common patent law, and free labor movements within the Community—have been implemented. Others are being worked on more aggressively following the signing by the 12 member states of the Single European Act in 1985. This act committed the Community to attain six major objectives by December 31, 1992. These are completion of a frontier free market, increased economic and social cohesion, a common scientific and technological development policy, further development of the European Monetary System, the emergence of a European social dimension, and coordinated action on the environment. The increased integration means additional sacrifices of national sovereignty, but the member states have indicated increased willingness to make such sacrifices. They have agreed to accept majority rather than unanimous voting in the adoption of many regulations and standards.

Under the Rome Treaty, association with the Community is open to all countries. The Community has association and preferential agreements with a number of European countries, including the EFTA "free-trade agreements" discussed in the next section. The Community also has a special relationship with 65 developing countries in Africa, the Caribbean, and the Pacific region, called the ACP countries. The Lome III convention, signed on December 8, 1984, represents an effort by the EC to assist the ACP developing countries and retain special commercial and financial relationships with their former colonies. The main instruments of cooperation are privileged trade arrangements, development assistance, a system for the stabilization of export earnings (STABEX), a special aid program for minerals (SYSMIN), and consultative institutions.[13]

---

[13] See Michael Blackwell, "Lome III: The Search for Greater Effectiveness," *Finance and Development,* September 1985, pp. 31–34.

European Free Trade Association (EFTA)

The *European Free Trade Association (EFTA)* was formed in 1960 by seven European nations that had a variety of reasons for not joining the European Community. These seven nations—Austria, Denmark, Norway, Portugal, Sweden, Switzerland, and the United Kingdom—were later joined by Finland and Iceland. As a free-trade area, EFTA abolished internal tariffs and quantitative import restrictions on intra-association trade, but each member continues to impose its own external tariffs. EFTA, therefore, has adopted *rules of origin*. Such rules ensure that only goods with a specified percent of export value produced in the area can benefit from the tariff reductions.

Britain and Denmark left EFTA in 1972 to join the EC. Similarly, Portugal resigned in 1986 to become an EC member. Britain's and Denmark's entry into the EC opened the way for the previously mentioned free-trade agreements between the individual EFTA countries and the EC. The agreements provide for the progressive elimination of customs duties for industrial products, with minor concessions for certain agricultural products. They do *not* provide for a customs union or for the obligation to harmonize legislation, however.

The formation of EFTA boosted trade among member countries. These gains have become overshadowed, however, by the large increase in trade with the EC after the conclusion of the free-trade agreements. The EC is EFTA's biggest trading partner.

COMECON and East-West Trade

The centrally planned economies of Eastern Europe formed the Council for Mutual Economic Cooperation (COMECON) in 1949 to coordinate their trade and other forms of economic relations. The council includes Bulgaria, Cuba, Czechoslovakia, East Germany, Hungary, Mongolia, Poland, Romania, Viet Nam, and the USSR. For a number of reasons unique to the centrally planned economies (as discussed in Chapter 14), COMECON has not become a vital component of the international trade framework.

The basic objective of COMECON is not trade liberalization, as in the case of GATT and the EC, but to establish an interbloc division of labor between its members in order to achieve specialization in production at low cost. The emphasis is on *autarky*, or self-sufficiency, and economic growth through central planning, with trade flows as a necessary fact of life rather than as a goal. The government normally exercises complete control over exports and imports, and various state trading organizations have full responsibility for buying and selling a particular product.

With the exception of emergency situations, foreign trade is managed in accordance with national economic plans rather than market-determined commercial opportunities. Political as well as economic factors prevail. The yardstick is the requirement of the total plan rather than the benefits and costs to the individual state enterprise. Under such conditions, tariffs and subsidies for controlling or stimulating trade are unnecessary and not used. World prices are normally the guide for international transactions within or outside the bloc, and import and export prices may have no relationship to domestic prices. Nor are the planners necessarily constrained by cost-price relationships.

The absence of any necessary link between the cost and price of a product makes it difficult to apply the trading rules of market-oriented organizations such as GATT to trade between COMECON countries and the market economies. For example, it is practically impossible to determine whether exports from a COMECON country are subsidized.

The currencies of the socialist countries are not freely convertible. Consequently, trade is frequently arranged on a barter basis or with clearing systems whereby sales are balanced with purchases from another country. This inconvertibility has encouraged bilateralism within the trade bloc. No socialist country is willing to run a surplus with another socialist nation because of the difficulties in spending the currency. As a result, each socialist country plans for a bilateral balance in its trade with every other socialist nation. For the same reasons, bilateral trading agreements are also common between the socialist countries and the Western World.

Regional Integration among Developing Countries

Most developing countries favor regional integration as a promising strategy for accelerating their development aspirations. Yet few of the many regional integration attempts have succeeded. Most of the 14 regional arrangements shown in Figure 7–1 are in the talking stage, in the process of being implemented, moribund, or defunct. Two exceptions as of the late 1980s are the Association of South East Asian Nations (ASEAN)—which includes Brunei, Indonesia, Malaysia, the Philippines, Singapore, and Thailand—and the Andean Pact—of which Bolivia, Colombia, Ecuador, Peru, and Venezuela are members.

ASEAN was formed in 1967, but because their economies were growing at very rapid rates during the 1970s and early 1980s, the ASEAN countries made little effort to achieve regional economic integration. With growth slowing down and protectionism increasing abroad, the ASEAN countries began in 1986 to consider taking new initiatives toward regional integration.[14]

During the 1970s, the Andean Pact countries achieved significant results in dismantling intra-regional tariffs and expanding intra-regional trade. But the international debt crisis of the 1980s, which affected all of the Andean countries, indefinitely delayed further integration efforts.

Unlike the free-trade motivations of the EC and EFTA members, the developing countries look to regional integration mainly as an aid to their industrialization efforts. They need market enlargement to support modern industries and achieve a more efficient use of their resources. Thus, trade diversion through substituting

---

[14] *The Economist*, February 15, 1986, pp. 72–73.

FIGURE 7-1 Regional and Trade Arrangements among Developing Countries

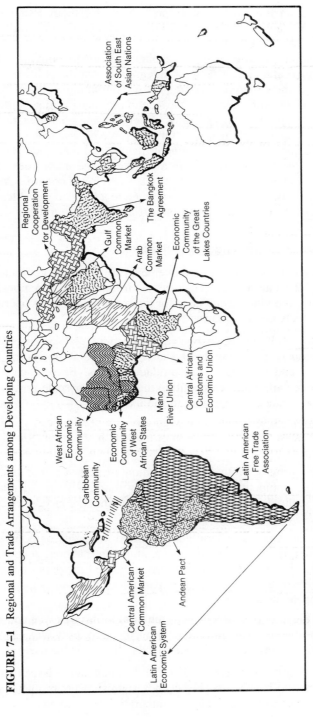

SOURCE: *IMF Survey*, July 4, 1977.

regional production for imports takes precedence for them over trade creation. The countries are determined to industrialize, and regional integration can reduce the inefficiency of such efforts.

The developing countries have encountered severe political and economic difficulties in their attempts at regional integration. On the political side, a major barrier has been the different and frequently conflicting political orientation of the countries being embraced. On the economic side, critical difficulties have arisen because the production structures of neighboring countries tend to be competitive rather than complementary. Other problems are that custom revenues are often the major source of government finance and that trade restrictions may be one of the few policy instruments available to the authorities. Still another serious barrier has been the concern of the least-developed countries in the group— such as Bolivia in the Andean Pact—that the more advanced countries will capture most of the gains from the improved industrialized opportunities.

Significance to International Business

Regional economic integration movements are certain to continue as a significant feature of the international business environment. And regional integration movements can have vital significance for international business operations. Some of the major effects are as follows:

1. Competitive conditions are changed as between internal and external producers. Firms previously exporting to the area may find it necessary to jump the trade barrier and establish local producing units. Firms located within the market can become more competitive through larger-scale producing units, if economies of scale are important to the industry.

2. Trade creation effects and more vigorous competition can stimulate growth rates and increase the attractiveness of markets in countries joining integration movements.

3. International firms established in common markets or free trade areas can become more competitive in third-country markets if the increased level of production secured within the home market permits reduced costs for exported goods.

4. Integration movements generally incorporate measures or policies that favor business enterprises from the area as against international enterprises of other nationalities. The EC, for example, has promoted mergers of European firms as a defensive measure against the expansion of U.S. and Japanese companies in the European area.

5. Changes in the rules of competition, such as adopting areawide antitrust policies, can cause problems for multinational firms that have previously given exclusive rights in specific member countries to subsidiaries or licensees.

For these and other business reasons, one of the challenging issues for the international manager is to be able to predict the establishment, probable success, and future development patterns of specific integration movements.

INTERNATIONAL COMMODITY ARRANGEMENTS

International commodity agreements and producer associations constitute another category of trading arrangements. Both types of arrangement attempt to control the terms of trade for specific commodities. They differ in that commodity agreements include both consuming and producing countries, whereas only producer countries are members of a producer's association.

The initiative for such agreements comes mainly from the developing countries. From their perspective, commodity trade (excluding petroleum) has traditionally been burdened by two problems: (1) the short-term instability of markets for primary products, and (2) the previously mentioned conviction that long-term trends have been adverse, as reflected in deteriorating terms of trade and sluggish growth in export earnings.

Short-term instability in commodity markets has resulted from both changing supply conditions stemming from the vagaries of climate, and fluctuating demand reflecting periodic recessions in the industrial nations. Such contingencies have caused sharp and damaging fluctuations in the export earnings of developing countries. As one example, Zambia was hit hard by the copper price boom and bust of the early 1970s. The price of copper peaked in April 1974, then fell to less than half its peak level before the end of the same year. Zambia's ability to purchase imports fell by 45 percent between 1974 and 1975, and its gross domestic product decreased by 15 percent.[15]

Three basic approaches have been followed in dealing with the instability of primary commodity markets—compensatory financing, international commodity agreements, and increased processing by developing countries of their own primary commodities.[16] The IMF compensatory financing facility created in 1963 extends credits to countries whose exports earnings fall dramatically because of a commodity price slump. The STABEX scheme of the EC performs a similar function for the community's associates in Africa, the Caribbean, and the Pacific. Both schemes are considered by the developing countries to be too restrictive in conditions and available funds—thus the continuing and growing emphasis on international commodity agreements.

International Commodity Agreements

The most common form of international commodity agreement is the *buffer stock system.* Under this agreement, the participating producer and consuming countries agree on fixed minimum and maximum prices for the commodity. The supply of the commodity is controlled by assigning export quotas to the producers. The demand for the commodity is influenced through the operation of a buffer stock financing facility. The manager of the buffer stock fund buys the commodity

---

[15] *The Economist,* April 19, 1980.

[16] See F. Gerard Adams and Sonia A. Klein, *Stabilizing World Commodity Markets* (Lexington, Mass.: D. C. Heath, 1978); A. I. MacBean and P. N. Snowden, *International Institutions in Trade and Finance* (London: George Allen & Unwin, 1981), pp. 111–21.

when international prices are close to the minimum mark and sells when they rise toward the maximum. The purpose is price stability in an intermediate area, guaranteeing a minimum price for exporters while safeguarding the importers against price surges.

Commodity agreements with market intervention provisions were in operation during the early 1980s in the case of tin, rubber, sugar, cocoa, and coffee. The coffee agreement does not have buffer stock financing but was designed to stabilize prices through adjustable quota restrictions on producers. As a whole, the commodity agreements have had only limited success. The buffer stock agreement on tin began operations in 1956 but finally collapsed in 1985 when the fund manager ran out of money trying to buy up surpluses on the open market (see Box 7–4). But despite the largely unsuccessful record, commodity agreements still continue as a priority item of the developing countries. The difficulties encountered in the agreements are looked upon as a challenge to improve the mechanism rather than as a deterrent.

The fundamental problem of the international commodity agreements is that the producers generally try to hold a price higher than one that would equalize

---

BOX 7–4
Collapse of the Tin Agreement

The International Tin Council (ITC) included among its 22 members 16 consumer countries. They had joined in the early days, after the Korean war, when tin was occasionally scarce and high priced. The United States was at one time a consumer member but dropped out in 1982.

The immediate—though certainly not fundamental—cause of the collapse of the ITC is that the buffer stock manager, besides purchasing physical stocks of tin, had bought large amounts of tin on forward contracts, on margin. When the price fell, he ran out of funds and couldn't honor those contracts, which amounted to an astonishing 60,000 metric tons of tin. (These would have been worth about $710 million at prices then prevailing.) He made these contracts in a futile attempt to hold the price above the ITC's floor of about $5.20 a pound or a London price of about £8,300 a ton.

When rescue attempts failed, the London Metal Exchange rather arbitrarily settled all of the outstanding contracts at £6,250 a ton. This compromise price entails heavy losses for many participants in the market, and doesn't fully reflect the price that the market now places on the metal. Tin recently has been trading in Kuala Lumpur at less than $2.85 a pound, or £4,000 a ton.

The ITC collapsed because the effort to hold a price higher than one that would equalize supply and demand eventually brought more supplies to the market and drove consumers to look for alternatives. New supplies came from nonmembers because the producer members didn't control all of the world's tin reservers.

SOURCE: Adapted from Willard D. Sharpe, "Tin Cartel Joins OPEC on the Crash List," *The Wall Street Journal*, April 7, 1986. © Dow Jones & Company, Inc., 1986. Used with permission. All rights reserved.

supply and demand. This encourages new producers who can gain handsomely by not being members of the agreement. They can undercut slightly the market price, and they are not restrained in how much they sell. In the case of tin, consumers economized on the use of the overpriced commodity, and plastic and aluminum substitutes were developed that reduced the demand for tin.

Trade arrangements to moderate short-term fluctuations in commodity export earnings have considerable international support, but commodity arrangements that attempt to shift the long-run terms of trade in favor of the producers do not. Changing the terms of trade is viewed as benefiting the producers at the expense of the consumers.

Buffer stocks of the stabilizing sort can be of practical benefit to consumers. Increasingly inflexible cost structures in the industrialized countries have meant that rises in commodity prices have a ratchet effect on inflation. Prices of final goods rise to reflect increases in raw material costs; they rarely fall in step once commodity prices start downward. On the producers' side, widely fluctuating possibilities in future prices hamper investment. Sustained periods of falling prices lead to stagnant production facilities, and periods of sharply increased demand lead to destabilizing commodity price increases, because production cannot be quickly expanded. Stabilization is, therefore, perceived by both exporters and importers as in their mutual interest.

Thus, there are sound reasons for supporting some commodity stabilization schemes. But the mechanism that has been developed through international commodity agreements may not support the burden of good intentions. Nevertheless, international commodity agreements are certain to persist as a component of the international trade framework.

Producer Associations

The Organization of Petroleum Exporting Countries (OPEC) is a leading example of a producer association. Although frequently referred to as such, OPEC is not a true export cartel. Its members have not given OPEC the power to enforce decisions on production quotas and market share allocations. OPEC serves as an information clearinghouse and as a meeting ground for making decisions on prices and production targets, but the compliance of member countries is voluntary.

Since its creation in 1960, OPEC has worked to obtain greater benefits for its members through raising and controlling petroleum prices in the international market. OPEC was slow to realize its goals, and the world price of petroleum hovered around $.75 to $1 a barrel from 1960 to 1970.[17] In the early 1970s, however, OPEC succeeded in taking control of world prices away from the major international oil companies and was able to initiate a spectacular escalation of oil prices, which by 1979 reached a level of $40 a barrel in the spot market.

---

[17] Suhayr Mikdashi, *The International Politics of Natural Resources* (Ithaca, N.Y.: Cornell University Press, 1976), p. 72; see also Fariborz Ghadar, *The Evolution of OPEC Strategy* (Lexington, Mass.: Lexington Books, 1977).

The shift in bargaining power occurred because the supply situation in world markets had become tight as a result of rapidly expanding demand and because the position of the major oil companies had been weakened by the entry of many similar U.S. and European oil companies into petroleum exploration and production—thus enlarging the options of the oil-producing countries.

The first major price escalation was prompted by the Israeli-Arab war of 1973, which caused the oil ministers of the Arab nations to use the "oil weapon" to support the Arab cause by imposing an embargo on sales to the United States and Netherlands.[18] The result was that oil prices, which had reached $2.60 a barrel in 1973, skyrocketed to almost $10 in 1974. This new level remained relatively stable until 1979, when the Iranian revolution interrupted oil supplies. Anxious buyers scrambled for oil and bid up prices in the spot market to a level of $40 a barrel.

But the OPEC victories sowed the seeds for subsequent defeat. Oil consumers throughout the world undertook intensive measures to conserve the use of petroleum and succeeded in greatly reducing demand. Consumers also turned to alternative sources of energy (such as coal, nuclear, solar, and wind energy), which had become more economic than oil. At the same time, the high oil prices stimulated unprecedented petroleum exploration and production activity that sharply increased the supply of oil available from non-OPEC members.

From 1980 to 1985, the reduced demand, the increased supplies, and generally slow economic growth trends caused OPEC to lower gradually the price of oil to the $30-a-barrel level. But in 1985, the full impact of the "seeds of destruction" hit, and OPEC was unable to get its members to agree on major production cutbacks. The market collapsed, and crude oil prices dropped from nearly $32 a barrel in November 1985 to $9.75 a barrel in April 1986, stabilizing in 1986 at between $15 and $20 a barrel. In December 1986, the OPEC members negotiated a new agreement to control production to maintain a price of $18 a barrel, but the future effectiveness of OPEC remained in doubt.

In a number of commodity areas other than oil, many producing countries have tried to emulate the OPEC model. Producer associations have been initiated in copper, bauxite, phosphate, and chromium but have not had any marked success. To be effective, such an association must consist of a relatively small number of countries that control a large share of world production. Also, world demand for the commodity must be strong and growing.

BILATERAL TRADING ARRANGEMENTS

To complete the picture of the international trade framework, mention should be made of bilateral trading arrangements. Many such agreements exist between the centrally planned and market economies. Another example of bilateral arrangements is the United States-Canada Automotive Products agreement concluded in

---

[18] Robert B. Stobaugh, "The Evolution of Iranian Oil Policy, 1925" in *Iran Under the Pahlavis,* ed. George Lenczowski (Stanford, Calif.: Hoover Institution Press, 1978), p. 244.

1965. At the time the agreement was signed, it was considered a model that might be widely followed for obtaining the benefits of specialization and large-scale production by creating broader markets for a specific industry.

The agreement permits the integration of Canadian and U.S. production of automobile parts and vehicles. Thus production units in each country can produce at efficient levels, and most vehicles and parts can cross the border duty-free in each direction. The selection of products and plants in each country was intended to result in an equitable trade balance between the countries in the automotive field.

THE PROS AND CONS OF PROTECTIONISM

"Protectionism" is a mildly pejorative label attached to national policies that shelter certain domestic activities from foreign competition by preventing imports in these fields or making them excessively expensive. The domestic producers and workers receiving protection generally attempt to identify their private gains as contributing to the national interests. Such national interests may be infant-industry protection, national security, the need to maintain domestic employment and income and reduce foreign exchange outflows, and the desirability of diversifying the domestic economy to improve economic stability and stimulate growth. Normally, domestic pressures for protection are resolved by political considerations and in favor of the domestic parties with the most political muscle. Yet the political debate invariably revolves around economic arguments, some of which have qualified validity while others are highly questionable from the standpoint of national interests.

Protectionist measures generally favor one group in a country at the expense of other sectors of the economy. Therefore, nations have to evaluate the trade-offs involved in protectionist policies and determine the net benefits or costs to the country. If the U.S. steel industry, for example, is given protection against foreign steel imports through tariffs, quotas, or so-called orderly market agreements, the direct benefits will be to the steel workers in terms of jobs, to the steel companies in terms of profits, and to the U.S. trade balance because of reduced imports.

On the cost side, because of resulting higher domestic prices for steel, other U.S. industries that use steel to produce machinery become less competitive in both foreign and domestic markets. Their profits, their workers, and their foreign exchange earnings for the country are likely to suffer. Domestic consumers of steel products will have to pay higher prices and, in effect, subsidize the protected industry. As an example, the United States was giving protection to the steel industry in 1984 against foreign competition in carbon steel. This protection cost consumers an estimated $6.8 billion in 1984, according to a study by Gary C. Hufbauer and Howard F. Rosen. Even more startling is the estimate that the protection cost consumers $750,000 for each job saved.[19]

---

[19] *Business Week*, April 7, 1986, p. 4.

Another factor is that foreign countries are likely to retaliate with their own protectionist measures, which could reduce exports, profits, and employment in other U.S. industries. Both the positive and negative effects will have different weights depending upon the economic situation of the country. Even where the net economic impact is negative, a nation may be willing to pay this price to satisfy long-run or noneconomic goals.

The infant-industry argument for protection can be a valid argument if the industry being protected has realistic possibilities of maturing into an adult that no longer requires protection. However, this justification has been used for initiating types of business activities that are likely to remain infants and require what amounts to a permanent subsidy. National security can also be a valid justification for protection and worth the cost to a country if the national-security goals to be served are consistent with a sound, modern security strategy. Likewise protectionist measures that encourage the diversification of the domestic economy may provide substantial long-term gains to a country that more than offset short-term costs.

Most of the other arguments for protection are questionable or invalid from an economic standpoint, even though they may have great emotional appeal that garners strong political support. Most common among these is the highly plausible but generally fallacious cheap-labor argument, which both industry and labor use to demand protection against "unfair" competition from low-wage workers in foreign countries. This argument has at least three fatal weaknesses.

First, the argument confuses wage rates and unit labor costs. Labor costs depend on labor productivity as well as wage rates. Productivity depends in turn on the other factors of production, such as capital, management, and technology, that are combined with labor in the process of producing goods and services. Assuming that all other factors are constant, low wages will mean lower labor costs. But in reality all other factors, including the skills of the workers themselves, are not constant; and high-wage industries in one country can, in fact, produce goods with lower labor costs *per unit of output* than competing industries in countries where wage costs are low.

Second, the low-wage argument for protection also assumes that the only important cost involved in the ability of businesses to be competitive is the cost of labor. Labor costs as a share of total costs vary greatly from industry to industry. Therefore, even if labor costs (irrespective of wage rates) are lower in some countries, the competitive advantage for a specific industry may be minor compared with variations in other production or distribution costs. The cost of electric power, for example, is much more significant in the production of aluminum than labor costs.

Third, one nation may have comparative advantages in large supplies of low-cost labor. Other nations may have their comparative advantages in low costs of raw materials, transportation, capital, or electric power. Labor costs are neither the only—nor the most important—competitive consideration.

Some proponents of protection broaden the low-wage argument to a general plea for equalizing all production costs between foreign and domestic producers on the grounds of "fair competition." Such a policy would violate whatever validity there is in the argument that a country should specialize in those fields in which it has a comparative advantage, as a result of differences in resource endowments, and trade with others. It would be just as valid or invalid for Japanese steel manufacturers to ask for protection against the lower prices that U.S. firms are able to pay for coking coal because the United States happens to have favorable resource endowments in these fields. In fact, if the argument for protection to equalize national differences in production costs were accepted, there would be no basis whatever for trade taking place.

The basic problem frequently underlying protectionism is that a country needs to make structural changes. It must move out of industries in which the nation is no longer competitive into other activities where it has a comparative advantage. Such structural changes are difficult to accomplish, particularly in periods of slow national growth.

SUMMARY

The large number of organizations and the complexity of the many trading arrangements suggest that a high degree of disarray exists in multinational trading. This is true in the sense that the multinational enterprise must keep informed about and even participate in numerous trade negotiations in many forums. In another sense, however, the picture is rather simple and clear-cut. There are "three worlds" involved, and each has its own objectives. The industrialized world favors free trade and specialization and has resisted basic changes in the structure of the world economy. The developing countries are not in favor of free trade and want to use trade arrangements to achieve structural changes in their own economies and in their economic relations with the rest of the world. The centrally planned world would like to expand its trading relations with the other two worlds but with a minimum of change in internal economic structures.

The multinational trade agreements "game" is one in which each of the participating groups—and each country within a group—is trying to move a few more steps toward its goals. The game cannot stop because of the growing interdependency of the three worlds. Also, there are usually enough mutual benefits involved to warrant the continuing search for new trade arrangements. The results of the negotiations depend, of course, on the respective bargaining power of the participants. The bargaining power keeps changing and involves geopolitical factors as well as economic considerations, such as growing world scarcities in certain natural resources.

Institutional arrangements frequently lag behind real needs and deal mainly with the problems of yesterday rather than those of today. This observation is relevant to the international trade framework. As one example, the relationship of the multinational enterprise and foreign direct investment to trade patterns has not yet been given proper recognition by the institutional arrangements that make up the international framework.

An underlying reality of the international trade framework is that the nation-states give lip service to the venerable concepts of the virtues of free trade, but in practice they are not willing in many situations to let free-market forces prevail. One of the most basic reasons (generally more implicit than explicit) motivating nations to influence international transfers is the fact that maximizing output for the world as a whole does not necessarily mean that each country will share these benefits in a satisfactory proportion. Thus, many controls and incentives to influence transfers have been designed by nations to attempt to increase their shares of the benefits.

EXERCISES AND DISCUSSION QUESTIONS

1. What policies do you think the United States should follow with regard to East-West trade? To what extent should the United States use pressure to influence policies of other Western nations in regard to trade with the socialist countries?
2. Distinguish between a free-trade area, a customs union, and a common market.
3. What is the significance of the principle of ''most-favored-nation'' treatment? Why has it not weakened significantly the bargaining position of individual countries in their tariff negotiations with other countries?
4. ''The time has come to create a GATT for investment. Trade negotiations must recognize that direct investment and foreign production are both alternatives and complements to traditional trade.'' Discuss.
5. Under what circumstances would you recommend that industrial consumer countries support moves by the developing producer countries for further commodity agreements?
6. ''Export promotion activities can produce just as much distortion to free trade as do tariffs; therefore, no nation should actively stimulate exports.'' If you disagree with this statement, compile a list of export promotion activities the United States should undertake and suggest how the limit should be determined for each activity.
7. ''The Ford Motor Co. finally joined forces with the United Auto Workers Union to formally request restrictions of shipments of Japanese-built cars and trucks to the United States. It filed a petition with the International Trade Commission for a temporary remedy to restrain Japanese imports, which it charged are causing serious injury to auto employment and investment in the United States.'' (*The Wall Street Journal*, August 5, 1980.) As a member of the ITC, how would you decide on this petition and why?
8. Why has the regional economic integration movement of the European Community (EC) been successful whereas most other regional integration efforts have not?
9. Why do many nations give lip service to the economic virtues of free trade and still adopt protectionist measures?

CHAPTER 8

The International Legal
Environment

The legal environment for international business consists principally of the laws and courts of the individual nation-states. As no single international commercial legal system exists, the international firm is confronted with as many legal environments as there are countries. The national systems differ significantly in philosophy and practice, and each nation-state maintains its own set of courts in complete independence of every other nation. The closest approximation to an international legal framework is a patchwork system of treaties, codes, and agreements among certain nations that apply to selected areas of international business activity.

Both business enterprises and national governments are often frustrated by the legal environment. As the effective domain of the multinational enterprise exceeds the legal jurisdiction of individual nations, the enterprise constantly faces uncertainties and conflicts as to which laws apply. At the same time, national governments are seriously troubled because of their perception that multinational firms can and do escape from national regulations and laws.

This chapter provides the international manager with some background on the labyrinth that comprises the international legal environment. It also identifies some of the principal legal issues that are likely to concern the international business firm.

INTERNATIONAL LAW AND INTERNATIONAL BUSINESS

Although contrary to the facts, there is a widely held impression that a rather precise system of international law exists for guiding business transactions across national boundaries. This impression is particularly strong as it relates to the protection of foreign-owned private property. It is common to hear businessmen and government officials assert that the expropriation of foreign property without prompt and adequate compensation is a violation of international law. Such wistful views have long been popular in the economically advanced investor countries, but they are not generally accepted around the world. In order for rules and principles to become international law, nation-states must consider such rules and principles legally binding upon them.

The only international court is the International Court of Justice at The Hague in the Netherlands. It is the principal organ of the United Nations, and all members of the United Nations are ipso facto parties to the statute establishing the court. The court's function is to pass judgment on disputes between member states, but only when each of the states involved agrees to accept the court's jurisdiction. Private persons or corporations do not have access to the International Court.

From the standpoint of international business, the most important international legal issues arise out of the growing number of treaties and conventions covering commercial and economic matters. Of special significance is the so-called Rome Treaty establishing the European Community (EC) and under which a vast amount of regional law is developing for most of Western Europe.

According to modern diplomatic usage, the more important international agreements are referred to as *treaties*. Those of lesser importance are called *conventions, agreements, protocols,* and *acts*. All of these forms are agreements between two or more nation-states that normally become legally enforceable through the internal courts—also referred to as *municipal courts*—of the participating countries.

The weakness of the structure of international commitments through treaties, codes, and agreements is its inadequate coverage for many ingredients of business operations that have grown in importance with the internationalization of business. Furthermore, the number of countries participating in particular agreements may be limited in comparison with the global horizon of the multinational enterprise.

European Community Law

A principal institution of the EC is the Court of Justice established to interpret and apply the provisions of the Rome Treaty.[1] The jurisdiction of the court involves every aspect of the Treaty. Its decisions take precedence over national laws throughout the Community, now ranging from Ireland to the Iberian Peninsula. The Court has been very active; and the treaty covers many economic and business issues such as the free movement of goods, workers, and capital as well as the right of establishment, transport policy, agricultural policy, and rules of competition. Consequently, the regional legal system emerging from the actions of the Court of Justice has great relevance to international business operations in Western Europe.

The Court of Justice has a broad jurisdiction; and it seeks to establish uniformity in the understanding, interpretation, and application of Community provisions within the member states. It "reviews" issues involving Community law that arose in cases before national courts and hears actions against member states, Community institutions, or the Community itself that are brought before it. National courts and national enforcement institutions are responsible for implementing judgments of the Court of Justice.

The Right of Establishment

Through bilateral commercial treaties, many governments seek to enlarge the opportunity for their nationals to transact business in foreign countries on a nondiscriminatory basis. The privilege of doing business in a foreign country and the conditions under which it is formally granted are the substance of a series of treaties known in the United States as Treaties of Friendship, Commerce, and Navigation. The objective of such commercial treaties is to secure for foreigners the right to trade, invest, or establish and operate a business in a country on a nondiscriminatory basis. The fundamental point underlying commercial treaties is that engaging in business transactions in a country other than one's own is a privilege and not a right. Usually, this privilege and the delineation of its conditions are worked out by negotiation between governments.[2]

Such treaties, of course, are not always observed. In the early 1960s, for example, the French government became greatly concerned because U.S. firms

---

[1] See Henry J. Steiner and Detlev F. Vagts, *Transnational Legal Problems, Third Edition* (Mineola, N.Y.: Foundation Press, 1986), pp. 1059–1122; Donald T. Wilson, *International Business Transactions, Second Edition* (St. Paul, Minn.: West Publishing Co., 1984), pp. 67–90.

[2] Steiner and Vagts, *Transnational Legal Problems,* pp. 637–38.

were attempting to take over a number of French companies, including France's largest manufacturer of computers (Machines Bull). The French response was to restrict U.S. direct investment through administrative delays and informal pressures. Although these restrictions violated France's Treaty of Establishment with the United States, the U.S. government never formally protested and apparently was not asked to do so by U.S. firms that were refused. But the French ban on new direct investment did not last long because other Common Market countries were anxious and willing to receive the U.S. companies.[3]

The Protection of Intellectual Property Rights

Most countries protect intellectual property rights—a term that includes patents, know-how, and trademarks. But patents are granted and trademarks are registered by national governments and are valid only within the territorial jurisdiction of the granting government. Consequently, foreign exploitation of a patent or trademark requires a parallel grant by foreign governments. As might be expected, the requirements for trademark registration and the patent systems of the various countries differ significantly.[4] And some countries have developed flourishing businesses by not having—or not enforcing—laws to protect intellectual property rights (see Box 8–1 and note the dates of the several items).

To protect its intellectual property rights, the international firm must file patent and trademark registration applications in every country in which these property rights are to be used. This requirement can be both burdensome and expensive. One large corporation estimated that the cost of obtaining foreign patents was running close to $2 million a year.

In many cases, companies have lost the foreign rights to trademarks and have had to pay royalties for their use or buy back these rights. An extreme example of trademark difficulties is the case of a U.S. citizen living in Mexico who registered in Mexico the brand names and trademarks of some 40 companies. These included such well-known names as "Carter's Little Liver Pills" and "Bromo Seltzer." Most of the companies succeeded in regaining control of their brand names, but lengthy litigation and official support of the U.S. government was required.[5]

Several international agreements have simplified the process of protecting intellectual property rights in foreign countries. The Convention of Paris is made up of a group of more than 90 nations, including the United States, that has agreed to provide national treatment for each other with regard to intellectual property rights. This means that each country grants to nationals of other member

---

[3] Christopher Layton, *Transatlantic Investments* (Boulogne-sur-Seine, France: Atlantic Institute, 1966), pp. 36–44.

[4] See Ethan Horwitz, *World Trademark Law and Practice* (Albany, N.Y.: Matthew Bender & Co., 1982).

[5] Philip R. Cateora, *International Marketing, 5th ed.* (Homewood, Ill.: Richard D. Irwin, 1983), p. 204.

BOX 8–1
Fighting the Pirates—Fast Action

Washington—The Reagan administration unveiled plans to protect American trademarks, copyrights and patents more aggressively, and proposed new legislation to help do the job.

The legislative package would revamp some existing trade and antitrust provisions to make it easier for government and businesses to prosecute foreign companies that have been caught counterfeiting or pirating U.S. goods or technology.

Officials said the administration also plans to intensify pressure on U.S. trading partners to protect U.S. copyrights, patents, and trademarks and to use existing laws more aggressively to help crack down on violations. Among other things, the United States might limit the special tariff preferences now given to developing countries, in cases where the Third World governments don't take steps to safeguard such U.S. "intellectual property."

SOURCE: *The Wall Street Journal,* April 8, 1986. © Dow Jones & Company, Inc., 1986. Reprinted by permission. All rights reserved.

The Tape Battle in Singapore

Singapore—Singapore is taking steps to change its image as an emporium of bootlegged music and films. It is introducing an intellectual property copyright bill, which is expected to become law by the end of the year. The Motion Picture Association of America reckons its members lose more than U.S. $11 million a year in profits because of videotapes illegally recorded in Singapore. Producers of recorded music say the city-state is the biggest exporter of pirated music and cassettes in the world.

The benefits the city-state receive under America's organized system of preferences for imported goods will, in future, depend in part on copyright safeguards.

SOURCE: Adapted from *The Economist,* April 12, 1986.

Book Piracy in Taiwan

The Taiwan government announced earlier this year that it would strengthen copyright protection for U.S. authors. While none of the pirates has yet been brought to court, most local publishers have stopped printing pirated versions of foreign books. For years, Taiwan publishers have produced copies of Western books, ranging from best-sellers to technical works, often within a month after they came off the press abroad. No royalties were paid to the author or the original publisher.

The book-piracy issue is part of a U.S. campaign to get Taiwan and other Asian countries to strengthen protection for "intellectual property rights."

SOURCE: *The Wall Street Journal,* May 6, 1986. © Dow Jones & Company, Inc., 1986. Used with permission. All rights reserved.

countries the same rights it affords to its own nationals. The European Patent Convention that became operational in 1978 permits a single European patent office to issue a patent that is effective in 11 European signatory countries. A Patent Cooperation Treaty, intended to simplify and expedite the patent application process through providing centralized international search reports, also became effective in 1978. Such reports can aid patent applicants in deciding whether patent protection should be sought in other countries.

Taxation Treaties

In a world of separate taxing authorities, problems arise because the entity being taxed, or parts of it, may fall under the jurisdiction of more than one taxing authority. An enterprise may have its legal residence in one country, do business in another country, and have headquarters in still another country. How is the enterprise to be taxed, and how can it avoid paying taxes on the same base to more than one of the taxing jurisdictions? The solution to this problem must recognize both the right of the enterprise to be free from excessive taxation and the right of the different authorities to tax revenues.

The right to levy and collect taxes is one of the most sacred rights of national sovereignty, but there is no clear or universally accepted theory of tax jurisdiction. Nor is there an international law that specifies who has the right to tax and that sets limits to the reach of any country's tax jurisdiction. Business transactions across national boundaries, therefore, can be greatly influenced in both positive and negative ways by the problems or opportunities resulting from varying taxation policies of overlapping national tax jurisdictions.

The tax systems of different countries vary significantly in the treatment of who is taxed—that is, in concepts of residence of the firm or individual—and in what sources of income are taxed.[6] As a result, two taxing jurisdictions may claim the right to tax the same property or income. This probability has caused governments to provide credits for taxes paid abroad and to negotiate bilateral tax treaties.[7] The United States has bilateral tax treaties with some 40 countries, all of which are intended to provide relief from double taxation. No multilateral tax treaties have been realized as yet; but the Model Double Taxation Convention on Income and Capital approved by the Organization for Economic Cooperation and Development (OECD) in 1977 has been influential as a guide to countries in their bilateral negotiations.

The tax credit feature in tax treaties has encouraged host countries of international business firms to impose taxes up to the rates imposed by the home countries of the international business firm. Such a policy can maximize the share received by the host country without increasing the total tax burden on a company. Another

---

[6] For example, see *Corporate Taxes: A Worldwide Summary* (New York: Price, Waterhouse, January 1982); *Differences in Tax Treatment of Foreign Investors: Domestic Subsidiaries and Domestic Branches,* ed. John I. Forry (Hingham, Mass.: Kluwer, 1984).

[7] Detlev F. Vagts, *Transnational Business Problems* (Mineola, N.Y.: The Foundation Press, 1986), pp. 84–97.

trend is for nations to use tax exemptions or low taxes as an attraction for international business activities. But the effectiveness of such government policy depends upon the willingness of the home governments of the international business firms to grant "tax sparing," that is, to allow tax credits as if full taxes were paid. The United States, for example, does not grant tax credit for taxes spared abroad. Thus, the advantage to U.S. firms of tax inducements in foreign countries may be offset by home-country taxation on the higher foreign profits resulting from the tax concessions.

Property Protection in Foreign Jurisdictions

The protection of property in foreign jurisdictions has long been a sensitive international legal issue. All nations assert the right to expropriate (take over) private property when the national welfare makes such a move desirable. In the United States, for example, governments can take over private property for a "public purpose" under the common law concepts of condemnation or eminent domain. The right of a sovereign government to expropriate is rarely in dispute, although national laws vary as to what is a public purpose. But international legal controversy frequently arises as to the matter of compensation; namely, what compensation rule should be followed and how should disputes be settled.

On the compensation issue, the positions of foreign investors and host countries are frequently in conflict. The developing nations assert the principle of supremacy of national law and jurisdiction. Foreign investors, however, are not willing to rely solely on local courts for the protection of foreign property. They are supported by the position of the industrialized countries—that international law imposes certain limitations on the exercise of national sovereignty and that its exercise can be further limited with binding effect by agreement.

The unhappy experiences of South American countries during the 19th century with diplomatic and military intervention on behalf of foreign investors led to the development of special South American attitudes towards the protection of aliens and their property. An Argentine jurist, Carlos Calvo, was active in this development; his name is attached to the Calvo Doctrine, which asserts that a foreigner by entering a country to do business implicitly consents to be treated as are national firms. This means that a foreign firm does not have the right to invoke the protection of its own government in investment disputes.

The Calvo Clause has been used in contracts with foreign investors. It also appears in statutes and even in some Latin American constitutions. The Calvo philosophy remains strong in Latin America, as evidenced by the unwillingness of the Latin American countries to become associated with the International Center for Settlement of Investment Disputes (ICSID), to be discussed below. But its importance has been diminished by recent trends, such as treating property protection matters under investment guarantee agreements.[8]

A more recent and broader assertion of the absolute supremacy of national

---

[8] Steiner and Vagts, *Transnational Legal Problems,* pp. 553–60.

laws and jurisdiction is the Charter of Economic Rights and Duties of States adopted by the United Nations in 1974. This UN Charter states (Article 2, Section 1) that "Every state has and shall freely exercise full permanent sovereignty, including possession, use and disposal, over all its wealth, natural resources and economic activities." Although not formally binding on member states, the Charter asserts untrammeled discretion and the *absolute supremacy* of national law and jurisdiction in matters of nationalization, compensation, and the revision or termination of contracts. The UN vote was 120 to 6 with 10 abstentions. The dissenters included five Western European countries and the United States. The abstentions were Canada, Israel, Japan, and seven Western European nations. In effect, the vote was a case of the developing nations versus the industrialized countries.

Foreign investors are reluctant to rely on local courts because they fear they may have great difficulty enforcing their rights. Under the Doctrine of Sovereign Immunity, the investor may be precluded from access to many national courts for litigating claims. Although many limitations on the sovereign immunity doctrine have evolved, the thinking underlying the concept is illustrated by the statement of Justice Holmes in a 1907 case that "there can be no legal right as against the authority that makes the law on which the right depends." A further hurdle may be the Act of State Doctrine, which is separate but closely related to the immunity doctrine. The Act of State Doctrine does not deny a court's jurisdiction. But it does preclude the court in an action before it from inquiring into the "validity" or "lawfulness" of public acts of a sovereign power committed within its own territory.[9] Implicit in the Act of State Doctrine is a form of reciprocity. It says, "I won't question the validity of what you do in your own backyard and the reverse applies to you."

Both the Sovereign Immunity and Act of State doctrines present special problems for U.S. firms engaged in international business. U.S. firms are most familiar with the largely private enterprise U.S. economy. But outside of the U.S. most governments are heavily involved in commercial activities, and commercial disputes frequently involve foreign governments. Fortunately, recent experience in applying these doctrines reflects a growing judicial recognition that a sovereign's commercial activities should be excepted from the benefit of these doctrines.

Still another problem may arise from the principle of parliamentary sovereignty. This doctrine implies that one parliament cannot bind its successor as far as legislative functions are concerned. Government policies, local laws, and even constitutional provisions may be altered unilaterally at some future date.

In the crucial matter of compensation for the taking of property, the views of investor and host countries may differ sharply. The rule as usually asserted by investor nations—that compensation must be prompt, adequate, and effective—

---

[9] See Henry P. de Vries, "The Enforcement of Economic Development Agreements within Foreign States," *University of Detroit Law Review*, Fall 1984, p. 13; Donald T. Wilson, *International Business Transactions*, pp. 335–82.

is not recognized by many developing and communist nations. Most developing countries take the philosophical position that "social" considerations may be paramount to the rights of the immediate property owners. Furthermore, the requirement for full and immediate payment would deny to poor countries the right to pursue a broad program of economic and social reform. In the communist nations, expropriation without compensation has been justified as the means of implementing a philosophy opposed in principle to private property.

Yet there has been a big gap between rhetoric and reality. At the same time that many nations were supporting the rhetoric of the UN Charter of Economic Rights, the same nations were entering into treaties with major investor nations that bind the contracting parties to specific substantive and procedural rules relating to foreign investments.[10] Such rules deal with the conditions under which nationalization may take place, standards of compensation, settlement of disputes, access to international arbitration, and the like. The reality is that many nations are anxious to attract foreign investment, and they are convinced that assurances are needed to interest foreign investors.

INTERNATIONAL ARBITRATION AND DISPUTE SETTLEMENT

Given the problems inherent in relying on national courts for dispute settlement, there has been a growing trend in international business to make use of international arbitration. In relying on national courts, there can be uncertainty about the country and the court in which a dispute may be heard, as illustrated by Box 8–2 on the Bhopal disaster. There can be uncertainty about the procedural and substantive rules to be applied, about the degree of publicity to be given to the proceedings, the time necessary to settle a dispute, and the effectiveness of the resulting judgment. Although arbitration may be costly and has other limitations, in most of the previous respects it is likely to be a preferred mechanism for dispute settlement.

It has become a common practice, therefore, for mutually agreed upon arbitration clauses to be included in investment guaranty treaties, economic development (concessions) agreements, and other agreements between foreign investors and host nations.[11] Similar clauses are common in international commercial agreements between business parties, such as a license agreement, sales contract, or distributorship contract.

The arbitration clauses normally specify the institutional arrangements and rules that will be used. The principal centers for international arbitration are Geneva, London, New York, Paris, and Stockholm, where international arbitration associations at such places have fairly settled rules for conducting arbitration.

---

[10] See the section on Foreign Risk Insurance in Chapter 12.

[11] See Henry P. de Vries, "International Commercial Arbitration: A Transnational View," *Journal of International Arbitration*, April 1984, pp. 7–20.

BOX 8–2
Whose Court Should Decide? The Bhopal India Case

On December 3, 1984, a storage tank erupted at a Union Carbide pesticide factory in Bhopal, India. More than 2,000 persons died from the spread of methyl isocyanate gas; and perhaps some 200,000 were injured, in some cases so severe as to be permanently disabled. The plant belonged to Union Carbide India, Ltd., a company organized under the laws of India but owned 51 percent by Union Carbide, a U.S. multinational.

In what has been called the "greatest ambulance chase in history," U.S. lawyers descended upon Bhopal and sought to enlist plaintiffs in suits against Union Carbide (U.S.). Various class actions calling for billions of dollars in damages, far more than the net worth of the company, were commenced in the United States and were ultimately consolidated before one federal judge in New York, who had to decide whether the damage claims should be heard in the United States or in India.

There's no doubt that U.S. courts have jurisdiction over the suits, for Union Carbide's headquarters are here. Nevertheless, the cases might be moved to India under the doctrine of forum non conveniens, which is supposed to prevent cases from being tried in locations so inconvenient as to be unacceptably burdensome to one of the parties.

The U.S. attorneys for the Bhopal victims want the U.S. courts to accept jurisdiction. They have been supported by the Indian government, which took the unusual step of asking for U.S. judicial involvement, maintaining that the case will flounder in India's overburdened legal system. Union Carbide (U.S.) has taken the position that the claims should be litigated in the Indian courts, asserting that its Indian unit is a separate business with an arm's length relationship to its parent.

The attraction of the U.S. courts to the plaintiffs is that tort liability in the U.S. is greater than it is in other countries. U.S. measures of damages (such as those for pain and suffering and punitive damages) increase manyfold the amount of potential judgments. Recoveries for personal injuries in India seldom exceed $8,000. Contingent-fee arrangements, illegal everywhere else in the world, make it legal for U.S. lawyers to get a sufficient share of the spoils for them to risk the cost of pursuing the case in the United States.

In June 1986, the federal judge dismissed all Bhopal-related federal court claims against Carbide-U.S. and ordered that the Bhopal cases be transferred to India, with the condition that Carbide accept certain ground rules. Among other things, he ordered that Carbide-U.S. agree to pay any future judgments against it in India and that Indian officials be allowed to use U.S. legal discovery procedures in pressing their claims against the company. Such U.S. rules, which govern the lawyers' access to witnesses and evidence, are far broader in scope than those available in India.

If this ruling is upheld on appeal to a higher U.S. court and all pending Bhopal-related state court claims against Carbide are dismissed, the role of plaintiffs' U.S. attorneys in the Bhopal case will end.

SOURCE: Various articles in the *New York Times; The Wall Street Journal,* and Vagts, *Transnational Business,* pp. 141–42.

London, for example, is the world center for international arbitration on maritime, insurance, and commodity matters. The Stockholm Arbitration Institute handles much of the arbitration dealing with East-West trade. In nonspecialized cases, the International Chamber of Commerce in Paris is one of the main institutions. In about 70 nations, including most commercial nations, the enforcement of arbitral awards in national courts is facilitated by the United Nations Convention on the Recognition and Enforcement of Foreign Arbitral Awards.

An international mechanism that offers arbitration and/or conciliation services in disputes where one of the parties is a state is the International Center for Settlement of Investment Disputes (ICSID). ICSID was founded in 1966 under the auspices of the World Bank. As of 1985, 83 governments were associated with ICSID. All of the industrialized countries are members, as are the Eastern European countries of Yugoslavia and Romania. Most of the developing nations in Africa and Asia are members, including the small less-developed countries that hope to improve their attraction to foreign investors. But through Calvo Doctrine eyes, the Latin American countries view ICSID as an infringement on national sovereignty; and only Ecuador, Paraguay, and El Salvador were contracting states as of 1984.[12] During the first 17 years of operation, ICSID had undertaken 22 proceedings.

INFRASTRUCTURE TREATIES AND CONVENTIONS

The international legal environment includes many areas of intergovernmental cooperation as well as conflict. An important area of cooperation is that of infrastructure, where a series of UN specialized agencies perform valuable services that facilitate business transactions across national boundaries. The international agreements and activities in the fields of communications and transportation are of special importance.

The International Civil Aviation Organization (ICAO) fosters safe, regular, and efficient international civil aviation through developing international specifications for air traffic, airports, telecommunications, charts, operations, airworthiness, and personnel that are adhered to by member countries. The International Telecommunications Union (ITU) controls and allocates radio frequencies and facilitates international telegraph and telephone communications. The Universal Postal Union, initially based on a convention of 1874 and presently a specialized agency of the United Nations, has established compulsory provisions for member countries governing international postal service and operates as a clearinghouse in the settlement of certain accounts. The International Labour Office (ILO) has adopted conventions on trade union rights and on the protection of the right of workers to organize and bargain collectively. The World Health Organization (WHO) works to improve health conditions and has various international duties relative to the standardization of drugs, epidemic control, and quarantine measures.

---

[12] Ibrahim F. I. Shihata, "Towards a Greater Depoliticization of Investment Disputes," *ICSID Review*, Spring 1986, pp. 1–25.

As new technologies are developed and new issues become of critical concern to nations, nations are stimulated to create new infrastructure agreements or institutions. Such has been the case in the fields of environmental control, which spawned a new specialized agency of the United Nations, access to deep sea mineral resources, harmonization of telecommunications technology, and the launching of communications satellites (see Box 8–3).

In the area of access to deep seabed mineral resources, a new international treaty sponsored by the United Nations was signed in 1982. The ocean contains vast quantities of manganese, copper, cobalt, and nickel strewn over much of

---

BOX 8–3
Third World Seeks Its Place in Space

Geneva—In the 22 years since the United States launched the first communications satellite, the so-called geostationary orbit 22,300 miles above the Equator has become the hottest property in space. At present, an estimated 138 satellites are in the orbit, relaying telephone calls, television pictures, and weather reports. About 160 more are in various stages of planning.

Not surprisingly, the competition between the industrialized countries and the Third World for the available positions and frequencies in space has caused resentment on earth. Most of the satellites belong to the United States, Canada, Japan, Western Europe, and the Soviet Union, or to Intelsat, the International Telecommunications Satellite Organisation.

A few developing countries have satellites. But many in the Third World fear that the geostationary orbit, where a satellite travels at the same rotational speed as the earth and is a fixed target for radio signals, will be crowded by the time they have the resources to launch a satellite. Satellites cannot be placed in lower or higher orbits because they would either go slower or faster than the earth's rotation.

So, more than 100 country members of the International Telecommunications Union, a United Nations agency, have been haggling for more than a month over who gets into the orbit and when. The delegates said they believed in the principle of "equitable" access, but they could not agree on what "equitable" meant. Finally, both sides appeared to accept a compromise offered by Australia.

The Australian plan, although supported by the developing nations, does not meet all their demands. In particular, the first-come, first-served custom would still apply to the still-vacant positions in the highly-used C-band, a frequency range about 40 times higher than that of an FM radio receiver. However, the Third World would be able to reserve slots in a C-band expansion made possible by better technology and in the higher frequency K-band, which is used heavily by the Soviet Union.

The Russians, who usually champion Third World causes, have been keeping a low profile at the conference. The United States, the biggest user of satellite communications, is grudgingly supporting the Australian plan.

SOURCE: Adapted from the *New York Times*, September 15, 1985.

the deep seabed beyond the limits of national jurisdictions. How should access to these resources be regulated? The United Nations General Assembly unanimously declared in 1970 that the deep seabed resources are the "common heritage of mankind" and therefore must be under international control.

The United Nations Convention on Law of the Sea becomes effective when ratified by 60 countries, still a long way off as of 1986. The treaty provides for the creation of an International Seabed Authority to administer a "parallel system." This will permit both private or state-owned mining companies and an international public enterprise to mine the deep seabed mineral resources. The enterprise, as proposed, would be the first completely internationally operated commercial institution. The treaty also covers many other issues of interest to international business, such as the rights of coastal states to govern offshore fishing and petroleum exploration (see Box 8–4).

An emerging issue of great importance to international business is transborder data flows. Computer communications allow instant access to vast stores of information without regard to physical distance—or national borders. Not surprisingly, therefore, a number of nations have become concerned about transborder data

---

BOX 8–4
Fishy Business in the Pacific

Several Pacific island nations, such as the Solomons, Kiribati, and Vanuatu, have all claimed "exclusive economic zones" of 200 miles around their coasts, as, in fact, have more than 100 countries around the world. The United Nations gave a seal of approval to these zones when the UN convention on the law of the sea was signed in 1982. But until the convention is ratified, it will not have the full force of international law.

The country that the islanders are most bitter about is America, because U.S. boats have long fished in the Pacific coastal waters and see no reason to stop. In June 1984, a light aircraft spotted a U.S. boat fishing within the Solomon's exclusive zone. Knowing that the Solomons had no navy to stop it, the boat carried on fishing. But, by chance, a privately owned armed Australian patrol boat was in the Solomons on a sales demonstration tour. Tally ho! The Australian boat, with a crew of Solomons police armed to the teeth, arrested the astonished U.S. "pirate."

The Solomons fined the owner and impounded his boat, whereupon the U.S. government stopped importing Solomons fish, a major part of its export trade. This sanction by America, which has its own 200-mile rigorously-guarded zones, infuriated the Solomons government, which is normally as Western-minded as the Statue of Liberty. For a while it considered doing a deal with the Russians. Eventually, however, the boat was sold back to its original U.S. owners for $700,000; and the U.S. import sanction was lifted. The U.S. government is now urging the Solomons to negotiate a deal with the U.S. tuna industry for permission to fish in Solomons waters.

SOURCE: Adapted from *The Economist*, November 16, 1985, pp. 37–8.

flows and have enacted laws that control or restrict the collection and processing of data. Of particular concern has been the "privacy" protection of personal information stored in automated networks or files. But other issues, still vaguely perceived, are being debated.

In early 1981, the 21-nation Council of Europe completed an international treaty to protect persons against abusive use of computer data and to regulate the flow of computerized data across borders. Most of these nations have data-protection laws that safeguard personal privacy. A major objective of the treaty is to prevent the emergence of "data havens," akin to tax havens, by preventing sensitive personal data being shipped to countries without data-protection laws.

In a sense, this treaty is only the tip of the iceberg. The need for regulating cross-border data flows has been argued from many other standpoints. As underlined in a United Nations study,

> The possession and capacity to utilize information resources are increasingly a form of national power. . . . the transborder-data-flows links are not only used to move data internationally, but also to shift such information resources as managerial and engineering skills, computer power, technological capacities, data-base management systems, specialized software and intelligence in general. Given the prevailing global distribution and administration of information resources and skills, transborder data flows thus tend to facilitate their concentration in developed countries.[13]

Proposals have been made to require disclosure of cross-border data transmissions to facilitate law enforcement. This reflects a concern that computer service networks can facilitate tax evasion by billing a company in whichever country suits the customer's convenience. Other concerns are that electronic funds transfers may fuel inflation by accelerating the velocity of money and that the greatly reduced cost of international transmissions of computer data by satellite is endangering the profitability of public telephone monopolies.[14] Several international organizations are studying the implications of transborder data flows, and important recommendations that may restrict international data flows are certain to result.

NATIONAL LEGAL SYSTEMS

The above review indicates that the regulatory framework for international business still rests predominantly on a multiplicity of national legal systems. Given the great diversity and complexity of national legal systems, the international firm will undoubtedly rely on specialized assistance for legal matters. Nevertheless, the international manager will find helpful a general understanding of the national legal systems and the types of legal problems likely to arise.

Most national legal systems are based on either the common law or the civil law system. Civil law prevails in most continental European countries, in their former colonies, and in a number of Asian and African countries. Supple-

---

[13] United Nations Centre on Transnational Corporations, *Transborder Data Flows and Brazil* (Amsterdam: North-Holland, 1984), p. 13.

[14] *The Economist*, May 23, 1981, p. 93.

mented by Islamic law, civil law also predominates in Middle Eastern countries. The common law system, developed in England during the Middle Ages, has been adopted by most countries where the English settled or have governed.

Civil-law countries embody their main rules of law in a legislative code, and government executives are responsible for interpreting the codes and developing detailed working rules for implementing legislative acts. In common-law countries, the judiciary is the ultimate interpreter and decision maker in the legal system; the judges are normally guided, not by a code, but by principles declared in previous decisions in similar or analogous cases.

In practice, the distinction between common and civil law is not clear-cut. Large parts of Anglo-American law are contained in statutes and codes. In civil law countries, large parts of the law have never been reduced to statutes or codes but have been developed by the courts. In general, however, civil-law countries place great reliance on the prestige of a career civil service as a counterpart to the judicial power in the Anglo-American system.

Differences in the formal structure of national legal systems are important. Equally crucial can be national differences in the legal process for resolving legal problems. The gap between the developed legal system and effective administration of justice will vary greatly among nations. In some countries, even the most advanced laws remain dead letters on the books because of a limited capacity to implement the laws or because an underdeveloped judicial system does not have the capability for an expeditious handling of litigation.

The U.S. society probably goes further than any other in translating issues into legal questions and expecting the courts and lawyers to resolve them. By way of contrast, Chinese and Japanese societies go to the other extreme: abhorrence of lawyers, laws, and, above all, litigation. "It is better to be vexed to the death than to bring a lawsuit," says a Chinese proverb. The Chinese and Japanese prefer conciliation and mediation to litigation. The aversion to litigation reflects a fear that legal rules are too impersonal and rigid to accommodate the realities of particular cases and a desire to avoid the disruptions of friendly relations attending a clear-cut victory and defeat in litigation.[15] In all of Japan, according to official statistics, there are about 12,000 lawyers. This compares with 30,000 in Washington, D.C., 64,000 in New York State, and nearly 600,000 in the United States, with twice Japan's population.[16]

SELECTED LEGAL PROBLEMS IN INTERNATIONAL BUSINESS

Jurisdiction in International Trade

International trade is based chiefly on the use of standardized forms and practices. The standardized instruments contain most of the rules governing the

---

[15] Steiner and Vagts, *Transnational Legal Problems,* p. 226.

[16] *The Wall Street Journal,* February 9, 1981.

parties. Sales memoranda, brokers' notes, bills of lading, charter parties, marine insurance policies, and letters of credit all embody familiar clauses that shipping clerks and bank tellers are trained to follow. Also, the import or export of goods can be, and usually is, arranged so as to involve the law of a single country. By including a "choice-of-law" clause in the contract, the parties can select the law that will govern their obligations on issues that lie within their contractual capacity—such as sufficiency of performance and excuse for nonperformance. But even with a choice-of-law clause, issues may arise that are outside the contractual capacity of the parties and on which the governing law is uncertain. In many cases an arbitration clause may supplement or substitute for a choice-of-law clause.

Translation Problems

A unique source of legal difficulties in the international business field is the problem of language translation. The problem is present in the drafting of contracts, in the preparation of corporate documents, in negotiation and settlement of disputes by arbitration or court proceedings, and in any reference to foreign laws or concepts. Legal instruments must be drafted with a view toward their meaning to a judge or arbitrator when foreign legal elements are involved. The translation problem expands the area of uncertainty not only because of the normal difficulties of translating the meanings of words from one language to another. The translation of legal language also involves a transfer of concepts rather than a mechanical matching of words. The vital issue for the international manager, according to one distinguished legal authority, is to make sure that the matter of translation is properly worked out during the period when the instrument is drafted.[17]

Whose Law Determines "Inc."?

In the present international legal environment, the business enterprise engaged in multinational operations cannot become an international corporation in a legal sense. No international agency has yet been created with the authority to grant international incorporation. Consequently, the multinational business enterprise must content itself with stringing together a series of corporations created by the laws of different nation-states. The legal complexities arising out of such a situation are immense. The presence of the same enterprise in many countries necessarily subjects it to different laws and legal climates, which in many situations may conflict.

In setting up multinational operations, one of the first considerations is to determine which country's laws will be applied to give life to the component

---

[17] Henry P. de Vries, "The Language Barrier," *Columbia Journal of World Business,* July–August 1969, pp. 79–80.

parts of the multinational enterprise. This issue has been posed by one legal authority as "Whose Law Determines Inc.""?[18] The legal test of nationality varies among countries. Like an individual, a corporation can have dual nationality. It can also be "stateless," thereby exposing the members of the corporation to individual liability. The question of nationality may have significant tax consequences. It may also determine whether an enterprise can benefit from government subsidy programs or engage in certain strategic businesses.

The underlying U.S. view for all corporations is that a corporation secures its life and existence from a grant of the sovereign, and the nationality of the corporation is that of the sovereign power making the grant. In many other countries, particularly civil law countries, a corporation is considered to be created by the contractual intent of its members rather than by a grant from the sovereign. The nationality of such a corporation is not necessarily that of the country in which it is constituted. In determining the law applicable to a corporation's existence and internal relations, several countries look at the place of incorporation. Others look to the center of management or the place of the registered head office. As a result of these variations, multiple incorporation in various countries may be necessary to protect stockholders from personal liability.

The problems and risk arising from different concepts of nationality can be illustrated by a recent case brought before the German courts. A suit was filed against the U.S. stockholders of a corporation organized in the State of Washington to conduct mining operations in Mexico but with the central management of the corporation meeting in Hamburg. Because the corporation was administered in Germany but not constituted pursuant to German law, the court held that it was an unincorporated association in Germany and that the stockholders were personally liable for corporate liabilities.

Choosing the Form of Business Organization

What form of business organization should be used in different legal jurisdictions? Tax consideration both at home and abroad may play a key role in the choice of legal form. The principal objective, however, normally will be that of insulating the parent organization or the investor from direct liability for obligations incurred in operations.

In the choice of legal form, a clear distinction exists between common-law countries and civil-law countries. As noted previously, in common-law countries a grant from the public authority gives life to the corporation. In civil law countries the corporation is created by a contract between two or more persons, and the root concept is that of "societe" or "Gesellschaft." Thus, the one-man corporation is a contradiction in terms; and most civil-law countries tend to reject the one-man corporation and the wholly owned subsidiary. In some countries, the acquisi-

---

[18] Henry P. de Vries, "The Problem of Identity: Whose Law Determines Inc.?", *Columbia Journal of World Business,* March–April 1969, pp. 76–78; Vagts, *International Business Problems,* pp. 364–81.

"I PLEDGE ALLEGIANCE TO THE FLAG OF THE COUNTRY
THAT GIVES ME THE BEST DEAL ...."

Conrad © 1975, Los Angeles Times. Reprinted with permission.

tion by one individual or legal entity of all the shares of a corporation may lead
to its automatic dissolution and to personal liability of the stockholder for the
corporation's liabilities.

In most countries, the choice of foreign business organization to operate as
a subsidiary or affiliate will be between two forms, both similar to the U.S.
corporation. The two forms are a *societe anonyme* (S.A.) or a *societe a responsibil-
ite limitee* (S.A.R.L.). In German-speaking countries the similar forms are the
Aktiegensellschaft (A.G.) or the *Gesellschaft mit beschrankter Haftung* (GmbH).
The S.A. or A.G. is the most common form of business organization for medium-
scale and large-scale businesses outside of the United States and British Commonwealth countries. However, the S.A.R.L., often referred to as Limitada in Latin
American practice, has gained in favor as the form of foreign subsidiaries.[19]

The establishment of a joint venture creates special legal problems because
the stresses and strains of the normal business operations may result in discord.

---

[19] Henry P. de Vries, "Legal Aspects of World Business," in *World Business,* ed. Courtney
C. Brown (New York: Macmillan, 1970), pp. 289–93.

In the choice of business form for a joint venture, the international enterprise should be alert to the problem of eventual liquidation and dissolution. The divorce may be far more complicated than the marriage, particularly where patents, trademarks, and the use of an internationally known firm name are involved.

Economic Development Agreements

The right of a multinational to engage in certain activities in a host country may be based on so-called *economic development agreements* (formerly referred to as concession agreements). In its most common form the development agreement involves an extractive enterprise. The provisions of the agreements, which specify a series of rights and obligations for both the enterprise and the government, vary widely among countries and industries, generally reflecting the relative bargaining power of the government and the investor.[20]

The development agreement is apt to be a unique instrument tailored to meet special needs. Furthermore, it may involve mineral rights or other interests controlled by the government and arrangements on matters, such as taxation, which are within a legislature's competence. These agreements often resemble special legislation governing relationships between the country and the international enterprise. For a variety of reasons, development agreements are likely to generate disputes between the parties. The long-run trends in many development contracts proceed through several identifiable stages.[21]

The first stage begins when a country suspects that it has natural resource possibilities that might attract foreign investors. But the existence of such resources—as in the case of petroleum—or the economic feasibility of production is not known. In this stage, the host government is negotiating from weakness because the risks as seen through the eyes of both parties are high.

A second stage begins when the investments have been made and the projects are successful. As judged by hindsight, the host government views the original concession agreement as excessively favorable to the foreign investor and begins to raise its sights regarding its share of the returns from the concession activities. With its bargaining power greatly strengthened, the host government tends to increase its demands in the form of taxation, requirements for foreign enterprise to provide educational and other public facilities, and in a number of other ways.

At a third stage, the government presses for greater linkage of the concessionaire's activities with the economic development aspirations for the local economy. For example, the foreign firm may be required to develop local sources of supplies for many types of equipment and services.

---

[20] See David N. Smith and L. T. Wells, Jr., *Negotiating Third World Mineral Agreements* (Cambridge, Mass.: Ballinger Publishing, 1975); Vagts, *Transnational Business Problems,* pp. 445–88.

[21] See Raymond Vernon, "Long-Run Trends in Concession Contracts," *Proceedings of the American Society of International Law at its Sixty-First Annual Meeting,* April 27–29, 1967 (Washington, D.C.: 1967), pp. 81–89.

At a fourth stage, local governments become interested in sharing in the ownership of the foreign enterprise or in the process of decision making or both. As concession agreements move through these stages, the relative bargaining power of the parties, generally economic but sometimes political, influences the patterns of conflict and resolution rather than conventional legal considerations.

Transnational Reach of Economic Regulation

Transnational reach, or the extension of one country's laws or regulations to actions outside of that country, can create vexing problems for the international enterprise. The international enterprise can adjust most aspects of its operations to differences in national laws. But the effect of some business policies or actions extend beyond the national boundaries of the country in which the decision or action is initiated. The policy or action may be legal in Country A, where initiated, but illegal in Country B, where the policy or action also has effects. As a result, Country B may take legal action in its jurisdiction that affects activities in Country A, where the law of Country B does not have jurisdiction. In this way, the international enterprise becomes the vehicle through which conflicts between nations arise.

The extraterritorial reach of national laws as related to international business has been a source of conflict between nations in such areas as antitrust, securities regulation, product liability, tax collections, and export controls. In some cases, the conflicts have had to be resolved through diplomatic negotiations. In the securities regulation field, the United States has intensified its efforts to negotiate treaties and agreements with nations whose bank-secrecy laws stymie prosecution of securities fraud, money laundering, and other crimes. And in still other situations, the legal issues remain unresolved.

Restrictive business practices have been illegal in the United States for many decades under various antitrust laws. Restrictive business practices are agreements among enterprises to fix prices, limit production, allocate markets, restrain the application of technology, or engage in similar schemes likely to reduce competition. More recently, other nations have developed similar policies, notably the European Community (EC) and its members. The EC assumed responsibility for regulating competition in its Common Market area based on articles 85 and 86 of the Rome Treaty (1958).

Although the jurisdiction of national laws is normally limited to the particular nation, the reality is that actions taken outside the national boundaries can affect competition within the national market. In recognition of this reality, the U.S. courts have extended the U.S. antitrust laws to actions abroad that "substantially affect" the commerce of the United States and competition in the U.S. market.[22]

---

[22] For an analysis of the impact on U.S. firms abroad, see James B. Townsend, *Extraterritorial Antitrust: The Sherman Antitrust Act and U.S. Business Abroad* (Boulder, Colo.: Westview Press, 1980); Philip Nelson and Louis Silva, "Antitrust Policy and Intra-Industry Direct Foreign Investment: Cause and Effect," in *Multinationals as Mutual Invaders,* ed. Asim Erdilek (New York: St. Martin's Press, 1985) pp. 97–123.

This has produced jurisdictional overlap, for the governments never abdicate control over the activities of their own citizens in their own territory. Sovereignty itself becomes an issue.

The enforcement of the U.S. antitrust laws was greatly relaxed during the 1980s, but a recent example of extraterritorial reach was a case still in the courts filed by the Zenith Electronics Corp. during the 1970s. Zenith had charged seven major Japanese manufacturers with conspiring to drive U.S. television makers out of business by selling merchandise in the U.S. at prices lower than in Japan. The Japanese defendants claim that they should be immune from U.S. antitrust laws because they were compelled by Japanese trade policy to set minimum prices and to limit sales to five U.S. companies each.

America is not the only country to contend that its laws have extraterritorial reach. In antitrust matters, West Germany and the EC have done the same. In a landmark case some years ago, the Court of Justice of the EC held the local subsidiaries of big foreign dye manufacturers responsible for a price-fixing cartel operated by their parent companies outside the Community. In doing so, the Court observed that the fact that a subsidiary company has its own legal personality does not rule out the possibility that its conduct is attributable to the parent company.

U.S. enforcement procedures have been another major conflict area. The legal procedures of one country can command a defendant in a law suit to deliver information to the state while laws of another country prohibit it. In a U.S. antitrust case, many documents and records may be needed by the government to determine whether an infringement has taken place. U.S. courts and regulatory commissions have exerted pressure on foreign firms with offices in the United States to produce documents and records from abroad. The pursuit of foreign documents and records became a major issue in an antitrust action brought by Westinghouse against the international uranium cartel for price fixing. The cartel was legal in the home country of the foreign companies and its formation was encouraged by the foreign governments to stimulate the search for uranium.[23] The response has been a wave of legislation by other trading nations prohibiting release of domestic business records in response to foreign judicial orders.

In another case, *Messerschmitt Bolkow Bloehm G.m.b.H. vs. Walker,* the West German aircraft maker was sued when a helicopter it made crashed in Texas. During the litigation, the survivors made 32 different requests for documents, many of which were located in West Germany. The West German government, in a brief filed with the U.S. Supreme Court, said that ''allowing courts to order, under threat of sanctions, the removal of documents located in Germany to the U.S. . . . . violates the Federal Republic of Germany's sovereignty.''[24]

The problem of extraterritoriality of national laws, or of transnational reach, is being worked on in several international forums, including the Organization

---

[23] See Thomas N. Gladwin and Ingo Walter, *Multinationals Under Fire* (New York: John Wiley & Sons, 1980), pp. 521–25.

[24] *The Wall Street Journal,* April 28, 1986.

for Economic Cooperation and Development in Paris. Still, the possibility that an international firm will find itself in the middle of conflict between sovereign nations is real.[25]

Selecting International Counsel

Just as legal systems vary greatly among nations, so does the role of the lawyer. When engaging legal representation in foreign countries, the U.S. international enterprise should not expect to find the counterpart of the U.S. lawyer. In the United States, the breadth of services the U.S. lawyer is permitted to offer is virtually unlimited—including participation in business operations, client decisions, contract negotiations, tax litigation, drafting of legal documents, and dealings with government authorities. In contrast to the all-embracing scope of legal services permitted to the U.S. lawyer, the tendency in many foreign countries, particularly in civil law jurisdictions, is to divide the legal profession into separate careers.

In Japan, there are five legal professions other than the advocate or practicing attorney: the judicial scrivener, who drafts legal documents; the patent lawyer; the tax lawyer; the public accountant; and the notary. In Great Britain there is the division between the barrister, who represents litigants in court, and the solicitor, who handles the office work part of the profession. In France, court practice is limited to a rather small corps of *avoues* and *avocats*.

In the United States, the in-house lawyer (corporate counsel) who works as a full-time employee of the business firm retains his status as a member of the Bar, and the head of the in-house legal staff is usually an officer of the company and often a member of the board of directors. The French *avocat*, until recently, was not permitted to accept membership on a board of directors or to represent a party in dealings with administrative authorities.

One important foreign legal practice that may surprise U.S. international managers is the prominent role of the notary public. In the United States notary publics perform only a minor function. In civil-law countries, the notary is a key figure. Trained as a lawyer, the notary gives conclusiveness in a legal sense to contractual instruments. The legal necessity to have virtually all legal instruments notarized requires time and may be considered excessive red tape by the U.S. manager. But in Latin America, Western Europe, and other countries, it is absolutely essential that a transaction is adequately recorded, preserved, and made firm and certain by being recorded with a notary. The importance of the notary may be illustrated by the case of at least one Latin American country, where the privilege of being a notary is granted only by the president of the republic and is considered the most lucrative of all political grants.

---

[25] Detlev F. Vagts, "Extraterritoriality: The General Theory," *Journal of Contemporary Business*, Autumn 1977, pp. 133–45.

SUMMARY

The international legal environment is in a transitional stage of adaptation to new international business patterns. The conduct of multinational business has many ingredients, in addition to the transfer of goods and money across national boundaries, that ideally would be governed and facilitated by an effective world government and international legal system. In the absence of such a system, treaties, codes, and agreements negotiated by nations on a bilateral or multilateral basis have been the principal tool for building a substitute framework. Normally, treaties are obeyed and agreements adhered to. In any event, they serve as an important guide for predicting the behavior of national governments.

Although paths are uncertain, the prospect is that a sizable number of countries will begin to evolve more comprehensive legal principles to govern the international corporation. There will also be forward movement by groups of countries—either by multilateral international treaties, the adoption of a uniform business law, or by some less formal and more unconventional approach—to evolve codes of legal principles for dealing better with the international business phenomenon. Progress will be uneven and novel approaches will have to be devised. But there are certain to be important changes in the regulatory environment. International business has become such an important component of the world economy that the international legal environment will have to adjust to this reality.

EXERCISES AND DISCUSSION QUESTIONS

1. "When a foreign firm does business in our country its local affiliate must legally become a national enterprise," explained the official of a host government. "As a national enterprise the affiliate is entitled to the full legal protection of our laws in case of expropriation, alleged breach of concessions contract, etc., in the same way as any other national enterprise. Why should the investor countries and the international business firms be insisting on additional legal protection for foreign investment through international investment codes or international organizations to arbitrate what are essentially national legal issues? Such proposals violate our national sovereignty and discriminate against purely national companies." Discuss. How does this Calvo Doctrine approach compare with the Indian government position in the Bhopal Case?

2. The legal doctrine "rebus sic stantibus" relates to the presumption in contracts that things will remain in the same condition as they were at the date of agreement. There is a difference of opinion among the authorities as to whether the principle of rebus sic stantibus is a recognized rule of international law. To what extent do you think that the principle should be clearly recognized in the settlement of disputes concerning concession contracts?

3. Assume that the United Nations is prepared to establish a new specialized agency with limited powers to improve the international legal environment for multinational business operations. As a representative of the international business sector, what specific activities would you recommend that this agency undertake? To what extent would you expect that your recommendations would be acceptable to host countries as well as to investor countries?

4. As the manager of a multinational enterprise, what strategies would you follow to

improve the international framework for the transfer of intellectual property rights and for expanding the network of tax treaties? Remember that your firm is operating in a number of countries and must appeal to the national interests of all governments.

5. "The Japanese contract is a reflection of Japanese values, and most Japanese view the contract as merely a piece of paper. Underlying this pragmatic view is the realization that the parties to a contract are human beings, and that human beings are fallible creatures who do not always live up to expectations. While the Western recourse to breach of contract tends to be purely legal, the Japanese prefer to discuss and work out differences. The penalty for failure to discharge one's responsibility and maintain harmony is dishonor." As a Western manager, how would you adjust to the Japanese view in negotiating with the Japanese?

6. "There are compelling reasons for limiting the extraterritorial application of American laws. One of the most sensitive nerves of a state is its territorial sovereignty. When a foreign government infringes that sovereignty by seeking to control the actions of corporations within the state, contrary to the state's economic and foreign affairs policies, a reaction may be expected." How do you view the actions of the U.S. in banning the sale of certain products to the Soviet Union by foreign subsidiaries of U.S. firms located in countries where such trade is legal and consistent with the country's foreign policies?

PART THREE

Global Business Strategy

Two prime tasks of top management in a multinational corporation are to determine the firm's overall global strategy and to shape the organization to achieve that strategy. This section of the book is concerned with how such a global strategy is built, and how the organization structure of a multinational is likely to affect its success in achieving its strategy.

A global strategy encompasses the planning, timing, and location of a firm's activities and resources as well as its strategies for how it will enter new markets, what it will own, and how it will manage the global operation. The construction of a global strategy on a rational basis requires a careful assessment of the global alternatives and the risks involved for each. A prototype approach for building a strategy in this way is set out in Chapter 9.

Assessments of the economic and demand environments of the different countries in which a multinational may locate its activities are basic inputs into its global strategy. These assessments are examined in Chapter 10. Environments are dynamic and constantly changing and future conditions are far more important to the strategy than the past situation described by historical data. Macroeconomic and market forecasting skills are, therefore, required in projecting the assessments that are needed.

The range of organizational structures that are used in multinationals is very wide. Chapter 11 classifies the structures by their predominant line of responsibility and examines their strengths and weaknesses. No structure is perfect. Each has its blind spots, and the performance of each is determined as much by the management processes with which it is supported as by the structure itself. Nevertheless, at different stages of international growth and facing different environmental and competitive stresses, different structures will have a major impact on performance.

CHAPTER 9

Building a Global Strategy

Most business firms become international by a process of creeping "incremental-ism" rather than by strategy choice. Their step-by-step moves toward global operations may have first been stimulated by unsolicited export orders, dependence on foreign sources of raw materials, opportunities to acquire foreign technology, etc. But rarely are these early moves part of a comprehensive global strategy. At a later stage, as pressures arise from international competition and from country control programs, and awareness of synergistic benefits increases, the firm begins to recognize the need for global planning procedures and a global strategy.

A global strategy is an enterprise's plan for maximizing its chosen objectives through geographical allocation of its limited resources, taking into account global competition, geographical opportunities, and alternative forecasts of the firm's external environment.[1] To build a global strategy, the decision maker must be free of any national blinders and consider world markets and world resource locations and not simply the markets or resources of a particular country in isolation. A global strategy aims to maximize results on a multinational basis rather than treat international activities as a portfolio of separate country businesses.

WHY A GLOBAL STRATEGY?

The basic reason for having a global strategy is that most product and factor markets extend beyond the boundaries of a single country. Thus, the competition that ultimately determines a firm's performance is not constrained to individual country markets. To be competitive, the strategy horizon for most firms must encompass threats and opportunities of both domestic and foreign origin.

If domestic competitors extend their horizons to include a broader sales base, the firm could find itself unable to maintain the same pace of research or product development given its smaller sales base. Even where domestic competition is not moving rapidly to other markets, foreign firms may be developing global strategies that pose a threat. European and U.S. firms in a number of industries were largely unprepared for the competitive challenge when the Japanese firms broke into their traditional markets on a significant scale. Automotive firms that had failed to build global coverage in the price segments the Japanese attacked were at an immediate cost disadvantage. In the color television industry, which originated in the United States, Japanese producers were able to take over the U.S. market. The number of color television manufacturers in the United States declined from 50 in 1970 to 14 in 1980, and 10 of the U.S. firms were owned by foreigners.[2]

Many U.S. firms did not need in the past to think globally in the early stages of a product's life because leadership coincided with achievement in the U.S. market. With its large population, high-wage rates, high discretionary spending power, and high propensity to innovate, the U.S. market was for many years the leader in adoption and growth rates for many products. Conversely, firms outside the United States had more need to plan globally from the beginning of any product development.

But as of the 1980s, with disposable incomes becoming comparable and life styles increasingly homogeneous in Western Europe, Japan, and the United

---

[1] Thomas H. Naylor, "International Strategy Matrix," *Columbia Journal of World Business*, Summer 1985, p. 11.

[2] William H. Davidson, *Global Strategic Management* (New York: John Wiley & Sons, 1982), p. 9.

States, U.S. firms encountered the same need as foreign enterprises to plan globally for many products.[3]

Absence of global thinking also shows up where firms have been left behind in the competitive race because they failed to tap the cheapest sources of supply. In still other cases, firms may have achieved global market share and cheapest supplies, but it was at the expense of their financial strength or flexibility relative to foreign competitors.

THE MULTINATIONAL'S BUSINESS MISSION

At the core of its corporate strategy, no firm should limit its business possibilities to its existing products or services. Instead, it should identify demand areas where its capability for performance against competitors is greatest, even though the specific customer needs that are to be met differ from those the firm has already been meeting.[4]

With so many countries in the world, against which markets should the multinational firm make this strategic evaluation and choice of its business mission? Should the strategic evaluation be carried out against one major single market, many single markets, or some segments of many markets? It must also decide how it is going to organize the responsibility for carrying through this strategic assessment. Will it be done by central headquarters, by multinational committees, or by national units?

In the major single market, or central market, approach, the firm selects its mission based on one national market, establishes a marketing mix, and later expands to other national markets. This approach reduces decision problems and can bring high profits because of the low marginal cost of geographic extensions. But which central market should the firm choose? Normally, the firm begins with its home market; but this may not be the best choice. Some Japanese and European firms have selected the high-income, sophisticated U.S. market for selected product lines. The size of the U.S. market has both advantages and disadvantages. Many Europeans see the cost of communications and coordination efforts in such a large market as a deterrent to marketing products first in the United States as part of their world product strategy.

The multiple market approach may be the best strategy either where local conditions require special products, such as fertilizers and insecticides, or where product usage patterns and customer attitudes are quite similar for many countries,

---

[3] Kenichi Ohmae, *Triad Power: The Coming Shape of Global Competition* (New York: The Free Press, 1985), p. 23.

[4] Kenneth Simmonds, "Removing the Chains from Product Strategy," *Journal of Management Studies*, February 1968, pp. 29–40; Richard M. Burton, "Variety in Strategic Planning," *Columbia Journal of World Business*, Winter 1984, pp. 92–98.

as in the case of semiconductors,[5] aluminum ingots, and many consumer goods. Where special products are required, this approach implies a high degree of decentralization. Where markets are similar across national boundaries, the best strategy may be to focus on competitive cost advantages through developing more economic production or distribution systems.

In the market segment approach, the firm identifies segments of national markets that could profitably be given separate treatment across national boundaries. Small market segments in individual countries may be insufficient for any one country unit to justify development of an appropriate product or to make the necessary investment in market development. Worldwide or for a number of countries, however, such a segment may readily justify the expense.

GLOBAL STANDARDIZATION VERSUS DIFFERENTIATION

Having made its choice as to general market focus, the multinational firm must still be concerned with identifying which segments of the global market should be treated differently. The advantages of product differentiation to meet the special needs of smaller segments of the market conflict with the advantages of reducing unit costs through standardization.[6] Standardization can bring great savings from production economies and from spreading such expenditures as research and development, advertising, promotion, and general management over a greatly expanded sales base. Consequently, an international firm's best strategy, if the local environment is not excessively unreceptive, could be to avoid major adjustments of its product to local markets and to act as a change agent transplanting its culture around the world.

The pressures toward differentiation, however, are great. The international firm usually considers individual countries as the basic building blocks for its organization and it prefers to identify with each country. One way to achieve this identification is to adjust products to fit country markets. In fact, the orthodox emphasis in marketing is to adjust the marketing mix against an assessment of each market's characteristics. The difficulty confronting the firm is to decide when market differences are sufficient to justify the loss of standardization.

The choice between standardization and differentiation of products rests on the impact of the alternatives on revenues and costs. Differentiation is easiest when the adjustments to individual markets are not costly and when the initial design of a product has taken important market differences into account.

The most costly elements to adjust in a product already designed are its physical characteristics. If agricultural equipment, for example, is designed to be marketed in many countries, it must be tested to withstand extremes in temperature and not simply for performance in one particular climate. Also, the design

---

[5] Claudia Bird Schoonhoven, "High Technology Firms: Where Strategy Really Pays Off," *Columbia Journal of World Business*, Winter 1984, p. 9.

[6] See Robert D. Buzzell, "Can You Standardize Multinational Marketing?", *Harvard Business Review*, November–December 1968, pp. 102–13.

should recognize variations in attitudes regarding repair and maintenance of machinery and variations in the availability of technicians and repair facilities, or else a design for the market of a developed country might produce equipment that is unusable in less developed areas.

Designing products for international performance is not an easy task. A large number of different cultural settings need to be examined for ways in which a product is purchased and used in order to develop a list of important design criteria. Even better guidance can be obtained if test samples can be made available to those concerned with selling in different countries and shown to outlets and users.

Despite the potential costs of failing to consider the global suitability of different product features at the design stage, the product design strategy of even globally oriented firms has generally been to focus heavily on establishing a product in just one market. This practice may result in major impediments to later expansion in other country markets. A marketing success in the initial market can unwisely reinforce the practice of not considering international performance criteria in the initial design work.

As compared with changes in physical attributes, changes in product title are more easily made. But a name change can be costly if the spillover from advertising into other areas is lost and brand loyalty must be established anew. Coca-Cola stands out as an example here. While the flavor can be easily adjusted to local palates, a change of name in any market would mean a great loss in an established market value. It becomes important, therefore, that the product title initially selected does not have any unfortunate meaning in any of the major languages. The Chevrolet Nova, for example, was rather unfortunately named, given that *"no va"* means "does not go" in Spanish.

A PROTOTYPE APPROACH TO GLOBAL STRATEGY

This section presents a prototype approach to building a global strategy. While it is adaptable for use in a wide range of businesses, it is presented here as though developed for an existing product already marketed multinationally and for which the firm carries out its own production and marketing globally. The reader should bear in mind, however, that this prototype is just one possible approach out of many. Furthermore, no single approach will *guarantee* a viable strategy. The very nature of competition within a changing and complex environment demands creativity and thought in arriving at a strategy. No procedure could ever replace the need for these two ingredients. The approach does, however, allow for consideration of the essential elements of a strategy in a step-by-step framework. The reader may feel that any step should be amended or discarded, but at least to start with the approach provides a consistent and rational basis for building a global strategy. The better the underlying structure against which decisions are made, the better the decisions might be.

The prototype approach includes 14 steps. These steps are enumerated in Figure 9–1 and elaborated below.

FIGURE 9–1   A Prototype Approach to Global Strategy

1. Select a horizon year.
2. Predict country demands for the product or service annually up to the horizon year.
3. Assess the firm's competitive strength overall and in each country.
4. Decide emphasis to be placed on developing competitive market position in each country, and the general approach to be used.
5. Set annual target sales for each country to horizon year.
6. List countries where production or other operations *must* be located to meet sales targets in horizon year.
7. List countries where production in horizon year is not required but probably economic.
8. Estimate costs of investment and operation for the set of alternative production sites, and the transport and tariff costs from these into alternative markets.
9. Calculate an optimum location and logistics pattern for horizon year.
10. Assess country risks.
11. Prepare schedules of annual additions to investment that meet the annual targets and the horizon patterns.
12. Calculate the expected cash flow and net present value.
13. Calculate limits to available investment.
14. Align investment plans and sales targets.

The Horizon for Global Strategy

How far into the future should the firm plot its strategy? This will depend on the time horizon of the decision maker. Given the inflexibility of investment once it has been committed, an early horizon may produce a supply pattern that is far from optimum for the subsequent market pattern. On the other hand, if the horizon is set far in the future, intermediate profits will be more likely to suffer, the market pattern may be more likely to vary from the prediction, the technology may become obsolete, and current management may be less likely to see the full fruits of its decision. In practice, a four- or five-year horizon is common.[7]

Market Assessment

The prototype approach is market based. It starts by formulating targets for individual markets and works backward to decide the location of activity and investment to achieve those targets. Although the prime objective may be to obtain the greatest return on invested capital, it is not reached by taking country after country and calculating the return from expansion in that country.

The selection of market targets in turn requires prediction of demand and competition in the different markets. With different rates and patterns of growth

---

[7] George A. Steiner and Warren M. Cannon, *Multinational Corporate Planning* (New York: Macmillan, 1966); James M. Hulbert, William K. Brandt, and Raimar Richers, "Multinational Planning in the Multinational Subsidiary: Practices and Problems," *Journal of Marketing* 44 (Summer 1980), pp. 7–15.

in each market, any simple extrapolation of the current situation would be inappropriate. A more refined prediction of market growth is needed. In making such predictions, a whole range of forecasting methods can be used, as discussed in Chapter 10.

Whatever the methodology, the basic data required will involve past measurements of actual demand, indicators or determinants of demand, and then estimates of how indicators or determinants will behave in the future. As the firm develops an international planning system, it can begin to rely on its foreign subsidiaries for much of this information. But in the initial stages, decentralized inputs are likely to be extremely slow because of the time required to receive information from around the world. Furthermore, consistent forecasts are probably more important than accurate forecasts when they are to be used for allocating emphasis among markets. To call for estimates from a wide range of sources is to invite major inconsistencies. Different individuals will have different biases in assessing future market growth for their areas. Initially, then, the firm may rely on market data sources centrally available, such as from international agencies.

Competitive Assessment

The essence of strategy is that it is competitive. There are opponents. Whatever objectives a firm adopts, their achievement will be relative to the achievement of other firms. In most cases the competition will be direct and immediate. For some lucky firms it may be indirect and with delayed impact, but it is always there. At its best, a global strategy will be devised so as to gain a significant and continued advantage over competitors. The strategist will be looking to identify the performance and strategic emphasis by country of the leading global competitors and to plan accordingly. The plan may give priority to areas where competition is absent; it may directly oppose a competitor in one place and leave it unopposed in another. Whatever form strategy takes, however, it will certainly not be the straightforward application of a formula but a creative plan based on competitive assessments.

Assessments of competition has received renewed emphasis in recent years as marketing and strategy literature have developed an industry perspective to explain why profitability differs among firms.[8] The concept of the experience curve lies at the heart of much of the writing.[9] The price experience curve plots the change in real price as industry experience in producing and marketing a product accumulates. Many empirical measurements have shown that, as accumu-

---

[8] Charles W. Hofer and Dan Schendel, *Strategy Formulation: Analytical Concepts* (St. Paul, Minn.: West Publishing, 1978); Michael E. Porter, *Competitive Strategy: Techniques for Analyzing Industries and Competitors* (New York: Free Press, Macmillan, 1980); Michael E. Porter, ed., *Competition in Global Industries* (Boston: Harvard Business School, 1986).

[9] Winfred B. Hirschmann, "Profit from the Learning Curve," *Harvard Business Review,* January–February 1964, pp. 125–39.

lated experience doubles, the unit price reduces in real terms by between 20 percent and 30 percent.[10] Of course, as experience builds up and demand stabilizes, the period it takes for accumulated experience to double gets longer; hence price reduction in real terms slows down.

Such a downward sloping price experience curve over time does not imply a move from industry profits to industry losses. Real cost reduction by individual firms in the industry underlies the price reduction. This cost reduction can come about in many ways, from productivity in manufacture, through redesign with consequent material savings, to economies of scale and increased efficiency in advertising and marketing. Moreover, a cross-section of an industry's experience on price and cost at a point in time is likely to show individual firms in different competitive positions because of their varying accumulated experience and varying success in cost reduction.

The firm preparing a global strategy will wish to monitor these varying competitive positions on an international basis. A competitor of the same nationality may be gaining greater volume and more accumulated experience through international expansion or be reducing costs through relocation of production or supply. Foreign competitors, too, may be building cost advantages outside the geographical limits of the firm's operations. The task may not be easy. The global strategist may have to estimate the costs of a competitor in a foreign location and perhaps attempt to decompose the cost structure of a complex multinational. It may also be necessary to forecast exchange fluctuations in order to predict how competitor costs will differ for delivery into a particular market.

Figure 9–2 shows graphically such a cross-section of industry cost and experience. Firm A has the highest accumulated experience and the greatest current market share. At the current price level of $11, A is also making the highest profit per unit of $3.65. Firm C has only 20 percent of the market and is taking a loss. It is likely to go out of business. Firm B, on the other hand, has managed to reduce costs to $9.66 per unit, even though, with 30 percent of the market, its accumulated experience amounts to only 3 million units. Perhaps Firm B has entered the market recently with a more efficient new plant and an effective promotion scheme to build market share quickly.

If both Firm A and Firm B now maintain their relative market shares and both manage to reduce costs with experience on 70 percent cost experience curves, then B poses a significant threat to A. By the time A's experience doubles to 16 million units, B would have added another 4.8 million units, that is, $\frac{30}{50}$ of A's. At this point, A's cost would be $5.15 per unit and B's would be $5.90 per unit. A needs to watch B very closely. At the current time, A has a major cost advantage and can control the market. Later, A's lead will not be so sure. Perhaps now is the time to reduce price in order to gain higher market share and with the increased volume build a more efficient plant.

---

[10] Patrick Conley, "Experience Curves as a Planning Tool," *IEEE Spectrum,* June 1970, pp. 63–68.

FIGURE 9-2   Accumulated Experience, Market Share, Unit Cost, and Unit Profit for Three
Competitors (log-log scale)

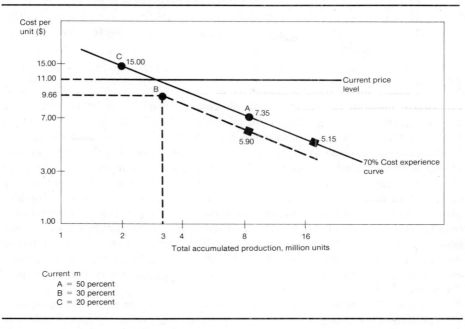

Market Emphasis

Once market demand and competitive assessments have been made, the
next and most important step in the prototype approach is to select a set of
decision rules against which the firm will allocate its efforts to different markets.
These rules reflect the essence of the firm's territorial attack on its competitors.

Such rules are best expressed as criteria for classifying markets according
to the emphasis to be placed on sales achievement. Examples of decision rules
expressed in this way are as follows:

Enter all markets with demand above $5 million and in which direct competitor
retaliation can be avoided.

Enter new markets only if necessary to match competitors X or Y, who
would otherwise build a strong position unchallenged.

Expand as fast as possible without actually incurring losses to buy market
share in all markets above $10 million with growth rates of more than
10 percent per annum over the next five years.

Expand through margin reductions in all markets in which competitor X
has a market share of more than 35 percent, our share is less than 5
percent, and margins are more than 30 percent.

Develop export agents in all markets estimated at between $2 million and $5 million per annum.

Withdraw from direct participation in all markets of less than $5 million demand and $100,000 actual sales and in which five-year growth rates are less than 5 percent per annum.

Pay no marketing attention to country markets below a country size of $2 million per annum.

The chosen rules should enable all country markets to be classified one way or another. Once classified, each market can then be allocated a sales target appropriate to the rule under which it falls. Such sales targets and the manner in which they are to be achieved, however, will be conditioned by the characteristics of the individual markets and the firm's existing position in those markets. For example, a decision by a capital goods firm to expand at a maximum rate in a particular market might require only a local agent to obtain inquiries for bids and maintain a local base for customer service. Yet for a firm manufacturing a branded consumer good, fastest possible expansion may require full local production, warehousing, and direct merchandising. Even then, the expansion rate possible may be limited if the firm has not earlier established a brand recognition among customers. Entry considerations and appropriate strategies are discussed in more detail later in this chapter.

It cannot be emphasized too much that the classification of markets according to the different emphases to be accorded them should express a strategy effective against competition. It may be helpful in achieving that if the decision rules for market emphasis are actually expressed in terms of how they will each affect competitive positioning. Alternatively, an overall strategic focus may be established first and then the emphasis rules developed from that concept. An approach that produces emphasis rules in this way has been suggested by Ayal and Zif.[11] Shown in Figure 9–3, they propose 10 feasible strategies based on three strategic considerations as follows:

Competitive Posture.   The posture may be either:

1. Defensive—to retain market share.
2. Offensive—to build market share.

Location of Competitive Action.   The market emphasis may be focused in one of three ways, on:

1. Home markets—where the firm has the advantage of being already well established.

[11] Igal Ayal and Jehiel Zif, "Competitive Market Choice Strategies in Multinational Marketing," *Columbia Journal of World Business* 13 (Fall 1978), pp. 72–81; and "Market Expansion Strategies in Multinational Marketing," *Journal of Marketing* 43 (Spring 1979), pp. 84–94.

FIGURE 9–3 Alternative International Strategies

	Location of Competitive Action		
	Home Market(s)	Neutral Territory	Competitor's Home Market(s)
		Offensive Strategies	
Concentration (few markets)	"Munitions factory" — Recommended for moving rapidly down experience curve for later international expansion, when home markets are large, developed, and with weaker competition than outside.	"Advance base" — Recommended for firms with insignificant product or cost advantages over competition and when home market is already dominated, small, or competitive, and therefore less attractive.	"Frontal assault" — Recommended for a strong firm trying to preempt an emerging competitor or weaken a failing one and when competitor's home market barriers are not high.
Diversification (many markets)	Not applicable	"Pincers movement" — Recommended for firms as under "Advance base" but with high resource availability and favorable product/market factors—e.g., low threshold at which neutral markets respond to marketing and low requirement for product adaptation.	"Broad sweep" — Includes neutral markets, too. Recommended for very strong firms with weak, fragmented opposition and when product/market factors overwhelmingly favorable.
		Defensive Strategies	
Concentration (few markets)	"Walled city" — Recommended for small firms without international competitive advantages when barriers exist or can be erected around small home market.	"Perimeter defense" — Recommended for weak firms at competitive disadvantage where preemption of neutral markets may avoid further competitor gains, hence protecting home market.	"Counter strike" — Recommended when a strong competitor has overstretched in attack and counteraction in competitor's home market will either weaken the attack or else yield cheap gains to offset losses to the competitor.
Diversification (many markets)	Not applicable	"Rear-guard action" — Recommended when stronger competition has launched a pincers movement and product/market factors do not overwhelmingly favor concentration. May be desirable even at a loss to hold competition from building strength with more costly later attacks.	"Guerrilla warfare" — Includes neutral markets, too. Recommended as for "Rear-guard action" but also as harassing action by strong firms facing strong competitors to force real fighting onto neutral territory.

SOURCE: Adapted from Igal Ayal and Jehiel Zif, "Competitive Market Choice Strategies in Multinational Marketing," *Columbia Journal of World Business 13* (Fall 1978), pp. 72–81.

2. Neutral territories—where the competitors are on roughly equal footing.

3. Competitor's home markets—where the competitor has prior-establishment advantages.

Expansion Mode.   Efforts to expand performance may be allocated through either:

1. Concentration—where the resources are concentrated on a few markets.

2. Diversification—where resources are spread over many markets.

Each of the 10 feasible strategies has been given a title appropriate to the mix of competitive posture, the markets on which the strategy focuses, and the degree of market concentration involved. Two alternatives are not classified, for it is not possible to focus on the firm's home market while at the same time following a diversified market strategy of expanding in many markets.

The conditions under which each of the 10 strategies should be adopted are summarized briefly in Figure 9–3. Size of the different markets, height of the entry barriers, and the strength within markets relative to competition are important. In addition, 10 product-market factors, as listed in Figure 9–4, are put forward as the basis for choice between concentration or diversification. It is possible that one of these factors alone might be strong enough to swing the decision between concentrating on one or two markets or diversifying effort across many markets. For example, if a very high advertising expenditure were necessary to gain a significant response from a market, it might pay to allocate all resources to that market. Normally, however, it will be a grouping of factors that reinforce each other in suggesting diversification or concentration.

Working backwards from an overall strategy chosen in this way, individual markets will still have to be allocated specific sales targets. These might be set directly, bearing in mind how a market might contribute to the overall concept; or, alternatively, they can be set after markets have been classified into groups

FIGURE 9–4   Major Product/Market Factors Affecting Choice between Diversification and Concentration

Product/Market Factor	Diversification Preferred if:	Concentration Preferred if:
1. Threshold of response to marketing effort	Low	High
2. Growth rate of each market	Low	High
3. Sales stability in each market	Low	High
4. Competitive lead time	Short	Long
5. "Goodwill" spillover effects	High	Low
6. Need for product adaptation	Low	High
7. Need for communications adaptation	Low	High
8. Economies of scale in distribution	Low	High
9. Program control requirements	Low	High
10. Extent of constraints	Low	High

SOURCE: Igal Ayal and Jehiel Zif, "Competitive Market Choice Strategies in Multinational Marketing, *Columbia Journal of World Business* 13 (Fall 1978), p. 73.

as already outlined. For example, from the role a market is given within the strategy its target might be set to:

1. Maximize sales growth.
2. Maintain sales.
3. Run down sales.
4. Give it no marketing attention.
5. Withdraw completely.

Location of Supply, Production, and Investment

While alternative sources of supply may have been loosely considered in setting the market sales targets, detailed planning of the sources of supply must wait until after targets have been set. It will then be possible to design a supply system from raw materials to final delivery to the customer that would minimize costs of achieving the targets. Few firms can determine supply independently for each market without throwing away significant economies from coordinating supply.

While it is theoretically possible to calculate a profit-maximizing pattern of supply and the consequent investment needed to meet market targets up to the horizon year, such calculations would invariably be too complicated for practical application. The number of alternative supply patterns is infinite. The ownership options are many and will influence the investment required. And the introduction of a sequence of changing targets for each market further complicates the issue. Here, again, the calculation may be simplified by adopting a set of rules that limit the alternatives considered without moving the result too far away from a best solution. Decision rules that might be used are:

1. Retention of existing locations as against new locations when sunk costs are high and an experienced labor force is a valuable asset.
2. Consideration of new sites when the local market is above a certain size, resource costs are below a certain figure, or tariffs exceed a certain level.

In some cases, too, the adoption of targets for particular markets will require local production or licensing because of the local regulations concerning access to the market. And in other cases, using external markets for purchasing materials and components may be more advantageous than internalizing production.[12]

With the reduced number of required and potential siting alternatives determined, the next step is to estimate the costs of investment and operation at alternative sites and from each the transport and tariff costs into alternative markets. For each possible alternative, the lowest cost of supplying the market targets in the horizon year might then be calculated.

---

[12] Davidson, *Global Strategic Management*, pp. 177–216.

The methodology used for calculating the costs of alternative sourcing patterns can become very advanced. It may, however, be possible to reduce the alternatives to a linear cost format and use a linear-programming model.[13]

Country Risk Allowances

Up to this point no direct allowance has been made for risks of losses that may arise because of the country locations of assets or activities. Losses can occur through expropriation or restrictions placed on capital assets, as well as through restrictions that reduce or remove the earning power from a market or increase costs in a country. An assessment of these risks is needed for each country likely to be incorporated in the global strategy.

This assessment may require the forecasting of government controls that affect transfers across the country's borders as well as controls aimed specifically at the operations of multinationals. Also needed may be an assessment of general political and economic conditions and the exchange rate for the country's currency. Chapter 16 deals specifically with control and political risk forecasts. Some methods of risk forecasting are designed to produce indices of country risk. The disadvantage of indices, however, is that they are difficult to integrate into decision approaches based on discounted cash flow or internal rate of return calculations. Imagine alternative investments in Egypt, Pakistan, or India, each with a calculated internal rate of return of 25 percent before allowing for country risk. How meaningful would it be to have a risk index of 120 for Egypt, 118 for Pakistan, or 110 for India? Furthermore, the organization or ownership structure of a particular investment may be such that the risk of loss is higher in a less risky country overall.

It is preferable to compile country risk assessments in a way that fits into the firm's approach to investment decisions. The global strategy prototype requires country risk assessments expressed in terms of their likely impact on specific costs or revenues and the probability of the impact occurring. From such assessments expected costs can be calculated and the cash flows from any strategy alternative reduced accordingly.

An example of risk assessments presented in this way is shown in Figure 9–5. The cost and revenue projections for an investment of $20 million in a new operation in Oceania are shown, along with the costs and probabilities of government actions that would affect these operating figures. Note that the probabilities have been assessed to indicate the probability of government action in any year, provided that the action has not been taken before. For example, we estimate that there is no probability of a tariff increase until year 3, when there is a 20 percent or 1 out of 5 chance of a loss of 4 percent (10 percent of the 40 percent

---

[13] Robert E. McGarrah, "Logistics for the International Manufacturer," *Harvard Business Review,* March–April 1966, pp. 154–66; David P. Rutenberg, *Stochastic Programming with Recourse for Planning Optimal Flexibility in Multinational Corporations* (Ph.D. dissertation, University of California, Berkeley, 1967); Ronald H. Ballou, "Dynamic Warehouse Location Analysis," *Journal of Marketing Research,* August 1968, pp. 271–76.

FIGURE 9–5   Proposed $20 Million Investment in Oceania

	Year				
	1	2	3	4	5
Operating projections ($ millions):					
Revenue	20	40	80	80	100
Costs (excluding depreciation)					
Imported materials	10	20	40	40	50
Local labor	8	12	20	20	25
Local expenses	4	6	8	8	8
	22	38	68	68	83
Profit	(2)	2	12	12	17
Local tax 30 percent	—	—	4	4	5
Net profit	(2)	2	8	8	12
Country risk projections:*					
Government price controls reducing revenue by 10 percent; probability	.1	.1	.1	.1	.1
Tariff imposition of 40 percent ad valorem; 90 percent can be passed on to customers; probability	—	—	.2	.3	.4
Profits tax levy on foreign-owned firms 10 percent; probability	—	.05	.05	.1	.2
Expropriation of foreign-owned plants with resulting total loss of net earnings. Compensation or insurance repayment $10 million; probability	—	—	—	.2	.2

* Probabilities assume actions from beginning of year.

tariff) that cannot be passed on to customers. In year 4, there is a .2 chance of the loss having arisen the previous year plus a .3 chance of its arising this year if it had not already arisen. This may seem a little complex, but it is simply .2 plus .3 times the .8 chance the tariff had not been imposed by the beginning of the year. In some situations, it might be easier to forecast directly the cumulative probability that an action will have been taken by that year. Note also that the various actions and their probabilities are independent of each other.

Based on these projections, Figure 9–6 presents a calculation of expected losses from government actions and a risk-adjusted cash flow. Note how the cash flow from the projected operations over the five years is both reduced by the risk and changed in pattern to show a peak of expected profit in year 3 instead of year 5. But for the certainty of compensation following expropriation, the cash flow would have been even more seriously reduced. For a more extended period than five years, however, the return would drop dramatically, given this high expectation of expropriation.

Incremental Net Present Value, Rationing, and Realignment

At this point the strategist following the prototype approach to global strategy will be able to compare cash flows adjusted for country risk of several possible sourcing and investment strategies, chosen initially on the basis of their costs in

FIGURE 9–6   Oceania: Cash-Flow Projection Adjusted for Country Risk ($ millions)

	Year				
	1	2	3	4	5
Revenue	20	40	80	80	100
Less price controls 10 percent	2	4	8	8	10
Cumulative probability	.1	.19	.27	.34	.41
Expected cost	.20	.76	1.96	2.72	4.10
Reduced revenue	19.80	39.24	78.04	77.28	95.90
Costs	22.00	38.00	68.00	68.00	83.00
Plus tariff increase:					
4 percent of imported materials (10% of 40%)	—	—	1.6	1.6	2.0
Cumulative probability	—	—	.2	.44	.66
Expected cost	—	—	.32	.70	1.32
Adjusted costs	22.00	38.00	68.32	68.70	84.32
Profit	(2.20)	1.24	9.72	8.58	11.58
Local tax:					
At 30 percent (losses c/fd.)*	—	—	2.62	2.57	3.47
Plus 10 percent increase	—	—	.88	.86	1.16
Cumulative probability	—	.05	.1	.19	.35
Expected cost	—	—	.09	.16	.41
Increased tax	—	—	2.71	2.73	3.88
Profit after tax	(2.20)	1.24	7.01	5.85	7.70
Expropriation allowance					
Compensation repayment $10 million:					
Probability occurs in this year	—	—	—	.2	.16
Expected recovery	—	—	—	2.00	1.60
Loss of profits:					
Cumulative probability	—	—	—	.2	.36
Expected cost	—	—	—	1.17	2.77
Expropriation cost	—	—	—	(.83) cr.	1.17
Cash flow adjusted for country risk	(2.20)	1.24	7.01	6.68	6.53

* Losses carried forward.

meeting the sales targets of the horizon year. The alternative with the highest present value of its cash flow up to the horizon year could be selected.

Most firms would require, however, that these strategic alternatives be related to the customary investment allocation procedures of a firm. How can this be done? First, the horizon investment requirement must be translated into annual investment requirements over the period up to the horizon year. The final investment may not all be needed in the first year. One practical decision rule would be to invest for each year in that portion of the additions ultimately needed to achieve the sales targets for the horizon year, which would minimize the cost of meeting the earlier year's targets.

Once the annual investment requirements have been established, it would be usual to calculate the net present value of the stream of earnings from each investment unit. The cash flow attributed to each unit is not so much what it produces directly as the incremental cash flow from the global system as a whole. This might be calculated on a marginal or opportunity cost basis and estimated further into the future than the horizon year if that is normally expected for net present value calculation. Expectations of changes in controls and other risks already prepared for the global strategy will also be available for this assessment.

Calculations of net present values will require a further discounting rate. Country risks have already been taken into account, so it may be argued that the use of the firm's normal cost of capital for discounting would take them into account twice. The cost of capital, however, is normally determined predominantly by risks inherent in the business operations themselves, so we suggest its use here. Readers wishing to pursue this point should consult international finance texts; but in any case, the refinement is unlikely to change the global strategy selected.[14]

Finally, each year's investment may be subject to a cut-off limit determined by the firm's capacity to expand. Firms frequently operate with expansion capacity limited by management's ability to cope with expansion. This capacity might be expressed as a maximum investment sum for any year that, together with reinvestment funds, is available to meet the schedule of investment opportunities. The firm then accepts these opportunities in decreasing order of net present value per unit of capital invested until the investment sum is fully committed. It is assumed that this sum is committed to projects for which the least attractive would show a high net present value using the cost of capital as the discount rate. Furthermore, the multinational firm's capacity to handle expansion is taken to limit investment in the short term and not the cost of capital. If the available investment is not used up, then the firm will raise its market targets and repeat the entire global planning process. Conversely, targets that cannot be met will have to be lowered.

The simplified global planning example presented in Figure 9–7 illustrates the choice of a logistics pattern for extending capacity and then shows how the extension might be assessed for incremental cash flow.

ENTRY STRATEGIES

The strategies or approaches adopted by a firm for entering and penetrating individual markets are often an important consideration in building global strategy and warrant more attention at this point. The firm has a choice of alternative approaches for penetrating new markets and for establishing new sources of supply. These alternatives imply different levels of commitment for the resources of the firm. They also have a time dimension and can operate as a building block or an obstacle to the achievement of long-term goals.

Moving from a minimum to a maximum commitment of company resources,

---

[14] See David K. Eiteman and Arthur I. Stonehill, *Multinational Business Finance,* 4th ed. (Reading, Mass.: Addison-Wesley Publishing, 1986), chap. 10, pp. 330–72.

FIGURE 9–7 A Simplified Application of the Prescriptive Model for Global Planning (given: demand, sales, and cost data)

	Seven Country Markets							
	A	B	C	D	E	F	G	Total
Market projection and sales targets in 00s units:								
Year 1 Market	260	400	320	800	250	470	510	3,010
(Target)	(60)	(90)	(80)	(160)	(100)	(80)	(110)	(680)
Year 2 Market	280	420	350	840	260	480	510	3,140
(Target)	(65)	(95)	(90)	(165)	(100)	(80)	(105)	(700)
Year 3 Market	310	420	390	880	270	490	480	3,240
(Target)	(70)	(100)	(110)	(175)	(100)	(90)	(105)	(750)
Year 4 Market	360	420	430	930	280	510	460	3,390
(Target)	(90)	(105)	(130)	(185)	(100)	(100)	(100)	(810)
Year 5 Market	410	440	470	930	290	560	460	3,560
(Target)	(110)	(105)	(150)	(195)	(100)	(110)	(100)	(870)
Market price per unit	$85	$100	$100	$90	$90	$95	$85	
Current annual production in 00s units	—	90	—	300	200	—	140	730
Production cost per unit with existing plant	—	$ 70	—	$65	$60	—	$60	
Cost of standard plant extension of 5,000 units annual capacity $250,000								
Production cost per unit from a new extension	—	$ 65	$ 75	$65	$55	$70	$55	
Transfer cost per unit (including transport and duty, in dollars)								
From A to:								
B	15	—	20	10	15	15	20	
C	20	25	—	10	15	15	5	
D	25	25	10	—	15	10	5	
E	20	25	15	20	—	10	5	
F	20	25	15	20	15	—	5	
G	25	25	15	15	15	15	—	

Simplifying Assumptions

1. Five-year horizon with plant extensions possible for year 3.
2. No change expected in sales prices.
3. Production cost per unit excludes plant cost and is taken as directly variable.
4. All transfer costs directly variable and no possibility of customs duty saving through manipulation of transfer prices.
5. Production strategy to be determined independently of corporation tax considerations.

Decision Analysis

Inspection of the following table shows that all expansion should be located at E to supply A's requirements and the balance of F. (Where one alternative is not so dominant a linear-program calculation would be needed to establish profits of the alternatives.) Extensions should be completed to increase capacity by a further 5,000 units in each of years 3, 4, and 5.

Incremental return can be based on the profit that would be foregone if the extension were not available. If this meant simply the elimination of sales to the least profitable market given the reduced supply system, it would be solely sales to A in years 3 and 4, but in year 5 production would be reallocated and 1,500 sales foregone in B, 1,000 in C, and 500 in F for a total lost revenue of $262,500.

Profits per Unit from Alternative Location of Plant Extensions (in dollars)

| | | | | | Destination | | | |
Source	A	B	C	D	E	F	G
A	—	35	15	15	10	15	—
B	5	5	25	10	5	10	10
C	-5	20	25	25	10	20	15
D	-5	20	30	15	35	30	25
E	10	5	15	—	5	25	10
F	-5	20	30	25	10	25	30
G	5						

213

entry strategies can be grouped into the following five categories: (1) licensing, (2) exporting, (3) local warehousing with direct sales staff, (4) local packaging and/or assembling operations, or (5) full-scale local production and marketing.

Within these categories, several options exist.[15] Direct export and sales through a local company sales organization, for example, can be done by setting up regional distribution centers or warehouses. Or the firm can create a regional sales branch office and/or subsidiary. Or it can organize an overseas franchise system with independent, or a combination of company and independent, franchises.

A similar set of entry strategies is available for initiating projects that are primarily a source of supply for the multinational enterprise. A minimum commitment of resources would be involved in establishing only a buying office in a foreign location. A maximum commitment of resources would be needed to invest in company-operated production facilities and in supporting infrastructure such as transportation, electric power, or housing, health, and educational facilities for employees. Many alternatives are available between these two extremes.

Given these many alternative entry strategies, what are the variables that determine the best choice for a company? For a market seeker, the decision variables will be both external and internal to the firm. Most of the decision variables apply also to the entry decision for supply projects.

External factors:
   Host-country policies and controls.
   Size and attractiveness of markets.
   Competitive conditions in the foreign market.
   Availability of local supply sources in the country.

Internal factors:
   Characteristics of technology and products.
   Enterprise-wide availability of productive capacity.
   Minimum economic size for producing units.
   Locational characteristics of production.
   Availability of capital and managerial resources.
   Company's willingness to assume risk.
   Long-term corporate goals.

In many cases, one or a few of the decision variables will dominate the decision on entry strategy and, in effect, sharply reduce the available options. Until recently, Japan followed severely restrictive policies regarding foreign investment. In many cases, the only practical options available to an international company for entering the Japanese market were licensing, exporting, and holding a minority position in a joint venture. In some instances, quota or tariff restrictions further reduce the options to only licensing. Or a less developed country attempting

---

[15] Business International Corporation, "Alternative Ways to Penetrate a Foreign Market," *201 Checklists: Decision Making in International Operations,* March 1980.

to encourage foreign direct investment may have such prohibitive import restrictions that the only realistic option for entering its market is to establish a foreign production subsidiary. Or the size of the market may be so small in relation to the minimum economic size required for efficient production that exporting is the only sensible initial entry strategy.

An interesting strategy used by some textile companies operating in Southeast Asia has been to establish local warehouses for raw materials and finished goods but to subcontract the manufacturing function to independent local companies. The international firm does the purchasing of supplies, the design and fashion work, and the international marketing—but not the actual manufacturing. Other strategies are to establish production facilities in free port or border industry areas, primarily to make use of lower labor costs in a foreign country.

For each project, the feasible alternatives will have to be sorted out and compared as to profitability and consequences for achieving the firm's long-term goals. In all cases, the firm should make sure that its initial entry strategy will not create future obstacles for achieving long-run objectives. Interim moves should be designed to achieve long-term goals.

Licensing is a relatively low-risk and low-cost entry strategy, available to both large and small firms that have something to sell. It is an option that allows a company to spread out the cost of its research and development and has the potential benefit of technology feedback. The conditions under which licensing may be a preferred strategy are discussed in Chapter 20 under "Managing International Technology Transfers."

OWNERSHIP STRATEGIES

Ownership strategies are another important component of overall global strategy. Should a foreign subsidiary be wholly owned, a joint venture in which ownership is shared with either private or government local interests, or a strategic partnership with another multinational firm? If the joint venture or strategic partnership approach is adopted, should the international firm seek a majority or minority participation? Ownership policies change investment requirements and other resource commitments for new projects. They also affect the extent to which individual subsidiaries participate in an enterprise-wide global strategy.[16]

International Joint Ventures

The reasons for entering into a joint venture generally fall into three categories: (a) government suasion or legislation, (b) need for the other partner's skills, and (c) need for the other partner's attributes or assets.[17] The primary skill required

---

[16] See Kathryn R. Harrigan, "Joint Ventures and Global Strategies," *Columbia Journal of World Business,* Summer 1984, pp. 7–16.

[17] J. Peter Killing, *Strategies for Joint Venture Success* (New York: Praeger, 1983), pp. 3–8.

of the local partner is its knowledge of the local economy, politics, and culture. Assets include such items as patents or finances, while attributes may be the local marketing know-how and managerial skills of an established local enterprise.

Some countries, mainly less developed countries, require all foreign firms to form joint ventures with local partners; and other countries may require joint ventures only in certain strategic sectors. The ownership strategy alternatives are limited in these countries, but in other situations, the multinational firm has considerable choice.

Even where governments do not insist on joint ventures, political considerations may be an important reason for having local partners. Sharing ownership with nationals can encourage national identification and reduce the appearance of foreignness and thus the risk of expropriation. Furthermore, local partners may in some cases be able to contribute political influence and protection against the possibility of increasingly severe national controls. The maximum local protection could be achieved by a joint venture with the national government, although where governments change with frequency even this strategy cannot be a complete defense. In terms of public-relations benefits, a wide distribution of shares among the investing public may be the best strategy.

The financial advantages of joint ventures may permit an international enterprise to enter into more foreign projects when its financial resources are limited. In some cases, local partners will accept the technological know-how, patent rights, or even the trade name of the international enterprise as a substitute for capital in payment for a share of the subsidiary's equity. Joint ventures also lessen the risk of foreign exchange losses by reducing the amount of investment at stake.

The disadvantages of joint ventures revolve largely around the desire and need of the multinational enterprise to retain control over the decisions of foreign subsidiaries.[18] This control issue can be the source of many conflicts between the international firm and its local partners. Where the special advantages of the multinational enterprise lie in a unification of markets and the rationalization of production, finance, and other functions on a regional or global basis, the interests of any subunit and the local partners are likely to conflict with global objectives and opportunities. As one example, in order to build volume the firm might prefer to adopt a transfer-pricing policy that would leave all profits in the marketing subsidiary but might be discouraged from doing so if the subsidiary is only part owned. Or local partners may prefer dividends rather than retaining earnings as a source of financing expansion.

In general, joint ventures are difficult to manage and frequently unstable. Several studies indicate a failure rate of 30 percent for joint ventures in developed countries and 45–50 percent in the less developed countries.[19] One study concludes

---

[18] John I. Reynolds, "The 'Pinched Shoe' Effect of International Joint Ventures," *Columbia Journal of World Business,* Summer 1984, pp. 23–29.

[19] Paul W. Beamish, "The Characteristics of Joint Ventures in Developed and Developing Countries," *Columbia Journal of World Business,* Fall 1985, p. 14.

that relatively equal joint ventures, where both parents play an active role, have a dramatically higher failure rate than ventures that are dominated by one parent.[20] Another study suggests that a multinational company's tolerance for joint ventures is closely related to its product strategy.[21] Where the firm specializes in a small number of products and services, and where marketing and production decisions need to be relatively centralized, the failure rate for joint ventures is high.

As in the case of entry strategies, the decision criteria that should influence ownership strategies will be a mixture of factors internal and external to the firm. The internal factors will be the product strategy of the firm, the availability of adequate financial and other managerial resources, the degree of operating experience it can command for new and different situations, and the speed with which it desires to initiate new projects for competitive or other reasons. The external factors will be the control policies of the host countries; the availability of local partners or of adequate financial markets where widely shared local ownership is desired; and the local competitive situation.

Strategic Partnerships

In recent years, a new form of joint venture—labelled *strategic partnerships*—has been growing in importance. In contrast to the traditional joint venture, which brought together a multinational firm and a local partner, the strategic alliance is a partnership of two or more multinationals that generally are competitors. A well-publicized example is the General Motors–Toyota partnership (NUMMI) to build small cars in the United States. Numerous other agreements among major competitors from the United States, Europe, and Japan now exist in telecommunications, computers, robots, biotechnology, and aerospace.

Whereas the traditional joint venture is usually a device to secure access to a protected national market, the strategic alliance is designed to aid the partners in serving global markets. These new ventures typically combine the technologies of two or more firms from industrialized countries (see Box 9–1) and have as their motivation increased research capability, cost reduction through joint production, and enlarged market access in order to face global competitors on more equal terms.

As strategic partnerships are relatively new, there is little historical evidence as to their long-run stability. The economic logic for cooperation is usually obvious, and the short-term advantages are quite clear. But a partnership between global competitors has built-in conflict potentials that may make the arrangement unstable over the long run.[22] Partnerships across national borders also have public policy

---

[20] J. Peter Killing, *Strategies for Joint Venture Success,* pp. 15–29.

[21] Lawrence G. Franko, "Joint Venture Divorce in the Multinational Company," *Columbia Journal of World Business,* May–June 1971, pp. 20–21; John M. Stopford and Louis T. Wells, Jr., *Managing the Multinational Enterprise* (New York: Basic Books, 1972), pp. 99–168.

[22] Gary Hamel and C. K. Prahalad, "Unexplored Routes to Competitiveness," *Harvard Business Review* (forthcoming).

BOX 9–1
Global Matchmaking

Motorola Inc. and the Toshiba Corporation, two of the world's largest semiconductor manufacturers, have announced plans to build a manufacturing facility in Japan and exchange a broad range of memory chip and microprocessor technology.

The Motorola–Toshiba deal, according to analysts, would help overcome critical deficiencies in both companies. Toshiba is strong in memory chip manufacturing and recently displaced Hitachi as Japan's No. 2 semiconductor maker. But it has stumbled in its efforts to develop microprocessors, the logic chips that form the core of most personal computers and work stations along with automobile and home appliance electronics.

Motorola, for its part, has developed its line of microprocessors into one of the strongest in the semiconductor industry. But along with most other U.S. manufacturers, the company has virtually abandoned the memory chip market. Motorola officials expect that the new agreement will aid their efforts to sell chips in Japan, where the company has been outspoken in charging that it was being excluded from the market.

Motorola's chief strength is in computer systems sold to the engineering and technical community. This is still an infant market in Japan, and with the new plant both companies should be able to exploit it.

The two companies said they would jointly own a new manufacturing facility in Sendai, Japan, that will initially produce memory chips and eventually microprocessors. Both Toshiba and Motorola deny that either company will invest in the other.

SOURCE: Adapted from *The New York Times,* November 26, 1986, p. D4.

---

implications for national governments.[23] From the U.S. point of view, it has been argued that such U.S. partnerships with Japanese competitors "give our future away."[24]

STRATEGY REVIEW AND UPDATING

As the planning process dictates, it is also important for the firm to make regular reviews of the particular business techniques being used in its different product and factor markets. Factors such as inter-regional shifts, urbanization and suburbanization, technology, transportation, competition, social pressures, local expertise, changing buying patterns and selling outlets, and government policies and regulation make periodic examinations essential if the company is to stay abreast of changing conditions. A firm that does not modify its style of

---

[23] Richard W. Moxon and J. Michael Geringer, "Multinational Ventures in the Commercial Aircraft Industry," *Columbia Journal of World Business,* Summer 1985, pp. 55–62.

[24] Robert B. Reich and Eric D. Mankin, "Joint Ventures With Japan Give Our Future Away," *Harvard Business Review,* March–April 1986, pp. 78–85.

operation according to changes in local conditions and laws may be passing up opportunities for great profits. None of the many possible routes to market penetration should be overlooked in a company's periodic review of its approaches. Likewise, possible new routes to reduce production costs and acquire new technology should not be overlooked.

The issue of ownership strategy has a time dimension. The point has been made that the stream of benefits of the foreign investment to the host country may decrease over time. Such a maturing of benefits and an increase in the alternatives open to a country can reduce the bargaining power of the foreign enterprise for maintaining 100 percent or even majority ownership.[25] And in a number of countries, the international firm may encounter national policies that require gradual divestment of foreign ownership over time, or what has been called a *fade-out policy*. Or the enterprise itself may want to change ownership patterns over time. A joint venture may have served the purpose of helping a firm acquire local experience in the initial entry stage but no longer serves this need at a later stage. The reverse can also be true; firms may develop preferences for joint ventures during mature stages of foreign market penetration. The point is simple. Conditions change; and firms must routinely review and adjust their plans, operating strategies, and ownership arrangements to compete most successfully in international markets.

A GLOBAL HABIT OF MIND

In the last analysis, developing a global strategy depends upon the way executives think about doing business around the world. The design and implementation of a global strategy require that managers in both headquarters and subsidiaries follow a worldwide approach that considers subsidiaries as neither satellites nor independent city-states but as parts of a whole, the focus of which is on worldwide as well as local objectives. And each part of the system makes its unique contribution with its unique competence. This approach, which Perlmutter has popularized as *geocentrism*, involves collaboration between subsidiaries and headquarters to establish universal standards and permissible local variations on the basis of which key decisions are made.[26] However, geocentrism requires a reward system for subsidiary managers that motivates them to work for worldwide goals and not just to defend country objectives.

Four general types of headquarters orientation toward subsidiaries in international enterprise have been described by Perlmutter. While they never appear in pure form, and there is some degree of each philosophy in most firms, they are clearly distinguishable as *ethnocentric* (home-country oriented); *polycentric*

[25] Peter Gabriel, "The Investment in the LDC: Assets with a Fixed Maturity," *Columbia Journal of World Business*, Summer 1966, pp. 109–19.

[26] Balaji S. Chakravarthy and Howard V. Perlmutter, "Strategic Planning for a Global Business," *Columbia Journal of World Business*, Summer 1985, pp. 3–10.

(host-country oriented); *regiocentric;* (region-oriented) and *geocentric* (world-oriented).[27]

The ethnocentric attitude can be characterized as: "We, the home-country nationals, are superior to, more trustworthy than, and more reliable than any foreigners in headquarters or the subsidiaries." In such firms, performance criteria and decision rules are generally based on home-country standards. Ethnocentrism works against a global strategy because of a lack of good feedback and because the experience and views of managers familiar with local conditions in the areas of operation do not carry appropriate weight in decision making.

Polycentric firms go to the other extreme by assuming that local people always know what is best for them and that the unit of the multinational enterprise located in a host country should be as local in identity and behavior as possible. A polycentric firm is more akin to a confederation of quasi-independent subsidiaries. A polycentric management philosophy is likely to sacrifice most of the unification and synergistic benefits of multinational operation. The costs of polycentrism are the waste from duplication of effort and inefficient use of home-country experience. The approach has the advantage of making intensive use of local resources and personnel but at the cost of global growth and efficiency.

Regiocentrism attempts to gain a not-quite-global perspective without sacrificing management control and effectiveness. But regionalism may have its limitations. Many areas of the world are far less homogeneous than regiocentrism assumes them to be. Also there are cost considerations in operating regional headquarters, and frequently the reward systems are for country rather than regional performance.[28]

Geocentrism also has costs, largely related to communication and travel expense, time spent in decision making because of the desire to educate personnel about global objectives and to secure consensus, and the expense of a relatively large headquarters bureaucracy. But the payoffs are a more objective total enterprise performance; worldwide utilization of resources; improvement of local company management; a greater sense of commitment to worldwide goals; and, last but not least, more profit. A globally oriented enterprise, of course, depends on having an adequate supply of managers who are globally oriented.

SUMMARY

Few, if any, companies are born with a global philosophy or a world-wide view. They normally become international by a process of creeping incrementalism, adding a series of international units to the parent company as isolated reactions

---

[27] For the interested reader, the relevance of this framework to international marketing strategies and decisions is discussed in Yoram Wind, Susan P. Douglas, and Howard V. Perlmutter, "Guidelines for Developing International Marketing Strategies," *Journal of Marketing* 37 (April 1973), pp. 14–23.

[28] David A. Heenan and Howard V. Perlmutter, *Multinational Organization Development* (Reading, Mass.: Addison-Wesley Publishing Co., 1979), pp. 71–86.

to perceived opportunities or competitive threats. But at some stage of international-ization, either as a result of growing experience or competitive pressures, the firm becomes aware of the need for a global strategy and a global decision model in order to benefit from the synergy potential of multinational operations and to maximize results on a worldwide basis. At this stage, if not before, the truly multinational enterprise engages in a system of international strategic and long-range planning.

The formulation of global strategy starts from the examination of global markets and identification of competitive position and works back to determine the location of supply and production activities and investments to achieve optimum performance in these markets. It requires decisions as to the best entry strategies for securing access to markets and foreign locations of resources or production. Another component of a global strategy is a company's decisions concerning ownership. Above all, the formulation and implementation of a global strategy requires managers with a global, or geocentric, state of mind.

EXERCISES AND DISCUSSION QUESTIONS

1. If a global strategy is required to maximize the special advantages and synergistic benefits of multinational operations, why have so many firms been successful in their international operations by responding to perceived opportunities and competitive threats without international strategic planning and global decision models?
2. How can an enterprise simplify the complexities of international possibilities and reduce to manageable proportions the variables it includes in its decision making?
3. Under what circumstances would global planning be desirable, even if the firm's international involvement is minor?
4. What decision rules other than those mentioned in the chapter might be used for choosing among alternative sources of supply?
5. "Global planning based on a sales horizon of four or five years and annual return on investment from those sales is in direct conflict with the normal return-on-investment calculations of financial management. But the top executive of the multinational firm will be measured on his five-year profit achievement before anything else." Comment.
6. "Entering a new market through licensing is generally the best strategy because market potentials can be tested with little or no investment." Comment.
7. "A multinational firm needs to have complete control over its subsidiaries in order to make optimum use of its resources and compete most effectively. This generally means 100 percent ownership." Comment.
8. "To interpret dissolution of a joint venture or a strategic partnership as failure overlooks the possibility that dissolution is a result of success: that is, both parties obtained their expected benefits and decided to discontinue."
Discuss. What might be some specific examples that support this view?

CHAPTER 10

Assessing and Forecasting National Economies and Demands

For the business firm newly venturing into international activities, the task of analyzing the economic and demand environment in many nations of widely varying characteristics will appear formidable. Nevertheless, the firm can reduce the task to manageable proportions. First, it must be selective and focus on those aspects of the environment of special importance to its field of business activity and its specific interest in a country as a market seeker, resource seeker, or production-efficiency seeker. Second, much of the needed information can be obtained from data and reports published by national and international agencies. And third, short-cut techniques are available for a preliminary scanning of the economic and demand environment in many countries to reduce the number of situations where in-depth analysis is required.

As the enterprise becomes multinational, the task of assessing and forecasting the economic and demand environment will be decentralized and shared among the various units of the system. The foreign subsidiaries will assume primary responsibilities for economic and market studies in their areas of operations. Headquarters staff can then limit its responsibilities to making cross-national comparisons, integrating national forecasts into an enterprise-wide forecast against which global policy decisions can be made, and assessing the international financial framework and trends in inter-nation relationships.

Much of the environment-forecasting activity of the subsidiaries will be to guide local operating decisions. But as part of a multinational system, the subsidiary will have to fulfill two additional requirements. First, it will have to follow a sufficiently standardized approach so that headquarters can make cross-country comparisons by combining individual country results into a broader mosaic. Second, each subsidiary will have to include sufficient information in its assessment so that the links can be made between the economic environment of the subsidiary and the rest of the multinational system.

At the headquarters level, the assessments of national economic and demand environments are needed for guiding strategy and operating decisions, for formulating systemwide policies, and for exercising a review function. When the firm expands into new countries where there is no subsidiary, headquarters will also have to assume full responsibility for the local environmental analysis.

The technical responsibility for assessing and forecasting will usually be handled by specialists. But in order to use such forecasts, international managers will need to have considerable familiarity with techniques and limitations. They must be aware of statistical perils, inaccurate perceptions, and the risks inherent in making cross-national comparisons or in integrating information based on different data bases.

ECONOMIC SCANNING

Economic scanning makes use of standard economic measurements to provide a general comparison of the potentials of different countries from the viewpoint of an international business. The indicators are primarily macroeconomic measures of economic size, income level, and growth trends; but they can also extend to indicators of sectoral growth and economic dependence.

Economic Size

The economic size of a nation is measured by its total gross national product (GNP) or by a similar measurement, gross domestic product (GDP). GDP measures the value of goods and services produced in a country without taking account of the nationality of those supplying the labor or the capital. When factor income received from abroad is added and factor income paid abroad is deducted, the resultant figure is GNP. Recent estimates by the World Bank of the GNP for countries are shown in Table 10–1.

In terms of total size, the United States is at the top of the economic ladder with a GNP of $3,915 billion (expressed in 1985 dollars). At the bottom of the scale are small countries with total GNPs of $700 million, such as the Central African Republic and Mauritania.

The attraction of the developed countries on the basis of economic size is

TABLE 10–1 Comparative Estimates of Gross National Product (GNP) and Population for 1985 (for countries with GNP of more than $500 million)*

Country	Gross National Product at Market Prices (U.S. $ millions)	Population (millions)
United States	3,915,350	238.8
Japan	1,366,040	120.6
Germany, Federal Republic of	667,970	61.1
France	526,630	55.1
United Kingdom	474,190	56.5
Italy	371,050	56.9
Canada	347,360	25.4
China, Peoples Republic of	318,920	1,041.1
Brazil	222,010	135.5
India	194,820	765.1
Australia	171,170	15.8
Spain	168,820	38.7
Mexico	163,790	78.8
Netherlands	132,920	14.5
Switzerland	105,180	6.4
Saudi Arabia	102,120	11.5
Sweden	99,050	8.3
Korea, Republic of	88,440	40.6
Indonesia	86,590	162.2
Belgium	83,230	9.8
Poland	78,960	37.3
Nigeria	75,940	99.6
Austria	69,060	7.5
South Africa	65,320	32.4
Argentina	65,080	30.5
Norway	57,580	4.1
Denmark	57,330	5.1

TABLE 10–1   *(continued)*

Country	Gross National Product at Market Prices (U.S. $ millions)	Population (millions)
Turkey	56,060	49.4
Algeria	55,230	21.8
Venezuela	53,800	17.3
Finland	53,450	4.9
Yugoslavia	47,900	23.1
Thailand	42,100	50.9
Colombia	37,610	28.4
Pakistan	36,230	94.9
Greece	35,250	9.9
Hong Kong	33,770	5.4
Philippines	32,630	54.7
Egypt	32,220	47.1
Malaysia	31,930	15.6
Libya	27,000	3.6
United Arab Emirates	26,400	1.3
Kuwait	24,760	1.7
New Zealand	23,720	3.2
Israel	21,140	4.3
Hungary	20,720	10.6
Portugal	20,140	10.2
Singapore	18,970	2.5
Peru	17,830	18.6
Ireland	17,250	3.5
Chile	17,230	12.0
Syrian Arab Republic	17,060	10.5
Puerto Rico	15,940	3.2
Bangladesh	14,770	100.6
Morocco	13,390	21.9
Ecuador	10,880	9.3
Guatemala	9,890	7.9
Tunisia	8,730	7.1
Oman	8,360	1.1
Cameroon	8,300	10.2
Sudan	7,350	21.9
Trinidad and Tobago	7,140	1.2
Burma	7,080	36.8
Sri Lanka	5,980	16.1
Kenya	5,960	20.4
Tanzania	5,840	22.2
Zimbabwe	5,450	8.4
Zaire	5,220	30.5
Qatar	5,110	.3
Dominican Republic	5,050	6.2
Uruguay	4,980	3.0
Ghana	4,960	12.7
Luxembourg	4,900	.3
Ethiopia	4,630	42.2
Panama	4,400	2.2
Yemen Arab Republic	4,140	7.9
Bahrain	4,040	.4
Jordan	4,010	3.5
El Salvador	3,940	5.5

TABLE 10–1   *(concluded)*

Country	Gross National Product at Market Prices (U.S. $ millions)	Population (millions)
Brunei	3,940	.2
Costa Rica	3,340	2.5
Gabon	3,330	.9
Honduras	3,190	4.3
Paraguay	3,180	3.3
Bolivia	3,010	6.3
Nicaragua	2,760	3.2
Cyprus	2,650	.6
Zambia	2,620	6.6
Nepal	2,610	16.5
Iceland	2,580	.2
Madagascar	2,510	10.2
Papua New Guinea	2,470	3.5
Senegal	2,400	6.5
Jamaica	2,090	2.2
Guinea	1,950	6.1
Congo	1,910	1.8
Haiti	1,900	5.4
Fiji	1,900	.7
Malta	1,900	.3
Rwanda	1,730	6.0
Bahamas	1,670	.2
Netherlands Antilles	1,610	.2
Somalia	1,450	5.3
Sierra Leone	1,380	3.7
French Polynesia	1,370	.2
Channel Islands	1,350	.1
Niger	1,250	6.3
Barbados	1,180	.2
Malawi	1,160	7.0
Yemen, Peoples Republic	1,130	2.1
Burundi	1,110	4.7
Mauritius	1,110	1.0
Benin	1,080	4.0
Mali	1,070	7.5
Liberia	1,040	2.2
Bermuda	1,030	.1
Virgin Islands	1,030	.1
Suriname	1,010	.4
Botswana	900	1.1
New Caledonia	860	.1
Togo	750	3.0
Lesotho	730	1.5
Central African Republic	700	2.5
Mauritania	700	1.7
Guam	670	.1
Guyana	460	.8

* GNP not available for about 30 countries, including Iran, Iraq, Lebanon, Taiwan, the USSR, and other centrally planned economies.

SOURCE: *The World Bank Atlas 1987* (Washington, D.C.: The World Bank, 1987), pp. 6–9.

highlighted by several comparisons. Germany's GNP is more than twice that of mainland China, even though China has 17 times Germany's population. Australia has about the same GNP as India, although India has 50 times as many people. Switzerland's total GNP is greater than that of Indonesia, even though Indonesia's population is 25 times as large.

Income Levels

GNP per capita—total GNP divided by total population—can be used as a rough guide to the purchasing power of a country. It does have many limitations, however, including its failure to allow for different patterns of income distribution.[1] From Table 10–2, it can be seen that the top-ranking GNP per capita is recorded for the United States ($16,400 per person), closely followed by Switzerland ($16,380). At the bottom come countries with GNP per capita of $150 or less, such as Ethiopia, Bangladesh, and Mali.

Countries are often classified as developed or developing countries based on average per capita GNP. Developing countries are also referred to as LDCs (less-developed countries). Although there is no general agreement as to where the dividing line should be, one representation of the gap between the LDCs and the economically advanced countries of the world is shown in Table 10–3. From this table, it can be quickly calculated that 75 percent of world population receives less than 20 percent of world GNP. Using estimates of GNP for all countries along with the internal distribution of income in each country, then 90 per cent of world population receives only 20 per cent of the world GNP.[2]

The development gap explains the aspirations of the LDCs for a greatly accelerated rate of economic progress, toward which international enterprise can make valuable contributions. At the same time, the development gap nourishes nationalistic feelings and defensive controls, which often make the LDCs unattractive to the international enterprise. Yet most of the world's population is in LDCs, and many are making remarkable economic progress; so they should receive careful consideration in the economic scanning of the globally oriented business enterprise.

Growth Trends

Data on economic size and income levels must be supplemented by recent trend data in order to secure a more dynamic picture of a country's economic attractiveness. Country A may have high income levels but be relatively stagnant. Country B may have lower levels of income but have more attraction to the

---

[1] See Hollis B. Chenery, "Poverty and Progress—Choices for the Developing World," *Finance and Development,* June 1, 1980, pp. 12–16.

[2] See Margaret E. Grosh and E. Wayne Nafziger, "The Computation of World Income Distribution," *Economic Development and Cultural Change* 34 (January 1986), pp. 347–59.

TABLE 10–2   Gross National Product per Capita for 1985, GNP Real Growth 1984–1985 and Population Growth 1973–1985 (for countries with more than 1 million population)

Country	GNP per Capita		Population Growth Rate 1973–85 (percent)
	Amount 1985 (U.S. $)	Real Growth Rate 1984–85 (percent)	
United States	16,400	2.0	1.0
Switzerland	16,380	4.1	0.1
Kuwait	14,270	−14.5	5.7
Norway	13,890	2.9	0.4
Canada	13,670	2.8	1.2
Sweden	11,890	2.8	0.2
Japan	11,330	4.5	0.9
Denmark	11,240	2.7	0.1
Germany, Federal Rep.	10,940	2.4	−0.1
Finland	10,870	1.7	0.4
Australia	10,840	2.5	1.3
France	9,550	0.7	0.5
Netherlands	9,180	1.5	0.6
Austria	9,150	2.8	0.0
Saudi Arabia	8,860	−10.5	4.8
Belgium	8,450	1.5	0.1
United Kingdom	8,390	3.0	0.0
Libya	7,500	−5.4	4.0
Singapore	7,420	−1.0	1.3
New Zealand	7,310	−0.7	0.6
Italy	6,520	2.3	0.3
Hong Kong	6,220	−0.4	2.3
Trinidad and Tobago	6,010	−7.7	1.6
Israel	4,920	−0.6	2.2
Puerto Rico	4,850	2.3	1.2
Ireland	4,840	−0.5	1.2
Spain	4,360	1.7	0.9
Greece	3,550	0.9	1.0
Venezuela	3,110	−3.2	3.3
Algeria	2,530	2.8	3.1
Korea, Republic of	2,180	3.8	1.5
Argentina	2,130	−5.3	1.6
Poland	2,120	4.2	0.9
Mexico	2,080	0.1	2.8
Yugoslavia	2,070	2.5	0.8
Malaysia	2,050	0.3	2.4
Panama	2,020	−0.2	2.3
South Africa	2,010	−4.0	2.4
Portugal	1,970	3.9	1.0
Hungary	1,940	−1.0	0.2
Uruguay	1,660	0.1	0.6
Brazil	1,640	5.9	2.3
Syrian Arab Republic	1,630	−3.7	3.4
Jordan	1,560	−1.4	2.9
Chile	1,440	−0.3	1.7
Colombia	1,320	0.2	1.9
Costa Rica	1,290	−1.3	2.3
Guatemala	1,240	−3.9	2.8
Tunisia	1,220	1.0	2.4
Ecuador	1,160	1.2	2.9

TABLE 10–2   *(continued)*

| Country | GNP per Capita | | Population Growth Rate 1973–85 (percent) |
	Amount 1985 (U.S. $)	Real Growth Rate 1984–85 (percent)	
Turkey	1,130	2.8	2.2
Congo, Peoples Rep. of	1,020	−5.7	3.1
Peru	960	2.7	2.4
Jamaica	940	−7.9	1.1
Paraguay	940	1.3	2.5
Nicaragua	850	−5.6	3.1
Thailand	830	2.2	2.2
Cameroon	810	5.1	3.2
Dominican Republic	810	−3.5	2.4
Nigeria	760	1.5	2.8
Honduras	730	−0.5	3.5
El Salvador	710	−1.4	3.0
Papua New Guinea	710	4.4	2.6
Egypt, Arab Rep. of	680	−2.1	2.6
Zimbabwe	650	0.9	3.2
Morocco	610	1.0	2.4
Yemen, Peoples Republic	540	−5.3	2.3
Indonesia	530	0.7	2.3
Yemen, Arab Republic	520	0.0	2.8
Lesotho	480	−0.3	2.4
Bolivia	470	−7.1	2.7
Liberia	470	−0.9	3.3
Mauritania	410	−4.1	2.1
Zambia	400	−1.0	3.2
Ghana	390	2.8	2.7
Pakistan	380	4.9	3.0
Senegal	370	0.1	2.8
Sierra Leone	370	−2.5	2.1
Sri Lanka	370	0.9	1.8
Haiti	350	0.0	1.7
Sudan	330	−8.9	2.9
Guinea	320	3.0	2.0
China, People's Republic of	310	9.7	1.4
Kenya	290	−0.2	4.0
Rwanda	290	0.2	3.3
Central African Republic	270	0.3	2.3
Benin	270	1.2	2.9
Somalia	270	1.1	2.8
Tanzania	270	−0.9	3.4
Togo	250	4.9	2.8
Madagascar	250	1.6	2.9
India	250	0.3	2.2
Burundi	240	4.8	2.3
Niger	200	4.0	3.0
Burma	190	4.2	2.0
Zaire	170	0.6	3.0
Malawi	170	−1.9	3.1
Nepal	160	0.2	2.6
Bhutan	160	2.7	2.0
Bangladesh	150	1.4	2.5
Mali	140	−1.2	2.5

TABLE 10–2   *(concluded)*

| | GNP per Capita | | |
| | Amount 1985 (U.S. $) | Real Growth Rate 1984–85 (percent) | Population Growth Rate 1973–85 (percent) |
Country			
Ethiopia	110	−7.6	2.7
GNP not available for:			
German Democratic Rep.			−0.1
Czechoslovakia			0.5
U.S.S.R.			0.9
Bulgaria			0.3
Iraq			3.6
Romania			0.8
Angola			3.1
Uganda			3.2
Mozambique			2.6
Chad			2.1
Albania			2.0
Cuba			0.8
Iran			3.1
Korea, Democratic Rep.			2.6
Lao, People's Democratic Rep.			1.6
Mongolia			2.8
Vietnam			2.6
Afghanistan			n.a.
Ivory Coast			n.a.
Lebanon			n.a.
Upper Volta			n.a.

SOURCE: *The World Bank Atlas 1987* (Washington, D.C.: The World Bank, 1987), pp. 6–9.

international enterprise because the economy is growing rapidly. Trend data for population and recent GNP per capita growth are also shown in Table 10–2.

Low rates of population growth are associated with higher GNP per capita with the exception of the oil countries of Brunei, Kuwait, Libya, Saudi Arabia, Oman, United Arab Emirates, and Venezuela, which have a very unequal income distribution, and the countries with a substantial immigrant increment over the

TABLE 10–3   Countries Grouped by 1985 GNP per Capita

GNP per Capita, 1985	Number of Countries	GNP 1985 (U.S. $000 millions)	Population 1985 (000)	GNP per Capita 1985 (U.S. $)
$400 and less	35	639	2,318,153	280
$401 to $1,635	47	525	672,211	780
$1,636 to $4,300	21	967	472,325	2,050
$4,300 and more	48	9,026	776,071	11,630
No data	33	n.a.	549,961	n.a.

SOURCE: *The World Bank Atlas 1987* (Washington, D.C.: The World Bank, 1987), p. 16.

1973–83 period, such as Israel and Hong Kong. It is particularly noticeable, too, that communist countries generally record significantly lower population growth rates than noncommunist countries with roughly similar GNP per capita. Most Middle Eastern countries plus Brazil and Ecuador have managed to maintain a high rate of growth in GNP per capita while population also expanded at high rates. The predominant relationship, however, is the opposite. At the bottom end of the scale are numerous poorer African countries with high population growth and actual decreases in real GNP per capita.

Historically, as a nation's income levels rise and urbanization increases, the rate of population increase slows down. Whether rapid increases in population are a burden on economic development efforts is still a controversial question in many countries. Yet the arithmetic is clear. The faster population expands, the larger is the overall rate of growth required to achieve per capita increases. Countries with rapid population growth normally have a large share of their population in the lower age groups. As a result, the potential labor force will be a relatively small share of total population. Expenditures required for education will be disproportionately large, and the heavy educational costs have to be borne by the relatively small share of the population that is productively employed.

Sectoral Trends

The multinational enterprise may need to extend its scanning of the economic environment into individual sectors of an economy. A firm whose markets lie in the agriculture sector, for example, may need to compare the size and trends of that sector in different countries. Sectoral data can also provide indications as to the overall potential for growth of individual countries.

Growth potentials are generally less for predominantly agrarian countries. More than in other sectors, growth in agriculture is constrained by low income elasticities in the demand for foodstuffs and by the rate at which new production techniques can be adopted. As industry approaches agriculture in size, countries become capable of more rapid growth, particularly during the period in which domestic manufacturing is substituting for imported goods.

Empirical studies have shown a regular pattern of change in economic structure associated with rising levels of income. As income increases, the shares spent by consumers for necessities decrease, while the shares for luxury goods, services, recreation, and other goods produced by the manufacturing (secondary) sector and the trade and services (tertiary) sectors increase. As a rough average, primary production, including agriculture, fishing, and forestry, falls continuously from around 50 percent of GNP in the least-developed countries to around 10 percent in the most developed.[3] Meanwhile, industry, including mining, grows from less than 10 percent to 40 percent of GNP. The remainder is accounted for by

---

[3] Hollis Chenery and Moises Syrquin, *Patterns of Development 1950–1970* (London: Oxford University Press, 1975), pp. 20–21; Bruce Herrick and Charles P. Kindleberger, *Economic Development,* 4th ed. (New York: McGraw-Hill Book Co., 1983), p. 81.

utilities, which grow from 5 percent to 10 percent, and services, which grow from 30 percent up to 45 percent then fall back again to 40 percent.

Structural changes within sectors also generally follow a regular pattern. For example, the manufacturing sector of low-income countries is likely to have a predominance of textile and food processing industries, whereas high-income countries have a heavy concentration in the manufacture of machinery and other technologically sophisticated products. The development pattern of a specific country will deviate in varying degrees from the normal pattern deduced from the empirical studies. Yet the normal patterns are still extremely useful in forecasting the growth prospects for industries or products closely related to the sectoral structure of a country.

External Dependence and Economic Integration

The degree to which a country's economy is dependent upon external forces can be another important indicator of the economic environment. The ratio of exports to GNP indicates a national economy's vulnerability to fluctuations in international trade. Thus Hong Kong, with exports representing the equivalent of around 90 percent of GNP, depends to a high degree on economic trends in the countries to which it is exporting. At the other extreme, a nation that has a closed or relatively self-sufficient economy, such as India, has maximum control over its economic future; and the forces influencing such trends will be predominantly domestic.

Another form of external dependence is a country's obligations to service and repay foreign loans. External debt and interest obligations can be compared to foreign exchange earnings as a measure of the capacity to repay. For many less-developed countries, annual public debt service and investment-income payments have risen to very high levels, some representing several hundred percent of foreign exchange earnings (see Box 10–1).[4] A high ratio of debt service to foreign exchange earnings is not necessarily an indication of crisis. The capital inflow may have been invested so as to increase future capacity to repay through increased exports or import substitution.

External dependence is not good or bad per se, but high external dependency means that a careful analysis of external forces must be included in assessing and forecasting a country's future prospects. A high degree of external dependence may mean a high foreign exchange earning capacity and an ability to secure a great deal of external stimulation to internal growth.

Sources of Economic Data

National economic statistics are published regularly by international agencies such as the United Nations, the World Bank, the International Monetary Fund, and the Organization for Economic Cooperation and Development (OECD). Of

---

[4] See section on "Focus on External Debt," *Finance and Development*, March 1987, pp. 2–22.

BOX 10–1
Debt Indicators

Simple ratios that relate a country's external debts to its ability to repay those debts (GNP or exports) are always misleading. However, do not throw them all out of the window. Use some simple precautions such as:

Relate debt to GNP rather than GDP. The latter omits remittances from nationals working abroad, which are sizable for many heavily indebted countries.

Remember that most measures of debt include only loans with an original maturity of more than one year. The true burden of servicing debts is often grossly understated.

Look at the composition of exports. A heavy concentration on a few commodities makes foreign currency earnings vulnerable to violent lurches.

Look at imports to see how much they can be squeezed without suffocating economic growth.

Do not ignore the level of official reserves. Three month's import bill is generally considered a minimum safety margin.

Remember that debt service ratios usually relate to actual rather than scheduled payments of debt. A debt service ratio may be low (good) only because a country has fallen behind on its payments (bad).

Do not be fooled by rising debt ratios over a number of years. It may be because of more comprehensive reporting or from turning (excluded) short-term debt into (included) long-term debt.

Distinguish between interest and principal. A creditworthy country can roll over its principal. Its ability to pay interest is a more appropriate indicator of its ability to remain creditworthy.

Look at the proportion of debt that is on floating rather than fixed interest rate terms. That shows the vulnerability of a country to rises in interest rates.

SOURCE: Extracted from *The Economist,* International Banking Survey, March 20, 1982, p. 99.

particular significance for economic scanning is the monthly OECD publication *Main Economic Indicators,* which provides a picture of recent changes in the economies of member countries. These sources also include data on the performance within individual sectors of economies.

NATIONAL ECONOMIC COMPARISON

Pitfalls in Translation Rates

Special problems arise in making comparisons between countries. Financial data expressed in national currencies must be converted to a common unit. Most commonly, current exchange rates are used to translate measures in local currencies to a common currency unit such as the U.S. dollar or the currency of the enterprise's home country.

Ideally, translations to a common currency should be derived from national currency figures on the basis of purchasing power parities or through direct real-product comparisons. However, such comparative data are available for only a limited number of countries and generally relate to different periods.

Those concerned with economic development have long recognized the deficiencies inherent in the exchange-rate approach to comparative income analysis and have been searching for better ways to compare countries' economic progress. The most ambitious effort undertaken in this area is the UN International Comparison Project (ICP).[5] The ICP has developed a highly sophisticated method for measuring total expenditure, which can be used to derive more reliable and directly comparable estimates of per capita income than previously possible.

The figures produced by this study illustrate how economic differences between countries can be overstated using current exchange rates, especially as between countries in the highest and lowest income categories. When the comparison was based on exchange rates, for example, the U.S. GNP per capita in 1975 exceeded that in India by a ratio of 50:1. But based on a purchasing power parity calculation, this ratio was reduced to 14:1.[6] For developed countries, the differences are much less.[7]

The reason for such different results lies primarily in the divergent price and product structures of different countries. Exchange rates equate at best the prices of only internationally traded goods and services. They may bear little relationship to the prices of goods and services not internationally traded, which in most countries form the large bulk of the total national product. Specifically, the prices of farm products and of services in less developed countries are in most cases considerably lower relative to industrial prices than in the more developed countries. Moreover, agricultural output generally accounts for the major part of overall national output in the LDCs, whereas the opposite is true in developed countries. As a result, the internal purchasing power of the currency of a low-income country will generally be greater than indicated by the exchange rate.

The use of exchange rates for converting national currency data into a common currency is further complicated by the fact that official or par value rates do not always constitute equilibrium rates. Economic history provides countless instances where an overvalued exchange rate has been maintained for a lengthy period of time. A straight conversion on the basis of the overvalued rates would overstate both absolute levels and changes over time. An additional problem arises when no single or unique rate of exchange exists. The international enterprise wishing

---

[5] A good summary of the ICP results is contained in Irving B. Kravis, "Comparative Studies of National Incomes and Prices," *Journal of Economic Literature* 22 (March 1984), pp. 1–39.

[6] See "Technical Note" in *World Bank Atlas* (Washington, D.C.: International Bank for Reconstruction and Development, 1977), p. 31.

[7] See Peter Hill, *Real Gross Product in OECD Countries and Associated Purchasing Power Parities* (Paris: OECD, 1984), p. 15.

to express national data in a selected currency is given the choice of free rates, controlled rates, preferential, basic, auction, nonpreferential rates, and so forth, depending on prevailing national policies.

To the extent that nations follow flexible exchange-rate policies, the problems of multiple and nonequilibrium rates are reduced. But no easy solution exists for the problem of inter-country comparisons.

Pitfalls in Comparability of Statistics

The likelihood of inaccurate perceptions of economic environments is always high because of variation in the concepts, coverage, and quality of national statistics. Also, a country's stage of development can result in statistical biases.

Biases frequently exist in GNP per capita. Although most nations use the same general concept,[8] the extent to which statistical estimates reflect the actual situation in different countries can vary significantly. In less developed countries, levels of economic activity are generally understated. Statistical coverage becomes increasingly comprehensive as economic levels rise and the availability and quality of data improves as a country becomes more affluent and develops more complex institutions and improved record keeping. Moreover, as an economy develops, an increasing share of economic activity passes through the marketplace and is counted as national output. For example, housewives purchase bread instead of baking it themselves.

But not all economic activity is recorded, even in developed countries. High progressive tax rates and other limitations on the accumulation of personal wealth have contributed to the buildup of substantial ''underground economies'' of unrecorded or underrecorded cash, barter, and offshore transactions. Such transactions can account for a significant proportion of an economy's growth.[9] Italy revised 1975–78 figures upward by about 10 percent. France, Germany, Japan, and Sweden have also made upward revisions.

Another statistical peril involves country variations in official definitions. The label ''manufacturing activity'' is an example. French statistics, unlike those of most other nations, include fishing and the quarrying of building materials as manufacturing, whereas wine production is classified as agriculture.

Even where definitions and statistical coverage are similar, statistics can vary greatly in quality among nations, among different items in the same country,

---

[8] This is not true for centrally planned economies. See M. A. Jansen, ''Problems of International Comparisons of National Accounting Aggregates between Countries with Different Economic Systems,'' *Review of Income and Wealth*, March 1973, pp. 69–77.

[9] Vito Tanzi, ''Underground Economy Built on Illicit Pursuits Is Growing Concern of Economic Policymakers,'' *IMF Survey*, February 4, 1980, pp. 34–37; Konstantin Simis, ''Russia's Underground Millionaires,'' *Fortune*, June 29, 1981, pp. 36–50; Adrian Smith, ''The Informal Economy,'' *Lloyd's Bank Review*, July 1981, pp. 45–61; Arne Jon Isachsen and Steiner Strom, ''The Size and Growth of the Hidden Economy in Norway,'' *The Review of Income and Wealth* (March 1985), pp. 21–38.

and among different statistical observations for the same item in a country. Variations in statistical quality among economic sectors result in large part from the
greater difficulty of collecting data in one area as against another. For example,
data on imports and exports are usually the best, while data on agricultural production are the weakest. The high quality of foreign trade statistics results from the
fact that imports and exports generally flow through a limited number of ports
of entry and involve some government surveillance for tax or control purposes.
Contrast this situation with the problem of collecting agricultural data from hundreds
of thousands (or millions) of reporting units widely separated geographically
and from an agrarian social group that frequently has low levels of education
and record-keeping experience.

For the international manager, the degree of error that can be tolerated depends
upon the decision being made. In many situations, a wide margin of error would
not seriously affect a decision. For example, national product estimates for a
country may understate the economic reality. Yet, if the statistical bias is rather
consistent from year to year, the business firm can draw a reasonable conclusion
as to whether a country is expanding and even as to the rate of expansion.
Likewise, cost-of-living data for a given country may be based on observations
in only one or two principal cities but they may provide a reasonable indicator
over time of general trends in price levels.

MACROECONOMIC FORECASTING

For many reasons, the international enterprise may require a deeper assessment
of a country's economic prospects than is involved in economic scanning.

Basic Economic Forecasts

Comprehensive long-range planning studies and economic forecasts are available for most countries and for regions and sectors.[10] Such planning studies
vary immensely in quality and in validity, particularly if prepared under political
control. In addition to local sources, planning studies are frequently available
from international organizations such as the OECD. The World Bank, in particular,
has sent economic survey missions to most of the LDCs, and many of the mission
reports are publicly available.

When acceptable country economic forecasts are not available, the international firm can build its own.[11] Seldom, though, will the international firm require
a comprehensive forecast of an entire economy. Beyond the general trends of

---

[10] Metra Consulting, *Handbook of National Development Plans* (London: Graham and Trotman, 1983).

[11] There is a comprehensive literature on macroeconomic forecasting. For example, see Charles R. Blitzer, Peter B. Clark, and Lance Taylor, eds., *Economy-Wide Models and Development Planning* (London: Oxford University Press, 1975).

economic growth, the usual need will be for specific forecasts of changes in price-levels (i.e., inflation), in the country's external accounts with the rest of the world, and in the international exchange rate for its currency. It must be remembered, however, that macroeconomic variables are not independent of each other. The price level, the balance of payments, and the exchange rate are closely interrelated. While it is possible to forecast each separately, forecasts obtained by examining a complete economic system are more soundly based.

Price-Level Forecasts

Inflationary pressures are of particular significance to the international enterprise because inflation may be the prelude to devaluation of the country's currency in the foreign exchange market. Furthermore, an inflationary environment requires special business strategies.

A standard source for data on past price levels is the monthly *International Financial Statistics* of the International Monetary Fund. For forecasts of future price-level changes, the analyst should also look to changes in monetary and fiscal policy, probable rates of change in labor costs and productivity, as well as any inflationary pressure particular to the country under consideration. Countries dependent on export earnings from raw materials or primary products can experience major inflationary pressures following increases in world prices for their exports.

The forecasting of monetary and fiscal policies is an art in itself. For short-term forecasts of price levels, however, it is possible to gain an indication of whether the quantity of money that the authorities have permitted will have further inflationary impact. Wage increases that outstrip productivity increases can also have a major impact. In developed countries particularly, the processes of wage adjustment can gain a momentum that carries wages upward even with no increase in productivity either before or after the increased wages.

Finally, it is necessary in price-level forecasting to examine the measures used to minimize or neutralize the effects of inflation.[12] Loans, savings accounts, pensions, or other fixed obligations, as well as wages and salaries, can include provisions for cost-of-living adjustments.

Balance-of-Payments Forecasts

The most practical way to proceed in balance-of-payments forecasting is to analyze each item in the balance-of-payments accounts.

Foreign Exchange Earnings Prospects. Future supplies of foreign exchange will depend upon exports of goods; sale of services (including tourism);

---

[12] P. T. Knight, F. D. McCarthy, and S. van Wijnberg, "Escaping Hyperinflation," *Finance and Development* 23 (December 1986), pp. 14–17.

unilateral transfers; and both short- and long-term capital inflows. Forecasting future export prospects involves conventional supply and demand analysis of a country's principal export products and prospective new exports. In the case of traditional exports, an examination of recent trends in both quantity and price of specific exports and growth trends in the principal buyer countries can provide considerable insight into future prospects. Additional considerations will be a country's capacity for increasing the supply of export goods, possible variations in supply conditions due to weather and related conditions, the price and income elasticity of demand for specific products, the competitive position of countries that are alternative sources of supply, and the possibilities for changes in tariff and quota regulations imposed by buyer countries.

Unrequited transfers can be either from foreign governments or from individuals. Foreign exchange inflows from development-assistance grants can be sizable, though the prospects of future flows will depend heavily on political and security policies of donor governments and the availability of resources from international development agencies. Private unrequited transfers are significant for some countries such as Israel, which has received sizable foreign donations; or countries such as Egypt, Turkey, and Greece where nationals have migrated to work in other countries and are sending regular remittances to families remaining at home, representing as much as 50 percent of exports.[13]

Capital inflows will depend on the interest of foreign firms in making direct investments and on the policies of the country toward encouraging or controlling foreign investment. Future prospects for inflows of portfolio investment, loan funds, and short-term deposits attracted by high-interest rates must also be analyzed.

Foreign Exchange Needs.   Set off against the forecast of future foreign exchange availability will be an estimate of foreign exchange needs for imports, for purchases of foreign services, and for servicing foreign debt and the capital accounts. The forecast of import requirements can begin with an analysis and a projection of recent trends in both quantities and prices of principal import items. The projections should then be modified to reflect significant future changes likely to occur. Such a change might be the discovery of new resources that will substitute for imports (for example, petroleum), or a one-time need for large imports of capital goods to initiate a major industrialization project, or a high demand for kinds of goods not being produced within the country stimulated by rapidly rising consumer incomes.

Exchange-Rate Forecasts

Foreign exchange forecasting has already been introduced in Chapter 4. Most textbook treatments of exchange-rate forecasting, however, deal at greater length with various theoretical relationships between national differences in interest

---

[13] Anand G. Chandavarkar, "Use of Migrants' Remittances in Labor-Exporting Countries," *Finance & Development* 17 (June 1980), pp. 36–39.

rates, forecast rates of inflation, and the forward exchange rate. While this literature provides a theoretical base for initial projections of exchange-rate changes, the forecaster must also take into account the motivations and pressures that affect the actions and timing of governments and other parties that may be able to affect exchange rates in the short term.

FORECASTING NATIONAL INSTITUTIONAL ENVIRONMENTS

The international firm may want to extend its investigation into aspects of the institutional environment that are of special importance for the activity being considered. The firm may need to know about local banking and other financial institutions, as well as the extent to which local capital markets operate effectively. Other significant factors may be the role of labor unions and patterns of labor-management relations, the importance of government enterprises and the business fields in which they are operating, the influence of economic planning agencies, the types of business regulation that will be encountered, and patterns of social-welfare programs.

In some situations, an assessment of the institutional environment may heavily influence the firm's decision to invest or initiate operations. For example, the prospective business opportunity may be in a field previously limited to government enterprise that is likely to be privatized. In other situations, assessing the institutional environment may not be critical for the investment decision but of primary importance in shaping the business project and in providing guidance for future operations.

Where rapidly changing dimensions of the institutional environment have to be projected into the future, the forecasting task can be difficult. Techniques for forecasting the institutional environment are not well developed. Furthermore, unlike the situation in economic forecasting, the international firm cannot look to international and national governmental and research organizations for a large flow of institutional forecasting studies.

Yet good forecasts are possible. In some cases, forecasting can be done by an analogy technique whereby patterns in one country can be projected on the basis of patterns in another country at a higher stage of development. Where institutional patterns clearly follow different evolutionary paths in different countries, forecasting will require more speculative techniques. For example, the role played by labor unions and patterns of labor-management relations has followed quite different patterns in Italy, Japan, and the United States. In such situations, the forecasting approach will have to identify in each country the particular factors that have been shaping institutional patterns and then attempt to forecast trends in the underlying factors.

Italian labor unions generally have a political affiliation and play an important, direct political role in the country. Furthermore, many of the issues that are normally resolved in the United States through collective bargaining, such as vacations and pensions, are resolved in Italy through governmental legislation. Consequently, a forecast of labor union patterns in Italy would require that considerable attention be given to the political situation and political trends.

FORECASTING THE DEVELOPMENT PROCESS

Some business firms have long been active in the less developed countries (LDCs) as resource seekers for supplies of petroleum, minerals, and agricultural products such as tea, cane sugar, and bananas. More recently, production-efficiency seekers have established feeder plants in the LDCs to produce textiles, apparel, and electronic components for export to the advanced countries.

As market seekers, international enterprises have shown only modest interest in the LDCs because of their small markets, low income levels, and perceived political risk. Yet the LDCs have most of the world's population, and many of the LDCs are achieving relatively high growth rates. As incomes rise, effective demand rises even faster for the kinds of advanced products that can be supplied by international firms. It is a reasonably safe forecast that the LDCs will have a much greater business attraction for the multinational enterprise in the future than they have had in the recent past.

As most international managers have acquired their international experience in the advanced countries, it is quite likely that their reservoir of experience and knowledge may be inadequate for assessing and forecasting the significantly different economic environments of the LDCs. A few brief comments should suffice to demonstrate the complexity of the development process and the need for considerable expertise on the part of the international enterprise in forecasting the economic conditions.

The LDCs almost universally give top priority to the achievement of rapid economic and social development. The challenge of trying to raise economic levels for such a large share of the world's population has stimulated considerable research on the development process. Theories have been advanced to account for low levels of economic activity, ranging from climate and natural resources endowment to cultural and social factors.[14] The various theories, however, are more complementary than contradictory and are gradually evolving toward a complex explanation that recognizes the need to move on many fronts in order to accelerate economic growth.

In terms of general strategy, the early approach of most nations was to emphasize capital as the prime mover. Increasing savings and stimulating capital

---

[14] The theoretical literature on economic development is vast. For a survey and synthesis, see Gerald M. Meier, *Leading Issues in Economic Development,* 4th ed. (New York: Oxford University Press, 1984); Everett E. Hagen, *The Economics of Development,* 4th ed. (Homewood, Ill.: Richard D. Irwin, 1986). For a different view pertinent to multinational enterprises, see Fernando Henrique Cardoso and Enzo Faletto, *Dependency and Development in Latin America* (Berkeley: University of California Press, 1979).

formation through domestic or foreign means were seen as the principal needs for accelerating economic growth. As experience and understanding increased, development strategies became broader and more complex. Capital continues to be recognized as a crucial bottleneck, but not necessarily the only one. Other issues are emphasized, such as increasing the absorptive capacity of a country for capital flows, the elimination of institutional blocks, investment in human resources, and international technology transfers. Foreign exchange as a constraint has also received considerable attention, leading to an emphasis in many nations on expanding exports and attracting more public and private transfers of capital. In virtually all cases, heavy reliance has been placed on national economic planning and on government enterprise as a source of entrepreneurship.

The development process requires much more than preparing economic blueprints or injecting more capital into a system. Many preconditions for investment must be established in order to secure significant results. Such preconditions may be a mixture of increasing the skills of people, improving the administrative capacity of private and public institutions, creating new technologies, and securing greater efficiency in the operations of political institutions and political decision making in a country. The detailed requirements for a specific country will vary, depending upon resources, the present state of the economic infrastructure such as transportation and communications facilities, soundness of economic policies, and so forth.

In most cases, development-minded countries give great emphasis to industrialization as a means of expanding national productivity and creating new employment. Industrialization strategies vary greatly. In many countries, industrialization policies are first directed toward opportunities for further processing of raw materials normally exported from the country. Import substitution industries will also be encouraged as an easy means of stimulating the industrialization process, because a domestic market will already be available, and because such industries hold the promise of saving foreign exchange. But the growth possibilities for import substitution industries appear to decline after an initial period.[15]

The agricultural sector traditionally receives a great deal of attention because it is generally the largest sector in the LDCs and because productivity is generally low. Land-reform proposals to increase output often face major opposition in this sector.

Conflict among economic, political, and social goals is a general phenomenon. Most countries have less developed regions such as the south of Italy or the northeast of Brazil where, for political reasons, development will have to receive special incentives. Geographic distribution to satisfy political goals may conflict with achieving rapid growth rates. From the social-welfare viewpoint, the issue invariably arises as to how increased economic gains should be distributed between increased consumption and increased investment. On the one hand, there is widespread desire for economic growth to be reflected quickly in improved living

---

[15] See Albert O. Hirschman, "The Political Economy of Import-Substituting Industrialization in Latin America," *Quarterly Journal of Economics,* February 1968, pp. 1–12.

conditions. On the other hand, increased consumption generally means the reduced availability of savings for new investment in further growth.

Conflicts also arise concerning the use of capital-intensive rather than labor-intensive technologies. Most of the LDCs have serious problems of unemployment and underemployment. Thus the preference is for adopting new technologies that will create maximum employment.[16] But in many situations, the only technology options available are capital-intensive ones developed in the advanced countries to fit the needs in such countries. In other cases, where the labor-intensive technology option is available, its adoption may make the enterprise less competitive than if capital-intensive technology is used.[17]

The advanced countries and the international agencies recognize the development gap between the LDCs and the advanced countries as a critical world problem and have established a wide range of governmental programs to transfer financial and technological resources to the LDCs. The United Nations concentrates a major share of its activities on development assistance. The World Bank has become a major multilateral source of development assistance. Many regional development banks such as the Asian Development Bank and the Inter-American Development Bank have also been created as multilateral agencies to support the development efforts of the poor countries.

The specific content and the size of bilateral and multilateral development-assistance programs change as a result of political forces and experience. Yet their importance to the international enterprise should continue. Development-assistance programs can play a key role in determining future economic trends in specific countries and can also be a source of financial resources and other types of support for a wide range of international business projects. The development role that can be played by international enterprise has been well recognized. Thus many development-assistance programs have included specific incentives to encourage the expansion of international business activities, and considerable attention has been devoted to finding ways to expand the flow of foreign private investment that are acceptable to the host countries.

MARKET DEMAND FORECASTING

Collecting the Basic Demand Data

In large part, market-demand forecasting requires the same skills and techniques whether it is directed to domestic markets or foreign markets. But there are differences. The multinational enterprise with a global strategy will want the

---

[16] Guy Pfeffermann, "Men and Machines in Africa," *Finance and Development*, March 1974, pp. 16–19.

[17] R. Hal Mason, "Some Observations on the Choice of Technology by Multinational Firms in Developing Countries," *Review of Economics and Statistics*, August 1973, pp. 349–55; Austin Robinson, ed., *Appropriate Technologies for Third World Development* (London: Macmillan Press Ltd., 1979).

market-demand studies for different countries to be sufficiently standardized so that cross-country comparisons can be made. From the standpoint of cost, relatively inexpensive techniques may be needed so that a large number of potentially interesting market opportunities can be appraised. Longer-range forecasts may also be needed where foreign opportunities involve initiating new operations and require a large commitment of resources, and where a high degree of risk is perceived because of limited familiarity with operations in a new country.

The American firm "going international" may have to make an especially large adjustment in its market-demand forecasting activity. Not only is the United States outstanding in the availability of data from government, trade associations, and other sources, but it has also accumulated an impressive stock of market research studies, market research organizations, and skilled personnel. Furthermore, the flowering of market research in the United States has been aided by a cultural variable that favors considerable openness concerning economic and business information as contrasted to the attitudes of secrecy prevailing in many other countries.

The first place to look for international demand data, therefore, is within the United States. Commercial sources may already have data available. Business International, Frost and Sullivan, and Predicasts are organizations with an extensive library of international market surveys. The U.S. Department of Commerce also makes available a wide range of market surveys prepared on a contract basis by private research organizations or by Commerce Department market research officers abroad.

The market demand for products and services will in many countries result directly or indirectly from governmental programs to expand infrastructure facilities and services such as transportation, electricity, education, housing, and health. In such areas, national government planning work is likely to provide excellent guidelines to future market demand. Where the LDCs are soliciting international financing from agencies such as the World Bank, market studies must normally be prepared as a component of the project proposal submitted for financing. Beware of overoptimistic government figures, however. Governments frequently adopt overambitious spending targets that are not realistic. In times of financial difficulty, LDC governments have tended to reduce spending on production and infrastructure projects by twice as much as they reduce spending on social programs.[18]

In many countries, particularly the LDCs, data problems will arise. Data on actual sales or variables that influence future demand may be outdated, unreliable, or simply not collected. Forecasts will often have to be based on fewer variables than would be desired. In some cases, data and relationships used for forecasting will have to be based on experience in other countries.

Where actual sales are not available for a country, it may be possible to

---

[18] Norman Hicks and Anne Kubisch, "Cutting Government Expenditures in LDCs," *Finance and Development,* September 1984, pp. 37–39.

estimate them from trade and production statistics. The United Nations now pub-lishes import-export data in great detail for most countries.[19] Market demand, also called *apparent consumption,* is estimated by combining local production and imports, and then making adjustments for exports and fluctuations in inventory levels.

Inventory data generally are not available in countries with underdeveloped statistical systems, but one way to compensate for short-term fluctuations is to use longer periods and calculate an annual average or a moving average. The resulting estimate, however, may not indicate current sales rates.

Extrapolating Past Demand Patterns

Market demand can be forecasted simply by extrapolating historical patterns of actual or apparent consumption. Nevertheless, where imports supply a large share of local market demand, an extrapolation of historical apparent consumption may understate future demand if imports have been controlled. Furthermore, when local production replaces imports, domestic demand may increase faster than suggested by import trends, merely because local facilities can provide quicker and more flexible service to customers.

While a straight extrapolation may be valid for a short time period and for a relatively mature economy, it assumes that future trends will follow the patterns of the historical past. This assumption is precarious for a low-income country that is expanding rapidly and undergoing structural changes.

Forecasting with Income Elasticities

In many situations, market-demand forecasting can be partially or wholly based on income elasticities. The concept of income elasticity measures the relation-ship between the change in demand for a product and changes in income. Symboli-cally, the formula below measures the income elasticity for commodity A where Q represents the quantity demanded, Y is the income, and $\triangle$ specifies a change in quantity demanded or income.

$$\frac{\dfrac{\Delta QA}{QA}}{\dfrac{\Delta Y}{Y}}$$

If demand increases at the same rate as income, a product would have an income elasticity of one. If demand increases only half as fast as income, the income elasticity of a product would be 0.5. Goods with values of more than one are income elastic. Goods with values of less than one are income inelastic. Income elasticities have been calculated for individual or family incomes and separately for various levels of income. Where detailed data on family and personal

---

[19] United Nations, *Yearbook of International Trade Statistics* (United Nations, N. Y.).

income distribution are not available, as in many LDCs, income elasticities have been calculated for a country as a whole in relation to average per capita income for the country. In the absence of better market information, the latter form of income elasticities can be a reasonably satisfactory approach to market-demand forecasting.

Market-demand forecasting by the income-elasticities method requires four steps. First, current levels of demand are determined. Second, average per capita income is forecast for the selected future period. Third, income elasticities are determined either from a country's own historical experience or cross-sectionally from the experience of other countries. Finally, future market demand is estimated as current demand times a factor derived by multiplying the projected increase in per capita income and the income elasticity for the commodity. If per capita income is expected to increase by 50 percent in the forecast period and the income elasticity of the product is 1.5, total demand should increase by 75 percent.

Income elasticities are widely used by economic planners for establishing development targets for a country. Consequently, a considerable amount of information has been developed on income elasticities.[20] In general, the empirical information follows the patterns suggested by Engel's law. The income elasticities for food and other necessities are generally less than one and for luxury goods more than one.

Several cautions in the use of income elasticities should be noted. High-income elasticity for a product does not necessarily mean a high-volume market. It merely indicates that demand will increase rapidly as incomes rise. In terms of volume, the large markets in most countries will be in necessities, even though the growth in these markets may be relatively slow. Furthermore, income elasticities indicate a constant relationship between demand changes and income changes. For specific products, such as consumer durables, the demand is likely to increase at an increasing rate after income reaches a certain level.

Prices also affect the elasticities in several ways. If prices in a country for the products of a new industry are relatively high, and if such prices fall as the industries become more mature, demand for such products will increase from a combination of price and income factors. As between countries, prices can vary greatly because of taxes, subsidies, and other factors. Such differences must be taken into account in using income elasticities. Thus, income elasticities are useful guides but not perfect substitutes for specific market research.

Estimating by Analogy

Patterns of demand in the more advanced countries can be used to estimate future market demand in later-developing economies. This approach assumes that product usage moves along a standard path as a country's stage of development

---

[20] Pan Yotopoulos and Jeffrey Nugent, *Economics of Development: Empirical Investigations* (New York: Harper & Row, 1976).

advances. The use of cross-sectional income elasticities to forecast demand is an example of estimation by analogy in this way.

Careful grouping of countries by similar characteristics can provide a basis for more refined comparison than simply grading countries by stage of development as indicated by their GNP per capita. Groupings can be arrived at easily by classifying countries that are reasonably similar over a range of specific characteristics—for example, dependence on agriculture, degree of urbanization, or level of education. Alternatively, the groupings could be arrived at more formally using cluster analysis.[21]

Blind reliance on analogy, however, can result in erroneous estimates. Differences in culture, tastes, and habits that dictate consumption patterns may limit the validity of analogies. Technical advances such as new inventions or substitute products may cause future patterns of consumption in late-developing countries to change sharply from the patterns of presently advanced countries. Price differences among countries—because of import tariffs, for example—can also cause errors. Nevertheless, used with caution, the method can be extremely useful where data are limited.

Regression Analysis

Regression analysis can be a powerful tool in forecasting market demand, especially for countries where data on current demand are scarce. Also, where estimates are made by income elasticities or by analogy, regression analysis provides a basis for checking the reasonableness of estimates.

Regression analysis is simply a statistical technique for determining the relationship between two or more variables. A regression equation can express the quantitative relationship between the demand for a specific product and a gross economic indicator. This relationship can be determined for Country B, or a number of countries, and then applied to Country A in which the firm is interested, even though information on current market demand for the product is not available in Country A. In such a case, the market-demand estimate is based on both regression analysis and analogy, as the relationship discovered for other countries is assumed to be applicable for the country in which the business firm is interested. Regression analysis can also be used, when data on current consumption are available for Country A, to compare market-demand patterns in Country A with the experience in other countries so that future forecasts can be verified or modified.

A linear regression model $(y = a + bx)$ with y as the amount of a product

---

[21] See, for example, S. Prakash Sethi, "Comparative Cluster Analysis for World Markets," *Journal of Marketing Research,* August 1971, pp. 348–54; S. Prakash Sethi and Richard H. Holton, "Country Typologies for the Multinational Corporation: A New Basic Approach," *California Management Review,* Spring 1973, pp. 105–18; and A Coskun Samli, "An Approach for Estimating Market Potential in East Europe," *Journal of International Business Studies* 8 (Fall–Winter 1977), pp. 49–53.

in use per thousand of population and x as per capita GNP is a simple way of predicting demand for consumer durables. More advanced predictions may allow for saturation of the market, life of the product, and replacement rates.[22] The data collection task for developing and for using more complex regression models is substantial. The selection of the minimum number of variables to include in the model requires considerable testing and judgment. For many firms, however, the cost of a solidly developed quantitative estimate of the potential in each market is justified by the need for long-range commitments to expensive production facilities. Detailed forecasts can have the additional benefit of producing information that can be used for guiding marketing and other operations once a project is established in the country being studied.

Input-Output Forecasting

Input-output tables can also be used for market-demand forecasting, particularly for industrial products where much of the demand will be derived from the growth of other industries. Input-output tables have been published for many countries, although many break down an entire economy into only a small number of broad industry groups and cannot provide much detail on specific products.

Conceptually, input-output tables recognize the interrelationships of each sector in an economy to all others (see Table 10-4). The total output of one sector reading across the rows in the transaction table—for example, agriculture— becomes the input of all sectors (including the agricultural sector itself). At the same time, reading down each column, each sector receives its inputs from the other sectors. The input into each sector can then be expressed as a proportion of the total input to give production coefficients, as shown in Table 10-5.

Where input-output tables are sufficiently detailed, one can trace the direct and indirect impact on the demand for one product of changes in demand for the products of other industries. The tables can show the extent to which sales are made to final users or consumed as intermediate goods. Also, input-output tables can provide information on the sectors that are users of the products from another sector. These can differ markedly between countries at different stages of development.

Input-output analysis has its limitations. Inadequate data and the lack of resources have often resulted in tables that are too general or too incomplete to be of great value for specific market-demand forecasting. Also, input-output tables normally use fixed technical coefficients which do not take into account the effects of changes in production processes or in production levels. There could be a variety of other dynamic changes, too.

---

[22] J. Scott Armstrong, "An Application of Econometric Methods to International Marketing," *Journal of Marketing Research* 7 (May 1970), pp. 190-98; Bertil C. Lindberg, "International Comparison of Growth in Demand for a New Durable Consumer Product," *Journal of Marketing Research* 19 (August 1982), pp. 364-71.

TABLE 10-4 Input-Output Transactions Table: Country A

From \ To	Intermediate Demand							Final Demand					Total Demand
	Agriculture	Food Processing	Textiles	Manufacturing	Transportation and Power	Construction	Services	Consumer Expenditures	Government Operations	Exports	Investment	Total	
Agriculture	60	80	40	12	10	8	5	320	—	200	—	520	735
Food processing	5	5	1	2	—	—	2	400	—	150	—	550	565
Textiles	2	3	2	2	—	—	1	80	—	100	—	180	190
Manufacturing	19	13	17	32	15	32	2	150	30	—	—	180	310
Transportation and power	2	3	3	7	—	—	—	65	35	—	—	100	115
Construction	—	—	—	—	—	—	—	—	50	—	80	130	130
Services	2	1	2	5	—	—	—	20	5	—	5	30	40
Value added:													
Wages and salaries	570	345	50	190	80	85	20	—	10	—	50	60	1,400
Imports	50	80	60	30	—	—	—	180	20	—	100	300	520
Profits, interest, depreciation, and taxes	25	35	15	30	10	5	10	—	—	—	10	10	140
Total value added	645	460	125	250	90	90	30	1,215	150	450	245	2,060	2,060
Total output	735	565	190	310	115	130	40						2,085

TABLE 10–5 Input-Output Production Coefficients: Country A

	Agriculture	Food Processing	Textiles	Manufacturing	Transportation and Power	Construction	Services
Agriculture	.082	.142	.210	.039	.087	.062	.125
Food Processing	.006	.009	.005	.006	—	—	.050
Textiles	.003	.005	.011	.006	—	—	.025
Manufacturing	.026	.022	.089	.103	.130	.246	.050
Transportation and power	.003	.005	.016	.023	—	—	—
Construction	—	—	—	—	—	—	—
Services	.003	.002	.011	.016	—	—	.500
Wages and salaries	.775	.611	.263	.613	.696	.654	—
Imports	.068	.142	.316	.097	—	—	—
Profits, interest, depreciation and taxes	.034	.062	.079	.097	.087	.038	.250
Total output	1.000	1.000	1.000	1.000	1.000	1.000	1.000

SUMMARY

International firms require assessments and forecasts of individual economies and their market demands for a variety of reasons and with varying requirements for precision and comparability. All the conventional limitations of forecasting the future that exist in domestic economic forecasting carry over in forecasting the economic dimensions of the international business environment. In addition, great variations in national patterns plus the influence of the inter-nation economic framework make the task more complex and difficult.

The forecasting of structural changes can be of major significance for a specific type of international business activity. This may require the forecasting of differential growth rates for different sectors of the economy. As the economic structure of national economies is certain to change with economic growth, an extrapolation of past trends would be almost certain to give misleading forecasts for the future. Analogies with other countries at a higher stage of development are one basis for such structural forecasting.

To the extent that national economies and markets are dependent upon external economic considerations—foreign markets or inflows of private investment or external development assistance—the economic forecasts will have to examine carefully such external forces and external future prospects.

In a growing number of countries, government planning reports or available market research studies can supply the international firm with sufficient information on which it can decide whether or not it will undertake a detailed business opportunity analysis for the country. In other situations, particularly in LDCs, the firm will need to make its own market-demand studies, using techniques that are not too costly and that can produce reasonable results where the availability of data is limited.

A number of such techniques have been suggested. In general, they make use of analogies and methods that relate the market demand for a product to one or more general economic or demographic indicators. As a subsequent step, in-depth field surveys will be required to examine the competitive and operating environment that the international firm will encounter in the promising markets.

EXERCISES AND DISCUSSION QUESTIONS

1. As an exercise in macroeconomic scanning, rank the first five African nations with a population of 1 million or more in terms of the total size of their economy. In terms of growth rates in per capita GNP, what are the five fastest growing Asian economies with a population of 1 million or more?
2. According to the normal pattern, what would you expect industry's contribution to total GNP to be in France, Malaysia, and Brazil? How do these expected patterns compare with the actual structure?
3. Would you have considered establishing operations in a country such as Brazil, experiencing high and increasing annual rates of inflation up to 1986? Why or why not? (Note that real GNP expanded at an average annual rate of 4 percent from 1973 to

1985.) If inflation were dramatically reduced along with growth and employment, would this make Brazil more attractive?

4. "A country may have a trade surplus, but still have an increasingly serious balance-of-payments deficit because of capital outflows or rising remittances. Careful assessment must be made of short-term versus long-term outflows." Discuss.

5. "Whatever the causes, rapid increases in prices mean a currency is depreciating internally—and an external depreciation may become necessary." Discuss. Under what circumstances would domestic inflation *not* lead to devaluation?

6. Compile a list of sources of economic and market data for a specified African nation other than South Africa.

7. Country A's GNP rose from $6 billion by a further $550 million during 1987 and its steel consumption, all imported, rose by 400,000 tons to 3.8 million tons. Population also increased from 10 million to 10.4 million. What is the income elasticity of demand for steel? Do you think this would provide a very accurate indicator for predicting steel usage over the ensuing five years?

8. Select a LDC (less-developed country) and for either textiles or metal manufactures determine the forecasting methods you think would have been most appropriate for forecasting demand at each of two dates within the last 20 years, separated by at least five years.

9. "It may be true that all European countries are travelling the same road towards what has been called salvation through industrialization and it may be possible, therefore, to forecast some of the probable changes in living habits as the process continues. Even so, there are still great differences between one place and another, between one nation and another, and in the rates at which they change. These differences reveal themselves in a great diversity of what people will buy. Economic development is certainly affecting culture and customs, habits and attitudes, traditions and mentality; but these, in turn, are reacting on what is going on in the economy—in production, consumption, and distribution. You may detect the general trend; but look around Western Europe and you will discover all sorts of subtle variations in the speed and character of the change. Here the emancipation of women may be moving more slowly. There peasant and aristocratic attitudes may persist."

   In the light of this extract, what types of products would you expect to follow dissimilar demand patterns over time in European countries? Of these, would you expect a country's past demand to provide a better basis for predicting demand than analogies with other countries at a more advanced stage?

10. Give your own definition of the market saturation point for a consumer durable, such as washing machines, and explain why the level may vary from country to country.

11. "Comparison of either total demand or per capita demand for different countries may be misleading for the purposes of formulating a global strategy, particularly if major variations occur within countries." Elaborate on this statement and suggest how the problem might be overcome.

12. You would expect to find some relationship between a country's demand for medical drugs and the numbers of doctors and hospital beds in the country. What other indicators might be used for forecasting the level of drug purchases? As the basis for a global marketing plan how would you go about predicting a country's spending on drugs five years hence?

13. Explain how demand for the output of a primary industry might be forecast using an input-output table. What are the limitations in the input-output method?

Organization of the Multinational

SUMMARY
EXERCISES AND DISCUSSION QUESTIONS

The organization structure of a firm doing business internationally is a vital determinant of success. It must provide an effective decision-making process and a smooth flow of communications between various parts of the enterprise. And because of the many special elements in international operations an organizational structure designed for purely domestic business is usually unsuitable for multinational operations.

The organization structures used by international firms are as diverse as the strategies they have been following in achieving growth abroad.[1] Few, if any, are identical; and no simple criteria exist for selecting the best organizational form. Yet a number of useful guidelines exist for resolving the organization problems as a firm develops from a domestic to a multinational enterprise.

STATUTORY AND MANAGERIAL ORGANIZATIONS

The international enterprise encompasses two distinct but interwoven component structures: the statutory, or legal, organization, and the managerial organization. The statutory organization exists on paper only. It is designed to conform to legal requirements while best meeting the objectives of the firm, for example, minimization of commercial restrictions or taxation. The managerial organization may cut right across the statutory structure and is concerned with the authority and responsibility of each executive and their lines of communication. It is also concerned with the information that flows along these lines of communication and the procedures for channeling and processing the information.

The statutory organization defines the legal and ownership structure that links the parent company with its various units. Each unit may have a different statutory status—branch, subsidiary, holding company, and so forth—depending in part on the legal requirements of the local jurisdiction. Holding companies in low-tax areas have often been used for the statutory organization but rarely serve as the operating center. In fact, some statutory centers consist of only a part-time local lawyer and a mail clerk. Thus, the statutory and managerial structures must be considered as separate entities. The lawyers and tax experts will be primarily responsible for designing the statutory structure. The international manager will be involved mainly in the design and function of the managerial structure—the subject of the rest of this chapter.

---

[1] See, for example, Michael G. Duerr and John M. Roach, *Organization and Control of International Operations* (New York: The Conference Board, 1973); Business International, *New Directions in Multinational Corporate Organization* (New York, 1981); John M. Stopford and Louis T. Wells, Jr., *Managing the Multinational Enterprise* (New York: Basic Books, 1972); Stanley M. Davis, *Managing and Organizing Multinational Corporations* (New York: Pergamon Press, 1979).

EVOLUTIONARY STAGES OF MULTINATIONAL ORGANIZATION

The evolution of the organizational structure of an enterprise can be viewed as a series of stages, with each stage a modification or adaptation of the structure in the previous stage. The speed of the process varies from company to company. Some tread cautiously and take one step at a time, whereas others rush through certain stages and bypass other stages.[2]

In the early stages of entering foreign markets through exports, a company may use an independent trading company. As foreign sales increase, the enterprise may establish an export department with some medium-level company official as export manager. Still concentrating on exports, the firm may go further and set up its own sales, service, and warehousing facilities abroad.[3] In the early stages, the basic organizational structure of the firm is left undisturbed.

Japanese firms, in entering foreign markets through exports, have been able to rely on the giant Japanese trading companies *(sogo shosha)* instead of forming their own export departments.[4] The Japanese general trading firms have few comparable counterparts in other countries. Their basic business is foreign trade, and they can handle many of the international business functions that U.S. and European companies normally perform for themselves. While there are several thousand trading companies, the nine largest handled 44 percent of Japan's exports and 68 percent of its imports in 1985.[5] Some Japanese firms, such as the major automobile and consumer electronics companies, have followed an evolutionary pattern similar to that of U.S. companies. Their products required consumer service facilities and other specialized attention that the giant trading companies could not provide.

As international operations change from exporting to a mix of exporting, licensing, and foreign production and become of more than incidental importance to the firm, conflicts of interest arise between internal units of the firm that are not easily handled by an export department type of organization. The export department may fail to recognize a need to establish production facilities in areas served by exports. Or it may prefer to continue with exports because foreign production may mean a loss of export sales attributed to the department. The usual organizational response by U.S. companies to such conflicting interests has been to create a full international division, which includes the previously independent export unit.

Some companies pass through an intermediate stage where the firm acts only as a holding company for largely autonomous foreign subsidiaries, without

---

[2] Stopford and Wells, *Managing the Multinational Enterprise,* p. 11.

[3] See James Greene, *Organizing for Exporting* (New York: National Industrial Conference Board, 1968).

[4] See Kiyoshi Kojima and Terutomo Ozawa, *Japan's General Trading Companies* (Paris: OECD, 1984).

[5] *The Wall Street Journal,* March 31, 1986.

making any significant changes in the organizational structure of the remainder of the company. It occurs where foreign ventures are first established, not as a result of planning but in response to a specific threat or opportunity. Because such first ventures are small, and because the parent firm has little international experience to contribute to the new foreign ventures, foreign managers are allowed virtually unlimited powers of decision and action. As one study explains, "The need for learning exceeds the desire for control."[6] The subsidiary will have loose financial ties to the parent financial officer, but its operating freedom will be great so long as the financial results of the venture are satisfactory.

The autonomous subsidiary phase may have a short life, particularly if the foreign units grow rapidly and accumulate significant resources. As their significance to the total enterprise increases, the international experience that the subsidiary has brought to the parent firm enables it to design and implement controls with more assurance. Furthermore, the prospects of economic gain from coordinating the foreign subsidiaries will generate pressures for organizational changes that permit a greater central control over the subsidiaries' decision making.

The establishment of an international division, generally of equal status to other major divisions, normally results from four factors. First, the international commitment of the firm has reached an absolute size and a relative importance within the enterprise to justify an organizational unit headed by a senior manager. Second, the complexity of international operations requires a single organization unit that can resolve within it such conflicts as the best means for entering foreign areas based on a broad view of the firm's international opportunities. Third, the firm has recognized the need for internal specialists to deal with the special features of international operations. And finally, the enterprise wants to develop an affirmative capability for scanning the global horizon for opportunities or competitive threats rather than simply responding to situations that are presented to the company.

As Clee and Sachtjen have observed, "The really decisive point in the transition to world enterprise is top management recognition that, to function effectively, the ultimate control of strategic planning and policy decisions must shift from decentralized subsidiaries or division locations to corporate headquarters, where a worldwide perspective can be brought to bear on the interests of the total enterprise."[7] Unless all components of the enterprise are judged on their performance worldwide, they will not be motivated to act in accordance with the worldwide interests of the enterprise.

At the global stage, responsibility for both foreign and domestic business is moved to the top echelons and new subdivisions are specified on either a functional, regional, or product basis. A simple global structure, however, is not the final stage in the development of organizational structures for a multinational

---

[6] Stopford and Wells, *Managing the Multinational Enterprise,* p. 20.

[7] Gilbert H. Clee and Wilbur M. Sachtjen, "Organizing a Worldwide Enterprise," *Harvard Business Review,* November–December 1964, p. 67.

enterprise. Simple global structures are based on the management principle of unity of command: one man having sole responsibility for a specified part of the business, either subdivided by function, product, or geographic areas, and accountable to a single superior officer. But the conflicting need for coordinating function, product, and geographic areas can still remain a serious problem. Some firms have adopted more complex structures in which managers have dual or multiple reporting relationships and where area, function, and product responsibilities overlap.

THE NATIONAL SUBSIDIARY STRUCTURE

In a national subsidiary structure, each foreign subsidiary reports directly to the president or main board of the parent, without intermediate layers of management either at regional headquarters or international division headquarters. In some cases, subsidiary management reports only to its local board of directors, although the parent company is usually represented on that board, and the parent company president may also be the subsidiary president.[8] The pattern is illustrated in Figure 11–1.

This pattern gives the subsidiary a considerable degree of autonomy. While there may be legal autonomy, however, in managerial terms there will usually be some common reporting and conferral requirements.[9] But headquarters' units will not have direct responsibility for the subsidiary, its functions, or its product sections.

The national subsidiary structure has been more common for European multinationals than for United States multinationals, which have tended to adopt it only as a passing phase. The structure of some of the European multinationals evolved before modern communications made a closely integrated organization possible. Others built from a small home-country market and from an early stage treated the foreign operations as of equal importance with the home unit.[10]

Strengths

Individual country affiliates can work as independent, responsible enterprises within their individual environments. They can make many decisions at the national level and adjust rapidly and with utmost sensitivity to local markets and governments. Local ownership is most easily accommodated with this structure, and it

---

[8] Jacques Picard, "Organizational Structures and Integrative Devices in European Multinational Corporations," *Columbia Journal of World Business* 15 (Spring 1980), pp. 30–35.

[9] G. Garnier, T. N. Osborn, F. Galicia, and R. Lecon, "Autonomy of the Mexican Affiliates of U.S. Multinational Corporations," *Columbia Journal of World Business* 14 (Spring 1979), pp. 78–90.

[10] See Hans Schollhammer, "Organizational Structures of Multinational Corporations," *Academy of Management Journal,* September 1971, pp. 345–65; Andrew J. Lombard, Jr., "How European Companies Organize Their International Operations," *European Business,* July 1969, p. 37; and Lawrence G. Franko, *The European Multinationals* (London: Harper & Row, 1976), chap. 7.

FIGURE 11–1   A National Subsidiary Structure

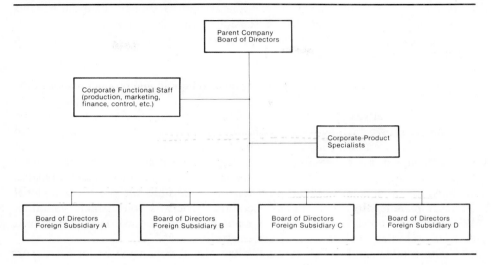

also permits a more complete career structure for local nationals within their own country. Local ownership and the use of nationals as managers can also reduce local tension against multinationals.

The individual affiliate's problems are directly visible at the highest levels of the multinational and less likely to be subordinated to the concerns of an intermediate regional, product, or functional layer. The advantages for top management of direct involvement at a country level are also marked. If parent company board members each hold responsibility for particular affiliates, they can bring multiple international perspectives built from direct experience into the highest decision-making levels. Direct top management involvement both elevates the importance of the local management and assists immeasurably in contacts and negotiations with senior government officials of the affiliate's country.

Weaknesses

Direct access to top management can, on the other hand, be a disadvantage. Top management's time can be used inefficiently; or, in the case of smaller affiliates, important questions can get completely overlooked. When an affiliate's top management interacts with numerous functional and product specialists at headquarters on a whole range of issues, there is also a danger of completely diffusing responsibility for international issues. The introduction of a regional level into the international organization can avoid most of these problems.

One potential weakness often claimed for the subsidiary structure is that decisions will tend to be taken in the light of the subsidiaries' particular horizons and individual interests. Instead of maximizing the worldwide performance of the overall system, the units will suboptimize. There are likely to be benefits to the multinational enterprise as a whole that are not perceived by the individual units.[11] There are ways, however, for central staff to arrange for these benefits to be translated into rewards to the subsidiary for taking the preferred action. So long as corporate staff can see the benefits clearly, there is an internal price mechanism for expressing them.

THE INTERNATIONAL DIVISION STRUCTURE

A representative organization diagram for a firm using an international division structure is shown in Figure 11–2. The international division is usually headed by a vice president who reports directly to the president or chief executive of the company. Some enterprises form a separate international company headed by a president, which plays essentially the same role as an international division. In most cases, the international division is responsible for policy and global strategic planning for international operations. There is considerable variation, however, in administrative practices for maintaining links between the international activities and the domestic side of the enterprise.

The international division usually has direct responsibility for all export and licensing activities of the parent company and is accountable, directly or indirectly, for the operations of overseas manufacturing and sales units. Its task is to coordinate all the international activities so as to raise the level of performance above that likely where subsidiaries are autonomous and other international functions, such as exporting and licensing, are dispersed within the firm. The division may be able to reduce the cost of capital for a subsidiary by borrowing in some other area or in international capital markets. It can transfer experience among subsidiaries. It may be able to reduce tax liability through transfer-pricing policies. In brief, it has responsibility for improving total performance through the unification or synergy potentials of multinational operations.

At an early stage, the corporate staff groups, except for finance and control, are likely to continue to be domestically oriented. The international division will rely mainly on its own staff. As policy and strategic planning shift to the corporate level, the marketing, manufacturing, research, personnel, and other corporate staff will become internationally oriented. Both patterns can occur while maintaining the international division or international company structure.

Strengths

For the firm extending its activities internationally from a large domestic market such as the United States that has dominated the company's attention, the international division provides an organizational umbrella for all foreign activi-

---

[11] Gunnar Hedlund, "Organization In-Between: The Evolution of the Mother-Daughter Structure of Managing Foreign Subsidiaries in Swedish MNCs," *Journal of International Business Studies* (Fall 1984), pp. 109–23.

FIGURE 11–2   An International Division Structure

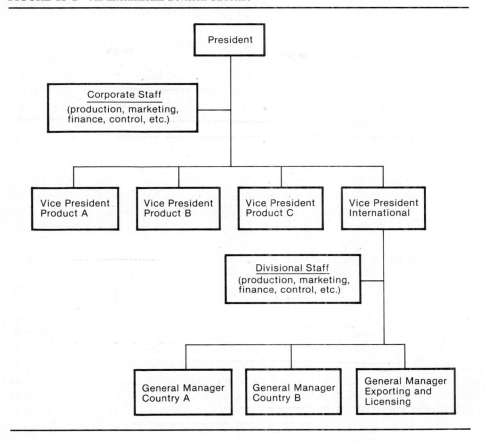

ties and a focus for learning about international operations. It permits centralized direction of a company's foreign operations, particularly during the developmental and expansion stages of the international program. It concentrates international know-how and skills in a separate unit detached from domestic responsibilities and makes possible a concentrated drive on market expansion and investment overseas.

Internationally experienced executives developed in an international division can be a positive strength to a company needing to make a rapid international impact. The team specializes in international issues and develops a multinational way of thinking and coordinating that would be difficult to create without this specialization. The skills built up in this way are also valuable when international staff is transferred to a domestic division.

An international division adds a champion of foreign activities to the top-management echelons and a strong voice for allocating the necessary resources.

Where the division has been built alongside an existing product organization, moreover, international also becomes an impartial arbiter between product divisions.

From a competitive strategy viewpoint, perhaps the major advantage of creating an international division is that it can overcome product divisions erecting a mental fence around the domestic market and failing to plan their strategy globally. Not all international divisions develop a strategic approach; but the need to decide which markets should be developed, and when, usually demands at least a cursory comparison with global competitors.

Weaknesses

Where the products manufactured or sold abroad are the products developed at home, as is normally the case, the international division is heavily dependent on the domestic product divisions. The international division normally does not have its own product development, engineering, and research and development staff, and the domestic divisions controlling these important components of the overseas operations are frequently reluctant to give priority to foreign needs because they are measured solely by their domestic performance. Thus the international division depends heavily on communication and cooperation procedures that are worked out with the domestic product divisions for making the specialized skills of the domestic units available to the international operations. As product divisions become more familiar with international needs, the effectiveness of the communication and cooperation devices can improve. But the inherent conflict between the goals of the domestic and international divisions is never completely eliminated.

There is always some conflict between international and domestic divisions on transfer pricing; this would not occur if domestic divisions were able to operate globally and receive directly the benefit of sales in foreign markets. This conflict may exist even if the transfer pricing rules adopted do in fact benefit the total multinational system.

Specialization and separate accountability often lead to a failure to use managerial know-how and potential to the utmost. Underutilized skills may rest in domestic divisions and never be turned to international problems they have already coped with domestically.

There is also the problem of product divisions forming a coalition against the international division. Not infrequently, the international division may be growing more rapidly than domestic divisions—on the back of the domestic experience—and may even become much larger than several of the domestic divisions combined. In such a situation, product division heads have sometimes formed a coalition to obtain more resources for their own growth. In some cases, product divisions go even further and instigate a move to break up the international division to allocate its growth and power across the product divisions.

The international division has constraints on its ability to assist the foreign subsidiaries. As a division, it normally does not have the resources to develop detailed knowledge about the environments and characteristics of large numbers of local areas and must heavily delegate direct operating responsibilities to the foreign subsidiaries. In general, the amount of decentralization will vary with the particular functions involved, product characteristics, the degree of expertise accumulated at the divisional level, the local competitive situation, and the time taken to refer matters to the division. Firms with a narrow line of mature goods with relatively stable technologies and markets, for example, tend to move farther in the direction of centralization than firms expanding into many different markets with diversified lines of new products involving rapidly changing technologies.

The fact that the international division structure remains dominant in many U.S. multinational companies, despite a strong move toward global structures and matrix arrangements, suggests that many firms have been able to work out informal arrangements or formal devices for resolving the problems inherent in dividing the international unit from the rest of the company. One outstanding example is the International Business Machines Corporation (IBM), which continues to handle its extensive international operations through its separate IBM World Trade Corporation while integrating basic research, product development, and manufacturing activities on a worldwide basis.

THE FUNCTIONAL STRUCTURE

The functional organization structure for international operations was the traditional form used by European companies. The division of responsibility at headquarters is organized by functions such as marketing, manufacturing, and finance; and the heads of these divisions have worldwide responsibilities as line executives (see Figure 11–3). The marketing or sales division, for example, has worldwide marketing responsibility, with direct control over all sales companies and distributors, wherever located. In addition, the division normally has staff responsibility for coordinating the marketing of manufacturing subsidiaries, which usually control sales of the goods they produce, except for exports that are handled directly by the marketing division. The manufacturing division usually has line control over domestic plants, staff responsibility for worldwide product standardization, product development, quality control, and research and development; and a mixture of staff responsibility over the foreign manufacturing subsidiaries.

Strengths

The functional structure has the advantage of concentrating management attention on the internal functions. If these are carried through well on a global scale, they may provide the key to advantage over competitors and, hence, strategic success. The structure is most appropriate for a company with a fairly narrow product line that has reached a rather stable plateau of global coverage and demand and does not face major changes in competitive attack. Mintzberg refers to this class of organization as a "machine bureaucracy," arguing, "Bureaucracy has become a dirty word. Yet this is the configuration that gets the products out

FIGURE 11–3   A Functional Organization Structure

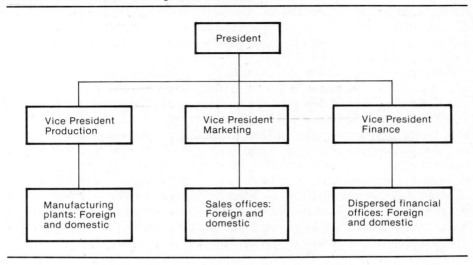

cheaply and efficiently.''[12] Knowledge and experience in the functional fields is concentrated and applied to the firm's activities and operations in all regions and product lines. One study of 92 U.S. multinationals from the *Fortune* 500 disclosed 10 operating a worldwide functional organization. They were all raw materials extractors, with heavy capital investment and 100% ownership of subsidiaries. Their key strategic need seemed to be coordination among functions.[13]

This structure enables a relatively small group of officers to maintain line control over an organization without much duplication. There is, moreover, no conflict between profit centers. The functional specialists at any level can devote their full attention to overall profitability of the organization as related to their specialist function.

Weaknesses

The disadvantages of a functional organization may quickly outweigh the advantages for a multinational with multiple product lines. The functional specialists either would need to have expertise in each product line or would have to specialize by product line within functions. This latter alternative would be unwieldy unless the organization moved to a product structure and grouped the functions by product line.

---

[12] Henry Mintzberg, "Organization Design: Fashion or Fit," *Harvard Business Review* 59 (January–February 1981), p. 109.

[13] John D. Daniels, Robert A. Pitts, and Marietta J. Tretter, "Strategy and Structure of U.S. Multinationals: An Exploratory Study," *Academy of Management Journal* 27:2 (1984), pp. 292–307.

FIGURE 11-4   A Regional Structure

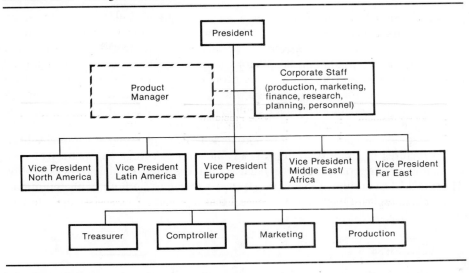

Another basic weakness is that sales and production tend to become separated in their objectives. Disputes that arise between production in one country and sales in several others, for example, would have to go to the highest levels for adjudication. Also, general managers of foreign subsidiaries may find themselves reporting to more than one person. Some European firms that have grown rapidly, have experienced difficulties with the hazy responsibility assignments of this organizational form and with breakdowns in the informal lines of communication and reporting.[14]

Finally, the structure results in tremendous duplication with regard to environmental inputs. Each of the functional divisions may need its own regional specialists and could be making different assumptions about future trends in the various areas of operations.

THE REGIONAL STRUCTURE

Under a regional structure, the primary operational responsibility is assigned to area managers, each being responsible for a specific region of the world, as shown in Figure 11-4. Corporate headquarters retains responsibility for worldwide strategic planning and control. Where the regional form of organization has replaced the international division in U.S. companies, the United States becomes simply one of a number of world markets. Each regional division has responsibility for all functions within its area and is able to coordinate marketing, production, finance, and so forth, within its region.

---

[14] Lombard, "How European Companies Organize International Operations," p. 38.

Strengths

The regional structure tends to give greater emphasis to the country subsidiary as an important profit center and as a unit for which product attributes and other elements of the marketing mix must be adapted. The structure is particularly appropriate where marketing adaptations require modest levels of technological skill. It is also a good structure where economies of scale in production call for a region-sized unit for basic production with minor feature, packaging, and communication adaptation for individual country markets. Food, pharmaceutical, and oil companies are examples of firms with these product characteristics.

A regional structure offers an improvement over functional or national subsidiary structures in simplifying top management's task. Regional matters of less-than-strategic importance can be dealt with more quickly and knowledgeably. There is also an argument that regional expertise can be built up, with appropriate regional strategies. Others, however, feel that regional cohesion is more a mirage than a reality.

Weaknesses

When the firm has a diverse product range, the regional structure does not easily handle the tasks of coordinating product variations, transferring new product ideas and production techniques from one country to another, and optimizing the flow of product from source to worldwide markets. One organizational response has been to create a global product manager at the corporate level with worldwide responsibilities for particular products or product lines. This requires molding a global product strategy and facilitating the transfer of experience from one area to another. But the operating relationships between the global product manager and the area managers who have line responsibility are likely to be ambiguous.

A regional structure usually requires a large number of internationally experienced executives to staff the various regional headquarters. It may result in too much information being screened from corporate headquarters and undue focus placed on the performance of the specific regions as opposed to the company's worldwide interest. It may also require considerable duplication of functional and product specialists within the enterprise. This can be very costly.

The very idea of regional identification, though, is perhaps the biggest handicap. A business that is large enough to have regions is in global competition. For this it needs a global strategy and does not want to have to fight to impose such a strategy on regional executives who are busy molding a regional character. All manner of barriers are likely to build between strong regions. When it comes to building one worldwide plant for some item, regional differences in standards, transfer pricing, and other internal bureaucracy may be difficult to surmount.

THE PRODUCT DIVISION STRUCTURE

The product division structure assigns worldwide product responsibility to product division executives as the primary line managers (see Figure 11–5). Overall goals and strategies for the company are set at corporate headquarters and, within

FIGURE 11–5   A Product Division

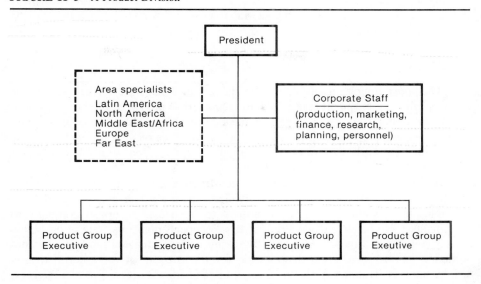

these corporate guidelines, the plans of each product group are reviewed and approved by top management. Each product group, however, has primary responsibility for planning and controlling all activities for its products on a worldwide basis. It is usual to have a top layer of functional staff management but less common to have a layer of regional specialists as indicated in the diagram. When this layer is added, their function is to provide area expertise and coordinate activity for all products in their area.

Strengths

The product structure works best when a company's product line is widely diversified, when products go into a variety of end-use markets, and when a relatively high technological capability is required. It is also advantageous when high shipping costs, tariffs, or other considerations dictate local manufacture of the product. The structure puts a prime emphasis on product market and production know-how, aiming at its exploitation worldwide. There is no conflict between domestic and foreign operation as with the international division structure, and those with skills are in a worldwide unit for exploiting those skills.[15]

The concept of global market performance comes through almost automatically with this structure. Certainly, if competition is attacking on a product front globally and picking individual country markets in which to do so—the product division

---

[15] See James R. Basche, Jr., *Shifting Patterns in International Organizations: U.S. Experiences in the 1970s* (New York: The Conference Board, September 1978), p. 10.

executive is in a position to see it and to react. There is perhaps more tendency, too, to look for international segments, and to design new products against markets other than the home market.

Weaknesses

The most important problem with the product structure is that worldwide responsibility is frequently assigned to managers with great product expertise whose experience has been largely domestic. Similar problems can arise at all levels when the personnel assigned are selected because of their product expertise and many have little experience and capability for dealing with the new kinds of problems that arise out of international operations.

Another problem inherent in the product structure is the difficulty of coordinating the activity of different product divisions in any given area. Suppose, for example, that Product Division A wanted to license a European company to manufacture Product A, while Product B's European plant was operating below capacity and could avoid a loss only by taking on an additional product. Without someone on the local scene responsible for the success of the enterprise as a whole, the two divisions might be unaware of each other's needs. Product Division A would incur the unnecessary expense of licensing the European plant. Product Division B would take a loss. The company as a whole would suffer.

The local coordination problem and the problem of weak local knowledge is partially overcome with the addition of some sort of country management. These managers do not have profit responsibility under this structure, however. They report to the appropriate product divisions for their shares of the local activity and perhaps to an area staff specialist for their "janitorial" role in maintaining the local presence.

Multidivisional plants are a classic problem under the product division structure. Allocation of costs and capacity can be a particular headache if there are major fluctuations in the demand for different products. One way out is to base any plant firmly within one division and have it operate on an arm's-length basis in contracting for the supply requirements of other divisions.

MATRIX STRUCTURES

A matrix organization is structured as a grid with intersecting responsibilities. There is a dual rather than a single chain of command and some managers report to two bosses rather than to one boss. It requires a move away from the traditional hierarchy of power and unity of command of the single-dimension structures to a balance of power and sharing of responsibility.

There are three roles in a matrix organization that differ from those in single-dimension structures. First, there are the managers who report to two different matrix bosses; then there are the matrix managers who share subordinates; and, finally, there is the top manager who must head the dual structure and balance and adjudicate disagreement. For each of these roles there are special requirements.

Matrix management is not new. It has been with organizations for 50 years since the matrix concept of brand managers and product managers first began developing in U.S. consumer goods firms.[16] There is, therefore, a great deal of expertise in managing matrices and developing their strengths. What is more recent, however, is the movement to incorporate matrices at a much higher level in multinational firms. The scale of the matrix is immediately enlarged many times.[17]

Most multinational firms that have adopted a matrix structure have organized with dual reporting along product and regional lines, where the region can be a national subsidiary, a world region, or international versus domestic. There is not just one matrix structure, however; combinations of two or even the three dominant dimensions of function, product, and region can be arranged at a variety of levels.

The structure adopted by General Electric Company is a good example of a product-regional matrix, as illustrated by this comment on how its strategic business units (SBU) plan product and country strategies:

> General Electric Company effectively joins product-related and geographic concerns. The firm is working toward a product SBU organization in which each SBU has worldwide strategic planning responsibility. GE has identified a number of priority countries. Each product SBU head sets forth what he plans to accomplish in each country within a certain time frame. The country executive develops a comprehensive country opportunity plan to cover all products and strategies. This is a difficult task, because the country manager lacks the expertise to decide authoritatively what is optimal for each product and strategy—but it is important that he contribute to the planning effort. The country plan is then compared with the individual product SBU plans for that country. The outcome is a merging of informational and strategic input from both sources. Conflicts are identified and proposals made for their solution. Some conflicts may be resolved at the country level, others at the area or even the sector level. Each party may push issues up its relevant hierarchy for higher-level review.[18]

Strengths

Each matrix pattern will have its own strengths and weaknesses according to the combination of dimensions adopted. There are, however, general strengths and weaknesses of the matrix approach.

The case for adoption of a matrix is strongest when there are strong pressures along more than one dimension simultaneously; and failure to take a dimensional pressure into account could be disastrous for the firm's performance. This is

---

[16] See, for example, Gordon H. Evans, *The Product Manager's Job* (New York: American Management Association, 1964).

[17] Thomas H. Naylor, *The Corporate Strategy Matrix* (New York: Basic Books, Inc., 1986), pp. 202–38.

[18] Business International, *New Directions in Multinational Corporate Organization*, p. 132.

precisely the situation for multinationals facing aggressive competitive attack through product or process-technology and at the same time strong pressures from individual countries to adapt to national objectives. The firm is torn between its product strategy and its global location strategy. If the firm under these pressures organizes on a single geographical dimension, the sum of the geographical units may not add up to maintaining its competitive performance. Alternatively, if the firm organizes on a product division basis, the growing country pressures may not be seen as they develop and the firm may find its global strategy crimped by loss of a market to a competitor or even expropriation of assets.

Under a matrix structure, the two viewpoints can be continually monitored and compared. Doz and associates describe the process well:

> Some managers, attuned to local needs and sensitive to the power of host governments and national interest groups, favor, on almost any issue, more subsidiary autonomy and greater freedom in responding to national demands. Other managers, more concerned with worldwide competitive strategies, strive to increase coordination and integration across geographic boundaries. In trying to gain power and in defending their own areas of responsibility, these managers unearth different facts, analyze them differently, and propose different strategic decisions. By confronting conflicting views constructively the organization can learn.[19]

The aim of a matrix structure is not, however, to seek out the actions on which opposing dimensions of the matrix can agree or readily compromise. The aim is to show up the conflicting viewpoints as clearly as possible and then to analyze objectively which, in the long run, is most justified. There is thus a greater emphasis on market, competition, and environmental facts and in their analysis than there is in unidimensional structures, where the data and recommendations come up a single hierarchy and are unlikely to be inconsistent.

The matrix shape makes it possible for the organization not only to diagnose the need for action along more than one dimension but to adjust between these dimensions.

Weaknesses

The main weakness of matrix organizations is that the pattern can be negated by managers who do not operate according to its requirements. Managers who have a strong drive for organizational power, for example, are likely to try to dominate the matrix organization at their level. They will generally fail to acknowledge the power of the analytical approach in justifying the best path for the overall organization. If they succeed, they destroy the matrix.[20] Others who are

---

[19] Yves L. Doz, Christopher A. Bartlett, and C. K. Prahalad, "Global Competitive Pressures and Host Country Demands," *California Management Review* 23 (Spring 1981), p. 66.

[20] Stanley M. Davis and Paul R. Lawrence, "Problems of Matrix Organizations," *Harvard Business Review* 56 (May–June 1978), pp. 131–42.

less tolerant of conflict but less dominating may continually seek for compromise and create the worst of all worlds—a nonstrategy.

If at any level of a matrix organization proper attention is not given to the detailed analysis of conflicts, it is very likely that the organization will be left with the structure and not the output. Managers reporting to dual superiors will quickly realize when careful analysis is not being carried through and may then proceed to operate in an anarchistic way with only perfunctory reporting of the real issues.

Matrices are intrinsically complex. Every effort, therefore, should be made to specify quite explicitly the detailed interrelationships and responsibilities. Matrix design, on the other hand, can run away with itself. When a multinational blossoms into matrices with conflicting specializations at different levels, the resolution of basic problems can be hampered. In one large multinational, the international personnel department developed its own matrix of training, personnel, industrial relations, and social relations, overlaid with regional specialists and functional specialists. The Western European marketing training manager certainly had an advanced specialization—but his interests did not make it easy for him to discuss the general training needs of the consumer appliances manager of the consumer division of the French national subsidiary.

Excessive internal meetings and discussions without decision and action are also a danger within matrices. The complexity of the relationships may lead to executives checking with base after base before acting only to find that a global competitor with a single line of command has beaten them to it.

As a result of these difficulties, according to one recent study, the use of worldwide matrix organizations with dual reporting is generally avoided by U.S. multinationals.[21] But the researchers go on to describe how some organizations enrich their unitary (i.e., non-matrix), structures by methods that approximate matrices, such as strengthening corporate staffs, rotating management, locating line and staff with overlapping responsibilities in physical proximity, developing ad hoc World Boards or strategy groups without line authority, and assigning executives to a double staff and line responsibility at the same time.

COMBINATION STRUCTURES

For very large multinational businesses it is possible, and in many cases desirable, to combine two or more of the standard organization designs. Different businesses with different patterns of global demand, supply, and competition—and for which different variables have been chosen as important to strategic success—demand different management structures. If the size of a business sector (or activity) is large enough, the multinational should consider setting up the activity as a separate global entity reporting to its top management more or less

---

[21] Robert A. Pitts and John D. Daniels, "Aftermath of the Matrix Mania," *Columbia Journal of World Business,* Summer 1984, pp. 48–54.

as a holding company. This approach would quickly end up with a patchwork global organization composed of different designs for each business. Superimposed over this patchwork would very likely be an international regional organization for liaison with governments at the highest level, and for servicing in combination those business units not large enough to justify their own global organization.

CHOOSING AMONG ALTERNATIVE ORGANIZATIONAL STRUCTURES

The basic organization problem common to all firms operating internationally can be summed up in three questions:

1. Should the corporation be divided into domestic and international divisions?
2. Should line responsibility be subdivided for management purposes according to major functions, major product lines, or major geographic areas?
3. What is the best way to provide for needed specialization and coordination according to the other two variables, or how should the three necessary inputs—functional, product, and geographic—be meshed?

Clearly, there is no one right way to organize, no perfect organizational structure, and no organization form that can remain static when once adopted. Successful companies are using various organizational patterns to manage their international business operations effectively.

Although there are no standard requirements, a relatively small number of variables can help in choosing an organizational form that best fits the needs of a given firm in a given set of circumstances.

1. The relative importance in the present and future of foreign and domestic markets to the firm's competitive strategy.
2. The historical background of a firm and its evolutionary stage in international operations.
3. The nature of a firm's business and its product strategy.
4. The management traits and management philosophy of the firm.
5. The availability of and willingness to invest in internationally experienced management personnel.
6. The capacity of an enterprise to adjust to major organizational changes.

The absolute size of international sales will determine the desirability of moving from an export-manager form of organization to an international division for most U.S. companies. The choice between an international division and a global structure will be influenced by the relative importance of international and domestic markets within the firm's competitive strategy. The benefits of having all senior managers experienced in the diversities of international business may be great.

But when a company's future is likely to be dominated by a large domestic market like the United States, the investment needed to man a global organization with internationally experienced personnel may not be warranted. Also, so long as domestic activities continue to be much larger than international operations, international concerns may continue to require special attention so that they do not become subordinated to domestic considerations.

The choice of organizational structure is inevitably influenced by a company's history and past experience. A company that has operated internationally for decades and possesses a top management experienced in dealing with worldwide problems will approach organizational change differently from a company that is a comparative neophyte on the international scene. During a firm's early stages of growth abroad, its organizational decisions are likely to be influenced by the need to encourage a concentrated drive on international opportunity by separating foreign from domestic activities. At a more advanced stage, organizational decisions will be increasingly motivated by the potential gains to be realized from coordinating all components of the enterprise on a worldwide scale.

As a firm's international activities become large relative to domestic business, the choice of organizational structure is closely related to the nature of the firm's business and its product strategy. Where there is little product diversity, and where the success of the firm is not heavily dependent on diverse trends in different geographic markets, a functional structure can be effective. Where there is a limited product line and great similarity in end-user markets and in marketing techniques and distribution channels, but where area expertise plays a major role, a regional or geographic structure operates well. In such cases, it is less costly to duplicate product and functional expertise than area expertise. Where product lines are diverse, have a high-technology component, and serve different end-user markets—and where production and sourcing can be advantageously rationalized on a worldwide basis—the product division structure has major advantages. The product structure facilitates the transfer of technology and sales support from producing divisions to international operations and can accelerate growth by forcing domestic divisions to become more aware of the markets and potentials of foreign areas.

Management traits and philosophies can be other key variables determining the organizational structure of a firm. Some managements are bold and willing to make frequent organizational changes. Others are cautious and make changes only when absolutely necessary.[22] The management philosophies and heritage of executive experience of European-based multinational companies favor structures that facilitate a potentially more centralized control over the totality of corporate operations by a few key executives, thus giving preference to functionally

---

[22] Christopher A. Bartlett, "MNCs: Get Off the Reorganization Merry-Go-Round," *Harvard Business Review* 61 (March–April 1983), pp. 138–46.

oriented organization structures. The management philosophy of U.S. firms is more likely to favor structures that provide greater opportunities for decentralized decision making, but with formal control devices such as the profit center concept that allow for more strict supervision, control, and coordination within the product-oriented or regionally oriented divisional activities.[23]

Another dimension of a firm's management philosophy is its orientation toward foreign people, ideas, and resources in headquarters and subsidiaries, and in host and home environments.[24] A polycentric firm would have something akin to a holding company structure with loose connections to quasi-independent subsidiaries. A geocentric philosophy leads to a global structure that permits a worldwide approach in both headquarters and subsidiaries.

But, even if a firm can determine the merits of one organizational form over another, the question arises of finding qualified managers. All global structures require an increase in the number of internationally experienced managers, and a shortage of such managers can be a serious barrier to adopting a global structure. As noted previously, the investment required to expand the international experience of the numerous managers needed for a global structure would have to be justified in terms of the future relative importance of international activities as compared to domestic business.

A final variable, related in part to management traits, is the capacity and willingness of an enterprise to adjust to organizational changes. Major organization realignments are likely to disrupt delicate working relationships. Executives of domestic divisions may be unwilling to accept new managerial roles until there is overwhelming evidence of the need for change. Or a forceful manager of a successful international division is likely to use his record of success to resist reorganization pressures that would dilute his responsibility and authority over international activities. Where the capacity and willingness of an enterprise to adjust to organizational change are limited, informal arrangements and devices other than a major organizational change may have to be adopted to secure some of the prospective benefits of a major change.

Organizational structures normally cannot be changed and operated effectively when they are imposed unilaterally by top management. The choice of structure must emerge out of a political process of group bargaining in which decisions are frequently reached by coalitions of groups. As one study of the process of structural change in multinational corporations emphasizes, "Although the choice of structure is ultimately the responsibility of top managers, they have the role of identifying a workable solution, persuading each group of its logic, and implementing the reorganization."[25]

---

[23] Schollhammer, "Organizational Structures of Multinational Corporations," pp. 352–53.

[24] David A. Heenan and Howard V. Perlmutter, *Multinational Organization Development* (Reading, Mass.: Addison-Wesley Publishing, 1979), pp. 17–21.

[25] Stopford and Wells, *Managing the Multinational Enterprise,* p. 75.

ORGANIZATION PROCESS WITHIN THE GLOBAL STRUCTURE

The formal organization structure of a multinational establishes the main lines of authority but on its own is not enough to guarantee viable operation in a complex and changing environment. Four other important organizational facets must be established and managed over time.

- First, there will need to be a set of conventions and instructions as to where decisions of different types are to be taken within the organization.
- Second, the type of data that is recorded and reported and the way it is used as the basis for decisions will significantly influence the organization's performance.
- Third, there is a need for top management to establish and foster informal communication channels to avoid organizational stasis which can result when the only paths for communication parallel the formal structure.
- Fourth, rules for temporary organization to cope with problems that cut across the organization's lines of authority will substantially influence flexibility.

Location of Decisions

The ideal relationship for implementing a global strategy is for corporate management to determine overall corporate objectives, to specify organization-wide strategies and policy guidelines, to decide on the allocation of corporate resources to the various operating divisions, and to institute effective systems of communications, coordination, and control. Within this framework, managers of individual units are supposed to be free to determine a specific course of action for achieving the expected contribution to corporate objectives.

But whatever the stated ideology and intentions of the company, complicated and contradictory pressures cause relationships to oscillate between varying levels of centralization. Among factors that determine the degree of centralization or decentralization are the age, size, and profitability of a specific subsidiary. Large, long-established, and profitable subsidiaries are likely to have a maximum degree of autonomy (see Box 11–1). Another important factor is the amount of confidence placed in subsidiary management. Still another force that can press for local autonomy is an environment with strong national governmental controls that requires frequent and unique local decisions. Factors that work toward centralization are the integration of multinational operations, rapid technological change, and the rapid development of global techniques, strategies, and communications.[26]

---

[26] Gerard Garnier, "The Autonomy of Foreign Subsidiaries: Environmental and National Influences," *Journal of General Management* 10 (Autumn 1984), pp. 57–82.

BOX 11–1
More Autonomy to Foreign Units

London—International Business Machines Corp. (IBM) said it is realigning its management structure to give more responsibility to local operating units outside the United States, especially in Europe. IBM's European operations accounted for about 30% of IBM's net income last year, and the computer company has been trying to shed its image of a U.S.-centered multinational.

In Europe, IBM will divide its subsidiaries into five operating groups. The major countries—France, Italy, West Germany, and Britain—will be treated as relatively autonomous divisions. The remaining smaller European subsidiaries will be combined into a separate division with a general manager based at IBM Europe Paris headquarters. Previously, IBM had closely run its European operations from Paris, with guidance from headquarters at Armonk, N.Y.

IBM said the changes will give division managers more authority. That will at least improve the image of local executives. An IBM manager who competes directly with heads of European computer makers said that he "felt like a flunky when he had to report his operation's head count to Paris."

IBM also is creating 13 "business area management" groups that will provide European product requirements to IBM manufacturing plants around the world.

Under the new plan, the European operating units will plot marketing strategy and select products on their own. They will report to Paris headquarters on a strategic level rather than on a day-to-day basis.

SOURCE: Adapted from *The Wall Street Journal,* June 5, 1984. © Dow Jones & Company, Inc., 1984. Used with permission. All rights reserved.

In virtually all cases, however, the relationship will vary by function. Corporate control will be strongest in those functional areas in which the suboptimization problem is likely to arise and where important economies of scale can be achieved by the joint utilization of high-cost specialized personnel. Depending, of course, on a firm's product strategy, the opportunities to optimize for the entire system may be in a regional or worldwide rationalization of production,[27] in the field of purchasing, or in research and development activities. Such functions tend to be centralized, whereas the marketing function tends to be most decentralized.

Of all the functions, it is finance over which the closest headquarters supervision is usually exercised. Partly, this continues the bias toward controlling businesses through their use of finance that is common in domestic firms. But also accounting standards are widely adhered to around the world and it is much easier to impose standard reporting requirements in finance than in, say, marketing where measurement practices vary widely. Tight central control is usually exercised

---

[27] Stephen R. Gates and William G. Egelhoff, "Centralization in Headquarters—Subsidiary Relationships," *Journal of International Business Studies* 17 (Summer 1986), pp. 71–92.

over capital spending, and often the levels that a subsidiary manager can commit on his own authority are very low indeed. Most companies also centralize the search and analysis of potential acquisitions, but some are beginning to involve subsidiaries in the process.

Apart from centralized control motivations, however, there are also pressures to centralize finance to gain economies. Central cash and capital management can often open up economies by reducing transfers and their associated costs and by reducing the money stocks that are required. Central expertise can also add a supranational protection of the value of assets and revenues against loss through exchange and other risks that national units could not engage in themselves.

The very design of matrix organization requires frequent adjudication at a level above that at which proposals are prepared in the matrix units. In fact, the "planned-conflict" design can produce so many directly opposed proposals from the opposing matrix units that a decision overload can be built up at top management level.[28] This is one reason why regional offices are advocated. The adjudication can be moved down a level and the less crucial conflicts sorted out before they reach the top of the organization.

Specification of Data and Its Decision Use

In all firms, the data that are required to be reported and the ways in which it is expected to be analyzed shape the organization's performance. Information and the release of its energy is the blood flow that gives life to the organization structure.

Careful specification of information requirements is of particular importance in multinationals in which global economies are large and where injudicious emphasis on the wrong countries can place the firm at a major competitive disadvantage. Information requirements are also important in matrix organizations where the rationale for the structure is to allocate responsibility for collecting, analyzing, and presenting the case for action along the dimensions on which the matrix is structured. Management must design reporting requirements so that conflicting views are effectively represented at the appropriate higher level for adjudication.

Because the conflict structure of a matrix involves adjudication rather than compromise, there inevitably will be managers whose case is not adopted. To avoid the sense of failure in these cases, many organizations have adopted procedures for review of conflicting plans and proposals in open meeting. With a consistent emphasis by top management on analysis to show the best decision for performance of the overall system, a climate can be created in which clear analysis of facts is the mark of the good executive. Management of the multinational

---

[28] Doz, Bartlett, and Prahalad, "Global Competitive Pressures and Host Country Demands," p. 68.

becomes more analytical and turns away from political protagonists encouraged to bias data and presentations to produce the most attractive case from their subunit viewpoint. Equally, with fewer nonparticipative adjudications from on high, decisions are seen less as "wins" and "losses," and the problem of alienated managers who are not committed to the decision is much reduced.

In shaping the way in which a multinational organization operates, the planning and budget instructions that specify the content, format, and review procedure are perhaps even more important than the formal organization structure. By changing the planning process, a top executive can change the entire shape of the decisions that emerge. Thus, in many multinationals, the basic outcome of conflicts is often established at the planning stage. If plans for a national subsidiary, for example, are approved independently of product divisions' plans, inherent conflicts might never be resolved as the subsidiary adheres steadfastly to the "contract" established by its plan.

Throughout the review process of a multinational, a very strong influence will be the personal values of top management in their approach to information and search for problem solutions. The values exhibited will color the ways in which decisions are implemented and future plans are presented. The process of review thus offers a formal platform to educate a multinational to the style of management that the top team is seeking.

Informal Communication Channels

No organization structure, however complex, can cover all the directions from which need for change may arise. Individual managers somewhere in an organization, however, will very quickly perceive threats or opportunities, even when they cut across their organizational responsibility. But distance, cultural barriers, and the formal organization structure itself are at work to hinder communication of such perceptions within the multinational. Specific actions to build informal communication channels and to soften the perceived responsibility boundaries are, therefore, widely advised as important supplements to organizational design. Such actions include meetings and conferences, ad hoc task groups of one type or another, and interchange of management within the structure. Bartlett outlines how Baxter-Travenol changed annual general managers' meetings at which regional and line managers listened to formal presentations of the year's results, corporate plans, and new products.[29] They were replaced with a senior management conference to which product and functional managers were also invited. The formal presentations gave way to discussions at which managers jointly identified and tried to resolve strategic and organizational issues. As a result of this experience, the participants formed strong bonds that endured far beyond the meeting. Pitts and Daniels' approaches for enriching a unitary structure towards a matrix awareness fall within this category, too.[30]

---

[29] Bartlett, "MNCs," pp. 143–44.

[30] Pitts, and Daniels, "Aftermath," pp. 51–52.

Temporary Initiatives

From time to time top management will find that any combination of organizational structure and processes, however appropriate to the bulk of decisions, will fail completely to face a decision or to change as soon as it should or in the direction it should. To overcome the difficulty, management must introduce temporary procedures that cut across the established patterns.[31] Suppose, for example, that an organization based on a matrix of geographical and product divisions is in an oversupply situation requiring a dramatic cost-cutting exercise. Neither national units nor product divisions want to initiate the scheme, all hoping for a future demand increase. To rely on functional control specialists to work through the organization against the wishes of the matrix managers to whom they report would be to invite only partial success. In this case, an alternative would be to establish a temporary task force to recommend and monitor cost reduction, reporting directly to top management and dominated by financial control executives.

Task forces and committees, as in this case, may have to be designed with a clear bias in their composition simply to offset the power of established groups. Even then, there may be little support for views that conflict with the dominant organization dimension, if members can see only personal career disadvantage in espousing recommendations that go against the organizational wishes and are not likely to be adopted.

Another type of temporary initiative is to build a cadre of trusted executives who can be transferred for short assignments within the organizational structure to bring about changes that go against the structure. Home-base or third-country nationals, for example, may be less inclined to take a suboptimizing national viewpoint to the detriment of the total firm.

Reliance on temporary initiatives, however, has its drawbacks. First, the need for action is likely to be recognized too late, after early diagnosis has been suppressed by the existing organization. Solutions are likely to be needed more to overcome the resulting weaknesses than to build on strengths. Ad hoc committees, moreover, may not be in a position to implement recommendations, nor want to do so. Temporary initiatives are also very expensive in their demands on top management time. Designing and composing groups takes time and much personal interaction. So does monitoring effectiveness, particularly if intervention is required in sensitive situations or to keep the initiative moving.

SUMMARY

An international commitment by a business enterprise normally requires significant changes in a firm's organizational structure. There is no one organizational structure that is ideal for multinational operations, and any structure once adopted

---

[31] Christopher A. Bartlett, "Multinational Structural Change: Evolution versus Reorganization," in *The Management of Headquarters—Subsidiary Relationships in Multinational Corporations,* ed. Lars Otterbeck (Aldershot, U.K.: Gower, 1981), p. 135.

must be continually reviewed and revised as internal and external factors keep changing. At the senior management level, the broad types of organization options for assigning responsibility and authority are relatively limited. But within the broad patterns, considerable diversity is possible.

The organizational structure of most international enterprises evolves over time in a series of stages. American companies have typically moved from an export unit structure to a separate international division or international company as operations are extended to foreign areas. As top management becomes increasingly interested in international opportunities, a global organization structure may be adopted. International companies based in Europe and Canada tend to skip the international division stage and move directly to a global structure because domestic markets are smaller and less important to their overall success. Global structures can be organized with primary emphasis on function, product, or geography. Some firms have attempted to build complex grid structures where managers have multiple reporting relationships, and function, product, and area responsibilities overlap.

The choice among alternative structures depends on a small number of variables. The key problem is the inherent conflict between three dimensions of a firm's activities—functional, product, and geographic. A functional structure has the benefits of integrating marketing, finance, and production, but at the cost of area coordination and difficulties in transferring product and technological expertise from the parent company to the subsidiaries and among foreign operations. The product structure reduces problems of transferring technology and new products among locations, but it incurs the costs of duplication in functional tasks and of coordinating all the interests of an enterprise in a foreign area. The area structure gives good coordination geographically, but at the cost of product coordination among areas and duplication in functional expertise. In the final analysis, the choice of organization structure will reflect management's choice between sets of problems.

The relationships between corporate headquarters and the foreign subsidiaries present another difficult organizational problem—namely, centralization versus decentralization. In general, the preference is for headquarters to be responsible for strategy and the final decisions on long-range goals, and for the subsidiaries to have maximum responsibility and authority for operations. Here again, a firm's product strategy becomes a key determinant. Where the product strategy may result in suboptimization by not taking advantage of enterprise-wide unification possibilities, such functions as manufacturing, research and development, and financial management are likely to be closely controlled or coordinated at the center. At the other extreme, where great diversity in products and in end-use markets exists, marketing is particularly likely to be decentralized.

EXERCISES AND DISCUSSION QUESTIONS

1. What are the principal considerations that make organizational structures that work well for domestic operations less suitable for multinational operations?
2. "There is no single best structure for all international companies. Each company's

operations are different, and each company has an almost unique set of needs to be served by its organizational structure.'' Discuss.

3. Select a multinational corporation and from its latest published annual report construct its international organization pattern. What do you think will be the chief weaknesses of this organization pattern in the current business situation?

4. Under what conditions would you recommend a functional structure at the topmost level as against a regional or international division structure?

5. Why do you think one of the major U.S. automobile companies retains an international division structure whereas a company like General Electric has a structure that emphasizes global business units?

6. ''The key to successful matrix organization in a multinational is the set of rules that are developed for compromise between the demands of national interests and the imperatives of worldwide competition in the firm's businesses.'' Discuss.

7. ''Within a tendency toward greater centralization of decision making, there is yet a discernible trend to greater individual independence for managers in multinational enterprises. Increased independence can accompany a reduction in the area of decision making by subsidiary managers.'' Discuss.

PART FOUR

The Nation-State and International Business

Business enterprises have become increasingly international, but the structure of world government has not moved along a similar path. Sovereign nation-states continue to be the dominant unit of government, and the number of states has increased phenomenally from about 65 at the end of World War II to more than 160 in 1988. Some observers argue that the nation-state is old-fashioned and not well adapted to serve the needs of the modern, complex world. Yet nation-states persist as the governmental unit with which international enterprises must coexist.

Each nation-state has its own nationalistic spirit and set of national goals. As a sovereign power, the nation-state sets the rules for governing business transactions within and across its national boundaries. In dealing with domestic business enterprises, governments normally feel competent to achieve their goals and do not consider their sovereignty threatened. In dealing with international business, and particularly with multinational enterprises, nation-states perceive special potentials for conflicts with national goals and threats to national sovereignty.

Such potential conflicts have little to do with good or bad intentions on the part of either international firms or nation-states. The potential exists because each has divergent goals that it is trying to maximize. It is the ineluctable result of the internationalization of business in a world of nation-states.

As nations have become more aware of the potential impact that multinational enterprises can have on national goals, they have responded by establishing control programs over the operations of multinational enterprises within their national boundaries. These responses and the objectives that nation-states are attempting to achieve with such controls are the subject of Chapter 12. And as a guide to the implementation of control programs, governments increasingly rely on techniques for measuring the benefits of international business projects to the nation. These techniques are presented in Chapter 13.

Doing business with the centrally planned economies is discussed separately in Chapter 14 because these countries present many unique issues of business-government relations. In dealing with governments, however, the multinational enterprise is not without some means of protecting itself against controls that threaten its own objectives and existence. Its countervailing power is considered in Chapter 15. As political environments keep changing and new risks can arise, Chapter 16 examines how a prudent multinational may form a view on the likelihood of political risks and national controls and take these into account in deciding its strategy.

CHAPTER 12

National Controls over International Business

Nation-states have developed a variety of ways to achieve national goals and protect national interests as far as international business transactions are concerned.

Traditionally, their method was to control the international transfers of goods. They followed with controls over transfers across national boundaries of money, personnel, technology, legal rights, and data.

The rise of the multinational enterprise, however, created a new set of challenges and opportunities for nation-states that are not met through transfer controls. With a growing conviction that something more is needed, most nations adopted additional measures specifically directed toward multinational business. Slowly but inevitably, both investor nations and host countries have been moving toward a general and coordinated national policy in this area. There have also been related control efforts at the regional and international levels aimed at reducing competition among host countries by agreeing on standard controls and establishing codes of conduct for multinational enterprises.

National control programs differ among nations reflecting variations in country characteristics, in national goals, and in levels of sensitivity to multinational enterprises. Furthermore, each nation's control policies are likely to change over time. Because of these variations, this chapter will not attempt to provide a comprehensive survey of the many national control programs. As the need arises, the international manager will want to make use of the standard references available in order to be currently informed on the details of a specific country's controls.[1]

Instead, this chapter will focus on the rationale underlying the various control measures. Even though national programs differ in detail, the underlying rationale is frequently similar. The chapter will also review the status of efforts to establish regional and international controls over multinational enterprises.

WHY NATIONS ADOPT CONTROLS

Why do nation-states feel the need for controls over international business? The basic issue is simple. Each nation state has its set of national goals. Each multinational enterprise has its set of supranational goals toward which it directs the corporate family of diverse nationalities under its control. Some, if not most, of the enterprise goals may be in harmony with the goals of a specific nation within which the firm is operating. But some of the enterprise goals may conflict with the goals of one or more nation-states. This potential for harmony or conflict, moreover, extends to all countries hosting an enterprise, including its home base.

Most discussions of control policies emphasize exclusively the conflict potentials and the negative curbs and constraints imposed by nations to protect their national interests. Nation-states, however, are also aware of the potential of multinational enterprises for advancing national goals and have introduced incentives to encourage those activities of multinational enterprises considered to be in harmony with national goals.

---

[1] A standard reference source is *Investment Laws of the World* (Dobbs Ferry, N.Y.: Oceana), a loose-leaf service prepared by the International Centre for Settlement of Investment Disputes. Other sources are the information guides for individual countries published periodically by accounting firms such as Price Waterhouse & Co. and Arthur Andersen & Co.

The potentials for both common advantage and potential conflicts can be illustrated by the example of employment impact. As firms expand internationally, they create employment opportunities in host countries. Host countries are generally anxious to have more local jobs available and frequently offer inducements to attract foreign industries. At the same time, labor unions in the home country may feel that overseas expansions result in a loss of jobs in the home country and press for negative curbs by the home country. Although anxious to secure more jobs, the host country is also interested in having as many as possible of these jobs filled by its nationals. It may therefore also use constraints, along with inducements, requiring that a specified share of the labor force, or technical personnel, be reserved for nationals.

Employment and job protection goals are just two of a complex pattern of goals that emerge from the interplay of interests and factions in each country. We have already detailed a number of other goals when examining the motivation for controls over transfers of goods in Chapter 7. They include government revenue needs, development aspirations, the need to balance a country's payments, health and safety, national security concerns, and international political goals. Each one can lead a nation to impose controls over international business.

CONTROLLING TRANSFERS OF MONEY

Foreign Exchange Controls

Foreign exchange controls are widely adopted by nations for resolving payments imbalances.[2] Such controls render a nation's currency inconvertible; that is, it is no longer freely transferable into other currencies. There can be degrees of inconvertibility, depending on the nature and extent of the exchange controls. The government normally requires that all receipts of foreign exchange be turned over to the central bank or some other designated government agency. Exchange can be bought only for specified purposes and in amounts determined by the government. A license is therefore required for the purchase of foreign exchange. Exchange controls can be limited to import and export transactions, or they can also cover transfer payments such as profit remittances and capital flows.

Effective functioning of an exchange-control system requires that all foreign exchange receipts by individuals, businesses, and government agencies be captured and directed into a central pool. Consequently, an export licensing and policing system is needed to assure that foreign exchange receipts are turned over to the government in exchange for local currency at fixed rates. At times, a so-called free market is allowed to operate alongside exchange controls, but only limited types of transactions are legal in the free market. Exporters may be allowed to keep a share of their export earnings, which they can sell at the higher rates

[2] International Monetary Fund, *Annual Report on Exchange Arrangements and Exchange Restrictions 1986* (Washington, D.C. 1986). This IMF report, published annually, describes current policies and practices of each member country of the IMF and is a valuable reference for international managers.

prevailing in the free market, and generally the free market is used by tourists for securing local currency.

Once exchange controls are established, the government determines the priorities and quotas for the allocation of foreign exchange, and the choice is often rather arbitrary. The system can vary from a simple allocation of available foreign exchange among domestic individuals or firms to a complex licensing system discriminating between many different categories of goods. Some exchange-control systems establish multiple exchange rates, which vary by category of goods and permit the import of high-priority goods at the lower rates and nonessential or luxury goods at the higher rates. Some systems also require importers to make substantial deposits in order to obtain an import license. The deposit requirement ties up funds that might otherwise be earning a return and thereby increases the cost of importing.

A major problem constantly confronting exchange-control authorities is the black market, where exchange is bought and sold in disregard of official regulations.[3] Depending upon the severity of the exchange controls and the administrative capacity of government agencies, black-market activities in foreign exchange and import licenses can be extensive. When the official rate is far below what it would be with a free rate, the opportunities for earning illicit profits are great, and extensive graft and corruption are almost certain to emerge.

Exchange controls may buy time while basic adjustments are undertaken to secure balance-of-payments equilibrium or to implement development programs. Nevertheless, the more serious the imbalance between supply and demand for local currency, the more difficult such a system is to administer effectively. Under all circumstances exchange controls require an honest and highly skilled administrative capacity. If exchange controls are substituted for policies to correct underlying imbalances and are maintained over long periods of time, illicit operations are inevitable, with their detrimental influence on business morality and the effectiveness of the controls. Yet while controls are at best a temporary measure, they frequently are retained as permanent fixtures. Even countries with a heavy balance of trade surplus have retained exchange controls. In January 1987, Taiwan, with holdings of $48 billion in foreign exchange, was just considering the possibility of allowing exporting firms to keep some exchange for direct investment in foreign projects.[4]

Capital Controls

Partial controls over flows of short-term and long-term capital are also common. Like foreign exchange controls, capital controls normally require approval by governmental authorities for international transfers of funds. The motivation for capital controls has most frequently been to attain balance-of-payments equilibrium at desired exchange-rate levels. But they have also been used to implement

---

[3] Michael Nowak, "Quantitative Controls and Unofficial Markets in Foreign Exchange," *IMF Staff Papers*, June 1984, pp. 404–31.

[4] *Financial Times*, January 24, 1987.

national development priorities, to influence the patterns and size of international business operations in a country, and to support varied foreign policy objectives.

Administration of capital controls may be simpler than a full-fledged exchange-controls program, with fewer parties involved in either capital inflows or outflows. Furthermore, such controls generally allow governmental authorities a great deal of discretion to meet changing circumstances. The disadvantage of capital controls, however, may be that short-term benefits in improving the balance-of-payments situation are secured at the expense of even greater long-term gains. Profitable direct investment, for example, can generate a continuing stream of return flows in the form of repatriated profits.

CONTROLLING TRANSFERS OF PERSONS

Controls affecting the movement of persons across national boundaries are crucially important to international business. Trade depends to a large extent on the ability of businessmen to move from nation to nation. The identification and exploitation of direct investment opportunities require even more that business executives be free to travel internationally. International business operations may be dependent upon the ability of management personnel or production workers to move across national boundaries.[5] The transfer of technology can also be significantly influenced by national policies toward the international movement of persons who possess the technical knowledge.

National policies for controlling the entry and exit of persons from a country generally are not motivated primarily by international business considerations. Broader political, economic, and social considerations usually underlie such policies, which generally distinguish between persons entering a country for a temporary stay such as tourists or, at the other end of the spectrum, persons who want to enter a country on a permanent basis. An intermediate category would be foreigners who enter for a period of employment but do not intend to become permanent residents of the country.

Passports and visas are the basic means for controlling the international movement of persons. Passports are issued to persons by the country of which they are a citizen or permanent resident. The issuing country can restrict movements by not authorizing passport holders to enter specified countries, as the United States forbade its citizens to travel in Lebanon in 1986. Visas are issued by the country into which persons desire to travel. Political considerations can be grounds either for refusing citizens a passport or for denying visas.

Generally speaking, restrictions on exit are regarded as morally less defensible than restrictions on entry. Apart from the communist bloc, only a few countries make it difficult to depart. Few make any attempt to charge departing individuals with the cost of their education, but limitations on the right to export capital other than this human capital are common. Nationals of India, for example,

---

[5] See John D. Daniels, "International Mobility of People," *South Carolina Essays in International Business,* no. 1, March 1980.

are not normally granted any foreign exchange facilities for emigration purposes.

Most countries, anxious to expand their tourist industry, impose minimum restrictions on the entry of persons on temporary visits. The most restrictive policies are applied to persons who wish to seek employment in a foreign country or become permanent residents. During certain periods of history, such as the late 19th and early 20th centuries, countries such as the United States encouraged immigration. Australia, Canada, Argentina, and Brazil have also had periods of relatively open immigration. But the general world pattern, except for internal movement in Western Europe and the Arab states, has become one of selective and limited immigration.

In Western Europe after about 1955, there was a greatly increased movement of workers across national borders. The major movements were northward, especially to Switzerland, Belgium, France, and Germany, first by Italians, and then by Greeks, Spaniards, Portuguese, and Turks. The mobility of workers in Europe tended to limit wage-rate variations and greatly improved the functioning of the European labor market. With economic downturn, however, "guest" workers have been treated less well than their co-workers.[6]

The size of the international flows of migrant labor is impressive. In 1975, there were more than 6 million migrant workers in Western and Northern Europe making up about 7 percent of total employment.[7] By 1980, there were about 3 million immigrant laborers in the oil-exporting countries of the Middle East, and that was projected to double by 1990.[8] In Kuwait, for instance, immigrant labor constituted 80 percent of total employment.

From the standpoint of international business, national controls over the transfer of persons are likely to be more burdensome than prohibitive. Yet there are cases where countries have not granted work permits to foreign managers and technical staff of an international enterprise, as part of a policy of reserving such positions for nationals. To meet this kind of a situation, a firm must plan its recruitment and training policy so that the nationalities of its managerial strength will match its future global need for these nationalities.

CONTROLLING TRANSFERS OF TECHNOLOGY

The concept of technology encompasses technical and managerial know-how that is embodied in physical and human capital and in published documents and that is transmitted across national boundaries in various ways.[9]

---

[6] Hermann Korte, "Political Rights and Foreign Workers," *Financial Times*, May 14, 1986, p. 25.

[7] Zafer Ecevit and K. C. Zachariah, "International Labor Migration," *Finance and Development*, December 1978, pp. 32–37.

[8] Naim A. Sherbini, "Expatriate Labor in Arab Oil-Producing Countries," *Finance and Development*, December 1984, pp. 34–37.

[9] Stefan H. Robock, *The International Technology Transfer Process* (Washington: National Academy of Sciences, 1980).

In the industrially advanced countries, technological progress is encouraged through a patent system that gives the owner of new technology ownership rights during a fixed number of years—17 years in the case of the United States. In most cases, these countries have applied no controls over the international transfer of technology or even over the price received for transfers. Notable exceptions, however, are the U.S. restriction on "trading with the enemy," which places statutory prohibition on technology transfer for security reasons, and foreign policy controls to further U.S. diplomatic objectives, applied under the Export Administration Act. Controls instituted under this latter Act are tabulated in Table 12–1. Although not all are concerned with technology, the main impact has been upon technologically advanced products.

Attitudes in the less developed countries (LDCs) differ markedly. They are predominantly buyers rather than sellers of technology. To them, the question is whether the adoption of a patent system will help or hinder the country's access to foreign technology on acceptable terms. Consequently, national patent systems for protection of rights over technology do not exist universally, and where they do exist, the right of foreigners to use the protection varies greatly. The LDCs are also making more and more attempts to control the transfer of technology across their borders.

The objectives of the LDCs are ambitious. They want to ensure that imported technology is appropriate to their needs, which generally means smaller-scale and labor-intensive technology, and that it will actually be transferred to local nationals. They want to ensure that charges for technology, either explicit or concealed, are as low as possible. Another common objective is to minimize the restraints in technology transfer agreements, such as limiting the markets in which the licensee can sell or the quantity that can be produced. Such restrictions have been common in order to protect the licensor from competition from the licensee or to ensure that the licensed subsidiary fits into a global strategy. Finally, and inconsistently, many countries also want to retain for their own country all rights arising from local development of technology.

Attempts to achieve these objectives commonly take the form of a technology transfer law, requiring the registration of all documents and agreements to do with payments to foreigners for patent rights, trademark authorization, technical knowledge, engineering, technical assistance, and so on. Agreements that are not registered are by statute neither valid nor enforceable. Moreover, the act usually states grounds on which registration can be refused, such as those listed in the 1972 Mexican law, set out in Figure 12–1 (see page 291).

The prima facie evidence is that such controls are effective from the country's standpoint. Firms can be thrown into a negotiating position with the government as their applications for registration are first rejected and then accepted after amendment. Royalty levels drop. The really important indicators of success, however, are more difficult to assess. Does the law perhaps reduce the priority that firms place on the country as a site for more advanced development? Do restrictions on the multinationals' rights to locally developed technology discourage local research and development? Does the control of royalty rates lead to reduction

TABLE 12–1   Primary Instances of Foreign Policy Controls, 1976–1986

Target (year)	Products Controlled	American MNCs Affected	Diplomatic Purpose
Soviet Union			
(1978)	Computers, energy exploration technology	Sperry Rand, Dresser	To protest the arrest of two Soviet dissidents
(1979)	Computers	Control Data	To protest the presence of Soviet troops in Cuba
(1980)	Grain, phosphates, high-technology	Cargill, IBM, Armco	To punish the Soviets for invading Afghanistan
(1981)	More restrictions on U.S. high-technology exports; Poland included as well	GE, Dresser, Fiat-Allis	To protest the imposition of martial law in Poland
(1982)	The 1981 technology controls are extended extra-territorially	MNC subsidiaries	To impede construction of the Yamal Pipeline
Uganda			
(1978)	Total trade ban	IBM, several oil MNCs	To undermine the regime of Idi Amin
Iran			
(1979)	Total trade ban and blocking of Iranian assets in U.S. banks	IBM, Ford Aerospace	To provide leverage in the American-Iranian hostage negotiations
Libya			
(1983)	Aircraft	Boeing	To protest Libyan support for international terrorism
(1986)	Total trade ban; ban on bank lending; ban on the performance of contracts	Occidental Petroleum, Amerada Hess, Brown and Root Inc.	To condemn Libyan support for terrorist attacks in Western Europe
Rhodesia			
(1977)	Total trade ban	Mobil, Colt	To promote majority rule
South Africa			
(1978 to 1982) and (1985)	Ban on the export and reexport of U.S.-origin products and technical data to the South African police, military and prisons. Ban on bank loans to South African Government	IBM, Burroughs, Control Data	To protest apartheid
Nicaragua			
(1985)	Total trade ban	IBM, Xerox, Exxon	Presidential determination that the actions of the Government of Nicaragua "constitute an unusual and extraordinary threat to the national security and foreign policy of the United States"

SOURCE: Adapted from Erik Lindell, "Foreign Policy Export Controls and American Multinational Corporations," *California Management Review* 28 (Summer 1986), pp. 27–39.

FIGURE 12–1   Grounds for Refusing to Register Contracts in the Mexican National Register
of Technology Transfer

I. When their purpose is the transfer of technology available in the country free of charge or
under more advantageous conditions than those governing its acquisition abroad, provided
the same technology is concerned.

II. When the price or the compensation is not related to the technology acquired, or it constitutes
an unfair or excessive levy on the national economy.

III. When clauses are included whereby the supplier is permitted to control or intervene, directly
or indirectly, in the administration of the party acquiring the technology.

IV. When the obligation is established to transfer, onerously or gratuitously, to the party providing
the technology, the patents, trademarks, innovations, or improvements which may be obtained
in the country.

V. When limitations are imposed on the research or technological development of the party
acquiring the technology.

VI. When the obligations are established to acquire equipment, tools, parts, or raw materials of
an exclusively determined origin.

VII. When the total prohibition is established on exportation or the possibilities of the party
acquiring the technology are limited with regard to exporting, in a manner contrary to the
interests of the country.

VIII. When the use of supplementary technologies is prohibited.

IX. When the obligations are established to sell on an exclusive basis to the supplier of the
technology the goods produced by the party acquiring the technology.

X. When the party acquiring the technology is obliged to permanently utilize the personnel
indicated by the supplier of the technology.

XI. When production volumes are limted or sales or resale prices are imposed for domestic
production or for the exports of the party acquiring the technology.

XII. When the party acquiring the technology is obliged to enter into selling contracts or exclusive
representation agreements with the supplier in Mexico.

XIII. When excessive validity periods are established. In no case can said periods exceed ten
years and be obligatory for the party acquiring the technology.

XIV. When presentation is made to foreign courts-of-law of the facts or resolution of the judgments
which may derive from the interpretation or compliance with the aforementioned memoranda,
contracts, or agreements.

SOURCE: Government of Mexico, *Diario Oficial*, December 30, 1972, Article 7.

in the quality of available technology or limit the terms of the agreement? With
limited investment to meet world-wide demands, the answers to these questions
are very likely in the affirmative.[10]

Some countries that operated fairly rigorous regulation of foreign technology
during the 1970s seem to have realized that overly strict measures may have
been counterproductive. In Korea, regulations were liberalized in 1978 and again
in 1979. Technology agreements between Korea and foreign companies rose
from 842 over the 1962–1977 period to 432 in 1984 alone. There were, however,
some negative effects. Repetitive acquisitions of foreign technologies increased,

---

[10] See *The Acquisition of Technology from Multinational Corporations by Developing Countries*,
(United Nations, N.Y., 1974), p. 43.

less consideration was given to technical evaluation of agreements leading to acquisition of outdated technologies, and higher royalty rates were paid for fairly standard technology.[11]

The developing countries have been attempting to improve the terms for international transfers of technology through pressures by UNCTAD, beginning in 1976, for a code of conduct. Some progress has been made toward a possible convention. The industrial countries, however, have resisted having the code apply to intrafirm transactions.[12]

CONTROLLING TRANSFERS OF RIGHTS

Governments can also regulate the international transfer of rights. Rights of nonnationals to own, hold concessions, or operate a business, for example, may be restricted either absolutely or for certain areas of the economy. Such restrictions are common for natural resources and land. A few countries expressly prohibit all foreign ownership of land, others extend the prohibition to only agricultural land or forestry rights. Concessions for mining radioactive materials, such as uranium or thorium, are restricted in some cases to domestic enterprises. Other areas in which restrictions apply are those with a strong national cultural and political impact, such as newspapers, magazines, and broadcasting; those that form an integral part of any national security network, such as telecommunications operation or military manufacturing; and those that are essentially part of the economic regulatory mechanism, such as major banks.

The motivations behind limitation of foreigners' access to local rights are partly xenophobic and partly reasoned economic, political, or security precautions. Where foreigners' rights are removed, the method used is quite likely to be public nationalization of the activity in question. Local private rights are removed at the same time so the action appears less like expropriation of foreign property. In fact, the underlying motivation may have little to do with a belief in state ownership of the particular field.

CONTROLLING TRANSFERS OF DATA

Laws governing the flow of data across national borders are recent phenomena in both developed and Third World countries. Initially, laws were enacted to protect privacy by excluding the possibility that foreign organizations, public or

---

[11] Katherin Marton, *Multinationals, Technology, and Industrialization* (Lexington, Mass.: Lexington Books, 1986), pp. 247–54.

[12] See Miquel S. Wionczek, "The Major Unresolved Issues in the Negotiations on the UNCTAD Code of Conduct for the Transfer of Technology," *CEPAL Review*, April 1980, pp. 94–102; Howard V. Perlmutter and Tagi Sagafi-nejad, *International Technology Transfer; Codes, Guidelines, and a Muffled Quadrilogue* (New York: Pergamon Press, 1981); see also Edward M. Graham, "The Terms of Transfer of Technology to the Developing Nations: A Survey of the Major Issues" in *North-South Technology Transfer: The Adjustments Ahead*, ed. J. H. Dunning, et al. (Paris: Organization for Economic Cooperation and Development, 1982), pp. 55–87.

private, could use international business records to build foreign data bases concerning their citizens. Some of this legislation extended beyond customer information. Under some of the regulations, it could be illegal, for example, to maintain a foreign central computer file on a multinational's local employees. For those countries in which locally incorporated firms are viewed as legal persons and are included within protective legislation, it could even be illegal to build a foreign computer file on the pricing and promotion actions of such a local competitor.

Some countries have further motivations for controlling data transfers. They do not wish to be dependent upon the data banks or processing skills of another country, to be held to ransom by a multinational corporation that will not release data about their own country, or to fail to obtain a share of the modern information processing business. President Mitterrand of France pointed out at the 1982 Versailles economic summit that concentration of information in a few firms in a small number of dominant countries could cause the rest to lose their sovereignty and jeopardize their freedom of thought and decision.[13] Such thinking leads quickly to legislation that circumscribes multinationals. Banks doing business in Canada, for example, are required under the 1980 Canadian Banking act to carry out the data processing of their customer records in Canada.

The OECD has published a set of voluntary guidelines on transborder data flow that corporations should follow when handling personal data. The aim in establishing clear guidelines was to avoid national restrictions on data flow and hence inefficiencies. Nevertheless, multinationals are likely to face a growing wall of legislation that will force them into duplication of records if not decentralization. While the United States is likely to remain very open as regards data flow, it has mainly been the beneficiary of inward data flows. It will be other nations that take the protective steps.

The United Nations Centre on Transnational Corporations has been very active in studying the issues, and it is possible, as discussed in Chapter 8, that an international code on transborder data flows will emerge that emphasizes data processing within individual nations.[14]

CONTROLLING OUTWARD DIRECT INVESTMENT

Incentives

Historically, the United States and several other major investor countries have adhered to a basic economic philosophy favoring the free flow of investment

---

[13] Martin D. J. Buss, "Legislative Threat to Transborder Data Flow," *Harvard Business Review,* May–June 1984, p. 113.

[14] See United Nations Centre on Transnational Corporations, *Transnational Corporations and Transborder Data Flows: Background and Overview* (Amsterdam: North-Holland Publishing Company, 1985).

and technology among countries. These nations have liberal policies that encourage outbound direct investment and impose few (if any) constraints on inbound direct investment by foreigners. The other major investor countries also have liberal policies to encourage outbound direct investment but, at the same time, impose screening or constraints on inbound investment.

The rationale for the liberal policies is the assumption that investment abroad increases trade and expands exports, jobs, markets, and government revenues for the investor country. These policies implicitly assume that the interests of the multinational enterprise and its home country are largely in harmony. To state the belief in a provocative way, the assumption is that "what's good for U.S. International, Inc., is good for the United States."[15]

In recent years, there has been growing skepticism concerning the domestic costs and benefits of the liberal policies, and some modifications in the policies of investor nations have resulted. These developments will be discussed below in the section on restraints over outward direct investment.

The prevailing situation is that many investor countries, including the United States, Canada, and West Germany, impose no restrictions whatever on outward direct investment. Some of the other investor countries have only formal regulations requiring that the government be notified of such investments. In support of their liberal policies, the major investor nations have incentive programs that generally include risk insurance, capital assistance, tax incentives, and, at times, political representation.

Foreign Risk Insurance.   All major investor nations now have insurance programs to cover major types of foreign investment risks. The geographic coverage varies from worldwide to investments in selected countries. The types of risks generally insurable are those of expropriation, war losses, and inability to transfer profits.[16] Some countries extend the insurance to exports of home-country goods, and Japan also insures investments in non-Japanese companies engaged in developing mineral resources for import into Japan.

The U.S. program was the earliest. It was started in 1948 to support the European Recovery Program by guaranteeing U.S. investments in Western Europe against restrictions on the conversion of currency. It was gradually expanded to cover investments in developing countries against all political risks. Since 1970, the program has been administered by the Overseas Private Investment Corporation (OPIC) "under the policy guidance of the Secretary of State."

OPIC has been the focus of considerable controversy that has resulted in major program modifications. It is now required to give priority to investments

---

[15] Stefan H. Robock, "U.S. Policies toward Transnationals," in *Transnational Corporations and China's Open Door Policy,* Weizao Teng and N. T. Wang, eds. (Lexington, Mass.: Lexington Books, 1988), pp. 109–20.

[16] See Felton Mc C. Johnston, "Political Risk Insurance," in *Assessing Corporate Political Risk,* ed. David M. Raddock (Totowa, N.J.: Rowan & Littlefield, 1986), pp. 186–96.

in truly low-income countries and special emphasis to U.S. small business firms in its foreign investment loan program.[17]

Associated with the insurance of investment risks, a number of countries have negotiated bilateral investment agreements with the governments of host countries. The general experience has been that the developing countries have been careful to avoid even minor breaches of the agreements. Agreements provide for an arbitration procedure. If a country is condemned under the arbitration procedure, it may lose international standing, which may lead to a loss of creditworthiness. Thus, in a not so subtle sense, insured investments carry with them an implicit hint that investor countries will be concerned about the imposition of controls and actions that will require insurance payments.

Both capital-exporting and capital-importing countries can offer a further incentive to direct investment through the Multilateral Investment Guarantee Agency (MIGA). Formed in 1985 by the World Bank, with capital subscribed by 20 countries, MIGA is an autonomous agency and investors who are nationals of member countries are eligible for coverage. This includes corporations whose principal places of business are in member countries or who have the majority of their capital owned by nationals of member countries. The Agency, however, will normally guarantee investments only in member countries with priority given to the lesser developed. Cover may, however, be offered for other countries where the investment is sponsored by a member country as trustee for the country of destination. The cover is for new medium to long-term investments and is intended to supplement rather than replace existing programs. Risks covered include host government restrictions on currency conversion and transfer, loss from legislation or administrative actions, and losses from war or civil unrest.

Capital Assistance.   Many investor nations have special funds or banks that make government loans to firms wishing to invest in developing countries.[18] Moreover, several countries have official export credit programs that help to finance equipment exports. The U.S. Export-Import Bank, for example, promotes investment overseas by making it easier and cheaper to buy the capital goods and machinery in the United States necessary to establish overseas subsidiaries.

Tax Incentives.   Steps to eliminate double taxation of foreign income, mainly through bilateral tax treaties, have been motivated to maintain a degree of equity rather than to encourage foreign operations. Some nations, however, do maintain lower tax rates, exemptions, or special deductions for income earned abroad. Two common provisions that may act as incentives to foreign investment are the tax deferral and tax credit provisions. Deferral provides that taxes will

---

[17] Alan C. Brennglass, *The Overseas Private Investment Corporation* (New York: Praeger Publishers, 1983).

[18] For further detail on capital assistance programs, see *Investing in Developing Countries,* 5th ed. (Paris: OECD, 1983).

not be levied by the home country until profits are repatriated. Tax credit provides that direct taxes paid to a foreign government will be credited against the tax liability to the home country. These two provisions have been part of U.S. legislation for more than 50 years but have come under considerable criticism for their purported subsidy of foreign investment.

Political Representation.   Investor countries have used their political influence to persuade host countries to relax their restrictions over inbound foreign business investment. For example, the United States has pressured Japan directly and through the OECD to liberalize its stringent limitations on foreign investment. Also, the U.S. Congress has given official government support to U.S. investors overseas by legislating quasi-automatic sanctions against governments that nationalize U.S. holdings without full compensation. These sanctions may be in the form of terminating U.S. foreign aid; denying eligibility for import privileges under the Generalized System of Preferences (GSP); or opposition to loans from international agencies.

Restraints

Virtually all investor countries, including the United States, have at times controlled capital exports for balance-of-payments reasons. But the objective is usually to limit balance-of-payments deficits rather than to promote certain national goals through foreign direct investment. In some cases, however, countries have used controls to support foreign policy goals such as protesting against apartheid policies in South Africa.

In contrast to the laissez-faire policies of other investor nations, Japan has a long history of controlling overseas investment by Japanese firms so as to achieve specific national goals. Before 1971, each overseas investment had to be approved by Japan's Ministry of International Trade and Industry (MITI). Since 1971, MITI has not reviewed overseas investments on a case-by-case basis. Nevertheless, the government maintains an industrial strategy policy that firms are expected to observe.

Sweden's control program governing outbound foreign direct investment became effective in 1974. It requires prospective investors to include in their applications to the government an analysis of the effects of their overseas project on domestic employment and industrial policies. Applicants are also required to include the views of the labor unions representing their workers. When necessary "to achieve the objectives of national economic policy," the government is authorized to block a foreign direct investment. In 1978, out of 1,145 applications for outward investment, 29 were refused.

In the United States, the belief that uncontrolled overseas direct investment is in the national interest began to be challenged by labor unions and others in the 1970s. The Burke-Hartke bill, introduced in the U.S. Congress in 1971 but never passed, would have established extensive controls over the foreign operations of U.S. firms.[19]

The economic arguments for controls stressed the economic costs to the investor country. According to this view, overseas investments have a negative impact on the home country through the loss of jobs, reduced foreign exchange earnings, and a steady erosion of the competitiveness of the United States in the world economy because of the export of technology to foreign subsidiaries.

The challenges to the conventional wisdom have provoked a flood of studies by business advocacy groups, labor unions, and government agencies that attempted to provide definitive answers to the economic questions being raised. Thus a considerable controversial literature exists on most of the economic questions but there are no clear and compelling answers. The challengers to established U.S. policies have not yet succeeded in persuading the Congress to establish controls over outbound direct investments.

Political impact arguments have also been raised in support of the demand for controls. They emphasize that a distinction must be made between the foreign policy interests of the home country and the specific interests of the multinational corporation. U.S. investments in foreign countries can have a negative as well as a positive impact on U.S. foreign policy.

In the past, the U.S. government often assumed responsibility for protecting the interests of international business firms with U.S. nationality, but this practice began to change in the early 1970s. In 1969 the government of Peru expropriated the assets and operations of the International Petroleum Company, a Canadian company whose shares were almost completely owned by Standard Oil of New Jersey (now EXXON).[20] In 1971 a new Marxist government in Chile expropriated the local subsidiaries of major U.S. copper companies.[21] In both cases, for reasons of foreign policy and political relations with Latin America, the United States backed away from a hard-line position and did not impose the retaliatory actions called for by law.

These cases raise the issue of the need for screening programs by investor nations that assume responsibility for protecting the nation's foreign policy interests in foreign areas. The political problem was bluntly raised as far back as 1962 by Secretary of State Dean Rusk, in testimony before the Foreign Relations Committee on the hearings of the Foreign Assistance Act of 1962:

---

[19] See Robert G. Hawkins and Bertram Finn, "Regulation of Multinational Firms' Foreign Activities: Home Country Policies and Concerns," *Journal of Contemporary Business* 6, no. 4 (Autumn 1977), pp. 7–30; Kent H. Hughes, *Trade, Taxes, and Transnationals: International Economic Decision Making in Congress* (New York: Praeger Publishers, 1979), on the Burke-Hartke controversy.

[20] See Adalberto J. Pinelo, *The Multinational Corporations as a Force in Latin American Politics: A Case Study of International Petroleum Company in Peru* (New York: Praeger Publishers, 1973).

[21] See Theodore Moran, *Multinational Corporations and the Politics of Dependence: Copper in Chile* (Princeton, N.J.: Princeton University Press, 1974).

I don't believe that the U.S. can afford to stake its interests in other countries on a particular private investment in a particular situation, because someone has to live with the results anyhow. . . . If we are to tie American policy by law to the private investor overseas, then I think that we, of necessity, must reassure ourselves as to the operations, the conduct, the financial structure, and other aspects of those private investors.[22]

One alternative for investor countries is a comprehensive screening program as was used by Japan. In the early 1970s, when Japan became concerned about rising resentment toward its business expansion, which was being viewed as neocolonialism in some Southeast Asian countries, it added a review of political impact to its examination of proposed outbound investments. Another alternative is to screen only those projects that apply for government risk insurance.

Still another alternative is for the home country to be neutral and require international business firms of its nationality to assume all of the risks of dealing with foreign governments. This may not be feasible, however, for countries where international firms are powerful domestic political forces and expect their government to give them protection. Furthermore, the activities of international firms may have significant repercussions for an investor country, even though such a nation is not anxious to assume responsibility for its international firms. Disputes may cause difficulties for the home country whether it likes it or not.

Will investor countries increase their controls over outbound investment in the future? Two underlying trends suggest that increased controls are likely. First, the long-prevailing view in investor countries that outbound investment always brings positive benefits has been successfully challenged. As a result, the policy debates are revolving more and more around technical studies and specific evidence rather than ideologies and beliefs. A second element is the burgeoning controls of host countries. These host-country controls are likely to create the need for investor countries to protect themselves against their own enterprises as these firms react to meet the demands of other nations.

CONTROLLING INWARD DIRECT INVESTMENT

Incentives

For obvious reasons, the LDCs and the less developed regions within an economically advanced country are most likely to be offering incentives to attract industry. But a country may offer attractive incentives at an early stage of development, and later reduce its incentives and even impose restraints. Or it may have a mixture of inducements for some fields and restraints in others. Normally, the incentives are available to either domestic or foreign firms—such as Italy's long-

---

[22] *Foreign Assistance Act of 1962. Hearings Before the Committee on Foreign Relations,* U.S. Senate, 87th Congress, 2d sess. (Washington, D.C.: U.S. Government Printing Office, 1962), p. 31.

standing effort to accelerate development of its poorer southern region. But in the case of the newly industrializing nations, where indigenous enterprise is weak or nonexistent, incentive programs are intended primarily to attract foreign business firms.

Incentives offered reflect a nation's stage of economic development, its specific development priorities, and its need to compensate for such business limitations as small local markets. Many small, newly independent countries with little local industry may offer a broad range of incentives that are not selective as to type of business activity. On the other hand, the semi-industrialized or even industrialized countries may direct their incentives to specific types of new activities.

Great ingenuity has been shown in developing incentives to fit the particular goals of individual countries, or individual states or provinces. Flexibility is increased, moreover, by a common practice of wording the enabling laws so as to leave considerable bargaining discretion for government administrators. As a result, incentives within one particular country might vary according to the location of the investment, the size of the investment, the industry, the employment created, or even, as in the case of India, according to the number of shifts worked. In some cases, usually through administrative discretion rather than published regulations, countries try to encourage a mix of nationalities for inbound investment so as to reduce the appearance or reality of foreign economic domination by one country.

Incentives offered generally fall into the following categories:

Tariff Protection. Potential import competition is reduced or eliminated by special high tariffs or import controls.

Duty-Free Imports. Equipment and sometimes future supplies of raw materials or components are allowed to enter the country duty-free or on special concessionary terms.

Financial Assistance. Short- and long-term loans, generally from government agencies, may be available at special low-interest rates.

Tax Concessions. Tax reductions, deferrals, and even 10-year tax holidays are being offered in certain countries.

Foreign Exchange Guarantees. Specific governmental guarantees that foreign exchange will be granted for profit remittances and capital repatriation.

Other Governmental Assistance. The government may assist in assembling parcels of land or agree to build roads or other public facilities needed to complement a project, or even provide subsidies for training personnel.

An important force in shaping incentive programs has been the competition among host countries, states, or provinces as potential locations for the international enterprise. This has been particularly important in relation to regional integration movements. With the elimination of internal tariff walls within the European Community, a foreign firm locating in any of the member countries gained free access to the markets of the others. Consequently, competition developed among the countries in attracting foreign investment. A similar pattern has developed within the United States in recent years. Competition among the states has resulted in extremely attractive inducements being offered to foreign investors.

The establishment of a free port, foreign trade zone, or border industry program can attract foreign investment by using a combination of incentives. In the case of free ports and foreign trade zones, goods may be imported, processed, or stored indefinitely duty-free, with payment of appropriate duties only when goods are shipped from the port or zone into the customs territory. In the case of the border industry program, industries are permitted to import materials and components duty-free, employ local labor to assemble them, and export the products, paying a duty on only value added.

Investment promotion efforts are not limited to the nonsocialist countries. Several Eastern European socialist countries have taken special steps to permit and encourage foreign private companies to make direct investments in their countries.[23] The investment promotion measures being used illustrate the reciprocal nature of inducements and restrictions because reductions in restrictions have operated as incentives.

Restraints

Host countries are at many different stages in devising policies and programs for restraining multinational business. A growing number of nations, having addressed themselves directly to the issue, have formulated a comprehensive set of policies and devised a coordinated set of control instruments.[24] Many other countries follow an evolutionary case-by-case approach in negotiating investment agreements.

Given the variations in national goals, national control programs differ in the aspects of multinational business on which they focus and the tools used. Tax measures, foreign exchange controls, and legal restrictions are used in varying proportions. A growing tendency has been to supplement restrictive measures over multinational firms with affirmative policies to strengthen domestic industries—through mergers, financial assistance for research and development, and other means. Where these incentives discriminate against foreign-owned firms, those firms are in effect penalized to the extent of the advantage accorded their competition.

From the standpoint of the international enterprise, it is important to note that control activities generally focus on new enterprises and new projects. The operations of established foreign enterprises, which may have an even greater impact on host-country goals, are frequently neglected.

---

[23] See Martin Schnitzer, *U.S. Business Involvement in Eastern Europe* (New York: Praeger Publishers, 1980).

[24] See Centre on Transnational Corporations. *National Legislation and Regulations Relating to Transnational Corporations* (New York: United Nations, 1978).

Entry and Takeover Controls

In most countries foreign investors must request approval for a new investment project or for takeovers of existing local firms. In France, foreign firms must apply to the Ministry of Finance for permission. In India, a Foreign Investment Board coordinates the review of foreign direct investment applications, but decision-making authority on separate features of a project is decentralized. The United States is almost unique in that no permission whatever is required. As one foreign firm entering the United States observed, "We were confused when we invested in the States. Every other country has a door that says 'Enter here to request permission.' We couldn't find any such door in the States."

The majority of developing countries and some advanced nations have established procedures for systematic screening of foreign investment. The investment laws in these countries generally specify broad criteria to be used in the evaluation of foreign investment requests. The criteria may be extremely general as in the case of Kenya—"projects furthering economic development or of benefit to Kenya, as determined by the Minister of Finance." In the case of Mexico, the criteria are "the importance of the activity to development, including export production, the use of domestic inputs, the effect on employment, wages, prices, and the balance of payments, the transfer of technology and the training of technical and managerial cadres, the diversification of investment, regional development, the respect of national and social values and a general identification with the national interest."[25]

By requiring a potential investor to gain approval, the host country throws onto the would-be investor a responsibility to describe operational, financial, and expansion plans in some detail and to justify the anticipated contributions to national goals. The reviewing authority is automatically placed in a position of power to open negotiations on adjustment of particular aspects of the proposal.

Where government authority is widely dispersed, where guidelines are vague, and where strict ethical standards do not prevail, the process of controlling the entry of foreign projects may involve crude or highly sophisticated forms of bribery and corruption.

If the host nation has signed a treaty of friendship, commerce, and navigation with the home country of the investor (see Chapter 8), it might technically be a breach of the treaty for the reviewing authority to withhold approval. The would-be investor should be accorded "national treatment" identical to the treatment of local firms. Delay in approval, however, is not a breach; and most investors would think it dangerous to establish a business against a host government's wishes.

Prohibition of Foreign Ownership

In numerous countries, foreigners are excluded from specific business fields. They are excluded from the tobacco and mining industries in Sweden; from

---

[25] Ibid., p. 212.

development of certain natural resources in Brazil, Finland, and Morocco; from retail trade in the Philippines; from Norway's textile and shipping industries; and from holding mining rights in Italy. Mexican exclusions are particularly sweeping. Mexico prohibits foreign ownership of land within 31 miles of the coastlines or 62 miles of the borders with other countries, and Mexican companies permitting foreign shareholders are not allowed to own land in the restricted zones. In accordance with the constitution, the petroleum industry, the generation and distribution of electric power, railroads, and telegraphic communications are legally reserved for the government. Private enterprise, whether domestic or foreign, is therefore restricted from these fields. Foreigners, except as minority investors, are not permitted to invest in Mexican banks or other credit institutions, or in insurance companies. Recent administrations have also required, but not retroactively, either 100 percent ownership or a majority of Mexican ownership in a wide range of industries, including radio and television broadcasting; production, distribution, and exhibition of motion pictures; all phases of the soft-drink industry; advertising and publishing; and fishing and packing of marine products.

Public-utility fields are widely restricted, either because of ideological preferences for public enterprise or because the activities are considered indispensable for national development. Governments generally restrict the communication fields such as television, radio, and news publications to domestic firms or the government for protection of vital national interests. As a Canadian government report explains, "Communications media lie at the heart of the technostructure of modern societies. Canadian ownership and control facilitate the expression of Canadian points of view."[26] Protecting national interests is also the rationale for prohibiting foreign ownership in the banking, insurance, and other financial fields. To quote the Canadian report again, "Financial institutions, because of their pervasiveness and their potential as bases for influence and control, constitute the commanding heights of the economy. Canadian ownership and control facilitate the exercise of Canadian economic policies."

Controls over Natural Resource Extraction

Host-country policies controlling international business activity in natural resource fields have a special ideological and even emotional flavor. In most countries of the world, subsurface mineral rights and often forestry resources are reserved by law as the *property of the nation as a whole*. This legal pattern results from the belief that resources provided by nature should be used for public benefit rather than private profit. Thus, the international business firm operating in the natural resource field is frequently dealing directly with government officials rather than with private owners of property, and with an issue that is of public rather than private concern. The situation is further complicated when

---

[26] "Foreign Ownership and Structure of Canadian Industry," *Report of the Task Force on the Structure of Canadian Industry* (Ottawa: Queen's Printer, 1968), p. 389.

the natural resource being exploited is exhaustible, and the nation cannot expect the project to continue indefinitely making its contribution to the national economy and public welfare.

The issue of controls over foreign firms does not arise, obviously, where countries restrict the exploitation of certain natural resources to government or domestic enterprises. But where foreign firms are allowed to operate, special controls or policies are generally imposed. The standard arrangement has been for a foreign company to purchase a concession giving it exclusive rights to explore in a particular area and to develop and produce the minerals or the petroleum found in that area for a stated number of years. The host government receives royalties on the materials extracted and income taxes on the net earnings of the concessionaire. The production of petroleum and minerals is generally for export, frequently to other foreign affiliates of the producing companies. Much of international business activity in resource exploitation is located in the less developed countries, and in these countries the resource industries are likely to be major sources of foreign exchange earnings, domestic employment, and economic growth. Consequently, host countries are especially anxious to secure a maximum share of the benefits by extending national controls over production, pricing, and marketing.

Specially negotiated concession agreements are intended to spell out the conditions under which foreign enterprises can operate. But in many of the countries, governments have changed with great frequency, and the new government may endeavor to alter or renegotiate the agreements.[27] In fact, the renegotiation of concession agreements is almost certain when foreign enterprises have secured unusually favorable arrangements and when the respective bargaining power of the two parties changes.

Over time, the degree of ownership and control by foreign firms is likely to decline because the unique contributions that the foreign firm makes to the domestic resource industries are also likely to decline. The bargaining power of the foreign firm is ultimately based on the degree to which its capital, technical skills, managerial ability, and marketing knowledge are needed by a foreign country. As the foreign enterprise earns profits for the country and trains local technical and operating personnel, it undercuts its own bargaining power by making less scarce the unique contributions that it had to offer initially.

Expropriation

Strictly used, the term *expropriation* refers to governmental action to dispossess someone of property, but with compensation. Government takeover without compensation is referred to as *confiscation,* as occurred with the takeover of foreign investment in Cuba in 1960. Distinction should also be made between

---

[27] William A. Stoevèr, *Renegotiations in International Business Transactions* (Lexington, Mass.: D.C. Heath, 1981).

expropriation and nationalization. Expropriation normally refers to the taking of a single property or business activity by the state. Nationalization usually means the taking of all activities or properties in a certain field—such as the nationalization of the steel industry in Great Britain, of the banks in France, and of petroleum exploration in Venezuela. Nationalization may involve a number of expropriations. Nationalization and expropriation are, however, frequently used interchangeably or even replaced with such terms as *indigenization* or *domestication*.[28]

Expropriation is in many ways the ultimate host-country control over foreign enterprises. The firm is forced to give up assets and profitable operations for which it risked capital. The compensation following expropriation has usually been less than the ''going concern'' value of the subsidiary to the parent firm. On some occasions, the loss of a subsidiary may mean the creation of a competitor.

The number of expropriations and nationalizations since World War II has been significant. One study identified 559 acts of takeover of foreign enterprises over the period from 1960 to 1979.[29] It appears, however, that the mid-1970s was a peak period for expropriations and that the trend has turned toward more limited use of this control strategy.

One reason for the trend reversal is that past expropriations of foreign investment in petroleum, mining, public utilities, insurance, and so on have left relatively little to expropriate. Nevertheless, one study has argued that selective expropriation has been remarkably rational and confined to those parts of economies in which foreign firms have ceased to contribute more than comparable local firms could contribute. Furthermore, they appear to have been managed so as to minimize the fall off of future potential investment inflows resulting from investors' fears of future expropriation.[30]

Nationalizaton risk has generally been considered to be limited to the developing and socialist countries. But patterns keep changing. As of the late 1970s and early 1980s, the advanced capitalistic countries of Canada and France were the most active areas for nationalization. Under Canada's federal system, provincial governments possess broad powers over local mineral resources. In 1978, Saskatchewan invoked these powers to nationalize much of its potash industry and reduce foreign ownership in this area. Quebec also moved to expropriate foreign investment in asbestos mining. The nationalization program of the Mitterand government in France was directed toward specific business areas and involved foreign as well as domestic investors. In the mid-1980s, nationalization has widely given way to denationalization.

---

[28] J. Frederick Truitt, *Expropriation of Private Foreign Investment* (Bloomington: Graduate School of Business, Indiana University, 1974), pp. 9–11.

[29] Stephen J. Kobrin, ''Expropriation as an Attempt to Control Foreign Firms in LDCs: Trends from 1960 to 1979,'' *International Studies Quarterly*, 1984 (28), pp. 329–48.

[30] P. Juhl, ''Economically Rational Design of Developing Countries' Expropriation Policies Towards Foreign Investment,'' *Management International Review* 25 (1985), pp. 44–52.

Limitation of Foreign Ownership

Policies to minimize the effects of foreign ownership are two-pronged. They can be designed to strengthen domestic enterprise or weaken the power of foreign firms. Sometimes, both objectives are accomplished in single actions. The Japanese government has long had a policy of encouraging licensing agreements with local firms rather than direct foreign investment. Such a policy can be effective if a country is extremely attractive to international business firms, and if the domestic industry sector is strong and has potential and resources for fully utilizing the technology part of the foreign business package without the accompanying investment and management resources.

Governments also attempt to minimize foreign domination by opposing or prohibiting the acquisition of domestic firms by international enterprises. Canada, for example, created its Foreign Investment Review Agency (FIRA) in 1973 to screen all foreign takeovers of existing Canadian firms. The yardstick used by FIRA for approval was that foreign ownership must provide "significant benefit to Canada."[31] With the same objective of restricting foreign investment, France followed the strategy of promoting and encouraging mergers on the assumption that larger and presumably more competitive domestic firms would reduce the competitive advantage of foreign firms.

Policies requiring that ownership and control of foreign business projects be shared with local firms are another means of reducing foreign control. Mexico, for example, has taken a hard line on having Mexicans share in the ownership of Mexican affiliates or subsidiaries of international business firms. Its Mexicanization policy is promoted through bargaining when permission is granted for foreign firms to establish business in the country and through policies that limit certain tax exemptions or export permits to companies at least 51 percent owned by Mexican nationals.

Performance Requirements

A major type of performance requirement imposed by some countries is so-called *local-content* policies.[32] Prospective investors are asked to commit themselves to a schedule of increasing the locally produced content of the final product over a stated period of time. Such local-content policies have been widely applied to automobile manufacturers who have expanded in Latin America, with the hope that the development impetus of new types of activity will continue over

---

[31] Charles J. McMillan, "The Regulation of Foreign Investment in Canada: Experience and Prospects," *Journal of Contemporary Business,* Autumn 1977, pp. 31–51; Alan M. Rugman, "The Regulation of Foreign Investment in Canada," *Journal of World Trade Law,* July/August 1977, pp. 322–33.

[32] See Stephen E. Guisinger and Associates, *Investment Incentives and Performance Requirements* (New York: Praeger Publishers, 1985).

time and be extended into other related areas of activity. But countries may have to pay a high price for having local content when local markets are not large enough to permit economic scale production for many parts and components.

Another way of increasing local benefits is through employment policies imposed on international enterprises. The labor law of Mexico provides that at least 90 percent of a foreign company's employees must be Mexican citizens. Executives are generally excluded in calculating this percentage. The immigration of foreigners for managerial and other positions is permitted only if qualified Mexicans are not available. Some countries also establish limits in relation to the total payroll.

Export strategies of multinational enterprises have become the focus of another set of controls. Countries have realized that the global strategies of multinational firms may not allow or encourage subsidiaries and affiliates to compete freely for export markets. Some countries thus make it a requirement for approval of all new operations that the units are completely free to export and earn foreign exchange. Some nations will even force divestiture if a specified proportion of output is not exported. And there are many pressures exerted for local processing of local materials before export.

Financial and Fiscal Controls

Balance-of-payments objectives are increasingly obvious in the development of controls over financing. Many host countries require external financing for new foreign investments and some limit the access of foreign firms to local sources of capital. Other common policies are control over remission of profits, repatriation of capital, and royalty payments to the home office of the foreign enterprise. To back these controls, however, more and more countries are realizing that they need additional controls to regulate transfer pricing for goods and services moving among units of the international enterprise.

REGIONAL AND INTERNATIONAL CONTROLS

While the controls that confront multinational firms are those of the individual nation states, some regional or international groupings of states have agreed to standardize controls.

The principal example of a common regional approach to foreign direct investment is the Andean Pact. Negotiated in 1971 by Bolivia, Chile, Colombia, Ecuador, and Peru and joined later by Venezuela, the Pact took a hard line toward foreign investors. Under Decision 24 of the Pact, new foreign investment was excluded from the areas of public utilities, the mass media, advertising, and banking. Existing firms in these areas were given three years to sell 80 percent of their stock to local nationals. The profit rate on invested foreign capital was limited to 14 percent for repatriation purposes and 5 percent for reinvestment. New foreign enterprises wishing to take advantage of tariff reductions were required to sell 51 percent ownership to national investors or governments over a period of 15 to 20 years.

The success of such a hard-line approach depends in large part on the attractiveness of the host countries to foreign investors and the relative bargaining strength of the countries and the foreign investors. While the common policy certainly reduced competition among the Andean countries, the net result has been to discourage foreign investment.[33] Chile withdrew from the Pact in 1976 because it considered the regulations to be too rigid and there had been recent steps by Ecuador and Peru to relax Decision 24.

At the international level, the international business community and some investor nations have long been pressing for a multilateral convention establishing a code for fair treatment and protection of foreign investment. Not too surprisingly, the codes proposed by the investors and investor countries focused heavily on the responsibilities and obligations of the host countries.

Most national governments were slow to join the movement for international codes of conduct. By the mid-1970s, however, the governments of the industrialized countries (through the OECD) and the developing countries (through the UN Commission on Transnational Corporations) began to demonstrate considerable enthusiasm for an international code.[34] But the difference between the concerns of multinational firms and those of governments became sharply apparent. To the international business community, international regulation means restraints on governments. To the governments, international regulation means restraints on multinational enterprises. Somewhat ironically, the movement for a code of fair treatment and protection of investors had become transformed into a movement for the fair treatment and protection of countries.

The first product of this new-found concern of governments was a Declaration on International Investment and Multinational Enterprises approved by OECD countries in 1976. The declaration includes rather detailed Guidelines for Multinational Enterprises that "aim at improving the international investment climate," at strengthening "confidence between multinational enterprises and states," and "at encouraging the positive contributions of multinational enterprises to economic and social progress and minimizing or resolving difficulties that may result from their activities."[35] Although an intergovernmental consultation procedure has been established, the guidelines are voluntary and the parties to the declaration do not include any of the developing countries.

What are the prospects for global agreement on standard controls? The issues to be resolved are not simple. If many countries benefit significantly, others are likely to perceive costs. As the vast majority of United Nations members are

---

[33] Robert E. Grosse, *Foreign Investment Codes and the Location of Direct Investment* (New York: Praeger Publishers, 1980).

[34] See John Robinson, *Multinationals and Political Control* (London: Gower Publishing Co. Ltd., 1983).

[35] OECD, *International Investment and Multinational Operations*, Revised Edition (Paris: 1984).

host countries only, their majority pressure for controls has been against the interests of the investor countries. The investor countries agree that multinational corporations should adhere to codes of good conduct, but they insist that governments as well as enterprises must respect obligations undertaken by them. As is suggested by one study, the apparent enthusiasm by both governments and some international managers for international codes "masks different conceptions of who is going to be controlled, who is going to do the controlling, and what the purposes of the control will be."[36]

Some internationally agreed upon measures are likely to emerge. But the forecasts are for only modest accomplishments at the international level. In 1980, after 10 years of discussion by members of the United Nations Conference on Trade and Development, the industrialized, developing, and communist nations adopted a set of guidelines for controlling restrictive business practices in international trade. The guidelines, however, will not affect national laws because they are voluntary. In 1987, the UN Commission on Transnational Corporations was still bogged down, with key issues unresolved, in its six-year effort to draft a code of conduct for multinational corporations. Consequently, the prevailing view is that "control" will continue to be exercised nationally rather than internationally.

SUMMARY

International business operates across and within the boundaries of many discrete sovereign nation-states. The business firm has its private goals that it pursues within a geographical area of its own choosing, which includes the sovereign domains of several or many national governments. Governments have their public purposes, some of which are in harmony with and others that may run counter to the private global goals of the international corporations. As sovereign nations, governments will exercise their power to influence the operating patterns of the enterprises. Through incentives, they encourage those activities considered to be in harmony with national goals. Through negative curbs, they try to constrain those activities likely to conflict with national goals. The multinational enterprise will try to thread its way through the multiple and often conflicting claims of many governments with the minimum of sacrifice to its goals.

The stimulus for national control programs does not come primarily from bad experience with multinationals, although many examples exist of what nations consider to be "negative behavior." National governments have long used controls over international transfers of goods, money flow, and persons to increase their share of national benefits from such international transactions. Similar controls over the operations of multinational enterprises have now been adopted by nations to increase a nation's share of the global benefits generated by these enterprises and to reduce the negative effects, such as a threat of economic domination and challenges to economic and political autonomy.

---

[36] C. Fred Bergsten, Thomas Horst, and Theodore H. Moran, *American Multinationals and American Interests* (Washington, D.C.: Brookings Institution, 1978), p. 398.

EXERCISES AND DISCUSSION QUESTIONS

1. What are the principal objectives of exchange-control systems and how do exchange controls serve these objectives?
2. "To prevent the outflow of direct private investment is to kill the goose that lays the golden eggs." Discuss.
3. "There is no cost in making technology available that has already been developed for other purposes; therefore an acquiring nation will maximize its benefits by strictly limiting the amount that can be charged for existing technology. The return permitted on investment associated with any technology transfer, however, should be set in a much different way." Comment on these statements and draw up a set of practical rules for a developing nation to use in controlling the returns going to foreigners for technology and investment.
4. "Investment-guaranty insurance merely encourages both investing companies and host governments to behave more irresponsibly, knowing that the investing company's government would bail the company out. Safeguards should be written into such schemes that would prevent a company claiming on the guarantee scheme if it had somehow provoked the host government into nationalization, for instance by bad labor practices or disguised political activity locally." Discuss.
5. The United States has a vital national-security interest in acquiring dependable foreign sources of critical minerals at a reasonable cost. Therefore, it should give maximum support and protection to the foreign direct investments of U.S. international resource industries in such fields as petroleum and copper, where U.S. domestic production is insufficient for U.S. needs. Discuss.
6. You have been retained by an industrialized country, such as France, to recommend strategy and policies for regulating the entry and continuing operations of foreign multinational companies in that country. What are the two or three most important issues that you would have to resolve? What information would you need to complete your assignment? In what ways would the key problems and the nature of your recommendations be different if you were working for a small LDC in Africa?
7. Host-country policies that require multinational companies to share ownership with nationals are frequently used to minimize the economic power of foreign interests. But such policies will also reduce the amount of foreign capital transfers to the host country and reduce the supply of local capital for domestic entrepreneurs. Why do you think so many host countries are insisting that foreign firms share ownership with locals?
8. Under what circumstances would you as a host country prohibit foreign companies from acquiring domestic companies? Why?
9. In formulating an investment promotion program to attract foreign direct investment to a less developed country, which incentives do you think would be most effective and why?
10. Alleging that the Japanese auto companies locating in the United States are making excessive use of imported parts, a New York congressman has introduced a bill in the U.S. Congress that would require 80 percent of the value added in cars assembled in U.S. foreign-trade zones to be American. As a lobbyist for the Japanese auto companies, what arguments would you use to oppose this use of performance requirements? (Hint: Would the law be a violation of GATT?)

CHAPTER 13

Measuring Benefits to Countries and Negotiating Agreements

Who benefits from the expansion of multinational enterprises? The international business community holds the view that the multinationals benefit both home and host countries. An opposing view argues that the multinationals are the agents of the capitalist-imperialist countries, producing and maintaining a pattern of inequality and dependency among the developing countries. Still another view, the global-reach position, argues that the effects of the multinationals are negative on home and host countries alike.

But while the ideological debate has waxed and waned, most host countries have been moving to a less ideological and more social cost-benefit approach to foreign direct investment. This approach recognizes that foreign investment has costs as well as benefits to the nation. Consequently, governments must evaluate each case in an effort to distinguish between the positive and negative effects, both actual and prospective.

This chapter discusses the major areas of controversy in the ideological debates, the concepts underlying social cost-benefit techniques, the approaches being used for measuring benefits to the nation-state, and the process of international negotiations.

THE IDEOLOGICAL DEBATES

The ideological debates on the vices and virtues of multinational enterprises have generated a vast academic and popular literature.[1] The neoimperialist view would recommend that host countries should not permit the entry of foreign direct investment because the multinationals are a tool for exploiting host countries to the exclusive benefit of their capitalist-imperialist home countries. As discussed in the next chapter, the position of the neoimperialists has been sabotaged by the pragmatic behavior of the Peoples Republic of China and the countries of Eastern Europe. These nations apparently recognize that they can benefit from collaboration with multinational enterprises.

The *dependencia* school, which has flourished in Latin American intellectual and government circles, pictures the world economy as consisting of the major capitalistic countries as the "center" and the underdeveloped countries as the "periphery."[2] It attributes the development problems of the periphery to an unbalanced relationship with the center. The result of this unbalanced relationship is that economic growth in the less developed countries has been distorted and limited by being subordinated to the economies of the major capitalist countries. Foreign investment may stimulate growth in the peripheral countries, but it is likely to be growth of the wrong products and industries. There may be growth of income, but for the elite who are allied with the multinationals, and not for the needy. But the dependency view has lost force in recent years. One factor has been considerable negative experience with nationalized enterprises.[3] Another

---

[1] For an in-depth discussion of these ideologies, see C. Fred Bergsten, Thomas Horst and Theodore H. Moran, *American Multinationals and American Interests* (Washington D.C.: Brookings Institution, 1978), pp. 309–53.

[2] See, for example, Andre Gunder Frank, *Capitalism and Underdevelopment in Latin America* (New York: Monthly Review Press, 1967); Osvaldo Sunkel, "Big Business and Dependencia, A Latin View," *Foreign Affairs,* April 1972, pp. 517–31.

[3] Paul E. Sigmund, *Multinationals in Latin America* (Madison: University of Wisconsin Press, 1980), pp. 256–301; Raymond Vernon, "Multinational Enterprises in Developing Countries: Issues in Dependency and Interdependency," in *The Multinational Corporation and Social Change,* ed. David E. Apter and Louis W. Goodman (New York: Praeger Publishers, 1976), pp. 40–62.

factor has been the growing realization that host countries have a great deal of power for shaping the participation of foreign enterprises in their economies.

The ideological debates have given way to pragmatism in many countries.[4] Yet a number of the issues raised by the debates are included in the evaluation process of social cost-benefit analysis. Some of the major areas where the costs and benefits of international business are open to debate are examined below.

THE IMPACT ON NATIONAL SOVEREIGNTY

The multinational enterprise is subject to the sovereign power of a nation-state over its business activities within that state's territory. But, unlike purely domestic firms, the multinational also responds to outside commands emanating from the parent, other family members, or even indirectly from other sovereign states. Furthermore, the local subsidiary can rely for support on the economic power of the entire system and at times on the political power of other sovereigns. The presence within a nation of an appendage of a powerful multinational system may thus generate local tensions and appear to be a threat to national sovereignty.[5]

The threat to sovereignty reflects considerations over and above the sum of the net benefits or costs of individual international business activities. As a result, any specific international business project may become subordinated to the broader issues and may not be evaluated as an independent event. International firms, therefore, should not ignore the more general nationalistic concerns in the cost-benefit analyses.

THE POLITICAL CHALLENGE

The history of foreign investment during the 19th and early 20th centuries contains many examples of foreign firms, particularly in the extractive industries, exercising their power to influence political events in host countries (see Box 13–1). However, direct attempts at political influence by multinational firms have steadily declined. The multinational now tends to face more subtle political problems in which it is unintentionally caught between opposing political interests of different nation-states.

To the host country, the local subsidiary of a multinational enterprise can be perceived as a political arm of the home-country government. Through its control over the parent company, home governments can and have interfered in the political affairs of another, or host country. Over certain periods, for example, the U.S. government has pressured U.S. subsidiaries in England and in Europe into turning away business from Cuba and Soviet-bloc countries, even though

---

[4] See Sanjaya Lall, "Transnationals and the Third World: Changing Perceptions," *National Westminster Bank Quarterly Review*, May 1984, pp. 2–16.

[5] The "threat to sovereignty," however, can also be an "extension of sovereignty" with the host country able to extend its sovereignty into the home country. See Joseph S. Nye, Jr., "Multinational Corporations in World Politics," *Foreign Affairs*, October 1974, p. 158.

BOX 13–1
Dollar Diplomacy, 1972 Style

I helped make Mexico safe for American oil interests in 1914. I helped make Haiti and Cuba a decent place (sic) for the National City Bank boys to collect revenue in. I helped purify Nicaragua for the international banking house of Brown Brothers. . . . I brought light to the Dominican Republic for American sugar interests in 1916. I helped make Honduras "right" for American fruit companies in 1903. Looking back on it, I might have given Al Capone a few hints.

Maj. Gen. Smedley D. Butler, USMC, 1931

By the time Smedley Butler pridefully described his role in Latin America, economic colonialism by the world's prosperous nations had come to be regarded almost as a matter of course. For nearly two and a half centuries, Britain's East India Co. had provided stunning evidence of just how far the practice could go by ruling one fifth of the world's population, maintaining its own standing army, and producing revenues that actually exceeded its homeland's. But if America was a latecomer, it quickly made up for lost time. Washington spent the first three decades of the 20th century wielding its big stick on behalf of U.S. business interests, intervening in Latin America alone an astounding 60 times.

* * * * *

Against this background, the recent charges that officials of International Telephone and Telegraph Corp. had conspired with the CIA to block the election of Chile's Marxist president, Salvador Allende Gossens, seemed evidence that, for all their low profile and talk of corporate good citizenship, some multinational corporations of 1972 may operate just as cynically as the United Fruit of 1928.

SOURCE: *Newsweek*, April 10, 1972.

---

the nations in which the subsidiaries are located have different policies.[6] Other conflicts with host countries have occurred, as discussed in Chapter 8, through the enforcement of U.S. antitrust laws, which has had the effect of banning activities in another country that are not against the laws of that country.

Still another type of political challenge to a host country occurs when the home country of the multinational parent assumes political responsibility for protecting the foreign interests of its citizens. Although foreign subsidiaries are normally incorporated within the countries in which they are operating and subject

---

[6] See Jack N. Behrman, "Export and Technology Controls," in *National Interests and the Multinational Enterprise* (Englewood Cliffs, N.J.: Prentice-Hall, 1970), pp. 101–13.

to national laws as a national corporation, home-country governments are not always willing to accept the results of expropriation under local law.

The multinational enterprise faces a complex and ambiguous situation in the political conflict area. It has little, if any, capability for reducing the political challenge it represents to host countries when it is used as a political arm of the home government and in cases involving extra-territoriality. It does not relish its role as a carrier of controls. At best, it can urge the conflicting nation-states to undertake bilateral negotiations or participate in intergovernmental programs to harmonize laws or mediate disputes.

In their relations with home countries, multinational companies have mixed and, at times, ambivalent views. Some companies would like to be independent of the political interests of a home country. Some have even expressed the desire to have an island somewhere in international waters as their home base. Other firms place a high value on having a home-country government that will protect their operations in a foreign country and represent their interests in intergovernmental negotiations on such matters as tariffs and trade policies. In still other cases, multinational enterprises would like to be politically free from their home country on some issues and yet be able to call for its political muscle on other issues.

REDUCTION IN ECONOMIC INDEPENDENCE

In any individual case, a multinational firm may offer sizable net benefits to a nation in which it is operating. But when a dominant share of the domestic economy comes under foreign ownership and control, the merits of the individual case become subordinated to a nation's broader concern for maintaining its economic independence. Over many decades, the new jobs and other benefits generated by foreign investment in Canada were sufficiently appealing to quiet national fears of foreign economic domination. But when 60 percent of Canada's manufacturing industry, 75 percent of her petroleum and natural gas industry, and 60 percent of her mining industry came under control of foreign corporations by the mid-1960s, national sovereignty tolerance levels were breached. As one Canadian scholar expressed this concern: "Once the most dynamic sectors of our economy have been lost, once most of the savings and investment is taking place in the hands of foreign capitalists, then the best prediction is a steady drift toward foreign control of the Canadian economy with the only certain upper limit being 100 percent."[7]

Nations also become agitated when foreign enterprises dominate key growth industries. Writing in 1901, a British author observed, "The most serious aspect of the American industrial invasion lies in the fact that these incomers have acquired control of almost every new industry created during the past fifteen

---

[7] Mel Watkins, in the preface to Kari Levitt, *Silent Surrender: The American Economic Empire in Canada* (New York: Liveright, 1971), p. xi.

years.''[8] Referring to the British, he concludes, ''We are becoming the hewers of wood and the drawers of water, while the most skilled, most profitable, and the easiest trades are becoming American.''[9]

Somewhat ironically, the necessary conditions for successful international business expansion can be responsible for creating national tensions. Foreign firms must have something to offer over and above what is available from domestic enterprise. In sophisticated technology and rapid growth areas such as computers, international firms have a competitive-advantage basis for entering foreign areas. Thus arises the national fear of becoming technologically dependent upon foreigners.

The multinational threat to national economic autonomy is perceived in many dimensions. As host nations may complain, the decision centers that control many of their key economic sectors are outside of the country and less subject to national controls. The multinational enterprise can shift resources within the system and thus reduce the effectiveness of national programs to control inflation, improve the balance of payments, or expand employment. The research centers for multinational enterprises are likely to remain in the home country, with the result that a host country becomes technologically dependent on outsiders. Foreign enterprises that command mammoth resources and have a head start in key growth areas are viewed as slowing the emergence of local entrepreneurship in these fields.

The LDCs, which can benefit most from the transfers of resources, management skills, and technology of the multinational enterprise, are especially sensitive to the economic domination issue. Foreign investment, as they see it, can change over time from a development stimulant to a retardant. As Hirschman has articulated the case, ''Foreign investment can be at its creative best by bringing in 'missing' factors of production, complementary to those available locally, in the early stages of development of a poor country. The possibility that it will play a stunting role arises later on, when the poor country has begun to generate . . . . its own entrepreneurs, technicians, and savers and could do even more along these lines.'' The increased domestic capacity for supplying missing factors may in large part be the contribution of multinational enterprise. But, as Hirschman argues, institutional inertia makes for continued importing of so-called scarce factors even when they become locally available. This line of thinking has resulted in proposals that foreign enterprises should be forced to withdraw, or disinvest, at the stage when the factors brought in by the multinational enterprise are no longer complementary to local factors but become competitive with them and prevent their growth.[10]

---

[8] Fred A. McKenzie, *The American Invaders* (New York: Street and Smith, 1901), p. 31.

[9] Ibid., p. 157.

[10] Albert O. Hirschman, *How to Divest in Latin America, and Why,* Princeton Essays in International Finance, no. 76 (Princeton N.J.: International Finance Section, Department of Economics, Princeton University, November 1969).

NET NATIONAL BENEFITS: UNDERLYING CONCEPTS

Most nations might agree in principle that the free movement of multinational enterprises across national boundaries can improve overall economic efficiency on a world basis. Yet this does not remove an active concern for how the global gains are distributed among individual nations. Thus the multinational enterprise must focus on individual national benefits rather than on world benefits.

In evaluating national benefits and costs, national authorities may consider political, social, or spiritual effects as well as economic effects. And they may value each effect explicitly or implicitly through the decisions they take. The mix of effects included in any evaluation, however, will vary from nation to nation and reflect differences in national priorities. The same effect will almost certainly be weighted differently by different nations, and the effects considered will change over time as national priorities change.

While these points may be readily grasped at the conceptual level, in practice, the quantification of costs and benefits remains a highly ambiguous subject, even in the economic area. How does a nation measure the value of a transfer of technological and managerial know-how to nationals of that country? What is the value of a foreign enterprise's contribution to national goals of economic and social modernization, or what are the costs of having prized cultural values changed? How much is it worth to have more competition injected into an economy or for indigenous entrepreneurship to be stimulated (or stunted) by the entry into a country of foreign firms? For the home as well as the host country, the quantification problem is equally formidable.[11] Yet, implicitly more often than explicitly, each nation-state makes such calculations, or intuitive leaps, in establishing and exercising controls over international business.

With each nation aiming for a surplus of benefits over costs from the operations of multinational enterprise, it might appear that the international firm is in the middle of an impossible situation. In order for one nation to have net gains, does another nation have to have net losses? Fortunately, two factors help to reduce the stress placed on the multinational enterprise in a world of nation-states. One is that the cost and benefit items have different values for different nations. A loss of jobs to a full-employment Swiss economy because of the establishment of overseas production facilities by a Swiss multinational enterprise will be valued as a small cost to Switzerland. But the same number of jobs will be valued as a great benefit by a host country with a high degree of unemployment that receives a new subsidiary. A second saving feature is that international business activity is not necessarily a zero-sum game in which one nation has to lose in order for another nation to gain. If international business results in a more efficient

---

[11] A major attempt at overall assessment of benefits accruing to the United States from its own multinationals is presented by: C. Fred Bergsten, Thomas Horst, and Theodore H. Moran, *American Multinationals and American Interests: The Economic and Political Effects and Proposals for a New Policy* (Washington, D.C.: Brookings Institution, 1978). See also Erik Hornell and Jan-Erik Valne, *Multinationals: The Swedish Case* (New York: St. Martin's Press, 1986).

use of world resources, all parties can secure increased benefits. Because the pie to be divided is larger, each nation can have a larger slice.

Conceptually, the final or "bottom line" calculation in measuring national benefits involves three steps that must be understood by the foreign firm. *First,* it is not benefits from business expansion per se that are being measured. Instead, the focus is on contributions by the foreign firm that would not otherwise be available to the nation. Only the net contributions over what might have been available from domestically controlled business activities really count. *Second,* costs as well as benefits are calculated and the foreign enterprise must provide a surplus of benefits over costs. *Third,* it is not enough for the benefits to be positive. The surplus must be greater than that for other alternatives available to the nation in order for significant common interests to exist between the enterprise and the specific nation-state. *very rational model, it is perceptions that count*

RESOURCE TRANSFER EFFECTS

A very important component in the calculation of net national benefits is the extent to which the multinational enterprise increases the availability of resources and the supply of productive facilities in the countries where it establishes operations.

In industrialized countries, the important resource transfers may be in the fields of technology, management, and skilled technical manpower. In the less developed countries, the range of resource transfers has generally been much broader. Outside capital has often been a major contribution. Where foreign exchange is a major constraint on growth, foreign capital can help to break this bottleneck. The transfer of technology and the import of management, marketing, and production skills may be valued even more highly than in the more advanced countries. To the extent that the inflow of resources consists of "missing factors," they may complement and effectively "increase" the supply of local factors heretofore idle or less productively used. Thus, the resource transfer effect may be both the net addition from the outside as well as the net increase in the effective value of domestic resources.

Resource transfers have a cost as well as a benefit side. The multinational enterprise may use local resources that are scarce rather than in excess supply. Although local management skills may be in short supply the foreign enterprise is frequently under pressure to hire nationals. It is then likely to be charged with the opportunity cost of preempting managers who otherwise would be available to initiate and direct indigenous enterprises. Or enterprises may be required by national policies to form joint ventures by enlisting local capital and may be charged on the cost side with preempting scarce local capital that should be available for local enterprises.

Whether such opportunity costs are valid costs in calculating net national benefits is a complex question. For example, foreign enterprises that use local capital may enlarge rather than reduce the total supply of that resource. In countries that are attempting to strengthen local capital markets, the selling of equity shares locally by a well-known and presumably financially secure and profitable international firm can increase local confidence in such institutions and thereby help in attracting more savings to capital markets for equity investment.

The profits earned by foreign enterprises can be considered an offsetting cost by a nation. To the extent that a multinational firm transfers profits out of the country, there is a foreign exchange cost. If the firm reinvests profits within the country, the cost to the nation may be that a larger amount of the national patrimony comes under foreign ownership. What is frequently overlooked by antagonists to foreign investment is that such profits come out of newly created increments to domestic GNP generated by the multinational enterprise, and that the profits are generally a small share of the total increment. The firm gains profits: the nation gains an even greater increment in GNP and employment.

Turning to a question posed earlier, if the host countries are gaining resources, aren't the home countries losing? This possibility exists, of course. The normal situation seems to be, however, that resources are being transferred from countries in which they are relatively abundant to areas where such factors are in relatively short supply, and that the opportunity cost to the home country of such resource outflows may be low. Offsetting these home-country costs are a flow of benefits such as repatriated profits, payments to the parent company for royalties and management services, increased exports to overseas subsidiaries, increased exports as an indirect result of expanding world output, and even return flows of technology.

It should be noted that the resource transfer capability of the multinational entrance extends far beyond that of bilateral transfers between home and host country. Operating with a global strategy, the firm can transfer resources among any of the nations in which it is operating.

In order to welcome international firms a nation must feel that the net value of resource transfers from such operations is positive. There may be cases, however, where a net cost is acceptable because of large indirect or linkage benefits. The establishment of an agricultural processing plant by a foreign firm may not in itself result in a net inflow of resources, but the stimulus of this plant to agricultural employment and farm output may be a more than offsetting indirect benefit.

Resource transfers, of course, have a time dimension. When a direct-investment project is initiated, benefits are greatest and certainly most spectacular. In the initial stages, capital flows in, plants are built, local workers are hired and trained, and local supply contracts are let. After a new project has been started, or a new product or process introduced, a steady decline in benefits is likely to set in. The benefits may never phase out completely. Yet over time they may lose much of their value to a nation.

The longer the enterprise operates on its original technological, organizational, and other resource transfer base, the smaller is the value placed on the original benefits by the host country. Where firms do not continue adding to or upgrading their initial technological, organization, or product contribution, the host country may question whether payments to the foreign investor should continue indefinitely since the net contribution to the nation has declined and may even cease over time.[12]

BALANCE-OF-PAYMENTS EFFECTS

The total impact of multinational business operations on either a host or an investor nation's balance of payments has long been a controversial issue. A number of scholarly studies have attempted to resolve the controversy but without success. The conflicting conclusions can be explained mainly by different assumptions as to what would have happened if the foreign investment had not been made and by the completeness of the effects that have been measured.

Host countries often only compare the initial capital inflow—usually a once-and-for-all effect—with the continuing outflows of dividends, interest, royalties, and administrative charges to the parent company. For example, over the 10-year period from 1960 to 1969, the net capital inflow to the less developed countries from U.S. multinationals averaged about $650 million per year. Over the same period, U.S. firms returned to the United States as repatriated earnings an average of $2,500 million per year, plus additional amounts as royalties and fees. From these data, the conclusion can be drawn that the host countries suffered a substantial net loss in foreign exchange from the operations of multinational enterprises and that the investor countries had a substantial net gain.

This type of calculation is misleading because it does not take into account the full range of effects, particularly the effects on the trade accounts—exports and imports—which generally overshadow the effects on capital inflows and repatriation outflows. The foreign firm can generate foreign exchange benefits for a country through expanding exports or substituting for goods and services previously imported. The net result can be a surplus of export earnings and import savings over the foreign exchange expenditures for raw materials or intermediate inputs that the multinational enterprise must import.

A more comprehensive evaluation of foreign exchange effects can be illustrated by a study of 132 projects financed by the Overseas Private Investment Corporation.[13] In fiscal 1976 these projects had a positive balance-of-payments effects for the host countries of $722 million annually. As benefits, the projects generated $837 million in import substitution savings plus $434 million in exports. As costs, the projects required $279 million for importing production inputs and $270 million for profit repatriation and other payments to the parent company.

---

[12] Thomas A. Poynter, "Managing Government Intervention: A Strategy for Defending the Subsidiary," *Columbia Journal of World Business,* Winter 1986, p. 58.

[13] See "U.S. and Development Effects Data Output Sheet for Groups of OPIC Assisted Investors," Report no. 18 (Overseas Private Investment Corporation, Washington, D.C., September 8, 1976; processed).

This study assumed that the same business activity would not have occurred without the foreign investment.

The importance of the assumption as to available alternatives is underlined by another study of 159 companies in six developing countries over a five- to seven-year period in the late 1960s.[14] This study concluded that the balance-of-payments impact of the multinational firms was negative for all countries except Kenya. The net negative effect, however, derived mainly from the assumption in this study that someone else would undertake the production in the absence of the foreign investor.

An important and often emotional issue relating to balance-of-payments effects is transfer pricing. The transfer price is the price at which a transfer or sale of goods takes place *within* a firm, regardless of whether the firm spans several countries. Intracompany transfer prices have tax and other implications, as discussed in Chapter 23 on multinational financial management. Insofar as transfer prices operate against the interests of any host country, such as the parent company charging high prices to its foreign subsidiary, the balance-of-payments gains from foreign investment are less, or losses more, than they would otherwise have been.

The role of the multinational enterprise in expanding export earnings will depend on its export strategy. The enterprise following a global strategy will attempt to supply its export demand from areas of lowest cost, or where excess capacity exists, or where national pressures or incentives for exporting are most effective. Thus, the subsidiary in any specific country may have a better or a worse chance, but not a free chance, of competing for all export markets. As an independent local company, the same operation would have a free, but probably worse, chance of expanding exports. With its ties to other affiliates in the multinational enterprise system, a local subsidiary may bring to a country special export advantages because the system provides an easy conduit to sales in other countries. But many different possibilities exist, and the conclusion will depend upon the specific case being considered. On the whole, the various studies available suggest that the multinational enterprise has been a means of expanding, rather than constraining, exports.[15]

Most certainly, foreign investments in raw materials industries are a major source of increased exports. But, here again, the evaluation of net foreign exchange benefits depends on whether these products would be produced and exported in the absence of foreign investment and at what price. As a result of technology transfers and the opportunity to accumulate capital that followed from multinational business operations, a reasonable assumption for many countries is that local

---

[14] S. Lall and P. Streeten, *Foreign Investment, Transnationals and Developing Countries* (London: Macmillan, 1977); see also Neil Hood and Stephen Young, *The Economics of Multinational Enterprise* (New York: Longman, 1979), pp. 212–15.

[15] *Foreign Ownership and the Structure of Canadian Industry,* Report of the Task Force on the Structure of Canadian Industry (Ottawa: Queen's Printer, 1968), pp. 203–7.

[handwritten margin note: what about domestic knowledge & contacts?]

production and export can take place without foreign investment. Some countries have hired foreign technology and management on service contracts that limit the foreign exchange costs in amount and for a fixed time period. Direct investment requires a continuing outflow of repatriated profits.

How about the home countries of the multinationals and the impact of outbound foreign direct investment on their balance of payments? As in the case of the host-country studies, the conclusions of the investor-country studies depend on the assumptions as to the alternatives available to the multinational enterprises.[16]

If an enterprise can be competitive in foreign markets through exports from the home country, the establishment of a foreign production facility will result in a net foreign exchange loss to the home country. The home country will earn some foreign exchange through the repatriation of profits and the export of components and services to the foreign subsidiary. But the size of these foreign exchange earnings will be much less than what could have been earned through the export of the final products. If, however, the foreign market is likely to be lost to local producers or other foreign competitors, the net balance-of-payments effect will be positive because there will be no loss from export substitution. Foreign production may also be the only feasible alternative where a country has established formidable quota or tariff barriers to force the establishment of local import-substituting industries.

If foreign production is for export back to the home country and substitutes for goods previously manufactured in the home country, there is a foreign exchange cost. If domestic producers have been losing the local market to foreign producers anyway, foreign production by a home-country enterprise may result in a net benefit because there is no loss on the trade account, and the repatriated profits are likely to more than compensate for the initial investment outflow on the capital account. Furthermore, in many cases the multinational enterprise raises some or all of its capital for foreign investment outside of the home country.

In the case of balance-of-payments effects, and the employment effects to be discussed below, the interests of the multinational firm and its home country may be in conflict. In some situations, the multinational company may be able to compete profitably in both home and foreign markets through home-country production. But the firm can make even greater profits through foreign production. In such cases, it is logical for the firm to maximize its profits. But the additional private gains to the enterprise may mean a loss in national benefits to the home country.

---

[16] See G. C. Hufbauer and F. M. Adler, *Overseas Manufacturing and the Balance of Payments* (Washington, D.C.: U.S. Treasury Department, 1968); *Implications of Multinational Firms for World Trade and Investment and for U.S. Trade and Labor*, Report to the Committee on Finance of the United States Senate, 93d Congress, 1st sess. (Washington, D.C.: U.S. Government Printing Office, 1973); M. D. Steuer et al., *The Impact of Foreign Direct Investment on the United Kingdom* (London: HMSO, 1973).

EMPLOYMENT EFFECTS

The employment effects of multinational business expansion are a major social cost-benefit issue in both home and host countries. In the home countries, labor unions are concerned about the export of jobs when firms expand overseas (see Box 13–2). In the host countries, the principal concern is that foreign firms do not create enough jobs because the technology being transferred is not "appropriate" to the factor endowments of the host countries.

In the United States, labor unions did not become sensitive to the employment implications of multinational business expansion by U.S. firms until the late 1960s. But in 1971, during a year of economic stagnation and increasing unemployment in the United States, the U.S. labor movement launched an attack on multinational enterprises for harming the national interest through exporting jobs.[17] In response to labor union pressures, the U.S. government commissioned several studies to determine whether the spread of multinational business had reduced U.S. employment.

The studies did not resolve the controversy. A broad study by the U.S. Tariff Commission concluded that the question could not be answered definitively.[18] Not surprisingly, the reason given was that "both the analysis and the answer must depend on crucial assumptions" about the extent to which foreign markets would have been lost if foreign production facilities had not been established. Another study commissioned by the U.S. Department of Commerce concluded that foreign investments did not result in an export of jobs from the United States.[19] This study examined in depth nine selected cases of foreign investment. The conclusion necessarily followed from the fact that in each case, according to the researchers, the companies were forced to invest overseas to preserve their markets. The Commerce study, however, was challenged on the grounds that the nine cases were not a "representative sample" from which a general conclusion could be drawn.

A number of business organizations have also sponsored studies that purport to show that foreign investment does not export jobs. As an example, a Business International study concludes that "the job-export theory is totally unfounded" by showing that a sample of 104 highly foreign-investment-oriented U.S. companies increased U.S. employment faster than other U.S. manufacturing firms over the 1970–79 period.[20]

The validity of this analysis, however, can be seriously questioned. The international companies are generally in high-technology and rapid-growth indus-

---

[17] Industrial Union Department, AFL–CIO, "New Breed of International Cat," *Viewpoint*, Summer 1971, pp. 10–15.

[18] *Implications of Multinational Firms for World Trade*, pp. 6–7.

[19] Robert B. Stobaugh, et al., *U.S. Multinational Enterprises and the U.S. Economy* (Boston: Harvard Business School, January 1972).

[20] Business International, *The Effects of U.S. Corporate Foreign Investment: 1970–79* (New York: June 1981), p. 21.

BOX 13–2
GM Union Leaders in Europe Demand Data on Firm's Plans
New Jobs in Some Countries Could Lead to Cutbacks in Others,
Workers Assert

Geneva—Union leaders for General Motors Corp. workers in Europe demanded that the company provide details of how GM's European expansion plans will affect employment.

The union representatives, at a conference organized by the International Metalworkers Federation, discussed company plans for five new European plants and the expansion of existing facilities involving an investment of $2.4 billion.

"While the company press relations department proudly produces a few figures promising new jobs in a few countries, it is as silent as a tomb on its present and projected disemployment plans," the federation's general secretary, Herman Rebhan, told the meeting.

He also asked: "How will the import of more than 600,000 engines from Australia, Brazil, and perhaps Japan affect our members? What are the consequences of the U.S.-European integrated product lines, involving increasing numbers of robots on terms of employment on both sides of the Atlantic?"

Mr. Rebhan said "all the important decisions are made in Detroit, in the office of the president." Workers can't "accept this Kafkaesque situation" in which a distant person "pulls the strings."

In Detroit, a GM spokesman declined comment.

SOURCE: *The Wall Street Journal*, May 21, 1980. © Dow Jones & Company, Inc. Reprinted permission. All rights reserved.

---

tries. Consequently, even though a multinational computer or telecommunications firm is expanding abroad, the same company should also be expected to be expanding at home more rapidly than traditional industries.

The limitations of the "job export" studies seem to suggest that the issue is best examined on a case-by-case basis. The crucial element is whether home-country production is a feasible alternative to foreign production for the firm. If the foreign investment is *desirable* to increase profits, rather than *necessary* for avoiding losses, the national interest of the home country might be better served by a trade-off of more local employment as against greater business profits.

In host countries, and particularly in the less developed nations, unemployment and underemployment is likely to be a major economic problem. As a result, host countries are anxious to secure as many new jobs as possible from every foreign investment project. If capital-intensive technology is imported into these countries by multinational firms, severe limits may be placed on the degree of labor absorption possible.

This problem raises the "appropriate technology" issue. The technology of the multinationals, in most cases, has been developed in the industrialized countries where labor has been relatively scarce and expensive and capital relatively abundant and cheap. Against this environment, new technology is normally capital-intensive and labor-saving. In contrast, labor is usually abundant and relatively cheap whereas capital is scarce and relatively expensive in the developing countries. Consequently, many host countries would like to have the foreign firms use a technology more appropriate to the factor endowments of their country—namely, more labor-intensive technology.

The appropriate technology issue, also called the *factor-proportions* problem, has been widely debated,[21] with sharp disagreement as to the availability of commercially competitive technology alternatives, as discussed in Chapter 20. Nevertheless, the multinational firm must be aware of the appropriate technology concern. To the extent that a more labor-intensive technology can be used without endangering the competitiveness of a project, the national benefits to the host country can be enlarged.[22]

SOCIAL COST-BENEFIT CALCULATIONS

The measurement of national social value is not a standardized procedure. In fact, it would be risky to use the same evaluation procedure for all assessments. Important effects could be left out or effects could be evaluated in a way inappropriate to the particular use for which the assessment is required. Each case in practice shapes its own format.

Common to all cases will be four stages in the evaluation procedure:

1. Identification by the country of the individual effects of a foreign investment project that are crucial for achieving national goals.
2. Measurement of these individual effects after adjusting for distortions in market prices that typically exist because competition is weak or because of government intervention in the marketplace through tariffs, minimum wage laws, etc.
3. Combine the individual effects into an overall quantitative assessment of the social value of the investment.
4. Supplement the quantitative results with qualitative evaluations of significant effects that do not lend themselves to quantification.

An insight into how such an overall assessment is commonly put together should help the international manager to marshal the data needed for a positive evaluation, or to adjust the proposal to match national goals more closely. As an example, an appraisal of a proposal from a multinational firm requesting permission to construct a new plant in a developing nation is presented in some

---

[21] Sanjaya Lall, "Transnationals and the Third World," p. 9; see also Nicolas Jequier and Gerard Blanc, *The World of Appropriate Technology* (Paris: Organization of Economic Co-Operation and Development, 1983).

[22] For cases where more might rationally have been done, see L. T. Wells, Jr., "Economic Man and Engineering Man: Choice of Technology in a Low Wage Country," *Public Policy*, Summer 1973, pp. 319–42.

detail below. The expertise in placing quantitative assessments on social value and social cost that is illustrated here falls within the field of project analysis. A considerable literature is available in this field.[23]

Nitrogene: A Worked Example

A European-based multinational firm has requested permission to construct a new plant in Asiatica for the production of Nitrogene, a chemical fertilizer based on a patented process. Although there are other foreign licensors, none shows any interest in submitting competitive proposals. The currency unit in Asiatica is the lira, and the proposed investment comprises an equity sum from foreign currency sources of 500,000 lira supported by local long-term financing within Asiatica of a further 500,000 lira at an interest rate of 12 percent per annum.

Annual costs and revenues from operating the proposed plant are estimated as shown in the first column of Table 13–1. The second column records adjustments to the operating estimates to register the social value of the proposal to Asiatica. In this case, there are five major types of adjustment as follows:

1. Gross Social Benefits.   Adjust the value of gross social benefits to eliminate the price distortion due to tariffs. The social value to Asiatica of the project (social opportunity cost) is the cost of securing the same output from the lowest cost alternative source if the project were not undertaken. In this case, the alternative would be imports and the *gross social benefit* would be the cost of the imports.

To attract the new industry, Asiatica has agreed to establish a tariff on imports to protect the new plant from foreign competition. As a result of the tariff, world market prices are 20 percent *below* the projected price of local production. Because local prices are certain to reflect the cost of imports plus the tariff, *the value of output, therefore, should be reduced by 20 percent* (2,000 × 20% = 400).

As a related point, it should be noted that without the tariff protection the sales revenue of the project would be reduced by 400,000 lira and the project would not be profitable to the enterprise.

2. Social Opportunity Costs.   Two kinds of adjustments are made to show the "real" costs to the country. First, where market prices are distorted, "shadow prices" or "social opportunity costs" are substituted. *Shadow prices* are the values that goods and services would yield in an alternative use under free market conditions. Second, costs to the firm that are not costs to the country are eliminated.

---

[23] See Louis T. Wells, Jr., "Social Cost-Benefit Analysis for MNCs," *Harvard Business Review,* March-April 1975, p. 40ff.; Anandarup Ray, *Cost-Benefit Analysis: Issues and Methodologies* (Baltimore: John Hopkins University Press, 1984); Lee A. Tavis and Roy L. Crum, "Performance-Based Strategies for MNC Portfolio Balancing," *Columbia Journal of World Business,* Winter 1984, pp. 85–94.

TABLE 13–1   Calculation of National Social Value for Proposed Nitrogene Investment in Asiatica (in thousands of lira)

	Annual Operating Estimates	Adjustments (numbers refer to written description)	National Social Value (+ = value, − = cost)
Sales (local)	2,000	$\begin{cases} -400\ (1) \\ +320\ (5) \end{cases}$	+1,920
Costs:			
Labor (including services)			
Local	500	−250 (2a)	− 250
Foreign	100	+ 20 (5)	− 120
Materials			
Local	200	—	− 200
Imported	700	$\begin{cases} -140\ (2b) \\ +112\ (5) \end{cases}$	− 672
Taxes			
Local	100	−100 (2c)	—
Capital charges			
Local interest	60	+ 90 (2d)	− 150
Depreciation	100	−100 (2e)	—
Total costs	1,760		−1,392
Net profit	240		
Taxation on profits	120	−120 (2c)	—
Profit after tax (remitted as dividends)	120	$\begin{cases} \text{record} \\ \text{as cost (3)} \\ + 24\ (5) \end{cases}$	− 144
Social externalities		+ 20 (4)	+ 20
Net social value			404

Such costs might be characterized as transfers from one pocket to another but in the same pair of pants.

a. Labor.   Union and statutory hiring rules require that labor be paid going rates although heavy unemployment among unskilled labor means that there is no social cost to Asiatica in providing unskilled labor input. The shadow price of unskilled labor is zero. For the Nitrogene production, unskilled labor represents 50 percent of labor costs. *Reduce local labor cost by 50 percent.*

b. Materials.   Imported costs include import duties levied at a tariff of 25 percent. Duties collected by the government are not a cost to the country. *Reduce imported material cost by 20 percent.*

c. Taxes.   Local tax payments do not reflect an additional cost to the country. *Eliminate local taxation payments.*

d. Interest.   The annual local interest cost of 12 percent to the firm understates the social value of using the local capital for alternative investments. The shadow price for alternative use of capital is calculated at 30 percent. *Increase interest cost to 30 percent.*

e. Depreciation. If remitted outside the country, depreciation would be a social cost. In this case, depreciation is planned to be retained for plant improvements. There is, therefore, no social cost. *Eliminate depreciation charges.*

3. Exported Benefits. Adjust the social value to record dividend remittance as a social cost. After-tax profits will be remitted from Asiatica annually as dividends and thus should appear as a social cost to the country. *Include profit after tax as a social cost.*

4. Externalities. Adjust the social value to record the value or cost of "externalities" not recorded in operating figures. The new operation will train managerial and technical labor and generally extend Asiatica's industrial capability in the chemical processing field. The social value of this training and development is assessed at a national figure of alternative cost of 20,000 lira per annum. *Add external social value of 20,000 lira.*

5. Foreign Exchange Adjustments. Adjust the social value to record the "real" lira value of entries involving foreign currency. For economic and political purposes, the official exchange rate has been maintained at a level that overvalues the Asiatican lira by about 20 percent. On a free market, it is estimated that instead of the official rate of 5 Asiatican lira = U.S. \$1, the market would clear at 6 Asiatican lira = U.S. \$1. *Increase the lira value of all foreign currency items by 20 percent.*

Social Profitability

After the adjustments have been made, the social profitability of the project can be summarized in several ways. For most purposes, the end result is the same no matter which method is used.

1. Net National Benefit. The net national benefit is the social benefits *minus* the social costs for all inputs. The Nitrogene project shows a positive annual net benefit or social value of 404,000 lira (1,940,000 − 1,536,000).

2. Benefit-Cost Ratio. The benefit-cost ratio is the social benefits *divided* by the social costs for all inputs. The Nitrogene project shows a benefit-cost ratio of 1.26 (1,940/1,536). The benefits are positive, of course, as long as the ratio is greater than 1.

3. Social Return. This method measures the social profit derived from the local capital utilized. The test is whether the return from this scarce local resource is greater than might be secured through alternative uses. Social return is the social benefits *minus* social costs other than capital, *divided* by the amount of local capital used.

The local capital in this case is 500,000 lira, with an opportunity cost of

30 percent, or 150,000 lira. By omitting this cost, the social benefits from this project become 554,000 lira instead of the 404,000 shown in Table 13–1. The social return from the local capital utilized is then 111 percent (554,000/500,000). By this measure, the project appears attractive to Asiatica because the social return greatly exceeds the opportunity cost of 30 percent for alternative uses of local capital.

4. Return on Domestic Resources.   This method compares the value of *all* domestic resources used in the project with the net foreign value of the production. The net foreign value is the foreign market value of the output less the cost of foreign inputs measured in foreign currency—say, U.S. dollars. The domestic resources used are valued in local currency, or lira. These two figures produce an implicit exchange rate, so many lira per dollar. The more lira of domestic resources it takes to produce what could be purchased abroad for a dollar, the less attractive is the project. If the implicit rate is below the actual exchange rate, presumably the local resources could be used to more account elsewhere.

The return-on-domestic-resources method appears to have growing appeal for host countries. It is useful, therefore, to follow through the calculation for the Nitrogene project. Net foreign value is $164,000 per annum, calculated as follows:

Sales (at world market price—1,600 lira @ 5 lira/U.S. $1)		$320,000
Less foreign costs translated at official rate		
Labor	$ 20,000	
Materials, before import duties	112,000	
Dividends	24,000	156,000
Net foreign value		$164,000

Domestic resource costs at their social cost levels are 580,000 lira:

Labor	250,000 lira
Materials	200,000
Capital charge	150,000
Externalities	−20,000
Total	580,000 lira

The implicit exchange rate that translates the foreign value into domestic revenue costs is 3.54 lira = U.S. $1 (580 ÷ 164). This compares to the estimated "real" or free market rate of 6 lira = U.S. $1. By this measure, the project also is worthwhile. Through local production, Asiatica secures $1 of foreign value by using only 3.54 lira of local resources, whereas Asiatica would otherwise have to spend 6 lira of local resources to get $1 of foreign value.

Some Limitations

Social cost-benefit measures are extremely useful for host countries, but they have their limitations. They are useful because they are quantitative, relatively simple in concept, easy to calculate and to explain. Furthermore, they provide a consistent basis for comparing multiple projects. In such comparisons, the test is not simply whether the social benefits are positive, but which project produces the largest surplus of social benefits.

The limitations are that the analysis is static, important factors that are non-quantifiable may be omitted, and the tests may not be sufficiently related to the country's development strategy. Nevertheless, the measurements may be extended to include a longer time horizon. The flow of costs and benefits may be analyzed for a longer period than one year. The method may also be adapted to take into account the time value of money through estimating the internal rate of return, payoff period, or discounted present value. The time horizon of the country's decision makers is often a crucial element. The political cost of slow achievement can be very high.

INTERNATIONAL NEGOTIATIONS

The Nitrogene example is useful for introducing the subject of international negotiations because many of the hypothetical elements included as ''given'' in the case would have been determined in real life by negotiations between the foreign investor and the host government. But the negotiation issue, it should be emphasized, is not limited to new investment commitments. The negotiation skills of international managers will be tested continuously in reaching agreements with foreign managers, workers, and governments on many international operations matters. In the case of joint ventures, negotiations will also include foreign partners or investors. Furthermore, many situations may arise where agreements have to be renegotiated.[24]

International business negotiations have many characteristics that distinguish them from domestic business negotiations. Domestically, some business firms will have periodic negotiations with the government. Internationally, virtually all negotiations will involve the host government. The cultural backgrounds of the negotiators are different. Negotiations normally take a great deal of time because of the scale of the projects and because the parties need time to get to know each other. And, as shown in the General Motors–Egypt case in Box 13–3, significant political factors can greatly complicate an international business negotiation.

---

[24] See William A. Stoever, *Renegotiations in International Business Transactions* (Lexington, Mass.: D. C. Heath & Co. 1981); Stan Reid, ''The Politics of Resource Negotiation: The Transnational Corporation and the Jamaican Bauxite Levy,'' *United Nations Natural Resources Forum 5* (1981), pp. 115–27.

BOX 13–3
GM's Grand Design in Egypt May Be a Mirage:
A Case Study in International Negotiations

Last March General Motors won permission from the Egyptian government to create a brand-new $700 million auto industry, beating out Japanese, Italian, and French rivals. GM agreed to modernize the aging factories of Nasr Automotive Manufacturing Co. (Nasco) and bring in more than 20 foreign-parts suppliers. One year later, the project hasn't gotten off the ground, and GM is still wrangling with Nasco on details of the joint venture.

Nasco officials complain that GM is making requests that "contradict their original proposal approved by the government." GM officials say they aren't making new demands, just trying to compensate for changing conditions. The biggest problem, according to GM, is that the cost of imported assembly kits from Spanish and West German subsidiaries have risen by 30% to 50% because of the devaluation of the U.S. dollar and the Egyptian pound. Along with the cost problems, GM may have trouble living up to its pledge to achieve 50% local content because of difficulties in persuading its suppliers to set up plants in Egypt.

GM got involved in Egypt partly because of politics. U.S. officials have been pushing the Egyptians to reform their economy by allowing inefficient public-sector companies to enter joint ventures with market-driven multinationals. Egyptian officials saw the GM deal as a way to solidify U.S.-Egyptian relations.

But Nasco executives were not even involved in the initial feasibility studies. "Politicians were involved," says an Egyptian banker, "not engineers and accountants. Now it's time to calculate the pennies, the salaries, and the prices. This is where the real decision will come."

If the GM deal falls apart, relations between the U.S. and Egyptian governments could suffer. And Egypt's hopes for export-oriented growth could fade.

SOURCE: *Business Week,* March 30, 1987, p. 47.

Changing Host Country Benefits

Returning to the Nitrogene case, some negotiation issues could be the following:

- The tariff on competing imports.
- The amount of local financing.
- The rate of interest on local financing.
- Special tax incentives.
- Permission to repatriate profits.
- Freedom to import materials and components.

Why do these features require negotiation? Simply because the international firm and the host government have different goals, and changes in the investment conditions will affect each party's goals differently. Some changes can have favorable results for one party and a negative outcome for the other. Suppose that Asiatica offered to establish a tariff on competing imports of only half the level used in the case, so that world market prices were 10 percent rather than 20 percent below the projected price for local production. This would reduce gross sales income by 200,000 lira to 1,800,000 lira and, ceteris paribus (other things being equal), net profit would be reduced from 240,000 lira to 40,000 before taxes and 20,000 after taxes. Concurrently, this modification would increase the national social value of the project to Asiatica by 340,000 to 744,000.[25] Thus Asiatica gains by its criterion of net social value and Nitrogene loses by its criterion of business profits. With a prospective return of only 20,000 lira on an investment of 500,000 lira, Nitrogene would almost certainly not establish the plant.

Other changes could produce additional benefits for both parties. Let us assume that Asiatica agrees to eliminate local taxes on the condition that Nitrogene increases production by 20 percent and exports that additional output. The exports would have to be sold at world prices and would produce total revenue of 320,000 lira (400,000 minus 20 percent). The elimination of local taxes (100,000 lira) would raise net profit on previous output to 340,000. The increased output, however, would produce a net loss of 12,000 lira for a total profit of 328,000 before taxes and 164,000 lira after taxes. The net social value of the project to Asiatica would increase by 44,000 lira. Thus the new agreement increases both the profitability of the project to Nitrogene by about 37 percent and the net social value to Asiatica by 10 percent.

As a continuation of the exercise on measuring social benefits, the student could experiment with other variables, such as the amount of local financing, interest rates on local and imported capital, wage rates slightly above local scales, pressure for more labor-intensive technology, and limits on profit remittances to see how the attractiveness of the project to the two parties changes. Such analysis is valuable preparation for negotiations.

The Negotiation Process

The simple objective of negotiation is to reach an agreement advantageous to both parties. To achieve this objective involves both an art and a science of negotiation. The "science" loosely means systematic analysis for problem solving. The "art" includes "interpersonal skills, the ability to convince and be convinced, the ability to employ a basketful of bargaining ploys, and the wisdom to know when and how to use them."[26] Clearly, the development of negotiating skills

---

[25] The tariff adjustment (1) would be −180 (10% of 1,800) instead of −400. Remitted profits would be a social cost of −24 (20 + 20% foreign exchange adjustment) instead of −144. Thus national social value would increase by 340 because of reduced social costs.

[26] Howard Raiffa, *The Art and Science of Negotiation* (Cambridge, Mass.: Harvard University Press, 1982), p. 8.

requires both instruction and guided experience in actual negotiation situations. Conceptually, the negotiation process has been characterized as occurring within a context of four "Cs": *common interests, conflicting interests, compromise, and criteria or objectives.*[27] In the Nitrogene case, the common interest of both the international firm and the host country is in having a new enterprise established. The conflicting interests arise from such matters as the degree of import tariff protection granted. The compromise aspect is to reach a decision that is advantageous to both parties even though it is ideal to neither. The criteria or objectives to the foreign investor are satisfactory profits with low risk and few restrictions. The objective to the host country is attractive net social benefits. Thus, international business negotiations are concerned with the balancing of freedom and restriction, benefits and costs, and profits and risk between the host country and the foreign investor.

In a specific negotiation, many other characteristics of the situation may become important. Are there more than two parties to the negotiation? If Asiatica were to insist on a joint venture, a local business firm or investor would become a third party to the negotiation. Are the parties monolithic? Each party might comprise people who are on the same side but whose values differ sharply. Does the negotiation create significant precedents for either party? The outcome of the negotiation may have important implications for other agreements the enterprise might make with other governments or the host country might make with other foreign investors. Are there linkage effects? If the project could result in encouraging new local industries that become suppliers of materials or distributors of the finished product, an astute negotiator can use these linkage effects to improve the investor's bargaining position.

Bargaining Power

In large part, the outcome of negotiated agreements will depend on the respective bargaining power of the parties. The following chapter on countervailing power discusses in detail several dimensions of the bargaining power of the multinationals. In general, and aside from the important element of bargaining skills, the deal that is struck between foreign investors and host governments reflects the need for and the scarcity of the resources offered by the two parties.[28] Implicitly, therefore, *bargaining power on both sides depends on the alternatives available to each.*

A foreign investor who can offer access to capital, technology, marketing know-how, managerial skills, and new jobs would be in a relatively strong bargaining position, *provided* other alternative sources for these benefits are not readily

---

[27] John Fayerweather and Ashok Kapoor, *Strategy and Negotiation for the International Corporation* (Cambridge, Mass.: Ballinger Publishing Co., 1976), pp. 29–45.

[28] See Nathan Fagre and Louis T. Wells, Jr., "Bargaining Power of Multinationals and Host Governments," *Journal of International Business Studies,* Fall 1982, pp. 9–23.

available. A country with a large market (if the multinational is a market seeker) or available and attractive human and natural resources (if the foreign investor is a production efficiency or resource seeker) would be in a relatively strong bargaining position. But as in the case of the foreign investor, the country's bargaining position can be limited by the attractiveness of opportunities in other host countries.

There is always a time dimension to bargaining power. The bargaining power of the multinational is likely to be greatest before it makes its initial commitment to invest, and its bargaining power may deteriorate once its capital is sunk in a country. If the technology for the project is dynamic, the bargaining power of the foreign firm can continue to be strong, because the competitiveness of the project will depend on a continuing flow of product and process innovation from the parent firm. Conversely, if the technology is old and static, the host country may find it easier to acquire the technology elsewhere or develop a local capability.

Negotiating Skills

Given the respective bargaining power of the negotiating parties, the decisive factor in determining the outcome of a specific bargaining situation is the negotiating skill of the people doing the negotiation. The so-called people problem is extremely complex, and many books have been written on the psychology and sociology of negotiations. They emphasize such issues as how people perceive each other, how they interact, how the ambience of negotiations can be altered, how confidence and trust can be established—and even how to threaten and intimidate others. All of these issues are present in international business negotiations along with additional complexities arising from the negotiators different economic, political and social environments, different cultural influences, and, in many cases, different languages.

Until quite recently, there was a widespread belief in the Third World that host countries were at a sharp disadvantage as to negotiation skills in dealing with the multinationals. But as the United Nations has observed, "The learning experience of host countries has on the whole improved over time."[29] As a reinforcement of this trend, several international agencies have been providing technical assistance to the developing countries in their negotiations with foreign investors. In some cases, host countries have sent government officials abroad to learn more about how multinationals operate by studying in business schools, thereby improving their negotiation skills.

On their side, multinationals have become increasingly aware of the need for improving their international business negotiation skills, and many special training programs have emerged for training international managers for negotiating cross-culturally and with foreign governments.

---

[29] United Nations, *Transnational Corporations in World Development: Third Survey* (New York: United Nations, 1983), p. 238.

The wide scope of the "art of negotiation" can be illustrated by citing some topics in a typical training program for managers. They include:

- How to prepare for negotiations.
- How to select the proper negotiating stance.
- How to use questions to control and direct your negotiations.
- Effective offensive/defensive strategies such as:
  - Bland withdrawal (Who, me?).
  - Reversal (go forward or backward).
  - Feinting (look right, go left).
  - Crossroads (intersect, entwine, entangle).
  - Agent with limited authority (OK, but I'll have to check it out with someone else).
  - Good guy-bad guy (feigned irrationality).
  - Low-balling (too low to be realistic).
  - Intentional misunderstanding.
- How to use non-oral communication techniques to read your opponent like a book and to understand hidden meanings in conversations.

Another way of illustrating the complexity of international business negotiations is to list the major mistakes commonly made. One authority in the field has identified at least 19 major mistakes—organized into four broad and interrelated categories of empathy, role of governments, decision-making characteristics, and organizing for negotiations. The list includes such mistakes as failure to put yourself in the other person's shoes, insufficient understanding of different ways of thinking, insufficient recognition of the perception by host countries of the role of multinational's home government in negotiations, insufficient allocation of time for negotiations, and insufficient recognition of the loci of decision-making authority.[30]

Probably the biggest gap that has to be bridged in international business negotiations is between the Japanese and Western multinationals from the United States and Western Europe. Western managers will encounter a different attitude toward the role of lawyers; litigation and contracts; and many cultural differences, such as consensus decision making, emphasis on harmony, concealment of emotions, reluctance to say "No," vagueness of responses, and emphasis on face and face-saving devices.[31]

Where the native language of the negotiators is different, negotiations take on an additional burden. Not only is time required for translation, but important

---

[30] Fayerweather and Kapoor, *Strategy,* pp. 47–49; See also John L. Graham and Roy A. Herberger, Jr., "Negotiators Abroad—Don't Shoot from the Hip," *Harvard Business Review,* July–August 1983, pp. 160–68.

[31] Rosalie L. Tung, *Business Negotiations with the Japanese* (Lexington, Mass.: D. C. Heath & Co., 1984), pp. 33–61. See also John L. Graham, "The Influence of Culture on the Process of Business Negotiations," *Journal of International Business Studies,* Spring 1985, pp. 81–96.

differences in the meaning of words can exist. Inadequate interpretation services can disrupt negotiations because the perspectives of both sides cannot be presented adequately. Besides helping in interpretation, bilingual members of a negotiation team familiar with the culture of the other party can also interpret facial expressions and body language.

SUMMARY

The international business community has long embraced the view that multinational enterprises are engines of development that provided developing countries with needed capital, technology, and know-how essential for the modernization of their economies. Thus, it came as a violent shock during the late 1960s to discover that many government officials, political leaders, and academic scholars were expressing serious misgivings about the economic, political, and cultural impact of the multinationals on the developing countries. Equally disturbing was the emergence of antagonistic views by groups in the home countries toward outbound foreign direct investment.

These misgivings were reflected in the spread of ideologies that espoused a negative view of the benefits of multinationals. But over time, the ideologies have lost influence as policy makers began to recognize that neither the automatic harmony of interests assumed by the advocates of free enterprise nor the inevitable conflict of interest espoused by the Marxists is an accurate description of the relation of multinational enterprises to the host and home countries. The result has been that the use of social cost-benefit analysis has spread.

The international manager will continue to encounter the various negative ideologies among certain groups in both home and host countries. Some familiarity with the ideologies and their limitations, therefore, is important. Also essential is an understanding of social cost-benefit analysis so as to be aware of how specific multinational operations impact on the national interests of home and host countries.

The matrix of common interests and potential conflicts in goals makes for a love-hate relationship between international corporations and nation-states. The countries love the benefits but hate the costs and the national tensions that accompany the benefits. Furthermore, the benefits may be greatest at the time of the wedding and steadily decline thereafter. On balance, the trade-off to both host and home countries appears to have been generally in favor of the benefits, as evidenced by the continued rapid expansion of international business activities. Yet the need to identify its common interests and potential areas of conflict with many different nation-states is a continuing and never-ending operating requirement for international enterprises.

The multinational enterprise must develop a capability for international negotiations and be prepared to deal with specific business situations in relation to specific national environments. A specific type of business activity may face one kind of response in Country A and a completely different type of response in Country B and Country C. The only certainties are that the situation will constantly be changing and that, in order to maintain its tenure, the international enterprise must be ever ready to justify to a nation-state not only its entry but its continued presence.

EXERCISES AND DISCUSSION QUESTIONS

1. "It is characteristic of direct-investment projects that their first-order benefits are greatest, certainly most spectacular, in the initial stages of the undertaking. On the other hand, the explicit costs of the foreign investment to the host economy generally behave in an opposite fashion." Explain what the writer meant by this statement and evaluate its validity.
2. Under what circumstances can an acquisition of an existing domestic business operation by a foreign multinational enterprise be justified as contributing national benefits to a country? Under what circumstances would it be difficult to justify an acquisition?
3. As a government official evaluating a proposal for investment by a foreign corporation that could have a 20-year life span, suggest how the streams of national benefits and national costs should be treated in reaching a decision.
4. "To control the export of American technology, much of which was financed by public funds and the export of American jobs, the government should regulate, supervise, and curb the export of technology and the substantial outflows of American capital for the investments of U.S. companies in foreign operations." Would you agree or disagree with this statement?
5. As an expert in negotiation, you have the task of preparing your company for negotiating approval for establishing the Nitrogene project in Asiatica. What would you recommend as to:
   a. The composition of the negotiating team?
   b. The background preparation for the negotiators?
   c. The importance of having a bilingual person on the team?
   d. The desirability of using a simulation exercise for preparing the negotiators?

CHAPTER 14

Doing Business with the Centrally Planned Economies

Doing business with the centrally planned economies warrants special attention. These countries account for a massive share of the world's population and a large share of the world's economic activity. And although the international business relations of the socialist nations have been modest in the past, there is a great potential for expansion. However, international enterprises accustomed to operating in Western market economies must develop a special expertise for achieving success in East-West trade and investment. Furthermore, political forces play a major role in assisting and/or constraining East-West business relations.

The Western enterprise must adjust to major differences in underlying economic and political philosophies, in institutional settings, and in the motivations and objectives of business decision makers. The centrally planned nations share many common features; but they also have significant differences in institutions, policies, and business practices. Consequently, the international manager will have to become familiar in-depth with the special features of the particular country of interest.

The subject of East-West business relations is too broad to be covered comprehensively in a brief chapter. As an introduction, this chapter presents an economic overview of the centrally planned economies and a brief treatise on differences in economic systems. The Soviet and Chinese models are described and contrasted as they relate to trade and investment. And some general guidelines are presented for trading, making direct investments, and entering into industrial cooperation agreements.

AN ECONOMIC OVERVIEW

Population

The most impressive feature of the centrally planned economies is that they contain 1.6 billion people and account for about 34 percent of the world's population. The Soviet Union and the People's Republic of China are the major countries in this group. China alone accounts for one out of every five persons in the world.

Another 18 countries are usually classified as centrally planned economies. In Eastern Europe they are Albania, Bulgaria, Czechoslovakia, East Germany, Hungary, Poland, Romania, and Yugoslavia. The other Asian countries are Afghanistan, North Korea, Laos, Mongolia, Viet Nam, and South Yemen. The African countries are Angola, Ethiopia, and Mozambique. Cuba in the Western Hemisphere also belongs to the group. All but Albania and China, as shown in Table 14–1, are members or have observer status in COMECON, the so-called Eastern Trading Bloc.

Economic Size

The total economic size of the centrally planned economies is difficult to estimate on an internationally comparable basis. Except for the countries that belong to the International Monetary Fund (Hungary, Romania, South Yemen,

TABLE 14–1   The Centrally Planned Economies

	Population		
COMECON Members	1985 Millions	Growth Rate 1973–85 (percent)	1980 GNP US$ (per capita)
1. Bulgaria	9.0	0.3	3,551
2. Cuba	10.1	0.8	n.a.
3. Czechoslovakia	15.5	0.5	4,740
4. Germany, Dem. Rep.	16.7	−0.1	5,910
5. Hungary	10.7	0.2	4,390
6. Mongolia	1.9	2.8	n.a.
7. Poland	37.3	0.9	3,730
8. Romania	22.9	0.8	2,680
9. USSR	277.6	0.9	4,190
10. Viet Nam	61.6	2.6	n.a.
COMECON Observer Status			
11. Afghanistan	16.3	2.6	n.a.
12. Angola	8.7	3.1	470
13. Ethiopia	42.2	2.7	110*
14. Korea, Dem. Peoples Rep.	20.4	2.6	n.a.
15. Lao, PDR	3.6	1.6	n.a.
16. Mozambique	13.8	2.6	270
17. South Yemen, PDR	2.1	2.3	540*
18. Yugoslavia	23.1	0.8	2,620
Other			
19. Albania	2.9	2.0	n.a.
20. China, Peoples Republic	1,041.1	1.4	310*
Total	1,637.5		
World total	4,788.8		

* Data are for 1985
n.a., not available

SOURCE: *World Bank Atlas 1987* for population data and 1985 GNP estimates; *World Bank Atlas 1981* for 1980 Angola and Mozambique GNP estimates. Paul Marer, *Dollar GNPs of the USSR and Eastern Europe* (Baltimore: Johns Hopkins Press, 1985), p. 7 for the 1980 per capita income estimate for the USSR and Eastern Europe.

Yugoslavia, and China), there is no official measurement of GNP or GDP as it is defined in the West.[1] A reasonable estimate of the total GNP of the centrally planned economies, however, might be about U.S. $2,000 billion, or between 15 and 20 percent of global activity as of the mid-1980s.

Economic levels vary greatly among the various countries. In 1980, per capita income ranged from a high of US$5,910 for East Germany to a low of $270 in Mozambique. In the same year, U.S. per capita income was estimated to be $11,360. But, as noted by the World Bank, the GNP estimates for the

---

[1] Paul Marer, *Dollar GNPs of the USSR and Eastern Europe* (Baltimore: Johns Hopkins Press, 1985), p. 6.

centrally planned economies must be treated as tentative because of differences between the concepts used for national accounts of market economies and centrally planned economies.[2]

International Business Activity

The international trade activity of the centrally planned economies is only one indicator of their international business importance. The relatively low level of trade, however, reflects both the ideological commitment to autarky or self-sufficiency (that appears to be changing) and trade barriers resulting from political considerations, particularly on the part of the United States. In 1984, the centrally planned economies had total exports of US$206 billion and imports totaling US$177 billion. This represented 10 percent of world exports and slightly more than 9 percent of world imports.[3] About half of the exports and 60 percent of imports were East-East trade. In terms of East-West trade, therefore, the countries were a market for about $70 billion of merchandise from the West.

Another international business indicator is the involvement of the centrally planned economies in foreign direct investment and in various forms of so-called industrial cooperation with market-economy enterprises. Overall quantitative measures are not available for describing these activities. But, as the United Nations has noted, East-West business relations, other than trade, have been expanding, particularly during the late 1970s through various forms of industrial cooperation.[4] Most of the new forms (to be described below) are contractual arrangements not involving direct investments or equity participation.

Many centrally planned economies have their own multinational enterprises, though they do not refer to them as such. One study identified nearly 500 companies with Soviet and Eastern European equity participation operating in 23 OECD countries at the end of 1983.[5] Most of these overseas ventures were related to trade; but a significant number were engaged in assembly and manufacturing, in local marketing, and in financial services.[6]

China, since its economic reform of 1978, has extended its business activities overseas by undertaking foreign projects to provide labor services; build bridges and highways; and even do landscaping of city gardens in the United States, the United Kingdom, and West Germany (see Box 14–1). Overseas construction, as of mid-1985, employed more than 500,000 Chinese workers and technicians in

---

[2] World Bank, *1981 World Bank Atlas* (Washington, D.C., 1982), p. 24.

[3] United Nations, *Monthly Bulletin of Statistics,* June 1985, p. xviii.

[4] United Nations, *Transnational Corporations in World Development: Third Survey* (New York, 1983), pp. 272–82.

[5] Carl H. McMillan, *Multinationals from the Second World* (London: Macmillan Press, 1987), pp. 29–47.

[6] Geoffrey Hamilton, ed., *Red Multinationals or Red Herrings?* (New York: St. Martin's Press, 1986), pp. 185–94.

BOX 14-1
Exporting Cooks, Fishermen, Tailors, and Chauffeurs

Between 1982 and 1984, Guangdong province of China undertook 42 construction, building materials and water conservancy projects in a dozen Asian, African and Latin American countries, and in Hong Kong and Macao. The contracts were valued at US$97.6 million. It also signed 68 labour service contracts on sending cooks, fishermen, tailors and chauffeurs to other countries—deals that were worth US $26.6 million.

SOURCE: Reprinted from the *Beijing Review*, July 1, 1985, p. 25.

---

71 countries, with the Middle East serving as China's largest contractual market. From 1980 to 1985, China established about 110 joint ventures in 30 foreign countries. About 70 percent of the partnerships were in developing countries. The combined investment in overseas ventures was US$200 million, two thirds of it from China.[7]

As a recipient of conventional direct investment from the West, the People's Republic of China has become a major area of activity, most commonly in the form of joint ventures. Beginning in 1979 and until the middle of 1985, direct investment by foreign firms in China totaled more than US$6 billion.[8] The Eastern European Countries of Bulgaria, Poland, Romania, Hungary, and Yugoslavia have adopted policies to allow equity joint ventures, as did the Soviet Union in 1986. But aside from Hungary and Yugoslavia, the number of such joint ventures has not been great. As of the end of 1980, Yugoslavia had signed 199 joint venture agreements.[9]

A BRIEF TREATISE ON ECONOMIC SYSTEMS

What are the major differences in economic philosophy between the East and the West to which international enterprises must adjust? Economic systems are commonly classified on the basis of who owns the means of production: *capitalism* (private ownership) and *socialism* (government ownership). An equally important classification basis is a country's method of resource allocation and control: *market economies* or *centrally planned command economies*.

---

[7] *China Daily*, June 18, 1985, and July 8, 1985.

[8] *Beijing Review*, August 26, 1985, p. 4.

[9] Patrick F. R. Artisien and Peter J. Buckley, "Joint Ventures in Yugoslavia: Opportunities and Constraints," *Journal of International Business Studies*, Spring 1985, pp. 111–35. See also Jerzy Cieslik and Boguslaw Sosnowski, "The Role of TNCs in Poland's East-West Trade," *Journal of International Business Studies*, Summer 1985, pp. 121–37.

The popular use of the label *mixed economies* reflects the reality that all countries have a mix of private and government ownership and a mix of government commands and reliance on markets in resource allocation. The classification problem is further confused by great ambiguity in the use of the *socialism* label (see Box 14–2). Poland considers itself a socialist country, even though agriculture is largely privately owned. France under President Francois Mitterrand had a socialist government, and many businesses were nationalized. Yet the economy is classified as market capitalism.

Although the dividing line is not crystal clear, the two groups are separable. In the market economies, property ownership is *mainly* private; and markets are *dominant* in resource allocation. In the centrally planned economies, property is *mainly* government-owned; and the commands of government planners are the *dominant* force in allocating resources. In the market economies, governments influence economic and business decisions in many ways, often owning some enterprises. Yet the enterprises independently determine what to produce and how much, in response to the market demands of other enterprises, final consumers, and the government. In the centrally planned economies, the managers are appointed by the state and determine what and how much to produce, to whom to sell, from whom to buy, and at what price, based on orders from the central planners.[10]

The institutional framework and the decision criteria in both systems derive directly from their ideological foundations. In the market system, the basic philosophy is that overall social welfare is maximized by allowing individuals and business firms to maximize their own well-being, whether in terms of profit or utility, but with a great deal of government intervention. Under the centrally planned system, the basic philosophy is that the *common good,* however defined, is best achieved by having a central authority make the major economic decisions. The *common good* may be equality or economic development.

The crucial significance of the different ideologies is that doing business with the centrally planned economies means dealing with governments and government enterprises where the decision maker on the other side of the table has different criteria and different motivations than the market-economy enterprise normally encounters. Furthermore, within the group of centrally planned economies, each country has many unique characteristics and policies; and patterns keep changing.[11]

The countries most permissive toward private ownership are Poland and Yugoslavia, where agricultural land and output is mainly in private hands. The countries with the most liberal policies toward foreign direct investment, joint ventures, or other forms of industrial cooperation with Western companies are

---

[10] See Franklyn D. Holzman, "Systemic Bases of the Unconventional Trade Practices of Centrally-Planned Economies," *Columbia Journal of World Business,* Winter 1983, pp. 4–9.

[11] Several international accounting firms publish periodic guides. See, for example, Price Waterhouse, *Doing Business in Eastern Europe,* October 1982.

BOX 14–2
Defining the Word Socialist

Few political definitions have engendered so much dispute as the meaning of the word Socialist.

Virtually all who call themselves Socialist favor redistributing wealth, income and power to the less well-off, particularly industrial workers. Socialists are generally seen as favoring common ownership of factories, banks and the land—"the means of production" is the common Socialist phrase—usually through the state.

But in recent years, many who call themselves Socialist have supported private ownership of even large industrial firms, favoring government ownership of only a few sectors of the economy. These moderate Socialists, whose views are often similar to those held by many in the American Democratic Party, support welfare and social security programs to redistribute income, and state planning of the economy without outright state control.

Although the Communist governments of Eastern Europe claim to be Socialist, the term is most often associated with the parties in Western Europe that call themselves Socialist, Social Democratic or Labor.

The confusion over the use of the word *Socialist* stems largely from the split in the world Socialist movement caused by Lenin in 1919. Parties that allied themselves with him eventually became known as Communist.

SOURCE: *New York Times,* November 30, 1983. Copyright © 1983/86 by the New York Times Company. Reprinted by permission.

Bulgaria, China, Hungary, Poland, Romania, and Yugoslavia. The countries that have established their own joint ventures or wholly owned enterprises abroad are China, Czechoslovakia, Hungary, Poland, Romania, the Soviet Union, and Yugoslavia.

THE SOVIET MODEL AND FOREIGN TRADE

Planning Foreign Trade

Under the Soviet model, the planners have the enormous task of determining output targets and balancing supply and demand for thousands of commodities. They are concerned with changes in demand, but such changes do not usually lead rapidly to changes in output and almost never are reflected in changes in prices. Since 1955, most Soviet prices have only been changed twice: in 1967 and in 1982. Prices are commonly described as "irrational" and play little, if any, role in resource allocation. But under the *perestroika* (reconstruction) plan initiated in the late 1980s, a major reform in prices is scheduled to take place. The expected result is that fewer prices will be centrally fixed and that some prices will be freed altogether.

The planners tell each firm where and when to ship its output and from which enterprises to order its inputs, and a number of control agencies supervise the carrying out of each plan. In the Soviet Union, GOSPLAN and its various subordinate planning groups have supervision responsibility and keep a running check on the progress of each plan.

The centrally planned countries have closed economies with the primary goal of autarky (self-sufficiency) rather than economic expansion through greater internationalization. The central planners include foreign trade in their plans when absolutely essential for achieving their material balances for each of thousands of commodities. They plan for imports of goods that are scarce domestically (grain) and for exports typically produced in excess of domestic needs (Soviet oil) to earn foreign exchange needed for imports. Unplanned exports are used to get rid of products when unexpected surpluses occur, and unplanned imports are used to fill sudden domestic shortages. Although planners use foreign trade on an *ad hoc* basis to correct planning imbalances, they do not permit unplanned exports of goods not in surplus. Such exports would disrupt the domestic commodity balances and create potentially large negative multiplier effects on several related sectors of the economy.

The sanctity of the central plan, the difficulties of integrating foreign trade into the plan, and problems of currency convertibility naturally lead to a preference for avoiding foreign trade when possible and, when it is not, to arrange trade through bilateral international trade agreements. Such bilateral agreements are difficult to arrange with the West, however, for governments cannot easily make commitments for their private importers and exporters as can socialist authorities with their nationalized enterprises.

Foreign Trade Organizations

The institutional framework in most centrally planned economies consists of a few dozen separate foreign trade organizations, each of which handles the exports and/or imports of a large group of goods and services. Domestic enterprises producing exports or using imports normally do not deal directly with foreign firms but operate through the offices of the foreign trade organization that actually carries out the international trade transaction. Some countries, however, have been attempting gradually to change over to direct contacts between producers and users (see Box 14–3).

Trade Problems

One major trade problem that results from the restriction on planned exports is *commodity inconvertibility*. The term means that foreign firms cannot use their foreign exchange to buy exportable goods unless the transaction has been planned in advance. Foreign importers are not allowed to compete with domestic enterprises for products that these enterprises are scheduled to receive under the plan.

Other special trade problems arise, such as the matter of prices and payments.

BOX 14–3
No Rush into Russia

To smooth the way for setting up profit-making joint ventures in the Soviet Union, Mr. Gorbachev has broken a stifling monopoly over imports and exports held by the powerful Ministry of Foreign Trade. For the first time, 21 other industries and 72 state enterprises can arrange their own business affairs with the noncommunist world.

The new policy has attracted hundreds of foreign companies with high hopes of cracking a market of 280 million potential customers. But many of the firms have found that—so far at least—actually doing business in the Soviet Union is a frustrating and unproductive process. At times, the ponderous Soviet bureaucracy seems to be trying to ignore Mr. Gorbachev's sweeping economic reforms. In some cases, ministries' turf-protective measures have blocked business proposals. And many Soviet trade and industrial officials don't understand basic Western business practices and concepts.

In an economic system where prices do not reflect the exchange value of a product or service, some other system has to be used to price exports and imports. Generally, the policy has been to use world prices rather than domestic prices.

In a system where the import and export of domestic currencies is legally forbidden and currencies are therefore not convertible, different forms of payment are required. Exchange rates do exist for all currencies of the centrally planned economies; but these are fixed by official decisions rather than determined by the demand and supply for such currencies, as is the basis in a floating rate regime.

The problem of not having a functional exchange rate is finessed in different ways. Intrabloc trade with the Eastern European countries is balanced in world prices in order to avoid holding another country's inconvertible currency. East-West trade is conducted at world prices and in convertible currencies. Trade is not balanced bilaterally, and each centrally planned economy is free to spend its convertible currency earnings in any other country. Thus, trade with the West is conducted multilaterally.

Compensation Agreements

In order to expand trade with the West beyond their ability to earn convertible currency through competition in foreign markets, Eastern European countries engage in compensation trading. This requires the Western supplier to accept payment for goods delivered, either wholly or partially, in kind. Compensation trading can be in the form of barter or arrangements for goods to be supplied by another trading company of the same country or goods from a third country. Frequently, as in the general case of countertrade, Western firms acquire goods for which they themselves have no use. A number of firms based in cities such as Vienna or Zurich, with close Eastern European connections, offer their services in selling compensation goods.

COMECON—The Eastern Trading Bloc

The objective of self-sufficiency has been extended to encompass the Eastern European countries as a group through the Council for Mutual Economic Assistance, usually referred to as COMECON or CMEA, previously discussed in the chapter on the international trade framework.[12] Trade between COMECON countries is basically regulated by five-year agreements on a quantity quota basis that assure user countries of an adequate supply of raw materials and energy. Each country's export and import quotas are reconciled with its anticipated production and requirements as determined by its own five-year plan. Thus, there is a partial coordination of economic planning between the COMECON countries. The trade agreement quotas are officially binding. They can be adjusted, however, during the period by mutual agreement between the concerned parties, to take account of changes in circumstances.

None of the Eastern European countries are members of any other trade bloc, although Romania and Yugoslavia have established formal relations with the European Community. Czechoslovakia, Hungary, Poland, Romania, and Yugoslavia have signed the GATT agreements; and Bulgaria has observer status.

Trade between the COMECON countries is priced in *transferable roubles* on the basis of approximate world market prices. In the case of raw materials, prices are based on the average world market prices during the previous five years. The transferable rouble is not a convertible currency, however; it is nothing more than an accounting device for clearing bilateral trade deals between member countries. Most trade within the bloc is conducted by agreement between two governments as if there were no other potential customers.

On the whole, the COMECON experience has not been a great success. The goal to create a single market of the Eastern European countries, within which different industries would be parcelled out (e.g., aircraft to the Soviet Union, buses to Hungary, computers to East Germany), has not been achieved. As one source concludes, "Eastern Europe remains a collection of individual markets" that are "open to sales of Western products, services and technologies."[13] The main limitation is the ability of these countries to earn hard currencies to pay for their desired imports.

---

[12] See also A. I. MacBean and N. Snowden, *International Institutions in Trade and Finance* (London: George Allen & Unwin, 1981), pp. 195–210.

[13] Business International, *Business Eastern Europe*, October 28, 1983, pp. 337–38.

THE CHINESE MODEL: FROM CENTRAL PLANNING TO MARKET SOCIALISM

The People's Republic of China (PRC) is a special case, both because of its massive population and because it recently reversed its century-old inward-looking and anti-Western stance to become an important participant in international business. Unlike the Soviet model that emphasizes self-sufficiency, China has shifted to a policy of vigorous encouragement of foreign trade and investment as a principal strategy for achieving its goal of economic modernization. It hopes to achieve its goals by creating its own unique model of market socialism.

The economic reforms adopted to support China's new posture date back only to the mid- and late 1970s.[14] But by the mid-1980s, considerable success had been achieved. *If* China is able to continue this success and avoid radical political change, it has prospects, according to a World Bank evaluation, of reaching a total gross national product of US$1,000,000,000,000 by the year 2000.[15] This is the equivalent of Japan's GNP as of 1980.

Some History

China's history underlines the need for accenting the big "if" of avoiding radical political change. The revolutionary overthrow of the Manchu Empire by Sun Yat Sen in October 1911 heralded almost *40 years* of political and military confusion in China. Japan exerted economic control over the country at different times and in different ways during this period. With the end of World War II in August 1945, the Japanese armies in China capitulated. Soon thereafter, civil war broke out between the nationalist government of Chiang Kai-shek and the forces of the Communist Party. With the Communist victory in 1949, the present PRC was established. But turbulence still continued.

In the early days of the PRC, the economy was organized with the aid of the USSR along the Soviet central planning model. By 1959, however, Sino-Soviet relations were broken, and Soviet assistance was completely withdrawn. Beginning in 1966, Mao Zedong initiated the Cultural Revolution, which lasted for a decade and nearly tore China apart. In 1977, after the death of Mao, Deng Xiaopeng returned to power and influenced the Party to adopt the reforms that are supposed to lead to a market socialist economy. Although the reforms have produced dramatic economic and social welfare gains, they have also resulted in numerous negative side-effects and ideological conflicts.[16]

---

[14] See N. T. Wang, *China's Modernization and Transnational Corporations* (Lexington, Mass.: D. C. Heath & Company, 1984), pp. 17–39 for background on the nature of the reforms.

[15] Edwin R. Lim et al., *China: Long-Term Development Issues and Options* (Baltimore: Johns Hopkins University Press, 1985), pp. 32–43.

[16] For example, see Orville Schell, *To Get Rich is Glorious: China in the Eighties* (New York: Pantheon Books, 1984).

What Is Market Socialism?

China does not have a blueprint for the market socialism system it hopes to achieve. Instead, the reforms of 1978 were a commitment to begin a pragmatic process of trying different methods of resource allocation and distribution. Under this program, experiments were conducted, evaluated, modified, and implemented on a national scale when judged beneficial, and changed or eliminated when found inappropriate. The rural reforms, for example, were introduced on an experimental basis in only two provinces and later extended nationally.

China remains a socialist country in the sense that the means of production are still mainly the property of the state. But the role of private enterprise has expanded significantly, and the production responsibility system adopted in agriculture resembles a private ownership system. China continues to have central planning. But the scope of mandatory planning has been narrowed, while that of guidance planning and reliance on markets has expanded.

Guidance planning concentrates on outlining the direction the economy should take and relies for implementation on macroeconomic policy instruments, such as correct price signals, taxation, credit and interest rates, profits, and wage differentials. Mandatory planning is restricted to major products (energy, steel, cement, etc.) that have a direct bearing on the national economy and the standard of living.[17]

Under the new "production responsibility" system in agriculture, land is contracted to a group of farmers, a household, or an individual. These contracts specify the amount of land to be cultivated, the amount and type of produce the contractor is to deliver to the state, and the required tax payments and contributions to the welfare and investment funds. The contracts can be passed on to the children and other beneficiaries or even sold with the permission of the commune. Beyond the contractual requirements, the farmer is free to dispose of excess production in free markets. Farmers are permitted to purchase tractors, trucks, and other production tools and to engage in long-distance transportation for marketing their produce. The rural reforms quickly resulted in greatly expanded agricultural output, improved economic conditions in the rural areas, and a large share of farm output being disposed of through free markets.

China's reform of the industrial sector began in October 1978, first in certain experimental factories in Sichuan Province and later in other parts of the country. The general thrust has been toward decentralization of economic decision making from the central government to the provinces and cities, and greater autonomy for the individual enterprise. The planners set broad policies, but the enterprises are increasingly responsible for their own profits and losses. A key element of the reform was the introduction of an income tax for state-owned enterprises

---

[17] Luc De Wuf, "Economic Reform in China," *Finance and Development,* March 1985, pp. 8–11; Luc De Wuf, "Financial Reform in China," *Finance and Development,* December 1985, pp. 19–22.

and a policy that allows enterprises that improve their profitability to retain the largest part of increased profits.

Other powers of the enterprises were expanded to include formulation of production plans, marketing of products, setting prices, purchases of production inputs, use of funds, disposal of assets, labor and personnel management, setting wages and bonuses, and merging. This has been characterized as a process of making the enterprises into relatively independent socialist commodity producers.

With respect to prices, the scope of state-controlled prices has been reduced, while that of prices agreed upon between buyers and sellers has expanded. The logic of the price reforms is to create a situation in which prices—whether state-controlled or not—will reflect production cost and take into account the supply and demand forces in the economy.

Another aspect of the reforms has been to permit private activity to take place and even to stimulate private enterprises. By the end of 1983, private enterprises (engaged principally in small-scale commerce, handicraft, catering, transport, and construction) accounted for a small but rapidly growing share of the total work force (about 2.3 million workers). As such, the role of the private sector has become firmly established in China, "and its contribution is recognized as an irreplaceable element in the continued improvement of China's living standards."[18]

Thus, as of the mid-1980s, the major elements of an economic transformation—work and profit incentives, markets cleared by price, private enterprise—were in place and generally accepted. But the precise balance between state control and the stimulus of market forces that China will consider acceptable for its market socialism model is still uncertain and will most certainly keep changing over time.

Trading with China

Until 1985, foreign trade with China was conducted exclusively through a small network of foreign trade corporations organized on the basis of commodities or services for which they were responsible. All of the corporations were under the Ministry of Trade and not subject to profit or loss constraints as a measure of their performance.

The foreign trade reforms adopted in 1985 were intended to separate government administration from enterprise management. MOFERT, the Ministry of Foreign Economic Relations and Trade, is responsible for overall planning and coordination of foreign trade. But instead of foreign trade being conducted exclusively by foreign trade corporations of MOFERT, other ministries and factories totaling more than 600 were authorized to establish foreign trade corporations. These corporations are supposed to have great management autonomy, secure

---

[18] Ibid., p. 11.

their revenue by ensuring commissions from trade, operate on an independent accounting system, and assume full responsibility for their profits and losses. They can expand their lines of activities and the provinces they represent. Clearly, an important step in trading with China is to determine which trading company or companies have jurisdiction over the commodities concerned.

FOREIGN INVESTMENT AND INDUSTRIAL COOPERATION AGREEMENTS

If the socialist countries strictly adhered to their ideology of government ownership and autarky, business relations with Western firms would be restricted to traditional importing and exporting. Yet most socialist countries have placed pragmatism ahead of ideology because of their desire to secure advanced technology, financial assistance, managerial know-how, greater access to Western markets, and other benefits available from Western multinationals (see Box 14–4).[19]

To achieve these benefits, the Eastern European countries have encouraged Western firms to participate in their economies through nonequity industrial cooperation agreements—the most numerous form of arrangement—and in many cases allow foreign direct investment in the form of equity joint ventures. China has gone the farthest in encouraging foreign direct investment, even allowing 100 percent foreign ownership in special cases.

Industrial Cooperation Agreements

The industrial cooperation agreements range from straightforward licensing, franchising, and management agreements to highly complex combinations with a wide variety of provisions. The number of such agreements in Eastern Europe, excluding Yugoslavia, totaled more than 2,500 at the end of 1980.[20] Nevertheless, an overall measure of the value of these arrangements is not available because of their heterogeneity.

The industrial cooperation agreements differ from barter and countertrade in that the agreements are for a longer time period and result in a degree of operational interdependence between the private firms of the West and the state enterprises. One arrangement is for the delivery of a turnkey plant and payment by the state enterprise in the form of output from the plant. Other relatively simple arrangements are contract manufacturing and subcontracting. Under contract manufacturing, the Western partner supplies all materials and design specifications while the Eastern partner assembles the product, using its labor and equipment, and ships it back to the Western partner.

---

[19] See Irene Lange and James F. Elliott, "U.S. Role in East-West Trade: An Appraisal," *Journal of International Business Studies*, Fall-Winter 1977, pp. 5–16; Marilyn L. Liebrenz, *Transfer of Technology: U.S. Multinationals and Eastern Europe* (New York: Praeger, 1982).

[20] See Carl H. McMillan, "Trends in East-West Industrial Cooperation," *Journal of International Business Studies*, Fall 1981, pp. 53–68; "Reciprocal Trading Arrangements in East-West Trade," *Economic Bulletin for Europe* (Oxford, England: Pergamon Press), June 1982, pp. 172–87.

BOX 14–4
Marxist Angola Welcomes Western Enterprises

Lucio Lara, regarded as an ideological leader within the Angolian politburo, talks of the problems of "exploitation" and "class consciousnes" and describes the ruling party as a "Marxist-Leninist party in ideology." But when it comes to dealing with foreign companies, the graying theorist says, "It is a question of business. They are business companies and they are very correct with us."

And Angola is correct with foreign companies. The government pays cash for its share of existing businesses and contributes its share of costs in joint ventures. Profits can be repatriated easily by foreign companies.

Undaunted by Marxist rhetoric, Western oil companies drilled 118 exploration wells in Angola from 1976 until 1983; and the country's oil reserves more than doubled to 1.7 billion barrels. The rewards for the companies have been considerable.

Oil isn't the only business. Conoco has been asked to launch an agricultural project. General Tire operates a manufacturing plant. A British company associated with the De Beers consortium manages the diamond mines in the northeastern part of Angola. Arthur D. Little & Co. serves as financial consultant and runs courses for Angolian technocrats.

Angola's effort to woo Western businessmen while relying on Cuban troops and keeping close ties to Moscow leads to incongruities.

SOURCE: Adapted from a news story by Steve Mufson in *The Wall Street Journal*, November 13, 1985. © Dow Jones & Company, Inc., 1985. Used with permission. All rights reserved.

Coproduction and *specialization agreements* are the most important forms of cooperation for many countries. Under coproduction, each partner supplies the other with certain components of the product, and each then assembles the product and markets it in its respective area. Specialization agreements take this process one step further, and each partner relies on the other for deliveries of certain final products. In many cases, coproduction and specialization agreements evolve from less sophisticated arrangements. They may present a solution when it becomes increasingly difficult to expand trade by compensation (barter) agreements.

A refinement of coproduction is *project cooperation*. In such arrangements a Western enterprise and an Eastern organization jointly undertake an investment project to serve customers located in the country of either of the partners or, more frequently in a third country, usually a developing country.

Joint Ventures

Equity joint ventures in Eastern Europe are most numerous in Yugoslavia and Hungary. Yugoslavia, as noted previously, had signed 199 joint venture agreements as of the end of 1980. Hungary had approved a total of 44 joint ventures as of mid-1985, 22 of which were established since 1982.[21] As of mid-1987, the Soviet Union's new joint-venture program had resulted in discussions with about 200 Western companies and the signing of several preliminary agreements; but no new ventures were yet in operation. With some exceptions, the Eastern European countries that permit joint ventures limit the foreign equity holdings to 49 percent. Some multinationals that entered into joint ventures are Citroen, Control Data, Corning Glass, Ciba-Geigy, Fujitsu, Siemens, and Volvo.[22]

Foreign Investment in China

China's drive to attract foreign direct investment began in early 1979, coincident with the establishment of formal diplomatic relations with the United States. In the early period, the program met with mixed success because China was neither prepared institutionally nor had negotiation experience. Over the next five years, however, China put in place much of the framework for dealing with foreign investment, such as a joint venture law, tax treaties, policies for international technology transfers, accounting standards, and some commercial laws. In addition, China created special economic zones and a number of so-called open cities along the coast, which can offer special tax and other incentive programs to attract foreign investment. Also, economic decision making in these areas has been decentralized.[23]

By the end of 1986, China had absorbed US$5.9 billion in foreign investment. The government reported that 7,300 new enterprises had been approved and that about 2,400 were in operation. One third of the total investment was to tap China's offshore oil resources. Of the new enterprises, 80 percent are in the coastal regions and cities.[24]

THE POLITICAL OVERLAY

A heavy political overlay covers and controls trade and other economic relations between the East and the West, particularly between the United States and USSR. As of the late 1980s, U.S.-Soviet political relations seemed to be improving but the outlook for increased U.S.-USSR trade was uncertain. The U.S. government still had in place a number of regulations controlling trade between the United States and the Soviet Union, including controls on exports, financing exports, and imports to the United States.

---

[21] *Nepszabadsag,* August 14, 1985, p. 10.

[22] United Nations, *Transnationals—Third Survey,* p. 274.

[23] An excellent guide for Western firms interested in investing in China is N. T. Wang, *China's Modernization and Transnational Corporations* (Lexington, Mass.: D. C. Heath & Co., 1984); see also Philip Wik, *How to do Business with the People's Republic of China* (Reston, Va.: Reston Publishing Co., 1984).

[24] *The Wall Street Journal,* December 18, 1986.

Export controls by the United States restrict the export of goods and technology that would prove detrimental to the national security of the United States. Export controls have also been used for punitive purposes, such as the partial embargo on the sale of grain to the Soviet Union imposed in 1980 (but discontinued in April 1981) in response to the Soviet invasion of Afghanistan. U.S. controls on the financing of exports to the Soviet Union prohibit the U.S. Export-Import Bank from financing trade with the USSR as long as the Soviet Union denies its citizens the right to emigrate. The import restrictions consist mainly of denying most-favored-nation status to the Soviet Union until it complies with the emigration provision noted above.[25]

With political issues playing such a negative role in the East-West business relations, why should the international firm commit resources to doing business with the socialist countries? One reason is that the political constraints have been most severe in U.S.-Soviet relations and are not as difficult a bar on trading and investing in the other Eastern European countries. The export controls related to national security apply also to China, but they have been administered in a liberal way and affect primarily trade in military goods. Thus, there is still wide scope for non-Soviet East-West economic relations.

Another factor is that U.S. policies keep changing, and there has been steady pressure from some government officials and from the business community to refrain from using trade as a political weapon.[26] In support of this position, it has been argued that boycotts have not been effective, that other Western countries have been willing to sell equipment to the Soviets which the United States would not supply.

BOX 14–5
If You Can't Lick the Competition

U.S. sales to Moscow are bigger than the bare figures show. Many U.S. multinationals ship parts to overseas affiliates that sell to the Soviet Union. FMC Corp. supplies packaging from its Italian subsidiary, and Paper Converting Machine Co. in Green Bay, Wisconsin, sold $20 million worth of equipment last year from its British subsidiary. In trade with the Soviets, some American companies have decided that if, because of U.S. restrictions, you can't lick Japanese and European competition, join them.

SOURCE: Adapted from *Business Week*, November 11, 1985, p. 106.

---

[25] See Michael V. Forrestal and James H. Giffen, "U.S.-Soviet Trade: Political Realities and Future Potential," *Columbia Journal of World Business*, Winter 1983, pp. 29–35.

[26] See R. D. Schmidt, "US-USSR Trade: An American Businessman's Viewpoint," *Columbia Journal of World Business*, Winter 1983, pp. 36–39.

Still another factor is the practice of many multinationals to channel their business activities through subsidiaries domiciled outside the home country, in nations that have a more flexible attitude toward East-West trade (see Box 14–5). For example, an interesting study by two Polish economists revealed that 75 percent of the value of purchases and 83 percent of the value of sales by the U.S. multinationals included in their study were channeled through foreign subsidiaries.[27]

SOME BUSINESS GUIDELINES

The most important guideline for Western enterprises when doing business in the centrally planned countries is to be constantly aware that they are dealing with a nation rather than with independent enterprises. This means that there is a lack of symmetry between the objectives of the foreign firm and the government of the host country that controls the actions of its enterprises. It also means that the home government of the Western enterprise by reason of its national objectives frequently imposes special constraints on such business relations.

In addition to this fundamental difference that pervades all East-West business relations, the Western enterprise must become familiar with unique institutional and structural factors of the centrally planned countries and become aware of cultural differences that affect negotiations.

Although the business environments in the centrally planned countries have much in common, great caution is necessary in applying experience gained in one country to doing business in another. Yugoslavia in particular regards itself as being outside the Soviet bloc, and, in Eastern Europe, Yugoslavia is often regarded as being part of the West. Nevertheless, the Yugoslav business environment differs significantly from Eastern Europe and the Western market economies.

Assymetry in Objectives

For a Western firm, the priorities and criteria that serve to shape its foreign business activities emerge from the self-interest of the enterprise. Potential ventures are normally judged on the basis of return to the enterprise on its investment. Aside from abiding by the laws of the land and government regulations in both host and home countries, the Western firm is free to pursue no higher purpose than enhancing its own well-being. Decisions are made at the enterprise level and in relation to the specific interests of the enterprise.

In contrast, the priorities and criteria applied by the state enterprises to foreign business transactions are based almost entirely on considerations that transcend the enterprise involved. The socialist doctrine and ideology regards

---

[27] Cieslik and Sosnowski, "The Role of TNCs," pp. 125–26.

productive capacity as the source of common benefit, not the individual gain of the enterprise. The enterprise is the State in microcosm and a vehicle for achieving its objectives. In practice, a specific set of priorities emerge from the State to influence the form and outcome of any proposed venture with Western firms.[28]

The criteria by which the centrally planned countries judge the merits of any proposal may give priority to such goals as providing technology transfer, earning foreign exchange, filling gaps in the domestic economy, and accelerating economic growth. To achieve these goals, the preferences of the socialist countries may be for industrial cooperation agreements and joint venture agreements rather than for straightforward sales and purchase agreements. In contrast, the Western firm may give priority to minimization of business risk in unfamiliar circumstances and a minimum commitment of funds and management resources, thus preferring sales and purchase arrangements rather than entering into joint ventures or direct investments.

The desire by the socialist countries to have ventures generate foreign exchange—or at least not cause its expenditure—raises special problems for the Western enterprise. It places restrictions on project financing and structure. It results in the socialist countries frequently offering investment "in kind" through the provision of land, labor, and infrastructure rather than funds directly to a project. At the downstream end, it results in the encouragement of nonmonetary compensation to the foreign partner through barter arrangements.

The assymetry of motives is illustrated by a study of the industrial cooperation experience of a large number of Swedish firms. As the researchers reported, "The most frequent motive among the Swedish firms is to promote exports. . . . The next most frequent motives are cost and availability advantages, and better utilization of existing capacity. The dominant Eastern motives, according to the Swedish firms, are to acquire technology, to reduce currency outlays for the technology, and to expand exports of resultant (and other) products. Except for promotion of exports, therefore, the partners have different motives for cooperation."[29]

Negotiation Styles

Individualism.   Western enterprises can normally make quick decisions with a minimum of outside consultation, in part because of their independence and in part because of the cultural trait of individualism. Negotiators for the socialist countries are influenced by the State and by an ideology that precludes actions taken on the basis of personal initiative. They consult frequently with

---

[28] Rudy L. Ruggles, Jr., "The Environment for American Business Ventures in the People's Republic of China," *The Columbia Journal of World Business,* Winter 1983, p. 68.

[29] Bengt Hogberg and Clas Wahlbin, "East-West Industrial Cooperation: The Swedish Case," *Journal of International Business Studies,* Spring/Summer 1984, pp. 66–67.

other officials, often introduce new demands in the course of negotiations, and may have limited authority to make concessions.[30]

Perceptions of Time.   Western managers are usually time-conscious and prefer events to be scheduled. They try to conduct negotiations quickly and efficiently. The socialist manager must deal with many government agencies and finds it difficult to meet exact schedules and to work efficiently, thus making negotiations very lengthy.

Perceptions of Risk.   Western managers are willing and able to take individual risks to achieve results. The socialist officials are risk averse. Responsibility is diffused by involving many parties in decision making. No one individual can approve a venture although many can disapprove it. The risk to the individual in *not* taking action may be minor. The risk of a failure when action is taken can be severe and result in a loss of status and personal benefits to the responsible decision makers.

Human Resources Constraints.   When assembling negotiation teams, Western firms are restrained by the availability of talent within the company and by the cost of hiring outside consultants. The socialist countries take a different view of human resources, and the government may be free to call on experts from all over the country. Although this may give them greater expertise, it makes the negotiating process more complex and time-consuming.

Negotiating Latitude.   While the Western firms have great freedom in defining the terms on which they wish to negotiate, the socialist representatives are constrained by rather strict policy limitations. They can bend the guidelines, but only slightly and with great care. This relatively rigid position of the socialist negotiators makes the negotiating process somewhat lopsided in favor of the socialist official when playing on their home ground.

Structural Factors.   When Western firms enter into joint ventures, industrial cooperation agreements, or direct investments in the centrally planned economies, the local arrangements for physical and human resources are under control of the government. Normally, there is no free market for choosing suppliers; nor are there free market prices for goods, services, and labor (see Box 14–6). All of these matters have to be negotiated with the possibility of conflicting pressure. For example, the government may want to assist certain suppliers in an early stage of getting experience, even though they are not the low-cost producers.

---

[30] See Edward Beliaev, Thomas Mullen, and Betty Jane Punnett, "Understanding the Cultural Environment: U.S.-U.S.S.R. Trade Negotiations," *California Management Review,* Winter 1985, pp. 100–112; Rosalie Tung, "U.S.-China Trade Negotiations: Practices, Procedures and Outcomes," *Journal of International Business Studies,* Fall 1982, pp. 25–37.

BOX 14-6
Protracted Negotiations

Antiaibo, China—With a roar from the exhaust of an earth-moving shovel, Occidental Petroleum Corp. inaugurated its partnerships in the Pingshuo open-pit mine, a U.S. $650 million project.

The bureaucratic problems of introducing advanced business and technical skills into a Chinese milieu have deterred many potential investors. And Occidental's protracted negotiations almost collapsed on several occasions.

For months, the Chinese insisted that the workers should be paid the equivalent of union wage scales in the United States, which would have worked out to more than $14 an hour, about 50 times the Chinese rate. As Chinese practice is to pay workers in "joint venture" undertakings at the local rate and retain the difference, the arrangement would have netted the Chinese principals a "profit" of more than $45 million a year.

After world coal prices sank more than $10 a ton from their 1982 high of more than $50, Occidental dug in. Eventually, the Chinese agreed to a compromise under which labor would be paid on the basis of each ton of coal mined.

SOURCE: Adapted from *International Herald Tribune*, July 8, 1985.

Preparation for Negotiations.   Given the vast difference between the East and the West in terms of cultural, ideological, political, and socio-economic systems, special preparation is usually required by Western firms when initiating business relations with the centrally planned countries. The published literature on East-West business experience has been expanding and can be an important aid in preparing for negotiations. Where the company does not have in-house facilities for training negotiators, it may be necessary to hire experts to assist on many matters. To some extent, home country governments such as the United States provide some support in the form of information for companies engaging in East-West trade and investment.[31]

SUMMARY

The centrally planned economies are important because they account for about a third of the world's population. Their past participation in international business activities has been modest as a result of their ideological commitment to self-sufficiency, East-West political conflicts, and other factors. For the future, however, there is reasonable possibility that East-West trade, investment, and industrial cooperation will expand greatly.

---

[31] See Robert D. Hisrich and Michael P. Peters, "East-West Trade: An Assessment by U.S. Manufacturers," *The Columbia Journal of World Business*, Winter 1983, pp. 44–50.

China has shifted to an open policy of encouraging trade and investment from the West. Within Eastern Europe, internal pressures have been intensifying for securing access to technology and other forms of know-how from Western multinationals. And political relations between the U.S. and the Soviet Union, which reached a low point in the mid-1980s and critically restrained economic relations, appeared to be improving in the late 1980s. But even in the environment of the 1970s and early 1980s, a number of Western enterprises developed profitable opportunities for trade and industrial cooperation with the centrally planned countries.

Doing business with the centrally planned economies requires major adjustments for enterprises attuned to the environment and business practices of market economies. Western firms must become familiar with differences in economic and political philosophy, institutional frameworks, motivations, and decision criteria that are involved in East-West business transactions.

EXERCISES AND DISCUSSION QUESTIONS

1. Should the United States link trade and credit concessions for the centrally planned countries to internal policies concerning human rights and emigration? Why or why not?
2. Wang Beiming, a Chinese manager working with a China-U.S. joint venture, made a series of recommendations for American firms operating in China. (*Wall Street Journal,* Sept. 26, 1986.) What problems and solutions do you see in adjusting to the following recommendations?
   a. Longer-term commitments by American executives, whose average term in China is shorter than three years.
   By contrast, the average term of a Japanese executive is 13 years, while German businessmen generally stay eight and one-half years, Australians eight years, the French seven years, and Britons six years.
   b. More American businessmen doing business in China should learn Chinese.
   Few speak either Mandarin, the national language, or any of the local dialects.
   By contrast, almost all Chinese businessmen in the United States speak English.
   c. An increase of interaction between employers and employees.
   Unlike American executives, who seldom mix with employees after work, Chinese managers spend much of their spare time with their workers. American managers should pay more attention to the attitudes local workers have toward their companies.
   d. Have more patience in arranging contracts, which most Americans complain are very difficult to negotiate.
   While Americans are relatively open toward foreigners, the Chinese are more guarded, for they remember the period from 1849 to 1945 when China was invaded again and again by foreign military powers.
3. How does COMECON differ from the European Economic Community as an economic integration movement?
4. In view of the argument below, should the foreign affiliates of socialist enterprises from the Eastern European centrally planned countries be exempt from the "rules of conduct" adopted by the OECD and being drafted by the United Nations? Why or why not?

''The branches of the socialist companies at present in the West can be called 'red multinationals,' but there is little point in using a concept fashioned in the West to refer to the product of a very different economic system. These companies are little more than insignificant trading companies unlikely to develop into part of a multinationally integrated production system.'' (Adapted from G. Hamilton, *Red Multinationals or Red Herrings?*)

5. What do the centrally planned companies want from the West and vice versa, in the area of international trade and foreign investment?

6. Would you encourage U.S. multinationals in high technology fields to invest in joint-venture projects in China? in the USSR? Why or why not?

CHAPTER 15

Using the Countervailing Power of International Business

International business is not without its own power for countering the impact of national controls. It is entitled to use legal means to avoid controls that may hinder attainment of its legitimate global business objectives. The experienced international enterprise goes even further. It will plan to avoid *future* controls. It will examine the existing strategies of relevant countries toward multinational business and international transfers, project the likely pattern of change, and adapt its own strategy accordingly. The firm is not an unprotected, misused pawn of omnipotent nations; it is a powerful player in the international business game.

The international firm may make adjustments to its business operations so that the costly effects of national controls are minimized.[1] The firm may involve others in its business situation, and through this support, deter a country from negative controls it might otherwise impose. The firm may take countervailing actions in direct confrontation with a nation-state in order to mitigate the effects of controls. Also, there are different styles of response a multinational may take in a conflict situation.

DEFENSIVE ADJUSTMENTS TO BUSINESS OPERATIONS

Changing the Business Activity

One of the most obvious ways for a firm to avoid controls is to change its type of activity. Confronted with restrictions concerning one area of business, the firm can quickly move to others. Most international corporations have many facets to their business and can develop those in which controls do not hamper achievement of the firm's objectives. When ITT's telephone company was bought out by the government of Peru in the late 1960s, the company shifted its Peruvian activities into more acceptable company lines, such as the construction of a Sheraton hotel (ITT subsidiary) and the manufacturing of electrical equipment. Where the compensation terms for the sale or expropriation of a company's assets require reinvestment for a period of time in the same country, such as in the case of ITT, the choice of new business activity will be influenced by the locational restriction.

The prime criteria in the selection of expansion opportunities will almost certainly be growth, risk, and return on capital. These criteria will favor expansion where capital and profits look least vulnerable to erosion by government controls. Public utilities presently have the highest degree of vulnerability to expropriation and national controls and are generally avoided for new investments. The extractive industries, particularly petroleum and mining, also have a high degree of risk. By using a high-risk factor in evaluating such investments, international firms weigh them less favorably as attractive choices for business activity. Lower vulnerability is likely to occur in intermediate production that buys from and sells to local entrepreneurs. Both supplier and customer can act as buffers against imposition of controls.

---

[1] See Yves L. Doz, *Government Control and Multinational Strategic Management* (New York: Praeger Publishers, 1979).

Changing Location and Dispersal of Operations

Some national controls attempt to increase the production level of local subsidiaries by requiring the subsidiaries to export and make greater use of higher cost local raw materials or components.[2] Such pressure to maximize production at any one location may make the firm less competitive in export markets and may vitiate the firm's potential to minimize production costs through a systemwide locational strategy that seeks economies of scale, reduced transportation costs, and minimum tariff burdens.

To the extent that the firm has flexibility in the location of its facilities, such flexibility can be a countervailing power. As soon as a nation's controls exceed those of alternative locations, the country becomes a less likely location for new investments or expansions of existing facilities by international firms. Conversely, when it reduces its control level, a country is more likely to be a recipient of future investment.

In some industries, firms have been known to maintain reserve production potential in several countries as a deterrent to individual nations imposing added controls. In the 1950s, for example, United Fruit kept large amounts of improved land prepared for banana planting but unplanted. The stated company objective was to have land reserves in case its plantations were exposed to diseases or other natural hazards. Another obvious advantage was the possibility of shifting the location of production as a defense against national controls.

Strength can be built against both home and host countries by setting up directly competing units within the same organization but located in different countries. Such an arrangement can be effective in limiting national controls if the subsidiaries directly compete for the same export markets. Any restraining controls applied locally might give the competing subsidiary an export advantage.

Yet another defense available to the multinational enterprise lies in adoption of a truly international production network in which each plant specializes in some part of the total process. This means that most subsidiaries will contribute export income to the country of residence. Any insistence by the local government on further local production could be demonstrated by the international corporation as likely to jeopardize exports to units elsewhere in the network. Furthermore, by breaking down its operations into small stages and spreading these across the globe, a multinational can reduce the incentive for a single nation to nationalize operations at one stage. First, the management of such a small unit might have difficulty managing a unit that depended on a complex system beyond its control; second, a small segment might be fairly readily replaced elsewhere; and third, the gains to the country would be minimal.

The location of management can be changed, as well as the location of

---

[2] See Stephen E. Guisinger and Associates, *Investment Incentives and Performance Requirements* (New York: Praeger Publishers, 1985).

production. The U.S. business community in Britain made strong representations to the British government in 1974 that the proposed imposition of high U.K. taxes on the unremitted foreign income of U.S. nationals in Britain would force them to leave. Some relaxation of the proposals was gained, but there was subsequently a significant transfer of multinationals' offices to Paris and other locations.[3]

Retaining Control of Intangible Assets

A powerful source of countervailing power for international firms is their ability to control the location of intangible business assets. These include research and development ability, technical, marketing, and management know-how. If the activity requires continual injections of updated research output, expropriation of purely production facilities could be self-defeating. More gradual attempts at creeping controls, such as limitation of profit remittances or permission to expand, could be offset by the firm through withholding new developments as a bargaining gambit. The same situation prevails when the international firm retains the production, marketing, and management expertise through the use of expatriate personnel rather than training nationals. This suggests, unfortunately, that countries perceived to be high-risk control areas are less likely to maximize the technology-transfer benefits from multinational enterprises.

Retaining Control of Markets

When production or extraction is located in one country and the consumer in another, the international firm can build a strong position through control of access to the market. If the firm owns the channels of distribution or has built an unassailable market position, controls imposed over production must not take the costs beyond those the marketing organization could obtain elsewhere. So long as no supplying country is in a monopoly position and supplying countries do not act in unison, any action by one will be checked by the failure of the others to act likewise. In some cases, international corporations have built themselves into virtually single-buyer positions from competing suppliers.

But just as a nation's bargaining position can be undercut by the availability of other sources of supply, so can the bargaining strength of an international enterprise be sapped when other companies are willing to do the marketing. In 1971 Guyana nationalized its bauxite mines owned by Alcan. Given a world oversupply of bauxite, Alcan was unlikely to have trouble finding other sources of supply. In the closely knit world of a small number of aluminum producers, it appeared that Guyana was going to have serious difficulty in selling its bauxite. To Alcan's dismay, Guyana demonstrated its own marketing capability by securing independent Swiss and British marketing agents and by actively searching out

---

[3] *Business Week,* March 10, 1975.

new markets in the USSR, China, and Yugoslavia.[4] With its market control eroded, Alcan agreed to a settlement that it considered much below the true value of its assets.

Even within one country, an international business firm likely to be hampered by creeping controls may build a stronger position by retaining dominance of the market. Manufacturers of internationally branded consumer goods, for example, have sometimes adopted a policy of purchasing supplies from a range of local suppliers while retaining all the marketing in their own hands. This limits the amount of investment required and at the same time builds added protection against controls. Small local producers without experience in marketing branded consumer products should act as a buffer against government interference.

Changing Sourcing and Movement of Funds and Profits

When governments restrict remittances and the use of local funds in order to improve their balance of payments, support domestic economic policies, or reduce excessive profit taking, the multinational firm is in a strong position to avoid much of the intent behind these controls. Using a variety of legal forms of incorporation, it can generally arrange to allocate the ownership control of its assets and activities to a preferred pattern of jurisdictions. It can use assets in one nation to support borrowing in another, obtain funds from outside a nation for inward remittances at a time when local firms would find great difficulty obtaining further capital, or adopt a range of other financial management policies discussed in Chapter 23. This strength has been used frequently in both home and host countries in times of inflation and tight monetary controls to build up a larger market share at a lower cost than would be the case were local competitors on the same footing.

The international movement of funds can also be carried out through a range of internal transactions that are difficult to police. Charges for royalties, interest, travel, training, research and development, corporate overheads, machinery, advice, use of overseas facilities, and so on endlessly, can be arranged in such a way that governments could effectively prevent significant transfers of funds only by stopping all business transactions. Then there are the more controllable, but still quite effective, possibilities of altering the transfer prices for components, raw materials, part assemblies, or finished goods.

All these actions affect the location of profit. They may thus equally be used for arranging the place at which profit is taken so that taxation is minimized. Where, however, the arrangement that would minimize taxation is not that which would locate the funds in the way the business would find optimal, the firm will have to choose between the objectives.

---

[4] J. Frederick Truitt, *Expropriation of Alcan's Bauxite Mining Subsidiary* (Boston: Intercollegiate Case Clearing House, 1974), Part D.

ACTIONS TO INVOLVE AND GAIN SUPPORT FROM OTHERS

Enlisting Home-Country Support

Investor countries vary in their willingness to lend official support to their international enterprises. But where support for private companies can be wrapped in the mantle of national interests, investor countries may be enticed to support the private interests of its citizens in foreign situations.

In 1971, for example, the United States used economic pressure on Chile after Chile's expropriation of U.S. copper companies. The U.S. Export-Import Bank announced that credit guarantees for purchase of American jet aircraft by the Chilean airline were being "postponed" pending resolution of the copper compensation question.[5] The U.S. government has also used its influence with the World Bank and the Inter-American Bank to deny financing to countries that had taken undesirable action against U.S. companies.

But the United States is not alone in lending its official support to counter host-country measures against multinational enterprises. When Libya expropriated the oil assets of British Petroleum in 1971, the British foreign office is reported to have approached other oil-importing nations, "expressing concern for BP's rights."[6] In some situations, home-country support can be more direct. In 1987, the drive by multinational financial institutions to gain access to the Japanese capital markets came to a head, with the United States threatening reduced access to Wall Street and the U.K. threatening reduced access to the City of London.[7]

Still another way in which the home country can give support to its multinational enterprises is through legal actions in the World Court, as discussed in Chapter 8. But such support through World Court litigation has not been an effective source of countervailing power.

When foreign projects are covered by home-country investment-guarantee schemes, the international enterprise may secure home-country support as well as risk insurance. Such programs, however, do not explicitly guarantee that the home country will intervene on behalf of the international enterprise.

Stimulating Local Enterprise

If the international firm accepts the hypothesis that a host country's receptivity varies inversely with the share of the total economy or of key sectors controlled by foreign interests, it can take steps to increase receptivity and deter controls

---

[5] Paul E. Sigmund, *Multinationals in Latin America* (Madison: University of Wisconsin Press, 1980), p. 153.

[6] *The Wall Street Journal*, December 31, 1971.

[7] Michael R. Sesit, "U.S. Lawmakers on Mission to Japan, to Press for Opening of Tokyo Markets," *The Wall Street Journal*, April 10, 1987, p. 19.

by stimulating growth of indigenous enterprise. It can, for example, plan and implement active programs for encouraging independent local firms to become suppliers, processors, further manufacturers, and sellers of the product of the venture. The benefits of stimulating domestic activity are much heralded by proponents of foreign investment, but, too frequently, the opportunities for domestic development are left to slow natural forces or are realized not by domestic business but by other foreign investors.

More by necessity than by design, Sears Roebuck de Mexico demonstrated more than four decades ago the effectiveness of policies to stimulate local enterprise in increasing host-country receptivity without prohibitive costs. In establishing its first large, modern department store in Mexico, Sears assumed that it would import about 70 percent of its merchandise from the United States. But in late 1947, less than a year after opening its first store, the company had to face a drastic change in the Mexican economic situation. As a result of foreign exchange difficulties, Mexico placed an embargo on a wide range of consumer imports. To meet this unexpected challenge, Sears responded by a mammoth program of encouraging new local enterprises as sources of supply. Within six years, and through cooperation with 1,300 local firms, Sears was able to buy in Mexico 80 percent of the merchandise it sold there.[8]

Developing Local Allies

Another interesting example of measures to deter national controls is the case of Firestone's rubber-growing operations in Liberia. As a planned strategy, Firestone initiated a comprehensive rubber-growers assistance program designed to help Liberians grow rubber on their own farms and even market their production.[9] Through assisting local enterprises, a number of which happen to be owned by political leaders and government officials, Firestone increased its supply of rubber while reducing its relative share of the local rubber-growing industry. It was also protecting itself against adverse government controls by helping many nationals secure a vested interest in favorable governmental actions toward rubber growing.

Sharing Ownership with Nationals

Probably the best known deterrent to host-country controls is the sharing of ownership in local subsidiaries with nationals. Although the decision to engage in joint ventures involves many considerations other than a defensive move against national controls, this strategy can have the multiple effect of reducing the apparent

---

[8] Richardson Wood and Virginia Keyser, *Sears Roebuck de Mexico, S.A.* (Washington D.C.: National Planning Association, 1953), p. 39.

[9] Wayne Chatfield Taylor, *The Firestone Operations in Liberia* (Washington, D.C.: National Planning Association 1956), p. 94.

threat of foreign domination, securing local allies, and enlarging the role of indigenous enterprise in the local economy.[10] Complete ownership of local subsidiaries gives the multinational enterprise greatest flexibility in such areas as organization, intercompany pricing, and dividend policy. Yet many firms find that divestment of some equity can provide more than offsetting benefits through protection against controls. The greater the proportion of ownership that is divested, the greater the gain in protection and the greater the loss of parent-company control.

The distribution as well as the share of the local ownership can be important. The advantage of having local ownership in the hands of a small number of local partners is that such partners are likely to take an active interest in protecting the profitability of their investment from erosion by government controls. The advantage of a wide dispersion of local ownership is that the international firm may be able to retain a degree of control greatly in excess of its ownership share.

With the local government as a partner, there is a negative incentive for controls or harassment—and, in some cases, an incentive for positive advantages. Moreover, a government usually has ample funds for desirable expansion, is less interested in profit distribution than in growth, and is generally uninterested in taking over the business itself or undertaking day-to-day management. Private partners frequently produce problems on each of these counts.

Selective Ownership Divestment

Another ownership strategy is selective divestment. The various parts of the business operation can be separated. The commercial or technical side can remain in the hands of the international enterprise and heavy local ownership may be arranged for the capital-intensive parts requiring physical assets. With a large share of the total investment in local hands the risk of expropriation is greatly reduced. Also, local investors may prefer to retain the pattern rather than become involved in a wider range of activities with which they are not familiar. United Fruit, a favorite leftist target in Latin America for many years, finally divested itself of its landholdings and banana growing. It then continued its activities in the banana business by concentrating on its marketing and transportation operations.[11]

Conversely, some international firms may find that retention of marketing activity by local entrepreneurs is advantageous. In many countries, the importer-distributor is a powerful political force. Working through such an outlet may ensure continued access to the market, even though the international company would be able to carry out much more effective distribution on its own account.

---

[10] For example, see Richard W. Wright, "Joint Venture Problems in Japan," *Columbia Journal of World Business,* Spring 1979, pp. 25–31.

[11] *Business Week,* November 22, 1969.

Introducing Multiple Foreign Ownership

The domination of the foreign business sector by firms of a single nationality may be an important stimulus for stronger national controls. One response to the fear of economic domination is for multinational enterprises to acquire multiple nationality. Both Royal Dutch Shell and Unilever have carefully nurtured the dual Dutch-British nationality of the parents because they have found the ambiguity to be useful. When Indonesia's Sukarno was unfriendly to the Dutch, these enterprises emphasized their British identity. When antagonism emerges against the British, it is the Dutch identity that comes to the fore.

Another response is for firms from several nations to join in undertaking a project. Consortia of international firms of different nationalities have been common in the field of mining. Some examples are the Fria bauxite project in Guinea, the Freeport nickel project in Indonesia, and iron ore mining projects in Australia. The theory is that the host country would act more circumspectly if tempted to repudiate the terms of an agreement when faced with the multinational "establishment."[12] A somewhat similar strategy practiced by firms in natural resource fields is to sell output forward to buyers in a number of countries in order to increase the problems that the host country would face if it attempted to expropriate.[13] Kennecott Copper worked out such a defense prior to Chilean nationalization in order to protect its compensation position.[14]

Bringing in Third Countries

The encouragement of competition between different countries is also an option open to the international firm if the nature of its business permits a number of alternative locations. For such firms it may be feasible to move from requesting permission to carry on business in a particular country to a solicitation of bids from competing countries. In some cases, the weakest countries will be adding taxation holidays, dividend-remittance guarantees, and other incentives to attract investment away from countries in which location is initially more attractive to the international investor.

The European Commission has been particularly concerned with the "beggar-my-neighbor" policies that result from corporations shopping around for the best European sites. The practice of "bidding-up" for mobile international investments, however, has been reduced by a landmark ruling of the Luxembourg court against

---

[12] Joseph S. Nye, Jr., "Multinational Corporations in World Politics," *Foreign Affairs* October 1974, p. 157.

[13] Theodore H. Moran, "Transnational Strategies of Protection and Defense by Multinational Corporations: Spreading the Risk and Raising the Cost for Nationalization in Natural Resources," *International Organization* 27, no. 2, Spring 1973, pp. 273–87.

[14] Theodore H. Moran, *Multinational Corporations and the Politics of Dependence: Copper in Chile* (Princeton, N.J.: Princeton University Press, 1975), pp. 132–36.

the level of aids that Philip Morris had received from the Dutch government.[15]

Whenever a business has something of value that can be offered to several nations, the limits on a nation's power to control are set by the weakest of the nations concerned. No other nation can impose on a firm a higher cost in terms of controls unless that cost is offset in some other way by higher profitability. In the same way, competition among firms can set limits on the countervailing power of the enterprise.

Forming Business Coalitions

There have been numerous examples of multinationals joining together to bargain with nation states. In the early 1970s, 63 major U.S. multinationals joined together to form The Emergency Committee for American Trade and lobbied successfully against the protectionist moves of the AFL-CIO, which had produced the Burke-Hartke bill. In Europe in 1983, a committee of multinationals was formed under the acronym of CRISIS (Committee to Restore an Internationally Stable Investment System) and lobbied against the unitary taxation moves of U.S. states.[16]

DIRECT COUNTERVAILING ACTIONS

Lobbying

The countervailing power of international companies includes the possibility of influencing governmental authorities through direct action and lobbying.[17] For an international enterprise there may always be some local interest that would identify with it and be prepared to lobby accordingly. And in some countries local interest groups exercise influence disproportionately to the importance of their claims. In fact, on many occasions international firms have decided not to use direct influence simply because the results might be so inequitable in their favor that a later backlash would be likely.

Sometimes the "lobbying" is quite open. In 1981, Renault of France quite openly threatened to reduce its Belgian car assembly operation if Belgium did not put further curbs on imports from Japan. In Britain, the Japanese typewriting group, Brother, stimulated newspaper stories that it was "worried" about its plans for future investment there. It implied, in effect, that a proposed EEC

---

[15] Giles Merritt, "How Europe's Governments are 'Aiding' the Multinationals" in *Multinational Info,* no. 7, February 1985, pp. 6–9.

[16] Clive Wolman, "*E.E.C.* Companies to Fight Double Taxation in U.S.," *Financial Times,* November 23, 1983.

[17] See Jack N. Behrman, J. J. Boddewyn, and Ashok Kapoor, *International Business-Government Communications* (Lexington, Mass.: D. C. Heath, 1975), chap. 4; Thomas A. Poynter, *Multinational Enterprises and Government Intervention* (New York: St. Martin's Press, 1985), pp. 75–78.

anti-dumping levy that might boost its costs 27% could "affect" its plans for further investment in the United Kingdom. The British government should, therefore, intercede on its behalf with the Brussels' authorities.

Negotiating

Faced with proposed controls, or even formal legislation, the multinational may decide that the best approach is to engage the governmental authorities in direct negotiation. It may use the threat of withdrawal or refusal to supply additional resources or skills in order to "de-escalate" a country's control proposals. It may also appeal to precedent in this country or others, reciprocity, or fair play. In short, the multinational attempts to view legislation as a starting point from which it will use the power of its alternatives, relative to those of the country, to negotiate a more favorable outcome.

The use of negotiation to make a trade-off on one national control against that on another may even enable a multinational to gain a local advantage over competition and end up ahead. Some multinational enterprises faced with Indian requirements to restrict foreign equity participation to 40% used such a strategy to negotiate a license to expand. India prohibits a firm from expanding capacity beyond agreed limits or entering new product lines without specific permission. Once a new license is gained, however, it serves as a barrier to competitors. Both Ciba-Geigy and Cheesebrough-Pond's were successful in obtaining expansion licenses as part of their "Indianization" moves. Cheesebrough-Pond's issued new equity exclusively to Indian investors, expanded its Indian plants from one to four over a five-year period, and began exporting 30% of its output.[18]

Their study of responses between 1977 and 1983 of 12 multinational corporations operating in India led Encarnation and Vachani to suggest that MNCs faced with changed controls should:

1. Look at the full range of strategic possibilities. If the firm doesn't, the competitor may.
2. Use the law to further the corporation's ends. By using controls creatively, the corporations built competitive barriers.
3. Create future bargaining chips. By meeting the country's requirements, corporations placed themselves in a stronger position for negotiations at the next stage. Their importance to the country became greater.

Renegotiating

Just as countries can attract international investment on the basis of a published set of conditions and a signed agreement and then later change their laws or insist on renegotiating the agreement, so, too, can multinational enterprises force renegotiation. Renegotiation is a two-way street.

---

[18] Denis J. Encarnation and Sushel Vachani, "Foreign Ownership: When Hosts Change the Rules," *Harvard Business Review,* September–October 1985, pp. 152–60.

An approach that has emerged in the past is for a multinational to enter into a minority partnership as specified by the country's rules regarding foreign investment, but with an agreement as to detailed plans for profit performance. When operation begins, however, the profits may not materialize as planned. At this point, the multinational may be the only party able and willing to advance further capital or expend more on research or management to overcome the problems that have emerged. Renegotiation is sought—and the country acknowledges its position as having weakened and relaxes the minority ownership requirement or some other control.

Resorting to Legal Defenses

The local subsidiaries of multinational firms generally can contest national control actions in the local courts. Two American copper companies, whose properties were nationalized by Chile in 1971, appealed the settlement offered by the government to a special tribunal created by the constitutional reform that permitted the nationalization of these properties. Although such appeals may take a long time to be decided and although the international companies are uncertain about success, in the judgment of the companies such resort to legal defense in local courts appears to warrant the effort.

Another related strategy has been to undertake legal action in the courts of nations other than the host country. One of the U.S. copper companies expropriated in Chile brought suit in a U.S. federal court in New York to block Chile's use of assets in the United States, pending resolution of the copper company's claim for compensation. Subsequently, Chile agreed to pay the copper company for a loan it made to its Chilean subsidiary for developing a copper mine in Chile. As reported by a U.S. newspaper, "There was some speculation that President Allende cleared payment to unfreeze the government's assets in the U.S."[19]

Boycotting

Where the output of multinational firms is exported from the host countries, international firms have used boycotts as an effective means of countervailing power. When Libya nationalized the local assets of British Petroleum (BP) in 1971, BP advertised in more than 100 newspapers around the world to advise potential purchasers that the company reserved its rights with regard to Libyan oil. Although both BP and the British government denied that they had organized a formal boycott of Libyan oil, other petroleum companies and oil-importing nations began to shun the purchase of crude oil from the expropriated properties.

Changing Nationality

A multinational enterprise may find that its greatest countervailing power lies in its ability to change its nationality, either to avoid home-country controls

---

[19] *The Wall Street Journal*, February 28, 1972.

or to be better received by host countries. A number of firms have switched domicile in recent years from the United Kingdom to Australia, Canada, and elsewhere. McDermott, the large U.S. engineering and contracting firm, emigrated from Delaware to Panama in 1983 by issuing stock in McDermott International of Panama in place of the stock in what then became the U.S. subsidiary. The motivation was clearly stated as tax avoidance.[20] Another large multinational, Jardine Matheson, emigrated from Hong Kong to Bermuda in 1984 primarily to avoid controls that China might place on the firm after Hong Kong sovereignty returns to China in 1997.[21]

Refusing to Participate

Refusal to participate is the simplest and most direct form of countervailing power available to the international enterprise. Where national controls make the business environment unattractive, the international firm can refuse to make new investments. And it can even divest and discontinue existing operations, as occurred in 1977 when IBM and Coca-Cola withdrew from India rather than consent to sell 60 percent ownership to local enterprises.

A nation's optimum strategy is to set its controls at a level that maximizes net national benefits. Above a control optimum, the nation will lose benefits from investments not made and business activities discontinued. With nationalistic enthusiasm, nations have frequently exceeded the control optimum and been forced to relax or abandon controls when they became aware of what they were losing in potential new investments and expansions or in terminated operations. In both developed and less developed countries, the loss of future foreign investments has operated as a constraint on national control policies.

DECIDING THE CORPORATE RESPONSE

The management of a multinational does not set out to use all its countervailing power to the utmost. In order to obtain the best possible outcome for itself, it may decide to be less assertive. It may also find that cooperation with the nation-state produces better results than an uncooperative approach. Thomas classified the combinations of assertiveness and cooperativeness that a multinational may adopt into five styles of conflict management, as shown in Exhibit 15–1.[22] Gladwin and Walter have added to this classification four situation variables—outcome stakes, relative power, interest interdependence, and relationship quality—which

---

[20] McDermott Incorporated, *Prospectus of Exchange Offer for Preferred Stock*, February 17, 1983.

[21] Les Nicholls, "1997 Fears Behind Move—Jardine's Holding Company Quits H.K." *South China Morning Post*, March 29, 1984.

[22] Kenneth W. Thomas, "Conflict and Conflict Management," in *Handbook of Industrial and Organization Psychology*, ed. Marvin D. Dunnette (Chicago: Rand McNally, 1976), pp. 889–935.

EXHIBIT 15–1   Styles of Conflict Management and Situation Determinants

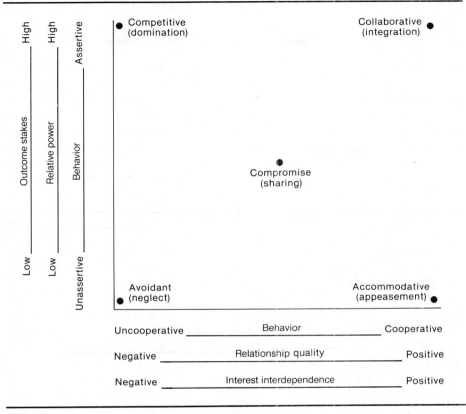

SOURCE: Gladwin and Walter, *Multinationals Under Fire*, 1980.

suggest the appropriate style to be used in a given conflict situation. Interpreting from Exhibit 15–1, the five styles are as follows:

Competitive.   Management adopting this style is assertive and uncooperative and competes head-on to overcome the opposition and achieve its own objective. This style is most appropriate when the amount at stake for the multinational is high and its power within the situation is high, but there is a negative interdependence between the interests of the multinational and the country and a negative relationship between the two.

Avoidant.   This style occurs when management is uncooperative yet unassertive and does nothing to combat the situation. The firm concedes the battle and reserves its energies for other things. It is useful when the multinational's stake and its power are relatively low and when the interest interdependence and quality of relationship between the firm and the nation-state are low.

Accommodative.   An accommodative style is adopted when management is unassertive but cooperative and does what it can to accommodate the nation-state. The strategy is one of appeasement. It makes sense when the firm's stakes and its power are low and when the interdependence of interests and quality of relationship with the nation-state are relatively positive. In such situations, the firm has little to lose from giving way and will lose even less if it cooperates.

Collaborative.   Management adopts this style when it is assertive and cooperative hoping through its positive action to meet both its own and the nation-state's objectives. It is best adopted when the firm's stakes and its power are relatively high and interest interdependence and relations with the nation-state are positive. Both the firm and the nation-state can gain—their conflict is only how to achieve the gain.

Compromise.   A compromise style emerges with management adopting an intermediate amount of assertion and cooperation to meet the nation-state halfway. It is likely to be used when stakes are moderate, power is relatively balanced and interest interdependence, and quality of relationship are mixed positive and negative. It is a bargaining style and can produce expedient solutions under pressure of time.

Conflict situations are dynamic and the issues often complex. The response required may also need to be complex and changing. The five styles of response to national control moves, therefore, are not necessarily exclusive choices for the one situation. They may appear in sequence or even be in use at the same time. Nevertheless, the style of response is an important consideration for the multinational. Recognition of its countervailing power alone will not gain it the most mileage in its defense against nations working unceasingly towards their own objectives.

SUMMARY

This chapter has shown that the international enterprise is not without protection against the nation-state. In fact, its countervailing power is much greater than suggested by the picture of sovereign nations and their control programs. The enterprise has a range of protective measures available that vary in effectiveness with its type of business operations and with the alternatives available to the host countries. Some of the measures, such as sharing ownership with local government or private interests, may imply an opportunity cost and reduced profitability. Yet the cost may be a reasonable price to pay for protection against future controls. In deciding its response, moreover, the enterprise must use its countervailing power judiciously. Style may be as important to the outcome as the power position itself.

EXERCISES AND DISCUSSION QUESTIONS

1. "The management of a multinational firm should in no way take it upon itself to decide what different contributions the firm will make to the various societies in which it operates. Within the external pressures and constraints surrounding the firm, management's first task is to ensure the firm's survival and beyond that to pursue the balanced interests of its owners, employees and customers." If you do not agree with this statement, what guidelines would you give to the management of multinational firms?

2. Discuss the following proposals: The chief executive of a multinational corporation *should not*:

   a. accept any politically motivated direction from the government of the corporation's home country that would limit the performance of a foreign subsidiary.

   b. seek partnership with a foreign government in order to gain privilege or protection for its operations.

   c. use power stemming from its domestic operation to lobby the home government to intercede on the firm's behalf with foreign governments under whose jurisdiction the firm's subsidiaries operate.

   d. select expatriates for the top management of foreign subsidiaries because they can be trusted to place the firm's interests ahead of the local environment.

3. "In order to protect their traditional international business operations some multinational firms monopolize distribution channels and effectively deny small producers in developing countries reasonable access to international markets. Such action is against the principles underlying U.S. commercial law and should not be permitted under U.S. law simply because those harmed fall outside its jurisdiction." Comment on this statement. Can you identify any firms to which you think this statement might apply?

4. It has been argued that one way a multinational firm should use its strength is to ensure that countries know they are really in direct competition for its new investment. If you agree, how would you suggest the firm go about ensuring this awareness and what risks do you see?

CHAPTER 16

Assessing Political Risk and National Controls

As firms expand internationally, they must deal with the fragmenting influence of many different political environments. The most cataclysmic political events affecting business operations have become referred to as political risks. But these are only the tip of the iceberg. Beneath the surface, less dramatic changes take place in day-to-day political and administrative policies and practices that even more frequently affect the viability of multinational operations and the achievement of corporate objectives. The dividing line between discontinuities and continuous change is difficult to mark precisely, yet there is enough difference in the political forces at play and the business response to warrant examining the two phenomena separately. The potential cost of both types of event must be assessed for each country incorporated in a firm's global strategy.

Political risk has long been a familiar term in the lexicon of international business, but political-risk assessment is relatively new as an established managerial function in international firms. A survey of U.S. firms made in the mid-1960s found no evidence of a systematic approach to political-risk assessment.[1] In contrast, a 1980 survey revealed that more than half of the 193 responding U.S. firms had taken some steps toward formal assignment for the function and over one third had established political assessment units.[2] Numerous consulting firms have also sprung up to provide both general political risk summaries and studies of specific projects. The recent surge of interest began with the unexpected fall of the Shah's regime in Iran (1979–80) and was reinforced by the overthrow of apparently secure regimes in Nicaragua and South Korea during the same period.

POLITICAL-RISK ASSESSMENT

Some General Observations

A Pervasive Factor.   The mention of political risk is most likely to bring to mind the notion of unstable, less-developed countries; bearded revolutionary leaders; and threats of expropriation. But political risk is a more pervasive influence, both geographically and in the ways it affects international enterprises. Political risk arises in host countries that are industrialized, such as France and Canada, as well as in the LDCs. It can also arise in the home countries of investors such as Sweden and the United States.

The 1980 election of Mitterrand in France brought a radical change in the French business environment with the adoption of a policy to nationalize a number of major industries, including ones involving foreign investors. In the same year, Canada sharply reversed its traditional welcome for foreign investment in the area of petroleum by adopting a new energy policy intended to reduce foreign participation in this field from 75 to 50 percent.

Home-country political risks have emerged in the form of political boycotts in the United States against national firms doing business in South Africa and with Soviet-bloc countries. In Sweden, domestic political forces were responsible for legislation prohibiting Swedish firms from investing in South Africa and Namibia (South-West Africa) and requiring them to cut back existing operations there.

---

[1] Franklin Root, "U.S. Business Abroad and Political Risks," *MSU Business Topics*, Winter 1968, pp. 73–80.

[2] Stephen Blank et al., *Assessing the Political Environment: An Emerging Function in International Companies* (New York: The Conference Board, 1980); see also Stephen J. Kobrin, *Managing Political Risk Assessment: Strategic Response to Environmental Change* (Berkeley: University of California Press, 1982).

Gains as Well as Losses.   Political risk usually connotes the possibility of losses. Yet, as in the case of other types of risk, political risk can result in gains as well as losses. For example, dramatic political changes that improved the business environment for foreign firms occurred in the 1970s in the People's Republic of China. The overthrow of the Allende government in Chile (1973) resulted in a return of expropriated foreign investments. And a 1983 change in Canada's ruling party was followed by a significant easing of restrictions on foreign investment.

The Need for Continuing Assessments.   Political assessments should serve management in two phases of decision making. Political assessments are needed in preinvestment decisions where political-risk assessments are integrated with parallel studies of marketing, production, logistics, and finance. They are also needed on a continuing basis to guide, protect, and nurture already established operations.

Sovereign Risk.   *Sovereign risk,* also referred to as *country risk,* should be differentiated from political risk, although the two are clearly related. Sovereign risk is a principal concern of financial institutions making loans to foreign governments or to foreign firms where the government guarantees repayment. The risk is labeled "sovereign" because the ultimate responsibility for repayment rests with a government and generally depends on the country's external liquidity.[3]

Sovereign risk exists even though the lender has no physical presence in the foreign country. In contrast, political risk refers to changes in a country's environment that affect the operations of a foreign firm within the country.

Defining Political Risk

Political-risk assessment for international business operations must start with a precise and operational definition. Although there is no general agreement on how to define political risk,[4] the following definition has become widely accepted. *Political risk is the likelihood that political forces will cause drastic changes in a country's business environment that affect the profit and other goals of a particular business enterprise.*[5] Thus, political risk includes four necessary elements:

---

[3] For further information on sovereign risk see Briance Mascarenhas and Ole Christian Sand, "Country-Risk Assessment Systems in Banks: Patterns and Performance," *Journal of International Business Studies,* Spring 1985, pp. 19–35; Shelagh A. Heffernan, *Sovereign Risk Analysis* (London: Allen & Unwin, 1986).

[4] For a summary of different political-risk definitions see Stephen J. Kobrin, "Political Risk: A Review and Reconsideration," *Journal of International Business Studies,* Spring/Summer 1979, pp. 67–70.

[5] Stefan H. Robock, "Political Risk: Identification and Assessment," *Columbia Journal of World Business,* July/August 1971, pp. 6–20.

1. Discontinuities—drastic changes in the business environment.
2. Uncertainty—changes that are difficult to anticipate.
3. Political forces—defined as power and authority relationships in the context of society at large.[6]
4. Business impact—potential for affecting significantly the profit or other goals of a particular business enterprise.

Political risk, therefore, focuses on discontinuities in the business environment. National-control forecasting, to be discussed below, focuses on changes in the business environment that reflect continuity in government policies and political forces and that can be anticipated with greater certainty. Tax laws, for example, are constantly changing. But most changes do not represent a radical departure from past trends and are not too difficult to anticipate.

Political risk and political instability are separate though related phenomena. Instability is a property of the environment. Risk is a measure of how that instability might affect the business enterprise. It follows that political fluctuations that do not affect the operating conditions for the firm do not represent political risk for international business. Furthermore, political risk is firm-specific. What is political risk for one firm may not be political risk for another.

Political scientists have done considerable research on the subject of political instability, and a number of empirical studies have attempted to analyze the relationship between selected indicators of political instability and foreign direct investment.[7] Although methodological problems cloud the results, it is clear from the studies that political instability is neither a necessary nor a sufficient condition for policy changes relevant to foreign enterprise. Discontinuities that affect international business can occur with or without major changes in political leadership. Conversely, major changes in political leadership can occur without greatly affecting the business environment.

Political and economic risk should be differentiated wherever possible because they have different sources and may require different managerial responses. Government decisions are always political—by definition. Yet the forces dictating the decisions may be purely economic. For example, political-risk insurance offered by the U.S. government for foreign investments includes currency inconvertibility as a political risk. Yet currency inconvertibility can occur for predominantly economic reasons in politically stable nations and at times when political systems and political leadership are not changing.

In some cases of currency inconvertibility, however, political rather than economic forces may be the dominant factors, or there may be an intermingling

---

[6] See David Easton, *The Political System* (New York: Alfred A. Knopf, 1968).

[7] See David A. Jodice, "Sources of Change in Third World Regimes for Foreign Direct Investment, 1968–76," *International Organization* 34 (Spring 1980), pp. 193–98; Stephen J. Kobrin, "The Environmental Determinants of Foreign Direct Manufacturing Investment: An Ex Post Empirical Analysis," *Journal of International Business Studies,* Fall–Winter 1976, pp. 29–42.

of political and economic motivations. Political uncertainties in some nations have stimulated large outflows of flight capital, which in turn caused a balance-of-payments crisis. Or internal political forces in opposition to foreign enterprise have compelled governments to limit the repatriation of profits and other financial transfers by foreign firms. An example of the intermingling of forces is the general strike that occurred in Tunis during 1978 that began as an economic event—a protest against wage restraint—and ended as a full challenge to the Bourguiba government. But even where considerable intermingling exists, the international firm may get useful results by trying to separate the political factors from the others.

Macro Political Risk.   The international business enterprise may encounter both macro and micro types of political risk. *Macro risk* occurs when *all* foreign enterprises are affected in much the same way by politically motivated discontinuities in the business environment. Micro risk occurs when the changes affect only selected industries, firms, or even projects.

Macro risk can be indirect and spasmodic. At times of political turmoil, foreign companies and foreign management personnel are tempting targets for political factions opposed to the regime in power. At other times foreign executives may be kidnapped by terrorist groups for financial reasons, as shown in Box 16–1.

Direct and relatively permanent macro risk can be illustrated by the takeover of private enterprise in 1959–60 by the Castro government in Cuba. Foreign enterprises were seized along with domestic firms. In part, the broad-sweep confiscation of foreign investment was explained by a basic change in political philosophy brought about by the Cuban revolution—a shift from a market to a socialist economy. Also, the large size of the foreign-owned sector of the economy and the domination by foreign firms of several strategic fields[8] of business activity supported pressures to end the "economic colonial" status of the country.

The Cuban case is not an isolated example of macro risk. International enterprises, along with domestic private enterprises, also felt the broadside of expropriation by socialist governments in Eastern Europe and China following World War II. More recently, however, the incidence of macro-risk situations appears to be declining. A study of expropriations in 79 LDCs from 1960 to 1979 concluded that ideologically motivated mass expropriations actually occurred in only 10 of the countries—Algeria, Angola, Chile, Ethiopia, Indonesia, Mozambique, Peru, Tanzania, Uganda, and Zambia.[9]

Macro-risk situations can also result from broad action taken against foreign enterprise as a political boycott. In the Middle East, various Arab countries began

---

[8] See Leland L. Johnson, *U.S. Private Investment in Latin America: Some Questions of National Policy,* Memorandum RM-4092 ISA (Santa Monica, Calif.: Rand Corporation, July 1964).

[9] Stephen J. Kobrin, "Expropriation as an Attempt to Control Foreign Firms in LDCs: Trends from 1960 to 1979," *International Studies Quarterly* 28 (1984), p. 331.

BOX 16–1
The Political Risk of Executive-Napping

Washington—Last year there were 67 terrorist attacks—including kidnappings—against business facilities or personnel abroad, about one third more than in each of the previous years, the State Department says. Although Mideast terrorism received the most media coverage, Latin America, where 35 of the attacks took place, holds the highest risk for American firms. In most cases, the kidnappings are for financial, not ideological, reasons.

On December 10, 1985, for instance, three executives working at a pumping station on an oil pipeline project in Colombia, near the Venezuelan border, were kidnapped by members of the Popular Liberation Army, a small Marxist group. A day later, according to U.S. sources, one of the three was returned with a message demanding $10 million ransom for the other two, a Fluor Corp. employee and a Bechtel Group Inc. executive. After months of negotiations a $2.2 million ransom was paid, the sources said.

U.S. terrorism experts are disturbed by signs that Latin American terrorist groups, which once had little to do with one another, have begun to coordinate activities. For example, the M-19, a Colombian group, has been training members of the Ecuadoran AVC terrorist group. . . . The U.S. experts say that along with the closer coordination comes a terrorist grapevine that can spread the word quickly about American companies that are willing to pay ransoms.

SOURCE: Adapted from *The Wall Street Journal,* December 22, 1986. © Dow Jones & Company, Inc., 1986. Used with permission. All rights reserved.

---

in 1955 to boycott companies that had branches in Israel or allowed use of their trade name there. Direct trade with Israel was ignored. But any permanent investment in that country, or any long-term agreements such as licensing arrangements or technical assistance, earned the company a place on the blacklist. The implementation of such policies, however, has been sporadic.

Micro Risk.   Macro political risk is dramatic. Micro political risk is more prevalent. With considerable frequency, the international manager is likely to encounter abrupt and politically motivated changes in the business environment that are selectively directed toward specific industries, firms, or projects. In technical jargon, *micro risk* is industry, firm, or project specific. The types of business operations with a high vulnerability to micro risk will vary from nation to nation and over time in the same nation. And vulnerability may vary with the product or service, level of technology, ownership structure, or management style.

At a particular point in time and for a specific country, it should be possible to rank types of business activities according to their degree of political risk vulnerability. Such rankings, however, keep changing. A few decades ago, public utility investments were popular with both host countries and investors. More recently, worldwide trends have been toward domestic—usually government—ownership of electricity, transportation, and communications enterprises because of national security and developmental goals. As a result, most of such enterprises owned by foreigners have been nationalized, and international firms have not been active in these fields.

In a current ranking of industry vulnerability, technologically dynamic industries dependent upon a continuing import of new technology from abroad would have a low degree of political risk. In contrast, natural resources projects and financial institutions have a high degree of political-risk vulnerability. Petroleum and mining projects in particular are frequently endangered by growing nationalistic feelings and a conviction that natural resource endowments should be developed for the welfare of all people in a nation rather than for private profit. Financial institutions are vulnerable because of "their pervasiveness and their potential as bases for influence and control."[10]

A number of factors can change the political-risk vulnerability of an industry over time. One is the dominance of foreign enterprise in a major industry sector. Vulnerability from industry dominance is illustrated by the previously mentioned case of Canada's 1980 policy reversal intended to reduce foreign ownership in its petroleum industry from 75 to 50 percent.

A second factor, the capacity of nationals to operate a business successfully, has a somewhat ironic aspect. At an early stage in a nation's development, foreign enterprises may be welcomed because they provide scarce capital, management know-how, and technical skills not available locally. Over time, countries manage to accumulate capital and local managerial and technical skills as a result of the successful operations of the foreign enterprise. As the value of foreign contributions erode and local personnel are trained for copper mining, running a tea plantation, or managing other types of businesses initiated by foreign firms, the political pressures for curtailing foreign enterprises are likely to increase.[11]

Other factors with risk implications are: changing priorities of a specific industry in national plans, emergence of indigenous firms in the same industry, increased access by local firms to foreign technology, the corporate image of the multinational, and new competition from other multinationals wishing to establish operations in the country.

Sources of Political Risk

What are the sources of political risk? The conceptual framework presented in Figure 16–1 suggests the major underlying political forces that can cause abrupt policy changes. The framework also indicates the groups or political actors

---

[10] *Foreign Ownership and the Structure of Canadian Industry: Report of the Task Force on the Structure of Canadian Industry* (Ottawa, Canada: Information Canada, 1970), p. 389.

[11] Fariborz Ghadar, "Political Risk and the Erosion of Control: The Case of the Oil Industry," *Columbia Journal of World Business,* Fall 1982, pp. 47–51.

FIGURE 16–1 Political Risk: A Conceptual Framework

Sources of Political Risk	Groups through which Political Risk Can Be Generated	Political-Risk Effects: Types of Influence on International Business Operations
Competing political philosophies (nationalism, socialism, communism)	Government in power and its operating agencies	Confiscation: loss of assets without compensation
Competing religious groups	Parliamentary opposition groups	Expropriation with compensation: loss of freedom to operate
Social unrest and disorder	Nonparliamentary opposition groups (e.g., anarchist or terrorist movements working from within or outside of country)	Operational restrictions: market shares, product characteristics, employment policies, locally shared ownership, and so forth
Vested interests of local business groups	Nonorganized common interest groups: students, workers, peasants, minorities, and so forth	Loss of transfer freedom: financial (for example, dividends, interest payments), goods, personnel, or ownership rights
Recent and impending political independence	Foreign governments or intergovernmental agencies such as the EC	Breaches or unilateral revisions in contracts and agreements
Armed conflicts, internal rebellions for political power, and terrorism	Foreign governments willing to enter into armed conflict or to support internal rebellion	Discrimination such as taxes, compulsory subcontracting
New international alliances		Damage to property or personnel (kidnapping from riots, insurrections, revolutions, wars, and terrorism

through which political risk can be generated, and the political-risk effects on international business operations. It should be noted that some of the specific effects shown in the far right column are not exclusively associated with political discontinuities. For example, pressure for local sharing of ownership can occur in relatively stable political situations. Also, the loss of financial transfer freedom may result from economic rather than political forces.

The seven general sources of political risk shown in Figure 16–1 are of particular importance to international business. The most frequently encountered risk arises from political forces hostile toward foreign enterprise for philosophical reasons that diverge sharply from prevailing government policies. Others are social unrest and disorder, the private vested interests of local business groups, recent or impending independence, new international alliances, and armed conflicts or terrorism. Less predictable, and political only in the sense that it is a tool of politicians, is the exposure of corruption or scandal. It is often linked to a government official who might well have provided influence for a foreign firm.

Latent Hostility.   Some latent hostility to foreign enterprises is present in most nations, including the United States. The potential strength of such hostile forces affects the degree of political risk. Numerous avenues are available for making such political strength effective in changing government policies. The basic form of government can be changed, as happened in Cuba. The leadership of government can change but the political system remains the same, as happened when Mitterrand succeeded Giscard d'Estaing in France. Or concessions can be exacted from the political parties and leaders in power without changes in the form or leadership of the existing government, as illustrated in Box 16–2.

The hostility of strong internal factions of a country to foreign enterprise may arise out of adherence to socialist or nationalist philosophies. They may also spring from attempts to achieve specific national goals, whether of security, welfare, or development.

Socialism commonly means government rather than private ownership of the means of production. Yet political labels can be misleading. "Socialism" as a label has been extremely popular in many parts of the world in recent decades. But the specific goals of political forces banded together under the socialism label vary greatly, as previously discussed in Chapter 14. Thus, the international enterprise must look behind labels for the specific goals of political groups in different countries.

The nationalistic philosophy generally asserts that control over a nation's economic destiny should be in the hands of nationals and that nationals should have preference over foreigners in benefiting from economic and business opportunities in the country. Both of these views can generate political risk for international business enterprises.

An example of national-welfare goals that can create political risk is the persistent pressure in many countries of the world for land reform. If land-reform measures are suddenly accelerated, as occurred in El Salvador and Nicaragua in the early 1980s with drastic changes in government, foreign as well as domestic business firms with landholdings are likely to be expropriated.

BOX 16–2
Garcia Dusts Off an Old Ploy: Expropriation

On December 28, with submachine gun-toting police surrounding the headquarters of HNG/InterNorth Inc.'s Belco Petroleum Corp, Peru's hard-charging President Alan Garcia summarily nationalized the Omaha energy company's Peruvian assets, worth $400 million. But the president of one of South America's poorest countries probably isn't on an expropriation binge. Rather, it looks as though he's playing a risky game to keep his political base from eroding.

At about the same time as the Belco takeover, Garcia awarded Occidental Petroleum Corp.—Peru's No. 1 oil producer—exploration rights to a vast Amazonian tract. The Oxy deal ensured the future of a highly successful exploration company that also produces half of Peru's 180,000-bbl.-a-day oil output. And that assurance apparently gave Garcia enough clout to move against producer No. 2.

"With the Oxy deal in his pocket," says an analyst in Lima, "he could show Peruvians he is shrewd. Then with the decision on Belco, he could show the left, his only opposition, that he is tough."

SOURCE: *Business Week,* January 13, 1986, p. 50.

National aspirations for economic development can create political risk for international business when the nation believes that the ultimate goal of development is to enlarge the domestic capacity for *self-generating* growth. This view implies that a country does not want to increase its dependence on outside forces any more than is necessary.[12]

Other Sources of Risk.   Social unrest and disorder may create political risk, not because of specific hostility to foreign enterprise, but because of general disruption of business activities. The causes of social unrest may range from the existence of extreme economic hardships, to racial disorders, religious disputes such as have occurred in India, and even student riots. Ineffective law enforcement can also be included in this category. It can result in risk to property and to persons and can greatly influence the costs of doing business and the efficiency of production, transportation, and communications.

The risk that can result from the political influence of local business interests that feel threatened by foreign enterprises should never be underestimated. In Japan, local business interests have been extremely successful in influencing government policies or decisions that restrict the activities of foreign enterprise.

Nations recently attaining independence, or about to do so, are likely to face great political uncertainty. In many cases, a nation secures widespread political cohesion on the issue of gaining independence but not on what policies should

---

[12] See Fernando H. Cardoso and Enzo Faletto, *Dependency and Development in Latin America* (Berkeley: University of California Press, 1979).

be followed after independence. In addition, new nations frequently lack experienced political leadership and undergo considerable turmoil while experience is gained and the policies and political power of various groups are tested. The role to be played by private enterprise and the attitudes toward foreign investment are not always clarified in the early stages of organizing a new nation.

Internal rebellion may be an extreme stage of social unrest and disorder. The situation in Central America during the early 1980s illustrates the kind of political risk that can occur. The effects on foreign business may be similar to those on domestic business or they may be accentuated because of the leverage that the opposing groups think they have in gaining support by putting pressure on foreign firms.

Armed conflicts between nations such as has occurred between Israel and the Arab states can greatly affect the feasibility and profitability of foreign business operations.

New international alliances would include the case where a country joins a common market or free-trade area and in the process agrees to give preference in certain ways to business activities of common market nationality. Or, as in the case of the Andean Common Market in Latin America, the member countries agreed to harmonize their policies toward foreign private investment. When such intergovernmental agreements are concluded, some national policies under which international enterprises are operating may drastically change.

Political-Risk Effects

Political-risk effects on international business operations fall into two categories. They can affect ownership of assets through expropriation or partial divestment. They can restrict operations and ultimately reduce cash flows or returns. Both types of effects have been discussed in the chapters on controls and the legal environment.

Concession agreements are especially vulnerable to political risk. The prevailing philosophy in many countries, particularly newly independent nations, is that agreements can be revoked or revised at the discretion of the host country if the national interests are no longer being adequately served. Such revisions are likely to occur when the goals of national governments change, when a new political regime feels that contract revisions will strengthen its domestic political support, and when key circumstances surrounding an agreement change.[13]

In September 1969, for example, a group of young military officers seized control of Libya, sweeping aside the monarchy of King Idris I, and established a "socialist republic." The announced goal of the new Qaddafi regime was to reduce foreign influences in the country. Shortly after the 1969 change in govern-

---

[13] See William A. Stoever, *Renegotiations In International Business Transactions* (Lexington, Mass.: D. C. Heath, 1981), for a detailed analysis of copper renegotiations in Zambia and petroleum renegotiations in Indonesia during the 1970s.

ment, Libya began to revise its agreements with the international oil companies.[14] One of the reported motivations was the need felt by the new regime to prove its toughness to the people by standing up to the oil companies, and the oil companies were blamed for corrupting the previous government with bribes.

To the sophisticated international enterprise, political risk, including expropriation risk, is not a bar to investment but an element to be weighed against prospective gains. Thus the time dimension is crucial. The firm may foresee high expropriation risk sometime in the future. Yet the profit possibilities up to the time when expropriation risk is high may be sufficiently attractive to make a project of interest. Such an approach has been characteristic of the petroleum industry.

Political-Risk Perceptions and Realities

To what extent are perceptions of "political instability" a reliable guide to political risk? The question deserves special attention because political instability is frequently cited as an obstacle to flows of private foreign investment, particularly to the less-developed countries.[15]

With a high sensitivity to political instability, inexperienced international enterprises may have missed attractive business opportunities because they perceived more political risk than actually existed. When international managers with limited background perceive political risk, it often means that they are not familiar with the political patterns and styles of a foreign country and would feel insecure trying to operate in a strange environment. In such cases, the problem is to come to terms with an unfamiliar rather than a hostile situation.

Another possibility is that international managers are applying ethnocentric standards, based on political systems with which they are familiar but that are not appropriate to the country being considered. And because the criteria for political stability are different for each political system, the perception does not fit the reality.

Most American managers have not been exposed to formal political training and are not familiar with politics as a process in the sense that they understand marketing, finance, or economics. Furthermore, as nationals of a large country where a single political system spans a continent, they have not had the advantage of close contact with a wide range of governments in a limited geographical area that European managers have had.

To interpret frequent changes in the leadership of governments as political risk can be highly misleading (see Box 16–3). The more fundamental question is whether strong factions are present with divergent views from those of the government on policies toward foreign business. Furthermore, the potential for

---

[14] Riad A Ajami, *Arab Response to the Multinationals* (New York: Praeger Publishers, 1979), pp. 110–11.

[15] See Douglas Nigh, "The Effect of Political Events on United States Direct Foreign Investment," *Journal of International Business Studies,* Spring 1985, p. 11.

BOX 16-3
Political Instability Doesn't Necessarily Mean Political Risk
El Salvador: U.S. Plants Hum along Despite Turmoil

U.S.-owned companies in El Salvador are operating relatively smoothly despite the political violence and economic sabotage there. Although a number of U.S. companies have left, those that still operate Salvadoran facilities—including Texas Instruments, Dataram, Chevron Oil, Phelps Dodge, and Kimberly Clark—report that disruptions have been minimal and that their employees are coming to work regularly. Notes the president of a U.S. electronics company with a factory there, "We missed less production in El Salvador because of that country's problems than we did in our plant in South Carolina because of snow."

U.S. executives cite several reasons why their factories in El Salvador continue to run smoothly. The most important is the work ethic of the Salvadorans—known as "the Japanese of Central America."

Most U.S.-owned factories in the country, like Dataram's, are assembly operations for export, with no local sales outlets and little need for local credit. Most are managed and staffed almost entirely by Salvadorans; fewer than 15 U.S. managers still work and live in the country full time. Many factories are in out-of-the-way locations and keep a low profile.

SOURCE: Adapted from *Business Week*, April 13, 1981, p. 60.

---

political risk in countries with centralized political control, sometimes headed by a military dictator, can also be great. One-man governments often behave erratically and generate underlying tensions. Considerable uncertainty may exist as to how an orderly transition to a successor will be possible.

Forecasting Political Risk

Corporate practices vary greatly among the international firms that have formalized the political risk assessment function. Political assessment "units" range from the part-time involvement of an assistant international treasurer to full-time staffs of political scientists, ex-foreign service officers, or other country specialists. The political assessment approach may involve no more than a checklist or an outline for a country study, or it may entail a relatively sophisticated system designed to gather and process expert-generated opinion. An example of the latter is a recent political risk analysis for Canada and Mexico that used a panel of 27 experts on Canada and 21 experts on Mexico in a two round Delphi methodology.[16] (See Chapter 25 for a description of the Delphi methodology.)

The state of the art for political risk forecasting is still greatly underdeveloped

---

[16] Richard Drobnick, *Political Risk Analysis for Canada and Mexico* (Los Angeles: Center for Futures Research, University of Southern California, February 1984).

compared with most economic and business forecasting functions.[17] The underdeveloped state of the art can be illustrated by a study of the pre-1978 published predictions for Iran based on the principal political risk models. Only two of the 10 models offered reasonably accurate forecasts of the impending 1978 Iranian revolution and the resulting massive expropriation of foreign direct investment.[18]

The task of political-risk forecasting involves four basic steps. First, a profound understanding is required of the type of government presently in power, its patterns of political behavior, and its norms for stability. Second, the characteristics of the multinational's own product and operations must be analyzed to determine the kinds of political risks likely to be encountered in particular areas. Third, the potential sources for these risks should be identified and evaluated. The fourth step is to project into the future the possibility of political risks in terms of probabilities and time horizons.

Throughout the process, the emphasis must be on political forces that can cause abrupt change in the environment for the business firm. What companies ultimately must know is not how stable a country will be, but how what happens in that country will affect its interests there.

Understanding the Political System.   The necessary background information on a country's political system goes far beyond a knowledge of the present administration's policies toward foreign private enterprise. The need is to understand within a nation's historical context its type of government, its political parties and forces, and their philosophies. The real challenge is to perceive the path along which policies and attitudes have been traveling, particularly those of political forces that are not shaping the policies of the present administration but are likely to do so.

Both internal and external sources can be used to develop this understanding. The most important internal sources are the managers of overseas subsidiaries. In addition, many companies secure the assistance of government and academic experts on the political systems of specific countries. Still another source of information and analysis is the growing number of political risk services.

The key features of the risk forecasting services are their periodic updates and their use of numerical indices to rank countries on several macro-level risk dimensions. Most of the services systematically collect opinions and data from panels of country experts and quantify these data to produce so-called risk indexes. Although the methodology gives the illusion of objectivity, it consists essentially of quantifying what are in fact subjectively-derived data.[19]

---

[17] Stephen J. Kobrin, "Political Assessment by International Firms: Models or Methodologies?" *Journal of Policy Modeling* 3, no. 2 (1981), pp. 251–71; see also David M. Raddock, *Assessing Corporate Political Risk* (Totowa, N.J.: Rowman & Littlefield, 1986).

[18] Charles R. Kennedy, Jr., "Multinational Corporations, Political Risk Models and the Iranian Revolution," Working Paper no. 81–10 (Austin: College of Business, University of Texas, April 1981).

[19] Wenlee Ting, *Multinational Risk Assessment and Management* (Westport, Conn.: Greenwood Press, 1988), chap. 7.

A major limitation of the services is that a broad and general ranking of a country's investment climate or stability cannot take into account the variation in risk exposure for different types of investment. Various types of investments and even individual firms are exposed in fundamentally different ways to political risk.

Analyzing Specific Risk Vulnerability.   The identification of the specific types of political risk that might be encountered requires an analysis of the enterprise's products and patterns of operation. Is the problem one of macro or micro risk? Is the project vulnerable to expropriation and loss of assets? Or are operational restrictions the principal risk? The answers to such questions as the following will be invaluable in this analysis:

Do nationals have the capability to operate the business successfully?

Are the foreign firm and its foreign managers highly visible in the local setting?

Are periodic external inputs of new technology required?

Will the project be competing strongly with local nationals who are in, or trying to enter, the same field?

Is the operation dependent on natural resources, particularly minerals or oil?

Does the investment put pressure on balance of payments?

Does the enterprise have a strong monopoly position in the local market?

Is the product socially essential and acceptable?

Does a social cost-benefit analysis of the project show attractive and continuing benefits to the country?

In general, projects or products that contribute strongly to national goals are likely to receive favorable political attention when first initiated. But as the projects become taken for granted over time and a local capacity is developed to operate such projects, political favoritism may shift to new fields.

Sources of Risk.   After the types of company-specific risks have been identified, the assessment procedure should examine the sources—factions and circumstances that influence the occurrence of the political risk event. The specific risk might be expropriation and the sources of this risk might be ideological shifts or the vested interest of local groups.

The easiest situation in which to evaluate risk is that of a parliamentary democracy where the opposition views can be determined from parliamentary debates or political platforms. Such was the case in the early 1980s with the political shifts in France and Canada. At the other extreme is the difficult task of determining views and weighing the political strength of antagonistic opposition forces in a dictatorship where considerable censorship occurs. In such cases, political forecasting should include an examination of the views of political exiles.

This step of identifying the sources of risk may result in a considerable amount of error and uncertainty. But over time, skill can be developed to accomplish this task within reasonable limits of probability.

NATIONAL-CONTROL FORECASTING

The most frequent changes in the business environment come not from political-risk discontinuities but from the ever-present desire of nations to increase national benefits from foreign investments. To predict changes in national controls emanating from this "natural" desire requires an underlying theory. This section attempts to develop a predictive theory of controls based on the interplay of the objectives and decision rules of representative firms and representative countries.

International Business as a Game

The imposition of controls over international business can be depicted as a vast international game. There are players, moves, strategies, and payoffs. The players are firms and countries. The moves of the firms can be changes in the location of business investments and operations. The moves of the countries can be changes in the nature and level of controls. The moves of the players interact to determine the payoff to each. For purposes of this theory, the players are depicted as representative firms acting to achieve payoffs of return on investment and representative countries acting to increase national benefits.

A simplifying assumption of rationality provides an efficient basis for prediction when applied to an aggregation of countries and firms over time. Yet for any individual firm, its investment pattern may not approximate a profit-maximizing one. And for any individual country, its policies at a specific point in time may not maximize national benefits.

The international business game proposed here is a non-zero-sum game. A gain by one player does not necessarily result in a loss by the same amount to the opposing player. Nevertheless, some of the objectives of the players are in definite conflict. Where this is the case, controls that increase the benefits to one country are likely to reduce the payoff to firms in some way. The same controls may also decrease the benefits to some other country.

The players are thus not arranged simply with countries on one side and firms on the other. Countries also compete with countries, and firms compete with firms. It is the competition among countries for shares of global business activity and among firms for foreign business opportunities that plays the major role in determining the pattern of controls. This formulation contrasts with the common view that controls may be explained by a narrow examination of conflict potentials between individual countries and individual firms.[20] This formulation has also been recognized by the United Nations, which reported as follows:

---

[20] See Charles P. Kindleberger, *American Business Abroad* (New Haven: Yale University Press, 1969), p. 150ff.; Raymond Vernon, "Conflict and Resolution between Foreign Direct Investors and Less Developed Countries," *Public Policy*, Fall 1968, pp. 333–51.

Unilateral measures relating to transnational corporations adopted by one developing country can no longer be assumed to have little effect on others. In some instances, the demands of a developing country for greater production may lead transnational corporations to divert some of their production from other developing countries rather than from industrialized home countries.[21]

The game is sequential and dynamic with continually evolving action and reaction. Players do not all disclose their hands at the same time before knowing their opponents' moves. With a large number of players competing under these conditions, it is not feasible to extend the formal presentation of the game to the point of proving optimum strategies. The prediction of strategies is based instead on the following simplified sequence of play:

1. International firms locate business activity for a "practical maximization" of expected net cash flow subject to allowances for the risk of potential controls.
2. Countries alter controls to maximize national benefits, bearing in mind the likely reactions of firms and ultimate reactions of other countries.
3. Firms realign existing operations and redirect new investment in the light of the changed controls.
4. Other countries feel indirect effects of the changed controls and move to alter their own controls.

The prime focus of the theory is the prediction of step 2 in the sequence— the strategies of countries. Step 4, of course, will be covered by the same prediction. This prediction is itself made against the backdrop prediction of where firms locate their activity with an existing set of controls and how they react to changes in controls. Firms' objectives are therefore the starting point for the analysis.

Objectives and Decision Rules of the Representative Firm

The representative international firm is defined as motivated toward a "practical maximization" of the present value of expected cash flows from its activities. It identifies market targets and location alternatives for supplying these markets through the global strategy approach developed in chapters 9 and 10. And it relies on national-control and political-risk forecasts for incorporating risk allowances in the firm's decision process.

A change in any control can alter the optimum location pattern for a firm's existing operations and possibly the ranking of its investment alternatives. As a general rule, at the margin, foreign business activity and investment will be discouraged when controls that decrease profitability are extended and encouraged when such controls are reduced.

When an adverse change in controls appears likely, the representative firm

---

[21] United Nations, *Transnational Corporations in World Development: A Re-Examination* (New York: United Nations, 1978), pp. 133–34.

may take protective steps to reduce the probability that controls will be changed. It may use some of the countervailing measures for reducing risk discussed in Chapter 15. An example would be to seek local associates who could act as a local buffer against pressures to increase controls. There is an incentive to arrange for protection when the estimated loss of profits that would result from the control change, multiplied by the probability that the change will occur, is greater than the cost of protection.

Objectives and Decision Rules of Representative Countries

A representative country for this theory is motivated toward maximization of net national benefits. As elaborated in Chapter 13, the costs to the country must be balanced against the gains to calculate net benefits. Moreover, only the incremental benefits over domestic or international alternatives open to the country should be included. It is assumed here that controls are independent and their individual benefits additive. Country control strategies can then be expressed in terms of a collection of separate controls.

The representative country acting rationally to maximize national benefits will set each individual control at its *control optimum*. This is defined as the level at which the control brings maximum net national benefit over some future time period. The national benefit from adjusting any control is the incremental benefit accruing as a result of the adjustment. A control change, for example, may increase national benefits from foreign business activity already established in the country. But the control change may also result in an opportunity loss of benefits by discouraging the entry of new foreign investments and future expansions of existing firms. A country's control optimum is exceeded when the opportunity loss of national benefits from discouraged international investment or business activity outweighs the gain from imposing the control.

Implicit in this definition of the control optimum for any control is an allowance for reactions by other countries, and reaction may be expected when alteration in controls will alter the control optimum of another country. The greater and the more immediate the effects on another country's business activity, the more likely the other country is to take matching action. With a fixed supply of international business investment, the lowering of controls by a less developed nation might siphon off a large proportion of the investment that another marginal recipient of such investment would have received. This second country might then move very quickly to offer the same or greater incentives.

In many cases, countries will be unable to predict what reactions their actions will produce from individual competitor countries. There are too many countries, too many investors, and too many controls for individual effects to be assessed accurately. The reaction of many other countries to change by one country is, moreover, likely to be a gradual process over time and best predicted as a decay in the benefit gained from a control as a function of time. Where it is clearly apparent that competition among countries can weaken each country's bargaining position and the number of such competing countries is relatively small, as in the case of the oil-producing countries, a possible strategy is to form a cartel and bargain as a group. This possibility, however, is limited to countries in an oligopoly situation as suppliers of raw materials.

General Features of Country Strategies

Some general features of country control strategies can be derived from the juxtaposition of country objectives and decision rules against prediction of strategies for representative firms. The control optima are likely to be high for those controls that produce a given gain in national benefits with the smallest reduction in expected profits of investors, or, what amounts to the same thing, where a given reduction in expected profits is accompanied by large gains in national benefits. This may occur when a control:

1. Results in a crucial contribution to the country's development.
2. Was anticipated by firms and, therefore, does not alter the expected cash flow to firms.
3. Takes effect a considerable time in the future.
4. Is not reflected in discounted cash-flow calculations.
5. Restricts access to the local market to gain power over location of production.

A requirement that foreign firms use nationals as local managers is an example of controls that could contribute greatly to national development with a small cost to foreign firms. Such controls may impose some immediate costs on foreign firms, but they can bring future offsetting benefits. Local management reduces the foreign image, adds personnel attuned to local culture, secures local allies, and may cost less than expatriates. For the country, the control contributes to development by increasing the supply of nationals with management experience.[22]

Certain controls may be anticipated by firms through effective forecasting or through messages that countries have relayed about future controls. In such cases, investment decisions will have already allowed for the risk and countries will have nothing to lose by imposing the anticipated controls. Also, the further in the future that increased controls begin to take effect, the less the discouragement to firms. Any control affecting an investor's cash flow after the first 10 years is likely to carry little weight in the investment decision. Its discounted cost would be infinitesimal, given the discounting rates commonly used for assessing international opportunities.

Controls that do not affect investors' discounted cash-flow calculations may

---

[22] Peter P. Gabriel, *The International Transfer of Corporate Skills* (Boston: Graduate School of Business Administration, Harvard University, 1967); Harry G. Johnson, "The Multinational Corporation as a Development Agent," *Columbia Journal of World Business,* May–June 1970, pp. 25–30; Frederick Harbison and Charles A. Myers, *Industrialism and Industrial Man: The Problems of Labor and Management in Industrial Growth* (Cambridge, Mass.: Harvard University Press, 1960).

also increase national benefits without having a strong negative effect on international business decisions. For example, by limiting the right of a foreign firm to expand into further business areas, a country can retain opportunities for national firms. Yet such a control is unlikely to be weighted heavily in a discounted cash-flow calculation for any investment that by itself is worth undertaking. Controls that limit the share of foreign ownership reduce foreign participation in a country's market but may not reduce the return to investing firms. Controls on transferring funds out of a country are also likely to create minimal discouragement to further initial investments if returns remain high and profitable local opportunities exist for local reinvestment.

Controls that restrict access to the local market to gain power over the location of production are also likely to have high control optima. Production for the home markets of many countries will not be located locally in the absence of controls, and production that has been located locally will tend for some to move to lower cost locations. Controls such as tariffs, import licensing, or local component requirements that would change firms' location decisions are thus likely to bring high national benefits, particularly for countries with large, advanced markets. While many economic studies have investigated the conditions under which reactions by other countries will eliminate any gains, the imperfections of the multilateral international business game are likely to mean that for individual countries the national benefits are not always eliminated.[23] And on the firms' side of the game, it may well be that investment required to supply the market from within the restricted areas remains profitable, further supporting the argument that the optimum level for these controls will be high for some countries.

What types of controls have low optimum control levels? Controls that threaten assets are likely to produce much greater negative reactions than other equally effective controls aimed at operations. The removal of the right to capital that is clearly recorded in the firm's books is more menacing than an equivalent reduction of potential earning capacity.[24]

Controls that can be avoided through an international firm's foreign ramifications will also have low control levels. Attempts by the United States to prevent foreign subsidiaries of U.S. firms from trading with the communist bloc countries were not very successful. French attempts to prevent the expansion of U.S. ownership in some industries have similarly been thwarted by the ease with which the same firms can locate in other European Community countries and then export to France.

Another dimension of country control strategies is that they will vary with the type of attraction the country has for foreign direct investment. Where potential

---

[23] Harry G. Johnson, "Optimum Tariffs and Retaliation," *Review of Economic Studies* 21, no. 55 (1953–54), pp. 142–53.

[24] National Industrial Conference Board, *Obstacles and Incentives to Private Foreign Investment 1967–1968.* (New York: Conference Board, 1969), p. 9: "An act of expropriation lingers long in the minds of potential foreign investors, swaying investment decisions for many years after the event."

foreign investors are market seekers, control patterns will emphasize increasing national benefits through encouraging as much production activity as is feasible to be undertaken locally. Where the principal potential investors are resource seekers, control patterns will try to increase the amount of processing of natural resources that is performed locally. Where the attraction of the country is mainly for production-efficiency seekers, controls are likely to facilitate such operations by measures such as permitting duty-free imports of raw materials and components.

Country Strategies over Time

Optimum control levels—and hence controls—can change over time. It can be argued, for example, that the following trends could permit optimum control levels to rise:

1. When a country's level of development increases significantly, its potential gains from foreign investment are reduced because the country is likely to have better local alternatives, whereas the potential returns to foreign firms increase with the growth in the country's market.

2. When low-technology types of foreign investment mature, such as mining, countries will have developed local skills and the necessary capital to do more with their own resources.

3. When the supply of prospective foreign investors increases, as occurred with the accelerated overseas expansion of German and Japanese firms after the mid-1960s, the bargaining power of host countries is correspondingly greater.

The control policies of Brazil in the case of the telecommunications industry can illustrate how control optima can change over time. Brazil is a large market that has experienced high growth rates. With this growth the market for telecommunications equipment, sold mainly to the government-owned telecommunications companies, expanded greatly. In the late 1970s, the government announced that it would purchase its telecommunications equipment only from companies that had majority national ownership. The market had become so important that companies like Ericsson of Sweden and ITT of the U.S. with great agony divested themselves of 51 percent ownership to nationals in order to retain access to it.

With optimum control levels changing over time, in part because countries do not have adequate information about firms' other investment opportunities, countries will be reduced to experimentation and adjustment as results are fed back. Over time, countries' control strategies should come nearer to their control optima—by definition, their best strategies.

This process of adjustment over time raises the question as to whether initial strategies will undervalue the optimum control levels. One likely hypothesis is that the greater the gap between a given country and the most advanced country, the higher are its unfilled aspirations and the greater is the likelihood it will increase controls beyond the control optima. As national benefits from additional business investment are high for relatively backward countries, there will be a tendency to add controls to achieve the maximum from international firms— only to produce the opposite effect. Conversely, more highly developed countries are likely to underestimate their control optima in the absence of a major lag in their development, particularly when their own international firms dominate the market.

It seems generally clear that the stronger hand in the international business game lies with the more developed country. The weaker a country's attraction to firms, the less it will find it worthwhile to impose controls to increase national benefits. While countries' strategic positions with respect to international business will vary markedly with such factors as population, business capabilities, agreements with other countries, ownership of international business, and level of gross national product, the strategies of countries in similar positions should have major similarities. Drawing on the elements of our outline theory, the strategies of four broad classes of country can be projected in sketch form.

Less-Developed Countries.   This group covers the great number of countries for which foreign investment is deemed to be of outstanding national benefit. Not only are the national benefits and hence the opportunity cost of foreign investment high for these countries, but elasticity of investment in response to controls is likely to be high. Except for investments in extractive resources, there will be many other countries almost as attractive to international investors and ready to replace those countries in which profitability is impaired in any way.

Countries in this situation (LDCs) are likely to avoid high controls because there will always be some other country not invoking equivalent restrictions which would gain the investment. A good initial strategy for the least-developed countries would be to present an environment as attractive as possible to international business with no hints of national animosity. On the other hand, nationalistic pressures against foreign ownership will frequently build up to produce controls in excess of these very low control levels. When this happens, the inflow of investment will slacken, and if the controls are high enough, or the nationalistic pressures seem likely to produce such controls, the inflow may dry up altogether. Interests from within the country that realize that investment is being forgone are then likely to begin advocating policies that will bring the country back toward its control optima, pointing out the national benefits from doing so.

As a country develops, it can gradually raise its controls. Until the debt crisis of the 1980s, Mexico was able to increase controls and yet successfully maintain capital inflow. Rapid and sustained growth, political and monetary stability, greater infrastructure to support local production activity, and less open hostility to foreign investment, all contributed to higher control optima. Moreover, the high controls on foreign ownership, foreign personnel, and local content that Mexico imposed may have discouraged less investment than would controls over capital and profit repatriation.

Countries with Their Own Foreign Investments.   For countries with significant foreign investment, their dual capacity as investors as well as recipients of foreign investments will influence their control strategies. Such countries as the United States, United Kingdom, Germany, France, and Switzerland are likely to avoid controls on inbound investment for which the national benefits might be offset by retaliatory controls over their own foreign investments.[25] The potential cost of retaliation can be high if other countries are prepared to escalate their response. Even a small amount of investment in another country gives that country scope for escalation.

To avoid retaliation, controls in this grouping of countries are more likely to be shaped as positive encouragement of desired patterns rather than negative restrictions. Such encouragement might be lower tax rates for foreign subsidiaries that have a high degree of local ownership. There is also likely to be more informal administration of controls than formal published regulations.

Positive steps may also be taken to strengthen a country's own international business operations, through such measures as subsidized political-risk insurance and loan programs for overseas investments. If indigenous international companies are not strong enough to compete in research and scale of operations with foreign multinationals, governments increasingly give their national firms a hand, perhaps through forced merger, government aid, or protected home markets. Such ideas are not new. The United Kingdom successfully created the Imperial Tobacco Company in 1902 to oppose the American Tobacco Company and in the interwar period created ICI to meet German and U.S. competition in chemicals.

Control policies that support the foreign operations of locally based firms are not likely to continue along a straight progression. As previously discussed, the possibilities for divergence between the objectives of firms and what is seen as maximizing national benefits are many indeed. As countries perceive a growing divergence of interests, the support policies are likely to change.

Investor countries can become greatly preoccupied with the need to retain their own international position. Retention of central head office functions, maintenance of financial centers, and preserving technical leadership through high spending in research and development will be advocated. Controls will be steadily oriented toward these "leadership" ends, quietly, positively, and not competitively—yet definitely using the multinational enterprise as an intermediary in the competition to stay ahead.[26]

The strategy for this class of countries, then, might be summarized as cautious

---

[25] "Insofar as multinational companies played a part in the formulation of taxation policy, the Treasury's objective was to encourage inward investment and prevent the most blatant forms of tax evasion, without taking stern measures which might provoke retaliation against the overseas subsidiaries of British companies." Michael Hodges, *Multinational Corporations and National Government* (Lexington, Mass.: D. C. Heath, 1974), p. 97.

[26] Both the United Kingdom and the United States have carried through government-financed studies that evidence major concern for technical leadership. For example, see chapter 3 in M. D. Steuer et al., *The Impact of Foreign Direct Investment on the United Kingdom* (London: Department of Trade and Industry, 1973).

discouragement of others' international activities, coupled with positive encouragement of desirable locally owned activities.

Minority Partner Countries.   These are small countries that are partners to economic integration agreements and that may be less preferred for major investments than their larger partners. The outstanding examples are the smaller European Community partners, Belgium, Holland, and Ireland. When a large number of such countries compete among themselves, or when the advantages of their larger partners appear large to foreign investors, competition to deescalate controls is likely, even to the extent of positive encouragement. Such a strategy has emerged in Belgium, somewhat to the detriment of France. Low-cost sites, capital, and interest subsidies, and various types of taxation remission have been offered.

If the partners to such trade agreements can also agree to eliminate competition in foreign investment controls, the optimum control level for the group as a whole will increase. But with divergent country interests, such agreements are difficult to achieve, as demonstrated by the Andean Common Market experience. A similar tendency to weaken controls also occurs within countries where states, provinces, regions, or cities have significant power to offer incentives.

Strong Government Countries.   Another type of strategy is appropriate for countries such as Japan and Korea. These countries have strong central control and strong approaches to foreign investment. They have evolved policies of securing foreign technology while excluding foreign direct investment or limiting it to minority participation. Such policies may have delayed the inflow of the most advanced technology, because multinational firms are likely to protect their technological supremacy by withholding the latest advances. On the other hand, when multinational corporations accept that they cannot gain majority ownership, they have often shown that they will settle for whatever participation they can get on the principle that something is better than nothing.

A corollary to this sort of strategy is that these countries develop their own local operations able to move into international attack. Initially, this attack aims at building export markets, and outgoing investment is largely to acquire outlets and market position. As their international attack meets with success, their strategy is likely to change to something like the global planning of our representative multinational firm.

Pressure to relax the restrictions on foreign investments in the home markets of these countries is unlikely to be effective until the reverse investments and exports of this group can be used as a lever. Yielding to repeated pressure, Japan reduced controls on inward investment beginning in the late 1960s. Nevertheless, entry by foreign multinationals has been slow. The Japanese industries have built up to international strength and are not easy to beat on their home ground.

In summary, the strategy pattern of this class of countries is predicted as limitation of foreign ownership with maximum acquisition of technological know-how, followed by international expansion that shapes them as investing countries.

RISK FORECASTING PROCEDURES

Projecting into the Future

As there is no way of forecasting the future with certainty, the assessment of risk is basically a process of developing a model and arriving at subjective probabilities for the variables, or events, in the model. Expert opinions are secured on the likelihood of the specific events occurring and the degree of confidence the experts hold concerning their predictions. Alternative scenarios can also be developed and evaluated. The probability assessments associated with each element or each scenario can then be combined into a consensus of opinions or a composite view for use by the decision maker. Such a composite view is referred to as an aggregate probability estimate.[27]

In actual practice, as the 1980 Conference Board study concluded:

> Quantification remains a distant—and debatable—goal, and even the achievement of such rigor as would be entailed in the development of structured formats for qualitative assessment still represents, for most firms, an aspiration rather than a reality. . . . Some of the most effective corporate analysts operate at a relatively low level of *technical* sophistication—which is not to say that they are unsophisticated—and several of the more technically sophisticated approaches to environmental assessment that have been offered to companies or tested by them are considered to be utterly nonsensical in the real business world.[28]

How One Company Forecasts

The ASPRO/SPAIR system was developed by Shell Oil Company and has been extended to a broader range of industries.[29] ASPRO is an acronym for Assessment of Probabilities. SPAIR is an acronym for Subjective Probabilities Assigned to Investment Risks.

The approach is structured because it involves developing an explicit model of the potential impact of the political environment on a specific project. As originally developed, the model defined risk in the context of an oil exploration/production contract and then constructed a causal model composed of independent events that could produce the specified risks.

---

[27] For more detail on the formal procedures available for combining expert opinions, see Alan R. Fusfeld and Richard N. Foster, "The Delphi Technique: Survey and Comment," *Business Horizons,* June 1971, pp. 63–74; D. W. Bunn and M. M. Mustafaoglu, "Forecasting Political Risk," *Management Science,* November 1978, pp. 1557–67.

[28] Blank et al., *Assessing the Political Environment,* pp. 61–62; see also Fariborz Ghadar, Stephen J. Kobrin, and Theodore H. Moran, eds., *Managing International Political Risk: Strategies and Techniques* (Washington: Ghadar & Associates, August 1983), pp. 167–70.

[29] C. A. Gebelien, C. E. Pearson, and M. Silbergh, "Assessing Political Risk of Oil Investment Ventures," *Journal of Petroleum Technology,* May 1978, pp. 725–30.

Risk is defined as the probability of not maintaining a concession contract that is considered to be equitable by both company and host country over a 10-year period. Risks are assumed to fall into two categories: those that result in a unilateral change in the initial contract so that the return is inadequate, and those that restrict the free flow of funds or oil entitlements out of the host country.

These two general contingencies are then decomposed into nine events that would increase the probability of risk to the project if they occurred. These events include civil disorders, sudden expropriation, taxation restrictions, restrictions on remittances, and oil export restrictions. In turn, a complete set of factors are specified for each political event that could increase the probability of the event occurring. For example, factors considered in evaluating the probability of sudden expropriation include ideological shift, strength of the economy, and the economic role of foreigners.

Expert panelists are recruited from a variety of backgrounds to review each factor for each event. Through interviews, the experts present their judgments as to the likelihood that the event will occur and indicate their degree of confidence in the judgment. A computer program then combines systematically the probability assessments for each factor into an aggregate probability estimate. The program uses the judgment and degree of confidence to generate a density function for the probability of the event occurring given the factor in question. Using Bayes' Theorem, the density functions are combined across factors to generate a panel assessment of the probability of the event occurring.

The ASPRO/SPAIR technique presents a number of problems. It involves a major and costly effort that restricts frequency of application. Its greatest value is for the specific project being assessed and much of its value is lost if more general assessments for a number of industries or projects are attempted. In addition, there is concern about the applicability of Bayes' theorem to combine the probabilities, including the actual degree of independence of the factors.

Minimizing Political and Control Risk

It is obvious that risk forecasting can be crucial to the international enterprise in reaching a "go" or "no go" decision on a particular project. It may be less obvious that risk identification and evaluation can guide the firm in reshaping a project so that a "no go" can become a modified "go." The international enterprise is not helpless in the face of political and control risk. To the contrary, it has a significant range of options for minimizing the magnitude and effects of such risks.[30] Some of the possibilities were discussed in Chapter 15.

---

[30] See Jean Boddewyn and Etienne F. Cracco, "The Political Game in World Business," *Columbia Journal of World Business*, January–February 1972, pp. 45–56; W. R. Hoskins, "How to Counter Expropriation," *Harvard Business Review*, September–October 1970; Ghadar et al., *Managing International Political Risk*, pp. 140–66.

SUMMARY

International firms must face the risk that political forces in both host and home countries will cause significant changes in the business environment. These forces affect the operations of multinational enterprises through abrupt changes, generally referred to as political risk, and through gradual changes in national-control policies intended to maximize a country's benefits from the participation of international firms in its local economy.

International firms have always been concerned about the impact of politics on their operations. Until recently, however, few companies had established formal systems to assess political factors in their multicountry business environments. The lack of a process for systematically evaluating political risks and evolving national controls increases the probability that the multinational enterprise will invest in countries when it should not, or refrain from investing when it should.

Considerable recent progress has been made in developing methodologies for political risk forecasting. Nevertheless, the state of the art for political risk forecasting is still underdeveloped compared with most other business forecasting functions. The major advance has been to make more objective the political risk elements included in decision making and to increase awareness of available means suitable for minimizing political risk.

The risks that result from changes in national-control strategies should be easier to forecast than political risk discontinuities. Given the concept of the international business game and an embryo terminology for analysis, the international manager should be able to anticipate, with a reasonable degree of accuracy, the pattern of controls that specific countries are likely to adopt to increase their national benefits. With such forecasts, the manager can develop cost and benefit calculations as a basis for business decisions. Such calculations will be limited by the assumptions made about the various interacting strategies, but control risk will be quantifiable. For any investment the cash flow can be reduced by the cost of controls multiplied by the expectation (probability) that they will occur.

EXERCISES AND DISCUSSION QUESTIONS

1. How would you define political risk? Would you consider a political risk the "inability to convert into dollars foreign currency representing earnings on, or return of, the investment or compensation for sale or disposition of the investment," one of the items included as political risk in the U.S. risk-guaranty program?

2. "Political stability is equated with democracy, with elections, with modernization, with a broad income distribution, with consensus, with participation, and so forth. This conception is derived from an ideologized model of what the American type of democracy is supposed to be like, projected on to other societies." Evaluate and discuss.

3. How would you rank types of business activities as to their political risk vulnerability? What is the basis for your ranking?

4. What is the relationship between political instability and political risk for international business? What criteria would you use to identify political instability?

5. How can a business project be modified to reduce political risk?
6. Numerous writers have observed an "inevitable tension" between multinational companies and nation-states and proposed ways for governments to control the operations of these firms. Is the conflict really between firms and countries, or simply between countries just as it has always been? What are the implications of this distinction for the sort of controls that might be recommended?
7. Select one country and, as a consultant to its current government, prepare an overall strategy for control of international business activities that fall within its jurisdiction.
8. What types of controls will be most likely to affect the performance of international firms as against simply being passed on by the firm to its customers? Does it make any difference?
9. Criticize the assumptions of the model that has been proposed in this chapter for forecasting controls.
10. As president of a U.S. company with a manufacturing subsidiary in South Africa, how would you respond to a home country campaign by students demanding that their universities divest their endowment funds of investments in companies with direct investments in South Africa?

PART FIVE

Multinational Operations
Management

Whatever a multinational firm's global strategy, it still requires sound operating management to achieve its objectives. This section of the book deals with basic issues that arise in the operations management of a multinational, paying particular attention to those aspects that are uniquely international.

Multinational management is, first and foremost, multicultural management. The first chapter in the section is accordingly devoted to the assessment of cultural differences and culture changes that will have an impact on the way in which a multinational is managed. Chapter 18 moves on to marketing management in a multinational setting, examining the ways in which marketing practices are standardized or differentiated across country boundaries. Because it is a major marketing activity, export management is given separate attention in Chapter 19. Chapter 20 deals with the considerations that arise in transferring technological expertise from country to country.

The next three chapters are devoted to the accounting and financial reporting and control of multinationals. Financial reporting, as examined in Chapter 21, has become a complex field, given the multiple purposes for which accounts are required, differences in national accounting practices, and fluctuating exchange rates. The design of internal information and control systems in multinationals is the subject of Chapter 22. Control measurements can have a major effect on the decisions taken by managers throughout a multinational. Badly designed control measures, for example, can lead managers of individual units within a multinational to take actions clearly opposed to those that would be best for the multinational as a whole.

With the added risk and opportunities introduced when operating within multiple currencies and capital markets, multinational financial management also requires a great deal of special attention within the multinational firm. Chapter 23 surveys the management of the finance function within the multinational.

The final chapter (Chapter 24) is concerned with multinational human resource management. Policies on nationality of executives, cross-national transfers, and differences in national compensation are among the thorniest of issues in many multinationals.

Cross-Cultural Management

Crossing national boundaries involves a step into different cultural environments. The enterprise that does business in one language and one culture will encounter many new problems when dealing with 2, 3, 4—or perhaps 50 languages and cultures. Groups of people, or societies, differ in their values and beliefs, in their aspirations and motivations, and in the ways they satisfy their desires. Such cultural differences pervasively influence all dimensions of international business activity.

THE MEANING OF CULTURE

By culture we mean the whole set of social norms and responses that condition a population's behavior. It is these that make one social environment different from another and give each a shape of its own. The basic discipline that is most relevant here is cultural anthropology.[1]

Culture is acquired and inculcated. It is the set of rules and behavior patterns that an individual learns but does not inherit at birth. For every society these norms and behavioral responses develop into a different cultural pattern that gets passed down through the generations with continual embellishment and adaptation, but with its own focus on aspects that are most highly developed.

For much cultural conditioning, the individual is unaware of the learning. The subtle process of inculcating culture through example and reward or punishment is generally much more powerful than direct instruction, and the individual unwittingly adopts the cultural norm. This process of learning a cultural pattern, called *enculturation,* conditions individuals so that a large proportion of their behavior fits the requirements of their culture yet is determined below the level of conscious thought.[2] To individuals, cultural conditioning is like an iceberg—they are unaware of nine tenths of it.

The concept of culture is so broad that some classification scheme is needed as a basic framework for grasping the cultural pattern. One such approach is Murdock's elaborate list of more than 70 cultural universals that occur in all cultures. Arranged in alphabetical order to emphasize their variety, these are listed in Figure 17–1. While this one-dimensional checklist has major limitations, it can nevertheless be of considerable value. The international firm selling razors and razor blades, for example, must be aware that it is dealing with the puberty customs of different cultures. Moreover, as most razors are given as gifts the seller is also dealing with gift giving, courtship, and family patterns. An examination of cultural patterns under each of these headings will certainly suggest differences in marketing strategy from country to country.

A sensitivity to differences in the elements of culture brings with it an ability to analyze any happening from its cultural perspective. What on the surface appears as a similar happening in different cultures may be composed of many different cultural elements. The apparently simple phenomenon of a family meal,

---

[1] See A. L. Kroeber and Clyde Kluckhohn, "Culture: A Critical Review of Concepts and Definitions," (Papers of the Peabody Museum of American Archaeology and Ethnology, Harvard University, Cambridge, Mass., 47. no. 1, 1952), pp. 1–223.

[2] Melville J. Herskovits, *Cultural Anthropology* (New York: Alfred A. Knopf, 1963), p. 326.

FIGURE 17–1   Cultural Universals

Age grading	Food taboos	Music
Athletic sports	Funeral rites	Mythology
Bodily adornment	Games	Numerals
Calendar	Gestures	Obstetrics
Cleanliness training	Gift giving	Penal sanctions
Community organization	Government	Personal names
Cooking	Greetings	Population policy
Cooperative labor	Hairstyles	Postnatal care
Cosmology	Hospitality	Pregnancy usages
Courtship	Housing hygiene	Property rights
Dancing	Incest taboos	Propitiation of
Decorative art	Inheritance rules	supernatural beings
Divination	Joking	Puberty customs
Division of labor	Kingroups	Religious rituals
Dream interpretation	Kinship nomenclature	Residence rules
Education	Language	Sexual restrictions
Eschatology (after life)	Law	Soul concepts
Ethics	Luck superstitions	Status differentiation
Ethnobotany	Magic	Surgery
Etiquette	Marriage	Tool making
Faith healing	Mealtimes	Trade
Family	Medicine	Visiting
Feasting	Modesty concerning	Weaning
Fire making	natural functions	Weather control
Folklore	Mourning	

SOURCE: George P. Murdock, "The Common Denominator of Cultures," in *The Science of Man in the World Crises*, ed. Ralph Linton (New York: Columbia University Press, 1945), pp. 123–42.

for instance, could be viewed as an extensive set of different rules concerning the time the meal is eaten, the seating arrangements, the roles played by each in initiating or ending conversation and in interrupting or changing the subject, the comments regarded as humorous, the facial expressions used, the values placed on different foods, the attitudes toward age, and so on. Moreover, the shape and size of the table will differ, as will the utensils, the way they are used, and how the people eat.

A language is inextricably linked with all aspects of a culture, and each culture reflects in its language what is of value to the people. Culture is largely inculcated through language—spoken or written. Language, then, becomes the embodiment of culture. It may even condition what we look for and therefore see. One anthropologist comparing the structure of languages pointed out that Eskimo languages have several different words for types of snow, while the English language has one, and Aztec uses the same basic word stem for snow, ice, and cold.[3]

---

[3] Paul Henle, *Language, Thought, and Culture* (Ann Arbor: University of Michigan Press, 1958).

CROSS-CULTURAL COMMUNICATION

Attempts to communicate meaning through the transmission of a message to someone from a different cultural background run into the danger that the cultural differences will lead to misunderstanding of the message. Communication is effective when the receiver ends up with the same meaning the sender intended to transmit. At each stage in the communication process, however, something may occur to confuse the meaning. The meaning may be encoded incorrectly into the elements that are used to transmit the message. But even if the message is encoded accurately, it may be transmitted inaccurately, received inaccurately, or decoded incorrectly. Across cultures, it is not untypical for a message to be encoded in the language and nonverbal elements of the sender's culture and decoded with the meaning that these give in the language of the receiver.

Communication does not always take the form of language. All behavior communicates and each culture may differ in the way it experiences and uses time, space, relationships, and a variety of other aspects of culture (see Box 17–1).[4] The use of time may convey quite different meanings in different cultures. To be 30 minutes late for an appointment with a business associate may be the height of rudeness in Culture A but in Culture B it may be early and unexpectedly reliable. Different messages may be conveyed by the amount of notice given for a meeting, the time of departure, invitations to future commitments, or the way in which a party agrees to the order of discussion at the meeting.

In a similar way, the use of space conveys different meanings. The distance one person stands away from another indicates the degree of relationship or interest and can dramatically influence what is said. Different cultures have different norms for the appropriate distance for a given type of interaction. Middle Easterners and Latin Americans, for example, stand much closer than Western Europeans. The size of an office in relation to other offices conveys a great deal about the status of a U.S. executive. In the Arab world, the size and location of an office are poor indicators of the importance of the person who occupies it.

An exhaustive listing of all the nonverbal methods of communication that might differ between cultures would be very long indeed. It would include gestures and facial expressions, stance and posture, use of touch, eye contact and direction of gaze, use of color and adornment, use of silence, and pauses in verbal behavior.[5] And they are important in every attempt at communication. It has been estimated, for example, that as much as 70 per cent of the message communicated during a conversation is nonverbal.[6]

---

[4] Edward T. Hall, *The Silent Language* (New York: Doubleday, 1959); *The Hidden Dimension* (New York: Doubleday, 1966); *Beyond Culture* (New York: Anchor Press/Doubleday, 1976).

[5] Philip R. Harris and Robert T. Moran, *Managing Cultural Differences,* 2d ed. (Houston: Gulf Publishing Co., 1987), pp. 25–53.

[6] R. L. Birdwhistell, *Kinetics and Context* (Philadelphia: University of Pennsylvania Press, 1970).

BOX 17–1
Breaking through the Cultural Barrier

Companies report much difficulty in training so-called primitive peoples, such as Eskimos and Australian aborigines, to accept basic working techniques or to stick to regular work routines. Professor Allen Ivey of the University of Massachusetts claims, however, that the problem is not idleness or stupidity as managers tend to assume but rather an entirely different cultural approach to problem solving.

"I found that managers in Australia kept complaining," said Ivey, "that their aboriginal workers were too slow in getting things done. What they didn't understand is that the aborigines are actually much more complex thinkers than we normally assume. Before they do anything, they like to think about all the implications of it. This may take a long time. What they interpret as stupidity or obstructiveness is most likely simply that the employee is still thinking about it."

One of the fundamental differences in communicating behavior turned out to be the way aborigines pay attention. Said Ivey: "I asked them, 'Show me how you attend.' They sat side-by-side instead of face-to-face and looked down. They then looked up and gazed slowly down the body of the person beside them. This would make a Westerner feel very uncomfortable."

The discomfort and embarrassment of the trainer was obvious to the aborigines, who became embarrassed themselves. The more embarrassed they became, the more difficult it was to teach them anything.

SOURCE: Extracted from a report by David Clutterbuck, senior editor, *International Management,* December, 1980, p. 41.

ADJUSTING TO CULTURAL DIFFERENCES

The international firm has a special need for cultural sensitivity and adjustment. It has an existence outside each local culture in which it operates and many of its actions, such as cross-national transfers of old products or standard company practices may represent a local innovation. And in many cases, the international firm may encounter unexpected problems because it is an unwitting agent for transplanting aspects of one culture into another.

The experienced international enterprise will try to accept the values of local culture patterns and, when culture change is necessary, seek to work within the accepted behavior patterns and customary goals that underlie these beliefs. As a general rule, national sensitivities tolerate less deviation from local standards by foreign firms than by native companies.

Lee suggests that three general classes of business adaptation are important—product, individual, and institutional—and that the degree of necessary adjustment ranges from none, or token, to comprehensive.[7] Adaptation is defined as the

---

[7] James A. Lee, "Cultural Analysis in Overseas Operations," *Harvard Business Review,* March–April 1966, pp. 106–14.

achievement of business goals with a minimum of problems and setbacks as a result of the various manifestations of cultural conflict.

Adaptation in product policies, which includes marketing strategies, can be illustrated by the experience of the Singer Sewing Machine Company in meeting different requirements of cultural patterns. In Moslem countries, the women's position had been a secluded and protected one, particularly with strangers. The practice of purdah, or wearing a veil so as to be screened from the sight of strangers, reflected this cultural pattern. Successful selling of sewing machines had been through sewing classes which Moslem women would not ordinarily be permitted to attend. In fact, at least one sewing machine salesman was sent to jail in Sudan for trying to encourage the wives to attend sewing classes. Singer overcame this problem by first selling the husbands, through demonstration classes, on how much additional work the women could do with sewing machines after taking sewing lessons. The men became convinced of the advantages and then ordered the wives to attend.

Individual adjustment is required of managers, and in the case of overseas personnel, of their spouses, and of their families. An expatriate manager who wishes to motivate natives in a host nation, not merely order them around, must first make some personal changes. The manager should learn the local language, make adjustments in the manner of dealing with people, and adapt to local behavior norms such as time patterns.

Institutional adaptation relates to changes in organizational structure and organizational policies to fit cultural differences. Hiring practices developed by a U.S. parent company, for example, may purposely overlook class distinctions and assume that people from different areas and factions will work well together. When operating in other countries, though, the same company might encounter serious difficulties in hiring members of different tribes or different religions to work side by side.

Adjustment of the multinational enterprise is needed at two levels—the national and the multinational. The issues at the national level might be characterized as bicultural. The situation is largely of a "we and they" type. The manager of a subsidiary must be aware of possible conflicts between local conditions and the cultural assumptions underlying the business practices being imported. Essentially these problems are two-sided, and management personnel of subsidiaries must be the bridge between the local situation and the international enterprise.

At the multinational level, or more specifically at global or regional headquarters, the international enterprise must coordinate and integrate business activities that are operating in many different cultural environments. Managers must deal with many languages and across many cultures. The problems are both horizontal—across many cultures—and vertical—between each subsidiary and headquarters. And the organizational structure and policies of the global enterprise must facilitate communications and the implementation of policies across many cultures in order to achieve global goals.

METHODOLOGY FOR CULTURAL ASSESSMENT

The impact of cultural differences on international business makes quite clear the need for the international manager to develop skills in assessing the key cultural elements that will have a direct bearing on his or her effectiveness. There is no one method to adopt in making cultural assessment a basis for specific business decisions. Business problems cover such a wide range that the methods used may extend from a narrow depth study of receptivity to a new management practice, through to broad assessment of a society's attitudes to spending.

Approaches for Assessing Cultural Differences and Similarities

Cross-cultural analysis for international business tends to emphasize differences because they are likely to create business problems. But to err by perceiving more differences than actually exist can also cause serious difficulties. Take the matter of managerial preferences for risk-taking. The American executive may see the Japanese as different, whereas some cross-cultural studies suggest that they are alike.[8] An American might needlessly overexplain a particular position, trying to convince the Japanese to be more adventuresome.[9] How the manager approaches a comparison conditions what the manager sees. If the mental set is to search for differences only, or for similarities only, these are all that will be found.[10]

Another general caveat is that observed cultural patterns may be representative of a national group yet not applicable to everyone in the group. What is usually being discussed is a modal pattern, and considerable variation from the mode will exist within a group or a subset of the group. In fact, for some cultural characteristics there may be a wider range within a given society than between societies. The manager should be careful always to define the limits of the group that is of interest and still be prepared to allow for individual differences.

The most common approach to cultural assessment is a partial approach confined to studying particular aspects of a culture that are believed to be of significance for a decision to be taken. Partial approaches are less powerful than comprehensive approaches that endeavor to identify and classify an entire range of cultural differences. The immense number of elements that can vary between

---

[8] Bernard M. Bass, *The American Adviser Abroad*, Technical Report 27, Management Research Center of the College of Business Administration (Rochester, N.Y.: University of Rochester, August 1969), p. 12.

[9] For a summary of the literature on Japanese cultural differences see Lane Kelly and Reginald Worthley, "The Role of Culture in Comparative Management," *Academy of Management Journal* 24 (1981), pp. 164–73.

[10] Nancy J. Adler, "A Typology of Management Studies Involving Culture," *Journal of International Business Studies 14*, Fall 1983, pp. 29–47.

cultures, however, makes overall approaches extremely unwieldy and costly to use. A compromise, often used by social anthropologists, is to compose a word picture of some constrained slice of behavior in the culture being examined, emphasizing, as would an artist, the more significant elements in the subject. Examples of such word pictures would be a description of a day in the life of a typical consumer,[11] or the motivation and thinking leading an employee to instigate a major confrontation with another worker.

Comprehensive approaches do have their value, however. Hofstede, for example, has carried out extensive research to identify attitudes that tend to be fairly consistent among the individuals from each country yet differ from attitudes of those from other countries.[12] He then uses these fundamental differences to explain variations in business practices among countries. Others, such as Hall[13] and Farmer and Richman,[14] present overall frameworks that incorporate many more aspects of culture and enable many dimensions of a business situation to be analyzed in a systematic way. The comprehensive approaches are examined more fully later in the chapter.

Numerous academics have also attempted to cluster countries according to cultural similarities. Ronen reviews nine such attempts and synthesizes country clusters that are titled as Anglo, Germanic, Nordic, Latin European, Latin American, Near East, Far East, Arabic, and Independent.[15] Turning such research to managerial use might lead a multinational to consider transfers of managers within clusters of countries as requiring only minimal cultural adjustment on the managers' part, while cross-cluster transfers should be made only after careful assessment and preparation of the individuals concerned. Again, however, the generalizations involved in clustering countries will tend to minimize the differences between countries placed in the same cluster and overemphasize differences between countries in different clusters.

Approaches for Assessing Culture Change

A cultural assessment may be either static or dynamic. A static assessment serves only to identify the differences in variables between cultures. A dynamic assessment seeks to indicate which variables will change and perhaps in what order and with what speed. For the international manager, the identification of

---

[11] Oscar Lewis, *Five Families: Mexican Case Studies in the Culture of Poverty* (New York: Basic Books, 1959).

[12] Geert Hofstede, *Culture's Consequences: International Differences in Work-Related Values* (Beverly Hills: Sage Publications, 1980).

[13] Edward T. Hall, *The Silent Language* (Garden City, N.Y.: Doubleday, 1959).

[14] Richard N. Farmer and Barry M. Richman, *Comparative Management and Economic Progress* (Homewood, Ill.: Richard D. Irwin, 1965).

[15] Simcha Ronen, *Comparative and Multinational Management* (New York: John Wiley & Sons, 1986), chap. 7.

what changes will be readily accepted and what will be rejected can mean the difference between success and failure.

Two approaches may be helpful in mapping culture change as a basis for business decisions. The first is a mapping of the way any change is expected to diffuse through the culture. The second is a mapping of the decision-making and influence process for the key individuals to be affected by the change at each stage. Such mappings make explicit the assumptions that are held about the change process. They also provide a necessary framework against which to specify actual research questions. Without some mapping of these two processes, any quantification on which to base a decision to introduce the change could hardly be soundly based.

Research into the pattern and speed of adoption, diffusion, or negative diffusion (i.e., elimination) of products or practices within cultures has received a great deal of attention in recent years.[16] An increasing tendency is to examine the process of change quantitatively over time.[17] The accumulated curve for numbers adopting a particular change has been widely shown to be S shaped. This basic shape holds for social changes in, for example, education, divorce, and career patterns, as well as for technological advances and changes in business practices. Moreover, a general logistic equation fits these diffusion curves almost as well whether the adopting units of the social system are individuals, families, firms, or governments.

The generality of these accumulated findings on diffusion suggests that quantitative analysis of change will be a valuable line of approach for the international manager. To date, most attention has been confined to demand forecasting of the direct adoption of products, but forecasting of social changes that influence the demand for a product should prove equally useful. Attempts to project ahead the rate of adoption of a new product, based on the rate of adoption at very early stages, have so far proved of only limited value, but precision increases as the degree of penetration expands.[18]

Approaches for Avoiding Cultural Bias

In all cases requiring cross-cultural assessment the problem of cultural bias will be present. Everyone tends unwittingly to bias their view of other cultures by unconscious acceptance of their own cultural conditioning. It takes a great deal of discipline to force the mind to see things that one's own culture ignores or places in low value.

---

[16] See Everett M. Rogers, *Diffusion of Innovations,* 3rd ed. (New York: Free Press/Macmillan, 1983).

[17] Robert Y. Hamblin, R. Brooke Jacobsen, and Jerry L. L. Miller, *A Mathematical Theory of Social Change* (New York: John Wiley & Sons, 1973).

[18] Frank M. Bass and Charles W. King, "The Theory of First Purchase of New Products," in *A New Measure of Responsibility for Marketing,* ed. Keith Cox and Ben M. Enis (Chicago: American Marketing Association, 1968).

Cultural bias can be reduced by using researchers from the culture to be studied and through the development of culturally sensitive management. Specific attempts to eliminate what Lee has called the "self-reference criterion" (SRC), however, can be built into the research approach.[19] The problems are first defined in terms of the cultural traits, habits, or norms of the home society, and then redefined, without value judgments, in terms of the foreign cultural traits, habits, and norms. The difference between these two specifications indicates the likely cultural bias, or SRC effect, which can then be isolated and carefully examined to see how it influences the concept of the problem. Following this examination, the problem is redefined with the bias removed. Such an approach can be used for a wide variety of business problems. Its value lies in forcing researchers or managers posing the problem to make very specific the assumptions held about the cultural elements affecting the problem and to question whether they hold for another culture.

In cross-cultural research there is a particular need to avoid misreading results because of a cultural bias in the phenomena focused on, in the ideas measured, or in the measurement instruments.[20]

Functional Equivalence.   The phenomena on which the research focuses may not fulfill the same function in each society. Bicycles, for example, provide basic transportation in some countries but are essentially for recreation and for children's use in others.

Conceptual Equivalence.   The concepts employed in describing or measuring behavior may not apply to all societies.[21] Some of the more esoteric constructs of consumer and organizational behavior, for example, are definitely culture-bound.

Instrument Equivalence.   The research instrument used to measure the phenomena in different societies may not provide an equally valid indication for each. Questionnaires aimed at identifying attitudes toward motherhood, for example, might have to ask quite different questions even if basic attitudes are the same because the cultures express these attitudes differently. Instruments may be classed as either "emic" or "etic."[22] Emic instruments are tests constructed to study a phenomenon within one culture only. Etic instruments are "culture-

---

[19] Lee, "Cultural Analysis in Overseas Operations."

[20] Nancy J. Adler, "Understanding the Ways of Understanding: Cross-Cultural Management Methodology Reviewed," in *Advances in International Comparative Management*, ed. Richard N. Farmer (Greenwich, Conn.: JAI Press Inc., 1984), vol. 1, pp. 31–67.

[21] R. Sears, "Transcultural Variables and Conceptual Equivalence," in *Studying Personality Cross-Culturally*, ed. Bert Kaplan (Evanston, Ill.: Row Peterson, 1961), pp. 445–55.

[22] R. Brislin, W. Lonner, and R. Thorndike, *Cross-Cultural Research Methods* (New York: John Wiley & Sons, 1973).

independent'' and the identical instrument, properly translated, can be employed in any number of societies. There are few etic tests in existence, however, and most research instruments require alteration to some extent for each society.[23]

PARTIAL CULTURAL ASSESSMENT: SOME KEY ASPECTS

This section briefly introduces some key cultural aspects that are fundamental to the way in which business is managed and yet vary greatly among cultures.

Attitudes toward Work and Achievement

The dominant view in a society toward wealth and material gain can have significant bearing on the types, qualities, and numbers of individuals who pursue entrepreneurial and management careers as well as on the way workers respond to material incentives. In most countries, wealth tends to be considered desirable and the prospect of material gain operates as a significant motivation. But there are societies where a worker will be on the job until he earns a certain amount of money and then be absent until these earnings are exhausted.

Variations among cultures in the dominant views toward achievement and work, which can be a vital determinant of management performance and productive efficiency, have been the subject of considerable research under the rubric of "achievement motivation."[24] The achievement motivation of an individual refers to a basic attitude toward life, namely, the willingness to commit oneself to the accomplishment of tasks considered by the person to be worthwhile and difficult. An achievement-motivated person makes accomplishment an end in itself. Tangible rewards are not rejected, but they are not essential.

Attitudes toward the Future

Some of the principal differences among cultures lie in assumptions and attitudes relating to man's ability to influence the future. For example, an assumption that people can substantially influence the future underlies much of U.S. management philosophy. Long-range planning becomes a worthwhile investment because of confidence that planning can influence what is to happen. In cultures where other attitudes prevail, management practices based on such assumptions are not likely to be effective. On the other hand, care must be taken not to overgeneralize. Despite a general view that Moslem cultures are fatalistic, Muna

---

[23] See, for example, Y. Tanaka, T. Oyama, and C. Osgood, "A Cross-Cultural and Cross Concept Study of the Generality of Semantic Space," *Journal of Verbal Learning and Verbal Behavior* 2 (December 1963), pp. 392–405.

[24] David C. McClelland, *The Achieving Society* (Princeton, N.J.: D. Van Nostrand, 1961). See also George W. England and Itzhak Harpaz, "Some Methodological and Analytic Considerations in Cross-National Comparative Research," *Journal of International Business Studies* 14 (Fall 1983), 14:2, pp. 49–59.

found Arab executives most amenable to planning, quoting a saying in the Moslem *Hadith* that admonishes man first to think and plan ahead then put his trust in God.[25] Some Moslem peasant groups may indeed be fatalistic, but this is probably not an irrational attitude on their part. For peasants operating at base subsistence level it may be a just estimation of the enormous, and discouraging, weight of the chancy factors that condition the success of their efforts.[26]

Whatever the explanation for varying attitudes, the critical issue for business operations is whether individuals believe that events will occur regardless of what they do and whether they can help shape future outcomes significantly. The self-determination or "master of destiny" attitude is generally qualified by the accompanying view that future aspirations must be realistic and that hard work is necessary to achieve future goals.

Patterns of Decision Making

Reliance on objective analysis in decision making varies greatly among cultures. In U.S. business, decisions are supposed to be based on objective analyses of facts, and all persons who can contribute relevant information are expected to do so. Such a norm leads to large collections of data and the development of impersonal decision-making techniques.

In other societies, the personal judgment of a senior executive may be the accepted basis for a decision. A request that the executive explain or give the rationale for his decision would be interpreted as a lack of confidence in the executive's judgment. Furthermore, it may be considered inappropriate for a senior executive to seek facts and consult others—especially juniors—on matters on which the senior is already presumed to be wise. In such cultures, hierarchical, emotional, and mystical considerations, rather than objective analyses, may dominate.

Attitudes toward Authority

The dominant view of authority in a society may range from an autocratic system at one extreme to a democratic-participative system at the other extreme. In autocratic systems, managerial decisions would typically be highly centralized with little delegation of authority. At the other extreme, managerial authority would be shared with subordinates and workers, and considerable decentralization in decision making would be typical of business enterprises.

It is not possible to say which forms of managerial authority along the continuum are best in terms of efficiency or in achieving other business goals. The forms vary greatly from Japan to West Germany and from the United States

---

[25] Farid A. Muna, *The Arab Executive* (London: Macmillan Press Ltd., 1980), p. 95.

[26] Maxime Rodinson, *Islam and Capitalism,* Eng. ed. (Harmondsworth, Middlesex: Penguin Books, 1974), p. 113.

to Yugoslavia. Yet each of these countries has had impressive records of business performance and economic growth. Whatever authority system prevails in a given country, the international enterprise will have to relate its managerial patterns to the expectations and traditions of local employees.

Authority systems are also highly relevant to marketing. It is important to know whether purchasing decisions within buying units are typically decentralized or reserved for the top-echelon executives. In negotiating with governments, the international manager will have to know whether decision authority resides with low-level bureaucrats or must be handled at the highest levels of government bureaucracy.

Expression of Disagreement

Differences among societies in frankness of expression and tolerance for personal differences affect interpersonal relations. In Far Eastern cultures it is traditional to value politeness over blunt truth. The Japanese business executive finds it inappropriate to say no in many situations. In dealing with an American, the Japanese may make all kinds of barely favorable noises and then maybe say, "I'll think about the matter." The Japanese has actually told the American no, but it is entirely possible that the American thinks that the answer was yes and later imagines that the Japanese was being deceptive.

In many countries, if a person expresses criticisms of a policy in order to improve the quality of decision making, such statements are likely to be interpreted as personal attacks. If a subordinate disagrees with the boss, the boss will most certainly feel insulted. Persons in subordinate positions are expected either to present information or judgments that support the ideas of senior officials or be silent.

Responsibility to Family

In some countries, businessmen operate as individuals independent of family.[27] In others, some version of the extended family prevails. Under this pattern large numbers of near as well as quite distant relatives are encompassed in a system of shared rights and obligations. All members of this group are interdependent, and it is the responsibility of the leaders to see that the resources are available to satisfy the needs of each member of the group. Writing about the Arab executive, Muna claims:

> The use of personal (family and friendship) ties and connections is not only widespread, but is also an important and necessary means of doing business. This approach is in direct contrast with the reliance upon official, institutional, or formal business channels for conducting business affairs. In the Arab world the use of such personal

---

[27] Peter Marris and Anthony Somerset, *African Businessmen* (London: Routledge and Kegan Paul, 1971), chap. 6.

ties and connections is evident in a wide range of activities. Typical examples that were provided by the executives include: *(a)* expediting and getting a work-permit, a passport or a visa, and generally bypassing or expediting most governmental formalities and paperwork; *(b)* obtaining referrals or employment; and *(c)* knowing about, negotiating, and eventually securing a multi-million dollar business contract.[28]

Strong and extended family ties can result in what has been characterized as patrimonial management.[29] Ownership and key positions in a business enterprise are held by family members. Nepotism is generally dominant in the full range of employment decisions, and business goals are oriented toward family interests and aspirations. Such patrimonial management has the advantages of encouraging teamwork, loyalty, and mutual interest. Family codes can enforce morality in financial and other matters, and family loyalty attracts and holds managers in situations where the supply of qualified managers is limited.

The extended family situation also has drawbacks. It emphasizes nepotism rather than competence. It can vitiate the will to work by limiting personal incentives. Family business may be run like an authoritarian household with little concern for considerations other than family goals. And family enterprises may suffer from a lack of invigorating ideas and innovations that can come from outsiders. Even where the family is not dominant within an organization, top executives in countries in which the extended family is important may expect and be expected to behave as the head of a family.

Family patterns can be extremely important from the standpoint of marketing as well as general management. In advanced societies, the husband and wife typically share decision making on family purchases, with children and other members of the family having a secondary vote. In the extended family, the family patriarch holds the key decision-making position, although this is declining with the monetization of the economy, the demise of family enterprises, and an increase in geographic and social mobility.

Social Structure

A final category of cultural elements can be grouped under the general heading of social structure. It includes such variables as interclass mobility, determinants of status, and patterns of education.

Few societies in the world assume that all individuals are equal. Instead, societies have traditional systems of ranking individuals and groups. Relative positions in the social hierarchy are based on ethnic, cultural, educational, and linguistic differences, as well as on economic position. Sometimes traditional social structures are fairly rigid, such as the caste system of India. Sometimes the distinctions are more fluid, and considerable interclass mobility is the rule.

---

[28] Muna, *The Arab Executive*, pp. 74–75.

[29] Frederick Harbison and Charles A. Myers, *Management in the Industrial World* (New York: McGraw-Hill, 1959), pp. 69–73.

In most countries of the world there is a distinction between the elite, who have political and economic control of the country, and the relatively underprivileged peasant groups.[30]

Two aspects of social structure are of special concern to the international enterprise—interclass mobility and the status assigned by a society to individuals who engage in business occupations. If a rigid social structure prevents a substantial number of individuals from moving into the ranks of management or other responsible business positions, managerial effectiveness is likely to be constrained. If the status assigned to business pursuits is low in the social structure, it will be difficult to attract adequate numbers of competent persons to business positions.

COMPREHENSIVE CULTURAL ASSESSMENT FOR MANAGEMENT

The international manager may have neither the time nor the need to build a comprehensive picture of a particular culture. Yet familiarity with ways to conceptualize the overall culture can provide the manager a checklist of elements that are important for particular business problems but likely to be overlooked. Two such approaches are briefly outlined here.

Four Fundamental-Difference Dimensions

Hofstede's approach is based on the identification of fundamental differences in the way people in different countries perceive and interpret their world.[31] From 150 questions in each of 116,000 questionnaires, 32 were identified that showed differences among countries. Grouping these answers, Hofstede derived four basic dimensions that explained half of the variance in countries' mean scores and correlated significantly with the findings of some 40 existing comparative studies examined. Hofstede's four dimensions are:

Individualism.   The extent to which the individual expects personal freedom versus the acceptance of responsibility to family, tribal, or national groups (i.e., collectivism).

Power Distance.   The degree of tolerance of inequality in wealth and power indicated by the extent to which centralization and autocratic power are permitted.

---

[30] Conrad M. Arensberg and Arthur M. Niehoff, *Introducing Social Change: A Manual for Americans Overseas* (Chicago: Aldine Publishing, 1964), p. 41.

[31] Geert Hofstede, "National Cultures in Four Dimensions: A Research-Based Theory of Cultural Differences Among Nations," *International Studies of Management and Organisation,* 13 (Spring–Summer 1983), pp. 46–74; Geert Hofstede, "The Cultural Relativity of Organizational Practices and Theories," *Journal of International Business Studies* 14 (Fall 1983), pp. 75–89.

Uncertainty Avoidance.   The extent to which the society avoids risk and creates security by emphasizing technology and buildings, laws and rules, and religion.

Masculinity.   The extent to which the society differentiates roles between the sexes and places emphasis on masculine values of performance and visible achievement.

Indices for each of these dimensions are reproduced in Figure 17–2 for 50 countries and three regions.

Each of these dimensions is reflected in national managerial approaches. The higher a country's index of individualism, the more its managerial concepts of leadership will be about leading individuals who are presumed to act for their ultimate self-interest. Interestingly, Great Britain, Australia, and the United States showed similar very high ratings on individualism. The lower the power distance, the more individuals will expect to participate in a leader's decision. The United States records a middle-level rating on power distance, but countries such as Denmark, Austria, and Israel record much lower. In these countries, subordinates will be unlikely to wait until their boss takes the initiative to let them participate. At the other extreme, employees in Third World countries generally do not expect to participate.

Hofstede uses the combination of power distance and uncertainty avoidance to explain prevalent models of organization in Great Britain, Germany, France, and India that fall into the four quadrants of a two-by-two matrix on these dimensions:

	Power Distance	Uncertainty Avoidance
Great Britain	Small	Weak
Germany	Small	Strong
France	Large	Strong
India	Large	Weak

The British model of organization seems to be that of a village market with no decisive hierarchy, flexible rules, and a resolution of problems by negotiating. The German model is more like a well-oiled machine. The exercise of personal command is largely unnecessary because the rules settle everything. The French model is more of a pyramidal hierarchy held together by unity of command issuing strong rules. Finally, the Indian model is more akin to the family with undisputed personal authority of the father and few formal rules.

A reasonably high masculinity index for the United States, associated with a low uncertainty avoidance index, shows clearly in prevalent approaches towards business motivation. The accepted wisdom is that as people are basically motivated by a desire to achieve something and have an inbuilt willingness to take some risks, management should simply make it possible for them to achieve by enriching

FIGURE 17–2 Index Values of 50 Countries and Three Regions on Four Cultural Dimensions

Country	Power Distance Index	Uncertainty Avoidance Index	Individualism Index	Masculinity Index
Argentina	49	86	46	56
Australia	36	51	90	61
Austria	11	70	55	79
Belgium	65	94	75	54
Brazil	69	76	38	49
Canada	39	48	80	52
Chile	63	86	23	28
Colombia	67	80	13	64
Costa Rica	35	86	15	21
Denmark	18	23	74	16
Equador	78	67	8	63
Finland	33	59	63	26
France	68	86	71	43
Germany (F.R.)	35	65	67	66
Great Britain	35	35	89	66
Greece	60	112	35	57
Guatemala	95	101	6	37
Hong Kong	68	29	25	57
Indonesia	78	48	14	46
India	77	40	48	56
Iran	58	59	41	43
Ireland	28	35	70	68
Israel	13	81	54	47
Italy	50	75	76	70
Jamaica	45	13	39	68
Japan	54	92	46	95
Korea (S.)	60	85	18	39
Malaysia	104	36	26	50
Mexico	81	82	30	69
Netherlands	38	53	80	14
Norway	31	50	69	8
New Zealand	22	49	79	58
Pakistan	55	70	14	50
Panama	95	86	11	44
Peru	64	87	16	42
Philippines	94	44	32	64
Portugal	63	104	27	31
South Africa	49	49	65	63
Salvador	66	94	19	40
Singapore	74	8	20	48
Spain	57	86	51	42
Sweden	31	29	71	5
Switzerland	34	58	68	70
Taiwan	58	69	17	45
Thailand	64	64	20	34
Turkey	66	85	37	45
Uruguay	61	100	36	38
U.S.A.	40	46	91	62
Venezuela	81	76	12	73
Yugoslavia	76	88	27	21
Regions:				
East Africa	64	52	27	41
West Africa	77	54	20	46
Arab countries	80	68	38	53

SOURCE: Geert Hofstede, "National Cultures in Four Dimensions: A Research-Theory of Cultural Differences Among Nations," *International Studies of Management and Organization,* 13 (Spring–Summer 1983), p. 52.

their jobs to give them a personal challenge. In other countries, such as Yugoslavia, which has a low masculinity index and strong uncertainty avoidance, there is more tendency to value interpersonal relations as a motivation and to take risks only if one is offered security in exchange. Although Japan is very masculine, it has a very high uncertainty avoidance index—yet this does not seem to have affected economic growth. General security of employment, however, is in marked contrast to U.S. practice.

The Primary Message Systems Matrix

Edward Hall presents his map of culture as a two-dimensional matrix composed of 10 aspects of human activity, which he calls Primary Message Systems.[32] These are shown in Figure 17–3. While each aspect can be examined alone, Hall shows how a grasp of the complex interrelationships of a culture can be obtained by commencing with any of the 10 aspects and studying its intersection with each of the others. In a matrix there will be two intersections of each pair of aspects.

For a direct application of Hall's matrix to international business, take the example of a large manufacturer of toys and games assessing opportunities in a new country. The firm will be directly engaged in the play aspect of the new culture, and it is certain that the cultural patterns with respect to play will differ from those the firm is currently dealing with.

Use of Hall's matrix would raise 18 categories of questions about play patterns in the new culture. Stemming from the intersection of play with the remaining primary message systems, the first two categories would ask about interaction in play and about play in interaction, the second two would ask about the associations—that is, organizations involved in play and games involving associations, and so on. Questions raised within the 18 categories are illustrated in Figure 17–4, but it must be clear that the map does not magically produce the right answers to even the right questions. This is simply one structured approach to investigating how a new culture may differ. The reader who rejects a structured approach, however, should be sure that an ad hoc alternative does develop an adequate sensitivity to the important cultural differences.

UNDERSTANDING CULTURE CHANGE

Acceptance and Resistance to Change

The manager operating cross-culturally needs an understanding of what aspects of a culture will resist change and how those will differ among cultures, how the process of change takes place in different cultures, and what the speed of

---

[32] Hall, *Silent Language,* especially chap. 3.

FIGURE 17–3   Primary Message Systems of Edward Hall's *The Silent Language*

Primary Message System	Depicts Attitudes and Cultural Rules for:
1. Interaction	The ordering of man's interaction with those around him through language, touch, noise, gesture, and so forth.
2. Association	The organization (grouping) and structuring of society and its components.
3. Subsistence	The ordering of man's activities in feeding, working, and making a living.
4. Bisexuality	The differentiation of roles, activities, and function along sex lines.
5. Territoriality	The possession, use, and defense of space and territory.
6. Temporality	The use, allocation, and division of time.
7. Learning	The adaptive process of learning and instruction.
8. Play	Relaxation, humor, recreation, and enjoyment.
9. Defense	Protection against man's environment, including medicine, warfare, and law.
10. Exploitation	Turning the environment to man's use through technology, construction, and extraction of materials.

SOURCE: Adapted from Edward T. Hall, *The Silent Language* (Garden City, N.Y.: Doubleday, 1959), pp. 61–81.

change will be. There are two seemingly contradictory forces within cultures. On the one hand, people attempt to protect and preserve their culture with an elaborate set of sanctions and laws invoked against those who deviate from their norms. On the other hand, the environment within which a culture exists is continually changing, and a culture must change in order to ensure its own continuity. Where a culture comes into contact with other cultures, this same dichotomy exists. There is, on the one hand, an ingrained belief, called *ethnocentrism,* that the ways of one's own culture are superior to those of other cultures, and on the other hand, a realization that a culture must be competitive if it is to retain its own identity.

These conflicting forces make some elements of culture highly resistant to change. Others immediately fall to innovations, even though some of them may give an impression that they are immutable. How can these elements be differentiated?

Edward Hall classifies cultural aspects into formal, informal, and technical, based primarily on differences in the way the cultural norm is learned, the culture's level of awareness of the norm, and the response to a deviation from the norm.

Formal rules are at the core of the culture and really determine its essence. They are taught through example and admonition as rules for which there is either right or wrong, with clear indication of when a mistake has been made. There is a formal awareness of the norm and a great deal of emotion if the norm is violated. Most societies, for example, have a formal rule that there

FIGURE 17–4 A Business Application of Edward Hall's Map of Culture

Intersections of Play and Other Primary Message Systems	Sample Questions Concerning Cultural Patterns Significant for Marketing Toys and Games
1. Interaction/Play	How do people interact during play as regards competitiveness, instigation, or leadership?
2. Play Interaction	What games are played involving acting, role playing, or other aspects of real-world interaction?
3. Association/Play	Who organizes play and how do the organization patterns differ?
4. Play/Association	What games are played about organization: for example, team competitions and games involving kings, judges, or leader-developed rules and penalties?
5. Subsistence/Play	What are the significant factors regarding people such as distributors, teachers, coaches, or publishers who make their livelihood from games?
6. Play/Subsistence	What games are played about work roles in society such as doctors, nurses, firemen?
7. Bisexuality/Play	What are the significant differences between the sexes in the sports, games, and toys enjoyed?
8. Play/Bisexuality	What games and toys involve bisexuality: for example, dolls, dressing up, dancing?
9. Territoriality/Play	Where are games played and what are the limits observed in houses, parks, streets, schools, and so forth?
10. Play/Territoriality	What games are played about space and ownership: for example, Monopoly?
11. Temporality/Play	At what ages and what times of the day and year are different games played?
12. Play/Temporality	What games are played about and involving time: for example, clocks, speed tests?
13. Learning/Play	What patterns of coaching, tuition, and training exist for learning games?
14. Play/Learning	What games are played about and involving learning and knowledge: for examples, quizzes?
15. Defense/Play	What are the safety rules for games, equipment, and toys?
16. Play/Defense	What war and defense games and toys are utilized?
17. Exploitation/Play	What resources and technology are permitted or utilized for games and sport: for example, hunting and fishing rules, use of parks, cameras, vehicles, and so forth?
18. Play/Exploitation	What games and toys about technology or exploitation are used: for example, scouting, chemical sets, microscopes?

should be no enjoyment from hurting others physically or from seeing them hurt. The rule is made clear from early childhood, and penalties are imposed for breaking it.

Informal rules are not taught so directly. Usually the learner picks them up by imitation and is unaware of learning them. The society is generally unconscious of the rules, and if one is violated, there would be only an expression of anxiety or some informally learned reaction. The average child does not receive direct instruction in how to play but is left to observe others and to do likewise. If the child attempts to dominate playmates, for example, the playmates will very likely develop ways of excluding the child. Thus, by experience rather than direct instruction, the child learns how to behave in groups.

Technical rules are usually taught by instruction in a logical and coherent manner. These are at the highest level of awareness as they are verbalized, reasoned, and explicit. Few emotions are attached to the violation of a technical rule. Breaking a rule by adopting a different training approach for an athletic sport, for example, would occasion intellectual interest but little emotion.

The aspects falling into each category differ from culture to culture. If we continue with a sporting example, for instance, we might find that the English regard acceptance of the referee's rulings as a fundamental principle of sportsmanship—a formal rule that would produce an emotional response from most of the population if they were confronted with a direct violation. On the other hand, the Germans may have a clear set of technical rules for when and how to object to rulings, while Americans adopt an informal approach that objections should be made as and when justified. Any aspect of culture could be compared between cultures in this way.

Attitudes toward change clearly differ for each of the three classes. Formal rules would be held with great tenacity, change very slowly, and be particularly resistant to any attempt to force change from outside. Informal rules can change more easily. There is room for more deviation by individuals and imitation can be selective in one direction or another. Change comes most easily with technical rules, because they are readily observed, talked about, transmitted, and accepted at a more or less rational level. The key to culture change seems to lie in the informal system. In a complex and changing environment, imitation of others will not be perfect. When some of the variants that emerge seem to work better than others, they are copied and eventually develop as technical rules.

Technical changes are most likely to deal with details of an activity—for example, the use of a new fertilizer or the introduction of a new type of motor. But a series of changes in technical rules, initially consonant with the existing formal systems, can cause more fundamental changes in the formal and informal systems. Technical and informal rules seem to surround each part of the formal system, and when these supports are removed, formal rules may eventually give way. This may explain why some parts of a culture reject change persistently only to collapse later on. Hall illustrates this sort of phenomena with the change in attitude toward premarital chastity in the United States.[33] Changes in women's social life, education, career patterns, and dress habits, and the widespread use of the private car removed many technical supports to the formal rule. After resisting change for many years, the rule eventually changed very rapidly.

Not all the new elements that evolve from within a culture, or are introduced from outside, are adopted by the culture. They have to fall on fertile ground in the sense that there is a perception of the need for the change and a broad acceptance of it. The social structure of the society and those who introduce the change or are aware of it will thus be important factors in its acceptance, as examined in the next section. Cultures also tend to develop a particular interest in some parts of their system—called a *cultural focus*. A culture is more likely to develop and adopt changes in those areas on which it places this emphasis. Conversely, less important areas will change less and there will be lower tolerance for change in them. The Arabs, for example, have regarded the "fellahin" engaged in agriculture as of very low status and have adopted few agricultural innovations in comparison with the Israelis who accord agriculture high status and reward successful agricultural innovation with almost national fame.

Social Dynamics of Culture Change

It is as important for the international manager to identify the roles different people will play in the change process as it is to identify what cultural aspects will resist change. Cultural change implies change in the pattern of behavior of the individuals adhering to that culture. The order in which persons with different characteristics adopt an innovation and the influences that affect their decision are thus of particular importance. The field of diffusion studies has a great deal to say about these.

Adopters of any innovation are conventionally classified into five groups, according to the order in which they adopt the innovation, as follows:[34]

Adopter Category	
Innovators	First 2.5%
Early Adopters	Next 13.5%
Early Majority	Next 34%
Late Majority	Next 34%
Laggards	Remaining 16%

The idea behind this classification is that common characteristics may be identified for the adopters of each stage.

"Innovators" are regarded by themselves and by others as deviants from

---

[33] Hall, *Silent Language*, p. 113.

[34] Rogers, *Diffusion of Innovations*, 3rd ed. Chapter 7 provides the references for most of the research generalizations that follow in this section.

the norms of their culture or subculture. They tend to have a characteristic venturesomeness and to have seen more of other cultures than later adopters. One study of firms commencing export activity showed almost all the innovators to have international backgrounds.[35] "Early adopters" tend to have a higher position in the social hierarchy than innovators and to rate high as opinion leaders. They may have a considerable influence on later adopters. The "early majority" seems to be characterized by their capacity for deliberation. They do not adopt until other respected persons have done so, seldom emerging as leaders. Contrasted with this, the dominant value of the people who make up the "late majority" is skepticism. They tend to wait until the weight of public opinion strongly favors the innovation before they proceed. "Laggards" tend to be older, to be suspicious of innovations, and to take the past and tradition as their point of reference.

Associated with the study of diffusion, and particularly relevant for cultural change, is the concept of an adoption process. This is conceived as a set of five mental stages through which an individual passes from first hearing about an innovation until finally adopting it. These are (1) awareness, (2) interest, (3) evaluation, (4) trial, and (5) adoption. Studies of each of these stages and the information and influence sources important at each stage have provided some significant generalizations about adoptions. It has been found that impersonal sources of information tend to be most influential at the awareness stage, and personal sources tend to be most influential at the evaluation stage. Commercial change agents, that is, advertising and selling, seem to be more important at the trial stage than at any other stage. In the earlier stages of the process, nonlocal sources of information tend to be most important. But in the later stages local sources take the command position. These findings may be very significant for firms planning the introduction of products into new cultural environments.

Social-class identification by groups within a culture can also affect the diffusion of an innovation. A social class, however defined, is likely to exhibit some common variants of the overall national culture, particularly if its members are grouped in the same living environment. One landmark study suggests that the cultural norms of a social class at the particular time were a significant factor in the acceptance or rejection of a particular innovation.[36] The pattern of interaction and influence that leads to adoption or rejection may also be largely carried on within one social class.[37] Changes may thus not trickle down the social scale with each class striving to copy classes above it. The international businessman must be prepared, therefore, to observe what happens within social groups as well as across a society as a whole.

---

[35] Kenneth Simmonds and Helen Smith, "The First Export Order: A Marketing Innovation," *British Journal of Marketing,* Summer 1968.

[36] Graham Saxon, "Class and Conservatism in the Adoption of Innovations," *Human Relations* 9, no. 1 (1956), pp. 91–100.

[37] Charles W. King, "Fashion Adoption: A Rebuttal of the 'Trickle Down Theory,' " in *Toward Scientific Marketing,* ed. Stephen A. Greyser (Chicago: American Marketing Association, 1963), pp. 108–25.

PROMOTING CULTURE CHANGE

In many situations, management will not passively adapt to the ever-changing patterns of cultural differences within which it operates but will endeavor to induce change in some aspect of a local culture. The most common targets for active attempts to induce change in this way are consumer buying patterns and employee work patterns. In most cases the attempt will be based on actual observation of the success of a culture change in another situation and will not stem merely from a management desire to "move ahead." Cultural transplants are more likely to be successful when an actual example of a similar culture change already exists.

The international enterprise may promote change, but it is the members of the foreign culture who have to accept change. The general strategy, therefore, must be to discover the ways and incentives characteristic of the culture that are likely to result in acceptance (see Box 17–2). The comparative business literature is replete with examples of unsuccessful attempts to induce cultural change. Yet the success stories are numerous also, and they provide considerable encouragement for the likely success of well-designed and well-informed efforts to promote cultural change.

Building on the Old.   Unless they produce dramatic benefits, the easiest way to have innovations accepted is to make sure they present no open conflict with traditional values and customs and to graft onto them. Medicine is one field in which problems have often occurred. In societies that have continued to

---

BOX 17–2
Educating the Unshaven

Tailoring its marketing to Third World tastes has become an important part of Gillette's growth strategy. But the toughest task for Gillette is convincing Third World men to shave. The company recently began dispatching portable theaters to remote villages to show movies and commercials that tout daily shaving.

In South African and Indonesian versions, a bewildered bearded man enters a locker room where clean-shaven friends show him how to shave. In the Mexican one, a handsome sheriff, tracking bandits who have kidnapped a woman, pauses on the trail to shave each morning. The camera lingers as he snaps a double-edged blade into his razor, lathers his face and strokes it carefully. In the end, of course, the smooth-faced sheriff gets the woman.

Such campaigns win few immediate converts, acknowledges Gillette's director of international marketing. Migration of peasants to the city does more to boost Gillette's sales.

SOURCE: Adapted from *The Wall Street Journal*, January 23, 1986. © Dow Jones & Company, Inc., 1986. Used with permission. All rights reserved.

rely on folk-medicine it has frequently been effective to relate new Western medical products to irrational traditional beliefs. Use of existing power and influence structures is also recommended, as Zaltman and Duncan have pointed out:

> Strategies that involve using existing power or influence structures such as midwives to disseminate birth-control pills or faith healers to distribute condoms do not cause a loss of pride or dignity among these often highly regarded individuals. To the contrary, their status, which is a source of their pride, is reinforced and enhanced.[38]

Identifying the Rational.   The straightforward approach of presenting information and rational argument assumes that individuals are guided by reason. Such a strategy, called a reeducative strategy,[39] is the most neutral of all strategies, and can be effective in many situations. Firms providing training and technical help to customers as part of their sales approach are adopting this sort of strategy. Nevertheless, education is a slow process, and what is rational to the protagonist of the change might not be what the change target believes is rational. Rationality, after all, does not exist independently of the objectives that are adopted. An individual's actions to protect an established status position against change may be very rational.

Avoiding the Unknown.   When the full nature of a change and its outcome are unknown, uncertainty and anxiety abound for those who perceive they may be affected. Resistance to the change then builds up as a protection against the unknown. The promoter of change should thus take great care to specify exactly what the change is and how it will work. Even prior to this stage, the development of awareness of the need for change may be desirable. Conceivably, an innovation may be brought about simply through providing the necessary tools with which to recognize the problem.

Recognizing the Influence of Others.   The attitudes of individuals toward change are influenced by those around them. Individuals may change because of a desire for recognition by others, prestige, or to emulate others with more status than themselves. If an individual is asked to change behavior in a way that will not be supported by others of significance to that individual, then the change is unlikely to come about.[40] The introduction of a change may have more chance of success, therefore, if its promoter works through opinion leaders who will influence others.[41]

---

[38] Gerald Zaltman and Robert Duncan, *Strategies for Planned Change* (New York: John Wiley & Sons, 1977), p. 71.

[39] Ibid., p. 111.

[40] Chris Argyris, *Interpersonal Competence and Organizational Effectiveness* (Chicago: Dorsey Press, 1962).

[41] Rogers, *Diffusion of Innovations,* 3rd ed., pp. 331–32.

Providing Support.   Anything new is likely to require further changes in using it. A change should not be introduced and dropped. It should be supported until it is thoroughly operational. Examples abound of modern equipment lying abandoned in fields, factories, homes, and offices because of lack of instruction on use or maintenance.

Compensating the Losers.   It is often argued that when a new gain results through change, nobody loses. In more cases than not, however, there will be net costs to some party affected. Measures to protect those affected adversely, from economic loss or from decreases in personal status and dignity, can go a great way toward smoothing the adoption of innovations. Firms within single nations have developed policies of compensating workers for adopting changes in technology. So, too, in multinational corporations will there be increased demands to compensate employees hurt economically by innovations, even though the same innovations have already been adopted in other parts of the multinational organization.

INTERNATIONAL BUSINESS AS A CHANGE AGENT

A final topic related to the cultural components of the international business environment is the role of international business as a change agent. Here we are referring to the cultural fallout as well as the deliberately promoted cultural changes. The concept of international business as a change agent usually has a favorable connotation in business circles and refers to such benefits as the transfer of technology and management skills,[42] the training of workers, and the social and economic modernization effects in the host country. All of these features of international business are generally assumed to be positive and desirable contributions to the countries in which international business activity takes place. But as the social scientists have observed, cultural change can have both positive and negative aspects for the members of a given society.

Some cultural changes for which international enterprises can claim credit are consistent with the goals of national leaders who are anxious to modernize and industrialize their society. The nature or the pace of other changes can provoke negative reactions to the international enterprise by government leaders or groups in the society. Because it is an agent of change, whether or not the change is intentional, the international enterprise should attempt to anticipate the changes for which it might be held responsible and the full chain of results from changes it is promoting. Such anticipation requires the international executive to construct a model, or description, of the changing society. The classification of socioeconomic effects of industrialization shown in Figure 17–5 might be usefully adapted for this purpose.

---

[42] See Karl P. Sauvant, ''The Potential of Multinational Enterprises as Vehicles for the Transmission of Business Culture,'' *Controlling Multinational Enterprises: Problems, Strategies, Counterstrategies,* ed. Karl P. Sauvant and Farid G. Lavipour (Boulder, Colo.: Westview Press, 1976), pp. 39–78.

FIGURE 17–5   Socioeconomic Effects of Industrialization

A. *Effects on Individuals:*
   Organization of production involves the movement of local inhabitants from self-contained village societies to an urban advanced economy. Personal adjustments include the transition from a rural to an urban existence, and from the timeless subsistence economy to an efficiency-oriented system geared to profit orientation.

   Relationship to work changes from that of the rural village work situation to that of an industrialized society. Differences include moving from a leisurely pace of production to the programmed efficiency of the MNC industrial environment. The diversified range of living skills indigenous to the rural village setting contrasts with the narrow, more repetitious skills resulting from the division of labor.

   Motivation and enterprise for the individual change with the move to an advanced society. The philosophy of cooperation inherent in the rural village setting fades into the competitive environment characteristic of modern industry. Responsibility for the acquisition of wealth and income now depends upon the individual's effort, not upon hereditary or seniority principles, as in the rural village.

B. *Population Effects:*
   The population shift from a rural to an urbanized economy is a key element in the westernization of an LDC's culture. First, there is an increase in the economically active population. Second, the population grows as a result of greater life expectancy and decreased infant mortality due to better health facilities.

C. *Effects on Economic Institutions:*
   Occupational aspects. Changes in occupational structure occur as workers entering the monetarized economy broaden the occupational base and move gradually away from their unskilled status. Education and training contribute to the upward movement of the local inhabitant in the occupational hierarchy.

   Savings and investments. The mobilization of savings and investments is an essential ingredient of industrialization. Investments by MNCs in manufacturing stimulate industrial growth and employment. MNCs in the financial sector help to mobilize savings for investment, and provide a stimulus for consumption through the hire-purchase mechanism.

   Consumption and distribution. As monetarization of the economy proceeds, more money is available for consumption purchases that, in turn, require additional distributive outlets. MNCs provide the expertise and organization required for a complex wholesaling and retailing setup.

D. *Effects on the Social Structure:*
   Kinship and family. Breakup of kinship and family patterns occurs as the geographically dispersed nuclear family supplants the extended family. The woman ceases to be the primary producer in the family unit, a role the man now assumes as he moves into industrial work. Arranged marriages give way to the Westernized free market courtship mechanism.

   Community organization and problems. Voluntary associates take the place of blood and kinship ties. The transition to urban life causes adjustment problems and a loss of emotional security, as urban Western values clash with a traditional rural village outlook. Increases in vandalism, alcoholism, and drug addiction can result. The severity of poverty also increases as the low wages of unskilled laborers prove insufficient in an environment where the consumption of many Western products becomes increasingly obligatory.

   Education and science. As industrialization progresses, institutions of higher learning in the LDC offer more vocationally oriented courses such as engineering, commerce and agricultural sciences. These courses are aimed toward supplying manufacturing units with local skilled labor, thus reducing the propensity to import labor.

   Communication and popular culture. Multinational corporations aid the development of a communications system occasionally through actual ownership of media, but more often through their commercial sponsorship of media. The media *(a)* provide vehicles through which the local population learns of Western lifestyles and consumption habits, *(b)* make accurate and permanent records more likely, *(c)* make timely reporting of major events

FIGURE 17–5 *(concluded)*

possible, *(d)* extend man's empathetic comprehension beyond his personal experiences, *(e)* coordinate the groups that constitute the personal contact network.

Interest groups and organizations. Affiliations with trade unions expand as the population becomes both more educated and more active in the monetarized economy. During early stages of economic development, however, labor remains largely unorganized and in an unadvantageous bargaining position.

Religious groups and organizations. Transition from rural village to urban life often results in a mixture of organized religion and witchcraft as religious beliefs.

Social stratification. The static rural village system, which ranks by heredity and seniority, is replaced in the industrial society by rankings on the bases of wealth, education, income, and occupation. The structure of society becomes more flexible and social mobility increases.

Organization of the state. As the LDC industrializes, the state may orient its functional parts to redressing the inequalities produced by the system (income, wealth, location of industry, etc.). As the MNCs undertake much of the private investment, the LDC's government focuses upon establishing an economic infrastructure and broadening educational opportunities.

SOURCE: Adapted from John S. Hill and Richard R. Still, "Cultural Effects of Technology Transfer by Multinational Corporations in Lesser Developed Countries," *Columbia Journal of World Business* (Summer 1980), pp. 40–51.

Where the changes are perceived as beneficial by local interests, the bargaining position of the enterprise is strengthened. Where the expected changes are likely to appear dysfunctional and be negatively received, the international enterprise may want to modify its operational patterns or prepare to meet local antagonism, for a while at least.

SUMMARY

When the business firm crosses national boundaries and begins to operate in a number of countries, it is faced with a wide range of cultural differences that can significantly affect the achievement of business objectives. The problem of identifying cultural differences is difficult because of the natural tendency for people to observe and evaluate behavior of others in terms of the cultural conditioning of their own country. Furthermore, cultural patterns are not static but constantly changing. The problems faced in the cultural field involve much more than an intellectual appreciation that differences exist. International managers must develop cultural sensitivity, frequently through living experience in different cultures. With cultural sensitivity, the enterprise will be aware of the need to identify cultural variables and to adjust its organization and its operations to cultural differences. In many situations, the enterprise will have to promote cultural change in order to achieve its business goals. In a broader sense, the international enterprise itself is a powerful change agent. It must anticipate the changes that it causes and the reception that such changes will receive in host countries.

EXERCISES AND DISCUSSION QUESTIONS

1. "Cultural anthropology has certainly spawned a lot of empirical research, but as far as theory is concerned it is barren. The few tested theories that are available, moreover, have to be stretched a long way to reach anything of value to inter-cultural business." Discuss.

2. Give your own definition of culture.

3. Some multinational firms issue a standard corporate manual for international use containing set organizational definitions and rules, personnel policies, and budget and accounting instructions. What limits on the types of standardized instructions would you recommend that a firm with operations in many countries adopt?

4. From whatever sources are available to you, build a comparison of the family decision-making process for a major consumer purchase in two different cultures. Specify the roles played by the different family members, the pattern over time of interaction among the family with respect to the purchase, the weighting placed upon different product characteristics by each family member, and the rules by which a consensus is finally reached.

5. Select one of the aspects of a culture—(1) the status ranking of different occupations, (2) the roles of the sexes, (3) the times of life with which different activities are associated, (4) the exercise of organizational authority, or (5) courtship patterns—in which you are aware of a change in the cultural norms and carry out the following activities:

   a. Describe the nature of the change.
   b. Give your opinion as to whether the culture regarded it formally, informally, or technically.
   c. Identify some distinguishing characteristics of the innovators and early adopters.
   d. Describe any role you think business played in stimulating the change.
   e. Describe the business significance of the changes for any foreign firm operating within the culture.

6. "The prime function of most executive development courses is not knowledge transmission but rather the transfer of a set of norms which conform with organizational objectives." Do you think it is acceptable for a U.S. top executive of a multinational firm to use executive-development courses to transfer to the management of foreign subsidiaries the norms that the executive has chosen?

CHAPTER 18

Multinational Marketing Management

Markets and marketing decisions play a crucial role in the development of a firm's global strategy, as discussed in Chapter 9. Marketing managers participate heavily in overall strategy formulation. They also have an operating responsibility for implementing the marketing dimension of the global strategy.

This chapter focuses on the marketing management function at both the strategy formulation and operational levels. It begins with the organizational issue of how marketing responsibility should be allocated between headquarters and country managers. It then considers the principal marketing functions of product strategies, marketing research, advertising, pricing, and channel management as these functions are affected when a firm extends its operations from its home market to a number of different national markets.

How does multinational marketing differ from domestic marketing? Both are similar in objectives, methods, and functions required. They differ in that the multinational firm operates simultaneously in a number of national markets that vary widely in economic, cultural, and competitive characteristics. Also, many governments with varied national interests—rather than a single government—are shaping the environment within which the marketers operate. As we shall see, the multinational setting expands manyfold the task of adjusting the marketing mix to the varied needs of the target markets.[1]

CENTRAL COORDINATION VERSUS LOCAL AUTHORITY

In multinational marketing, how should the function be divided between corporate headquarters and the foreign subsidiaries? A traditional view has been that most of the marketing responsibility should be handled at the local level because subsidiary managers are most familiar with the special characteristics of their markets. Where products and marketing approaches are extended from the central market to foreign areas with little or no adaptation, a contribution by headquarters is not needed. And where major adaptations are required, the managers closest to these markets are best able to make these adjustments.[2] As a result, marketing more than any other function is often conspicuous by its absence from the functions performed at corporate headquarters.

In other cases, an increased role by headquarters has taken the form of "interactive market planning."[3] One reason for this approach is that headquarters can better fulfill its role in strategic planning and controlling performance by participating in the marketing function. Another reason is that headquarters can perform certain operational functions more effectively than can be done at the subsidiary level. National markets have similarities as well as differences, and this creates opportunities for the enterprise to benefit from applying some common marketing policies in the different markets. The degree of headquarters participation will vary, of course, by marketing function, by industry, by company, and over time.[4]

At the operational level, headquarters staff normally play a significant role in standardizing some parts of the marketing strategy while the subsidiaries have principal responsibility for handling the differences and unique factors. In one study of major U.S. and European companies in four consumer industries, headquarters participation was greatest in decisions on product policies such as physical

[1] See Robert Bartels, "Are Domestic and International Marketing Dissimilar?" *Journal of Marketing* 32 (July 1968), pp. 56–61.

[2] Warren J. Keegan, "Multinational Marketing: The Headquarters Role," *Columbia Journal of World Business*, January–February 1971, pp. 85–90.

[3] Robert D. Buzzell, "Can You Standardize Multinational Marketing?" *Harvard Business Review*, November–December 1968, pp. 102–13.

[4] R. J. Aylmer, "Who Makes Marketing Decisions in the Multinational Firm?" *Journal of Marketing*, October 1970, pp. 26–27.

characteristics of the product, brand name, packaging, and product line.[5] Headquarters participation was far lower in decisions on pricing, distribution, and advertising and promotion. By industry, centralized decision making was stronger for nonfood than for food products, the latter perceived to be more "culture bound."

To carry out its strategic planning responsibility, headquarters must be adequately informed concerning markets and competition. Headquarters, therefore, should standardize certain measures so that market potential and marketing performance in different national markets can be compared. The extent of headquarters involvement will depend, of course, on an assessment of the benefits from such involvement compared to the costs in terms of personnel, information flows, and standardized approaches.

An interactive process is two-way. Headquarters must also make affirmative marketing contributions to the local subsidiaries. It can make available experience that has succeeded in one country to other countries when comparable conditions prevail. It may discover opportunities in market segments in different countries that country subsidiaries individually consider too small to warrant development. It can supervise marketing experiments in selected areas and make the results available to all units in the system. As an example, where there is uncertainty about the relative effectiveness of advertising versus personal selling, headquarters could experiment in Country A with 75 percent of the communications budget for advertising and 25 percent for personal selling and reverse these proportions in Country B, where both countries were preselected as reasonably comparable in other marketing dimensions.

Another contribution of headquarters staff can be to make certain that individual markets are developed in ways that fit the longer-term strategy of the firm, so that performance in those markets can fit without problems into later stages of the global plan. It may be necessary, for example, to choose outlets not initially the best for a small range of products selling in low volumes but that are preferred for later planned expansion. The brand image may also be important for carrying future lines and require special attention when products are first introduced.

One of the more common ways of placing responsibility at the level of those closest to the customer and the competition, yet still retaining central control over the marketing function, is through the use of a standard annual plan and review routine. Plans are requested in a standard format working from an assessment of the market environment toward specific action proposals and budgeted profit performance and resource requirements. These are then subjected to careful scrutiny and related to the overall plan for global performance. Any clashes or omissions discovered can then be raised before actions are taken.

This method of central control also acts as a major implement in educating the international organization in the use of marketing. A good grasp of marketing cannot be assumed to exist throughout any international organization. The ideas

---

[5] Ulrich Wiechmann, "Integrating Multinational Marketing Activities," *Columbia Journal of World Business* 9 (Winter 1974), pp. 7–16.

are alien to many cultures and frequently opposed to the message of the programs under which many international executives have been educated. Furthermore, foreign countries do not have a product management system as developed as that in the United States.[6]

The decisive question is not where ultimate control of strategy should lie, for this inevitably must rest with top management. The real question is the extent to which headquarters executives should be involved in the marketing-planning process. In the absence of headquarters involvement in the individual subsidiary planning processes, it is difficult, indeed impossible, for headquarters to impose global considerations effectively. On the other hand, in the absence of subsidiary involvement at a strategic level, the requirements of a particular market may be overlooked.

As a general rule, headquarters should be involved in subsidiary planning processes to the extent necessary to keep informed of the nature of basic opportunities and threats globally. Also, headquarters involvement should be measured against the degree to which it stimulates or contributes to subsidiary planning efforts. Alternatively, a check should be kept on the extent to which it may detract from initiative and enterprise on the part of subsidiary managers. The organizational form must facilitate the task of multinational marketing, particularly where marketing skills are important as a key element in the competitive advantage of the international company.

Of course, the relationship between headquarters and subsidiary on the marketing front seldom operates without some problems. Some are to be expected because of the obvious conflicts of interest built into matrix organizations and the differences in the cultural background and training of the marketers themselves. Wiechmann and Pringle identified 23 key problems as seen by headquarters executives of 40 European and United States multinationals and 22 key problems as seen by subsidiary executives.[7] These are reproduced in Figure 18–1. The multinational marketer, however, may find it more constructive to regard these issues less as problems and more as indicators of the ongoing need for management flexibility and involvement in a complex coordination task.

INTERNATIONAL PRODUCT STRATEGIES

The product strategy of an international firm generally falls somewhere between the extremes of central market focus and decentralized development, as discussed in Chapter 9, and between the extremes of marketing-mix standardization

---

[6] Alladi Venkatesh and David Wilemon, "American and European Product Managers: A Comparison," *Columbia Journal of World Business* 15 (Fall 1980), pp. 67–74.

[7] Ulrich E. Wiechmann and Lewis G. Pringle, "Problems That Plague Multinational Marketers," *Harvard Business Review* 57 (July–August 1979), pp. 118–24. A similar set of problems emerged from research into the management of North American, European, and Japanese multinationals operating in Brazil. See James M. Hulbert, William K. Brandt, and Raimar Richers, "Marketing Planning in the Multinational Subsidiary: Practices and Problems," *Journal of Marketing* 44 (Summer 1980), pp. 7–15.

FIGURE 18–1

Key Problems Identified by Headquarters Executives

Lack of qualified international personnel:
Getting qualified international personnel is difficult.
It is difficult to find enough qualified local managers for the subsidiaries.
The company can't find enough capable people willing to move to different countries.
There isn't enough manpower at headquarters to make the necessary visits to local operations.

Lack of strategic thinking and long-range planning at the subsidiary level:
Subsidiary managers are preoccupied with purely operational problems and don't think enough about long-range strategy.
Subsidiary managers don't do a good job of analyzing and forecasting their business.
There is too much emphasis in the subsidiary on short-term financial performance. This is an obstacle to the development of long-term marketing strategies.

Lack of marketing expertise at the subsidiary level:
The company lacks marketing competence at the subsidiary level.
The subsidiaries don't give their advertising agencies proper direction.
The company doesn't understand consumers in the countries where it operates.
Many subsidiaries don't gather enough marketing intelligence.
The subsidiary does a poor job of defining targets for its product marketing.

Too little relevant communication between headquarters and the subsidiaries:
The subsidiaries don't inform headquarters about their problems until the last minute.
The subsidiaries do not get enough consulting service from headquarters.
There is a communications gap between headquarters and the subsidiaries.
The subsidiaries provide headquarters with too little feedback.

Insufficient utilization of multinational marketing experience:
The company is a national company with international business; there is too much focus on domestic operations.
Subsidiary managers don't benefit from marketing experience available at headquarters and vice versa.
The company does not take advantage of its experience with product introductions in one country for use in other countries.
The company lacks central coordination of its marketing efforts.

Restricted headquarters control of the subsidiaries:
The headquarters staff is too small to exercise the proper control over the subsidiaries.
Subsidiary managers resist direction from headquarters.
Subsidiaries have profit responsibility and therefore resist any restraints on their decision-making authority.

Key Problems Identified by Subsidiary Executives

Insensitivity of headquarters to local market differences:

Headquarters management feels that what works in one market should also work in other markets.

Headquarters makes decisions without thorough knowledge of marketing conditions in the subsidiary's country.

Marketing strategies developed at headquarters don't reflect the fact that the subsidiary's position may be significantly different in its market.

The attempt to standardize marketing programs across borders neglects the fact that our company has different market shares and market acceptance in each country.

Shortage of useful information from headquarters:

The company doesn't have a good training program for its international managers.

New product information doesn't come from headquarters often enough.

The company has an inadequate procedure for sharing information among its subsidiaries.

There is very little cross-fertilization with respect to ideas and problem solving among functional groups within the company.

Lack of multinational orientation at headquarters:

Headquarters is too home-country oriented.

Headquarters managers are not truly multinational personnel.

Excessive headquarters control procedures:

Reaching a decision takes too long because we must get approval from headquarters.

There is too much bureaucracy in the organization.

Too much paperwork has to be sent to headquarters.

Headquarters staff and subsidiary management differ about which problems are important.

Headquarters tries to control its subsidiaries too tightly.

Excessive financial and marketing constraints:

The emphasis on short-term financial performance is an obstacle to the development of long-term marketing strategies for local markets.

The subsidiary must increase sales to meet corporate profit objectives even though it operates with many marketing constraints imposed by headquarters.

Headquarters expects a profit return each year without investing more money in the local company.

Insufficient participation of subsidiaries in product decisions:

The subsidiary is too dependent on headquarters for new product development.

Headquarters is unresponsive to the subsidiaries' requests for product modifications.

New products are developed centrally and are not geared to the specific needs of the local market.

Domestic operations have priority in product and resource allocation; subsidiaries rank second.

source: Ulrich E. Wiechmann and Lewis G. Pringle, "Problems That Plague Multinational Marketers," *Harvard Business Review* 57 (July–August 1979). Copyright © 1979 by the President & Fellows of Harvard College; all rights reserved.

441

or mix adaptation. The choices available can be illustrated by the five alternative strategies for product features and communications approaches summarized in Table 18–1.[8]

Strategy One: One Product, One Message—Worldwide

The easiest and most profitable strategy is that of product and communications extension. The same product or service is sold worldwide using the same sales message. International cosmetics firms sell the same products worldwide and use the same advertising and promotional appeals that are used in their central markets. They find little variation from country to country in target consumer groups, product usage patterns, and consumer attitudes. As one executive explained:

> A woman is a woman is a woman,
> irrespective of where she lives. . . .
> Even in Japan we use the same copy,
> with American models and English words.[9]

The "product-communications extension" strategy has great appeal to most international companies because of the enormous cost savings associated with this approach. Important among these are the substantial economies resulting from the standardization of marketing communications. The cost of designing print and video films for each market covered by a worldwide operation is extremely high.

This strategy is widely used in marketing advanced-technology producer goods. As Holton has noted, "The world of advanced technology is more nearly a single world than is the world of consumer goods."[10] A firm selling equipment to commercial television stations, for example, normally does not find specifications varying as much across markets as is likely to occur in the case of consumer goods. Even in the less developed countries, the technological specifications for producers goods generally follow those developed in the advanced countries.

Unfortunately, the product communications extension strategy does not work for all products. When Campbell Soup, for example, tried to sell its U.S. tomato soup formulation to the British, it discovered after considerable losses that the English prefer a more bitter taste.

---

[8] This section is based largely on Warren J. Keegan, "Multinational Product Planning: Strategic Alternatives," *Journal of Marketing*, January 1969, pp. 58–62.

[9] Ulrich Wiechmann, "Integrating Multinational Marketing Activities," *Columbia Journal of World Business*, Winter 1974, p. 12.

[10] Richard H. Holton, "Marketing Policies in Multinational Corporations," *Journal of International Business Studies*, Summer 1970, p. 18.

TABLE 18-1 Multinational Product Communications Mix: Strategic Alternatives

Strat-egy	Product Function or Need Satisfied	Conditions of Product Use	Ability to Buy Product	Recommended Product Strategy	Recommended Communications Strategy	Relative Cost of Adjustments	Product Examples
1	Same	Same	Yes	Extension	Extension	1	Soft drinks
2	Different	Same	Yes	Extension	Adaptation	2	Bicycles, motorscooters
3	Same	Different	Yes	Adaptation	Extension	3	Gasoline, detergents
4	Different	Different	Yes	Adaptation	Adaptation	4	Clothing, greeting cards
5	Same	—	No	Invention	New design	5	Motor vehicles

SOURCE: Warren J. Keegan, "Multinational Product Planning, Strategic Alternatives," *Journal of Marketing*, January 1969, p. 59.

Strategy Two: Product Extension— Communications Adaptation

When a product or service fills a different need or serves a different function under use conditions identical with or similar to those in the central market, the only adjustment required is in marketing communications. Bicycles, for example, satisfy needs mainly for recreation in the United States but provide basic transportation in countries like India. The appeal of the "product extension-communications adaptation" strategy is that savings in manufacturing, research and development, and inventory costs can still result. The only additional costs are in identifying the different functions the firm's offering will service in foreign markets and in reformulating advertising, sales promotion, and other dimensions of market communications around the newly identified functions.

Strategy Three: Product Adaptation— Communications Extension

A third international product strategy is to extend without change the basic communications strategy developed for the central market but to adapt the product to different use conditions. The "product adaptation-communications extension" strategy assumes that the product will serve the same function in foreign markets under different use conditions. McDonald's followed this approach when it adapted the physical characteristics of its hamburgers to the different taste and user conditions of different countries while continuing to advertise on a standard basis the invitation to join Ronald McDonald under the golden arch. International companies in the soap and detergent fields have adjusted their product formulation to meet local water conditions and the characteristics of local washing machines, with no change in the companies' basic communications approach. Firms selling chemicals to the construction industry internationally have done likewise because cement characteristics vary from country to country.

Strategy Four: Dual Adaptation

Strategy four is to adapt both the product and the communications approach when differences exist in environmental conditions of use and in the needs that are filled. In essence, this is a combination of strategies two and three. U.S. greeting-card companies have faced these circumstances in Europe, where the occasions for using greeting cards differ from those in the United States. Also, in Europe the function of a greeting card has been to provide a space for the sender to write a special message, in contrast to the U.S. situation, where cards usually contain prepared messages. Even with dual adaptation, though, all the benefits of standardization may not be lost. Many basic attributes may remain constant, bringing economies of scale in the functions concerned with those attributes.

Strategy Five: Product Invention

A final strategy is that of product invention. When potential customers cannot afford one of the firm's products or services, an opportunity may exist to invent or design an entirely new offering that satisfies the identified need at a price that the consumer can afford. If product-development costs are not excessive, this may be a potentially rewarding product strategy for the mass markets in the LDCs.

The choice among these five product and communications strategies in international marketing is a function of three key factors:

1. The need the product or service is intended to meet in a particular market.
2. The market conditions under which the product or service is used, including customer preferences and their ability to buy the product in question.
3. The competitive position of a company and its relative costs of adaptation and manufacture or delivery.

Only through analysis of the product-market fit, and the company's capabilities and costs, will the most profitable international product strategy be identified.

INTERNATIONAL MARKETING RESEARCH

National forecasts of aggregate demand, the subject of Chapter 10, are often a starting point for international marketing research. But much more detailed market data are usually needed. National aggregates can hide major sectoral differences. Potential demand, for example, can vary dramatically between agricultural and industrialized sectors and between urban and rural districts. There are also major regional disparities in the United States. California is not Appalachia. Italy divides into an industrialized north and a backward Messogiorno. Global strategy might thus be developed with greater precision and a changed emphasis if subnational data are available. In fact, for marketing decisions that have a locational element, such as advertising allocation or retail location, almost no unit of analysis is too small.

The smaller the size of the basic geographical unit for which statistics are published, the more precisely can market segments be targeted. But homogeneity within these basic units may be even more important than size.[11] In the United Kingdom, for example, few statistics are published for smaller areas than the 11 U.K. standard regions that themselves are not usably homogeneous units. They each contain a mixture of urban and rural areas and industry and agriculture.

Published statistics, however, will seldom fulfill all international marketing

---

[11] W. N. Barnes, "International Marketing Indicators," *European Journal of Marketing* 14, no. 2 (1980), p. 98.

needs. Decisions to adjust elements of the marketing mix to suit individual markets ideally require factual information about customer motivation, attitudes, and usage of the product or service, and local market and distribution conditions. As Mayer has pointed out, "Most major multinational marketing failures result from neglecting to recognize that a specific product can be viewed completely differently in different cultures."[12]

The Research Task

When undertaking the costly task of collecting detailed consumer data, the international market researcher must specify carefully and with discrimination the questions to be answered. The questions listed in Figure 18–2, although originally designed for decisions on international advertising, may also be used for decisions on the standardization of other marketing variables. The questions attempt to uncover national similarities. If sufficient similarity is discovered, there is a case for standardized marketing; otherwise, local adjustment is required.

The aim of international market research should not be to identify national stereotypes of persons or behavior in purchasing a particular product or service. National stereotyping not only tends to emphasize differences rather than similarities between countries but also tends to minimize the importance of differences in behavior patterns within a country.[13] National stereotypes are not very useful for international marketers who are looking for segment similarities that permit some standardization across national boundaries. Much cross-national market research, therefore, should be designed to identify customer subgroups in different countries that have similar behavior patterns.[14]

Deciding whether adequate customer similarity exists is a difficult problem in multinational market research. Representative cross-country samples of national and subnational populations are difficult to design. Careful design of research aimed at determining the similarity of potential buyers will include more nonusers in the samples for countries with low penetration. Nonusers, however, may find it very difficult to provide any reasonable assessment of their likelihood of purchasing a product that they may not even have considered. Opinions about product features might be equally suspect.

Sample sizes may also have to be limited by cost factors. Where sample sizes are limited, the researcher may be left with something that could only be validly titled "a comparison of a small sample of New York housewives with a small sample of Parisian housewives." To draw conclusions from such a limited

---

[12] Charles S. Mayer, "The Lessons of Multinational Marketing Research," *Business Horizons,* December 1978, p. 8.

[13] Susan P. Douglas, "Cross-National Comparisons and Consumer Stereotypes: A Case Study of Working and Non-working Wives in the U.S. and France," *Journal of Consumer Research* 3 (June 1976), pp. 12–20.

[14] For an attempt to do just this see Helmut Becker, "Is There a Cosmopolitan Information Seeker," *Journal of International Business Studies* 7 (Spring 1976), pp. 77–89.

FIGURE 18–2   Basic Market Research Questions for Determining International Marketing Standardization

Consumption Patterns

Pattern of purchase:
1. Is the product or service purchased by relatively the same consumer income group?
2. Do the same family members motivate the purchase?
3. Do the same family members dictate brand choice?
4. Do most consumers expect a product to have the same appearance?
5. Is the purchase rate the same?
6. Are most purchases made at the same kind of retail outlet?
7. Do most consumers spend the same amount of time making the purchase?

Pattern of Usage:
8. Do most consumers use the product or service for the same purpose or purposes?
9. Is the usage rate or quantity of usage the same?
10. Is the method of preparation the same?
11. Are the products or services used in conjunction similar?

Psychosocial Characteristics

Attitudes toward the product or service:
1. Are the basic psychological, social, and economic factors motivating purchase and use the same?
2. Are the advantages and disadvantages of the product or service in the minds of consumers basically the same?
3. Is the symbolic content of the product or service the same?
4. Is the psychic cost of purchasing or using the product or service the same?
5. Is the appeal of the product or service the same for a cosmopolitan sector?

Attitudes towards the brand:
6. Is the brand name equally known and accepted?
7. Are customer attitudes toward the package basically the same?
8. Are customer attitudes toward pricing basically the same?
9. Is brand loyalty the same?
10. Will images from past advertising conflict with a standardized approach?
11. Are the media suitable for a standardized advertising approach?

Cultural Criteria

1. Does society restrict the purchase or use of the product or service to particular sex, age, religious, or educated groups?
2. Is there a stigma attached to the product or service, brand name, advertising content, or artwork?
3. Does usage of the product or service suggested by advertising interfere with tradition in any country?

SOURCE: Adapted from Stewart Henderson Britt, "Standardizing Marketing for the International Market," *Columbia Journal of World Business* 9 (Winter 1974), pp. 39–45.

study as to basic similarities or differences between U.S. and French consumers would be both presumptuous and dangerous.[15]

Linguistic and conceptual differences can create distortions, even with the use of the same questionnaire and with careful translation and back-translation. Differences can occur in the administration of the questionnaires. Thus, the reliabil-

---

[15] Jean J. Boddewyn, "Comparative Marketing: The First Twenty-five Years," *Journal of International Business Studies*, Spring–Summer 1981, p. 67.

ity of findings may vary as between samples, and the power of the usual tests of statistical significance may be greatly reduced. Consequently, international marketers must be ever sensitive to reliability variations and the need to make appropriate adjustments before accepting cross-national sample readings as indicators of real similarities or differences.[16] Even where customer differences rather than similarities are identified, such differences may simply reflect country differences in product availability or in distribution channels rather than differences in underlying attitudes or preferences.

Not all international market research should be aimed at establishing similarity or differences between market or segment averages. For products or services at different stages of diffusion in different markets, the research should attempt to identify the characteristics and buying motivations of the next tranche of buyers within each market, whether they be innovators, opinion leaders, laggards, or whatever.[17] The marketing mix for a market where diffusion is almost complete and potential buyers have long been familiar with the product concept cannot be effectively transferred into a market in which no one is familiar with the product concept. Pricing, for example, would probably have to be higher in the new market to allow for adequate advertising expense to build demand and still leave adequate profit margins for the outlets during the low volume stages of market buildup. The special value of this type of research is that it recognizes that markets are not static and that researchers need to be aware of the dynamics of cultural change as discussed in Chapter 17.

Data Collection

In many countries, market researchers may have to collect their own primary data because what they need is not available from existing sources. This task has many pitfalls in foreign countries.[18]

To begin with, large segments of many foreign populations are virtually unreachable for marketing research purposes. Culture patterns may proscribe the interviewing of women, even by women interviewers. Or women may be extremely reluctant to discuss details of family purchasing. Males, too, may be reticent in replying to questioners or questionnaires. They may fear that information they give may be turned against the giver, or they may feel that it is undignified to discuss details of personal preferences in such things as food, clothing, toiletries, or household goods.

---

[16] Harry L. Davis, Susan P. Douglas, and Alvin J. Silk, "Measure Unreliability: A Hidden Threat to Cross-National Marketing Research," *Journal of Marketing* 45 (Spring 1981), pp. 98–109.

[17] Stephen C. Cosmas and Jagdish N. Sheth, "Identification of Opinion Leaders Across Cultures: An Assessment for Use in the Diffusion of Innovations and Ideas," *Journal of International Business Studies* 11 (Spring–Summer 1980), pp. 66–73.

[18] For a fuller development, see Philip R. Cateora, *International Marketing*, 6th ed. (Homewood, Ill.: Richard D. Irwin, 1987), chap. 11.

Even where there is no such reticence, locating the potential consumers may be difficult. Many areas have no telephone books, no address lists, few telephones, and inadequate postal systems. These limitations severely hamper the design and administration of a sample survey. Even where these media are available, comparative research that relied on telephone ownership might, for example, end up sampling the top 6 percent in one country against 60 percent in another country. Where the literacy rate is low or where dialects are spoken, written questionnaires can also eliminate many possible purchasers. Even where respondents are reached, the surveys may not be directed to the actual decision makers in the family. In countries where husbands make more decisions, a research design aimed at wives would automatically build in a bias.[19]

INTERNATIONAL ADVERTISING

Should advertising themes and advertisements be uniform internationally or developed specifically for individual national markets? Increasingly, advertising experts have been accepting the view that the advertising task is essentially the same in most markets—namely, to communicate information and persuasive appeals effectively. Therefore, the same approach to communication can be used in every country, but the specific advertising messages and media strategy may have to vary from country to country.[20]

Any component making up an advertisement—the words used, the symbols, the illustrations, and so on—may have to be changed. While the nature and motives of people are more or less universal, the ways in which they satisfy their needs are not. Cultural and socioeconomic differences play an important part in shaping the demand for specific goods and services and in determining what promotional appeals are best. The age of a product user depicted in an illustration might appear just right in one culture yet young and immature in another. The overall message that an advertisement conveys might also be changed for different cultures (see Box 18–1). The product image that would most influence purchasing will differ in many ways from country to country. Finally, media characteristics vary from country to country.

Good advertising built specifically for a given culture will usually be superior to that imported from abroad. For this reason, there is an initial bias in favor of separate advertising in each country. Good advertising campaigns, however, are expensive to produce. When they have proved effective in one culture, it seems worthwhile testing them in others before starting at the beginning again to develop

---

[19] Robert T. Green and Isabella C. M. Cunningham, "Family Purchasing Roles in Two Countries," *Journal of International Business Studies* 11 (Spring–Summer 1980), pp. 92–97.

[20] See Gordon E. Miracle, "International Advertising Principles and Strategies," *MSU Business Topics,* Autumn 1968, pp. 29–36; and Jacob Hornik, "Comparative Evaluation of International vs. National Advertising Strategies," *Columbia Journal of World Business,* Spring 1980, pp. 36–46.

BOX 18–1
Tokyo Trauma or an American Advertising Man in Japan

The Japanese are different. Ambiguity floats like a fine mist around all but the most intimate relationships. Little wonder, then, that marketing and advertising men, "professional communicators," unravel sooner than most other foreigners in such an alien atmosphere.

The first copy review session can be a shattering experience. You struggle in vain to get your mind around the English translation of the headline for your new product launch: "Set your gaze toward the morning horizon with a refreshed heart." And the illustration: A cowboy, one foot in the stirrup, stares dreamily out across Marlboroland. You remonstrate.

"But we're selling electric shavers, for Godsakes. Where's the product?" (In the saddle bag.) "And why a cowboy?" (John Wayne, Clint Eastwood—big box office in Japan.) "And what's all this twaddle about horizons and what kind of hearts?" (Refreshed.) "Yeh, well, we're a long way from where we ought to be."

All you ever learned about product positioning, marketing strategy, and consumer psychology convinces you that inscrutability never moved any product off the shelf. You want to believe, to leave it up to them. But how do you explain it all to headquarters? Unless you have some notion yourself of how the Japanese communicate, you haven't a prayer.

SOURCE: Adapted from *Advertising Age,* May 20, 1974.

separate campaigns for each culture. As the head of a Swedish advertising agency said years ago, "Why should three artists in three different countries sit drawing the same electric iron and three copywriters write about what after all is largely the same copy for the same iron?"[21] The economic arguments for using a standard appeal in international media are great, particularly in new markets that do not warrant the cost involved in developing entirely new material.

In developing a standard appeal to fit different markets from the outset, the compromise sought is that which will maximize total sales across markets. The model used by Ford of Europe to decide on a common European campaign when launching the Ford Granada is a good example of how such an optimum might be identified.[22] A complex model was used that developed data by country on buyers' preferences, after different levels of exposure to advertising, for the attributes of Ford's product against those of its competitors. With this data it was possible to simulate buying preferences between competing products in each

---

[21] Eric Elinder, "International Advertisers Must Devise Universal Ads: Dump Separate National Ones, Swedish Adman Avers," *Advertising Age,* November 27, 1961, p. 91.

[22] Michael Colvin, Roger Heeler, and Jim Thorpe, "Developing International Advertising Strategy," *Journal of Marketing* 44 (Fall 1980), pp. 73–79.

country and then estimate how total sales will be affected by heavy exposure advertising of selected attributes.

There have been numerous successful attempts to carry one message internationally. But even where the basic advertising approach is feasible, the advertiser must choose with care the symbols used in advertisement for a market. Colors as one form of visual symbol may have a different significance in one culture as compared to another. In China, yellow has always been the imperial color and is not used extensively except for religious purposes. In many countries, to illustrate women in power roles working closely with men even incidentally may raise antagonism from both men and women. Illustrations for the same product may have to differ from country to country. In Germany, an advertisement for cheese might show a large, foaming glass of beer, but in France, the advertisement would substitute a glass of red wine.

Another important consideration in international advertising is the national and supranational image of the product. Nations hold stereotyped impressions of the products of other nations, and the ratings by different nationalities of a nation's product, on a variety of attribute scales, will differ significantly.[23] These differences, moreover, show even when respondents have not purchased a nation's products. They are widely believed to influence purchasing,[24] can vary among purchasing agents of different nationalities employed in the same multinational purchasing unit,[25] and change over time. Many advertising campaigns directly or indirectly emphasize the "nationality" of products or services, so awareness of the implied stereotype is important. Japanese manufacturers in the United States have moved their advertising emphasis over time from themes that emphasized Japanese performance and origin to themes that emphasize the worldwide marketing performance.[26] A message such as "Number One Worldwide" is clearly contributing to a supranational image that may have a payoff superior to even a highly positive national image. It is possible, moreover, that both national and supranational images could be successfully combined in the one message.

In the area of media selection, considerable deviation from home-country patterns may be required, particularly for U.S. companies. In many countries, ownership of radio and television media is in the hands of the government and no commercials are allowed. Radio is also barred to advertisers in much of

---

[23] Akira Nagashima, "A Comparative Made in Product Image Survey among Japanese Businessmen," *Journal of Marketing* 41 (July 1977), pp. 95–100; see also Chem L. Narayana, "Aggregate Images of American and Japanese Products: Implications on International Marketing," *Columbia Journal of World Business* 16 (Summer 1981), pp. 31–35.

[24] T. V. Greer, "British Purchasing Agents and the European Economic Community," *Journal of Purchasing* 7 (1971), pp. 56–63.

[25] Brian Toyne, "Procurement-Related Perceptions of Corporate-Based and Foreign-Based Purchasing Managers," *Journal of International Business Studies* 9 (Winter 1978), pp. 39–54.

[26] Norihiko Suzuki, "The Changing Pattern of Advertising Strategy by Japanese Business Firms in the U.S. Market: Content Analysis," *Journal of International Business Studies* 11 (Winter 1980), pp. 63–72.

Europe. Except for these media restrictions, the availability and capability of media in foreign countries are similar to those in the United States. But the coverage and relative economic cost of foreign media are different and require adaptation.

In summary, the principles underlying communication by advertising are the same in all nations; but the specific methods, techniques, and symbols sometimes must be varied to take account of diverse environmental conditions. Uniform advertising for various market segments, whether national or international, has tremendous economic advantages for the firm. The critical questions for the multinational firm are *when* and *when not* to make adjustments. The best strategy is to try to take into account the international differences when preparing an advertising campaign and to export the same advertising approach to as many different markets as possible. But final decisions on copy or media should be handled by personnel who have intimate knowledge of foreign markets.

INTERNATIONAL PRICING

Price is only one of many variables in the marketing mix requiring careful consideration and monitoring. Yet it is the variable that normally produces the most direct and most rapid change in customer value and competitive impact. Hence the selection of price relative to competition is important and justifiably highlighted.

Pricing decisions must take into account the interests of many factions within the multinational enterprise frequently with conflicting price objectives.[27] The director of international marketing and the managers of foreign subsidiaries seek prices that will be competitive in the marketplace. But the managers of the divisions that produce and supply products or components to other divisions for merchandising will be pressing for prices that maximize the profits of their own division. The tax manager is concerned with the implications of pricing decisions on the total tax liability of the corporation, tax deferral opportunities, and government regulations on transfer pricing. With these and other sectors of the enterprise crucially affected by pricing decisions, top management invariably assumes substantial responsibility for formulating pricing policies and strategies. The implementation of these policies, however, may be widely diffused throughout the organization.[28] Inevitably, transfer pricing will be a contentious issue and the rules adopted will shape market performance. This issue, however, will be left until Chapters 22 and 23, and the attention here will be on appropriate market prices.

---

[27] *Solving International Pricing Problems* (New York: Business International, 1965).

[28] For an example of how the responsibility for pricing is distributed among the various units of an international company in the pharmaceuticals and chemicals field, see Enid Baird Lovell, *The Changing Role of the International Executive* (New York: National Industrial Conference Board, 1966), p. 52.

The need for price decisions differs for different types of goods and from market to market. In the case of standardized or relatively undifferentiated products, the market sets the price and the seller has little control over the level of prices. The same will be true of situations where government price controls prevail or prices are fixed through patent-licensing agreements. But for differentiated products selling in nonregulated markets, the producer has genuine alternatives in setting prices. And much international business activity is based on differentiated products and oligopoly elements.

In setting its pricing policies, the company has two basic choices. It may use prices as an active instrument for accomplishing market objectives. Or it may consider prices as a static element in business decisions. American companies generally regard price as an important variable in their marketing decisions. Japanese companies are probably even more aggressive in pricing and often use low pricing strategies. Their newly established foreign subsidiaries generally have sales growth as their prime target. And low-price strategies are used to achieve their sales goals, assuming that profits will come in due course.[29] Their strategy is similar to that advocated by some consulting firms that advise companies to set market share as the objective in the early stages of a product life cycle.[30] Profits are then expected to come from later market share leadership when the demand has grown and stabilized.

In using pricing as part of the strategic product mix, the international company will develop a pricing system and pricing policies that recognize the diversity of national markets in three basic dimensions—cost, competition, and demand. For any individual country market there is an optimum price, usually above the cost of sourcing the product, which is a function of the local demand curve for the product and its cost. Pricing, however, will have to be consistent with a number of international constraints such as dumping legislation, resale price-maintenance legislation, and governmental price controls where they exist. Another constraint may be multinational customers who demand equal price treatment regardless of location.

Firms must decide whether they are going to use marginal costs or full costs in calculating the payoff from alternative pricing decisions. The logic for using marginal or incremental costs may be that foreign sales are incidental to a company's main operations and any returns over the marginal costs are a bonus contribution to net profit, or that the firm has to price more competitively to enter a foreign market or to meet local competition. But companies selling products in foreign markets at lower prices than in domestic markets are subject to charges of "dumping," which may subject the company to antidumping tariffs or penalties.

---

[29] William K. Brandt and James M. Hulbert, "Marketing Strategies of American, European and Japanese Multinational Subsidiaries," (Paper presented at the Academy of International Business Meetings, Fontainebleau, France, July 7–9, 1975).

[30] Boston Consulting Group, *Perspectives on Experience* (Boston: Boston Consulting Group, 1968), chap. 13.

The firmly established global enterprise is more likely to measure results from individual markets after meeting full costs. The determination of full costs is again not a clear-cut matter. How much of general administrative, research and development costs, and other overhead items should be included in intracorporate transfer prices? What share of marketing, sales, and advertising costs incurred in the domestic market, but that generate marketing approaches that can be extended abroad, should be included in the cost to foreign subsidiaries? Where capital is tied up for longer periods because of the time lags inherent in international transactions, and where foreign exchange risks are involved, how should these financing and risk costs be incorporated into the pricing decisions? And innumerable other cost uncertainties exist, depending on the market, the product, and the situation.

A cost-plus pricing strategy has the advantage of simplicity as information on competitive or market conditions is not required for its implementation. It is widely used for export pricing and can be designed with some flexibility for adjusting the markup over costs to fit different market conditions. But it has the serious disadvantage that it is not directed toward maximizing the company's sales and revenues or profits in each national market.

Without ignoring the realities of cost, a market-pricing strategy gives principal emphasis to the demand and supply conditions of each market and the state of competition. The example in the appendix to this chapter shows how different demand elasticities in different markets can result in advantages from different price policies for subsidiaries in each market. Through the separate adjustment of prices for each market, a greater profit can be achieved for the total system than by any choice of a common price for both markets. A common, final price policy, however, may be necessary in order to minimize country-to-country arbitrage by intermediaries who are not controlled by the international firm and who can purchase in one market and sell in another.

A powerful argument that U.S. multinational firms have tended to restrict their worldwide performance through overpricing in LDCs has been propounded by Leff.[31] He argues that marketing practices in LDCs have been adopted with the U.S. bias toward nonprice forms of competition. Faced with low levels of per capita income and small sales levels in LDCs, marketing executives have tried to enlarge their sales with advertising and promotion, unaware of the highly price-elastic nature of market demand at low prices. While individual families might not buy more at low prices—that is, household demand is inelastic—at a low enough price many more families become able to purchase. If firms planned from the outset for large production runs and low merchandising support they could adopt a penetration rather than a skimming strategy. They would make goods that are mass-consumption goods in developed countries also mass-consumption goods in less-developed areas. Too often they now position goods in the luxury or semiluxury class in LDCs.

---

[31] Nathaniel H. Leff, "Multinational Corporate Pricing Strategy in the Developing Countries," *Journal of International Business Studies* 6 (Fall 1975), pp. 55–64.

INTERNATIONAL CHANNEL MANAGEMENT

In the marketing literature dealing with the choice of distribution channels, the message is clear that the distribution product mix for reaching consumers must be carefully selected against an assessment of merchandising needs, the longer-term strategy for the product line and characteristics of the channels that are available or can be built.[32] Channels cannot be changed frequently, and moves are usually not reversible. Alternatives foregone may not remain open, and outlets that have been dropped in the past may not be again willing to carry the line.

International channel management is intimately related to many other dimensions of marketing management and global strategy. If the best strategy for entering a given market appears to be through licensing, the primary responsibility for developing and managing distribution channels becomes that of the licensee. Likewise, if the indicated strategy is to serve a market through exports, the channel decision may be a choice among exporting indirectly through export merchants or middlemen, exporting directly to an importer in the market area, or establishing overseas sales branches, subsidiaries, or foreign warehouse facilities.[33] If the entry strategy is through foreign production as a joint venture or wholly owned subsidiary, then the channel management problem is largely a domestic business question.

No matter what the initial entry strategy, the choice of channels must be evaluated against the longer-range goals as well as the immediate goals of the company in the specific market. Will the channels be sufficiently effective to develop the scale of sales in the country that will permit the company to move at a later stage to local production? Or will the channels be a barrier to the expansion of direct selling activities in the area when such a channel strategy becomes economic and desirable? Or will the channels be an efficient transmitter of information to the producer that will help it to match its product policies to changing consumer demands?

As a first step after identifying attractive markets and their potentials, the marketing manager should specify the functions that the channel system is expected to accomplish.[34] These functions will be determined both by the nature of the product mix and by the characteristics of the markets. Necessary functions that must often be performed by the channels of distribution are the carrying of an adequate inventory in order to stimulate sales, the provision of consumer financing, and after-sales service and repairs.

The next step is to understand the channel alternatives available and the

---

[32] For a good survey of literature on distribution channels, see L. W. Stern and A. I. El-Ansary, *Marketing Channels* (Englewood Cliffs, N.J.: Prentice-Hall, 1977).

[33] See Franklin R. Root, *Strategic Planning for Export Marketing* (Scranton, Pa.: International Textbook, 1964), pp. 72–88.

[34] For more detailed discussions of international channel management, see Warren J. Keegan, *Multinational Marketing Management*, 3rd ed. (Englewood Cliffs, N.J.: Prentice-Hall, 1984), pp. 373–94.

BOX 18–2
Japan: A Nation of Wholesalers

Japan has more shops and wholesalers per head of population than any other big industrial nation. Productivity per worker in Japanese distribution is very low, while in Japanese manufacturing it is very high. This has annoying consequences for foreign countries.

Japanese goods sometimes sell more cheaply in suburban London than in suburban Tokyo. This is not because of Japanese dumping. The goods leave efficient Japanese factories at the same price for abroad or for home. They then suffer a bigger markup while traveling a few miles down Japan's convoluted distribution system than they do while crossing half the world and reaching British shops through Britain's efficient distribution system. Meanwhile goods leaving less-efficient British factories can cost four times as much in Tokyo as in London because they have to pass through Japan's inefficient distribution system on the way.

There are almost as many retail outlets and wholesalers in Japan as in twice-as-populous America. Despite the explosion of supermarkets in the past decade, by 1979 60 percent of Japanese retail outlets still employed no more than two people and 45 percent of wholesalers employed four people or less. The Japanese are as sentimental about their tiny shops as the French are about their peasants and the British about their old industries. Small Japanese shops are the centers of village neighborhoods in big cities. The survival of small stores has kept the wholesalers who supply them in business.

New tastes and fads, and the ease with which wholesalers can start peddling goods on a small scale, have brought nearly 50,000 new wholesalers into business since 1975, 80 percent of them with a capital of less than $40,000. This suggests that Japan's multitude of wholesalers survive because people want their services, rather than as crusty remnants from the past.

How do foreign firms find a way in? Successes and failures of foreign products in weaving through the distribution system are repeated like parables in Japan. Traders who have given up hope of finding competitive inlets generally say the best policy is to secure a Japanese partner with a powerful, established place in the distribution system.

SOURCE: Adapted from *The Economist*, September 19, 1981.

---

characteristics of the institutions in their particular environment (see Box 18–2). In most areas the distribution system is in process of change, and the selection of channels must take into account the process of change. Retailers and wholesalers are middlemen, not only in the flow of goods, but also in the whole process of satisfying the material needs and desires of a society. Consequently, their effectiveness will be largely determined by the changing environment in which they stand.[35]

---

[35] Understanding of the forces leading to change in channel structure is still in its infancy. For a challenging survey see Louis W. Stern and Torger Reve, "Distribution Channels as Political Economies: A Framework for Comparative Analysis," *Journal of Marketing* 44 (Summer 1980), pp. 52–64.

The key elements in decisions as to a distribution system are (1) the availability of middlemen, (2) the ability and effectiveness of the alternatives in performing the necessary functions, (3) the cost of their services, and (4) the extent of control that the multinational enterprise can exert over the middlemen's activities. The multinational is searching for the system that will provide the optimum pattern of function, cost, and control. Variations among nations, however, may indicate different solutions to channel distribution needs for various market areas.

The broad alternatives available for exporting are the manufacturer's own sales and distribution network, agent middlemen, or merchant middlemen. In general, the manufacturer retains most control over subsequent marketing decisions the further it can justify extending its own distribution system down the international chain of distribution. The scale of operations, however, may not justify the firm's extending its own system right up to the point at which final consumers buy, or even building a system to cover any stages at all. At some point in the international distribution chain it is, therefore, usual to turn to agents or merchant middlemen. Merchants purchase for their own account and bear the majority of the trading risks for the products handled. Agents do not take title to the merchandise but work on a commission basis. The firm therefore retains more control over prices and other aspects of the distribution function through agents. But this control does not extend more than one further stage in the chain as agents invariably sell to merchants at the next stage.

Middlemen tend to avoid expenditure on developing product brands and instead devote their resources to the sales of those brands or items that sell without merchandising effort. This tendency puts small firms with unestablished products in double jeopardy. To establish their product, they may have to opt for the more costly direct sales approach at the time they can least afford it. It is not uncommon for firms to move from a direct approach adopted at the beginning of international expansion to later use of outside middlemen after the demand has been established. A halfway approach that is less expensive initially is to reimburse or subsidize middlemen for promotion expenditure or the time of their sales force spent on selling the product.

A diagram in Figure 18–3 shows the potential stages in the international distribution chain to which the manufacturer may extend its own network in reaching toward the eventual foreign consumer. At the very extreme, it might operate its own retail stores, mail order operation, or even door-to-door sales force. It is possible, too, for the firm to use agents at intermediate stages and then enter back into the chain at a later stage. A firm whose sales depend heavily on consumer promotion might employ distributors as agents to export, to store, and to distribute goods while it operates its own sales force to foreign retailers.

The further down the distribution chain the manufacturer retains its own system, the more technical exporting and international marketing expertise is required. If the manufacturer turns to home-country middlemen, it is adopting indirect exporting. Foreign sales are handled in essentially the same way as domestic sales, and a minimum of international marketing know-how is required by the firm. For U.S. firms, the indirect approach generally means that the enterprise is small and that its international commitment and potential is limited. For a

FIGURE 18–3 Potential Stages of Entry into the External International Distribution Chain

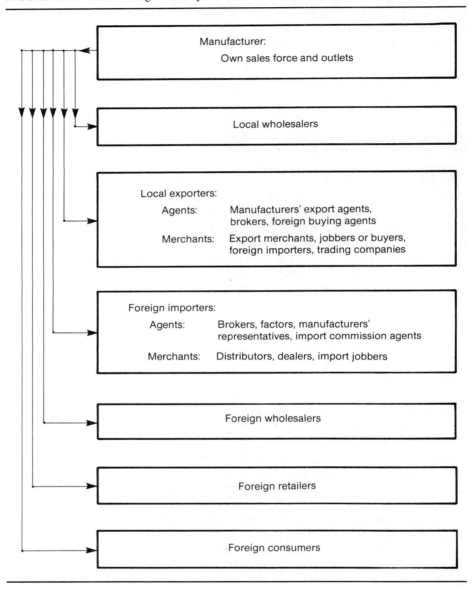

Japanese company, on the other hand, the use of the indirect approach may be explained by the availability of large and experienced international trading firms that have a significant comparative advantage in foreign selling even over direct operations by large enterprises. In direct exporting, the firm retains the complete responsibility for identifying markets, physical distribution, export documentation, pricing, and so on.

Within the foreign country, the wholesale distribution function can be handled by foreign importers, by the companies own overseas facilities, or by independent wholesalers. A wholesaler is a middleman who sells to retailers or industrial users and whose chief functions are negotiating for the buyer, buying, selling, and storing. Wholesalers may also offer other services such as financing or servicing.

In the LDCs, because a large share of industrial goods is imported and the volume of any one item may be small, the distribution of industrial goods is generally handled by importers who deal in a wide range of products in order to generate enough sales to support their operations. The smaller the market, the wider the range of products the wholesaler must carry. This feature reduces the choice of alternatives and frequently means that a wholesaler handles goods of several competing firms in the same field.

The retail distribution systems vary greatly among countries in the size of distribution units, in the services they perform, and in the assortment of goods they handle (see Box 18–2). In many LDCs, for example, retail distribution is characterized by large numbers of little shops with small capital investments, much imitation, low turnovers, high margins, and high mortality.

In summary, international channel management requires the design of a structure of distribution units that will perform the physical distribution task, provide service and other functions, and provide an effective transmission system for returning necessary market information to the company. The alternatives vary tremendously with the environment and are in a process of change around the world. Starting from its market targets and an understanding of the functions that the distribution system must perform for each product or group of products, the marketing manager must design a system that not only serves present needs but also has a flexibility to permit changes in the channel structure over time.

How is the international channel-management responsibility shared between headquarters and the subsidiaries in a multinational company? Obviously, in the case of foreign production, the responsibility must be highly decentralized. But headquarters has a role in monitoring and transferring experience from one area to another. Some of the experience also may indicate changes that should be made in the product mix in order to permit distribution channels to be more effective. Where distribution channels are having difficulty in providing postsales service, for example, product redesigns that reduce or simplify the service requirement add to the effectiveness of the available channels.

The need to develop working relationships with outside channels in a different cultural background presents further problems in the international firm. Particular concepts will often not be directly translatable, and the approach to market assessment is likely to have many cultural biases. One way of overcoming some of the problems is to develop representatives with preparation in both liaison with channels and the peculiarities of particular cultures. As early as the 1960s, Caterpillar, for example, developed a range of international representatives with language and area courses and special training for aiding distributors in solving inventory, financial, and merchandising problems.

SUMMARY

The basic marketing functions involved are the same for both domestic and international markets, but the implementation can be quite different because of environmental differences. Consequently, the international firm faces many special problems in selecting its marketing mission and in adjusting its mix of marketing actions. Throughout most dimensions of the marketing function, there is a conflict between differentiation to meet the needs of market segments and international standardization to reduce costs. The conflict relates to product strategies, pricing, advertising, and the way in which the marketing activity is organized. Unfortunately, there are no general or fixed rules for resolving this conflict. The international marketing manager must therefore be constantly alert to the impact on the corporation as a whole from decisions for any unit in the multinational system.

Appendix

Table 18A–1 illustrates how different price elasticities will lead to different price policies for subsidiaries in different markets where each obtains its supplies at the same unit cost and acts to maximize its profit. At a transfer price of £50 from the supplying unit, Country A would sell at £75 and Country B at £90. An increased transfer price, however, would lead to increased prices in both countries.

Given that the selling subsidiaries are motivated to maximize their profits, they will price so that their marginal revenue just equals the marginal cost to them. The greatest system profit will then emerge if a unit is charged a transfer price equal to the cost of supplying a unit, which in most cases can be taken to be the variable cost of production and distribution. The nearer the transfer price is to this variable cost, the closer a subsidiary's pricing policy will bring the firm to maximizing its contribution over and above this variable cost. Table 18A–2 illustrates how the system profits increase as the transfer price is brought down to variable cost in this way.

Suppose now that the firm were to fix the final market price in order to maintain uniform world prices. Inevitably this would lead to a decreased system contribution because, in this case, one subsidiary or both would be forced away from an optimal adjustment to the particular situation ruling in its market. Comparing Table 18A–3 with Table 18A–2, it can be seen that no choice of a common price level for the two markets would produce a contribution for any given variable cost that is as high as that possible when the prices are adjusted separately.

TABLE 18A–1

	Market Price (in £)							
	100	*95*	*90*	*85*	*80*	*75*	*70*	*65*
Sales volume that would result:								
Country A (units)	900	1,400	2,000	2,600	3,300	4,000	4,500	5,000
Country B (units)	1,200	1,400	1,600	1,800	2,000	2,200	2,400	2,600
Total revenue:								
Country A (£000s)	90	133	180	221	264	300	315	325
Country B (£000s)	120	133	144	153	160	165	168	169
Contribution when transfer price = £50								
Country A (£000s)	45	63	80	91	99	100*	90	75
Country B (£000s)	60	63	64*	63	60	55	48	39
£60								
Country A (£000s)	36	49	60	65	66*	60	45	25
Country B (£000s)	48	49*	48	45	40	33	24	13
£70								
Country A (£000s)	27	35	40*	39	33	20	—	—
Country B (£000s)	36*	35	32	27	20	11	—	—

* Indicates greatest contribution for a given transfer price.

TABLE 18A–2

	Sales Volume to Maximize Contributions				System Contribution when Variable Cost =		
Transfer Price	Country A (units)	Country B (units)	Total Units	Total Revenue (£000s)	£40 (£000s)	£50 (£000s)	£60 (£000s)
£40	4,000	1,800	5,800	453	221*	—	—
£50	4,000	1,600	5,600	444	220	164*	—
£60	3,300	1,400	4,700	397	209	162	115*
£70	2,000	1,200	3,200	300	172	140	108

* Indicates transfer price bringing greatest contribution for a given variable cost.

TABLE 18A–3

Common Market Price (£)	Combined Volume Country A + B (units)	Contribution when Variable Cost =		
		£40 (£000s)	£50 (£000s)	£60 (£000s)
100	2,100	126	105	84
95	2,800	154	126	98
90	3,600	180	144	108
85	4,400	198	154	110*
80	5,300	212	159*	106
75	6,200	217*	154	93
70	6,900	207	138	69
65	7,600	190	114	38

* Indicates price bringing greatest contribution for a given variable cost.

EXERCISES AND DISCUSSION QUESTIONS

1. "Until we achieve One World, there is no such thing as international marketing—only local marketing around the world." Do you agree or disagree and why?

2. The food division headquarters of a U.S. multinational with subsidiaries throughout OECD countries is considering the design of a standardized range of salad dressings worldwide. Until now, it has sold salad dressings in a range of flavors mainly in the United States with a few exports. What market research data do you think they should collect?

3. "There is a movement on the part of European companies for greater standardization and guidance of marketing policies in U.S. operations, particularly in relatively low-technology, high-market-saturation product areas such as petroleum, paper, and various sorts of consumer goods." In what ways do you think the type of product influences the degree of centralization and standardization?

4. Do products sold primarily on the basis of objective physical characteristics, such as razor blades and automobile tires, lend themselves to uniform international advertising strategies more than products such as foods or clothing? If so, why?

5. Examine Tables 18A–2 and 18A–3 and explain why no choice of a common price level for the two markets will contribute as much to profits as is possible when prices are adjusted separately.

6. Why do national differences in distribution channels frequently result in gaps in market coverage?

7. In what ways does a strategy of joint ventures rather than wholly owned subsidiaries place constraints on the task of managing the international product mix?

CHAPTER 19

Export Management and
Global Logistics

As new strategy alternatives emerged over recent decades, the venerable export/import option for engaging in international business has declined in *relative* importance. Yet, in *absolute* terms exports of goods and services have expanded steadily and continue to account for a massive share of international business activity. World exports of goods have grown to a level of about $2,000 billion annually, and world trade in services is estimated to be in the range of $400–500 billion a year.[1]

    The ways in which business firms use the export/import option, however,

---

[1] Helena Stalson, *U.S. Service Exports and Foreign Barriers* (Washington D.C.; National Planning Association, 1985), p. v.

have been changing. Many final products that once were exported are now being supplied to foreign markets through foreign production. For some firms, exporting or importing still involves a simple discrete transaction between an unaffiliated buyer and seller, each located in a different country. But for many firms, the export/import option is integrated with other options, such as foreign production, into an international logistics strategy where exports and imports are movements across national boundaries but between different units of the same enterprise. Also the international sale of services, has become a major international trade activity.

This chapter examines the various circumstances under which enterprises use the export/import option. It also introduces some of the special know-how and mechanical details required for strategy implementation. As previously noted in Chapter 12, international logistics management necessarily involves adjusting to many national controls over international transfers.

THE STRATEGY DECISION

The use of the export/import option can be illustrated by six different sets of circumstances. A specific enterprise may move from one situation to another, of course, as a result of changes in its horizons, its factor costs, new national controls, and gains in international experience.

Case 1. Domestic Horizons: The Casual Exporter/Importer

Many firms operate almost exclusively with domestic horizons as to both markets and sources of raw materials and components. Particularly in a large country such as the United States, firms can achieve production economies of scale and become successful without being aware of, or interested in, foreign markets or potential foreign suppliers. Such firms will not have an export department or an international division.

If the firm experiences a temporary recession in its domestic market or a supply shortage, it might be stimulated to become a casual exporter or importer on an ad hoc basis. An external initiative from some foreign buyer or seller may also prompt the enterprise to do incidental exporting or importing. In such situations, the firm can leave the implementation to an export/import agent or a trading company. But if the casual experience is successful, it may be a first step in the internationalization of the enterprise.

Case 2. Domestic Markets: Global Sourcing

Many retailers, such as major department stores, sell in the domestic market but buy their merchandise from foreign as well as domestic suppliers. Some firms considered to be manufacturers may also have a global sourcing strategy. Nike, the U.S. producer of sport shoes, for example, secures more than 90 percent of its production by contracting with foreign suppliers, mainly in Asia.

BOX 19–1
Nike: The Trials and Tribulations of Global Sourcing

Canton, China—Philip H. Knight, Chairman of Beaverton, Oregon-based Nike, Inc., feared it wouldn't be easy when his company began contracting out shoe production in China. He was right.

One of the factories, in Tianjin, was so filthy that workers couldn't consistently turn out a clean white shoe. In desperation, the factory's Chinese manager proposed a face-saving plan: "Why don't we just make gray shoes?" he suggested. Nike moved to another Chinese plant.

"You've got to have a sense of humor if you're doing business in China," says Mr. Knight. "Otherwise you're in big trouble."

Nike's four years of experience in China illustrate the problems and benefits for foreign companies that set up export processing arrangements in foreign countries instead of full-fledged joint ventures. Despite the problems encountered, Nike's shoe production in China has doubled during the past year, and today, four Chinese factories churn out a total of 250,000 pairs of Nike-brand sports shoes a month—about 5 percent of Nike's worldwide production.

Furthermore, Nike plans to shift more manufacturing to China from South Korea and Taiwan, which make 60 percent and 17 percent, respectively, of Nike's shoes.

SOURCE: Adapted from a news story by Adi Ignatius in *The Wall Street Journal*, December 11, 1985. © Dow Jones & Company, Inc., 1985. Used with permission. All rights reserved.

Nike, however, has expanded beyond its home market and increased foreign sales to almost 20 percent of its total turnover.

A global sourcing strategy may be passive in that purchases are made from import agents and negotiations take place in home country currencies. A more aggressive strategy may be to have buyers travelling overseas seeking out sources of supply or to have purchasing offices located in foreign countries. Overseas personnel may be responsible for quality control, product design, and for supplying materials to foreign fabricators as well as for purchasing and shipping (see Box 19–1).

The implementation of a global sourcing strategy requires appropriate organizational support, global research on supply sources, and personnel experienced in many dimensions of international trade. Buyers must be familiar with foreign exchange risk, tariffs, quotas, international transportation, differences in cultural environment, and many other import issues.

Case 3. Global Markets: Domestic Production Horizon

Resource industries—mining, fisheries, forestry, petroleum, and so on—frequently have global marketing horizons; but their production location alternatives are limited to the areas where the resources exist. For still other reasons, many manufacturing firms also fall into this category. The Hong Kong exporter of apparel must produce at home where labor costs are low in order to have a competitive advantage. The Japanese exporter of automobiles for many years produced at home for world markets, initially because government controls did not permit foreign direct investments and later because of the production efficiency achieved in Japan through a mix of competitive advantages in labor costs, quality control, labor-management relations, and supplier networks. The U.S. aircraft industry is another example of home-country production and global marketing, explained mainly by the large scale of production required to achieve efficiency. In the case of both Japanese automobiles and U.S. aircraft, protectionist pressures and national local content policies have more recently forced modifications in production location strategies.

This export strategy requires manufacturing industries to develop a global product strategy and undertake global market research.[2] The firm will have the usual set of alternatives for handling its exports, ranging from an export agent or a trading company to establishing its own international or export division. In all cases, the firm has to deal with export pricing decisions. And in many instances, it has to develop a global network for supplying parts and service. Many Japanese companies began their international business activities by using the Japanese trading companies as their export department but later assumed direct marketing responsibility because the trading companies were not equipped to supply parts and service.

Case 4. Global Markets: Partial Foreign Production

Firms that produce at home and export abroad create national benefits for the home country in terms of jobs and foreign exchange earnings. Importing countries frequently would like to have a share of these national benefits and adopt import substitution policies that restrict imports and encourage local production. Firms desiring access to such foreign markets will have to locate part of their production process abroad. In some cases, local production will be only the assembly of imported components or the packaging of imported bulk materials. Local production may not be cost effective, but it becomes profitable because higher local prices can be charged as a result of tariff and/or quota protection.

In countries where imports compete with nationally owned industries, protectionist laws—or the threat of adopting protectionist measures—may cause foreign firms to establish local production operations. Japanese automobile firms began to produce cars in the United States during the 1980s while continuing to supply the U.S. market (mainly through exports from Japan). The U.S. plants still relied heavily on components produced in Japan, but the creation of jobs in the United States—and the reduced pressure on the U.S. balance of trade by having a significant amount of local content—were expected to moderate protectionist pressures.

---

[2] See Warren J. Bilkey, "Development of Export Marketing Guidelines," *International Marketing Review*, Spring 1985, pp. 31–40.

Vertically integrated enterprises using foreign natural resources may be pressed to do more local processing by national governments attempting to increase their national benefits. In the case of aluminum producers, for example, national governments have attempted with some success to have the processing of bauxite into alumina completed locally. Many oil-producing countries require that some petroleum refining be undertaken locally, whereas the integrated international enterprise would have found market locations more economically efficient for the location of refineries.

The special export/import characteristic of the partial foreign producer is that the movements across national boundaries may be largely movements between different units of the same enterprise rather than traditional exports between unaffiliated parties. One implication is that the enterprise must be organized and staffed with personnel familiar with both international trade and foreign production. The issue of distribution channels becomes of minor importance, and the setting of prices on intra-firm transactions may allow for considerable flexibility and for the strategic use of transfer pricing.

Case 5. Global Logistics

The multinational enterprise with a global strategy will normally manage the sourcing of its target markets from a centralized system perspective. Rather than determining supply sources independently for each market, the enterprise can seek to strengthen its competitive position by considering all markets simultaneously and by designing a least-cost supply strategy for the system as a whole.[3] It may rationalize its manufacturing operations by having an integrated network of plants, each specializing in one or more products or components and each serving a world or a regional market. Plants can also be specialized by stages in the production process and can be located in different countries according to location advantages.[4] Extensive transshipments of components and finished products between subsidiaries in different countries result from such a global logistics strategy.

The integration strategy can reduce unit costs in industries where economies of scale are significant and not fully exploited within the size of national markets. An example of an integrated manufacturing network on a regional basis is IBM, whose European affiliates each export a significant share of their sales to each other. But integration also has disadvantages. As one example, currency fluctuations can affect sourcing costs, and market shifts can leave existing facilities outmoded.[5]

Once each subsidiary no longer manufactures a full product line, the manage-

---

[3] See Chapter 9, "Building a Global Strategy," p. 207.

[4] Yves L. Doz, "Strategic Management in Multinational Companies, *Sloan Management Review*, Winter 1980, pp. 27–28.

[5] William H. Davidson, *Global Strategic Management* (New York: John Wiley & Sons, 1982), p. 181.

ment of export activities becomes extremely important. Export orders have to be directed to the center and then allocated to the appropriate subsidiary. Not only does the enterprise need export/import expertise, but this capability must be exercised in close harmony with the management of foreign production.

Case 6. The Reluctant Exporter/Importer

Countries with chronic foreign exchange shortages often require foreign exporters to accept local merchandise in payment either as barter or countertrade. Thus the firm becomes a reluctant importer of foreign goods to its home country or an exporter to a third country market. Where the foreign firm has an operating subsidiary in such host countries, the subsidiary may be required to earn enough foreign exchange through exports either to pay for the materials and components it imports or to provide foreign exchange for the repatriation of profits.

In one case, a multinational chemical company with an Indian subsidiary that serves the local market went into the shrimp fishing and exporting business to produce the foreign exchange needed to supply imported materials for its chemical operations. Western firms doing business with the centrally planned economies commonly must accept goods rather than currency in payment, as discussed in Chapter 14.

EXPORT OPERATIONS

The global strategy issues discussed in Chapter 9, such as choice of markets, standardization or diversification of products, competitive assessment, and market emphasis are all crucial for export operations. In addition, export operations involve special export issues such as export pricing, the mechanics of payment, import/export financing, transportation choices, and distribution strategies.

Export Pricing

In what currency should exports be priced? Should quoted prices be FOB (free on board), where the buyer assumes all costs such as insurance and freight from the seller's point of shipment, or CIF (cost, insurance, and freight), where these three cost items are covered by the seller for delivery to a foreign port? Should prices be uniform in all markets, except for differences in delivery costs, or should the seller establish different prices for different markets, as discussed in Chapter 18?

Local production by a foreign firm normally is priced in the local currency. Exported goods, however, offer options as to the currency in which the goods are priced.[6] Pricing in the home country currency permits the seller to avoid

---

[6] Vern Terpstra, *International Marketing Management*, 4th ed. (New York: The Dryden Press, 1987), pp. 528–32.

foreign exchange risk. Pricing in the currency of the foreign buyer, on the other hand, reduces the buyer's foreign exchange risk and may increase sales or be necessary to meet competition.

FOB pricing usually favors the seller, whereas CIF pricing might normally be preferred by the buyer. CIF pricing makes it easier to compare the prices of different exporters. Again, the choice will depend largely upon competitive conditions and the impact of the pricing method on sales potentials.

Where exports are movements between affiliates of the same enterprise, the choice of currencies for billing can shift the foreign exchange risk from one subsidiary to another but not eliminate it. The currency decision should, however, be coordinated with the leads and lags strategy for reducing foreign exchange exposure discussed in Chapter 23. Also the pricing of intra-firm transactions involves all of the elements that have to be considered in transfer pricing, also discussed in Chapter 23.

For enterprises with a global strategy, the pricing policy for exports will, of course, be a component of the overall pricing strategy. There are special elements, however, in the export pricing decision. Where exports can be supplied to a separate national market from existing production facilities that have unused capacity and significant economies of scale, the firm may have great latitude for marginal cost pricing.

Another consideration in export pricing is the price escalation that usually occurs before the product reaches the ultimate consumer because of such costs as transportation, custom duty, and distributor margins. In fact, there may be as many as 20 specific costs in addition to the export price from the factory, such as storage, transfer, document verification, loading, unloading, insurance, demurrage, and duty, which add greatly to the landed cost.[7] This escalation is then multiplied when the distributor's margins are based on the landed costs.[8] In price-elastic markets, price escalation may reduce demand significantly.[9]

A market-pricing strategy that establishes different prices for each market depending upon local demand and supply conditions and the state of competition can increase profits for the system, as discussed in Chapter 18. Certain constraints or hazards must be observed, however, in following a policy of separate prices for different markets. Some countries have antidumping legislation, which imposes penalties on importers if they sell at prices below those usually prevailing in the home market (see Box 19–2). Where firms have higher prices in foreign markets, so-called gray markets may flourish if buyers can have easy access to the markets with lower prices. In 1984, for example, most German auto makers did

[7] C. G. Alexandrides and George P. Moschis, *Export Marketing Management* (New York: Praeger Publishers, 1977), pp. 61–63.

[8] See Warren J. Keegan, *Multinational Marketing Management*, 3rd ed. (Englewood Cliffs, N.J.: Prentice-Hall, 1984), pp. 343–45 for an example of how a retail price in Paraguay reaches 212 percent of the FOB Kansas City price.

[9] Subhash C. Jain. *International Marketing Management* (Boston: Kent Publishing Company, 1984), pp. 398–99.

BOX 19–2
The Risk of Anti-Dumping Levies

Ottawa—Canada's Department of National Revenue, Customs and Excise ruled that XTEK Piping Systems Inc., Cincinnati, dumped wear-resistant steel pipe on the Canadian market.

The pipe is used by the mining and oil industries to move slurries and tailings. Dumping occurs when goods are sold on an export market at prices lower than those usually prevailing on their home market.

The complainant in the case is North American Speciality Pipe Ltd., a Calgary-based concern that said it was the only Canadian producer of wear-resistant pipe.

The case has been referred to the Anti-Dumping Tribunal, which will determine whether the dumping has hurt Canadian production. Pending the tribunal's ruling, provisional antidumping levies will be imposed on XTEK's wear-resistant pipe.

SOURCE: *The Wall Street Journal,* November 16, 1984. © Dow Jones & Company, Inc., 1984. Used with permission. All rights reserved.

---

not reduce their U.S. prices when the U.S. dollar reached record levels. As a result, many Americans went to Germany to buy their BMW or Mercedes-Benz at German prices and made substantial savings.

The Mechanics of Payment

Selling is one thing. Getting paid is another. Normally the terms of sale in an export transaction are a matter of prior arrangement between the buyer and the seller. Usually the collection of payment for goods sold abroad is accomplished through the international facilities of a commercial bank. The choice of payment method, or financial instrument, depends on such factors as the credit standing of the buyer (importer); the exchange restrictions, if any, that exist in the buyer's country; and the competition the seller faces.

Except for cash in advance, the export letter of credit affords the seller the highest degree of protection among all the commonly used methods of receiving payment. A letter of credit is essentially a declaration by a bank that it will make certain payments on behalf of a specified party under specified conditions. It is called a "letter" because it takes the form of a notification to the party or parties likely to be the recipients of the payments. The letter of credit usually authorizes the exporter to receive funds upon presenting to the bank the prescribed shipping documents (see Exhibit 19–1).

The principal types of documents involved in export transactions are the commercial invoice, bills of lading, and insurance certification. The invoice shows the price of the sale. The bill of lading is evidence of the merchandise being shipped. The insurance certificate is evidence of insurance coverage for the goods shipped.

EXHIBIT 19–1   Example of a Commercial Letter of Credit

BANK OF AMERICA

World Banking Division Service Center #661
Place: P.O. Box 37020, San Francisco, California 94137

Cable Address: BankAmerica   7
Date: January 15, 19XX

❶ IRREVOCABLE
❷ NEGOTIATION LETTER OF CREDIT

All drafts must be marked:
"Drawn under Bank of America
credit no. 78910"

Advising bank reference no.

Advising bank	For account of
Brazil Bank 44 Rue Primeira Rio de Janeiro, Brazil	Gourmet Food Importers Inc. 300 Main Street San Francisco, CA 94000

To beneficiary	Amount
Noz Exportador Ltda 52 Avenida Sauchiz Miranda Rio de Janeiro, Brazil	U.S. $50,000.00 (Fifty Thousand U.S. Dollars) Expiration date March 15, 19XX

Gentlemen: ☐ This refers to preliminary cable advice of this credit.
We hereby establish our irrevocable letter of credit in your favor available by your drafts drawn at Sight
on Us
and accompanied by documents specified below covering full invoice value of merchandise to be described
in invoice as: 100,000 lbs. Brazil Nuts, packed in 100 lbs. new gunnybags,
            19XX crop at U.S. $0.50 per lb. C.I.F. San Francisco.

Documents Required:
1. Commercial Invoice in duplicate.
2. Special U.S. Customs Invoice.
3. Marine & War Risk Insurance Policy or Certificate in
   duplicate.
4. Packing List.
5. Inspection Certificate issued by General Superintendence
   Co. certifying shipment of nuts free of foreign matter.
6. Sole original clean, on board, Ocean Bill of Lading, (full
   set required if more than one original has been issued) to
   order of shipper, blank endorsed, marked:

           "Notify S.F. Customs Clearing Agent, 100 Main Street
           San Francisco, CA 94116 and Freight Prepaid".

❸

SPECIMEN

Shipment from	Santos, Brazil	to	San Francisco, California

Shipment latest	March 5, 19XX	Partial shipments ☐ Permitted ☒ Not permitted	Transshipment ☐ Permitted ☒ Not permitted

Documents must be presented to the negotiating or paying bank no later than 10 days after date of shipping document
(On Board validation applicable for ocean shipment) but prior to expiration date of this credit.

We hereby agree with bona fide holders that all drafts drawn under
and in compliance with the terms of this credit shall meet with due
honor upon presentation and delivery of documents as specified
to the drawee if drawn and presented for negotiation on or before
expiration date of this credit.
The amount and date of each negotiation must be endorsed on the
back hereof by the negotiating bank.
Negotiating bank charges are for account of beneficiary.

Advising bank's notification

❹

Sincerely yours,

Shirley Dunal   *P.R. Lee*

Authorized counter signature   Authorized signature

Place, date, name and signature of the advising bank

FX 152n (4 80) Bank of America NT&SA

❺

(left margin, vertical) ❻ PROVISIONS APPLICABLE TO THIS CREDIT: "This credit is subject to the Uniform Customs and Practice for Documentary Credits (1974 Revision) International Chamber of Commerce, Publication No 290"

(left margin, vertical) Please examine this instrument carefully. If you are unable to comply with the terms or conditions, please communicate with your buyer to arrange for an amendment. This procedure will facilitate prompt handling when documents are presented.

SOURCE: Bank of America, San Francisco, Calif. Used with permission.

Some export letters of credit provide that drawings will be by time drafts. This means that payment is not to be made until some specified period after presentation—such as 30, 60, 90, or even 180 days. When accepted by the bank issuing the letter of credit, these drafts can be discounted readily at the prevailing rate for prime bankers acceptances. Thus exporters can get their money immediately.

A special form of payment increasingly used in trade with communist and some developing countries is the use of clearing currencies within the framework of currency-clearing arrangements between two countries. In the case of an export switch, the importer in a communist or developing country market pays the exporter from a clearing balance held against a third country. The exporter then has the possibility, with the assistance of specialized agents (mainly in Austria, Germany, the Netherlands, and Switzerland), to use the clearing funds in the country holding the balance or to sell bilateral funds at a discount.

Import and Export Financing

In the traditional field of importing and exporting, an extensive range of financial services has been developed for financing international transactions. Whether for transactions within an international firm or with suppliers or customers, these offer the international manager important opportunities for extending the available funds.[10]

There are two broad categories of credits. *Supplier credit* is extended by the exporter to the foreign importer, and the exporter in turn is refinanced with credit from external sources. *Buyer credit* is granted directly to the foreign buyer to be used for stipulated imports. Supplier credit generally covers short-term credits and some medium-term transactions. Buyer credit is usually available only for medium and long-term credits of large amounts, normally for purchasing capital goods.

In extending supplier credit, the seller is primarily concerned with credit risk, the protection of export proceeds against currency fluctuations, and political risk. In recent years, many countries have developed export credit insurance-guarantee programs to expand the country's export earnings by reducing these risks. Export-guaranteed paper may then be financed more easily and at a lower financing cost.

Financing may be with or without recourse. If the importer fails to pay the note or the bill when due, the financing institution may or may not have recourse to the exporter for the amount due. Most export credit is granted with recourse to the exporter. However, an insurance policy or guarantee issued by a government export credit insurance agency limits the financing without recourse to the extent that risks and losses are covered by the insurance.

---

[10] See Harry M. Venedikian and Gerald A. Warfield, *Export-Import Financing*. 2nd ed. (New York: John Wiley & Sons, 1987).

Commercial banks are the principal source of short-term export financing. Private commercial finance firms are also important in export financing, but the growth of export guarantees has encouraged the use of commercial banks because private finance houses usually charge more than banks. Traditionally, commercial banks have been reluctant to grant medium-term financing; but as a result of government guarantee programs, export promotion incentives, and sponsorship of new institutions, the role of commercial banks and other private sources for medium-term financing has been increasing rapidly.

International trade is highly competitive and the financing terms are an important element in the competition. Most industrialized countries have government programs to assist their exporters in providing attractive terms.[11] The Export-Import Bank (Eximbank) is the U.S. agency authorized to provide loans, guarantees, and insurance to facilitate U.S. exports. In these activities, it is meant to supplement but not compete with private financing sources. It is particularly important for long- and medium-term financing.

The Foreign Credit Insurance Association (FCIA) is a joint enterprise of some 50 insurance companies in the United States that is affiliated with Eximbank. FCIA provides insurance—mainly for exporting but in some cases for banks—against risks involved in extending credit in foreign sales. On the basis of FCIA insurance, the exporter normally is able to obtain sales financing from a bank or other lender.

As might be expected, in periods of intensive export competition, governments have been prone to make credit available at lower interest rates and for longer terms for national exporters. This tendency has started export credit wars that have led to periodic efforts by the industrial countries to negotiate international agreements on minimum credit terms.[12] But such agreements have been circumvented by the use of "mixed credit" export-financing arrangements that combine foreign aid funds with export-financing money to provide especially generous terms for domestic borrowers. And the wars continue, as shown in Box 19–3.

Choice of Distribution Channels

What distribution channels should exporters choose to get their products to the buyers at the desired time and place? The choice of distribution channels must handle two basic flows: (1) the ownership flow that transfers ownership to the final buyer and (2) the physical flow that moves the product to the final buyer through a sequence of physical movements and storage points. The alternatives for the exporter range along a continuum with the assignment to an outside unit of complete responsibility for distribution at one extreme and the establishment

---

[11] The *Chase Guide to Government Export Credit Agencies* (New York: The Chase Manhattan Bank, 1985) identifies more than 30 countries that have export credit programs.

[12] David M. Cheney, "The OECD Export Credits Agreement," *Finance & Development,* September 1985, pp. 35–38.

BOX 19–3
The Export Credit "War"

The Credit War Begins

In an undeclared trade war, tactical surprise can be just as effective as in any other battle. Late last May, General Electric Co. and the U.S. government were caught unawares by the Japanese.

The U.S. multinational, Fuji Electric Co. of Japan, and other companies were in the final stages of assembling bids to build generators for the proposed Mae Moh power plant in Thailand. GE considered itself the leading candidate. Thai officials had called its equipment technically the best.

But on May 21, only 10 hours before the deadline for the bids, Japan's export-finance agency said it was offering the Thais subsidized loans and a U.S. $8 million grant to help them pay for the project. Although Bangkok hasn't announced a decision, GE expects the so-called mixed credit to win the U.S. $36 million contract for Fuji Electric. Moreover, GE has lost other contracts to foreign competitors offering mixed credits.

SOURCE: Adapted from *The Wall Street Journal*, September 19, 1985, p. 1.

The Counterattack

"I will not stand and watch American businesses fail because of unfair trading practices abroad." So said President Reagan when he asked Congress to approve a $300 million war chest to fight predatory export tactics by foreign governments.

The Export-Import Bank (Ex-Im) is already waging war against a foreign export-credit ploy that is a rising threat to U.S. competitiveness. The United States wants an international agreement to curb mixed credits, but until such a pact is worked out, Ex-Im intends to make the credit war more costly.

As a beginning, Ex-Im is using existing funds to offer unusually low-interest loans for six transportation, power, and computer projects, potentially worth more than $250 million in U.S. exports.

SOURCE: *Business Week*, November 18, 1985, p. 50.

---

by the exporter of its own complete distribution system with foreign sales agents and warehouses at the other extreme.

The choice depends on the size of export sales and their importance to the firm, the degree of internationalization of the enterprise, the nature of the products exported, and the characteristics of specific markets being served. The casual exporter will most likely assign total responsibility to an outside firm specializing in export distribution. The firm would not have the necessary exporting know-how, nor would the size and intermittent nature of the activity warrant creating an export department. As the firm evolves towards becoming a multinational enterprise with a mix of exporting, licensing, and foreign production, the firm may establish its own distribution system shaped by an overall international channel strategy, as discussed in Chapter 18.

Where the firm remains essentially an exporter with global markets but home-country production, the nature of the product will greatly influence the choice of distribution channels. This can be illustrated by the case of the U.S. commercial aircraft industry. Because the product is technologically sophisticated, the manufacturer normally will have its own sales engineers in the field who are well prepared with product and technical information. Furthermore, quick access to spare parts and repair facilities are crucial for the buyer, and the exporter must have such facilities easily available as part of its distribution channels. Exporters of automobiles, industrial machinery, and other similar products must likewise give great importance to customer repair and service facilities as a component of their distribution channels. In contrast, exporters of food products, textiles, apparel, and so on do not have a similar need.

The choice of distribution channels for each country will be influenced by the characteristics of the export market and of the wholesale and retail distribution facilities available. However, if the exporter is selling to markets where the government buys all imports, such as in most centrally planned economies, the exporter does not have to worry about choosing among alternative distribution channels. The only choice is whether or not to sell.

The appropriate choice of distribution channels, of course, will change over time as the firm becomes more internationally involved. The exporter, therefore, must try to establish channels that will not be an impediment if the firm at a later stage moves towards foreign production. Many channels cannot be changed frequently, and moves are usually not easily reversible.

Where the exporter chooses indirect channels of distribution, the export management company (EMC) and the trading companies are among the major alternatives to be considered. There are many types of EMCs, some of which provide a full range of services to the manufacturer and handle the entire export function.[13] The most famous general trading companies are the Japanese "Sogo Shoshas" previously mentioned, which handle about half of Japan's total foreign trade and provide global market information, financing, foreign exchange risk bearing and sales negotiating functions as well as physical distribution.[14]

The great success of the Japanese Sogo Shoshas has stimulated Korea to

---

[13] See John J. Brasch, "Using Export Specialists to Develop Overseas Sales," *Harvard Business Review*, May–June 1981, pp. 6–8; Daniel C. Bello and Nicholas C. Williamson, "Contractual Arrangement and Marketing Practices in the Indirect Export Channel," *Journal of International Business Studies*, Summer 1985, pp. 65–82.

[14] Stefan H. Robock and Kichiro Hayashi, "The Uncertain Future of Japanese General Trading Companies," in *Strategic Management in the United States and Japan*, ed. Rosalie L. Tung, (Cambridge, Mass.: Ballinger Publishing Co., 1986), pp. 33–45; Kiyoshi Kojima and Terutomo Ozawa, *Japan's General Trading Companies* (Paris: OECD, 1984).

emulate this model with the development of its own huge trading companies such as Samsung, Hyundai, and Daewoo.[15] The United States has also attempted to encourage the development of major export trading companies with the Export Trading Act of 1982. The new law gives antitrust protection to competitors that join together for exporting and permits banking institutions to have ownership interests in these exporting ventures. The Japanese trading companies are uniquely related to the Japanese environment and have a long history of operations. It is highly uncertain, therefore, that their example can be followed successfully by U.S. firms in a short period of time.[16] Although the principal business of the Japanese Sogo Shoshas has been to serve Japanese exporters and importers, these companies have expanded their activities and have taken on the export function for manufacturers in other countries.

Physical Distribution

The physical movement of the exporter's product and its storage at appropriate points is the second flow that must be handled by the distribution channel. This flow involves issues of transportation, warehousing, and inventories, all of which should be integrated in a systems approach as in the case of domestic distribution. If the number of warehouses is increased, transport costs can be decreased with bulk shipment. But inventory costs will increase because inventory will be duplicated at more places. Similarly, if an attempt is made to decrease inventory costs by reducing the number of warehouses and inventory levels, transportation costs will go up. A systems approach must recognize the trade-offs and will often lead to the use of more expensive air freight rather than less expensive ocean shipping because of savings in warehousing and inventory costs.[17]

The principal differences between international and domestic physical distribution are that goods can be out of the exporter's control for longer periods of time, more documentation is required, packing may be more costly, shipping insurance is more expensive, and transportation alternatives include ocean shipping and containerization as well as air freight, air express, and parcel post.

The trend for establishing foreign-trade zones (FTZs) may be of special interest for physical distribution. There are hundreds of FTZs worldwide, and if trends continue FTZs may soon account for as much as 20 percent of world trade.[18] A foreign-trade zone isn't a place as much as a special tariff status granted by a

[15] Dong-Sung Cho, *The General Trading Company* (Lexington, Mass.: D. C. Heath & Co., 1987), pp. 40–58.

[16] Ravi Sarathy, "Japanese Trading Companies: Can They Be Copied?" *Journal of International Business Studies,* Summer 1985, pp. 101–19.

[17] Philip R. Cateora, *International Marketing,* 6th ed. (Homewood, Ill: Richard D. Irwin, 1987), pp. 587–90.

[18] Nicholas Papadopoulos, "The Free Trade Zone as a Strategic Element in International Business," *The Canadian Business Review,* Spring 1985, pp. 51–55; Fernando Robles and George C. Hozier, Jr., "Understanding Foreign Trade Zones," *International Marketing Review,* Summer 1986, pp. 44–54.

BOX 19–4
Foreign Trade Zones Become Battle Zones

The nation's fast-growing foreign-trade zones are turning into battle zones. On the one side are the trade-zone operators and the companies and communities benefiting from the tariff breaks that the zones offer. Manning the opposing trenches are many U.S. companies fighting bids by foreign competitors or U.S.-foreign joint ventures to win trade-zone status for new plants. In addition, more and more critics in Congress, labor unions, trade groups, and elsewhere argue that trade zones are worsening the U.S. trade deficit by favoring imports over exports. They also say that the zones cost more American jobs than they create and give foreign companies a type of subsidy by U.S. taxpayers.

Scattered among 47 states and Puerto Rico are a total of 247 general-purpose zones and subzones for individual plants granted by the U.S. Department of Commerce—up from 27 in 1975. A typical case is a Coastal Corp. subsidiary that refines imported oil in a Corpus Christi, Texas, foreign-trade subzone. If the subsidiary exports finished products, it doesn't pay any import duty at all. But even if nothing is exported, the company saves at least $280,000 a year in the zone from, among other things, interest earned by postponing duty payments.

One of the battles surrounds Toyota Motor Corp.'s efforts to get subzone status for a new plant in Kentucky. The subzone would allow Toyota to bypass duties—averaging 3.3 percent—on imported parts and then just pay the lower duty on the finished product—in this case 2.5 percent. The opponents contend that trade zones help foreign more than American auto makers because foreign cars use a higher percentage of imported parts. Japanese producers dispute this, but Toyota estimates that a zone would save it between $30 and close to $40 a car. By contrast, General Motors says a trade zone saves it $4 to $5 a car; Chrysler says $5.

SOURCE: Adapted from *The Wall Street Journal,* September 30, 1987. © Dow Jones & Company, Inc., 1987. Used with permission. All rights reserved.

government—the Department of Commerce in case of the United States. Typically, a company imports parts duty-free into a zone, where it assembles them into a finished product that can be exported from the zone duty-free or can enter the country at a lower rate than had the parts come in separately. Companies also use zones for warehousing, repackaging bulk shipments, and displaying goods where showroom space is provided. Because a duty isn't due until a product leaves the zone—with most imports, it is due when they arrive in the country— zones can slow an importer's cash outlays and increase cash flows (see Box 19–4).

IMPORTS AND GLOBAL SOURCING

The enterprise that does global sourcing for its domestic market must develop importing channels. As in the case of exporting, the channels can be indirect, where the importer relies completely on outside units. At the other extreme, the importer can have its own buying offices in sourcing countries and handle all importing steps such as transportation and customs clearance with its own organization.[19]

The extent of involvement by the importer in establishing importing channels will vary inversely with the degree of responsibility assumed by the foreign supplier for its export operations. When sourcing in some newly industrializing countries (NICs) such as Hong Kong, Taiwan, and South Korea, many buyers or importers began by assuming full responsibility for setting product specifications, quality control, importing, and marketing. But as foreign producers acquired experience, they assumed ever-increasing responsibility, even to the point of establishing their own warehouses in the market countries.[20]

SUMMARY

Virtually all international business firms do some exporting and/or importing. The importance of this function, however, will vary with the degree of internationalization of the enterprise, the products being sold, and the firm's marketing and production logistics strategy. For many firms, the export/import activity will consist exclusively of selling to or buying from independent foreign parties. But for the multinational enterprise with a global strategy and foreign production units, the export/import activity is likely to consist largely of intra-firm movements of materials and components across national boundaries.

Export and import management requires considerable specialized expertise. There is a payments problem because the trading parties, either independent or foreign units of the same enterprise, deal in different currencies. There are special pricing issues, such as the use of transfer pricing in intra-firm transactions or the potentials for differentiated prices when selling in separate markets. The firm will have to choose among distribution channel alternatives that differ greatly from country to country. And choices have to be made in physical distribution among transportation means, the use of warehouses, and inventory policies. Also the role of governments can be a crucial competitive element, especially in export financing.

Export management can be handled in a passive way by assigning the complete responsibility to an outside unit specializing in export operation, such as an export management company or a general trading company. Likewise, the importer can deal exclusively with import agents or representatives of foreign suppliers that appear on the importer's doorsteps. The more aggressive approach is for the international enterprise to establish its own export/import organizational unit and develop its own distribution and sourcing network.

---

[19] See Ruel Kahler, *International Marketing, 5th, ed.* (Cincinnati, Ohio: South-Western Publishing Co., 1983), pp. 303–16.

[20] Lawrence H. Wortzel and Heidi Vernon Wortzel, "Export Marketing Strategies for NIC and LDC-Based Firms," *Columbia Journal of World Business,* Spring 1981, pp. 51–60.

EXERCISE AND DISCUSSION QUESTIONS

1. When Honda began to export motorcycles from Japan, the company had to choose between using the Japanese trading companies or establishing its own direct distribution channels. Which choice would you recommend and why?
2. " 'Mixed credits' which combine foreign aid with export financing are justified because they help poor nations pay for needed imports," according to a French government official. Do you agree with this argument? Why or why not?
3. As compared to domestic distribution what additional distribution elements are involved when goods cross national boundaries?
4. Under what circumstances should an exporter take advantage of the possibilities for establishing different prices in separate national markets?
5. Why is air transportation and air express so widely used in exporting when ocean transportation is so much cheaper?
6. The importer with a global sourcing strategy often has to choose between contracting with foreign producers or establishing a wholly owned or joint venture foreign production unit. What factors might be involved in such a sourcing decision?

CHAPTER 20

Managing International Technology Transfers

THE NATURE OF TECHNOLOGY AND THE TRANSFER
PROCESS
 Technology: A Definition
 Classification Schemes
 The Transfer Process
 Modes of Technology Transfer
 Expediters and Controllers of the Transfer Process
INTERNATIONAL TECHNOLOGY ISSUES FOR THE
MULTINATIONAL FIRM
 Foreign Technology Acquisitions
 Maintaining the Technology Advantage
 Locating R&D Facilities Abroad
 Technology Transfer Strategies
 Choice of Technology
 Pricing of International Technology Transfers
NATIONAL AND INTERNATIONAL CONTROL ENVIRONMENT
SUMMARY
EXERCISES AND DISCUSSION QUESTIONS

International technology transfers have become recognized as one of the most important—and controversial—components of international business activity. For many years following World War II, the role of multinational enterprises as vehicles for international transfers of capital was given more attention. A global shortage of capital existed. Furthermore, both government officials and experts in development perceived increased capital inputs as the magic key to rapid economic growth. But as capital steadily became more easily available, and as many development efforts based almost solely on capital inputs produced disappointing results, the strategic importance of technology for stimulating economic expansion became ever more apparent. As a result, the technology transfer role of the international firm moved to the forefront as an issue for international managers and for both host and home countries.

The subject of international technology transfers, however, has a broad setting that extends beyond the field of international business. And many national policies concerning technology that affect international business actually involve broader development issues. While international firms account for a large share of the international technology transfers and most of the commercial transfers, many noncommercial organizations are also responsible for international technology transfers.

The importance of the broader setting can be illustrated by the controversy that has emerged over the cost of technology transfers to the developing countries. International firms encounter difficulties in some countries because local officials believe their countries are paying "too much" for foreign technology imports. This may or may not be true, depending on what is acceptable as the appropriate measuring stick. In any event, the international manager should be aware that such beliefs usually stem from focusing exclusively on commercial transfers and neglecting the many technology transfers by governments and others that require little or no payment by the recipients.

This chapter will not attempt to cover the broad field. It will be limited to international technology transfers in international business activity. As necessary background, it will discuss the nature of technology, the international technology transfer process, and the various modes of transfer. It will then consider the international technology transfer issues facing the firm and the constraints and incentives of host and home governments as they affect the management of international technology transfers. The control issues have already been introduced in Chapter 12.

THE NATURE OF TECHNOLOGY AND THE TRANSFER PROCESS

In controversial areas, it is vital to have a clear definition of terms. Unfortunately, much discussion and controversy over technology transfers occurs where the parties are using different definitions and are not aware that others have a different concept in mind.

Technology: A Definition

A comprehensive definition of *technology* might be as follows:

Technology is a perishable resource comprising knowledge, skills, and the means for using and controlling factors of production for the purpose of producing, delivering to users, and maintaining goods and service for which there is an economic and/or social demand.[1]

---

[1] Stefan H. Robock, *The International Technology Transfer Process* (Washington, D.C.: National Academy of Sciences, 1980), p. 2.

Technology is distinguished from science in that science "organizes and explains data and observations by means of theoretical relationships . . . technology translates scientific and empirical relationships into practical use."[2]

The proposed definition includes social as well as economic goods. "Development" has come to mean "improving the quality of life" rather than simply "increased economic output." Therefore, technology transfers in the social sector such as education, health, and public administration are encompassed.

The definition recognizes that distribution factors can be a barrier to development as easily as can lack of production enterprise.[3] The definition, therefore, includes the knowedge, skills, and other means for the distribution of goods and services, as well as their production. The capacity to create new technology and to maintain existing technology is also included. Technology transfers can contribute to the ability of a receiving country to develop new technology and to the capacity for maintaining existing machinery, equipment, or tools.

Classification Schemes

Some of the more useful classifications of technology distinguish between (1) hard and soft, (2) proprietary and nonproprietary, (3) front-end and obsolete, and (4) bundled and unbundled technology. Although such groupings are presented as dichotomous classes, they are often simply divisions into two groups falling on the different sides of some point on a continuous scale. Moreover, the technologies are frequently interrelated. Thus, hard technology often requires accompanying soft technology, such as in the case of computers.

Capital goods, blueprints, technical specifications, and knowledge and assistance necessary for the efficient utilization of such hardware are characterized as *hard technology*. *Soft technology* refers to management, marketing, financial organization, administrative techniques, and computer programs. Proprietary technology is owned or controlled by particular individuals or organizations. It may be held as a trade secret, or it may be published as a patent. Nonproprietary technology includes knowledge contained in technical literature, hardware, and services that can be imitated or reproduced by observation and through reverse engineering without infringement of the proprietary rights. "Reverse engineering" simply means to learn how to reproduce equipment by taking it apart.

Front-end technology is the latest available technology, while *old technology* in some cases is obsolete. *Bundled technology* refers to controlled technology that the owner is willing to transfer only as part of a package, generally including

---

[2] G. R. Hall and R. E. Johnson, "Transfers of United States Aerospace Technology to Japan," in *The Technology Factor in International Trade,* ed. Raymond Vernon (New York: Columbia University Press, 1970), p. 306.

[3] See Sandy B. Conners, A. C. Samli, and Erdener Kaynak, "Transfer of Food Retail Technology into Less Developed Countries," in *Technology Transfer,* ed. A. Coskun Samli (Westport, Conn.; Quorum Books, 1985), pp. 27–44.

an ownership interest in the foreign affiliate using the technology. Unbundled technology is made available independent of the technology supplier's total package of resources.

The Transfer Process

Technology is not a self-contained physical object that is stored on a warehouse shelf and shipped as a package from the supplier to the user. Technology is a body of knowledge transferred by a learning process. When the transfer is from one national environment to another, it can be complex, time-consuming, and costly, even when transfers are between units of the same multinational enterprise.[4] Many transfer modes are available, and many participate in the process.

The complexity of the actual transfer process between affiliated parties has been illustrated by recent studies.[5] Many distinct phases are involved, ranging from planning and the design of products and facilities to personnel training, engineering for quality control, and technical support for local suppliers. The transfers usually require documentation, instruction programs, personnel exchanges, and continued communication on whatever problems arise.

Transfers made to nonaffiliated parties through licensing agreements can also require that the licensor show the licensee how to use the knowledge or equipment.[6] In the case of cross-licensing, the principal objective of the parties may be to permit free exchange of information under an umbrella agreement, rather than to simply permit the use of each other's existing patents.

The time required, the expense necessary, and the effectiveness of technology transfers will vary with such factors as (1) the nature of the technology being transferred, (2) the characteristics, capabilities, and objectives of the parties involved, and (3) the absorptive capability of specific economic and social sectors within the recipient country. A transfer of electronic technology from a U.S. firm to a Japanese company could occur rapidly, effectively, and relatively inexpensively, while a similar transfer to a developing country with a limited supply of trained and experienced personnel might not.

Modes of Technology Transfer

Technology may be transferred in many ways. The principal noncommercial modes are foreign study in regular university programs, government-to-government agreements in such realms as nuclear energy and space research, and development

---

[4] David Teece, *The Multinational Corporation and the Resource Cost of International Technology Transfer* (Cambridge, Mass.: Ballinger, 1978).

[5] See, for example, Jack Behrman and Harvey Wallender, *Transfer of Manufacturing Technology within Multinational Enterprises* (Cambridge, Mass.: Ballinger, 1976).

[6] See J. Davidson Frame, *International Business and Global Technology* (Lexington, Mass.: Lexington Books, 1983), pp. 110–18.

assistance under bilateral and multilateral aid programs. In the commercial area, the principal modes are:

- Foreign direct investment—establishing a foreign operation.
- Turnkey projects—all the necessary elements for an operating plant are provided in one package for an inclusive price.
- Trade in goods and services—sale of equipment, tools, and products, materials, and consulting services.
- Contracts and agreements—licensing of patents, trademarks, tradenames, and know-how; management contracts for equipment maintenance and service facilities; franchising.
- Research and development—location of R&D operations in foreign countries, research subcontracting, joint R&D projects.
- Personnel—employment of nationals by foreign firms; employment of foreign technicians (see Box 20–1); migration of trained personnel; internal training programs of business firms; commercial training programs of professional associations, educational institutions, and research institutes.
- Other—investment in or acquisition of foreign companies, transfers through international tender invitations, industrial espionage.

BOX 20–1
A "Moonlighting" Strategy for Technology Transfer

Seoul—Every Friday evening, dozens of young and middle-aged men leave their offices in Tokyo, head for the airport, and arrive here in South Korea a few hours later. They are Japanese engineers who have come to spend the weekend quietly moonlighting at Korean companies.

Among them are engineering professors, partners in technical firms, and employees of major Japanese corporations. Some are exporting their skills on the sly without the consent of their bosses. "Some of these engineers are working at big personal risk", says Nobuhiro Nakamura, whose Tokyo consulting firm last year recruited 250 Japanese technical experts for part-time work in Korea for various lengths of stay.

Their Korean sponsors range from small auto-parts makers to the biggest conglomerates. They typically meet the Japanese at the airport, put them up in good hotels, provide interpreters, and pay them the equivalent of U.S. $250 a day. Some even lend the Japanese money to help buy houses back in Japan.

The moonlighting engineers are just a small part of a larger Korean strategy. South Korea desperately wants to go high-tech but is badly lacking in the plans, people, and processes needed to get there alone. "We're very weak in design technology", says Yu Hee Yol, the head of technology transfer at the Ministry of Science and technology, "So we import what we can't create."

SOURCE: Adapted from *The Wall Street Journal*, January 7, 1986. © Dow Jones & Company, Inc., 1986. Used with permission. All rights reserved.

Much existing technology is nonproprietary and freely available. Whether a potential user is able to exploit that technology depends upon a number of factors. The user must be able to define the need for the technology. The user must have qualified personnel available with access to scientific and technical publications and an ability to apply that information. Also, the receiving country must have an infrastructure adequate to support the absorption, translation, and utilization of the technology.

The transfer of technology through international tender offers is an especially interesting mode. Thus, a Middle Eastern country invited tenders for a contract to install a national communications system. The potential value of the contract—hundreds of millions of dollars—prompted many multinational companies and consortia to invest millions of dollars in designing systems they hoped would win the contract. In the process of negotiating and awarding the contract, the responsible officials of the purchasing country received a massive amount of transferred technology.

Expediters and Controllers of the Transfer Process

International transfers frequently involve participants other than the suppliers and users of technology. A range of government and private groups, for example, perform expediting and controlling functions. These expediters and controllers can have a major influence on the timing, kinds of transfers, and terms negotiated. National patent authorities, assisted by national patent laws and international treaties and conventions, aid in expediting international technology transfers.[7] International standards organizations also act as technology transfer expediters and controllers. Thus, the International Civil Aviation Organization (ICAO) promotes international standards and regulations in civil aviation. The International Telecommunications Union (ITU) has similar responsibilities in radio, telegraph, telephone, and space communications. The objectives of these agencies are primarily safety and uniformity.

The most extensive control activities are those of national governments. These have been discussed in Chapter 12 and will be examined further below.

INTERNATIONAL TECHNOLOGY ISSUES FOR THE MULTINATIONAL FIRM

What special technology issues are encountered by the firm in international operations? Certain issues arise when the firm's motivation for "going international" is to acquire foreign technology. Other issues arise when the motivation for international expansion is to exploit technology advantages.

When the firm's competitive advantage abroad is based on technology, it

---

[7] See Sigmund Timberg, "The Role of the International Patent System in the International Transfer and Control of Technology," in *Controlling International Technology Transfers,* ed. T. Sagafi-Nejad, R. W. Moxon, and H. V. Perlmutter (New York: Pergamon Press, 1981), pp. 64–84.

faces such issues as how to maintain its technological advantage over time, which strategy to choose for profiting from the technology advantage, and how to price the technology. If the strategy chosen is to invest directly in foreign production, the firm must choose the technology alternative that best fits the foreign environment. And in all these managerial decisions the present and future control environment in both home and host countries must be considered. But let us first turn to the matter of foreign technology acquisitions.

Foreign Technology Acquisitions

Although technology is highly concentrated in the industrialized countries, these nations differ in the areas of technology in which they lead. The United States has been a leader in computer technology. Germany and Switzerland have a long tradition of advanced research in chemicals and pharmaceuticals. European and Japanese firms have been leaders in fuel-economy transportation vehicles, in large part because heavy government taxation in their countries kept gasoline prices much higher than in the United States. These national differences have been a motivation for many types of international business expansions, including foreign technology acquisitions through direct investment, joint ventures for research cooperation, and cross-licensing agreements.

An interesting example of technology acquisition through direct investment is the case of a leading Japanese computer company (Fujitsu) and a U.S. computer company (Amdahl). In 1970, a former chief scientist of IBM founded the Amdahl Corporation to produce large-scale, general purpose mainframes. The new firm had difficulty raising capital from U.S. sources. The U.S. stock market was depressed at the time. Also, U.S. investors were not anxious to risk their capital in a new company that would have to compete with IBM to be successful. But Fujitsu, Limited, was willing to provide capital by taking a substantial equity position in the Amdahl Corporation.

Fujitsu was developing its own technology and having difficulty producing large computers. The investment in Amdahl gave Fujitsu access to large computer technology and resulted in arrangements for joint development, cross-licensing, coproduction, and joint-venture sales agreements. It has been estimated that this investment enabled Fujitsu to close a three- to five-year technological gap between it and U.S. industry.[8]

Other examples include the acquisition by a Dutch company of a substantial equity interest in a U.S. company to gain access to pollution control technology, a joint French-U.S. venture established in the United States as a result of the French firm's desire to acquire process technology for making soft contact lenses,[9] and a large investment by Corning Glass of the United States in a small British

---

[8] Jack Baranson, *Technology and the Multinationals* (Lexington, Mass.: Lexington Books, 1978), pp. 75–84.

[9] U.S. Department of Commerce, *Foreign Direct Investment in the United States*, vol. 1 (Washington, D.C.: U.S. Government Printing Office, April 1976), pp. 201–6.

company that invented a revolutionary biotechnology for producing antibodies. In the British case, the new technology was given television publicity in the United Kingdom, but only one British offer of finance was forthcoming—and that on onerous terms. So the new company turned to a U.S. investor that now owns 49 percent of the venture.[10]

The acquisition of technology through foreign operations has been a frequent occurrence in international business. And such foreign expansions are not limited to the acquisition of product and process technology. A major European consumer-products firm established operations in the United States to gain firsthand knowledge and experience in marketing. Such technology was then made available to other units of the multinational enterprise in other foreign countries.

Maintaining the Technology Advantage

Where foreign operations are based on technology advantage, it is crucial for the international firm to maintain that advantage over time. Technology is perishable, and advantages can easily erode. Furthermore, the foreign firm must maintain a large enough technology advantage over potential local producers to more than offset the additional costs and disadvantages of operating in a foreign country. The foreign enterprise also needs to maintain its advantage in order to retain bargaining power against national control policies. This latter need is particularly important for firms operating in developing countries. The ever-present nationalism means that local enterprises are preferred and that foreign firms are usually viewed by the host country as a second-best choice unless they have something special to offer.

The need to maintain a technology advantage in the future applies to resource seekers as well as market seekers. Many international firms with foreign mining projects have been forced to divest or share ownership locally as their initial technology contribution has been absorbed locally and their technology advantage has eroded. The same need is present in foreign licensing arrangements. As will be discussed below, the licensor's ability to supply new technology can be a key factor in maintaining and profiting from arrangements with licensees.

How does the firm maintain its technology advantage over time? One way is to keep its unique know-how secret. Coca-Cola has done this with considerable success by safeguarding the mixture formula of its syrup. Another way is through reliance on trademarks. These are normally granted by law in perpetuity, whereas patent monopolies expire after a fixed number of years. The most effective means, however, is to have a research capability to develop new technologies and technological improvements.

Locating R&D Facilities Abroad

In many situations, the true source of a company's technology advantage is not its current technology assets but its research and development capability. In

---

[10] *The Economist*, April 21, 1979, p. 124.

international business operations, this reality raises the issue of where R&D facilities should be located. Multinational enterprises are frequently under pressure by host countries to locate R&D facilities abroad, along with production facilities. And a number of firms have deviated, with successful results, from the usual pattern of keeping R&D operations in the home country. As a survey of the experience of several U.S. multinationals concluded, foreign R&D units made these firms more competitive in both foreign and U.S. markets than if they had performed R&D only in the United States.[11]

A more ambitious study (undertaken in 1978) of 31 American and 18 European multinationals revealed a surprising amount of foreign R&D activity. In total, the group had more than 200 active foreign R&D units, many of which had their origin in pressures from host countries.[12]

What are the motivations for establishing foreign R&D units? At a minimum, such units can assist in the process of technology transfer, make product and process adaptations to local conditions, and strengthen the subsidiary's competitive position by providing technical services to customers. A more ambitious mission for such units, and even more crucial for maintaining a technology advantage in the future, is to develop new and improved products and processes expressly for foreign markets, after identifying opportunities different from those perceived in the home country. Still another motivation is to take advantage of a concentration of knowledge and talent in a foreign area.

The adaptation function can be illustrated by the agricultural chemical firm that needs to test and adapt its product to the climatic, soil, and other conditions in the foreign markets it is serving. Similarly, U.S. pharmaceutical firms have European formulation laboratories to meet European drug administration practices that differ from those in the United States.

The motivation of better serving distinctive foreign markets through foreign R&D units has been explained by the following underlying philosophy:

> Scientists in one country are not good at answering the specific market needs of another country. . . .
>
> We believe that the best way to overcome this problem is to have subsidiaries in important markets away from the parent company develop their own complete R&D organizations to take full and direct advantage of the opportunities peculiar to their environment.[13]

The French subsidiary of the Otis Elevator Company, as an example, was missing out in a major market for small elevators to be installed in low-rise buildings.

---

[11] Robert C. Ronstadt, "International R&D: The Establishment and Evolution of Research and Development Abroad by Seven U.S. Multinationals," *Journal of International Business Studies,* Spring–Summer 1978, pp. 7–24.

[12] Jack N. Behrman and William A. Fischer, "Transnational Corporations: Market Orientation and R&D Abroad," *Columbia Journal of World Business,* Fall 1980, pp. 55–60.

[13] Rosemarie Van Rumker, "Multinational R&D in Practice: Chemagro Corporation," *Research Management,* January 1971, p. 52.

Otis had not entered this market in the United States and did not have technology to transfer abroad. A unit established in Europe was able to develop technology for the small-elevator market.[14]

The desire to benefit from a highly favorable research environment is illustrated by the decision of many foreign firms to locate R&D facilities in the United States. R&D expenditures by U.S. affiliates of foreign firms totaled almost $1 billion in 1974. As explained by the foreign firms, the basis for their extensive R&D activity in the United States is the size and advanced nature of the U.S. market and the special attractiveness of the U.S. environment for R&D.[15]

The decision to locate R&D in a specific foreign country will depend, of course, on other practical considerations such as host government controls and incentives, whether an economic size research unit can be justified, the availability of adequate infrastructure and universities, and the foreign supply of needed technical skills.

Technology Transfer Strategies

Another important decision in managing international technology transfers is the strategy chosen by the firm for appropriating the potential returns from its technology advantage. As in the case of other sources of competitive advantage, the two broad strategy options are to internalize by extending its own operations or to use external markets. The decision variables affecting this choice were discussed in Chapter 3.[16] But two specific forms of using external markets— licensing and selling "turnkey projects"—deserve special attention as they relate to technology transfers. These strategies have gained in importance as government policies in many countries have become increasingly restrictive against direct investment.

Turnkey Projects.   Numerous firms in the United States and elsewhere specialize in the design, construction, and startup of "turnkey plants." In such transactions, the contractor agrees to handle every detail of the project, including the training of operating personnel. At the completion of the contract, the customer is handed the key to a completed plant that is fully ready for operations. In some cases, the contractor may take an equity interest in the project.

Japanese firms, in particular, have been using this strategy; and plant exports on a turnkey basis have been accounting for an increasingly large portion of Japan's trade. For example, in 1982, the giant trading company, Mitsubishi Corporation, was constructing four oil refineries and gas plants, in cooperation with several other Japanese firms, in a Middle Eastern oil-producing country. The size of this export business is illustrated by the fact that an oil refinery with a

---

[14] Ronstadt, "International R&D," p. 12.

[15] U.S. Department of Commerce, *Foreign Direct Investment in the United States*, p. 197.

[16] See Chapter 3, pp. 45–47.

BOX 20–2
Exporting Technolgoy

Kawasaki Steel Corp., Japan's fourth largest steelmaker, is taking that nation's edge in steel-producing technology both to new heights and to non-Western foreign markets in an unusually aggressive fashion. A new president is pressing Kawasaki's 800 scientists and engineers in Japan to come up with new, more sophisticated methods of making steel products used in everything from bridges to buses. At the same time, Kawasaki's sales representatives in the field are stalking overseas markets to export steelmaking technology as well as steel products.

Kawasaki is expanding its efforts to export technology because the emerging countries increasingly want their own steelmaking facilities, rather than relying on imports. Within five years, Kawasaki expects to double the contribution of technology exports to at least 10 percent of sales.

A drawback to Kawasaki's technology-exporting drive would seem to be that the plants it helps build elsewhere will become competition for the company's own production. The potential threat, however, does not worry the president. He is confident that his company's engineers will keep coming up with new break-throughs. "By the time the exported steel plant comes on stream, our technology will have advanced, so we will still be ahead."

SOURCE: *Business Week,* January 29, 1979, pp. 119–20.

---

daily capacity of 100,000 barrels would cost $450 million (in 1982 prices); and some Middle Eastern countries were planning refineries with a daily capacity of as much as 250,000 barrels.[17]

The strategy of selling technology in the form of turnkey plant export is used extensively in the chemical, pharmaceutical, and petroleum-refining industries. A large number of U.S. and other international companies have as their main business the selling of newly developed technology for these industries, rather than the sale of end products from the use of the technology. These firms reinvest a share of their profits in developing new generations of technology and have little concern for the potential competition from technology purchasers.[18]

International companies in the business of selling end products normally profit from their proprietary technology when it is commercialized into end products. In such cases, the direct sale of technology has the disadvantage of creating competitors and reducing the seller's competitive advantage in the marketplace. Nevertheless, end-product companies can use the turnkey strategy with success in certain special circumstances, as shown in Box 20–2.

---

[17] Mitsubishi Corporation, *Tokyo Newsletter,* January 1982.

[18] See Baranson, *Technology and the Multinationals,* pp. 115–42, for several case studies of international turnkey projects.

Licensing. Although long considered an inferior strategy, the licensing alternative is uniquely significant for international technology transfers and appears to be gaining in importance. In many selected situations licensing is not only very profitable but superior in a net risk-adjusted comparision with alternatives. Licensing has special advantages for small companies that lack capital, management, and the necessary experience for expanding internationally through direct investment. Many large firms also make extensive use of licensing, both with their foreign affiliates and with unaffiliated parties.[19]

A frequent argument against licensing unaffiliated parties is that the licensor may in time lose its competitive edge to the licensee and be barred in the future from direct expansion in overseas areas served by the licensee. This argument, however, usually assumes a simple and discrete relationship between the licensor and the licensee. But licensing can be a part of a multifaceted strategy that permits the licensor to take an ownership interest in the foreign venture. Also, trademarks remain the property of the licensor in perpetuity, whereas licenses normally have a finite period.

In many cases, the licensing firm retains considerable bargaining power because of the perishable nature of technology and the licensor's ability to supply new technology in the future to the licensee. Where reciprocal licensing is involved, the licensing firm may actually improve its competitive position through the benefits received from technological exchanges.[20]

The circumstances under which licensing may be a preferred strategy can be summarized as follows:[21]

- Where host countries restrict imports and/or direct investment.
- Where a specific foreign market is small.
- Where prospects of technology feedback are high.
- Where licensing is a way of testing and developing a market that can later be exploited by direct investment.
- Where the pace of technology change is sufficiently rapid that the seller can remain technologically superior.
- Where opportunities exist for licensing auxiliary processes without having to license basic product technologies.
- Where small companies have limited resources and expertise for direct foreign expansion.

---

[19] Farok J. Contractor, *Licensing in International Strategy: A Guide for Planning and Negotiations* (Westport, Conn.: Greenwood Press, 1985).

[20] Piero Telesio, *Technology Licensing and Multinational Enterprises* (New York: Praeger, 1979), p. 22–24.

[21] Farok J. Contractor, "The Role of Licensing in International Strategy," *Columbia Journal of World Business,* Winter 1981, pp. 73–83.

BOX 20–3
An International Technology Licensing Success Story

"Heli-Coil" industrial fasteners (screw thread inserts) were developed during World War II to meet aircraft and military needs for stronger threaded connections in aluminum and light metal alloys. After the war, the company (now the Heli-Coil Division of MITE Corp., Danbury, Connecticut) developed civilian industry sales and began to expand abroad through licensing.

Through an international program involving 10 licensees, the company achieved overseas sales of $15 million (in 1976) from a base of zero in 1950. Eighty percent of the royalty-paying sales involve product applications developed abroad. On top of royalties, an annual six-figure Heli-Coil export volume has grown because foreign licensees find it more economical to import certain U.S.-made items.

Another benefit has been technology feedback, now available to all licensees. The Japanese licensee conducted studies and succeeded in applying Heli-Coil fasteners in iron and steel. The English licensee developed power tools for automatically installing the fasteners. The French licensee adapted designs for applications in wood and developed production gauges used in the United States and by licensees in other countries.

The German licensee devised compound fasteners—a new product for themselves and all members of the Heli-Coil enterprise. Finally, the Indian licensee designed equipment that could be efficiently employed for short-run production, making it economically feasible to set up operations in other developing countries.

SOURCE: Adapted from the *Congressional Record*, June 1, 1972, p. E5919.

In general, the advantages of the licensing strategy will depend upon the specific technology, size of firm, product maturity, extent of internal experience of the firm, and environmental constraints in host countries. As shown in Box 20–3, licensing can be an attractive strategy for generating a flow of royalties, export sales, and valuable technology feedback.

Choice of Technology

When a firm decides to internalize its competitive advantage through establishing foreign production, it must make a choice as to the technology it intends to use. When the firm expands from one industrialized country to another industrialized country, the choice-of-technology decision has few special international elements. Normally the same technology as that used in the home country will be transferred, but with minor adaptations for differences that may exist in foreign supply sources and markets.

In contrast, where foreign production is established in developing countries, the choice-of-technology decision must take into consideration the controversy over "appropriate" technology. Many developing countries believe, as discussed in Chapter 13, that the technology imported in foreign firms should not be the same as that used in capital-rich countries with large markets but should be appropriate to the factor endowments of the host country. This usually means that imported technology should be labor-intensive and smaller-scale.

The appropriate technology controversy raises several key questions for the international manager. To what extent are commercially feasible alternative technologies readily available? If not available, can the cost of developing more appropriate technology be justified? And, what mix of factors other than differences in the relative cost of labor and capital should influence the managerial decision?

Availability of Technology Alternatives.   The question of alternative technologies has both an availability and a commercial feasibility dimension, and the experts differ on both issues. Based on a series of field studies, the ILO (International Labour Office) has concluded that the range of technologies available is "larger than earlier believed" and that "the scope for choice is considerable."[22] But according to another view, "the commercial competitiveness of alternative, highly labor intensive technology has not been established. Truly appropriate technology does not exist (outside the traditional sectors) and its development (if at all possible) could be extremely expensive." Consequently, the debate has become largely academic as most policy makers in Third World countries have opted for adapted versions of advanced technologies in manufacturing industries.[23]

In general, the nature of a process or product can determine the extent to which technology alternatives might be available.[24] In the textile industry, the manufacturing process is composed of a number of discrete processing steps, each performed by one or a group of machines. Consequently, the choice of technology and equipment on the basis of labor/capital trade-offs can be made for each of these processing steps independently from the choice for the other steps. In the chemical industry, the transformation of raw materials is achieved through the interaction of chemicals, heat, and pressure; and there is little room for manual intervention in the continuous transformation process. Trade-offs between capital and labor are available in the choice of manual or automatic controls but not in the choice of the basic processing equipment.

The nature of the industry or product also influences the cost and availability of technical information on alternative technologies needed by the firm to make its technology choices. In mechanical process industries, alternative technologies are embodied in standardized equipment that is available on an "off-the-shelf" basis. Thus alternatives and their characteristics can be known at little or no

---

[22] International Labour Office, *Technology Choice and Employment Generation by Multinational Enterprises in Developing Countries* (Geneva, 1984), p. 9.

[23] Sanjaya Lall, "Transnationals and the Third World: Some Changing Perceptions," *National Westminster Bank Quarterly Review,* May 1984, p. 9.

[24] See Michel A. Amsalem, *Technology Choice in Developing Countries* (Cambridge, Mass.: MIT Press, 1983).

cost. In chemical process industries, equipment is normally custom-made for each plant; and the decision maker may have to make a substantial investment in engineering and design work to secure the technical data needed to evaluate the technology alternatives. In general, information on capital-intensive equipment is more likely to be available to decision makers, for information flows usually run from developed to developing countries rather than between developing countries.

Technology Decision Criteria.   Contrary to the implicit assumption of many advocates of appropriate technology, the trade-off between capital and labor cannot be the sole criterion in the management decision on alternative technologies. As one writer suggests, management variables are often "the forgotten factor in technology choice."[25] Considerations that often tip the decision to more automated methods are quality control, maintenance, waste minimization, response to market-demand fluctuations, labor training costs, labor relations problems, and the prestige of having the latest equipment.[26]

Host government policies can also push the decision toward the capital-intensive alternative. Such policies include making investment capital available at below-the-market rates, restricting the import of used machinery, and adopting worker-welfare and labor-relations legislation that is viewed by business firms as excessively burdensome. When host countries protect local firms from competitive pressures through tariffs and import control and by limiting the number of producers, they greatly weaken the competitive incentive to reduce production costs by adapting technology to different capital/labor cost situations.

Pricing of International Technology Transfers

The pricing decision for technology transfers, whether domestic or international, can be complex. The market for technology is highly imperfect, and relatively little pricing information is publicly available to guide the negotiating parties. Furthermore, the compensation package may include many types of payments. A simple agreement might provide for a lump-sum payment and/or specified royalties over a fixed period of time. Under a more comprehensive agreement, the licensor might also receive compensation in the form of fees for technical assistance and other services performed, dividends from an equity share granted by the licensee, profits on goods supplied or received by the licensor, valuable technology feedback, and tax savings arising out of the arrangement.

---

[25] Michel A. Amsalem, "Management: The Forgotten Factor in Technology Choice," in *Technology Assessment and Development,* ed. Magalain Srinivasan (New York: Praeger Publishers, 1982); see also International Labour Office, *Technology Choice and Employment Generation,* p. 27.

[26] Farok F. Contractor and Taji Sagafi-Nejad, "International Technology Transfer: Major Issues and Policy Responses", *Journal of International Business Studies,* Fall 1981, p. 122; Donald J. LeCraw, "Choice of Technology in Thailand," in *Technology Crossing Borders,* ed. Robert Stobaugh and Louis T. Wells, Jr. (Harvard Business School Press, 1984), pp. 99–100.

As in the case of technology choice, special factors arise in pricing the technology for transfers to developing countries. Increasingly, host governments are intervening in the negotiation of agreements on technology payments. They are generally aware that payments to parent companies by controlled foreign affiliates are likely to be shaped by the various elements of transfer pricing strategies discussed in Chapter 23.[27] There is also a general presumption that the prices paid for technology are "too high."

Many host countries believe that the weak negotiating position of developing countries has resulted in higher technology prices than for similar transfers to industrial countries. They also argue that technology is generally protected by a patent monopoly that inherently permits the technology seller to extract an excessive monopoly price.[28] Still another argument is that the technology development costs have previously been amortized over home market sales. Consequently, international transfers need not be compensated at much more than the incremental cost of the transfer.

Broad empirical evidence on the pricing of international technology transfers is difficult to develop because of the combination of payments that might be involved. In any event, the expanding exchange of information among national agencies has better prepared host countries for preventing discriminatory pricing.

The monopoly pricing argument confuses the concept of a patent as a monopoly with monopoly power in the marketplace. Patented technology can face competition in the market where substitutable technology is available. In recent years, even in high-technology areas such as pharmaceuticals, computers, and petrochemicals, several sources of substitutable technology have typically become available.[29] Thus potential users in developing countries generally have several technology suppliers competing against each other.

The "sunk cost" argument is rejected by business firms on several grounds. They believe that the sale of present technology should not only cover sunk costs but also provide revenue to fund future research and development.[30] Furthermore, some governmental tax authorities, such as the U.S. Internal Revenue Service, have policies requiring that R&D expenditure be shared by all users of the resulting technology. This policy attempts to protect home-country income tax revenues from being reduced by expensing all R&D expenditures in the home country.

In summary, the international firm has no standard model available for pricing

---

[27] See G. Koptis, "Intrafirm Royalties Crossing Frontiers and Transfer-Pricing Behaviour," *Economic Journal,* December 1976, pp. 791–803.

[28] See Constantine Vaitsos, *Intercountry Income Distribution and Transnational Corporations* (New York: Oxford University Press, 1974).

[29] See Nathaniel H. Leff, "Technology Transfer and U.S. Foreign Policy: The Developing Countries," *Orbis,* Spring 1979, p. 146.

[30] Isaiah Frank, *Foreign Enterprise in Developing Countries* (Baltimore: Johns Hopkins University Press, 1980), p. 81.

international technology transfers. In practice, the pricing for nonaffiliated foreign buyers will be a negotiated price that reflects the bargaining power and skills of the parties.[31] The lower price limit will be set by the costs of effecting the transfer. The upper limit will be either the value of the technology to the buyer, a limit imposed by host-government policies, or terms offered by a competitor.

NATIONAL AND INTERNATIONAL CONTROL ENVIRONMENT

National controls over international technology transfers are certain to continue into the future. As is true for other control measures, they reflect the reality that the private interests of the buyers and sellers can diverge from the national interests of the countries. At the international level, the developing countries can be expected to continue their pressure for an international code to govern technology transfers. But universal agreement on such a code is difficult to achieve. Each of the participating countries is a sovereign power, and the national interests of the participants diverge sharply in a number of respects. Thus, the principal controls of concern to the international manager will be at the national level.

Home countries will continue to control technology transfers for national security reasons and to protect tax revenues. The broader concern for losing international competitiveness through foreign technology transfers will persist as a government policy issue. But retaining international competitiveness is only one element of a complex economic adjustment problem that many countries are facing as a result of a changing world economy. Also, the national costs of controlling international transfers may exceed the benefits.[32] In any event, it is difficult to envision controls intended to protect a nation's international competitiveness that are feasible and effective.

On the host-country side, the developing countries can be expected to become even more active in the national monitoring of international technology transfers. And the competence of national agencies should steadily increase with experience and with more information becoming available. The specific instruments used to press for reduced payments, more appropriate technology, more local R&D, and so on, will change as countries appraise their past experience with controls and as new strategies are conceived. But the determination to increase national benefits from technology transfers is not likely to weaken.

---

[31] Franklin R. Root, "The Pricing of International Technology Transfers via Non-Affiliate Licensing Arrangements," in *Controlling International Technology Transfer*, ed. T. Sagafi-Nejad et al., pp. 120–33.

[32] See John H. Dunning, "The Consequences of International Transfer of Technology by Multinational Enterprises: Some Home Country Implications," in *International Production and the Multinational Enterprise*, ed. J. H. Dunning (London: George Allen & Unwin, 1981), pp. 321–63; R. G. Hawkins and T. N. Gladwin, "Conflicts in the International Transfer Technology: A U.S. Home-Country View," in *Controlling International Technology Transfer*, ed. T. Sagafi-Nejad et al., pp. 212–62.

What are the implications of the suggested future control scenario to the international manager? First, the manager must be constantly aware that the negotiation of international technology agreements is what has been called a "quadrilogue," meaning that it involves four parties: the seller, the buyer, the home country, and the host country.[33] In managing international technology transfers, therefore, the manager must be informed, attempt to understand the motivation, and even forecast the national control policies that must be recognized in managerial decision making. It may also be incumbent on the manager to participate in national policymaking by contributing relevant information and views.

A second implication is that the manager should remain open to the possibility that control pressures may not be a zero-sum game. The pressure of host governments to have local R&D facilities may benefit the firm with expanded opportunities for developing technology and for maintaining its technology advantage in local markets.

Still another implication is that the manager should be exploring the feasibility and benefits of alternative strategies for transferring technology. This may mean a shift by some firms to more arm's-length licensing. It may also mean technology-sharing with host countries through cross-licensing agreements or cooperative projects for technological development.

SUMMARY

The management of international technology transfers has become a major aspect of international business activity and promises to become even more critical in the future. As a management function, technology transfers that cross national boundaries raise a series of special international issues. In particular, the international enterprise is likely to encounter substantial involvement by governments of developing countries that are technology recipients.

EXERCISES AND DISCUSSION QUESTIONS

1. You are seeking governmental approval in a Third World country for a licensing agreement. The government officials want to reduce the agreed-upon royalty rate on the grounds that "technology is the common heritage of mankind." What logical counterargument would you make?
2. What criteria should the international firm use in selecting its strategy for overseas expansion to profit from a competitive technology advantage?
3. A Swedish firm has a central staff charged with developing processes specifically for use in Third World countries. Under what circumstances would you recommend that your international company follow this same pattern?
4. "The export of U.S. technology, much of which has been financed by government funds, should be controlled so as to protect U.S. international competitiveness and protect U.S. jobs." Do you agree or disagree and why?

---

[33] Howard V. Perlmutter and Tagi Sagafi-Nejad, *International Technology Transfer: Codes, Guidelines and a Muffled Quadrilogue* (New York: Pergamon Press, 1981).

5. In negotiating an international licensing agreement, how would you try to protect your U.S. firm so that it would not be foreclosed in the future from expanding in the market area of the licensee? Take into account the U.S. antitrust law, which makes illegal any licensing provisions that restrict the geographic area in which the licensee can compete.

6. Under what circumstances is it advantageous for a multinational to locate some of its R&D facilities abroad?

Multinational Accounting

An accounting system for multinational enterprises must fulfill several requirements simultaneously.[1] It must provide financial data for information and decision purposes to the local management of the particular unit. At the enterprise level, the system must provide internal statements that can be compared and used for decisions involving more than one country. The system must also provide financial statements that can be consolidated on an enterprise-wide basis. Finally, the accounting for the total enterprise and the individual subunits of the firm must respond to external reporting requirements, particularly those of the different countries in which the

---

[1] See Hanns-Martin W. Schoenfield, "International Accounting: Development, Issues, and Future Directions," *Journal of International Business Studies,* Fall 1981, pp. 83–100.

firm operates. As no single set of accounts can fulfill all these needs, multinationals have little choice other than to maintain parallel sets of accounting records.

A more detailed examination of these multiple requirements of accounting systems follows, along with an outline of the various national and international accounting standards and practices that have evolved to guide and regulate the ways in which accounts are presented. Managers need to be familiar with these standards if they are to interpret successfully the messages contained in a multinational's accounts. They should also understand how accounts based on different accounting standards and expressed in different currencies are restated onto a consistent basis for consolidation and then translated into a common currency. The technical details of translation, which are discussed in the final section of the chapter, can make a considerable difference to a firm's annual profit performance—particularly under fluctuating exchange rates.

REQUIREMENTS OF MULTINATIONAL ACCOUNTING

Subsidiary Reporting Requirements

At the subsidiary level, understandability of financial reports must be guaranteed within the national environment. National accounting standards and procedures, prescribed either by law or by local professional organizations, must be followed so that financial reports can be understood by tax and other government officials. Firms domiciled in countries operating under the so-called civil code law system are required to present financial statements in a form specified by law. The format of these legal accounts is far removed from the format expected for public financial reportings. In some countries, subsidiaries may also be subjected to unusually stringent demands because of the foreign nationality of the parent.

Adherence to national accounting standards permits each local manager to manage on the basis of familiar data and concepts, to compare performance with that of local competitors, and to evaluate results against local rather than parent-company standards. Furthermore, many managerial decisions are dependent on local conditions and have to be based on local data. For example, local inflationary conditions may require price-level adjustments for company expenses or sales for different time periods, even though such accounting practices are not typical in the country of the parent.

Given the multiple purposes served by financial reporting, the national operating units often find it necessary to prepare three or four different sets of financial statements. One set is based on nationally accepted accounting principles. A second set complies with the accounting principles and the translation methods that are accepted in the country of the home office. Still another set may be prepared to comply with the regulations of the various tax authorities involved. And, finally, separate financial statements may be prepared that present a picture of the enterprise for management. In the internal enterprise statement, for example, uniform valuation methods for assets of all subsidiaries might be used, regardless of the different legal regulations or locally accepted accounting practices.

Corporate Reporting Requirements

At multinational headquarters, comparability between accounts of subsidiaries is likely to be an important requirement. Allocation of resources and management attention is frequently based on comparative performance. The central accounting staff must also produce parent company financial statements and consolidated financial statements that meet the requirements of the jurisdiction in which the parent is incorporated, the requirements of regulatory bodies such as the U.S. Securities and Exchange Commission (SEC), and their own external audit requirements. Statement No. 14 of the U.S. Financial Accounting Standards Board, in particular, requires separate disclosure of figures for the United States and for foreign operations by geographic area, including revenue, sales to unaffiliated customers, operating profit or loss, and identifiable assets.

The multinational enterprise may also have to report beyond its country of incorporation. External reporting requirements are particularly extensive for firms raising capital in the U.S. or having shares listed on the U.S. stock exchanges. Many European firms have great difficulties with the U.S. requirements because they are unaccustomed by national tradition to making so much detailed information publicly available. An important force for greater disclosure is the growing practice of following the U.S. norms of the SEC when raising capital in the Eurobond markets.

Where shareholdings are multinational, and a single set of financial statements could cause communications difficulties, the Accountants International Study Group (AISG) has recommended "secondary" financial statements.[2] Some Dutch and Japanese multinationals, for example, report both according to their home accounting principles and U.S. principles with statements in English. Unilever records its salient figures in British pounds, Dutch florins, Austrian schillings, Belgian francs, French francs, German marks, Swiss francs, and U.S. dollars.

The broadest pressure for external reporting has been the movement to establish guidelines for multinational enterprises discussed in Chapter 12. The guidelines agreed to by the OECD countries are not substantially broader than U.S. requirements (Figure 21–1) but they extend the requirements to all OECD-based multinationals.

The guidelines are voluntary and require implementing national legislation in the OECD countries to be compulsory. Yet the existence of the "voluntary" guidelines exerts strong pressure on the multinationals to comply. The requirements to disclose intergroup pricing policies and geographical information on operations, performance, and employment go one step further toward strengthening national controls over activities that span country boundaries.[3] The United Nations Centre on Transnational Corporations has also been active in promoting international

---

[2] Accountants International Study Group, *International Financial Reporting*, Study no. 11 (Toronto: AISG, 1975).

[3] See Karl P. Sauvant and Farid G. Lavipour, eds., *Controlling Multinational Enterprises: Problems, Strategies, Counterstrategies* (Boulder, Colo.: Westview Press, 1976).

FIGURE 21-1   OECD Guidelines for Multinational Enterprise

Disclosure of Information

Enterprises should, having due regard to their nature and relative size in the economic context of their operations and to requirements of business confidentiality and to cost, publish in a form suited to improve public understanding a sufficient body of factual information on the structure, activities, and policies of the enterprise as a whole, as a supplement, insofar as necessary for this purpose, to information to be disclosed under the national law of the individual countries in which they operate. To this end, they should publish within reasonable time limits, on a regular basis, but at least annually, financial statements and other pertinent information relating to the enterprise as a whole, comprising in particular:

1. The structure of the enterprise, showing the name and location of the parent company, its main affiliates, its percentage ownership, direct and indirect, in these affiliates, including shareholdings between them.
2. The geographic areas* where operations are carried out and the principal activities carried on therein by the parent company and the main affiliates.
3. The operating results and sales by geographical area and the sales in the major lines of business for the enterprise as a whole.
4. Significant new capital investment by geographical area and, as far as practicable, by major lines of business for the enterprise as a whole.
5. A statement of the sources and uses of funds by the enterprise as a whole.
6. The average number of employees in each geographic area.
7. Research and development expenditure for the enterprise as a whole.
8. The policies followed in respect of intragroup pricing.
9. The accounting policies, including those on consolidation, observed in compiling the published information.

* For the purposes of the guideline on disclosure of information the term *geographic area* means groups of countries or individual countries as each enterprise determines is appropriate in its particular circumstances. While no single method of grouping is appropriate for all enterprises or for all purposes, the factors to be considered by an enterprise would include the significance of operations carried out in individual countries or areas as well as the effects on its competitiveness, geographic proximity, economic affinity, similarities in business environments and the nature, scale, and degree of interrelationships of the enterprises' operations in the various countries.

SOURCE: Organization for Economic Cooperations and Development, *International Investment and Multinational Enterprises* (Paris, 1976), pp. 14–15.

standards of accounting and reporting. Extensive recommendations were made by a U.N. Group of Experts in 1977 but not formally adopted as many countries felt that the United Nations was not the appropriate forum for setting accounting standards.[4]

Another important trend has been growing demand and expectations that business firms act in a socially responsible fashion.[5] In the future, there is a

[4] See United Nations, *International Standards of Accounting and Reporting for Transnational Corporations* (New York, 1977) (E./C.10/33); N. T. Wang, "The Design of International Standards of Accounting and Reporting for Transnational Corporations," *The Journal of International Law and Economics 2* (1977), pp. 447–64.

[5] Isaiah A. Litvak and Christopher J. Maule, "Foreign Corporate Social Responsibility in Less Developed Economies," *Journal of World Trade Law,* March–April 1975; and Melvin Anshen, ed., *Managing the Socially Responsible Corporation* (New York: Macmillan, 1974).

strong probability that multinational firms may have to publish a social audit and report on their relationship to the social environment and the effects of this relationship. As some business leaders have predicted, "In addition to their independently audited annual statements, firms will some day be legally obliged to submit audited social utility accounts—even if the definitive form of such accounts is not yet clear."[6]

Consolidation Requirements

The accounting treatment for consolidated financial statements recommended by the International Accounting Standard No. 3 and adopted in the United States and other countries is as follows:

Foreign subsidiaries: Financial statements must be consolidated line-by-line with the parent company and other subsidiaries.

Foreign associates: Not consolidated but recorded under the *equity method* in the parent company books. The equity method requires that the value of the investment in the parent company's books be increased or decreased to recognize the parent's share of profits or losses since the acquisition. To calculate this profit or loss, though, a foreign associate's financial statements must be translated into U.S. currency, as described later, with the translation profit or loss specified.

Investments: Recorded under the *cost method*. They are retained at cost on the parent company's books and income is recognized only to the extent that dividends are paid from profits rising after the date of acquisition.

Subsidiaries are entities over which the parent exercises control. Control is indicated by ownership of a majority of the equity capital, or control of the board. But control may occur below 51 percent ownership. Associates are companies in which the investment interest is substantial and over which the investor has the power to exercise significant influence. Power to exercise significant influence, however, is not presumed to exist below a holding of 20 percent voting power. Investments are all equity holdings not in subsidiaries or associates.

Another set of consolidation requirements of multinationals is in the process of being formed within the European Community (EC). The proposals are contained in the "Proposal for a Seventh Directive" published by the EC Commission which becomes mandatory on January 1, 1990. Article 6 of the proposal requires preparation of consolidated EC accounts for every "dominant undertaking," that is, a company controlling another, with its registered office in the EC wherever its subsidiaries are located. There is no exemption if this undertaking is itself a subsidiary of a foreign multinational preparing consolidated accounts. Even further,

---

[6] Jeffrey S. Arpan and Lee H. Radebaugh, *International Accounting and Multinational Enterprises*, 2nd ed. (New York: John Wiley & Sons, 1985), pp. 31–39.

there is a requirement to consolidate separate "dependent undertakings" within the EC reporting to the same dominant undertaking outside the EC. Thus a U.S. multinational with separate German, United Kingdom, and Greek subsidiaries would have to present consolidated EC accounts for these three operations.

NATIONAL ACCOUNTING STANDARDS AND PRACTICES

Accounting standards have been issued in most countries. In the United States, the Financial Accounting Standards Board (FASB) is the principal rule-making body. FASB standards are recognized by the American Institute of Certified Public Accountants (AICPA), which in effect sets auditing standards, and by the Securities and Exchange Commission (SEC), which requires compliance with the standards for all corporations with public issues of securities in the United States. The FASB is independent of the AICPA and other accounting associations, although it seeks their comments on "exposure drafts" of all proposed standards before they are finally announced. In most other countries recommendations as to accounting standards are issued by the professional accounting associations. In some countries, though, there is more than the one association issuing such recommendations.

Members of national accounting associations will usually adhere to the local standards both in preparing and auditing financial statements, but within-country variations in practice are common. Few, if any, national standards are set out as a comprehensive code of rigid rules. The local standard may indicate preferred alternatives, but leave the choice to the discretion of the practitioner. There is also an overriding requirement to give a true and fair view that on occasions may justify departure from a standard. Normally, such departures would be indicated in notes accompanying the financial statements, making it important for the cross-national user to examine entire statements and not just the accounting figures. Nor are most standards supported by a statutory requirement. Most go well beyond the requirements of corporation law or other statutes. Consequently, little can be done to enforce a standard, particularly if practicing accountants and auditors are outside the discipline of the standard-setting accounting association.

National accounting standards tend to have common elements because most national associations are members of the International Federation of Accountants (IFAC). The national associations may also be members of regional accounting associations. But international contacts do not mean that national standards are identical—not by a long way. Local standards have developed over the years out of varying social, political, and economic influences interacting with the current accounting practices and theories.[7] For example, where there has been widespread public ownership of corporate securities and a felt need to offset insider advantage, as in the United States, there has been a strong move toward

---

[7] Stephen A. Zeff, *Forging Accounting Principles in Five Countries: A History and an Analysis of Trends* (Champaign, Ill.: Stripes, Publishing, 1972).

BOX 21–1
Swiss Disclosure Reforms Blocked

Swiss government plans for imposing improved reporting standards on Swiss companies have run into strong opposition from a parliamentary committee that wants substantial amendments to the government proposals to preserve the competitive advantage that secrecy offers Swiss businesses.

The so-called national council commission has decided to oppose compulsory disclosure of cash flow and proposed requirements that would do away with hidden reserves. It has come out against the compulsory disclosure of the details of companies' major activities. It also wants to restrict consolidation to the largest groups, though it does favor arrangements for the canceling-out of profits and losses in the profit and loss accounts of companies that form part of a group.

The commission rests its recommendations on the need to "retain Swiss companies' competitive ability."

One expert on Swiss disclosure practice commented: "The feeling is that the new regulations are not going to be implemented in the next two or three years.

"Basically, Swiss accounting is very flexible as far as being conservative is concerned. You can understate your assets as much as you like. There are no reporting formats except for banks. That means that there are no statutory reporting requirements. The whole purpose is to keep as many things as secret as possible."

SOURCE: Adapted from "Report by Stuart Mansell," *Accountancy Age,* June 13, 1985, p. 3.

---

standardization, consistency, and much disclosure. On the other hand, Swiss accounting practices have grown up requiring minimum disclosure in an environment that favors conservatism and that has sought to shelter more closely held corporations and their owners from external political action. Accounting practice is not an end in itself. It is a service justified by the extent to which it reflects the needs of its environment and adapts as those needs change. A move toward international standards may thus run counter to maximum usefulness.[8] The Swiss clearly agree with this, as Box 21–1 illustrates.

The situation is not as bad as it seems, however, because national accounting practices can be clustered into less than a dozen groups.[9] National differences in accounting standards have been minor where practices have evolved from a common base or a country has adopted the practices of a more advanced country. Perhaps the most useful classification is that of Nobes, which is based on a hierarchy of characteristics as depicted in Figure 21–2.

The cross-national user of financial reports will on many occasions need to

---

[8] Irving L. Fantl, "The Case against International Uniformity," *Management Accounting,* May 1971.

[9] Frederick D. S. Choi and Gerhard G. Mueller, *International Accounting,* 2nd ed. (Englewood Cliffs, N.J.: Prentice-Hall, 1984), pp. 32–41.

FIGURE 21–2 The Nobes Hierarchical Classification of National Accounting Practices

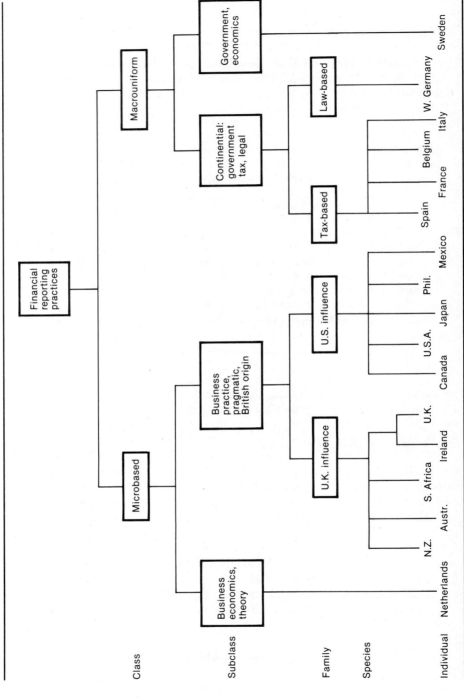

SOURCE: C. W. Nobes, "A Judgemental International Classification of Financial Reporting Practices," *Journal of Business Finance and Accounting*, Spring 1983, p. 7.

know specifically how national standards and practices differ in order to compare reports on a common basis. Two comprehensive reference works that provide such details are the American Institute of Certified Public Accountants, *Professional Accounting in 30 Countries,*[10] and Price Waterhouse's *International Survey of Accounting Principles and Reporting Practices.*[11] This second publication is in English, French, German and Spanish. Four examples of differences in accounting practices that serve to illustrate the lack of comparability are as follows:

Valuation of Inventories

In countries as diverse as Argentina, India, and the Philippines, exchange losses arising on foreign currency liabilities incurred for purchase of goods may be added to the cost of the goods in inventory when the losses are incurred, instead of being written off as an expense for the period in which they arise. Valuation at the lower of cost or market value still applies, but with the cost including the exchange losses. Furthermore, while many countries require inventory valuation based on first-in, first-out (FIFO), others, such as Canada, United States, Japan, and France permit the firm to select LIFO or other methods.

Valuation of Liabilities

German and Swiss practice takes a conservative approach to contingent liabilities and permits them to be overestimated, hence creating secret reserves. In other countries, hidden reserves are created by provision for taxes contingent on the distribution of funds when distribution is not intended. On the other hand, material rental commitments on long-term leases are not required to be disclosed in a wide range of countries—for example, Argentina, Australia, Brazil, France, Germany, and Japan.

Capital Gains and Losses

In the United Kingdom, Ireland, Australia, and New Zealand, as well as Peru, capital gains can be carried directly to capital reserve accounts without passing the credit through the income account as required in other countries. For the same countries, too, there is no requirement to amortize goodwill.

Price-Level Adjustments

In the 1970s, high inflation rates worldwide focused a great deal of attention on accounting methods of adjusting for inflation. Debates waged fiercely over different approaches. The resulting compromise patchwork of approved, recom-

---

[10] New York: AICPA, 1975, (792 pp.)

[11] R. D. Fitzgerald, A. D. Stickler, and T. R. Watts, eds. (Scarborough, Ontario: Price Waterhouse International, 1979).

mended, and required approaches introduced many national differences into accounts.[12] Major variations in national inflation rates are likely to continue. When combined with variations in accounting treatment, inflation will be a prime area for potential distortion in comparability of financial reports. Three main types of price-level adjustment may be encountered:

1. Appropriations of Income or Retained Earnings.   The least refined approach is to appropriate some current income, or retained earnings from past years, to a reserve for the increased replacement cost of the firm's assets. It is usually resorted to when the depreciation charges based on the historical cost of assets would be inadequate to finance the replacement of those assets. The idea is to reduce the funds viewed as available for dividend declaration and prevent the firm paying out its real capital. The appropriation, however, may be quite an arbitrary amount and is likely to be more influenced by available "profits" than by actual price changes. The user of financial statements, moreover, may be unable to tell on what basis the appropriation has been calculated. Appropriations out of retained earnings have been made quite frequently in the past, even in the United States. Charges direct to current earnings are less common but still arise in many countries.

2. Revaluations of Assets.   This approach revalues assets to approximate current replacement costs, either directly against the market or through use of an appropriate price-level index. If depreciation is then deducted on the revalued assets, operating income will reflect inflation more accurately. In many countries, revaluation is allowed if noted. In other countries, maximum revaluation levels are established and, in yet others, such as Brazil, companies are required to revalue assets each year using a government price index.

3. Comprehensive Adjustment for Price-Level Changes.   This method adjusts all items in the financial statements—assets, liabilities, costs, and revenues. Either a general price index can be used that retains historical cost as the basis or specific adjustments can be made to bring each item to its current market or replacement value. The United Kingdom took the lead in this field and in March 1980 adopted a comprehensive Current Cost Accounting solution. The details were specified in the U. K. Statement of Standard Accounting Practice No. 16. The standard was not made compulsory, however, and most corporations after providing the data for some years have now ceased to do so.

INTERNATIONAL ACCOUNTING STANDARDS

Differences in national accounting principles and practices can be justified in terms of local needs. But an opposing case can be made for uniform international

---

[12] Choi and Mueller, *International Accounting,* chapter 5.

FIGURE 21–3 Fun with Numbers: News Corp. Ltd. (U.S. $)

Australia	*United States*
Murdoch's earnings, as reported	
In Australia, News Corp. reporting a tremendous profit for the year ending June 30, 1985, breaking the $100 million barrier. **$101.3 million** **(75 cents per share)**	Under U.S. accounting rules, though, News Corp. made hardly any money because of currency losses and amortizing goodwill. **$29.8 million** **(23 cents per share)**
Murdoch's earnings, as they would have been	
In Australia, News Corp. would have shown a small loss had it owned the six TV stations Murdoch is after and Twentieth Century-Fox all year. **−$19.6 million** **(−14 cents per share)**	In the U.S., News Corp. would have shown a huge loss because it would have had to write off more than $100 million in goodwill. **−$263.2 million** **(−$2.09 per share)**
Murdoch's balance sheet, as reported	
In Australia, News Corp., which wrote up the value of its properties in 1984, had a very conservative debt-to-equity ratio on Sept. 30. **0.8 to 1**	In the U.S., where News Corp. isn't allowed to write up assets, the balance sheet is far from conservative. **3.4 to 1**
Murdoch's balance sheet, as it would have been	
In Australia, News Corp.'s ratio would have been conservative even with its new properties, because preferred stock counts as equity. **0.9 to 1**	In the U.S., meanwhile, with the preferred as debt and without the benefit of written-up assets, the balance sheet is horrendous. **11.6 to 1**

SOURCE: Reproduced from: Allan Sloan, "Understanding Murdoch—The Numbers Aren't What Really Matters," *Forbes*, March 10, 1986, p. 116.

standards. International standards reduce problems that arise from cross-national use of reports produced to different standards. Differences in accounting principles can affect performance comparisons and bias competitive decisions and allocations of resources.

There is substantial evidence that the FAS 8 requirement that U.S. multinationals show exchange translation gains or losses in the revenue account discouraged some investments, accelerated dividend payments from subsidiaries,[13] and nega-

---

[13] T. G. Evans, W. R. Folks, and M. Jilling, *The Impact of Statement of Financial Accounting Standards No. 8 on the Foreign Exchange Risk Management Practices of American Multinationals: An Economic Impact Study* (New York: Financial Accounting Standards Board, 1978).

BOX 21–2
Extract from General Electric Company
Annual Report 1985

Statement of Financial Responsibility

To Share Owners of General Electric Company. The financial information in this Report, including the audited financial statements, has been prepared by General Electric management. Preparation of these statements and data involves estimates and the use of judgment. Accounting principles underlying the financial statements are generally accepted in the United States and are consistent with standards issued by the International Accounting Standards Committee. However, in a few important instances, which are commented on in note 1 on page 38, there is no single specified accounting principle or standard. Where management makes a choice from reasonable, accepted alternatives, it uses methods which it believes are prudent for GE.

---

tively impacted valuation on Wall Street[14] (see later in this chapter). Differences in accounting practices between Australia and the United States are also argued to have helped Rupert Murdoch in his acquisition of 14 magazines from Ziff-Davis for $350 million, Twentieth-Century Fox for $575 million, and six T.V. stations fom Metromedia Broadcasting for $1.65 billion. Figure 21–3 shows the effect caused by decisions in the Australian parent's accounts to defer currency losses, not to amortize goodwill, to revalue assets, and to count preferred stock as equity.

The most significant move toward a set of international standards was made with the establishment of the International Accounting Standards Committee (IASC) in June 1973. The committee is comprised of representatives from professional accountancy associations of some 13 countries and operates through a secretariat in London. The member associations have pledged to support the standards promulgated by the committee and to use their best endeavors to ensure that published financial statements and audit statements comply with the standards or that there is disclosure of the extent to which they do not. They also pledge action to persuade governments, authorities controlling securities, and the business community to comply with these standards. The International Federation of Stock Exchanges, for example, has adopted a resolution that its members will require conformance with IASC standards in their listing requirements. General Electric Company has taken the lead in the United States in declaring that its financial statements are consistent with IASC standards (see Box 21–2). A number of leading European and Japanese multinationals do likewise.

---

[14] David A. Ziebart and David H. Kim, "An Examination of the Market Reactions Associated with SFAS No. 8 and SFAS No. 52," *The Accounting Review*, April 1987, pp. 343–57.

FIGURE 21–4   International Accounting Standards (as of March 1, 1987)

IAS 1	Disclosure of Accounting Policies
IAS 2	Valuation and Presentation of Inventories in the Context of the Historical Cost System
IAS 3	Consolidated Financial Statements
IAS 4	Depreciation Accounting
IAS 5	Information to Be Disclosed in Financial Statements
IAS 6	Accounting Responses to Changing Prices (superseded by IAS 15)
IAS 7	Statements of Changes in Financial Position
IAS 8	Unusual and Prior Period Items and Changes in Accounting Policies
IAS 9	Accounting for Research and Development Activities
IAS 10	Contingencies and Events Occurring after the Balance Sheet Date
IAS 11	Accounting for Construction Contracts
IAS 12	Accounting for Taxes on Income
IAS 13	Presentation of Current Assets and Current Liabilities
IAS 14	Reporting Financial Information by Segment
IAS 15	Information Reflecting the Effects of Changes in Prices
IAS 16	Accounting for Property, Plant, and Equipment
IAS 17	Accounting for Leases
IAS 18	Revenue Recognition
IAS 19	Accounting for Retirement Benefits in the Financial Statements of Employers
IAS 20	Accounting for Government Grants and Disclosure of Government Assistance
IAS 21	Accounting for the Effects of Changes in Foreign Exchange Rates
IAS 22	Accounting for Business Combinations
IAS 23	Capitalization of Borrowing Costs
IAS 24	Related Party Disclosures
IAS 25	Accounting for Investments
IAS 26	Accounting and Reporting by Retirement Benefit Plans

The IASC moves toward its standards through committee study of accounting topics that leads to exposure drafts that are circulated for comments and then restudied before final issuance of International Accounting standards. Figure 21–4 lists the standards published up until March 1987.

A variety of other bodies are concerned with recommending or legislating international standards of one sort or another.[15] In fact, there are so many interested parties, both politically as users and professionally as preparers, that pressure for change and arguments about how changes are to be specified are likely to proceed for generations.[16]

RESTATEMENT OF ACCOUNTS

The restatement of accounts is the process of adjusting financial reports, as stated in foreign currencies, to meet home-country accounting standards. After such adjustments, local currencies are translated into home-country currency amounts.

[15] Joseph P. Cummings and William L. Rogers, "Developments in International Accounting," *CPA Journal*, May 1978.

[16] S. J. Gray, J. C. Shaw, and L. B. McSweeney, "Accounting Standards and Multinational Corporations," *Journal of International Business Studies*, 10 (Spring–Summer 1981), pp. 121–36.

The process of restatement brings accounts onto a basis deemed suitable for consolidation purposes. But it does not necessarily produce an ideal common comparison base—and can raise as many problems as it solves. The financial statements to be consolidated have a domicile in terms of an underlying set of accounting principles, and such domicile orientation cannot be easily changed through adjustments to the financial statements themselves. For example, financial statements prepared in Argentina according to local accounting practices and then restated to a Canadian basis would differ markedly from those resulting if the Argentine operation had taken place in Canada and been accounted for originally in terms of Canadian practices.

Consolidation raises such problems as the treatment of reserves for future taxes on repatriated profits. A conservative accounting approach that includes such reserves in a consolidation, even though it is unlikely that the taxes will be paid, can be misleading as to the profitability of a foreign operation. A similar problem can arise in the treatment of depreciation expenses. To secure comparability among subsidiaries, a uniform rate of depreciation may be used. But to reduce current taxes and increase cash flows, the most rapid rate of depreciation allowed for local tax purposes should be taken. Faster depreciation for a subsidiary in a country where tax laws permit will increase cash flows but decrease net income in the short run.

The alignment of price-level adjustments also requires special attention. The aim of consolidation is to bring financial statements onto a common basis of valuation. If this is not achieved, consolidated financial statements become an amalgam of different price-level approaches without conceptual meaning. The asset values and revenue disclosed in the consolidated statements cannot be said to reflect any standard concept of asset valuation.

When a change is made in the date at which an asset valuation is set, the date of the exchange rate used for translation should also be changed. After all, an exchange rate roughly equates the relative purchasing power of two currencies at a given date. When an asset is revalued to a new date, there will be a new exchange rate reflecting the relative change in the inflation rates of the two currencies between the two dates. Thus, historical cost valuations should be translated at the appropriate historical exchange rate. But historical costs that have been revalued to approximate current costs should be translated at the current exchange rate. Techniques of translation are dealt with in more detail in the next section. It is important to remember, though, that restatement and translation must be consistent in the exchange rates chosen.

It is also recommended that restatement for price-level differences be carried out before translation into the currency of consolidation. This permits some concept of valuation pertinent to the country of origin. Above all, it would be quite unacceptable to translate first and then to restate in the new currency, using the inflation rate recorded for that new currency. The asset remains in the first country and the inflation rate there since the date at which the translation is set may have been quite different. An example of restatement of a subsidiary's accounts is shown in Figure 21–5. Three adjustments are made: to add back profit margin

FIGURE 21–5   Restatement of a Subsidiary's Financial Statements for Consolidation Purposes

	Before Adjustment (000 guilders)	Adjustments (000 guilders)	Restatement (000 guilders)
Revenue accounts:			
Sales	3,600	—	3,600
Less cost of sales	2,400	−120	2,280
Gross margin	1,200	120	1,320
Less expenses	1,075	− 80	995
Profit before tax	125	200	325
Taxation provision	25	137	162
Net profit	100	63	163
Assets and liabilities:			
Cash	50		50
Accounts receivables	850		850
Inventories	700		700
Current assets	1,600		1,600
Current liabilities	1,100	137	1,237
Working capital	500	−137	363
Fixed assets	600	80	680
	1,100	− 57	1,043
Long-term liabilities	300	—	300
Net worth	800	− 57	743
Capital	600	—	600

Adjustments are required as follows:

1. Reduce cost of sales by 120,000 guilders representing parent-company margin eliminated from last year's consolidation.
2. Reduce depreciation by 80,000 guilders to express it at standard rates used by parent company.
3. Increase taxation provision from 20 percent to 50 percent to allow for tax on future profit remittances.

eliminated from last year's consolidation (this margin was originally taken as profit when goods were transferred within the multinational system, but as they were not sold outside by balance date had to be deducted from last year's profit and added to this year's); to reduce excessive local depreciation to the home-country standard; and to increase the tax allowance to the level required if profits were remitted.

CURRENCY TRANSLATION

Translation is the term applied to reexpressing, in any required currency, financial statements expressed in another. This process is sometimes loosely referred to as conversion, but conversion should be reserved for actual physical exchange of one currency for another. Conversion takes place at a specific market rate at a specific time. Translation is a notional reexpression, and the exchange rate used should be chosen to produce the equivalent value in the new currency.

Alternative Translation Methods

Revenues and expenses, with the exception of depreciation and amortization charges, are usually translated at an average exchange rate for the period over which the revenue statement extends. For balance sheet items and depreciation on those items, however, four clearly distinguishable methods might be used. These are tabulated in Figure 21–6.

The *current-noncurrent* method translates current assets (for example, cash, receivables, and inventories) and current liabilities at the current rate of exchange—that is, the spot exchange rate on the balance sheet date. All other assets and liabilities are translated at the historical rate prevailing when assets were acquired and liabilities incurred. The only conceptual justification for favoring or disfavoring current assets and liabilities with the current rate of exchange is that their dating does not have to be recorded and the translation calculation is simplified. Significant fluctuations in current rates will produce translation profits or losses that distort the operating results even if the value of current assets and liabilities in the base currency remains constant. Also, the inherent advantages in the event of a devaluation of holding inventory in preference to cash or receivables, and in financing by local long-term borrowing, are not recognized. The method assumes that in the event of a devaluation assets held as inventory will suffer the same degree of foreign exchange loss as the holding of cash and receivables, an assumption that is generally not valid.

The *monetary-nonmonetary* method applies the current exchange rate to all financial assets and all liabilities, both current and long term. Physical, or nonmonetary, assets are translated at historical rates. This method is more defensible if all physical items are stated at historical cost. But if physical items have already been revalued at current market prices, translation at historical exchange rates will produce questionable results. In comparison with the current-noncurrent method, this method rewards holding of physical assets under devaluation. The implication is that physical assets will appreciate in local currency to the extent that the exchange value of that currency depreciates.

FIGURE 21–6   Four Currency Translation Methods

	Items Translated at	
	Current Rate	*Historical Rate*
1. Current-noncurrent	Current assets and current liabilities	Fixed assets and long-term liabilities Common stock
2. Monetary-nonmonetary	Financial assets and all liabilities	Physical assets Common stock
3. Temporal	Financial assets and all liabilities and physical assets valued at current prices	Physical assets valued at historical cost Common stock
4. Current rate	All assets and all liabilities and common stock	—

The *temporal* method differs from the monetary-nonmonetary only in the treatment of physical assets that have been revalued. It is based on the temporal principle, which states: "Money, receivables, and payables measured at the amounts promised should be translated at the foreign exchange rate in effect at the balance sheet date. Assets and liabilities measured at money prices should be translated at the foreign exchange rate in effect at the dates to which the money prices pertain." Cash, receivables, and payables are translated at the current rate, along with physical assets carried at current values. Assets carried at historical cost are recorded at the historical rate. The method thus produces similar results to the monetary-nonmonetary method when physical assets are valued at historical cost. The advantage of this method, then, is that it gives the best indication of real performance in the translated currency when assets are valued on a mixed basis of historical cost and market price. As we shall see later, though, it does have drawbacks.

The fourth method is called the *current-rate* method, the *closing-rate* method, or sometimes the *net-assets* method. All of a foreign subsidiary's assets and liabilities are translated at the current rate of exchange. The use of the current rate throughout ignores the idea that there will be appreciation in assets to offset currency devaluation, or depreciation to offset revaluation. In fact, it seldom follows that appreciation is directly in step with devaluation. The method is simple and produces the same result as the temporal method when assets are carried at current prices. Moreover, there is no change in the balance sheet ratios on translation, as occurs when historical and current rates are mixed.

These four named methods are not the only approaches. Hybrid methods are also possible. Two variations of the monetary-nonmonetary approach, for example, are: (1) translate inventories at current, or (2) translate long-term debt at an historical rate. Translation of inventories at current rate would be an acceptable practice when the inventories have been revalued at current market values. The use of current rate would also make sense following a devaluation if the market value of inventories would not rise proportionately and use of an historical rate would postpone recognition of an unrealized loss. Translation of long-term debt at an historical rate would avoid recording translation gains or losses on an item that does not have to be repaid for many years, yet for which translation gains or losses under a fluctuating exchange rate might obscure what is really happening on operations.

The different translation methods can lead to major variations in translated balance sheet figures with significant differences in the translation gain or loss. These variations are illustrated in Figure 21–7, where a 16.7 percent devaluation in the peseta produces gains from $266,000 to losses of $200,000—a range equal to nearly 40 percent of the equity invested in the subsidiary concerned:

> Current-noncurrent method. The net working capital position determines the accounting exposure to exchange fluctuation under this method because the current rate is applied only to current, or working capital, items. In the example, a positive net working capital of $800,000 existed before

FIGURE 21–7 Translation Gains and Losses Following a Foreign Currency Devaluation: Four Alternative Methods*

Foreign Subsidiary's Balance Sheet	Local Currency (pesetas millions)	Historical Rate pts. 100 = $1 ($000s)	Translated U.S. $ Equivalents New Current Rate Pts. 120 = $1			
			Current-Noncurrent ($000s)	Monetary-Nonmonetary ($000s)	Temporal ($000s)	Current Rate ($000s)
Assets:						
Cash	40	400	333c	333c	333c	333c
Accounts receivable	40	400	333c	333c	333c	333c
Inventories: (Cost 120 pts. millions)						
Market	80	800	667c	800	667c	667c
Fixed assets	200	2,000	2,000	2,000	2,000	1,667c
	360	3,600	3,333	3,466	3,333	3,000
Liabilities:						
Current liabilities	80	800	667c	667c	667c	667c
Long-term debt	160	1,600	1,600	1,333c	1,333c	1,333c
	240	2,400	2,267	2,000	2,000	2,000
Shareholder's equity	120	1,200	1,200	1,200	1,200	1,200
Translation gain (loss)			(134)	266	133	(200)
	360	3,600	3,332	3,466	3,333	3,000

* c indicates translation at current rate.

devaluation. Hence a 16.7 percent devaluation shows a translation loss of $134,000.

Monetary-nonmonetary method. The firm's accounting exposure is measured by its net monetary asset position. This is negative, that is, −$1,600,000. Consequently, the firm records a gain on devaluation of 16.7 percent or $266,000.

Temporal method. Inventories are valued at market rates so must be translated at the current rate and added into the exposure. The negative exposure is reduced to $800,000, and the gain on devaluation is halved to $133,000.

Current-rate method. Since all assets and liabilities are translated at the current rate, the firm's accounting exposure is equal to the net asset figure of $1,200,000. This gives a 16.7 percent devaluation loss of $200,000.

Required Translation Methods

Prior to 1976, U.S. corporations were permitted to choose among alternative translation procedures. From 1960, the American Institute of Certified Public Accountants (AICPA) advocated the monetary-nonmonetary approach; but corporations still widely used the current-noncurrent method, which had been advocated previously, and the two hybrid methods mentioned in the previous section. The latitude in selection of the translation method, however, was removed in 1975. From 1976, all U.S. public corporations and foreign corporations that issued securities in the United States were required to adopt the temporal method, as embodied in Statement No. 8 of the Financial Accounting Standards Board (FAS 8).

FAS 8 required that translation gains and losses be carried directly into the revenue account. They could not, as was previously the case, be charged to a foreign exchange reserve account that made it possible to smooth the impact of foreign exchange fluctuations upon reported earnings. As a result, "accounting exposure," in the sense of the net amount of assets that were exposed to foreign exchange fluctuations, became an important consideration. All items translated at current prices are "exposed" to fluctuations in the spot exchange rate, the greater the net exposure, the greater the exchange gain or loss that was required to be recorded against earnings.

There was widespread discontent with FAS 8 among U.S. multinationals.[17] And by late 1981, after several exposure drafts, the FASB issued a new statement—FAS 52—to take effect from December 1982.[18] FAS 52 adopts the *current-rate*

---

[17] Frederick D. S. Choi, Howard D. Lowe, and Reginald Worthley, "Accountors, Accountants, and Standard No. 8," *Journal of International Business Studies* 9 (Fall 1978), p. 85; Helen Gernon, "The Effect of Translation on Multinational Corporations' Internal Performance Evaluation," *Journal of International Business Studies,* Spring/Summer 1983, pp. 103–12.

[18] See Deloitte Haskins & Sells, "Foreign Currency Translation: FASB Statement No. 52," in *International Finance,* ed. Gerald D. Gay and Robert W. Kolb (Richmond, Va.: Robert F. Dame, Inc., 1983), pp. 579–619.

method and removes the translation gain or loss from reported earnings by recording it in the balance sheet in a new subsection of shareholders' equity. Under FAS 52, all items on the foreign subsidiary's balance sheet are calculated at the current value of their historical cost in the "functional currency," in effect adjusting for inflation. The change in net worth calculated on this basis is then translated at the current exchange rate to provide the translation gain or loss. The functional currency for a self-contained subsidiary is that in which it transacts most of its business—in other words, its local currency. For foreign branches that are really an extension of a parent unit in some other country, the functional currency is that of the parent.

The retention of historical cost—although adjusted for inflation—produces a problem in hyperinflation currencies. FAS 52 has allowed for this with an arbitrary rule that any currency that inflates by more than 100 percent in three years is not stable enough to be accepted as a functional currency. Dollar reporting must be used instead.

Analysts point out that they must now work with two numbers in place of the earnings figure they analyzed under FAS 8. Now they have earnings per share and a fluctuating book value per share reflecting currency changes. Some firms, of course, object to the fact that translation gains can never be incorporated into earnings until a subsidiary is closed or sold.

Outside the United States, use of the temporal method was never widespread. In some countries, the monetary-nonmonetary method predominates, in others the current-noncurrent method, but in those with most overseas investment the current-rate method has been more common—for example, France, Japan, the Netherlands, and the United Kingdom. The United Kingdom has now adopted SSAP 20, very similar to FAS 52. Also, the International Accounting Standard, IAS 21, became effective in January 1985 and follows the same lines.

Selecting the Translation Exchange Rates

The guiding principle in selection of exchange rates is to choose the rate that best reflects the business reality. Hence, if the firm has actually engaged in capital conversion from one currency to the other, it is the actual rate for the conversion that would be used—even if that rate is obtained at a high official rate level or a subsidized level. Most translations of financial statements, however, are purely notional calculations. In these cases, the preferred rate is the quoted spot buying rate on the free market. Such a rate will frequently differ from government official exchange rates, and it may be difficult because of exchange controls and regulations to transfer funds obtained at such a rate into and out of the country in question. But official rates may not reflect the underlying currency value and the firm may have no intention of converting its capital investment at those controlled rates.

Because many exchange rates fluctuate by the hour, some authorities recommend the use of a bookkeeping rate that approximates the current exchange rate and is changed only when there has been a significant move in the exchange rate. While simplifying both calculation and the recording of exchange rates, this approach introduces an arbitrary decision into translation practice.

SUMMARY

The multinational faces a wide array of requirements for financial disclosure both at subsidiary and corporate level. Many of these requirements seek different information. Frequently, too, the accounting practices and standards under which the accounts of a multinational's unit are prepared will differ. The firm's accountants, therefore, may have to make many adjustments to restate basic figures before they can be consolidated. With fluctuating exchange rates, translation of restated financial statements into a single currency also requires a great deal of care. Throughout this process, the accountants will be faced with the need to meet a growing body of international and national accounting standards, each with detailed rules and guidelines.

EXERCISES AND DISCUSSION QUESTIONS

1. Choose a large U.S. multinational and from its last annual report identify adjustments that have been made in subsidiary statements to make them consistent with U.S. reporting standards. Are there any balance sheet notes that are included to meet special requirements of non-U.S. users?
2. Explain in your own words why historical cost valuation should be translated at historical exchange rates and current valuations at current exchange rates.
3. Translate the restated figures for the subsidiary shown in Figure 21–5 into U.S. dollars using the four alternative translation methods. Assume that the historical rate was U.S. $1 = 1.5 guilders, the rate at balance sheet date is U.S. $1 = 2 guilders, the average rate is U.S. $1 = 1.75 guilders, and inventories are valued at end-of-year market prices.
4. What in your opinion are the strengths and weaknesses of the four major translation methods?
5. Present an argued case against the requirement of FAS 52 to record translation gains and losses only in the balance sheet and never against earnings.

CHAPTER 22

Management Information and Control in the Multinational

The need for a formal planning and control system is not uniquely related to international operations. Nevertheless, the most frequently cited examples of advanced planning and control practices are those of multinational firms. This reflects the special importance in multinational operations of an effective planning and control system as a tool for knitting the entity together across national boundaries.

This chapter describes the objectives and operation of the overall control process in the multinational and then goes on to examine the accounting rules adopted for internal budgeting and financial reports. Exchange fluctuations introduce special difficulties not faced in the control of domestic units. The firm's internal audit procedures must also be viewed as an integral part of the control system. Internal auditing holds the control system together by ensuring that the quality of data, reports, and operating procedures are maintained at acceptable levels throughout the organization. The final section takes a brief look at the special problems of controlling joint ventures where the legal power to exercise complete control over decisions is limited.

OBJECTIVES OF CONTROL IN MULTINATIONALS

A good multinational control system will fulfill three objectives. It will supply adequate data for top management to monitor, evaluate, and adjust as necessary the global strategy of the enterprise. It will provide the means for coordinating the units of the enterprise so that they work toward a common objective. It will also provide the basis for evaluating the performance of managers at each level of the organization.

For strategy evaluation, the information system should deliver data from the organizational units on the business environment, customer demand, and competitive developments that the units are facing. For coordination purposes, the control system should be structured to show where multinational economies can be realized and to discourage units from following independent suboptimization patterns. The firm that fails to achieve multinational economies by expanding competition to a global level is likely to be left behind in the global competitive race.[1] For performance evaluation, the system must measure the achievements of managers toward corporate objectives against those elements that each manager can control.

The presumption that a control system is needed rests on a belief that the units of a multinational organization will not automatically act to achieve the same goals nor act most appropriately even when goals are agreed. The different parts of a multinational have specialized knowledge of their individual environments. In coping with those environments, each unit will tend to develop different objectives and suboptimize to its own advantage.[2] Individual units are also likely to struggle with one another for power and status, forming and reforming coalitions in the process. The control system must recognize both tendencies. It is the primary method for achieving collaboration among the individual units.[3]

APPROACHES TO CONTROL

In establishing a control system, an organization has to determine the relative emphasis it will place on input, or behavioral, controls and output controls at

---

[1] See C. H. Prahalad and Yves L. Doz, "An Approach to Strategic Control in MNCs," *Sloan Management Review,* Summer 1981, pp. 5–13.

[2] See P. R. Lawrence and J. W. Lorsch, *Organization and Environment* (Cambridge, Mass.: Harvard University Graduate School of Business Administration, 1967).

[3] Michel Crozier, *The Bureaucratic Phenomenon* (Chicago: Chicago University Press, 1964).

each level.[4] Input controls create control "ex ante" and operate through behavioral interaction. Guidance and direction are extended to subordinates through personal oversight—and the expectations so communicated are given in advance of the action. There are implications of reward or punishment according to whether the expectations are met. Behavior is thus modified before the event. Output control, on the other hand, operates "ex post," feeding back indicators of performance with less personal interaction, such as performance against budget or cost variances.

Input control works best where an organization is small and relatively homogeneous and the effects of actions are fairly clear. Output control is better in large complex organizations where standard measures can convey a picture of what is happening in a relatively objective way and give some basis for making comparisons.

In a multinational, one would expect to find output measures being given more attention at higher levels in the organization. At the higher levels, the tasks being reviewed are more complex and heterogeneous, and it is less clear what the effects of specific actions would be for any unit.

Not only do multinationals exhibit differences in the emphasis they place on input and output control, they also exhibit differences in the extent and degree of explicitness of the rules through which control is exercised. A triangular continuum of approaches labeled *market, rules,* or *corporate culture* has been derived from the work of Ouchi by Lebas and Weigenstein:[5]

The Market Approach.   Under this approach, external market forces are left to control the behavior of management within the units of the multinational. Typically, the organization is decentralized and transfer prices are set by freely negotiating units. Each unit, moreover, is free to buy or sell inside or outside the multinational system. The market determines the wisdom of each unit's decisions and alone indicates to managers whether they need to change their behavior. The control orientation for a firm managed on such a market basis therefore rests predominantly on output controls.

The Rules Approach.   A rules-oriented organization replaces market feedback with strongly imposed rules and procedures. It will usually have highly developed planning and budgeting systems with extensive formal reporting. Its drawback, of course, is that it does not necessarily react quickly to changes in the environment. On the other hand, given identification of the need to change, a change of rules can be quickly implemented. This type of control uses both

---

[4] W. G. Ouchi and M. A. Maguire, "Organizational Control—Two Functions," *Administrative Science Quarterly,* 20 (1975), pp. 559–69; W. G. Ouchi, "Markets, Bureaucracies and Clans," *Administrative Science Quarterly* 25 (1980), pp. 129–41.

[5] Michael Lebas and Jane Weigenstein, "Management Control: The Role of Rules, Markets, and Culture," *Journal of Management Studies* 23(May 1986), pp. 259–72.

input and output controls in a highly formalized way. The multinational's control manual will undoubtedly be a weighty volume of great detail.

The Corporate Culture Approach.   The culture-controlled organization has internalized its goals by developing a strong set of beliefs and values which condition its operations. It has strong norms of behavior, but these are informal and less explicit and allow members of the organization to extrapolate and develop as new situations arise. Like national cultures, the corporate culture is constantly evolving, although it may take some time to adjust when the environmental change is major. The control process commences with an individual's introduction into the values, beliefs, myths, norms, and practices of the organization as well as through formal training, and through initiation into the rituals and ceremonies of the organization, such as annual conferences and planning reviews. The culture approach usually rests more strongly on input controls through its emphasis on inculcation into "the way we do things around here."

THE INFLUENCE OF NATIONAL CULTURAL TRAITS

In designing and adjusting the control mix used within a multinational—that is, the mix of input, output, market, rules, and corporate culture—it must also be borne in mind that attitudes towards control systems may vary among national cultures.

The designer of a multinational control system should, therefore, be alert to potential differences in management approaches to such aspects as budget preparation, the horizon against which a budget is prepared, the importance of achieving or exceeding budgets, and reaction to feedback. Daley and associates, for example, found in a comparison between Japanese and U.S. controllers and managers that Japanese controllers and managers had a longer-term planning bias and viewed budgets more highly as a communication device than their American counterparts.[6]

While one control approach may work very well within a given national culture, it may actually impede performance within another. The challenge is thus to recognize where such differences may arise and build a control system to accommodate national cultural differences. By and large, the designer wishes to avoid a system that allows many national peculiarities. Such a system tends to weaken control and comparability and possibly reduce the opportunities for unlocking economies across national boundaries. Methods of identifying and interpreting substantial differences in attitudes to control are, therefore, of some importance to the control system designer.

One such method for classifying national cultures has been advanced by

---

[6] Lane Daley, James Jiambalvo, Gary L. Sundem, and Yasumasa Kondo, "Attitudes Toward Financial Control Systems in the United States and Japan," *Journal of International Business Studies*, Fall 1985, pp. 91–110.

Hofstede[7] and was described in Chapter 17. His four dimensions vary across national cultures. Each has important implications for design and operation of an effective control system.

Power Distance. Hofstede defines power distance as the degree to which a culture accepts unequal distribution of power and privileges and the exercise of personal absolute authority. In a country such as France, where inequality is accepted and hierarchical authority is valued, a strong rules approach to control is likely to work best. There would be minimal lateral relationships in the organization and a strong dependence on the chain of command and rules set by superiors. In Sweden, however, the power distance is smaller, with a much greater wish to minimize inequality. The organizational structure is likely to be flatter and decentralized, with participation and teamwork prized and hierarchical interference minimal. The French culture would accept a more rules-oriented approach and the Swedish culture a corporate-culture approach.

Uncertainty Avoidance. This is a measure of the extent to which a society is risk averse. A risk-averse society tends to establish more formal rules and be less tolerant of deviant behavior. The preferred control system is thus likely to be more rules-based as the risk averseness and power distance increase.

Individualism-Collectivism. This dimension describes the extent to which the social norms constrain individuals—that is, how much individualistic behavior is accepted. In an individualistic society with an emphasis on initiative and action, adaptability to change and a fast reaction time are essential. A market approach to control appears most appropriate. In a collectivist society in which group norms control individual behavior, the control emphasis would be more on maintaining group coherence and participation. A corporate culture approach would be more appropriate. The obedience conditioning so typical of many Japanese management development programs illustrates the importance placed on corporate culture inculcation within Japan.

Masculinity-Femininity. The fourth dimension identified by Hofstede classifies national cultures on a scale according to their adoption of ''masculine'' values (such as assertiveness, acquisitiveness, and money-value orientation) as against ''feminine' values (such as concern for others and quality-of-life orientation). A ''masculine'' national culture would be more likely to produce a market approach or a rules approach to control. A ''feminine'' culture would be more likely to adopt a corporate culture approach with stronger norms for group coherence.

---

[7] G. Hofstede, *Culture's Consequences: International Differences in Work-Related Values* (Beverly Hills: Sage Publications, 1980).

In using Hofstede's four dimensional classification, it seems more appropriate to examine a national culture for its general positioning under each of the four dimensions than try to classify each nation into a category defined along four dimensions. The approach then becomes more of a diagnostic tool than an attempt at formal classification.

In the case of France, to continue the example introduced above, not only is the power-distance large but there also appears to be strong uncertainty avoidance with an absence of informal activities. These two dimensions point in the same direction towards a rules-based approach to control. The remaining two dimensions, however, shade the expectation more towards a market approach to control. The French are a strongly individualistic nation with each striving towards his or her own objectives. Moreover, masculine values in terms of personal assertiveness and orientation towards income and ownership are also strongly held. On the triangular continuum, then, France would be placed somewhere along the line between rules- and market-oriented approaches. It is interesting that a comparison by Cray of control exercised by U.S. multinationals over 27 subsidiaries in Great Britain and 30 subsidiaries in France found that "subsidiaries located in France were significantly more likely to operate under high levels of control."[8] Moreover, the control differences seemed not to result from difference in language or problems in communication.

Cultural traits of the multinational's parent nation also appear to have influenced control systems. Egelhoff compared control patterns of U.S., U.K., and European multinationals.[9] Although he (unfortunately) failed to specify the exact national composition of "European," he nevertheless found significant differences between the U.S. and European multinationals in type of control utilized, with U.K. firms generally lying between the two. U.S. multinationals tended to measure more quantifiable and objective aspects of a foreign subsidiary and its environment, while European multinationals tended to measure more qualitative aspects. The European multinationals also filled a significantly higher percentage of key marketing and manufacturing positions in foreign subsidiaries with parent company nationals than either the U.S. or U.K. multinationals. They thus leant more heavily on input control.

These findings confirm those of an earlier study by Brandt and Hulbert in which U.S. multinationals employed local nationals for managerial positions in their subsidiaries more frequently than did either European or Japanese firms. On the other hand, communication patterns between the parent and the subsidiaries also differed. Most U.S. companies held annual meetings for the chief executive officers of their affiliates, whereas fewer than half of the European and Japanese

---

[8] David Cray, "Control and Coordination in Multinational Corporations," *Journal of International Business Studies,* Fall 1984, pp. 85–98.

[9] William G. Egelhoff, "Patterns of Control in U.S., U.K., and European Multinational Corporations," *Journal of International Business Studies,* Fall 1984, pp. 73–83.

firms held such meetings annually. Also, visits between the head of the Brazilian subsidiary and his or her home office superior averaged 4.8 times per year for the U.S. firms, compared with 3.4 and 2.9 for the European and Japanese companies, respectively.[10]

THE CONTROL PROCESS

The Annual Planning Cycle

The formal control process is usually constructed around an annual planning cycle, beginning with the submission to the subsidiaries of planning guidelines from the central office. These guidelines often emerge from the development of a global strategy, as discussed in Chapter 9. The guidelines will vary in amount of detail, depending on the firm's managerial philosophy. Some companies believe that extensive corporate guidelines, even to the extent of specific sales targets, provide "better coordination between regions, better execution of plans after they have been approved, better allocation of capital spending, and the acceptance of more ambitious goals by units in the field."[11] Others take the view that "bottom-up" planning, which relies heavily on local initiative, encourages better performance from local units because they best understand their own capabilities. In the latter case, guidelines are minimal, and the subsequent global strategy assessment process at the center is used to highlight those units whose plans seem to be out of line.

After receiving the guidelines, subsidiary managers prepare their own plans, usually in a format specified in a standard planning or budget manual. The trend has been to increase the central requirements for detailed information on markets and competitors and to move away from internal accounting figures as the sole focus of the planning.[12] The subsidiary management's plan, including an assessment of the competitive situation and proposed actions, is then subjected to critical central review.

Some corporations have formal review meetings that pit the functional specialists at headquarters against the line managers who have submitted the plans. At such meetings, the chief executive may play the role of grand inquisitor cum adjudicator. In the case of ITT, somewhat of a legendary example in this respect,

---

[10] William K. Brandt and James M. Hulbert, "Patterns of Communications in the Multinational Corporation: An Empirical Study," *Journal of International Business Studies,* Spring 1976, pp. 17–30.

[11] Michael Duerr and John M. Roach, *Organization and Control of International Operations* (New York: Conference Board, 1973), p. 22.

[12] Specification of the contents of Business Unit Plans can be found in David S. Hopkins, *The Marketing Plan* (New York: Conference Board, 1981); Derek F. Channon and Michael Jalland, *Multinational Strategic Planning* (London: Macmillan, 1979), pp. 70–71.

the review sessions were traditionally attended by the top managers of other subsidiaries.[13] The purpose of such attendance is to facilitate coordination between the subsidiaries or divisions, avoid repetition of similar planning problems, and generally raise the standard of planning. The transfer of standards obtained in this way can be particularly valuable when subsidiaries are of comparable size and situation.

The formal acceptance of plans gives the line manager a license to implement the proposals in the plans and acknowledges the targets as reasonable expectations of achievement. Seldom are plans formally rejected. They may, however, be referred back for amendment or review. In this way, the planning cycle tries to avoid any implication of failure.[14]

Reporting and Achievement Reviews

Periodic reporting and review of progress during the year are standard requirements. Most firms require monthly reports on sales and certain financial items. Other types of reports may be required quarterly or semiannually.[15]

Several channels are used for reporting within the multinational system. The prime channel is reporting by managers up the line ultimately to the chief executive officer. In addition, controllers or financial officers, production managers, chief engineers, and directors of research and development frequently report directly to their headquarters counterpart on certain aspects of performance without going through their own chief executive. As a headquarters official of ITT explained, "On every company we get four or five inputs and the problems can't fail to surface."[16]

In some companies, the various reports are an input for periodic or monthly management meetings where progress is evaluated and trouble spots identified. When problems have been identified, plans may be revised or, when appropriate, a task force may be dispatched from headquarters or some other subsidiary to make repairs. Subsidiary managements hold more positive attitudes toward international reporting when the frequency, quantity, and quality of feedback are higher.[17] Low-quality feedback would include, for example, clarification on accounting definitions while high-quality feedback would include relevant questions on strategy

---

[13] *Business Week,* November 3, 1973, p. 46.

[14] Michael Z. Brooke and H. Lee Remmers, *The Strategy of Multinational Enterprise,* 2nd ed. (London: Pitman, 1978), pp. 85–126.

[15] See Jeffrey S. Arpan and Lee H. Radebaugh, *International Accounting and Multinational Enterprises,* 2nd ed. (New York: John Wiley & Sons, 1985), pp. 264–70.

[16] *Business Week,* November 3, 1973, p. 46.

[17] Laurent Leksell, "The Design and Function of the Financial Reporting System in Multinational Companies," in *The Management of Headquarters—Subsidiary Relationships in Multinational Corporations,* ed. Lars Otterbeck (Aldershot, England: Gower, 1981), pp. 205–32.

and the changing competitive environment. When the chief executive asks specific questions, such as on inventory levels for a specific product, subsidiary managers tend to feel that top management is well informed and there is a strong impact on the subsidiary managers behavior.[18] Such questioning from headquarters, however, may have unwanted effects. As one executive vice president of a Swedish multinational stated:

> I am very careful in asking subsidiary presidents overly specific questions regarding their operating efficiency. If you repeat the same question too often, they start to believe it's the most important evaluation criterion. Instead, I try to stick to their budgets and some specific performance goals.[19]

Attitudes toward feedback may also vary among cultures. Brandt and Hulbert's study of Brazilian subsidiaries of multinationals showed that most of the U.S. subsidiaries received monthly feedback, whereas fewer than 10 percent of the European and Japanese subsidiaries received regular feedback.[20]

Control through Communication

Formal control procedures are only one part of the overall control process. Formal control communications are supplemented by many more informal exchanges via telephone and telex, and at meetings. In many cases, the informal communications will even bypass the organizational hierarchy.

Where operations are in different countries and managers have different cultural and language backgrounds, control through programs of "corporate acculturation" and "people transfer" can be important and effective. *Corporate acculturation* is the process of training subsidiary managers extensively so that they understand and generally accept the company's way of doing business.[21] Part of this process is to have key subsidiary personnel spend part of their career at the head office. Likewise, headquarters personnel should have some experience working in the subsidiaries. A serious problem can arise, however, when short-term people transfers are viewed by the subsidiaries as a "half-spying" tactic.

Personnel contacts through either short-term or long-term people transfers greatly increase the ability of managers with diverse backgrounds to understand each other's viewpoints. In the Brandt and Hulbert study, two factors that strongly influenced the effectiveness of communications with headquarters were (1) whether a superior at headquarters had worked in the Brazilian subsidiary, and (2) the tenure with the company of the chief executive officer of the subsidiary.

---

[18] Ibid., p. 219.

[19] Ibid., p. 224.

[20] Brandt and Hulbert, "Patterns of Communications."

[21] Ulrich Wiechmann, "Integrating Multinational Marketing Activities," *Columbia Journal of World Business,* Winter 1974, pp. 13–14.

ACCOUNTING ASPECTS OF THE MULTINATIONAL CONTROL SYSTEM

Most multinational enterprises are relatively sophisticated in obtaining the internal accounting information they use in planning and control.[22] A uniform system for planning, budgeting, and performance reporting provides headquarters with comparable data from all parts of the enterprise. It ensures that all managers, regardless of background or nationality, speak a common "company language" when discussing business. In designing such a uniform system, however, many decisions have to be made as to exactly how the data are to be recorded. And, once recorded, there are many pitfalls in interpreting standard data from what will certainly be nonstandard situations.

Income Measurement

The design problems begin with the measurement of net income. Headquarters frequently charges royalties, service fees, and allocations of headquarters and research expenses to the subsidiaries. Generally, the headquarters management reserves final authority in such matters and attempts to reach systemwide optimization. Financial performance of a subsidiary may thus be determined as much by headquarters decisions as by local management.

On occasion, the performance of the foreign subsidiary will have been determined when it was first set up in order to reinforce performance elsewhere in the system. A reserve production unit established with replaced equipment, or a unit deliberately saddled with very high debt to provide funds to be used elsewhere in the multinational system, would be examples. Taxation can add yet further complications. A low local tax rate may encourage the multinational to charge only low amounts of central overhead. Both before-tax income and after-tax income would be affected.

Such headquarters' decisions can complicate immeasurably the task of adjusting a subsidiary's net income so as to make a fair comparison of the intrinsic profitability of individual units. In fact, recorded profitability as a basis for performance evaluation might even have to be abandoned and replaced with realized profit before charges and tax. Alternatively, some measurement of notional profit might be developed to reflect profit taken elsewhere in the system. Efforts to evaluate managers' performance on what is within their control and indicative of their real impact on the objectives set for them are, however, generally worth the cost and complexity involved.

Investment Measurement

Many multinationals wish to use more than income measurement and measure performance by relating income to the investment utilized. In such cases, care

---

[22] F. D. S. Choi and I. J. Czechowicz, "Assessing Foreign Subsidiary Performance: A Multinational Comparison," *Management International Review* 23 (1983–84), pp. 14–25.

is again needed in specifying the investment base. The choice of what is to be included and how it is to be valued can have a major influence on the behavior of managers. If, for example, the firm does not incorporate inflation adjustments in its control measures, investment will be understated and favor managers in countries with the highest inflation rates. As a result, these managers may tend to underprice and to expand volume and investment beyond what would be considered optimal if performance were measured in real terms.

Standard return-on-investment measures used companywide are not uncommon.[23] Because of the many difficulties in providing an equitable comparison, however, most managers prefer that return-on-investment measurements be replaced with performance measures designed to reflect the specific objectives and environmental conditions of each subsidiary. Full participation in the establishment of objectives by subsidiary management whose performance is to be measured will contribute to a spirit of cooperation and responsibility for achievement.

The Measurement Currency

Many multinationals require that all data—from market-demand assessments to profit and balance-sheet items—be presented in one "corporate" currency. In such cases, the rules used for exchange translation can have a significant effect on reported results. For example, a subsidiary's performance in a high-inflation country will look better (or worse) than it should if the exchange value of the subsidiary's currency depreciates less (or more) in relation to the corporate currency than relative inflation rates would indicate.

A significant school of thought considers that subsidiary performance should be judged solely in terms of the subsidiary's local currency. The subsidiary manager's performance can then be evaluated on operating efficiency, uncomplicated by any gain or loss from fluctuating currency values. Nevertheless, many multinationals use the home-country currency as the basis for budgets and for monitoring performance against those budgets. The choice of currency exchange rates, therefore, will shape the performance shown in the corporate currency and influence managerial behavior.

There are three ways of handling the translation of a budget into the corporate currency:

1. The current spot rate at the time of the budget can be used. This is called the *initial rate*.
2. A spot rate can be forecast for the end of the budget period. This is called the *projected rate,* and of course raises considerable forecasting difficulties.
3. The budget itself is translated at the rate current whenever a comparison is made. This is called the *ending rate method*.

The same three alternatives can be used for translating the actual performance figures for comparison against the budget. As illustrated in Figure 22–1, the

---

[23] See Wagdy M. Abdallah and Donald E. Keller, "Measuring the Multinational's Performance," *Management Accounting,* October 1985, pp. 26–30, 56.

FIGURE 22–1   Possible Combinations of Exchange Rates in the Control Process

Rate used to translate actual performance for comparison with budget

	Initial (I)	Projected (P)	Ending (E)
Rate used for translating budget Initial (I)	(II) Budget at initial Actual at initial	Budget at initial Actual at projected	(IE) Budget at initial Actual at ending
Projected (P)	Budget at projected Actual at initial	(PP) Budget at projected Actual at projected	(PE) Budget at projected Actual at ending
Ending (E)	Budget at ending Actual at initial	Budget at ending Actual at projected	(EE) Budget at ending Actual at ending

three alternatives imply nine possible combinations of exchange rates that might be used in the budgeting and control process. Of these nine, five seem reasonable. The remaining four, shaded in the figure, are illogical because actual performance is translated neither at the rate used in translating the budget nor at the exchange rate current when the comparison is made.

Under the three combinations (II, PP, EE), in which the same exchange rate is used for translating both budget figures and actual performance, a change in exchange rates creates no variance for the manager concerned. Thus, the responsibility for exchange-rate variations rests with the central corporate treasury. In only one of these three cases (PP) does the operating manager have to deal with an exchange-rate forecast. This is when a projected rate is used to translate both the budget and the actual performance. The projected rates under this combination are termed "internal forward rates" (IFRs). They produce the effect of the corporate treasurer acting as a banker to buy forward receipts in foreign currencies at a guaranteed rate. Besides its elimination of exchange-rate variation from measurement of management, the PP combination has the additional advantage of being able to incorporate the internal forward rate most appropriate to the corporation's position when the budget is being made. The manager assembling the budget will base the budget on the most profitable alternatives, bearing in mind the internal forward rate that is set. This rate may well be different from the best forecast of what the actual rate may be, if the firm wishes to bias its business in favor of or against the particular currency.[24]

---

[24] Donald Lessard and Peter Lorange, "Currency Changes and Management Control: Resolving the Centralization/Decentralization Dilemma," *Accounting Review*, July 1977, p. 634.

The remaining two combinations (IE, PE) leave the exchange risk with the operating manager. This risk is somewhat reduced when the budget is based on a projected rate (PE) rather than on the rate ruling at the time of the budget. The manager to be measured on actual performance translated at the ending rate will under both combinations be tempted to take steps to cover against the risk. In a large multinational, numerous managers acting in this way could produce significant costs with little gain to the multinational. While the best combination seems on balance to be (PP) "Budget at Projected—Actual at Projected," this is only a poor second in terms of general usage. A survey of 100 U.S. multinationals in 1977 reported the use of the various combinations as follows:[25]

Method	Approximate percent of firms
(PE) Budget at Projected—Actual at Ending	50
(PP) Budget at Projected—Actual at Projected	20
(II) Budget at Initial —Actual at Initial	12½
(IE) Budget at Initial —Actual at Ending	12½
(EE) Budget at Ending —Actual at Ending	5

The most common method does save some accounting costs, but it also makes the operating manager responsible for discrepancies between the projected and final exchange rate. If the projected rate were forecast by the corporate treasury, the manager's results would vary according to the quality of someone else's forecasts.

In translating balance sheet items for internal control purposes, the multinational may use any of the translation methods discussed in Chapter 21. It is not essential that the method used be identical to that used for external financial reporting. Theoretically, an external reporting requirement should have no effect on internal reporting. In fact, 60 per cent of U.S. multinationals surveyed in 1978 when FAS 8 had required use of the temporal method of translation had chosen also to use that method for internal evaluation—many switching simply because of the FASB requirement.[26] But the majority of the reporting companies excluded translation gains and losses from the income figure used to evaluate the foreign subsidiary manager.

Measurement under High Inflation

For subsidiaries operating under conditions of hypoinflation (high) or hyperinflation (very high), performance is likely to be distorted from period to period if

[25] Business International, "Evaluating Foreign Operations: The Appropriate Rates for Comparing Results with Budgets," *Business International Money Report,* May 20, 1977, pp. 153–54; Business International, *Assessing Foreign Subsidiary Performance—Systems and Practices of Leading Multinational Companies* (New York: Business International Corporation, 1982), p. 78.

[26] Helen Gernon, "The Effect of Translation on Multinational Corporations' Internal Performance Evaluation," *Journal of International Business Studies,* Spring/Summer 1983, pp. 103–12.

the actual or projected official exchange rate is needed for translation under any of the methods outlined in the previous section. Devaluation is unlikely to closely parallel the difference in inflation rates between the country of the parent and that of the subsidiary. Countries under high inflation tend to delay devaluation of their currency as long as possible, and sometimes they retain an overvalued currency even after devaluation. Moreover, there are frequently large steps in exchange rate changes.

As a result of such translation distortions, subsidiary managements may make decisions that are less appropriate than if a "truer" adjustment of the exchange rate had taken place. In particular, subsidiary managements may be likely to avoid borrowing in hard currency because subsequent devaluation will throw a large translation loss against their operating performance. Yet under high inflation it is often optimal for a subsidiary to seek additional foreign finance. Local prices are often controlled and increases held below the real inflation rate. In order to hold market share, the subsidiary would need further funding. At the same time, local interest rates can be excessively high. The temptation is for the local management to retrench and avoid a subsequent translation loss— rather than to see it as a cost of holding market position.

A refinement to the translation procedure that would reduce such temptations is to use a notional exchange rate based on Purchasing Power Parity, rather than the actual, official rate.[27] The final exchange rate is adjusted by the percentage difference between the inflation rates in the countries of the parent and the subsidiary over the period, less whatever percentage has already been accounted for by changes in the exchange rate during the period. Performance of a subsidiary measured at a notional PPP rate in this way would be insulated from fluctuations caused by exchange rate swings. The translated figures would reflect more accurately the underlying performance in terms of the measurement currency.

INTRACOMPANY TRANSFER PRICING

Intracompany transfer prices—that is, prices for goods and services exchanged within the corporate family—have an important effect upon performance and control. Not only are there difficulties in setting a fair price when there is not a free market; but when transactions between units of the same enterprise are subject to different customs duties, tax rates, and currency risks, adjustments in transfer prices can also be used to advance various enterprise goals and increase overall enterprise profits.[28]

Firms operating foreign units as profit centers, however, confront difficulties in manipulating transfer prices. If foreign units are made profit centers for purposes of monitoring their performance and financially rewarding their managers, goods must be transferred at competitive and relatively uniform prices between units

---

[27] For a fuller description see Laurent L. Jacque and Peter Lorange, "The International Control Conundrum: The Case of 'Hyperinflationary' Subsidiaries," *Journal of International Business Studies,* Fall 1984, pp. 185–201.

[28] See the discussion in Chapter 23.

in the system whose performance is being compared. On the other hand, there are techniques that can be used to maximize total system profits through manipulating transfer prices while still retaining the profit-center concept. One method is to share the total realized profits of the company between the parent and foreign subsidiary on the basis of assets used, costs incurred, or on a more subjective basis of equitable treatment.[29] Another way is to keep two sets of accounts— official accounts for tax and other local purposes and another set for management control purposes. Still another is to take account of transfer-price manipulations in the budget and measure performance against planned results, even if a loss were intended. But each of these techniques has drawbacks. The practices verge on the unethical, and it is doubtful whether the gains from manipulating transfer prices more than offset the resulting cost and complexity of judging performance. In fact, the evidence suggests that firms that use transfer pricing as an instrument for the enhancement of overall corporate profit place less emphasis on profit-oriented measures in evaluating performance of subsidiary managers.[30]

INTERNAL AUDITING IN THE MULTINATIONAL

Internal auditing performs a number of important functions in the control system of the multinational corporation. First, the internal auditing system establishes monitoring procedures for safeguarding the firm's assets, whether physical, monetary, or intangible. Second, the internal audit staff has the function of controlling the control system itself. Someone in the multinational organization is required to ensure that procedures for planning, reporting, and financial accounting are carried out as they should be. The good internal audit staff, however, will not confine itself to financial procedures, but will also extend its monitoring across the range of the firm's operations. At its very best, the internal audit function becomes a feedback link in appraising operating performance.

The firsthand knowledge of the local situation acquired by internal auditors can add significantly to the understanding at corporate headquarters and lead to modifications in plans and procedures. Equally, the external perspective of the internal auditor exposed to a wider range of the multinational's operations can be of value to local management, who may tend to see problems solely in terms of the local environment. The internal audit staff can act in a management services capacity, transferring best practices throughout the multinational organization.

Feedback to both local and corporate management is important for the multinational internal auditor. Without a reporting requirement directly to the corporate level, the credibility and power of the auditor to influence local management

---

[29] James Greene and Michael G. Duerr, *Intercompany Transactions in the Multinational Company* (New York: National Industrial Conference Board, 1970), p. 10.

[30] Penelope J. Yunker, "A Survey Study of Subsidiary Autonomy, Performance Evaluation and Transfer Pricing in Multinational Corporations," *Columbia Journal of World Business,* Fall 1983, pp. 51–64.

would be lower. The internal auditor's reports could be conditioned by allegiance to the local management group. Above all, any local management inclined to misrepresent the situation in business reports might be more tempted to do so if audit reports came solely through them, and if they had power and time to question a report and cover their position. Where national management in a subsidiary has a strongly independent leaning with nationalistic bias, an internal audit staff reporting directly to corporate headquarters can prevent the loss of control that can happen all too quickly when reports are biased, sketchy, and provided after the event.

Responsibility to report to local management as well as to corporate headquarters, however, goes some way toward avoiding the image of internal auditors as corporate spies. Where they can be viewed as a supportive part of the local management team, rather than as an external threat to be guarded against, the internal audit staff is likely to find out more, to find it out earlier, and to bring about change before potential troubles escalate. With the increasing complexity of on-line systems and multiple-terminal data entry, the current trend is to have more audit involvement before an amendment is incorporated. Audit involvement with local staff in system design and adaptation is not regarded as compromising the auditor's objectivity.

Many multinationals find that to maintain headquarters-based internal audit staff as traveling auditors is too expensive, both monetarily and in the personal costs to the audit staff of continual foreign travel. There are also the language and communication problems. Thus, it is not uncommon to base internal audit staff within local subsidiaries and even to use local nationals in these posts. The local identity problems are greately reduced in these cases; but, conversely, there is an increased need to keep the direct reporting channels to corporate headquarters wide open, and to rotate the internal audit staff regularly.

The Foreign Corrupt Practices Act of 1977 brought an added importance to internal auditing procedures of U.S. multinationals. The act focused on bribe payments to foreign governments, politicians, or political parties to obtain or retain business and provided for fines of up to $1 million on a corporation and fines of up to $10,000 and imprisonment of up to five years for individuals. The act, however, goes beyond the direct concern with bribery to specify requirements for record keeping and internal accounting control, presumably with the intent of limiting bribery. The result is that for the first time the internal control of U.S. corporations was made a question of law, not simply one of technical proficiency.[31] The requirements of the act apply to every publicly held U.S. corporation and require that the company shall:

1. Make and keep books, records, and accounts, which accurately and fairly reflect the transactions and dispositions of the assets of the company.

---

[31] See David N. Ricchiute, "Illegal Payments, Deception of Auditors, and Reports on Internal Control," *MSU Business Topics,* Spring 1980, 57–62.

2. Devise and maintain an adequate system of material accounting controls sufficient to provide reasonable assurances that—

   a. transactions are executed in accordance with management's general or specific authorization;

   b. transactions are recorded as necessary (1) to permit preparation of financial statements in conformity with generally accepted accounting principles or any other criteria applicable to such statements and (2) to maintain accountability for assets;

   c. access to assets is permitted only in accordance with management's authorization; and

   d. the recorded accountability for assets is compared with the existing assets at reasonable intervals and appropriate action is taken with respect to any differences.

CONTROLLING JOINT VENTURES

Joint ventures present a special control problem in multinational business operations. By desire or by necessity, multinational firms commonly have joint-venture affiliates as part of their multinational operations. And if the firm tries to implement a global strategy and realize the special advantages of multinational operations, it has to deal with conflicts that may arise between the interests of the local partners and the global objectives and opportunities for the enterprise. Frequently, joint ventures are located in the less developed countries, where the governments enforce a joint-venture policy as a means of increasing local control over business decisions to ensure that these decisions are compatible with national objectives.[32]

The experience of Japanese multinationals with joint ventures is of special interest because Japanese firms have had a much higher ratio of joint ventures than U.S., European, or Canadian firms. The extent to which a joint-venture subsidiary can be controlled by the parent, according to one study, depends upon the control that the parent has over key resources required by the subsidiary.[33] These key resources are informational (technology and management know-how); financial; and input-output leverage. The informational resources are controlled through technical assistance contracts and through placing parent-company personnel in subsidiary managerial positions. The so-called input-output leverage exists when the subsidiary is dependent upon the parent for securing components, equipment, and replacement parts or for marketing a significant share of the subsidiary's output.

For Japanese firms, the most important source of control has been the technical

---

[32] Richard W. Wright and Colin S. Russel, "Joint Ventures in Developing Countries: Realities and Responses," *Columbia Journal of World Business,* Summer 1975, pp. 74–80.

[33] Kichiro Hayashi, "Japanese Management of Multinational Operations: Sources and Means of Control" (Paper presented at the annual meetings of the Academy of International Business in Dallas, Texas, December 1975).

assistance contract and information and know-how flows. The second most important means has been the placing of home-country personnel in the subsidiary. The production manager position has been more heavily relied upon than the financial manager position as a means of control.

Control through home-country personnel frequently ran into difficulties because of the desire of foreign countries to have local nationals in managerial posts. Host governments in Malaysia, Singapore, Indonesia, and Thailand, for example, have at times been unwilling to issue visas or work permits to financial officers from Japan. The country motivation was not only to promote local financial talent but also to try to make accounting information more accessible so that local demands for higher wages could be supported. At one time Malaysia and Singapore also attempted to control the assignment of home-country engineers and technical personnel, but they had to reverse this policy because qualified local personnel were not available.[34]

Control problems are less likely to arise when the joint venture has been clearly thought through and agreement has been reached from the outset on business strategy, degree of autonomy, financial and accounting policies, and so on.[35] There is also some evidence that these problems are only marginally less than for wholly owned affiliates.[36] But there is no easy solution to the joint-venture control problem. In some cases, multinational firms have had to resolve the difficulties and frustrations associated with control attempts by increasing their ownership position or by selling out to local interests.

SUMMARY

The complexity, scale, and diversity of multinational operations make the control function in multinational business both extremely important and unusually difficult. Because information systems cross national boundaries and varied cultures, special efforts are required to improve the effectiveness of communications. It is difficult to develop performance standards that are meaningful and that do not interfere significantly with operating objectives. The environments and the ground rules for operations change rapidly in both the home and host countries. Control systems, therefore, must be flexible and continuously adapted to new circumstances.

Great care should be taken to avoid leading subsidiaries to take inappropriate actions simply because of the rules of the internal accounting system by which they are measured. In particular, practices adopted for translating budgets and accounts into a common currency can distort performance and lead managers to

---

[34] Ibid., pp. 16–17.

[35] Richard H. Holton, "Making International Joint Ventures Work," in *The Management of Headquarters,* ed. Otterbeck, pp. 255–67.

[36] Lars Otterbeck, "The Management of Joint Ventures," in *The Management of Headquarters,* p. 279.

cover themselves against exchange risk. Transfer pricing raises further problems. To ignore opportunities for increasing system performance through managerial transfer prices might place the multinational at a disadvantage against competition. Yet every changed transfer price will alter the recorded performance on either side of the transaction.

Internal auditing is an integral part of the control system. Properly managed internal auditing ensures a well-functioning and accurate system. The Foreign Corrupt Practices Act, moreover, has now made proper internal audit a legal requirement for U.S. multinationals.

Finally, the concept of control must be adapted to joint ventures and partly owned operations. The same principles of control apply, but, where statutory obligation is absent, there will be a greater premium on personal contact and persuasion to meet the goals of the multinational.

EXERCISES AND DISCUSSION QUESTIONS

1. The principles, procedures, and general problems of planning, information systems, and control appear to be fundamentally the same for operating in one or many national environments. Discuss.
2. Enumerate and discuss the relative advantages and disadvantages of giving subsidiaries detailed indications of what they should include as planned achievements in their annual plans.
3. "The performance of subsidiary businesses should never be measured by one overall return-on-investment figure; therefore, such figures should not be calculated and certainly not circulated." Discuss.
4. In choosing performance criteria, what are examples of potential conflicts of interest among units of the enterprise that must be considered?
5. Different combinations of exchange rates for translating budget and actual performance either leave exchange risk with the subsidiary manager or transfer it to the corporate center. Explain why you think it is good or bad to leave the risk with a subsidiary manager.
6. A foreign subsidiary is considering an expansion that will require a 50-million-francs investment and that is budgeted to perform over the next year as follows:

	(million francs)
Sales	100
Cost of sales and operating expenses	85
Operating profit	15

The current exchange rate is 8 frs. = US$1 but there is an equal chance that the exchange rate at the end of the first year will have remained at 8 frs. = $1 or will have dropped to 10 frs. = $1. As a consequency, the projected future exchange rate is 9 frs. = $1. Assuming that any change in exchange rate will not affect the local currency operating results, and that there will be no income taxes, show the comparisons of budget and operating performance in dollars under each of the five feasible methods in Figure 22–2. Where the rate at the end of the year is used, show alternatives for 8 frs. and 10 frs. = $1. Calculate the variance from budget performance and any exchange loss on the exposed investment of 50 million francs. Under which alternative would you be tempted to cover yourself against exchange loss if you were managing the subsidiary, and for how much?

7. Draw up a set of instructions for the reporting responsibility of an internal auditor based with a foreign subsidiary.

Multinational Financial Management

Multinational, as compared with domestic, financial management involves new environmental considerations, new sources of risk, and new opportunities for economies and efficiencies. The new risks arise out of fluctuations in foreign currency values, changes in tax liabilities as funds move across national boundaries, and the impact of national controls on financial flows. New opportunities arise with the access to multiple capital markets and the possibilities for achieving financial benefits in one part of the system from activities in another part.

As essential background, the multinational financial manager must be thoroughly familiar with the institutional setting for international financial transactions. The main components of the international framework—the international monetary system, foreign exchange markets, and international money markets—have already been introduced in Part II. The financial manager also needs a continuing flow of meaningful reports from units of the enterprise and on international financial markets. The development of an effective global intelligence system requires an understanding of the special features of multinational accounting, discussed in chapters 21 and 22.

This chapter recasts the international environmental elements into a managerial framework. It relates them to the functions of organizing the financial management activity, managing foreign exchange risk, and making decisions on long-run investments, financing techniques, financial structures, and management of working capital. The scope of this chapter, however, is limited to the multinational financial function in industrial and commercial firms. Financial intermediaries, such as banks and insurance companies, have their own financial problems, which will not be considered here.

ORGANIZING THE MULTINATIONAL FINANCIAL MANAGEMENT FUNCTION

The financial management function is a key element in achieving global corporate goals. Thus pressure usually builds up for strong central guidance from corporate headquarters and systemwide optimization. Ideally, the financial management function of a multinational enterprise would have three goals:

1. To take advantage of the potentials in multinational operations for reducing financial costs and increasing efficiency.
2. To adapt to environmental constraints at the national and regional level.
3. To protect the value of assets and revenues so that the benefits of multinational operations are not eroded through financial risks.

The efficiency contribution can occur through the ability of the multinational enterprise to secure capital at a lower cost since it has access to many different sources and can achieve economies of scale in financing. The adaptation responsibility is one of meeting national constraints in both home and host countries on moving funds across national boundaries. The protective function is to avoid losses through foreign exchange devaluations or revaluations, or through differential rates of inflation.

To achieve these goals the principal U.S. international companies follow three basic patterns in organizing the management of the international financial function.[1] The international functions of both policy making and performance of financial services may be:

1. Centralized at corporate headquarters.

2. Centralized at the headquarters of the international management unit with only overall guidance from corporate headquarters.

3. Split between corporate headquarters and some subordinate headquarters (that is, central international unit, regional headquarters, product division headquarters, and so forth).

The important determinants of organizational patterns and the resulting financial behavior have been the size of an international company and its degree of international involvement. Small firms, defined as having foreign sales of about $50 million, typically run a decentralized operation with an "every tub on its own bottom" policy. Headquarters provides little direction, few decision rules, and makes little effort to move toward optimum financing for the entire system. In fact, each subsidiary may be viewed as an independent financial operation.

Medium-sized firms typically run a centralized operation with strong direction from headquarters and substantial concern for the net cost of an action to the total system. Medium-sized firms more nearly approach the economists' concept of one "economic man" running the enterprise from headquarters.[2]

Large multinational enterprises strongly favor systemwide optimization but are too large and too complex to attempt an overall system approach even with modern computer systems. As a result of this complexity, headquarters' management uses a variety of rules of thumb to assist them in decision making, for example, setting equity equal to fixed assets in forming a new subsidiary. Even if the large multinational enterprise were to calculate an overall systems optimum, it could not take actions that might jeopardize its position in a foreign country.

The different patterns of organization and of financial policy behavior that prevail among U.S. international firms undoubtedly represent different stages of evolution along the path toward following global strategies and integrated management policies. They also reflect the state of knowledge in optimizing complex systems and the likely constraints on such optimization because of potential conflicts between optimization on a world basis and the interests of nation-states. As increasingly sophisticated organization and management techniques emerge, organizational patterns for the international financial function will continue to change.

---

[1] Irene W. Meister, *Managing the International Financial Function* (New York: National Industrial Conference Board, 1970), p. 5; Business International Corporation, *Organizing for International Finance* (New York: BIC, 1981).

[2] This section is a summary of Robert B. Stobaugh, Jr., "Financing Foreign Subsidiaries of U.S.-Controlled Multinational Enterprises," *Journal of International Business Studies,* Summer 1970, pp. 43–64.

LONG-RUN INVESTMENT AND FINANCING STRATEGIES

Investment decisions represent ultimate control over the operating subsidiaries and a principal means of implementing global strategy. Investment decisions to establish new operations or expand existing ones are based on a mix of strategic, behavioral, and economic considerations. They are not exclusively financial decisions. Yet the financial manager plays a key role by being responsible for analyzing the financial implications and comparing the expected returns and other financial features of alternative proposals.

Capital Budgeting

The financial manager's responsibility in decision making on long-term investments is normally performed within a capital-budgeting framework. *Capital budgeting* is a process of matching advantages from possible uses of funds against the cost of alternative ways to obtain the needed resources. In domestic business, capital budgeting has become highly developed with sophisticated analytical approaches available for investment decisions.[3] In the international field, the use of capital budgeting techniques has also developed despite a variety of complications and uncertainties that must be handled when national boundaries are crossed.[4]

Capital budgeting analysis for foreign as compared to domestic projects introduces the following complications:

1. Cash flows to a project and to the parent must be differentiated.
2. National differences in tax systems, financial institutions, and financial norms and in constraints on financial flows must be recognized.
3. Different inflation rates can affect profitability and the competitive position of an affiliate.
4. Foreign exchange-rate changes can alter the competitive position of a foreign affiliate and the value of cash flows between the affiliate and the parent.
5. Segmented capital markets create opportunities for financial gains or they may cause additional costs.
6. Political risk can significantly change the value of a foreign investment.

The additional international elements to be considered arise at each of three stages in investment appraisal. In the first stage, the estimated receipts and disbursements for the project are analyzed by including problems of exchange rates,

---

[3] See Lawrence J. Gitman, *Principles of Managerial Finance,* 3rd ed. (New York: Harper & Row, 1982), pp. 407–42.

[4] Alan C. Shapiro, *Multinational Financial Management* (Boston: Allyn and Bacon, 1982), pp. 402–10; Laurence D. Booth, "Capital Budgeting Frameworks for the Multinational Corporation," *Journal of International Business Studies,* Fall 1982, pp. 113–23.

financial costs, and risk measurement. In the second stage, the analysis moves from the subsidiary to the headquarters level. This requires estimating (1) what amounts will be transferred, at what time and in what form, from the subsidiary to the parent company, (2) what taxes and other expenses will be incurred due to these transfers, and (3) what incremental revenues and costs will result elsewhere in the system. In a third and last stage, the project is evaluated and compared with other investment projects on the basis of incremental net cash flow accruing to the system as a return on the investment.[5]

The projection of receipts and disbursements begins, of course, with the market forecasts, including export possibilities from the project. A unique requirement for a foreign project is the need to develop schedules of relevant, anticipated exchange rates for each type of transaction involved. This task goes beyond the general requirement for foreign exchange forecasting. Some countries have both an official and a free rate of exchange, each applying to different transactions. Many transactions involving foreign exchange are subject to duties, special taxes, and exemptions. Equipment exports, for example, may be exempted or receive exchange rate concessions. In some instances, foreign exchange rates are subject to negotiations between the government and the international enterprise. Consequently, the international financial manager may need separate projections over time of exchange rates for equipment imports, raw material imports, and export sales, and the importance of such rates to the revenues and costs of the project will have to be evaluated.

A second international consideration may be the need to consider alternative financial structures for the proposed project, which in turn will affect projected receipts and disbursements. Local debt financing, for example, tends to reduce both foreign exchange and inflation risk. But the availability of local credit for international enterprises varies greatly among countries for national policy or other reasons. Certain less developed countries (LDCs) require the international firm to finance up to certain limits by local sales of equity. Or the country may offer special incentives if external rather than local financing is used for imported equipment, in order to encourage foreign investment inflows. Consequently, the firm may want to develop separate receipts and disbursement forecasts for several alternative financial plans that are feasible for a particular national situation.

Still another international consideration is the need to include risk elements of a political- or national-controls nature in the investment analysis. As an extreme example, high probabilities of expropriation or confiscation can markedly change the projections of receipts and disbursements. These risks have been discussed in Chapter 9, where techniques for adjusting cash flow for country risk are illustrated. In addition to their impact on a project analyzed at a national level, these risk elements must be considered at the headquarters level from the standpoint

---

[5] See David K. Eiteman and Arthur I. Stonehill, *Multinational Business Finance*, 4th ed. (Reading, Mass.: Addison-Wesley Publishing, 1986), pp. 336–70, for a detailed case example of capital budgeting for a foreign project.

of how they might affect income flows such as dividend remittances and royalty payments available to the parent and the rest of the system.

In the second stage, where the analysis moves to the headquarters level, the principal additional issues become the availability to headquarters of income flows from the project and the net incremental benefits, if any, to the system. In many countries, particularly the LDCs, the repatriation of cash flows above a certain percentage return is blocked or is heavily taxed, and forecasts of remittance policies are required in such cases. Profits that are freely available to the parent concern have a different value than profits that must be reinvested. Forced reinvestment may, however, have desirable and beneficial results in cases where opportunities are growing or where the firm has initially set up a new venture on a narrow financial base to minimize its exposure. In any event, the firm will have to decide whether it should assign lower values to project flows that cannot be converted into home-country currency or transferred freely to other countries, or whether all earnings from the project should be considered as available inflows to the parent company. It will also have to take into account the tax and other costs of transferring income to the parent companies. The estimated inflows must also be translated into home-country currency units on the basis of foreign exchange forecasts over the planning period.

The incremental benefits to the rest of the system should be imputed as additional available income from the proposed project. These can be profits from increased export sales from the parent company; payments of license fees, royalties, or management services; or even transfers of technological or marketing know-how available to the rest of the system from the activities of the new venture.

In practice, the majority of U.S. multinationals continue to evaluate projects from both the parent and subsidiary viewpoint, according to several surveys that did not differentiate by location of the investment.[6] Another survey that examined geographical differences reported that companies investing in LDCs were particularly concerned with cash flows to the parent whereas firms investing in Europe were not as concerned about funds being available for repatriation.[7]

At the third and last stage, the alternative investment projects are compared with each other and ranked on the basis of expected return on investment, in which order they will be accepted up to the limit of the investment sums considered available for the capital budgeting period. One of the issues at this stage may be the method used for comparing projects. Another will be the criterion used for the cost of capital.

U.S. multinationals commonly use two or more methods for evaluating investments. The *internal rate of return* (IRR) clearly dominates as the primary method;

[6] Vinod B. Bavishi, "Capital Budgeting Practices of Multinationals," *Management Accounting,* August 1981, p. 34; Marjorie T. Stanley and Stanley B. Block, "A Survey of Multinational Capital Budgeting," *Financial Review,* March 1984, p. 48.

[7] Marie E. W. Kelley and George C. Philippatos, "Comparative Analysis of the Foreign Investment Evaluation Practices by U. S. Based Manufacturing Multinational Companies," *Journal of International Business Studies,* Winter 1982, p. 26.

and the *payback* (PB) *method* is the most important secondary approach. The *net present value* (NPV) *method,* often preferred in the academic literature, is infrequently used as the primary method.[8] The PB method is the number of years required to recover the initial investment. The IRR and NPV methods are more sophisticated and give explicit consideration to the time value of money.

Policies on cost of capital may range from a single weighted average cost for the enterprise to separate costs for each country of operation or each project. The weighted average cost is computed by combining the cost of equity with the cost of debt in proportion to the weight of each in the firm's optimal long-term financial structure. A single cost is the easiest to apply. But separate target rates are appropriate for specific projects where special sources of financing are available, such as local financial incentives or project-specific loans at concessionary rates, or where the financial structure of the subsidiary differs markedly from that of the parent.[9]

The principal international risk elements—foreign exchange, national controls, and political risk—have already been incorporated into the analysis. The recommended risk-adjustment procedures are to analyze the specific sources of risk and through the use of subjective probabilities to estimate the specific impact of the possible outcomes on the expected return from the investment. In making a final selection, the enterprise will have its estimates of the net present value of available inflows and a measure of risk for each alternative. The alternatives may consist of different projects or the same projects financed in different ways. The final choices from the financial point of view will then depend upon the firm's attitudes toward taking risks.[10]

Financial Structures of Foreign Affiliates

The choice of financial structure and financing plan, as previously noted, can greatly influence the attractiveness of new projects and expansions. At the enterprise level, the overall exposure of the firm to foreign exchange and political risk can also be affected. The options will differ, of course, for a wholly owned subsidiary and a joint venture.

In choosing optimal financing plans for foreign affiliates, the financial manager will have to decide such questions as the appropriate mix of debt and equity and the extent to which debt should be local or imported. The alternatives will depend on the local and foreign sources of capital available for financing projects in specific countries, national governmental regulations regarding financing and ownership arrangements, relative costs of the various options, and other factors.

---

[8] Bavishi, *Capital Budgeting,* p. 34; Stanley, *A Survey,* p. 41.

[9] See Marjorie T. Stanley, "Capital Structure and Cost of Capital for the Multinational Firm," *Journal of International Business Studies,* Spring/Summer 1981, pp. 103–20.

[10] See Donald R. Lessard, "Diversification and Regional Rates of Return," in Eiteman and Stonehill, *Multinational Business Finance,* pp. 464–73.

What constitutes an appropriate mix of debt and equity for U.S. firms has long been debated by financial experts. But the international manager discovers very early that equity-debt ratios differ markedly from country to country as a result of differences in national environments.[11] *Equity financing* is the sale of ownership rights. The suppliers of equity assume the business and financial risks of the enterprise and share in its profits or losses. *Debt financing* is a fixed obligation to pay interest and repay principal regardless of business success or failure. Thus, heavy debt financing can give the suppliers of equity leverage for maximizing earnings, or lead to bankruptcy if the company is not profitable. In the case of foreign subsidiaries, however, the bankruptcy risk is not a constraint unless the parent is willing to let the subsidiary default on its debt.[12]

To what extent should an international firm be guided by different country debt-ratio norms? Conforming to host-country debt norms has some advantages, particulary if it does not involve a cost penalty but merely replacement of debt in one affiliate by debt in another. One advantage is that management can more easily evaluate its return on equity relative to local competitors in the same industry. As a general policy, however, a multinational firm should probably borrow at the lowest cost anywhere in the world, without regard to the cosmetic impact on the financial structure of any particular affiliate.[13]

The choice of financial structure for affiliates must, of course, consider the effect on the total enterprise, where the parent's and affiliates' financial statements will be consolidated. If the consolidated balance sheet shows a higher debt ratio than is considered appropriate in the country of the parent, the cost of financing for the parent company is increased.

Local debt financing in weak-currency countries tends to reduce devaluation, inflation and political risks. When devaluations occur, the amount of local currency required to meet interest payments and retire principal is not affected. Local debt can reduce inflation risk in that repayment obligations may remain fixed in local currency while revenues and profits rise along with inflation. In other words, debt is being paid off with "cheaper" money. Political risk can be reduced because the subsidiary is likely to default on all loans from local sources in the event of expropriation. For these reasons, firms are frequently willing to borrow locally even though the cost is higher than for imported funds. The additional

[11] Arthur Stonehill, Theo Beekhuisen, Richard Wright, Lee Remmers, Norman Toy, Antonio Pares, Alan Shapiro, Douglas Egan, and Thomas Bates, "Financial Goals and Debt Ratio Determinants: A Survey of Practice in Five Countries," *Financial Management,* Autumn 1975, pp. 27–41; see also R. Aggarwal, "International Differences in Capital Structure Norms," *Management International Review* 21 (1981), pp. 75–88.

[12] Michael Adler, "The Cost of Capital and Valuation of a Two-Country Firm," *Journal of Finance,* March 1974, pp. 119–32; Sadahiko Suzuki and Richard W. Wright, "Financial Structure and Bankruptcy Risk in Japanese Companies," *Journal of International Business Studies,* Spring 1985, pp. 97–110.

[13] Eiteman and Stonehill, *Multinational Business Finance,* p. 456.

cost is considered an insurance payment against devaluation, inflation, and political risk.

Debt imported from strong-currency countries has the disadvantage that the amount of local currency required to meet interest and repayment obligations will increase in the case of devaluation. But even where devaluations are anticipated, nonlocal debt may have the advantage of providing greater freedom for foreign remittances where exchange controls prevail. Most countries give preference in the allocation of foreign exchange to remittances of interest and debt repayment over the remittance of dividends on equity.

The enterprise should determine its financial structure preferences for affiliates, but it should recognize that in some countries these preferences cannot be implemented. Companies prefer to use locally borrowed funds in areas that appear to be politically and economically unstable. Yet the risky areas chronically lack loan capital. Furthermore, certain countries restrict local borrowing by foreign companies on the ground that foreign firms should increase total local investment by bringing in capital. There is a feeling that the growth of local enterprise should not be stunted by having to compete for scarce funds with large, profitable, and well-known international enterprises that have easier access to outside capital markets. Some less developed countries that are concerned with their balance-of-payments situation object to high debt proportions when it appears that such a financial structure is intended to support high levels of foreign exchange remittances to the parent companies.

Some parent firms prefer to supply a minimum amount of equity to a foreign subsidiary. But the desire to minimize equity is not characteristic of internationally committed enterprises. They typically use a guideline such as ''let equity equal fixed assets'' in order that host countries do not become concerned about excessive local borrowing or unduly high dividend remittances. This strong equity base facilitates local borrowing after the subsidiary has become established and gives it greater independence in the future from the parent's central source of funds.

The decision to enter into a joint-venture arrangement with a group of local partners or to sell equity shares in the subsidiary locally can also reduce the financial burden on the multinational enterprise and increase access to other local sources of capital. If the outside ownership groups have similar expectations, equity costs would be unaffected. But where expectations are dissimilar among the participants, equity costs of the financial plan can be increased. Outside shareholders, for example, may expect to receive larger dividends than are traditional for the international enterprise. If so, the larger (or smaller) return expectations should be included explicitly in the flow projections used to appraise the desirability of a project.

Financing Sources and Techniques

Until recent years, the sources of funds for international enterprises were generally limited to the parent's home country, the local country in which a project was being established, or funds generated internally by its foreign affiliates.

But with the internationalization of money markets, described in Chapter 4, most international firms have come to consider an ever widening variety of global sources and financing techniques in their financing decisions.[14]

The multiplicity of sources and new techniques greatly enlarges the financial manager's task. The manager must follow world financial markets and local markets in the countries in which the firm operates. The sources include foreign as well as domestic commercial and investment banks, together with government financial institutions, export financing agencies, development banks, insurance companies, and pension funds. The new techniques keep proliferating and include lease financing, dual currency issues, and swaps in addition to traditional loans and the issue of securities.[15]

The evaluation of alternatives must be a continuing activity and the evaluation process must consider foreign exchange risk, tax effects, and political risk in choosing among alternatives.[16] As a general principle, the manager should go to the markets for funds when the markets are attractive, and not necessarily when the funds are required by the company. Surplus funds can be managed so as to attain high yields and still be available when needed.

The Eurocurrency and Eurobond markets are the most important uniquely international sources of financing. The freedom from taxation, the diversification opportunities for both borrowers and currencies, and the absence of interference by national governments are features of the Eurobond market that appeal to investors. From the standpoint of the borrower, many of the attractive features are similar. In addition to offering a choice of currencies, interest rates in the Eurobond market have generally been at levels little different from the prevailing rates in the home country of the currency.

INTERNATIONAL MONEY MANAGEMENT

The multinational financial manager plays a major role in the management of a firm's cash and near-cash assets. This function, referred to as international money management or working capital management, has the potential for decreasing the overall cost of funds to the enterprise and the overall risk to company assets. It can also increase the availability of funds and the overall return on available funds. These potentials emerge when the enterprise works toward optimizing the financial function on a systemwide basis, rather than having each subsidiary operate independently.

---

[14] For detailed current information on financing techniques, sources for cross-border financing, and the domestic financing situation in a large number of countries, see the monthly service, *Financing Foreign Operations* of Business International, or other similar services.

[15] See Gunter Dufey and Ian H. Giddy, "Innovation in the International Financial Markets," *Journal of International Business Studies*, Fall 1981, pp. 33–51.

[16] See for example Alan C. Shapiro, "The Impact of Taxation on the Currency-of-Denomination Decision for Long-Term Foreign Borrowing and Lending," *Journal of International Business Studies*, Spring/Summer 1984, pp. 15–23.

International money management can be considered as comprising a series of interrelated subsystems that perform the following functions: (1) positioning of funds—choice of location and currency of denomination for all liquid funds; (2) pool funds internationally; (3) keep costs of intercompany funds transfers at a minimum; (4) increase the speed with which funds are transferred internationally between corporate units; (5) manage foreign exchange exposure; and (6) improve returns on liquid funds.[17]

International Cash Management

Pooling.   The control of liquidity—liquid assets and short-term debt or credit facilities—is based largely on the concept of pooling. *Pooling* is a system for making the best use of liquid assets available on a regional or global basis. It attempts to optimize the use of corporate resources by making the surplus funds of cash-rich affiliates available to cash-poor affiliates. Any net surplus or deficit for the pool as a whole can be directed into short-term investments or financed by drawing on central credit facilities.

The pooling procedures call for the affiliates to hold only minimum cash balances for transaction purposes. With all reserve balances in a central pool, the size of the total pool for the multinational system can be reduced without any loss in the level of protection. Another advantage of pooling is that one affiliate will not borrow at high rates while another holds surplus funds or is investing them at low rates.

A pooling arrangement normally requires some degree of centralized financial control. It also requires a flow of information so that the financial manager is appraised of all intercompany transactions as well as of each affiliate's liquidity position and its local money market conditions. When pooling is attempted on a multicountry, multicurrency basis, tax considerations and exchange controls may preclude the actual pooling of funds in communal accounts. Indirect financing between affiliates can be achieved, however, through the leading and lagging of intercompany payments—usually trade, but sometimes dividends, royalties, fees, and loan repayments.

Funds Transfers.   International transfers of funds can require considerable time during which funds in transit cannot be used and may be exposed to undesired currency risk. By accelerating payments, less working capital is required and sizable savings can be realized. Improvements in this area may require changes in transfer means—cable rather than mail transfers—and improving the efficiency of the banking system being used.

The cost of international transfers can be reduced by decreasing the number of payments transactions and by minimizing foreign exchange costs. By analyzing

---

[17] See David B. Zenoff, *Management Principles for Finance in the Multinational* (London: Euromoney Publications, 1980), pp. 171–75.

the transactions of every affiliate with other units in the system, a central controller can arrange for the affiliates to remit or receive only their net debit or credit positions. This process is called *netting* or multicurrency clearing, where transactions can be offset on either a bilateral or a multilateral basis. The volume of actual transfers is cut sharply, with a consequent reduction in working capital requirements and foreign exchange costs and commissions.[18]

Protection against Inflation.   In managing working capital and controlling liquidity, the international manager will be particularly concerned with the problem of protecting assets in countries with high rates of inflation. Physical assets such as property, plant, and equipment generally maintain their value in real terms during inflation. But the value of working capital, particularly cash and receivables, is highly vulnerable to erosion through inflation. And the international financial manager is concerned about profits and the value of assets as measured in the home-country currency or some other strong convertible currency.

The traditional local strategy for protecting working capital in an inflationary situation is to operate with a minimum amount of liquidity by minimizing cash balances, reducing receivables, lagging in the payment of local expenses, and maximizing local borrowing. Where the penalties for tax delinquency are low, some companies try to lag as much as possible in local tax payments. The value of inventories, particularly imported goods, is less likely to suffer from inflation. Where a local unit is part of a multinational system, it has additional possibilities for protecting assets by accelerating cash remittances to the parent company or elsewhere in the system where inflation rates are lower and by delaying the receipt of payments from low-inflation countries. Such policies of taking advantage of leads and lags are similar to the strategy for protection against devaluation to be discussed below.

Subsidiary Remittance Policies

Dividend remittances are probably the most common way that funds are transferred from affiliate to parent. The remittance decision should be made in relation to all the other facets of international money management. It should take into account the subsidiary's future financing requirements, the host country's concern about retaining an adequate equity base, tax considerations, foreign currency exposure management, alternative means of remitting funds, and international cash management objectives. Although many variables are involved in remittance policy, companies can relatively quickly and inexpensively compute the effect of remittance alternatives. Through sensitivity analysis—that is, using a variety

---

[18] See Goran Bergendahl, "Multi-Currency Netting in a Multi-National Firm," in *International Financial Management,* ed. Goran Bergendahl (Stockholm: P. A. Norstedt & Söners förlag, 1982), pp. 149–73; Venkat Srinivasan and Yong H. Kim, "Payments Netting in International Cash Management: A Network Optimization Approach," *Journal of International Business Studies,* Summer 1986, pp. 1–20.

of scenarios—they can evaluate these alternatives under differing assumptions about the business performance and the external environment.[19]

In the interests of administrative simplicity, many companies overlook the opportunities in remittance policies and adopt general policies in this area. The dividend policy may require the subsidiaries to remit a specific percentage of their earnings to the parent. Such regular remittances help the parent company meet its dividend payments to stockholders. They improve the chances for continuing to remit during difficult balance-of-payment periods in the operating country, because there is a record of regular remittances. Regular remittances also remind local managers that the parent company supplied the capital and that controlling objectives are set by headquarters.

When the local subsidiary is a joint venture with local shareholders, the problem of remittances becomes more complicated. When dividends are declared by local subsidiaries, the funds remitted to headquarters may still be available wholly or net of taxation to the multinational enterprise. But dividends paid locally will generally leave the system and come back only through new financing. Also, it is not uncommon for local shareholders to expect high dividends, whereas the multinational enterprise may prefer to reinvest a large share of earnings and declare only modest dividends.

Transfer Pricing

An exceptionally sensitive area of multinational financial management is that of intracompany transfer pricing. A multinational firm normally has many transactions in goods and services between the parent and a foreign affiliate or between foreign affiliates. The prices established for these transactions within the corporate family are referred to as transfer prices. When transactions take place across national frontiers—and the units of the same enterprise are subject to different custom duties, tax rates, currency risks, and foreign exchange controls— transfer prices can be adjusted (or, as critics charge, "manipulated") to achieve a wide variety of results that will further the overall goals of the enterprise.

Transfer price setting can be used for positioning funds within an enterprise. As units in a multinational enterprise system may both buy and sell to each other, funds can be moved out of a particular country by charging high prices for goods and services sold to the affiliate in that country and paying low prices for purchases. Conversely, funds can be positioned in the country by the opposite policy of low selling and high buying prices. The movements can be between affiliates as well as between the parent and a particular affiliate.

What might the firm gain by moving funds out of a particular country through transfer pricing policies? The enterprise may reduce its tax liabilities by shifting earnings from a high-tax to a low-tax country. It may reduce its exposure to

---

[19] David B. Zenoff and Jack Zwick, *International Financial Management* (Englewood Cliffs, N.J.: Prentice-Hall, 1969), p. 438.

currency devaluation by changing the currency in which enterprise assets are held. It may increase the flow of funds to the parent or another affiliate when financial transfers in the form of dividend remittances are restricted. The firm may want to show lower earnings in a particular country because high profits might encourage local authorities to ask for price reductions or labor unions to press for wage increases.

What might the firm gain by the reverse policy of positioning more funds in a country through transfer pricing? Low import prices can reduce customs duties where duties are ad valorem—that is, assessed as a percentage of value. Low import prices can reduce import deposit requirements where they exist, and allow the importer to bring in a greater quantity where import quotas are established in terms of value. Another objective might be to help a subsidiary show a profit during a startup period and thereby improve its ability to get local credit.

Given the opportunities to shift funds and profits by the transfer-pricing mechanism, how extensively is the instrument used by multinational companies? Pricing policies are inevitably a sensitive area where management seldom gives out factual information. If companies are using international transfer prices to achieve some particular end, they do not announce that fact. A survey completed in 1980 of many multinationals of different nationalities reported that "few transnationals admitted to the use of transfers at other than arm's-length prices." Also, many firms insisted that "the extent of manipulative practices has been exaggerated." Yet, at the same time, most companies claimed to "have no idea" how common non-arm's-length transfer pricing is because of a lack of "firsthand knowledge."[20]

Another survey, limited to U.S. multinationals, ranked marketing considerations in the foreign country as the most important variables influencing transfer pricing decisions. These were followed by a reasonable profit for the subsidiary and U.S. tax considerations.[21] But the survey did not differentiate by countries. In contrast, still another survey with special focus on the developing countries reported that the desire to avoid foreign exchange controls and restrictions on profit repatriation ranked highest among company motivations for using transfer prices. Changing income tax liability was ranked only as a minor factor.[22]

The developing countries have been reluctant to accept the declarations of "innocence" and have made transfer pricing a major issue to be included in the proposed UN Code of Conduct for the multinationals and in the work of the United Nations Centre on Transnational Corporations. They are aware that the

---

[20] Isaiah Frank, *Foreign Enterprise in Developing Countries* (Baltimore: Johns Hopkins University Press, 1980), p. 97.

[21] Jane O. Burns, "Transfer Pricing Policies in U.S. Multinational Corporations," *Journal of International Business Studies*, Fall 1980, p. 25.

[22] Seung H. Kim and Stephen W. Miller, "Constituents of the International Transfer Pricing Decision," *Columbia Journal of World Business*, Spring 1979, pp. 69–77.

controls prevailing in many developing countries make the rewards to the enterprise from manipulating transfer prices extremely attractive. They fear that transfer-pricing policies can undercut their national objectives, and they cite several studies in support of this concern.[23]

Although conclusive evidence is not available, it is probably a fair conclusion that most multinational enterprises use transfer prices to switch funds at one time or another, depending on the particular investment involved and the particular host country. In any event, the tax authorities of the advanced countries continue to demonstrate a concern about the prevalence of transfer pricing, together with the use of tax havens, as a means of reducing tax liabilities. The developing countries also continue to list transfer pricing as a top priority conflict issue in their relations with multinational enterprises.

The use of transfer pricing is limited by both internal and external factors. If foreign units are made profit centers for purposes of monitoring their performance and financially rewarding their managers, goods must be transferred at competitive and relatively uniform prices between units whose performance is being compared. Several techniques, however, can be used to maximize total system profits through manipulating transfer prices while retaining the profit center concept.[24]

Another major constraint on transfer-pricing policies has been the rapidly expanding surveillance of tax and custom authorities. The transfer-price review program of the U.S. Treasury is perhaps the most advanced in the world today. It includes not only the sale of tangible property but also the pricing of money, services, the use of tangible property, and the transfer of intangible property such as patents and trademarks. Section 482 of the Internal Revenue Code (1954) and the regulations promulgated by the Treasury in 1968 to govern international pricing practices are intended to insure that the U.S. government gets its fair share of the taxes on income earned by the multinational corporate system. The general rule of the Treasury governing the pricing of controlled intracompany transactions is that transfer prices should be set at a level comparable to prices where the two parties are relatively independent and "bargaining at arm's length."

Although more and more limits are being imposed on transfer-pricing policies by governmental tax and customs regulations in home and host countries, within these limits there is frequently latitude for pricing to meet market and competitive factors. Even the U.S. regulations appear to leave an opening for a company to lower its transfer price for the purposes of entering a new market or meeting competition in an existing market. Consequently, for most companies the opportunity to support marketing goals and to increase systemwide profits by alternative transfer-pricing strategies should be an element in international pricing strategy, as discussed in Chapter 18.

---

[23] U.N. Centre on Transnational Corporations, *Transnational Corporations and International Trade: Selected Issues* (New York: U.N., 1985), p. 14.

[24] See, for example, M. Edgar Barrett, "Case of the Tangled Transfer Price," *Harvard Business Review*, May–June 1977, pp. 20–36, 176–78.

MANAGING FOREIGN EXCHANGE RISK

For many multinationals, managing foreign exchange exposures—that is, responding to anticipated changes in exchange rates—is the most important international financial challenge. Changes in the value of currencies, both devaluations and revaluations, have been frequent and significant in amount. Even more frequent have been the number of false alarms, which must be considered and dealt with.

Foreign exchange risk is not limited to companies with foreign operations. Any company with a receivable or payable to be collected or paid in a foreign currency is exposed to foreign exchange risk. As a dramatic example, let us assume that an American firm whose only foreign business is exporting sold $10,000 in merchandise in early February 1982 to a Mexican buyer and agreed to accept payment in Mexican pesos within 30 days. At the time, the exchange rate was fixed at 26.80 pesos to the U.S. dollar, so the sale price was 268,000 pesos. On February 18, 1982, Mexico devalued the peso and allowed it to float. By March 5, the peso had declined to 45.20 to the dollar. Thus the 268,000 pesos received by the U.S. company had to be exchanged for only US$5,929 at the March 5 rate, or an exchange loss of about 40 percent. If the sale had been denominated in U.S. dollars, the Mexican importer would have had to pay 452,000 pesos instead of 268,000 pesos, or almost 70 percent more.

The exposure of the multinational enterprise is far more complex. Changes in relative foreign exchange values affect the value of transactions, cash flows, assets, liabilities, and current and future earnings as measured by the yardstick or reference currency—normally the currency of the parent's home country. Changes in currency values also affect a company's competitive position in its home market and abroad, and may cause a change in the national control environment as governments adopt new policies to correct payments imbalances.

There are five components to managing foreign exchange risk. First, the enterprise must specify and analyze through an exposure audit all aspects of its operations that have foreign exchange implications. Second, it must identify and measure the types of exposure it has to changes in currency values. Third, it must have a strategy for exposure management. Fourth, it must develop a procedure for forecasting the amount, timing, pattern, and probability of changes in foreign exchange rates. Finally, it must develop a system to implement its exposure strategy.[25]

The Exchange Audit

The importance of having a comprehensive understanding of the implications of foreign currency changes on a company's operations cannot be overstressed. The audit should include an analysis of:

---

[25] For general background see Laurent L. Jacque, "Management of Foreign Exchange Risk: A Review Article," *Journal of International Business Studies,* Spring–Summer 1981, pp. 81–101.

1. The types of transactions that are affected.
2. How each unit in the system both at home and abroad is affected.
3. How elements of corporate strategy are affected.
4. How each function of management is affected, that is, marketing, production, personnel, and so on.

The implications of currency changes can be extensive.[26] A compensation policy for company personnel of different nationalities and located in different countries can be equitable at one exchange rate and inequitable when currency values change. Or even more fundamentally, the best strategy for serving a foreign market can change from exporting to foreign production, or vice versa, as a result of major changes in exchange rates.

Foreign Exchange Exposure

The formulation of an appropriate strategy depends on how management defines and measures its exposure to changes in currency values. The types of exposure are generally defined as transactions, economic, translation, and tax exposure.

Transactions Exposure.   *Transactions exposure* is the extent to which near-term cash flows of current business operations are affected by fluctuations in foreign exchange values. Such exposure includes obligations for purchase or sale of goods and services, as well as the borrowing or lending of funds in foreign currencies. Transactions exposure is the uncertain value to the firm of its open position in cross-currency commitments. Transactions exposure can result in real, as contrasted to bookkeeping, gains and losses.

Economic Exposure.   *Economic exposure* measures the extent to which a company's *future* international business earning power is affected by changes in currency values. It is concerned with the impact of currency changes on future sales, prices, and costs. In technical terms, it reflects the extent to which the net present value of expected after-tax flows will be affected as exchange rates change. From the standpoint of the long-run health of an enterprise, economic exposure is far more important than either transactions or translation exposure.

Translation Exposure.   *Translation exposure,* also referred to as *accounting exposure,* measures the impact of currency changes on the reported consolidated results and balance sheet of a company. Translation exposure is essentially concerned with present measures of past events, and the accounting gains or losses

---

[26] See Zenoff, *Management Principles for Finance in the Multinational,* pp. 106–8; and Richard M. Levich and Clas G. Wihlborg, *Exchange Risk and Exposure* (Lexington, Mass.: Lexington Books, 1980).

in translation are said to be unrealized. To report consolidated worldwide operations, the financial statements must be translated from the local currencies in which they are recorded to the measurement currency used by headquarters. This translation, as explained in Chapter 21, follows rules set by the government of the parent firm, an accounting association, or the firm itself.

The amount of translation exposure will depend upon which of the alternative translation methods discussed in Chapter 21 are used. The significance of translation exposure depends upon how the company's reported results are evaluated by the investment community, shareholders, financial institutions, and so on.

Tax Exposure.   Changes in foreign exchange values generally have income tax implications. As a rule, only realized gains or losses affect the income tax liability of a company. Translation losses or gains are normally not realized and are not taken into account in tax liability. Some steps taken to reduce exposure, such as entering into forward exchange contracts, can create losses or gains that enter into tax liability. Other steps that can be taken have no income tax implications.

To summarize, transactions exposure refers to the immediate or near-term effects on cash flows. Economic exposure refers to the same types of effect on cash flows over the long term. Translation exposure is the accounting reflection of a change in position that has not yet been realized.

Exposure Reports

In order to evaluate and analyze the foreign exchange position of the firm's overseas operations, the financial manager requires monthly foreign exchange exposure and flow-of-funds reports from each subsidiary. These reports, plus balance sheet and income statements, provide the necessary information base for currency decisions related to short-term transactions and translation exposure. They are not oriented, however, to economic exposure.

A *foreign exchange exposure report* is similar to a balance sheet, but it differs in three respects. It omits balance sheet items that are not considered exposed in an accounting sense. Which items are omitted will depend on the translation method being used. It includes off-balance sheet items such as foreign exchange contracts and future commitments such as lease payments or purchase and sales contracts. And, most important, the exposure report states all assets and liabilities in the currencies in which they are denominated. The currency distinction is crucial. A receivable in Mexican pesos, for example, is unlikely to have the same future value as a receivable in German marks, even though they had the same value at the time of sale.

The *flow-of-funds report* shows on a monthly or quarterly basis expected cash flows over a future period—say, a year—for each of the currencies in which the subsidiary does business. The expected flows are based on such factors as estimated sales during the forthcoming year, and assumptions about receivables collection. Such a report is really a cash budget subdivided by type of currency.

The funds-flow report may reveal that exposures in the different currencies vary dramatically over time. It may also show that the static balance sheet exposure is insignificant as compared to the exposure generated by the flows of an ongoing business. With the added information from the funds-flow report, the international financial manager can evaluate how various means of protection against foreign exchange risk affect exposure to accounting and cash-flow losses over time.[27]

Exposure Management Strategy

Each enterprise must formulate its objectives and strategy for exposure management to provide guidance to its managers responsible for making correct and timely decisions. And senior management must be involved in the formulation and approval process. Normally it is impossible to insure against all foreign exchange risk and prohibitively expensive to insure against some risks. How much risk is the enterprise willing to accept? If management's goal is to maximize long-run stockholder wealth, protection against economic exposure is a first priority. If management feels that its performance is judged mainly on short-term results, it will give priority to protection against transactions and translation exposure.[28]

Senior management must also develop an appropriate approach for what might be termed speculation. There is always a temptation to seek speculative profits in foreign currency transactions. But most companies avoid outright speculation on the grounds that the main focus of foreign exchange management should be directed to protecting corporate earnings at a minimum cost. Furthermore, governments and commercial banks are likely to disapprove of outright speculative activity not legitimately related to the firm's principal business activity.

Reacting to Economic Exposure

Reacting to economic exposure can require strategic changes that transcend the financial manager's function and encompass virtually every decision area, including marketing, production, sourcing, and plant location. The experience of Volkswagen (VW) of West Germany during the 1970s illustrates the potential impact of economic exposure and the variety of responses that a firm can make.[29]

In the late 1960s, VW was the largest automobile exporter in the world,

---

[27] For illustrations of exposure reports see Eiteman and Stonehill, *Multinational Business Finance,* 4th ed., pp. 182–91.

[28] An excellent example of corporate guidelines is Robert S. Einzig, "Foreign Currency Exposure Management in Transamerica," in *International Finance and Trade,* vol. 2, ed. Marshall Sarnat and Giorgio P. Szego (Cambridge, Mass.: Ballinger, 1979), pp. 117–34; see also Michel Ghertman, "The Behaviour of French Firms toward Foreign Exchange Risk," in *Recent Research in the Internationalization of Business,* ed. L. G. Mattsson and F. Wiedersheim-Paul (Stockholm: Almqvist & Wiksell International, 1979), pp. 278–93.

[29] The Volkswagen example is summarized from S. L. Srinivasulu, "Strategic Response to Foreign Exchange Risks," *Columbia Journal of World Business,* Spring 1981, pp. 13–23.

and its primary export market was the United States. In October 1969, and again in 1971 and 1972, the German mark (DM) was revalued against the U.S. dollar and other major currencies. Over the three-year period, the DM gained in value relative to the U.S. dollar by more than 40 percent. In absolute terms, the exchange rate was 4.00 DM = US$1 in 1969 and 2.7 DM = US$1 at the end of 1972.

The revaluation made VW noncompetitive in the U.S. market, where its sales declined from 570,000 vehicles in 1968 to 200,000 in 1976. The revaluation made it increasingly difficult to compete in the United Kingdom, France, and Italy. At the same time, VW had to face increased competition within the West German market from Renault of France and Fiat of Italy, as a result of the weakening of the franc and the lira vis-à-vis the DM. The net earnings of VW's overall operations dropped from a profit of DM 330 million in 1969 to a loss of DM 807 million in 1973.

How could VW cope with the economic exposure? VW had little price flexibility because of competition and price sensitivity of the market segment to which it was catering. Tactical responses such as hedging; leads and lags (discussed below); and swaps provided no solution to the basic problem. The company needed to match cash inflows in a specific currency with cash outflows in that (or a similar) currency in order to insulate itself from the economic exposure. VW had dollar revenues from its business in the United States but DM costs. When the DM was revalued, VW's revenues in DM declined but its costs in DM remained the same.

Through a series of strategic responses, VW was able to reduce its economic exposure in the U.S. market. It shifted from a policy of having all of its loans in DMs to a diversification policy where a portion of its loans were in U.S. dollars. Thus if VW's revenues in DM went down because of revaluations against the U.S. dollar, its cost of debt servicing went down and partially offset the revenue lost. VW converted other costs to U.S. dollars by setting up a production facility in the United States and by buying parts and components in the United States. As a general strategy, VW stepped up intersubsidiary linkages that required subsidiaries in revaluing countries to buy from subsidiaries in devaluing countries. This diversification in financing, changed production siting, and sourcing—activated in large part by the major economic exposure the firm had encountered—transformed VW's strategic profile.

Reacting to Transactions and Translation Exposure

Techniques to minimize transactions and translation exposure center around the concepts of hedging.[30] A *hedge* is a contract or arrangement that provides

---

[30] See David F. Babbel, "Determining the Optimum Strategy for Hedging Currency Exposure," *Journal of International Business Studies,* Spring/Summer, 1983, pp. 133–39; Chuck C. Y. Kwok, "Hedging Foreign Exchange Exposures: Independent vs Integrative Approaches," *Journal of International Business Studies,* Summer 1987, pp. 33–52.

defense against the risk of loss from a change in foreign exchange rates. Several forms of hedging have already been discussed in Chapter 4, including currency and credit swaps.

Leads and Lags. Firms can reduce their foreign exchange exposure by *leading* and *lagging* payables and receivables—that is, paying early or late. This can be achieved by accelerating payments from soft-currency to hard-currency countries and by delaying inflows from hard-currency to soft-currency countries. As an example, suppose a multinational enterprise had anticipated the February 1982 Mexican peso devaluation. In January, the parent had the subsidiary make early payment to the parent for goods, services, interest, loan amortization, and dividends, even though such payments were initially scheduled for later in the year. At the same time, the parent firm delayed a dollar loan to the subsidiary intended for expansion until after the devaluation. The early peso payments were converted into more U.S. dollars and the delayed dollar loan into more pesos than if payments had been made as originally scheduled. Leading and lagging can be used most easily between units of the same enterprise, but the technique can also be used with independent firms.

When the firm makes use of leads and lags, it must adjust its performance measures of the units and managers that are cooperating in the maneuver. The leads and lags can distort the profitability of individual units. Also, because the use of leads and lags is a well-known technique for minimizing foreign exchange exposure and because it has the effect of putting pressures on a weak currency, most governments impose some limits on leads and lags. For example, certain countries set 180 days as a limit for receiving payments for exports or making payments for imports.

Forward Exchange Market Hedge. The use of forward markets and foreign exchange futures as protection against foreign exchange risk was already discussed at some length in Chapter 4. A *foreign exchange market hedge* is a present agreement on an exchange rate for a foreign exchange transaction to take place at a specified future date. The rate agreed upon may turn out to be lower or higher than the spot rate at the future date. But the advantage of the hedge is that the firm can be certain of the value in its yardstick, or reference currency, of foreign currencies it is scheduled to receive or to pay in the future. The hedge may be used for amounts receivable in foreign currencies (selling forward), or for amounts payable in foreign currencies in the future (buying forward). The forward purchase or sale of foreign exchange for a future date is the easiest method of hedging to put in place or to remove. The method can be used, however, only when forward markets exist for the specific currency of interest to the firm.

Money Market Hedge. A *money market hedge* also involves a contract and a source of funds to fulfill the contract. The contract is a loan agreement. The firm using a money market hedge borrows in one currency and converts the proceeds into another currency. Funds to repay the loan may be generated from business operations, in which event the hedge is covered. Or funds to repay the loan may be purchased in the foreign exchange market at the spot rate when the loan matures. The latter is an "uncovered" or open hedge.

The cost of the money market hedge is determined by differential interest rates. The cost of the forward market hedge is a function of the forward exchange quotations, called the *forward premium.*[31]

Balance Sheet Hedge.   A *balance sheet hedge* is carried out by bringing exposed assets equal to exposed liabilities. If the objective is to minimize translation exposure, the usual procedure is to have monetary assets in a specific currency equal monetary liabilities in that currency. If the objective is protection against economic exposure or transactions exposure, the procedure is to denominate debt in a currency whose change in value will offset the change in value of future cash receipts.

Foreign Exchange Forecasting

A fourth dimension to exposure management is foreign exchange forecasting. Ideally such forecasts should produce estimates of the amount, timing, pattern, and probability of changes in exchange rates. The forecasts should suggest the magnitude of possible gains or losses from given levels of exposure. Thus, they provide an indispensable ingredient in calculating whether it pays to buy protection against given exposures. The development of forecasts should be guided by the specific needs of the enterprise. These include the time period for which the forecast is required, the degree of precision needed by managers using the forecasts, the company's criteria for a correct/useful forecast, and the cost of an incorrect forecast.

The current state of currency forecasting, as discussed in Chapter 4, is relatively modest. The international economy is extremely complex and the best of currency forecasts will be on target only part of the time. Yet with all their shortcomings, foreign currency forecasts are still an essential component of foreign exchange management. Implicitly, if not explicitly, forecasts underlie many decisions ranging from basic strategy formulation and investment decisions to managing existing operations and setting policies for dividend remittances.

Implementation

A final exposure component is the implementation system. Given the analysis of the firm's exposure and the forecast of foreign exchange rates, the financial manager can work out a protection strategy, making use of the growing body of

---

[31] See Boris Antl and A. C. Henry, "The Cost and Implications of Two Hedging Techniques," *Euromoney,* June 1979.

quantitative and model-building work available on managing foreign exchange risk.[32]

After calculating the types and amount of exposure, the financial manager will work out the reduction of exposure through financing alternatives and leads and lags. The rest of the exposure can be covered by the forward exchange market, providing the cost of such cover compares favorably with the prospective loss.

In some cases the cost of insurance will be too high, or nonfinancial considerations such as local goodwill are involved so that the company itself will absorb the foreign exchange loss. To use a simple example, suppose that the forecaster gives an estimated devaluation size of 20 percent and a probability of occurrence of 75 percent, and suppose the forecaster has been wrong 10 percent of the time. These three factors multiplied together ($0.20 \times 0.75 \times 1.10$) equal 16.5 percent. This result is multiplied by the company treasurer's safety factor, which reflects the company's willingness to accept risk—say, a 15 percent safety factor. Then, 16.5 percent multiplied by 1.15 equals 18.98 percent. This number can be compared with the market cost of cover to reach a decision. Suppose the annual market discount rate on forward contracts is 15 percent. The treasurer would spin off the risk because the cover cost is less than the expected loss indicated by the analysis. If the market price of cover is 22 percent, the company would self-insure because the cost of the cover would be more expensive than the probable loss.[33]

THE TAX VARIABLE

In a world of independent taxing authorities, the multinational enterprise encounters an almost infinite variety of types of taxes, levels of tax burdens, tax incentives, patterns of tax administration, and possible overlaps in tax systems. The tax variable is important in virtually all business decisions, and as tax systems are highly technical and change frequently, the enterprise needs the services of tax experts to anticipate tax burdens, minimize tax obligations within legal limits, and supervise compliance.

At the subsidiary level, the tax issue is to become informed on national differences and their impact on the profitability of operations in that country. At the multinational level, the firm must cope with overlapping tax jurisdictions,

---

[32] For example, see Alan C. Shapiro and David P. Rutenberg, "Managing Exchange Risks in a Floating World," *Financial Management,* Summer 1976, pp. 48–58; Raj Aggarwal, *The Management of Foreign Exchange: Optimal Policies for the Multinational Corporation* (New York: Praeger Publishers, 1976); Robert Z. Aliber, *Exchange Risk and Corporate International Finance* (New York: John Wiley & Sons, 1978); see also Pål Korsvold, "The Futility of Currency Hedging Models," in *International Financial Management,* ed. Goran Bergendahl, pp. 102–27.

[33] R. B. Shulman, "Are Foreign Exchange Risks Measurable?", *Columbia Journal of World Business,* May–June 1970, pp. 59–60.

possible double taxation, and differential treatment of cross-border money flows. At the global level, another major issue is the use of tax havens.

National Tax Environments

National differences in taxation can change greatly the profitability of similar operations in different foreign subsidiaries.[34] Nations vary in the relative importance given to direct versus indirect taxes, in corporate income tax rates, and in the treatment of depreciation and many other expense items. The United States relies heavily at the federal level on direct taxes, mainly personal and corporate income taxes. In contrast, European countries rely heavily on indirect or turnover taxes, such as the value-added tax. The value-added tax has been adopted as the main source of revenue from indirect taxation by the European Community.

The LDCs rely more on indirect taxes than personal or corporate income taxes. Indirect taxes are relatively easy to administer. In contrast, income taxes are difficult to administer efficiently. Extensive record-keeping is required of individuals and companies, and an effective system of penalties is needed to secure reasonable compliance.

Among the industrial nations, some countries differentiate between retained and distributed earnings, charging a lower rate on distributed profits. Germany and Japan, for example, tax distributed earnings at a lower rate.[35] Under such a system, corporations are under pressure to meet their needs for additional capital through new financing rather than through retained earnings.

The less developed countries fall into three tax categories. The first category consists of countries such as Mexico and Singapore that have been attractive areas for foreign investment and have been able to raise their income tax rates to the 40 percent level. A second group of countries use moderate income tax rates and tax incentives to encourage private investment, such as the Philippines and Taiwan. The third category includes the so-called tax haven countries that assess low (or no) corporate taxes to affiliates of foreign companies. Some countries that impose no income tax are the Bahamas, Cayman Islands, and Bermuda. Countries such as Panama and Liberia have special tax exemptions for foreign companies.

The Multinational Tax Environment

The tax variable becomes increasingly complex when profits are transferred from the subsidiary to the parent or to other units of the multinational enterprise.

---

[34] Various tax guides are published periodically by international accounting firms such as Price Waterhouse Co. and Arthur Andersen Co. These give detailed information on the tax treatment of foreign income and related matters and are available for most countries where international business is a significant activity.

[35] See Price Waterhouse & Co., *Corporate Taxes: A Worldwide Summary* (New York, 1984).

Countries differ in their treatment of foreign-source income earned by their own multinationals. The policies of the major industrial countries range from complete exemption of repatriated foreign income to full taxation at domestic rates. The United States taxes the worldwide income of its citizens, residents, and domestic corporations, but double taxation is mitigated by allowing a direct credit against U.S. taxes for foreign taxes paid.

In the tax field, as previously discussed in Chapter 8, governments have taken steps to avoid double taxation through bilateral treaties. Under such treaties, a country agrees to share with another on a prearranged basis the taxes imposed on business operations in the territory of one country by nationals of another country. Tax treaties may also provide for information exchanges between the governments that will aid each other in tax collection. The negotiation of a network of tax treaties has resulted in more tax uniformity among countries.

The topic of "tax sparing" was also discussed in Chapter 8. The special tax incentives provided by some countries to attract foreign investment offer little advantage to the business enterprise if the income is taxable at the same or higher rate in the home country of the parent company. Some countries permit a tax credit for taxes that have been spared in a foreign country. But others, particularly the United States, do not. The effect of policies such as that of the United States is to reduce or cancel the attractiveness of foreign tax incentives in influencing the investment decisions of multinational enterprises.

The matter of "tax havens" continues to be an extremely sensitive tax issue, although the use of tax havens is not limited to multinational enterprises. Tax havens are attractive as a means of avoiding or deferring home country taxes where the home country does not tax the income of foreign subsidiaries until the income is repatriated as a result of dividends, liquidation, and so forth. A nonoperating subsidiary established in a low-tax or no-tax country can be used to "book" financial transactions of operating subsidiaries of the same parent so as to concentrate as much taxable income as possible in the tax-haven country. Thus, taxes on foreign earnings could be avoided indefinitely. Such a subsidiary could even loan funds to the parent. But as one recent study observes, tax havens "are faced with a steady barrage of anti-tax avoidance laws to reduce further the haven's attractions."[36]

As a general rule, the tax policy of an investor nation should be neutral. It should not favor or penalize foreign as against domestic investment. Whether the U.S. tax system is neutral or favors foreign investment has been periodically debated in the United States with inconclusive results. The labor unions, in particular, have argued that the tax system favors foreign investment and that such measures as the foreign tax credit, which is a direct reduction against tax liabilities, should be replaced by allowing foreign taxes as an expense. Other parties have

---

[36] Caroline Doggart, *Tax Havens and Their Uses 1987* (London: Economist Intelligence Unit, 1987), p. 80.

BOX 23–1
New Tune for Corporate Tax Fiddlers

Multinational companies fiddle their accounts and evade taxes. Right? Well, yes—and quite a few of them are getting better at it. Through the 1970s, the world's tax authorities tried to stop multinationals laundering profits through low-tax, and no-tax, countries. The new powers they sought (and got) were aimed at curbing legal, but costly, tax avoidance—mostly on the assumption that multinational companies were playing it straight and not stooping to illegal evasion. At the same time, most multinationals developed worthy policies—some real, some not—that ruled out tax fiddling. The baddies carried on as before, and some of the goodies lost their haloes. When the inevitable crackdown on transfer pricing manipulation arrives, many of the world's most respectable companies will be caught cheating.

In a windowless Paris conference room in February this year, 60 tax inspectors from industrial countries met for three days to talk about ways of plugging international tax leakage. This was the fourth in a series of confidential meetings (with more to come), under the wing of the OECD committee on fiscal affairs, to discuss the detection of tax avoidance and evasion. The 60 are all actively involved in auditing multinationals' accounts. They discussed, according to a terse statement, "questions related to the selection of cases for in-depth audit, transfer prices for exchanges of goods, research and development, capital and services, and the different opportunities available to tax administrations to cooperate with other countries through exchanging information, simultaneous audits and joint audits."

SOURCE: *The Economist,* June 20, 1981, p. 108.

concluded that U.S. tax policy provides a "surprising close approximation to neutrality."[37] The debate is likely to continue.

In summary, tax planning is a complex and highly technical subject that requires the input of tax experts. The financial manager must have familiarity with national tax environments in which the enterprise operates as well as understand the tax philosophy and policies of the parent country.[38] Important considerations are how the home country views tax neutrality, tax deferral, foreign tax credits, tax havens, and intercompany transactions.

SUMMARY

International financial management is primarily concerned with the maximization of profits after taxes for the multinational system as a whole, within the

---

[37] Thomas Horst, "American Taxation of Multinational Firms," *American Economic Review,* June 1977, pp. 376–89.

[38] See Michael Adler, "U.S. Taxation of U.S. Multinational Corporations: A Manual of Computation Techniques and Managerial Decision Rules," in *International Finance and Trade,* vol. 2, eds. M. Sarnat and G. P. Szego (Cambridge, Mass.: Ballinger, 1979), pp. 157–210.

framework of a wider pursuit of corporate objectives. International operations add many complexities to the financial management function, ranging from the difficulties of developing an adequate financial information system, where the initial data input into the system must necessarily be shaped by varying patterns in national accounting systems, to the problems of dealing in multiple currencies and managing foreign exchange risks. At the same time, a multinational system affords opportunities to minimize interest costs, tax liabilities, and the effects of differential inflation rates among countries, and to reduce working capital needs through pooling liquidity among affiliates.

Thus, the major challenge and opportunity in international financial management is to optimize on a systemwide basis. Toward this end, major progress has been achieved in the development of concepts and tools for complex strategies that reveal profit-taking opportunities that normally do not become apparent under simple strategies focused on subgoals of financial management. But the use of complex and sophisticated techniques can be expensive in terms of required data, personnel, and experience. Given these cost and other limitations, many international firms deal with each subsidiary as an independent operation and make little or no effort to optimize the financial function on a system-wide basis.

Under most circumstances, however, the investment and capital-budgeting decisions above certain financial limits are a centralized responsibility for the multinational firm. The international financial manager has also become increasingly involved in decisions on financial structures of affiliates, financing techniques, and management of foreign exchange risk. The management of cash flows and liquidity on an international basis has been growing rapidly as an international financial management function.

The financial structure of affiliates will depend on the willingness of the parent company to assume equity risk. Although many companies prefer to minimize their equity commitments, for new foreign projects or expansions the hard-core financing will have to come from within the multinational enterprise. It must show a willingness to risk its own funds in order to tap external sources. A common pattern has been to finance fixed assets with company funds and long-term loan capital, and for working capital to use local borrowings to the maximum extent. The mix between local and imported debt depends on local availability, the relative costs of alternative sources, the degree of operating freedom associated with funds from different sources, and local government constraints on excessive debt ratios. Where local money costs exceed imported costs, a company will have to decide how much it wants to pay for risk avoidance. Tax factors and the effect of the financing plan on both the financial situation of the parent company and the total system will be additional considerations.

Appendix: A Systems Approach to Financial Optimization: An Example

The possibilities for gains through a systems approach are illustrated in Figure 23A–1. If each company in the system raised capital from the cheapest source (Country B) and paid local taxes, the net cost after taxes would be 4.0 percent for A (i.e., 8 percent less 50 percent taxes); 6.4 percent for B; and 4.8 percent for C. The average cost for

FIGURE 23A–1   A Systems Approach to Financial Optimization (an example)

Characteristics of the multinational system (by country):

	Three Fully Owned System Companies		
	A	B	C
Local corporation tax rates	50%	20%	40%
Import duty rates for system transfers	10	30	80
Local interest rates (After adjustment for forecast exchange rate change)	12	8	10

Each company transfers some production to the other two.
Each company has local profits and incurs corporation tax.

Possibilities for system savings over independent operation:
1. *Alter source of capital.*
   Independent decision: Raise capital from cheapest source (B) and pay local taxes.
   Net cost = (A) 4.0 percent; (B) 6.4 percent; (C) 4.8 percent.
   System decision: Company with highest tax rate (A) to raise capital from cheapest source and advance interest free to others. Net cost = (A,B,C,) 4.0 percent.
2. *Alter transfer prices.*
   Independent decision: Price somewhere between supplier company cost and receiving company revenue.
   System decision: Adjust prices as indicated on the table below. Gains would continue until lowered prices reached zero and increased prices eliminated all the profits of the receiving company, but there will be practical limitations in the real world.

Goods Transferred From:	Direction of Price Change	Gains from $100 Change			
		Source Country Tax ($)	Destination Country Tax ($)	Import Duty ($)	Net System Gain ($)
A to B	Lower	+50	−20	+30	+60
B to C	Lower	+20	−40	+80	+60
C to A	Adjust to give desired company profits				0
A to C	Lower	+50	−40	+80	+90
C to B	Lower	+40	−20	+30	+50
B to A	Raise	−20	+50	−10	+20

3. *Alter royalty charges and transfer prices:*
   Independent decision: Combined total to fall between supplier company cost and receiving company revenue.
   System decision: Lower *all* transfer prices to minimize import duties, and charge royalties from lowest taxed company to minimize corporation tax.

the system would be 5.06 percent. But if the subsidiary with the highest tax rate (A) raised all the capital needed by the system from the cheapest source (B) and advanced the funds interest-free to the other units, the cost to the system would be only 4.0 percent.

The advantages of the system for altering transfer prices for materials, services, and components from one unit of the system to the others are also illustrated. For every $100 that A lowers its transfer prices to B, there will be a net gain of $60 to the system. Half of this gain, $30, will be in taxes because profits are taxed at only a 20 percent rate in B as against a 50 percent rate in A. There will be another $30 gained in import duties because the price on which the 30 percent duty is charged has been lowered.

EXERCISES AND DISCUSSION QUESTIONS

1. Why might a multinational firm decide to invest in a project that shows a low expected rate of return on the basis of the first-level analysis at the local country level?
2. Which source of funds would be the cheaper—a loan in the United Kingdom at 11 percent annually on an overdraft basis or a loan from a U.S. bank at 9 percent annually but with the requirement of a 20 percent compensating balance?
3. A U.S. multinational enterprise has three subsidiaries, each located in a different European country. The British subsidiary imports semifinished products from its Dutch affiliate for further processing and distribution. Part of the British subsidiary's output is exported to its German affiliate, and the rest is sold in the British home market. Normal trade credit terms on all transactions are 60 days. In anticipation of British sterling depreciation during 1983, the British subsidiary was directed to give its German affiliate 110 days to pay and to reduce its liabilities to the Dutch affiliate to zero; that is, to pay for its imports COD. How can such tactics provide a hedge against one-time exchange losses?
4. The chief financial officer of a U.S. multinational company says, "Our foreign exchange strategy is to avoid risk. We pursue the practice of offsetting all balance sheet exposures with foreign exchange hedges, thus neutralizing the exposures." Comment on the wisdom of such a strategy.
5. How does the tax variable enter into decisions on transfer pricing, capital budgeting, remittance policies, and the financial structure of affiliates?
6. Why is the pricing of products and services between affiliates of the same company of prime importance to government tax officials of the parent country? of the host country?
7. How does netting work? How is it beneficial to the company?
8. Define *transaction, translation,* and *economic exposure.* Which is likely to have the greatest impact on the long-term profitability of the enterprise? And why?
9. If a company follows the local pattern of high debt ratios in the financial structure of a subsidiary, how would this affect the (a) capital budgeting decision, (b) production decisions, and (c) costs?

CHAPTER 24

Multinational Human Resource Management

The quality of a firm's executives is usually the single most important determinant of its success in international business. In the words of one international executive,

"Virtually any type of international problem in the final analysis, is either created by people or must be solved by people. Hence, having the right people in the right place at the right time emerges as the key to a company's international growth. If we are successful in solving that problem, I am confident we can cope with all others."[1]

Multinational business brings with it many unique problems in the management of human resources, the most fundamental of which is the necessity for managers raised and experienced in one culture to play bicultural or multicultural roles. The managers of foreign subsidiaries play a boundary or middleman role between two sets of cultural patterns.[2] To their subordinates and customers, they are "the company" and represent headquarters. To headquarters, they are the "local manager" who belongs to the subsidiary. They must know the local culture and language and they must understand the foreign cultural assumptions underlying the technology and business practices being introduced into the local environment. Whether a national or an expatriate, local managers are always sandwiched between two cultures, and for some, neither culture may be their own.

At headquarters or the regional level, managers play a multicultural role. They must integrate and coordinate activities taking place in many cultural environments that are being directed by managers with diverse cultural orientations. Furthermore, they must deal with the natural tendency of local managers to identify with the national interests of their unit.

Another set of management problems arises when employees are transferred across cultural and national boundaries. The selection of those who are to be transferred involves a choice among the various nationalities involved; raises questions concerning desirable characteristics, education, and remuneration; and requires procedures to facilitate the adjustment of those who switch cultures and residences.

Finally, the international extension of a firm involves wide variations in the skills and supply of workers, different patterns of labor-management relations, the possibility that the firm may have to face international union collaboration for multinational bargaining, and strong pressures to observe the voluntary codes of conduct for industrial relations promulgated by intergovernmental agencies.

MATCHING STRATEGY AND HUMAN RESOURCES

An aggressive global strategy implies managerial resources of a caliber to think out and implement such a strategy. Thus human resources planning must be viewed as part of the overall planning process so that the recruitment and development of human resources matches the firm's global strategy.[3] The failure

---

[1] Michael G. Duerr, "International Business Management: Its Four Tasks," *Conference Board Record,* October 1968, p. 43.

[2] See Chapter 17.

[3] Anders Edstrom and Peter Lorange, "Matching Strategy and Human Resources in Multinational Corporations," *Journal of International Business Studies,* Fall 1984, pp. 125–37.

to have an appropriate human resources strategy that provides the necessary managers for international operations is likely to result in overall strategies being compromised or falling short of expectations.

The human resources function for multinational operations is quite different from that needed for domestic operations. In domestic operations, the principal concern is technical competence. In multinational operations, other important criteria are involved, such as ability to empathize with foreign cultures and the adaptability of a manager's family to foreign countries in the case of international transfers.[4] Furthermore, when managers come from different cultural backgrounds, their values and behavior patterns can vary greatly. And it becomes especially important to match the company's strategies with the goals, competence, and motivations of key managers. Unless individual managers see that it is in their own best interest to commit themselves to the firm's strategy, realistic implementation may be hard to achieve.

EXECUTIVE NATIONALITY POLICIES

What nationality policy should the multinational firm adopt for the recruitment and development of international executives? Essentially, the firm can choose from three policies for staffing management positions, or else adopt no standard policy and build a patchwork approach.[5] It can fill key positions everywhere in the world with personnel from the home country of the parent company—an ethnocentric policy. It can use local nationals to manage foreign subsidiaries and home-country nationals as headquarters managers—a polycentric policy. Or it can recruit and develop the best persons without regard to nationality for key positions anywhere in the multinational system—a geocentric policy. Each of the alternatives has advantages and disadvantages.

An International Executive Cadre

At first glance, the most effective policy appears to be a *geocentric* one, where the best person is sought for a job, regardless of the person's nationality and the location of the job. Such a policy would be consistent with the unique strength of multinational business, namely, its ability to rationalize on an international basis the use of natural resources, financial resources, and technology. Why shouldn't it also rationalize on an international basis the use of managerial resources? To some degree and for a period of time, expatriate managers might be handicapped by not being fully immersed in the national cultural, political, and economic situation. But these disadvantages would be more than offset by their superior ability and experience. Even more important, the tendency of national

---

[4] Rosalie L. Tung, "Human Resource Planning in Japanese Multinationals: A Model for U.S. Firms?" *Journal of International Business Studies,* Fall 1984, pp. 139–49.

[5] David A. Heenan and Howard V. Perlmutter, *Multinational Organizational Development* (Reading, Mass.: Addison-Wesley Publishing, 1979), chap. 2.

identification of managers with individual units of the system would be reduced so that the firm would be better able to realize its mutinational potential.

Yet there have been only modest beginnings by a relatively few international firms toward developing a truly international executive force. Several factors combine to limit the popularity of a geocentric policy. First, host countries want foreign subsidiaries to be staffed by their local nationals and frequently they adopt national controls to achieve this goal. Second, an international executive policy can be expensive. It requires widespread recruitment, a substantial investment in language training and cultural orientation programs for managers and their families, substantial costs in transferring executives and their families into and away from foreign posts, and salary levels that are significantly higher than national levels in many countries. Third, such a pattern requires a high degree of centralization in the control of personnel and their career patterns, and undercuts the cherished prerogative of local managers to choose their own personnel. A fourth reason is that the policy would take a long time to implement.

For firms wishing to build an international management cadre, promotion policies and practice must make it very clear that cross-national service is important to the firm. And in order to recruit promising executives to work with the subsidiaries, the firm must also have a policy of open career opportunities for top-management positions. The view of many ambitious and able young foreign nationals was expressed as follows by an international manager; albeit with marked sexual bias:

> He must feel that if he has the ability he can aspire to any job in the company, apart perhaps from the presidency. It may be that when he is faced with the prospect of going on the main board, and so spending the rest of his working life outside his home country he will decide to reject the opportunity. If so, that will be his decision. But he must feel that his nationality does not, of itself, disqualify him from aiming for the stars.[6]

National Executives within Each Unit

Hiring nationals has many obvious advantages, which are mainly the obverse of the disadvantages of an international executive cadre. Hiring nationals largely eliminates the language barriers, expensive training periods, and cross-cultural adjustment problems of managers and their families. It lowers the profile of a foreign firm in sensitive political situations. It permits the firm to take advantage of lower national salary levels, while still paying a premium over local norms to attract high-quality personnel. And because the career of nationals will be in their home country, they will give continuity to the management of foreign subsidiaries.

---

[6] Christopher Tugendhat. *The Multinationals* (London: Eyre & Spottiswoode, 1971), p. 197; see also John D. Daniels, "The Non-American Manager, Especially as Third Country National in U.S. Multinationals: A Separate but Equal Doctrine?" *Journal of International Business Studies,* Fall 1974, pp. 25–40.

Nevertheless, there is a price to be paid in following a policy of hiring nationals. Nationals are likely to have difficulties in bridging the gap between the subsidiary and the rest of the system. The education, business experience, and cultural environment to which they have been exposed all their lives may not have prepared them to work as part of a multinational enterprise. They may experience cross-cultural problems because of different concepts as to business practices, differences in personal values such as reluctance to "dirty one's hands," and many other cultural variables. They may identify with their country as against the spirit and advantages of multinationalism. They are not likely to be fully knowledgeable about the management techniques, products, and technology developed in the parent firm's home country on which the firm's international expansion is based.

There is an inbuilt immobility. Once foreign managers reach the top position in the overseas subsidiary, they have nowhere to go. The narrow focus of their career can affect their own morale and block the promotion of those underneath them. In turn, some of the most promising foreign nationals may be difficult to recruit and to retain because of limited promotion possibilities within the total enterprise. Also, many nationals are interested in only a limited tour of duty with foreign firms in order to get training and experience.

Japanese multinationals, because their international business language is generally Japanese, have unusual difficulties in finding nationals with the necessary language ability. Even if the language gap is bridged by hiring nationals of Japanese ancestry, the culture gap may still remain. As a Japanese executive complained about his company's experience in Brazil, where there is a large nisei population, "They look Japanese, they speak Japanese, but they think Brazilian."

A policy of employing nationals makes it difficult for young executives from headquarters or from foreign subsidiaries to get experience working outside of their home country and to develop their capacity to communicate, coordinate, and supervise effectively in a multicultural setting. Such a policy is unlikely to create a body of international executives able to switch between units of the multinational firm as the need arises. It also reinforces the dominance of home-country executives, frequently with little foreign experience, in the higher corporate posts dealing with strategy and capital allocation decisions between subsidiary units dominated by local nationals.[7]

Retention of top corporate management at headquarters in the hands of nationals of the parent country has a number of advantages. The executives come from a reasonably similar cultural background and have little trouble in communicating with each other. They are likely to have experienced the buildup of the parent unit and to have developed skills and evolved a working pattern in the

---

[7] Kenneth Simmonds, "Multinational? Well, Not Quite," *Columbia Journal of World Business,* Fall 1966, pp. 115–22; Kenneth Simmonds and Richard Connell, "Breaking the Boardroom Barrier: The Importance of Being British," *Journal of Management Studies,* May 1974, pp. 85–95.

BOX 24–1
Innocents Abroad: GM's Overseas Drive Continues to Sputter after
Three-Year Push

Detroit—Three years ago, General Motors Corp. declared war on the overseas operations of Ford Motor Co. Bursting with optimism, Elliott M. Estes, then the president, vowed GM would blow the doors off its cross-town rival in overseas competition. But in fact, it is GM's doors that have been blown off.

One GM success abroad has been a turnaround at its Vauxhall Motors subsidiary in Luton, England. In other areas, however, GM still has a long way to go. It has had a particularly tough time, for instance, persuading bright young managers to accept overseas assignments. Because the company formerly used its foreign operations as a dumping ground for washed-up executives, some employees still attach that stigma to foreign transfers, "International was like the black hole," says a former GM executive. "People were sent abroad, and you never heard from them again." Only 300 of GM's 200,000 foreign employees are Americans. In the past year, GM has cut back overseas transfers for economic reasons, a source says, as such transfers cost an average of $100,000.

A long-term consequence of GM's inability to groom executives overseas is a shortage of international savvy at the top of the corporation. None of the five members of GM's powerful executive committee has ever served abroad (one did work in Canada); and no one of them speaks a foreign language. By comparison, five of the seven top executives at Ford have put in time abroad; and several are fluent in more than one foreign language.

If GM's high executives haven't much knowledge of markets abroad, they also seem less than interested in learning. . . . both Roger Smith and F. James McDonald, the current chairman and president, are homebodies. Each has taken only one foreign trip since assuming his post 19 months ago. Mr. McDonald says he saw a lot of the world when he was in the Navy, although "that was mostly through a periscope."

SOURCE: Adapted from *The Wall Street Journal,* July 19, 1982. © Dow Jones & Company, Inc., 1982. Used with permission. All rights reserved.

management of an international operation. In the longer run, however, a firm with this sort of management pattern can become a grouping of virtually independent national units with executives of the parent unit, who are not sufficiently prepared for this task, carrying the prime responsibility for transfer of ideas and for general cohesion (see Box 24–1).

Parent Company Executives Everywhere

An ethnocentric policy of placing home-country nationals in key executive posts everywhere seems directly contradictory to current trends toward nationalism and equality of opportunity. Yet it is surprisingly widespread. Some companies still feel that they must have a home-country "presence" in each foreign subsidiary. For U.S. firms that follow such a policy, this presence is usually the local general manager or chief finance officer. Some companies go even further in insisting on home-company personnel as essential for transferring technological strength from the parent company and feedback from the subsidiaries. As one manager of a European company claimed, "There should be a European at the head of the U.S. operation. I have a rapport with our parent that dates back over 33 years. This rapport is terribly useful for communication back and forth. How could an American develop such a rapport . . . particularly with a French mother company."[8]

In the early stages of internationalization, the use of home-country nationals may be the best approach. After all, most firms at this stage are involved in transplanting some part of the business that has worked in the home country, and detailed knowledge of that part is the critical factor. But disadvantages can quickly appear. The policy must mean blocked promotion for local executives. In addition, there are the high cost disadvantages and a much greater tendency to import into subsidiaries the management style of the parent company and its home-country cultural biases.

Mixed Policies

Clearly, none of the three "pure" policies provides a complete answer to the complexities of managing multinational enterprises. Most multinational firms favor hiring local nationals for foreign subsidiaries, home-country nationals at headquarters, and, where a regional organization exists, a mix of foreign and home-country managers for regional positions. Within this general approach, the nationality mix will vary with the nature of a firm's business and its product strategy. Where area expertise plays a major role, as in the case of consumer goods and/or a limited product line, the use of home-country personnel for overseas assignments will be minimal. Where product expertise is highly important and/ or industrial markets are being served, home-country personnel will be used more extensively for foreign assignments because they generally have quick access to the home-country sources of supply and technical information. Service industries also tend to have more home-country personnel in foreign posts, particularly where the firm is serving home-country multinationals in foreign areas, as has been the case in banking.

MULTINATIONAL MANAGEMENT RECRUITMENT

If a firm is to develop a management team with truly international capability, the best place to start is with recruitment policies. When a firm takes its first

---

[8] *European Strategies in the United States* (Geneva: Business International, S.A., 1971), p. 42.

steps toward becoming international, it normally does not have a cadre of international managers. Thus at such an early stage, managers for international operations have been mainly recruited from within the organization without having had any previous experience in foreign operations. Where international expansion occurred through acquisitions, some firms were able to add key executives of the acquired companies to their international management staff. A third source may have been "buy-ins," or experienced international managers hired from outside the company.

Such makeshift methods, however, inevitably lead to surpluses and shortages that can be minimized with a planned approach to international recruitment. Such an approach begins with a forecast of future management manpower needs on an annual basis for at least a five-year period. Given the long lead time necessary to develop top and middle management within an enterprise, even 15-year forecasts are not too short.

With recruitment targets specified as to positions to be filled, their location, and the type of personnel required, the international firm can follow conventional recruitment practices, except for several additional international complications.[9] It must decide:

1. In what countries the company should recruit.
2. What new techniques and sources will have to be used when recruitment is planned outside the home country.
3. Whether recruitment activities and decisions should be centralized in the parent company or decentralized in foreign subsidiaries.

A fruitful source of future subsidiary executives who are both highly selected and already sensitized to the parent company culture are foreign students graduating from business schools in the home country.[10] But recruitment for international managers should extend beyond the universities or business schools of the developed countries and include universities where the firm operates. Outside the United States, management training is a relatively new educational field; but the amount and quality of such academic training has expanded rapidly in most developed countries and in numerous less developed countries. In many countries, universities have not yet developed adequate facilities for assisting firms in their recruitment. In such cases, recruitment techniques may have to rely heavily on newspaper advertising, executive recruitment companies, or special efforts to contact young people when they finish their military service.

An underutilized source of managerial talent for international operations

---

[9] Jean E. Heller, "Criteria for Selecting an International Manager," *Personnel,* May/June 1980, pp. 47–55; Simcha Ronen, *Comparative and Multinational Management* (New York: John Wiley & Sons, 1986), pp. 529–40.

[10] G. Alpander, "Foreign MBA: Potential Managers for American International Corporations," *Journal of International Business Studies,* Spring 1973, pp. 1–13.

has been female candidates from either the home or host country. A survey made in the early 1980s of 686 Canadian and American multinationals revealed that fewer than 3 percent of their more than 13,000 expatriate managers were women. Although personnel managers recognized that qualified women were available for international business careers, they listed foreigners' prejudice, dual-career marriages, and resistance within their own companies as major barriers to increased participation by women in international management. Given the increasing internationalization of many business firms and more experience with sending women managers overseas, the number of female international managers is likely to increase.[11]

An enterprise-wide executive recruitment program will necessarily be a cooperative effort between the foreign subsidiaries and regional and global headquarters. This will mean the surrender of some power to make independent appointments on the part of individual units of the organization. Actual recruitment activities, however, can be decentralized and the managers of foreign subsidiaries should have a voice in the final decision on the hiring of personnel who will work under their direction. A company like Procter & Gamble has its subsidiaries establish their recruitment needs, which are then consolidated at the division level—for example, the European Division, which has responsibility for recruitment. Foreign nationals studying in the United States are recruited by the parent company for the foreign subsidiaries, but only up to a preselection phase. Such candidates are then interviewed by the manager of the division or the subsidiary that makes the final offer. In some cases, the prospective candidate may even be flown back to his or her home country at company expense so that the local manager can interview the person and make the final decision.

MANAGEMENT DEVELOPMENT AND TRAINING

Whatever policy or combination of management recruitment policies is adopted, the international firm must also have a long-range and continuing program of management development that is integrated with its global strategy and business planning.[12] It needs to work constantly toward internationalizing the experience and outlook of all executive personnel including the higher echelons of corporate power. The most compelling argument for developing multinational executives is that it will avoid inbreeding and narrowness at the top.

Promising managerial talent must be discovered early so that young managers can secure cross-national experience and be available in the middle of their careers for general management posts where this experience is needed. For the larger

---

[11] Nancy J. Adler, "Expecting International Success: Female Managers Overseas," *Columbia Journal of World Business,* Fall 1984, pp. 79–85.

[12] Lawrence G. Franko, "Who Manages Multinational Enterprises?" *Columbia Journal of World Business,* Summer 1973, pp. 30–42.

corporation, a central inventory of international executives will be needed to assure that promising executives do not become lost in a foreign posting. A central inventory will lead to further surrender of power to make appointments on the part of individual units of the organization. Unless there is a central voice in appointments, continued career development of the international executive might be sacrificed to the interests of individual units or jeopardized by preferred promotion of those known locally.

Such a management development program is usually supported by a range of training programs with a cross-national focus. There is no substitute for training in a multinational company. It transfers knowledge; it improves communications and it helps impart the parent company's way of operating. For all employees, whether at headquarters or working in foreign subsidiaries, training is also a means of increasing their sensitivity to cultural patterns that are foreign to their own experience and values. Some multinationals, therefore, try to extend the opportunity for foreign experience as widely as possible. Cummins Engine Co., for example, offers evening language courses open to all employees and seeks to arrange foreign business trips for more than the "privileged management elite" so that large numbers of employees build a foreign awareness.[13]

Training for culture sensitivity should have at least two dimensions. It should develop in the individual an awareness of his or her own cultural assumptions and the nature of his or her cultural conditioning. It should also develop a special kind of intellectual and emotional radar that alerts the manager to situations where cultural assumptions other than his or her own are present. If culture sensitivity could be achieved simply through intellectual awareness that cultural patterns differ, the task of developing cultural sensitivity might be accomplished through readings and lectures. But the problem is more difficult. Human reactions are likely to be emotional, visceral, or psychological motor responses. One can be fully aware in an intellectual sense that time has a different meaning and value in Latin America, and yet have unkind and unfriendly reactions when forced to wait hours rather than minutes beyond the previously fixed time for an appointment.

The most lasting means of achieving culture sensitivity comes through a sustained experience of living and working in one or more foreign environments. Why then should the firm bother with training programs for those employees who are to be moved between countries? The answer is, of course, the high failure rate associated with cross-national transfers. Training may be an imperfect substitute for actual foreign living experience. Yet it has great value if it can reduce the often painful and agonizing experience of transferring into another culture and avoid the great damage that culture shock and cultural misunderstanding can do to a firm's operating relationships.

Training to meet the specific needs of multinational management can be

---

[13] Jeffrey L. Blue and Ulrich Haynes, Jr., "Preparation for the Overseas Assignment," *Business Horizons,* June 1977, pp. 61–67.

carried out through external programs, internal programs, or on-the-job internal training. Each approach has characteristic advantages.[14]

External programs are those not tailored to a specific organization, and are used to broaden managers' horizons beyond the immediate concerns of their individual organizations. Programs covering foreign language and culture, for example, may be extremely valuable for developing cultural sensitivity, yet may never touch on the terminology or customs specific to the particular business. It is possible, however, to find external programs that are designed for those in similar situations so that rather specific learning can take place from the experience of others.[15] A course on transfer pricing in multinationals would be a good example. External programs such as this can expose managers to the most recent developments and to leading thinkers in an area. Some business schools have specific international management programs as well. On the other hand, general management programs are much more numerous and many multinational firms prefer to send managers to such programs run in a country to which a manager may be moving. Local programs can provide the manager with a more focused training in the business culture of a particular country.

Internal programs can be tailored to the specific needs of the individual multinational. They can also be easily changed as the organization learns and is confronted by different problems. Generally speaking, the impact of such training is more identifiable and more immediate. Participants from the one organization with different national and cultural backgrounds can be led together in the building of a common language to describe common problems. As the result of skillfully designed internal programs, persistent problems are often quickly surmounted—as much because of the stronger and common perception of the problem as because of the solutions discussed during the program. Internal participants also get to know each other and their individual points of view and it is quite possible to focus directly on problems of subunit identification that hold back overall performance of the multinational organization. With internal programs, the participants usually become more involved and more committed because topics have a closer relationship to their own work and the current problems of the organization.

Internal on-the-job training is usually tailored to requirements of individual managers and their specific job assignments, although some large multinationals do have general training schemes involving international job rotation

---

[14] See, for example, Yoram Zeira, "Management Development in Ethnocentric Multinational Corporations," *California Management Review,* Summer 1976, pp. 34–42; Yoram Zeira and Asya Pazy, "Crossing National Borders to Get Trained," *Training and Development Journal,* October 1985, pp. 53–57.

[15] See Nancy G. McNulty, ed., *International Directory of Executive Education* (Elmsford, N.Y.: Pergamon Press, 1985).

experience. On-the-job training has the advantage that actual performance in the real situation is monitored, usually by a more experienced superior. Moreover, the learning is real and not just an intellectual experience. For cultural conditioning, on-the-job training is unsurpassed. It also has the advantage of time. Programs, whether internal or external, are generally time-constrained—yet real sensitivity training takes a long time.

CROSS-NATIONAL TRANSFERS

All multinationals, whatever their policy on executive nationality, transfer employees across national and cultural boundaries to some extent. Some transfers may be permanent postings, some are designed to meet temporary needs, and others are part of an international career-development program.[16] Managers assigned to foreign posts for extended periods are likely to encounter special problems of working in a foreign environment, living in a different culture, and maintaining satisfactory relations with the parent company. Selection for such postings should not be taken lightly.

Adapting at Work

Transferred executives have to establish new working relationships within a cultural environment vastly different from the one to which they are accustomed. The executives will have to be aware of cultural variations as they affect local patterns of decision making, issuing and accepting instructions, and conducting many other day-to-day aspects of management and business operations. They must deal with local foreign personnel with different backgrounds, languages, attitudes, values, and points of view;[17] adapt technical and managerial know-how to an unfamiliar environment; and cope with economic and political conditions that are unfamiliar and often more complicated than those encountered at home. Anecdotes and case examples abound of the problems encountered in cross-national assignments. But the emphasis on problems, as Skinner cautions, "should in no sense imply that all men sent abroad fail to perform well, that most assignments abroad are unhappy ones, or that expatriate managers always present difficult and absorbing problems for executives in the home office. This is not so."[18]

Nevertheless, studies have disclosed patterns of suboptimal performance from expatriates at the beginning of foreign postings, followed by a gradual improvement

---

[16] Daniel Ondrack, "International Transfers of Managers in North American and European MNEs," *Journal of International Business Studies,* Fall 1985, pp. 1–19.

[17] See, for example, Richard B. Peterson and Hermann F. Schwind, "A Comparative Study of Personnel Problems in International Companies and Joint Ventures in Japan," *Journal of International Business Studies,* Spring–Summer 1977, pp. 45–55.

[18] See Wickham Skinner, *American Industry in Developing Economies* (New York: John Wiley & Sons, 1968), pp. 222.

as they adapt to their new situations. Managers posted from a parent company to head established subsidiaries, for example, often adopt an individualistic management style at the outset, shielding their decision making from their immediate subordinates. Furthermore, the new manager is likely to impose management patterns on the subsidiary that worked well in other environments but that do not suit the local situation. Such behavior may stem from a temptation to demonstrate a managerial superiority in the new post and to justify being chosen ahead of the local nationals who are the immediate subordinates. The behavior may also reflect a wish to prevent these subordinates from seeing the manager's limited comprehension of the new situation. Predictably, the relations between the manager and the local team will be strained, producing mutual mistrust and morale problems. Over time, the exposure of the manager to the new culture and interaction with its members will usually temper such an initial insensitivity to the differences. It has been observed, for example, that managers' perceptions of the differences in capabilities between themselves and their subordinates are reduced with the length of time they work overseas.[19]

Social Adaptation

Outside the work situation, foreign executives and their families encounter environmental differences that are even more marked than the on-the-job differences.[20] Social contacts may be severely curtailed, for example, if an expatriate's spouse cannot speak the local language. Wives of local business and social acquaintances are unlikely to speak anything other than the local language, and significant relationships are not likely to be built up across a language barrier. A broad study of almost 2,000 employees of a multinational firm on cross-national assignments, of whom about 20 percent were of American nationality, concluded that a male employee's satisfaction with his foreign assignment depended mainly on his wife's adjustment to the assignment. The wife's satisfaction ranked as the most important element among the American group, and only slightly lower than job-related elements in the total group.[21]

The stress of cross-national transfers on executives and their families may produce behavior patterns that prejudice the manager's job performance. Rejection of the new culture and glorification of the old is not uncommon. Frequently referred to as *culture shock*, this can result in the establishment of tight groups

---

[19] Edwin L. Miller, "Managerial Qualifications of Personnel Occupying Overseas Management Positions as Perceived by American Expatriate Managers," *Journal of International Business Studies,* Spring–Summer 1977, pp. 57–69.

[20] Michael G. Harvey, "The Executive Family: An Overlooked Variable in International Assignments," *Columbia Journal of World Business,* Spring 1985, pp. 84–92; Rosalie L. Tung, "Corporate Executives and Their Families in China," *Columbia Journal of World Business,* Spring 1986, pp. 21–25.

[21] Gillian Purcer-Smith, *Studies of International Mobility (in IBM World Trade Corp.),* mimeographed (New York: National Foreign Trade Council, 1971), NFTC ref. no. M-9936.

of home-country personnel who devote themselves to re-creating the home culture and dwelling on the "weaker" points of that in which they reside. This is what a Shell executive calls "those bloody people" syndrome.

> The expatriate goes young and fresh to his first "new" country and he makes a big effort to integrate. He learns about local culture, he travels the country, and he tries to learn the language. Then he is moved. The next country is a little more difficult. Those people in his first overseas assignment were pretty unreliable anyway. The new lot are worse. He makes some kind of effort, but it's not such a big effort. By the fourth or fifth country, he may have given up. He locks himself up with expatriate colleagues and he doesn't want to see anything of the local scene except when he is actually working. That man, I submit, is a major liability in any multinational operation . . . for him, they are only "those bloody people."[22]

Selection for Transfer

How should enterprises select managers for cross-national postings? Some criteria, such as technical competence, eagerness to acquire foreign experience and proficiency in the host country's language, are relatively easy to assess.[23] But the most difficult problem is to evaluate the ability of the manager and his or her family to adjust to foreign cultures. Because of the difficulties in predicting the relationship of behavior patterns of the expatriate to subsequent acculturation and overseas success, the failure rate can be high, and the costs of even a small number of family relocations can be exorbitant.[24]

Despite considerable research in the area, the acculturation process is not yet well enough understood to create satisfactory selection methods. Some psychological tests and tests for personal stress tendencies are available and sometimes used. Yet formal testing is not considered to be reliable enough to be used as a major tool for selection. Long interviews with the candidate and the candidate's spouse are perhaps the best means of drawing out potential problems.[25]

The chances of success in cross-national postings can be greatly improved

---

[22] Donald N. Leich, *Transnational Executive Development in the Royal Dutch Shell Group of Companies*, mimeographed (New York: National Foreign Trade Council, February 1970), NFTC ref. no. M-9293.

[23] Yoram Zeira and Moshe Banai, "Selection of Expatriate Managers in MNCs: The Host-Environment Point of View," *International Studies of Management and Organization* 15 (1985), pp. 33–51.

[24] Mark Mendenhall and Gary Oddou, "Acculturation Profiles of Expatriate Managers: Implications for Cross-Cultural Training Programs," *Columbia Journal of World Business*, Winter 1986, pp. 73–79.

[25] See William Alexander, Jr., "Mobil's Four Hour Environmental Interview," *Worldwide P & I Planning*, January–February 1970, pp. 18–27. Alexander reported that Mobil had "only 5 complete failures out of 750 employees placed abroad"; E. J. Karras, Roy F. McMillan, and Thomas R. Williamson, "Interviewing for Cultural Match," *Personnel Journal*, April 1971, pp. 276–79.

by predeparture training. The depth of the training should be a function of length of stay, type of involvement in the culture, the culture gap between the host country and the expatriate's home country, the position of the person in the subsidiary's hierarchy, and the likelihood of the manager needing cross-cultural skills in his or her future career.

Repatriation

Unless international assignments are part of a planned cross-pollination program—that is, the process of moving high-potential professionals between foreign affiliates for management-development purposes—the executives who undertake a foreign assignment may experience amplified feelings of insecurity and concern over their future career. As the distance and time away from headquarters increase, an "exile complex" may develop, and the manager will begin to ask such questions as: "Will I be forgotten at the home office?" and "Where is my next assignment going to be?" Concern about reentry may arise even if the manager is scheduled to return to the parent company or the home subsidiary.

To reduce the potential dissatisfaction of executives being transferred, the international firm should have a policy for repatriation. Some firms make it clear that those going overseas do so on a career basis and will be returned only if they are asked to take another position in the firm. Other firms argue that even the more successful and experienced managers within the firm will have failures in foreign posts resulting from factors outside their control, and that these managers are worth retaining despite the cost of repatriation. If the firm always repatriates executives when they wish to return and finds them a post with equally high status in their home company, the cost can be high. Not only are transfer costs large, but the foreign unit they leave must find a replacement with additional transfer costs and lack of continuity in the job. Nor is it always easy to find a job for a returning expatriate at the precise time that the person is ready to return.[26]

The return can produce another collection of problems. The disappearance of the high compensation and benefits that often accompany a foreign assignment can leave executives a long way below their overseas level of living. House prices may have risen so much that they cannot afford to buy a level of housing equal to their peers who stayed at home. Worse still, they may have been passed in promotion by executives of the same age who stayed home. And if their new job is a corporate post, it is also likely to give them less personal autonomy than they have had in a foreign subsidiary. All these experiences, together with schooling and adjustment problems for a family, can lead to reverse culture shock and the loss of experienced international talent as the executive turns to the job market to solve the problems. Careful counseling and repatriation services

---

[26] Michael C. Harvey, "The Other Side of Foreign Assignments: Dealing with the Repatriation Dilemma," *Columbia Journal of World Business,* Spring 1982, pp. 53–59.

such as housing search and financial aid, however, can go a long way toward diluting the shock of reentry and avoiding the costly loss of executive talent it can bring.

INTERNATIONAL COMPENSATION POLICIES

Executive Compensation

Compensation policies can produce some of the sharpest international conflicts within an international firm. They can also influence promotion patterns that executives seek within the corporation. Overpaid posts in peripheral foreign activity, for example, might attract good executives away from more important but lower-paid posts in the mainstream of the firm's development, or worse still, discourage them from returning to mainstream jobs later on (see Box 24–2). International compensation policies thus deserve the careful attention of top management.[27]

Why is it difficult to develop a satisfactory international compensation policy? The problem stems from the fact that salary levels and reward expectations differ among countries. Not only do reward patterns differ, but management is also motivated to behave differently. In the average British firm, for example, job performance is rewarded more than potential, and a high level of managerial effort is consequently directed toward job performance. In France, on the other hand, the reward arises more from the educational achievement before joining the firm and more managerial work effort is directed toward recognition outside the firm.[28] It would be a very foolish multinational that attempted to impose reward policies that did not fit national culture and managerial expectations.

A firm that attempts to maintain the same salary levels in all countries will cost itself out of markets where lower salary levels prevail and will not be able to attract managers in high-salary countries. Thus salary rates for roughly comparable jobs will differ between nations. But what policy should be followed when executives are transferred? Executives on the higher rates will not want any reduction when transferred. If they continue to receive their national salary level (plus allowances), they will be higher paid in the new post than local nationals with comparable responsibilities. If executives going to higher-wage areas are remunerated at the high-level rates, problems arise when they return to their home country. Do they revert to their old salary scales?

These fundamental questions of compensation policy have no one answer. The compensation policy is not an end in itself but a means of achieving company

---

[27] For surveys of the practices and problems of international companies in the compensation field, see *Worldwide Executive Compensation and Human Resources Planning* (New York: Business International, 1982).

[28] David Granick, "International Differences in Executive Reward Systems; Extent, Explanation and Significance," *Columbia Journal of World Business,* Summer 1978, pp. 45–55.

BOX 24–2
Executives in Indonesia Find Money Eases the Way

Jakarta, Indonesia—It must be tough being a foreign executive in Indonesia.

It costs almost $100,000 a year to keep a senior expatriate executive, his spouse and three school-age children happy in Jakarta, the Indonesian capital, according to an annual survey by Price Waterhouse & Co., the accounting firm. And that $100,000 is in addition to salary.

The average expatriate executive in Jakarta employs four servants at home: a cook, cleaning woman, houseboy and watchman/gardener.

Companies provide their senior executives in Jakarta with a car and driver. The average annual cost of the car was $26,814, while the driver's salary was $235 a month.

Practically all the executives receive company-paid annual home leave and local leave, as well as membership in a recreation club.

Not surprisingly, two-thirds of those surveyed said they would take another assignment in Indonesia.

---

objectives. An effective compensation policy for expatriates, therefore, should strive to meet the following objectives:

1. Attract and retain employees qualified for overseas service.
2. Facilitate transfers between foreign affiliates and between home-country and foreign affiliates.
3. Establish and maintain a consistent and reasonable relationship between the compensation of all employees of any affiliate, whether posted at home or abroad, and between affiliates.
4. Arrange reasonable compensation, in the various locations, in relation to the practices of leading competitors.

Components of Expatriate Compensation

Most U.S. companies construct their international compensation policies for expatriates with three components: base salary, premiums to work overseas, and overseas allowances.

Base Salaries.   Most expatriates are originally hired in their home countries at salaries paid for domestic assignments. When expatriates are transferred cross-nationally, the base salary continues to be that of their home country. The basic underlying philosophy is to facilitate reassimilation into the home-base company.

When managers are transferred to countries where the going rate for their position is higher than the base salary, most firms will raise the salary, although some will retain the base salary as a notional reference for repatriation. Few firms, though, will lower salaries to a local level. As a result, expatriates of different nationalities may find themselves working side by side for different compensation, and each of them on a higher rate than local nationals.

Fluctuating exchange rates can also cause problems when base salaries are retained. Expatriates can find themselves with lower incomes if their home currency falls against the currency of the country in which they are posted. The problem becomes more complex if part of the expatriate's salary is paid in the home currency. The home-currency payment is often arranged to minimize tax or exchange control difficulties for an employee who naturally wants savings to be available in the home currency.

Premiums.   Two types of premiums or inducements are commonly used: those to encourage mobility and those to compensate for the hardship of living in an undesirable location. Generally, the places where hardship premiums must be paid are not numerous and have few nonlocal employees. More important is the premium paid to encourage overseas mobility. This premium is usually a fixed percentage of base salary (10 to 20 percent) and is paid for the duration of a foreign assignment.

The disadvantage of continuing the mobility premium payment as long as the employee is assigned abroad is that the employee has no financial incentive to move from one foreign country to another, and that moves back to the parent country usually mean a substantial reduction in income. Several approaches have been adopted by companies to resolve these problems and to increase the mobility of international personnel. One approach is the "premium phase-out," whereby after x years (usually, three to five) the premium is phased out in increments. Another approach is the single payment "mobility premium," which ties the premium to the move instead of to the assignment. In both cases, the premium is paid each time a move is made. If the company's objective is to keep employees abroad for long assignments, it makes sense to pay a continuous premium. On the other hand, if the company is aiming at mobility and rapid movement, it will prefer the single-payment or phase-out premium.

Allowances.   Allowances are intended to assist personnel assigned to foreign posts to continue their normal pattern of living. The most common allowances are for cost of living, housing, education, and tax protection. The two largest items are usually taxes and housing.

With taxes, many international firms follow a policy of deducting taxes at the rate for residents in the employee's home country and then paying the actual tax assessment. Exemptions for income earned while overseas, however, can give a very low home-country tax—or none at all for nationals of some countries who are absentees longer than a specified period. Equalization to the home tax level can thus give a substantial bonus—unless the calculation is made as though the employee were still based at home. Generally speaking, it is only worth equalizing taxes if the differences are more than marginal and the differences in benefits, such as lower medical costs in the United Kingdom, fail to account for most of the variation. If double taxation problems arise for which the firm is responsible through the timing of its transfer, the firm should reduce an employee's tax obligation to that of residence in one country or the other.

In the case of other allowances, most U.S. companies adopt in varying degrees the allowance program of the U.S. Department of State. There are many problems, however, in developing international comparisons of the cost of living on which allowances are based, including changing exchange rates. Also, as companies increase their mix of third-country nationals in foreign posts, the allowance schedules of the parent country become less relevant. The latter problem is handled in some companies by using the United Nations allowance system, which has been designed for professionals of many nationalities stationed throughout the world.

International Wage and Benefit Policies

As they do for managerial salaries, multinationals usually pay the going wage rates for each country in which they operate. To raise all employees to the level of the highest wage country would raise the firm's cost above those of the competition. Furthermore, wage differentials for different jobs and skills differ markedly among countries, and within each country there are major pressures to maintain these differentials.[29] The same arguments apply to employment benefits. The types and levels of benefits that are customary can differ dramatically from country to country. Not only do individual benefits differ for such things as travel, holidays, insurance, and housing, but also the sum total of benefits can range from a small percent of the monetary wage to as much as 200 percent. Many benefits, too, are statutorily imposed. In West Germany a fired worker may get up to 18 months' salary. It would be an economically naive personnel function, therefore, that attempted to standardize wages or all benefits internationally.

This does not mean that a multinational should make no attempt to standardize wages and benefits. First, the firm may adopt the view that certain minimum standards are required for all its employees and that it must be able to meet the cost involved. For example, company liability for work-related injury, or for maintaining retired workers, may be viewed as a supranational responsibility. Second, there may be instances where international standardization may provide the same benefits at lower cost and save problems when employees are transferred between countries. Insurance cover is a case in point, as multinational insurance firms begin to offer worldwide programs.

---

[29] See Christopher Saunders and David Marsden, *Pay Inequalities in the European Communities* (London: Butterworths, 1981).

LABOR RELATIONS AND THE MULTINATIONAL FIRM

Centralized versus Decentralized Policies

Labor relations patterns differ markedly among countries.[30] The varying patterns reflect the unique cultural, legal, and institutional settings in different nations that affect labor relations through varying social values, psychic needs of workers, the peculiar industrial relations lore, pertinent legal intricacies, and so forth. In recognition of these realities, multinational firms have generally delegated the task of work-force management to the managers of foreign subsidiaries.

In the view of one experienced multinational company, the affiliated companies must have continuing responsibility and authority for handling industrial relations. "Without this responsibility it would be extremely difficult, if not impossible, for the affiliates to develop and maintain the kinds of relationships with their employees and employee representatives that are a key factor to the success of their operations."[31] Such a policy assumes, of course, that local managers have been competently trained for administering labor affairs.

There are strong arguments, though, for international management exercising some central coordination. In new units acquired as going concerns, local management experience in labor management may not be extensive nor up to the standard expected of a multinational corporation. Also, agreements made in one country may affect the international plans of the corporation or create precedents for negotiations in other countries. The more unions cooperate across country boundaries, the more need there will be for the firm to present a consistent front. The case for central labor relations coordination is thus strong, but such coordination should involve full participation by local management and infringe as little as possible on local autonomy.

Coordination does not necessarily mean that the international firm should have common policies in all countries. A whole range of elements may differ from environment to environment, leading to different arrangements in each. Any attempt to impose parent-company polices on new situations where they do not fit would be wrong. To have a world-wide policy to avoid unionization simply because this had worked in the parent company would be one example. Many companies that are not unionized in the parent unit have successfully followed unionization in subsidiaries and vice versa.

To fulfill its coordination role and manage its own responsibilities, headquarters staff needs a considerable understanding of national labor-management patterns and a continuing flow of information. Assessments and forecasts of national

---

[30] See R. Bean, *Comparative Industrial Relations* (New York: St. Martin's Press, 1985); Frances Bairstow, "A Trend Toward Centralized Bargaining—A Patchwork Quilt of International Diversity," *Columbia Journal of World Business,* Spring 1985, pp. 75–83.

[31] Malcolm L. Denise, "Industrial Relations and the Multinational Corporation: The Ford Experience," in *Bargaining Without Boundaries,* ed. Robert J. Flanagan and Arnold R. Weber (Chicago: University of Chicago Press, 1974), p. 140.

labor relations conditions are crucial to decisions on the location and expansion of facilities and for evaluating the performance of subsidiaries and local managers. Where transnational sourcing patterns have been developed and a subsidiary in one country relies on a subsidiary in another country as a source of components or as a user of its output, labor relations throughout the system become of direct importance to central management for maintaining its global production strategy.

The Union View of the Multinationals' Power

A major reason for headquarters involvement in labor-management affairs has been the move toward internationalization of the labor movement, in itself a direct reaction to the growth of the multinational corporation. Unions around the world have felt increasingly threatened by powerful multinational employers.[32] In essence, their situation parallels that of national governments. They are national institutions facing an international challenge.

Although many multinationals claim that authority in labor relations rests entirely with the local management of the subsidiary, union leaders point out that on all important matters the power rests with central headquarters. Furthermore, central headquarters may be working toward global goals or perhaps home-country goals that override local considerations.

Bargaining is inevitably more difficult when a union cannot deal directly with final decision makers. Some union leaders complain because the headquarters management is beyond the reach of a local trade union dealing with a subsidiary. Others feel seriously handicapped because of what they describe as a floating and invisible decision center for labor relations matters. Subsidiary companies, so the complaint goes, claim that decisions are made at central headquarters, and central headquarters responds that decisions are made by their subsidiaries.

Some union leaders believe that many multinationals have adopted dual sourcing policies as a deliberate strategy for reducing the impact of national strikes and for weakening the bargaining position of a national union.[33] They also recognize that a multinational can also operate an "investment strike" by refusing to invest anything further in a site. Before long, the plant would become obsolete and uneconomic and labor might be forced to lower its demands in order to retain any employment at all.

Finally, unions argue that multinationals have a size advantage not matched by national unions. Their worldwide financial resources enable them to weather strikes and continue to make a profit, even though a union may shut down operations completely in one country.

[32] See International Labour Office, *Tripartite Declaration of Principles concerning Multinational Enterprises and Social Policy* (Geneva: ILO., 1977).

[33] Duane Kujawa, ed., *American Labor and Multinational Corporations* (New York: Praeger Publishers, 1973), p. 226.

Multinational Union Organization

Membership of unions is limited to the employees within a particular country. Despite the use of "International" in the title of many unions, no union has the authority to bargain internationally for all the workers of a multinational corporation. Many unions, however, have affiliated themselves with International Trade Secretariats (ITSs), most of which are headquartered in Geneva and structured along trade and industry lines.

Unions have also joined into international federations outside their industry groupings. The most important are the International Confederation of Free Trade Unions (ICFTU) and the European Trade Union Confederation (ETUC). Both of these organizations have as members national confederations of trade unions. The British Trades Union Congress (TUC), for example, is a member of both. The American AFL-CIO was a member of the ICFTU but withdrew in 1969. These international organizations serve as forums for discussion of union policies and as pressure groups within the International Labour Office (ILO), the Organization for Economic Cooperation and Development (OECD), the United Nations, and the European Community (EC).

The ITSs are loose federations, leaving their national affiliates with complete autonomy. They generally have limited finances and small staffs. Of the 19 functioning ITSs, only 5 or 6 have taken an active interest in the operations of multinational enterprises. The rest either have a small membership, are concerned with specialized fields such as journalism, or represent public services workers.[34] The four that have been most important from the standpoint of multinational business are the International Metalworkers Federation (IMF); International Federation of Chemical, Energy and General Workers' Unions (ICEF); International Union of Food and Allied Workers Association (IUF); and the International Federation of Commercial, Clerical, Professional and Technical Employees (FIET).[35]

About 1960, several of the ITSs became aware of the expanding multinationals and began to explore ways of assuming a new role in relation to these companies. They collected and disseminated information to all national union centers on the finances, wages, benefits, and working conditions of individual multinationals. They created "company councils" to bring together unions representing employees of the same company in different countries (see Box 24–3). They sought consultation arrangements with headquarters management of the multinational firms and aspired to achieve transnational bargaining, in the sense of one world-wide agreement with a company. But by the mid-1970s, union officials came to recognize that their ambitious goals could not be achieved; and their main efforts turned toward representing the interests of their affiliates before intergovernmental bodies, particularly in the formulation of codes of conduct.

---

[34] Geoffrey W. Latta and Janice R. Bellace, "Making the Corporation Transparent: Prelude to Multinational Bargaining," *Columbia Journal of World Business,* Summer 1983, p. 77.

[35] Roy B. Helfgott, "American Unions and Multinational Companies: A Case of Misplaced Emphasis," *Columbia Journal of World Business,* Summer 1983, p. 82; United Nations, *The CTC Reporter,* Autumn 1984, p. 50.

BOX 24–3
Graduates of the World, UNITE

IBM is the big multinational that most frustrates trade unions. They have had almost no success in signing up its workers. That is mostly because IBM employees— or "graduates," as they call themselves—see little advantage in joining a union. The company pays them well, and maintains that it is sticking to its full-employment policy.

On January 12–13, three international trade secretariats ran a conference in London to persuade more IBM employees to sign up. They have compiled a dossier on the company which they say shows that it is antiunion. They plan to set up free telephone lines to advise IBM employees on joining unions and to nurture the few groups that have appeared.

While union leaders may dream of harmonizing wage bargaining from Detroit to Dusseldorf, their international aims are more prosaic. Presently, international trade secretariats spend most of their time collecting information. In the future the secretariats hope to expand the use of electronic communications (such as facsimile machines) to coordinate union branches at multinational's plants around the world.

Trade-unionists in many countries, however, still look no further than their own ports. Sometimes they have no choice. Britain, for example, has made strikes to aid workers elsewhere illegal. Only one of Britain's three biggest unions has a full-time officer dealing with international affairs.

SOURCE: Adapted from *The Economist*, January 24, 1987, p. 60.

Codes of Conduct and Industrial Relations

Responding to pressures from both national governments and the trade unions, the Organization for Economic Cooperation and Development (OECD) adopted in 1976 a voluntary code of conduct for multinationals that included guidelines for industrial relations.[36] The International Labour Office (ILO) followed in 1977 with a Tripartite Declaration of Principles concerning Multinational Enterprises and Social Policy. The European Community does not have a specific code of conduct, but a series of EC policy decisions supported by labor representatives have strengthened the unions in dealing with the multinationals. The United Nations was negotiating still another code as of 1987 that includes guidelines on industrial relations.

As to industrial relations, the OECD guidelines and the ILO "Principles" differ somewhat in their substance and complaint procedure, but their overall thrust is the same. Both seek greater acceptance by multinational enterprises of the workers' rights to join unions and engage in collective bargaining. They extend the scope of bargaining to include issues such as new investment decisions. Both aim for greater disclosure of company information to unions, disclosure

---

[36] See Chapter 12, p. 307.

which on many items should be followed by consultation "with a view of reaching agreement." In addition, there are certain provisions, such as restriction on transferring employees across borders during a strike, that essentially attempt to reduce the multinationals' economic power in bargaining.[37]

Although the voluntary codes are not legally enforceable and were criticized by labor for not going far enough, they are significant in shaping industrial relations patterns because they have been agreed upon by member governments and publicly accepted by leading multinationals. Furthermore, a quasi-legal practice has emerged of governments referring disagreements under the OECD code to the OECD Committee on International Investments and Multinational Enterprises (CIME). A notable referral was the case of a Raytheon (US) subsidiary in Belgium, the Badger Company, which went into bankruptcy. The parent company was influenced by a CIME ruling to meet the cost of termination payments to Badger employees even though Raytheon claimed that it had no liability. A more recent case (1981) was a referral involving the closure of an unprofitable subsidiary in the Netherlands by Ford Motor Company that was opposed by the Dutch unions. However, the matter was legally resolved at the national level, and Ford was allowed to proceed with the closure.[38]

The greatest challenge to the voluntary nature of the Guidelines has arisen most forcefully outside the OECD and at the level of the European Community. The so-called Vredling Directive would establish as Community law the rights of workers to regular information on the operations of the group of companies to which their employers belonged—that is, the multinational enterprise as a whole—and the right to consultations in the event of a company decision affecting their livelihood (such as a plant closure). As of this writing, the directive had not been approved.

Prospects for Multinational Bargaining

Those associated with international labor movements have as an ultimate objective the achievement of multinational bargaining. Unions, however, are basically nationalistic; and strong political and ideological cleavages exist between different national labor movements.[39] If the issue involved concerns the relocation of production activity, there will be a built-in conflict between the interests of the national union losing jobs and the interests of the national union gaining jobs. Furthermore, national governments will not always identify with their own

---

[37] Richard L. Rowan and Duncan C. Campbell, "The Attempt to Regulate Industrial Relations through International Codes of Conduct," *Columbia Journal of World Business,* Summer 1983, pp. 64–72.

[38] Ibid., pp. 67–70.

[39] See Gerard B. J. Bomers and Richard B. Peterson, "Multinational Corporations and Industrial Relations: The Case of West Germany and the Netherlands," *British Journal of Industrial Relations,* March 1977, pp. 45–62.

national union.[40] Governments realize that there may come a time when certain jobs should migrate, with their place taken by other trades more appropriate to the changed economic environment. For all these reasons, multinational bargaining is presently virtually nonexistent and unlikely to become a reality in the near future.[41]

The industrial relations behavior of the multinationals will continue to be closely monitored by intergovernmental agencies. The international unions have focused on codes and guidelines as a strategy for improving their bargaining position and eventually achieving multinational bargaining. Thus, codes of conduct will continue to be a fact of life, and the multinationals will have a strong vested interest in being involved in the drafting and implementing of these codes.

Codetermination and the Multinationals

The codetermination movement in Western Europe is another industrial relations trend of significance to the multinationals. Based on the philosophy that labor as well as shareholders have a vested interest in the business enterprise, national laws in a number of countries give workers a voice in management through workers' councils and representation on the board of directors. Thus, in codetermination countries, workers participate in management decisions affecting both the global operations of locally-based multinationals and the local operations of foreign-owned subsidiaries.

The system in force in West Germany is one of the best-known forms of worker participation in management.[42] Companies characteristically have a two-tier management structure. A supervisory board (*aufsichtsrat*) exercises policy guidance and supervision of the activities of the company. It approves decisions of major importance, such as the closure of plants, the opening of new factories, major production changes, and investments above a certain level. It does not meet more than four or five times a year, and elects the management board (*vorstand*) that is responsible for the daily operations of the enterprise.

Under this system, the workers select a number of members of the supervisory board equal to the number appointed by the shareholders—generally five each. An additional member is appointed jointly by the two sides. Two of the worker members—one wage earner and one salaried employee—come from within the company and are elected by the works council of the company. The remaining

[40] Franklin R. Root and Bernard Mennis, "How U.S. Multinational Corporations, Unions and Government View Each Other and the Direction of U.S. Policies," *Journal of International Business Studies,* Spring 1976, pp. 17–30.

[41] Herbert R. Northrup and Richard L. Rowan, *Multinational Collective Bargaining Attempts* (Philadelphia: Industrial Research Unit, University of Pennsylvania, 1979), pp. 533–64.

[42] See Trevor Bain, "German Codetermination and Employment Adjustments in the Steel and Auto Industries," *Columbia Journal of World Business,* Summer 1983, pp. 40–47; International Labour Office, *Workers' Participation in Decisions Within Undertakings* (Geneva, 1981), pp. 85–91.

BOX 24–4
The Rosenthal Experience

"We found that the major argument against codetermination—that it would lessen management's decision-making capability—was wrong. The fact that I had to explain to employee board members why we were doing something actually sometimes improved decisions. And sometimes decisions were carried through much more easily from the workers' side than they otherwise might have been."

These were the words of Philip Rosenthal, head of Rosenthal AG of Selb West Germany. Rosenthal was one of the first in Germany to put workers on its board, even before the legal requirement to do so. The firm also led in encouraging worker ownership by distributing shares instead of cash bonuses. Currently 90 percent of Rosenthal's 2,000-plus German employees own shares. With average individual holdings worth $1,700, workers as a group control 10 percent of the stock, compared with 4.5 percent held by the Rosenthal family.

Rosenthal reported: "We have less illness, fewer strikes, less trouble, and more contribution from our workers than the average."

Rosenthal's market share increased from 12.9 percent to 19.6 percent in fine china and from zero to 7 percent in glassware. At the same time it had become the largest producer in Europe of industrial ceramics and an important producer of furniture. Best of all, in Rosenthal's view, were the company's continuing productivity gains. From 1974 to 1979, productivity gains averaged 12 percent a year. In the past two years they averaged 7 percent a year.

Rosenthal admitted that much of the gain resulted from an extensive plant modernization, but added: "Without employee cooperation, the modernization program could not have been so successful."

SOURCE: Excerpted from Jean A. Briggs, "Is This an Answer?" *Forbes*, June 7, 1982, pp. 52–55.

---

worker members do not have to be and usually are not employees of the company. Normally they are appointed by the trade union concerned after consultation with the works council. The system as introduced in 1951 applied to the mining and iron and steel industries employing at least 1,000 workers. It was extended in 1976 to all companies employing more than 2,000 workers.

The *works councils* are committees composed of employer and employee representatives at the plant level. These councils have an equal say with management on such issues as job evaluation, overtime, holiday schedules, recruitment, selection, training, safety, and the like. Strikes over these matters are banned, with disputes usually resolved through arbitration.

Other European countries have followed Germany. Legislation on employee directors exists in Austria, Denmark, Luxemburg, Norway, and Sweden. In the Netherlands, works councils have the right to nominate and to veto candidates for the supervisory board; but neither the employees nor officials of a union represented in the enterprise are eligible for election to the board. At the EC level, a proposed directive requiring employee board representation has been proposed but not accepted. Britain itself rejected the suggestions of the 1977 Bullock report, which proposed employee directors; and during the late 1980s, Western Europe generally seemed to be moving away from union power.

How well has the codetermination system worked? West German companies report that employee membership on the supervisory board does not prevent management from working effectively. In fact, as shown in Box 24–4, the efforts taken to communicate with employee representatives and through them to the workforce have tended to improve workforce relationships and to loosen union control somewhat. From the workers' viewpoint, one study suggests that those workers who have actually participated in works councils are relatively more satisfied with their ability to influence decisions affecting their work conditions.[43]

For multinationals, the codetermination system presents several challenges. A major concern is that, in West Germany, the Aufsichtsrat interposes a group with strongly national interests between the subsidiary operating management and the parent company. This subsidiary board could oppose head-office wishes on the remittance of funds for investment elsewhere. Since the Aufsichtsrat usually determines management appointments and salaries, Vorstand members may be less inclined to upset the employee directors by taking obvious sides—hence limiting the power of the parent management. The parent management may also find it difficult to remove intransigent executives from the subsidiary. For multinationals with employee directors on the parent-company board it is likely that the pattern of transferring production to foreign, lower-cost sites as the product matures will be more severely questioned. The decision of Volkswagen to build its American plant was delayed several years by just this problem.[44]

TREATMENT OF DISADVANTAGED GROUPS

Generally speaking, pressure to change policies to help disadvantaged groups is limited to a concern for those within the confines of a single nation. Concern for inequality tends to be limited by a more dominant principle of national identity. Hence those opposing discrimination against women in the United States (see Box 24–5) would not usually concern themselves with positive discrimination against women in Japan.

In a few cases, general concern for disadvantaged groups crosses national boundaries. In these cases, the multinational is the obvious target for pressure from those concerned with the plight of the disadvantaged in some other country. The most outstanding case to date has been pressure on multinationals to mitigate the effects of apartheid on South Africa. U.S. activist groups, however, have

[43] J. B. Dworkin, C. J. Hobson, E. Frieling, and D. M. Oakes, "How German Workers View Their Jobs," *Columbia Journal of World Business,* Summer, 1983, p. 53.

[44] George S. McIsaac and Hubert Henzler, "Codetermination: A Hidden Noose for MNC's," *Columbia Journal of World Business,* Winter 1974, p. 70.

BOX 24–5
Sex Bias

New York—Sumitomo Corp. of America agreed to settle a sex-bias case at a total cost of more than U.S. $2.6 million over the next three years.

The company agreed to pay past and current female employees more than U.S. $1.2 million in cash, spend U.S. $1 million on career development, increase the salaries of women employees this year by an aggregate 16.5%, and provide incentive pay over three years of U.S. $375,000.

The settlement ends 10 years of litigation brought by female clerical workers, who claimed that the company discriminated on the basis of race, sex, and national origin.

Their complaint led to a 1982 U.S. Supreme Court ruling in which the justices found that the U.S. arm of the huge Japanese trading company couldn't be exempt from U.S. employment laws. Since that decision, the two sides have been working out their settlement.

SOURCE: *The Wall Street Journal,* January 9, 1987. © Dow Jones & Company, Inc., 1987. Used with permission. All rights reserved.

Some Background

In the court case, Sumitomo claimed that it is guaranteed freedom to hire whom it likes by the 1952 Japan-American trade treaty. At U.S. insistence, the treaty allowed U.S. and Japanese companies to hire "technical experts, executive personnel and other specialists of their choice" in the other country's territory.

The court ruled that the treaty was meant to protect foreign firms against restrictive hiring rules that might discriminate against them, not to exempt them from laws that apply to local companies.

---

also raised questions about labor practices followed by such multinationals as Gulf & Western in the Dominican Republic, Del Monte in the Philippines, United Brands and Castle & Cooke in Central America, Coca-Cola in Guatemala, and Motorola in South Korea.[45]

The policy of separate and unequal treatment for the black South African is openly fostered by the South African government. Pressure brought to bear on foreign multinationals is thus aimed at breaking the intent of the local government, if not the actual law. Multinationals often welcome such pressure as it reinforces their case against the local situation. On the other hand, if the pressure forces them to withdraw and changes the local situation little, it may be the disadvantaged workers themselves who suffer most.

The approach most widely adopted by activists has been to ask as shareholders

---

[45] Thomas N. Gladwin and Ingo Walter, *Multinationals Under Fire* (New York: John Wiley & Sons, 1980), pp. 414–16.

for disclosure of the multinational's employment and labor relations practices. Several considerations lie behind this approach. First, motions for disclosure are more readily passed than shareholder directives. Second, the process of collecting information focuses management attention on the practices. Third, the threat of disclosure provides a powerful incentive to change practices that the firm would not be proud to publicize. And, last, the information itself can provide the basis for specific pressures.

Partly as a result of a disclosure campaign mounted by a coalition of Protestant denominations in the United States (the Church Project on U.S. Investments in South Africa) between 1972 and 1976, leading U.S. multinationals grouped together in 1977 to affirm a set of operating principles for South Africa that called for desegregated workplaces; equal employment practices; equal pay; training for nonwhites; aggressive promotion of blacks; and spending on housing, education, and other social services. These were named the "Sullivan Principles" after the Reverend Leon Sullivan, an American black minister, who, as a board member of General Motors, led the campaign. A majority of U.S. companies operating in South Africa followed the principles; but after a decade of this pressure, apartheid still prevailed, and Reverend Sullivan called for a mass corporate exodus and broad economic sanctions against the country.[46] This position was generally consistent with the 1986 recommendations of a United Nations Panel of Eminent Persons.[47]

SUMMARY

In international business, as in most other activities, human resources are the critical elements. The peculiar problem that international firms face is that people are usually raised, educated, and rewarded in one culture, whereas international business management requires cross-cultural communication, coordination, and supervision. The challenge is to develop managers who can think globally or at least biculturally.

The multinational firm has various options in choosing a policy that will develop international managers with this ability. If it follows a policy of hiring local nationals to manage its subsidiaries, it will have to rely on training programs to internationalize its personnel. Training programs are also needed to prepare executives and their families for cross-national transfers. One of the most perplexing problems faced by multinational companies has been the matter of compensation policies, but with increasing experience most companies have been able to work out reasonably satisfactory solutions even for handling cross-national transfers.

The management of labor relations must necessarily be delegated largely to local management because of innumerable local variations in worker attitudes,

---

[46] *The New York Times*, June 4, 1987, p. 1.

[47] United Nations, *The CTC Reporter*, Spring 1986, pp. 3–13.

labor union roles, and the degree of governmental participation in labor-management affairs. However, the internationalization of the labor movement, in response to a perceived threat from the multinational enterprise, has tended to bring headquarters management increasingly into the formulation and implementation of labor strategies.

Also, the labor relations patterns of multinationals will continue to be closely monitored by intergovernmental agencies, such as the OECD, ILO, EC, and the United Nations. Headquarters management, therefore, has a significant role to play in the drafting and implementation of the codes of conduct formulated by these agencies.

EXERCISES AND DISCUSSION QUESTIONS

1. What are the advantages and limitations of a policy that favors hiring nationals as managers of subsidiaries?
2. Many international companies recruit potential managers for their home-country domestic operations and later look to this staff for their international managers, particularly at headquarters. Under what conditions, if any, would you advise a company to do specialized outside recruiting for its international management personnel?
3. Interview an American executive who has recently returned from a foreign posting. Record and analyze the executive's generalizations about the foreign employees with whom he or she worked. Or interview the wife of such an executive and record and analyze her experience in adjusting to life in the foreign country.
4. You have been asked to design an orientation program for personnel being transferred on a two-year assignment to a less developed country (you select the country). The program must be completed by the participants in three weeks of full-time study. What are the several most important subjects that should be included in the program and why?
5. How would the local labor situation affect your location decision for a new foreign plant that produced a product whose characteristics or technology would have to change rapidly to meet competitive conditions?
6. How would you answer the fear of labor unions that the multinational corporation can easily transfer its operations to a different country if it feels that the demands of labor unions in a specific area of operations are "unreasonable"?
7. The OECD guidelines for multinational enterprises with regard to employment and industrial relations state:

   > Enterprises should, within the framework of law, regulations and prevailing labor relations and employment practices, in each of the countries in which they operate,
   >
   > 1) respect the right of their employees, to be represented by trade unions . . . and engage in constructive negotiations . . . with a view to reaching agreements on employment conditions.

   What would you advise an American corporation that has to date actively opposed unions in the United States? Would your advice differ for (*a*) multiple unions in the United Kingdom, or (*b*) fully representative black unions in South Africa?
8. "In the United States, the industrial democracy idea has been considered both by management and organized labor to be fundamentally inferior to hard-nosed profit-

maximizing behavior of management coupled with equally hard-nosed and adversary collective bargaining by labor.'' Do you agree with this statement? Why or why not? How would you advise an American multinational in the consumer electrical goods field to organize the appointments to the Aufsichtsrat and Vorstand of its German manufacturing subsidiary?

9. Many multinationals perceive serious limitations on using female managers for foreign assignments. Yet a growing number of female managers are having successful overseas tours of duty. How would you explain this discrepancy?

PART SIX
Emerging Issues

All of our decisions are about the future.
All of our knowledge is about the past.

No one can really predict the future. Human knowledge is tentative and forecasting what will happen an uncertain exercise. Projections, not being predictions, indicate at most what is likely to happen. They can be fallible, as some past errors in demographic projections have illustrated. Nevertheless, scientific methods, by uniting rational thought and empirical facts in a systematic and explicit manner, are the only reliable bases for anticipating what will be the probable developments in the future.[1]

---

[1] Rafael M. Salas, *Reflections on Population,* 2nd ed. (New York: Pergamon Press, 1985), p. 107.

CHAPTER 25

Looking into the Future

Astrologers, mystics, chiromancers (palmists), prophets, psychics, haruspices (diviners from the entrails of animals), and other kinds of seers traditionally have had a corner on forecasting the future. Even today these "professionals" are by far the most numerous of all those who divine the future. The situation is not likely to change, and the international manager should be careful to recognize the role of astrology that is so prevalent in business and government decision making in many societies (see Boxes 25–1 and 25–2).

In recent decades, however, new competition has emerged in the futures field. It comes from the "Futures Movement," which has been directed toward making forecasting less of an art and more of a science.[1] Futures forecasting

---

[1] See *Futures Research Directory: Individuals* (Bethesda, Md.: World Futures Society, 1987), a listing of nearly 800 individuals professionally involved in the study of the future.

BOX 25–1
Future Shocks for Virgo

While Europe was having economic problems in 1982, one of its leaders was looking at the stars. Mr. Gaston Thorn, the EC commission president, was intrigued by a recent astrological report that gazed into EC's future and looked at the prospects of several world leaders.

A Parisian astrologer warned that the predictions were hardly reassuring and that they formed part of a deep and ''more or less brutal'' cycle that would continue until 1984. There would, however, be some more positive moments: ''islands of calm and harmony in the general, rather agitated climate.'' The happier occasions may include April 2, when the trigon between Venus and Pluto will bring an ''enrichment'' in international relations. On August 8 a conjuncture of Jupiter and Mars will be especially favorable for ''magistrates and ecclesiatics'' and for agreements on armaments, but it may provoke a speculative run on international money markets.

Mr. Thorn (Virgo) was also supplied with the horoscopes of Mr. Helmut Schmidt (Capricorn), West Germany itself (Gemini), and President Ronald Reagan (Aquarius).

What Mr. Thorn made of all this is anybody's guess. At best his astrological advice may have helped choose the right moment to try to resolve the tricky problems of Britain's EC budget contribution or for a breakthrough in the Spanish entry negotiations.

SOURCE: Adapted from *The Economist*, February 13, 1982, p. 48.

---

has become a growth industry in which many business and consulting firms have become established.

Forecasting the future is a brave—and hazardous—undertaking, unless the forecast is sufficiently in the future so that its accuracy cannot be verified during the lifetime of the forecaster. A plethora of erroneous forecasts can be cited in the areas of economics, business, and technology. To mention just one example in the international business field, in a famous book published in 1968 the distinguished French journalist-politician, J. J. Servan-Schreiber, made the following forecast:

> Fifteen years from now it is quite possible that the world's third greatest industrial power, just after the United States and Russia, will not be Europe, but *American industry in Europe*.[2]

Contrast this forecast with the situation in the forecast year of 1983, when Japan had become the second largest industrial power; the output of the European Community had matched that of the United States, and many Americans were concerned

---

[2] J. J. Servan-Schreiber, *The American Challenge* (New York: Atheneum Publishers, 1968), p. 3.

BOX 25–2
White House Confirms Reagans Follow Astrology, Up to a Point

President Reagan and his wife, Nancy, are both deeply interested in astrology, the White House spokesman said today, and two former White House officials said Mrs. Reagan's concerns had influenced the scheduling of important events.

A California astrologer claims she had been consulted by the Reagans regarding key White House decisions, but Mr. Reagan said astrology had not influenced policy.

Various reports today said the Reagans had used astrology to set several dates, including the signing of the treaty banning intermediate missiles last December and the Moscow summit this month.

SOURCE: Adapted from *The New York Times,* May 4, 1988, p. 1.

---

about the rapidly expanding size of the foreign-owned industry sector in the United States.

The numerous forecasting failures may have discredited the forecasters but not the value of "future studies." It should be accepted that none of us can foresee the future. Yet business firms, governments, and others have discovered great value in systematically formulating "alternative future scenarios" and doing advance thinking on actions to be undertaken as any of the alternatives become future realities.

As an introduction to futures studies, this chapter will discuss the principal methodologies being used and make reference to several major futures studies recently published. Some of the forecasts of direct relevance to international business will be summarized, and their implications to the international manager will be noted.

FUTURES METHODOLOGIES

Familiarity with the principal forecasting techniques helps to evaluate the many forecasts being made. The four most widely used techniques are:[3]

1. Extrapolation: projecting historical trends.
2. Econometric models: such as input-output.
3. Delphi: using informed judgment.
4. Alternative futures scenarios.

The *extrapolation method* consists essentially of extending historical trends into the future. Extrapolation can be based on simple or complex mathematical relationships, such as regression analysis and envelope curves. The core assumption

---

[3] See S. Encel, P. K. Marstrand, and W. Page, eds., *The Art of Anticipation: Values and Methods in Forecasting* (London: Robinson, 1975), chap. 8, pp. 63–91; C. W. J. Granger, *Forecasting in Business and Economics* (New York: Academic Press, 1979).

of extrapolation is that a mathematical relationship existing between two parameters in the past will hold for the period of the forecast. The method can be useful for short time periods and for relatively stable situations. It can be seriously defective for situations where significant structural changes are occurring. Many electric power utilities, for example, have relied on extrapolation methods to forecast future power demand and the need for expansion of facilities. With the dramatic escalation of energy prices in the 1970s and the widespread adoption of energy conservation that followed, most of the firms in the United States found themselves in the 1980s with substantial and expensive excess capacity.

The *econometric models* are of various types. They are more complex and can handle changing relationships between parameters. They can be regarded as an analytic tool as well as a forecasting technique. Econometric models are systems of simultaneous regression equations used primarily for forecasting macroseries such as gross national product, consumption, investment, and so on. An interesting and significant example of the use of an econometric model for futures study is the United Nations report prepared under the direction of Wassily Leontief, who received the Nobel prize for his work on input-output techniques.[4] The objective of the study was to investigate the interrelationships between future economic growth and prospective economic issues, including the availability of natural resources and measures needed to close the income gap between the advanced and the developing countries.

The *Delphi Approach* is commonly used in forecasting future technological developments. It involves a panel of experts in a given field who answer a series of questionnaires about situations to be forecasted. The individual assessments are combined and returned to the participants, who are asked to respond once more with the benefit of the feedback. The process continues until a consensus is reached or the dispersion of predictions no longer narrows. The basic assumption of the method is that useful forecasts lie hidden away in the collective subjectivity of a group of people knowledgeable in the area of interest.

The Rand Corporation pioneered with the Delphi method in a 1964 forecast of important scientific breakthroughs expected in the next 30 years or so.[5] About two thirds of the events forecasted to occur by 1970 had actually occurred by then. But more important, perhaps, many scientific breakthroughs had occurred that were not included in the original forecast.

The technique of *alternative scenarios* has become the most popular methodology. It attempts to identify possible rather than predicted paths into the future. It asks the question of how might the hypothetical situations come about, and it attempts to identify the alternatives for various actors to prevent, divert, or facilitate

---

[4] Wassily Leontief et al., *The Future of the World Economy* (New York: Oxford University Press, 1977).

[5] See H. Sackman, *Delphi Assessment: Expert Opinion, Forecasting and Group Process* (Santa Monica, Calif.: Rand Corporation, April 1974); See also Joseph P. Martino, *Technological Forecasting for Decision Making,* 2nd Ed. (New York: Elsevier Science Publishing Co., 1983), pp. 17–38.

the process. As an example, a world forecast by the late Herman Kahn worked with three major scenarios: world A or a "surprise-free" scenario, world B—a high-growth scenario, and world C—a low-growth scenario.[6]

The key issue in scenario methodologies is the plausibility of the intuitively selected scenarios. To the extent that scenarios open up new horizons to decision makers and provide a broader framework within which to make decisions, they are a valuable futures methodology. Scenarios may also have an advantage over many other techniques, particularly those involving mathematical methods, in their ability to communicate ideas about the future.

SOME MAJOR FUTURES STUDIES

A landmark study in the futures field was the *Limits to Growth* report (1972) sponsored by the Club of Rome.[7] The club is a private association of about 100 individuals in different countries. The *Limits to Growth* study, based on a computer model, concluded that the future growth of the world would be severely constrained by raw material shortages. This gloomy forecast provoked a stream of other studies that presented widely diverging "images of the future."

Probably the most relevant studies for international business are the *Interfutures* (1979) study of the OECD,[8] the *Global 2000 Report* (1980) by the U.S. government,[9] and *The Resourceful Earth* (1984), edited by Julian L. Simon and the late Herman Kahn.[10] The OECD study focuses on the future economic relationships of the developed and developing countries, using the alternative scenario method. It analyzes physical limits to growth, trade patterns, industrialization trends, and technological possibilities; and it makes alternative forecasts in each of these fields.

The *Global 2000* study reached conclusions similar to the Club of Rome report and sketched a future in which scarcity of food and raw materials as well as environmental degradation were highly probable. *The Resourceful Earth* was a response to the *Global 2000* report and presents a countercase as to natural resources, food, and the environment.

Why are the forecasts so different? One explanation is that some forecasts are directed toward supporting policy recommendations such as proposals for reforestration and increased use of solar energy. Another explanation is that the

---

[6] Herman Kahn, *World Economic Development: 1979 and Beyond* (Boulder, Colo. Westview Press, 1979).

[7] D. Meadows et al., *The Limits to Growth* (New York: Universe Books, 1972).

[8] Organization for Economic Cooperation and Development: *Interfutures* (Paris, 1979).

[9] Council on Environmental Quality and the Department of State, *The Global 2000 Report to the President: Entering the Twenty-First Century,* in three volumes (Washington, D.C.: U.S. Government Printing Office, 1980).

[10] (London: Basil Blackwell, 1984).

"basic data needed to understand where we are and where we are going are simply unavailable, or analysts are talking past each other, proceeding on different assumptions and selecting the data according to different criteria."[11]

SOME FORECASTS OF THE INTERNATIONAL ENVIRONMENT

The various futures studies deal mainly with economic trends and all are concerned with population, natural resources, food, and technology.

Population

The world's population passed the 5 billion mark in July 1987 and is estimated to reach 6.2 billion in the year 2000 and 8.2 billion by 2025.[12] The population growth rate has been declining and is projected to reach 1.44 percent annually in the year 2000, compared with 1.70 percent in 1985. Yet in terms of sheer numbers, the world's population is estimated to increase by almost 100 million annually in the year 2000.

Several major details of the forecasts have special significance for international business. The most striking feature is that 90 percent of the growth is estimated to occur in the poorest countries. By the year 2000, an estimated 80 percent of the world's population will be living in the LDCs (less developed countries). Asia's 58 percent share of the total is not expected to increase, as a result of low growth rates in China and Japan. But rapid population growth in Africa is projected to increase that region's share of world population from 12 percent in 1985 to 14.3 percent in the year 2000. In contrast, the U.S. share is forecast to drop from 4.9 percent in 1985 to 4.2 percent by the year 2000.

Continued rapid urbanization is another feature of the population projections. By the year 2000, an estimated 50 percent of the world's population will be in towns and cities; and 12 of the 15 largest metropolitan areas are expected to be in the developing countries. The largest city is projected to be Mexico City, with a population in the year 2000 of slightly more than 30 million.

Still another population trend is the expected aging of the population. The over-65 population is growing much faster than the total population—and in many countries, even faster growth is occurring among the over-80 population.

Natural Resources

Will the future availability of natural resources cause nations to halt or slow down their growth? This likelihood was forecast by the 1972 *Limits to*

---

[11] See Barry B. Hughes, *World Futures: A Critical Analysis of Alternatives* (Baltimore: The Johns Hopkins Press, 1985), p. 24.

[12] My T. Yu, *World Population Projections, 1985* (Baltimore: Johns Hopkins University Press, 1985), pp. xiii–xv.

Growth study. But many subsequent studies take a more optimistic view. They recognize that some specific resources are likely to be scarce and that certain regions of the world may have special resource problems, such as the ground water supply in Africa. At the same time, they argue that great potentials exist for improving resource availability through improved efficiency in the use of resources, through the development of substitutes, and through new technologies. Sustainable development requires, however, that appropriate resource management programs be implemented.[13]

Food

Does the world have the future potential to feed its expanding population? The answer to this question by one of the most authoritative studies is that the world possesses the potential to feed a population of more than 6 billion by the year 2000 moderately better than it fed 4.3 billion in 1980. To realize this potential, however, will require large investments to improve the infrastructure of agriculture, increased investments in research and education to stimulate development, and application of productivity-enhancing technologies, public policies that offer greater economic incentives to farmers in many developing countries, and expanded international trade. This study projects that some 85 percent of the increased production will come from productivity increases and only 15 percent from expanding the cultivated land base.[14]

Nevertheless, large numbers of people in the developing countries will be unable to share in the improved food situation and continue to be undernourished. Access to food by a family has become primarily dependent on the family's income and not on the availability of food to be purchased. As one study reported, "the food crisis of 1973–74 was not caused by food shortages as such, but by poverty. In that year 400 million tons of grain were fed to livestock; 2 million of those would have been enough to feed malnourished people."[15]

Technology

All these facets of the future are intertwined, and technology especially so. The decades since the end of World War II have been an unusually prolific period of technological development. The main futures question is whether the world has moved into a new cycle in which the rate of technological innovation

---

[13] Robert C. Repetto, *The Global Possible: Resources, Development, and the New Century* (New Haven: Yale University Press, 1985).

[14] Resources for the Future, "Feeding a Hungry World," in *Resources*, Spring 1984, p. 19; See also D. Gale Johnson, "World Food and Agriculture," in Simon and Kahn, *The Resourceful Earth*, pp. 67–112.

[15] Martin McLaughlin, "Food Security for Nations and People," *A Society for International Development: Prospectus 1984*, ed. Ann Mattis (Durham, N.C.: Duke University Press, 1983), p. 162.

will slow down. Most forecasters say "No." The OECD *Interfutures* study, for example, concludes that "up to the end of the century, a substantial slowdown of growth from lack of technological innovation seems unlikely. Nor does it seem that in the longer term the capacity for scientific discovery or even technological potential as such will set limits to growth.[16]

What are the major technological developments that might be expected? A recent study selected the following areas as technological frontiers for the next 10–15 years:[17]

New Materials: New characteristics being sought are special magnetic properties. A variety of multifunctional materials can be foreseen. Improved processing or fabrication methods are likely to reduce costs and enhance performance.

Computers: Important changes will be in the development of easy-to-use computers, the incorporation of microcomputers into a wide variety of factory, office and household equipment, and continuing dramatic decline in computational costs.

Telecommunications: Continued dramatic technological change is expected, particularly in the area of optical or lightwave communication systems and satellite communications.

Biotechnology: Biogenetic engineering is most likely to experience technological breakthroughs by the mid-1990s. The most promising application areas are health care and agriculture.

The longer-range predictions of "futurists" and science fiction writers should also be noted. In this genre, a recent writer has made such predictions as the following:[18]

In 2081, a voyage of a few days to a space colony will be as commonplace as a Caribbean cruise is today.

Long before 2081, computers that understand speech, so that orders can be given by those without special training, will have gone "mini" and will be accessible to most people.

By 2081, any major central computer will have rapid access to at least a hundred million million (100,000,000,000,000) words of memory and be no larger than a suitcase.

Still another writer forecasts for the nearer future—2019—baseball pitchers with bionic implants throwing 120 mph fastballs and a house that, sensing your mood, adjusts the blinds, selects music, and brews coffee with just the right amount of caffeine.[19]

---

[16] OECD, *Interfutures*, p. 113.

[17] Anne G. Keatley, ed., *Technological Frontiers and Foreign Relations* (Washington: National Academy Press, 1985).

[18] Gerard K. O'Neill, *2081: A Hopeful View of the Human Nature* (New York: Simon and Shuster, 1981).

[19] Arthur C. Clarke, *Arthur C. Clarke's July 20, 2019* (New York: Macmillan, 1987).

SOME FORECASTS OF ECONOMIC TRENDS

The growing interdependence of the world economy is the most fundamental feature of future economic patterns. Any forecast of economic trends for the low-income and middle-income countries depends on what happens in the advanced industrialized countries and vice versa. Thus, the outcome of any future growth scenarios will be shaped by policies adopted in the centrally planned economies, the industrialized market economies, and to a lesser extent in the developing countries.

In the late 1980s, the many existing uncertainties made most economic forecasters reluctant to make projections of long-term global economic trends. As the United Nations observed, "Since the unwinding of the major global imbalances is still ahead, it is quite possible that dramatic changes will occur before 1990. In this sense, the world economy is in uncharted waters."[20] The UN survey added that the prevailing uncertainties pointed downward and that the simultaneous occurrence of only some of the latent negative influences could move the world economy into global recession.

An optimistic scenario is that a sharp recession will coerce nations into undertaking the necessary major economic restructuring. Some of the actions needed to support continued healthy growth of the world economy are coordinated national policies to improve the multilateral trading system (which has been eroded by bilateralism and managed trade); reduce excessive instability in foreign exchange markets; resolve the debt crisis of the developing nations; and establish better controls on international financial markets.

With great caution, the World Bank in 1984 postulated two growth scenarios of the world economy for the decade up to 1995, both of which suggest a continued slower growth rate for the advanced countries than for the low-income and middle-income countries.[21] The Low Case scenario shows an annual GDP growth rate for the industrial countries of 2.5 percent and 4.7 percent for the LDCs. The High Case scenario suggests an annual GDP growth rate of 4.3 percent for the industrial nations and 5.5 percent for the developing countries. Each scenario depends critically on the future policies adopted by the countries, particularly the United States.

The global transformation of the global-industrial map can be expected to continue for several decades with the migration of traditional industries from the North (industrial countries) to the South (developing countries), as a number of the LDCs, such as China, South Korea, Taiwan, Mexico, Brazil, and others, assume leading roles in world industry. Another industrial growth area may be the centrally planned economies of the USSR and Eastern Europe that are emulating the Chinese experience of trying to implement reforms that will decentralize economic decisions and place greater emphasis on markets in place of central

---

[20] United Nations, *World Economic Survey 1987* (New York, 1987), p. 7.

[21] World Bank, *World Development Report 1984* (New York: Oxford University Press, 1984), pp. 34–50.

planning. In the case of both China and Eastern Europe, the success of the reforms will depend mainly on the ability of top government leaders to overcome bureaucratic, political, and ideological resistance to a loss of power.

As the traditional industries migrate from the North to the South, a new generation of technology-intensive industries will be the poles of economic growth in the North. The common feature of these new industries is that they are global from the start; their products (commonly services) have high unit values, which reduces the importance of transportation costs in international trade. Furthermore, because the new industries are knowledge/service-intensive rather than resource-intensive, they have great locational freedom.[22]

Future Trade Patterns

What are the likely scenarios for world trade? The big markets of the world will continue to be the industrialized countries, even though growth rates are expected to slow down in these markets. But even in the various slow-growth scenarios, the exports of manufactured goods from developing countries to these markets are projected to continue increasing. The big uncertainty is the issue of protectionism. This, in turn, depends on the ability and willingness of the industrialized countries to adjust their economic structure to permit the more efficient production from the developing countries to enter their markets.

A deterrent to growing protectionism may be the matter of economic interdependence. A number of the middle-income countries that are having external debt problems have been large export markets for such countries as the United States and Japan. Protectionist measures that reduce the export possibilities for these countries will reduce their potential for importing as well as for earning foreign exchange to service and repay their debts.

An interesting trade question for the future is whether technological developments will on the whole inhibit or foster the growth of international trade. New materials, if they can be produced from domestic raw materials, will reduce the demand for imported raw materials. Developments in telecommunications can widen the span of managerial control, and computer-aided design may reduce the optimum scale of production facilities. Taken together, these developments could result in both decentralized production close to foreign markets and centralized financial control. This situation would reduce foreign trade but increase direct investment.[23]

Pushing in the direction of greater trade, cheap telecommunications will permit long-distance selling and direct orders from distant sources. Lower transpor-

---

[22] Franklin R. Root, "Some Trends in the World Economy and Their Implications for International Business Strategy," *Journal of International Business Studies,* Winter 1984, pp. 21–22.

[23] See Richard N. Cooper and Ann L. Hollick, "International Relations in a Technologically Advanced Future," in Keatley, *Technological Frontiers,* pp. 244–45.

tation costs will also encourage trade. Although there are different views as to whether the trade-inhibiting or the trade-promoting tendencies will be the stronger, it is most likely that international trade will continue to grow more rapidly than world output—although the gap between the two may be less.

Future Direct Investment Patterns

International direct investment by multinationals has been a key contributor to the growing interdependence of the world economy. And as the globalization of competition has become the rule rather than the exception in so many industries, foreign direct investment can be expected to expand significantly in the future. The pace of such expansion will depend on growth trends in the world economy and changing business strategies. The factors shaping future trends, however, will differ for North–North flows between the advanced economies, North–South flows between the developed and the developing countries, and East–West flows between the market economies and the centrally planned countries.

The major share of future direct investment is quite certain to be flows between the industrialized countries. A driving force is the accelerated merging of the advanced country markets. As one writer has observed, "These countries are now inextricably tied to each other through the thread of international competition." "In some industries it is possible to have a single sales force that travels to the buyer's country and back again. . . . More typically, however, the firm must locate the capabilities to perform downstream activities in each of the countries in which it operates."[24] The same strategy is recommended by a Japanese authority, namely that it is vital for the firm "to become an insider" in each of the developed regions of Japan, North America, and Western Europe.[25] In many cases the foreign presence may be in the form of a new project jointly owned by major multinationals of different nationalities—a so-called strategic alliance.

Large expansion potentials exist in the developing countries and many LDCs have become quite receptive to foreign direct investment. The debt problem of many LDCs is an inhibiting factor, in the sense that national economic growth has been retarded. But the debt problem also has positive implications for foreign direct investment. A preference for securing investment funds through foreign borrowing rather than through foreign direct investment seems to have been reversed, because the pressure on a country's balance of payments for profit repatriation can be less than for servicing and repaying foreign loans. Still another development is that some indebted countries have promoted debt-equity conversion

---

[24] Michael E. Porter, *Competition in Global Industries* (Boston: Harvard Business School Press, 1986), pp. 1, 3.

[25] Kenichi Ohmae, *Beyond National Borders* (Homewood, Ill.: Dow Jones-Irwin, 1987), p. 97.

programs whereby foreign investors can secure local funds for investment at favorable terms in exchange for hard currency that can be used to repay foreign debts.

Among the centrally planned economies, the policy of encouraging foreign direct investment initiated by China has spread to the USSR and other Eastern European countries. The inflows to China ebbed in the late 1980s while China struggled to improve the environment for foreign joint ventures. It may be reasonable to assume that China will succeed in reducing the bureaucratic and other difficulties and that inflows will accelerate over the next decade. The USSR put out the welcome mat in 1987 for foreign investment but had not received many guests as of the late 1980s. The Soviets are anxious to gain by exposure to Western management and the transfer of technology. It is likely, therefore, that over the next decade, the USSR will be able to modify its regulations and create the necessary incentives to secure significant inflows of foreign direct investment.

The nationality mix of the foreign direct investment patterns will continue to change. The dominant position held by U.S. multinationals will continue to erode with the more rapid expansion of Japanese, Western Europe, and more recently, Korean multinationals. The United States will most likely continue to receive large inflows of foreign direct investment. The strategy of a "cheap" dollar, which is expected to reduce exports and help to reduce the U.S. trade deficit, favors shifting from exports to direct investment as a means of competing in the U.S. market.

THE INTERNATIONAL ENVIRONMENT FOR BUSINESS

Institutional and policy trends at the international and national levels, as well as economic forces, shape the future international environment for business. Although alternative future scenarios are difficult to postulate, a number of key areas can be identified where changes of major significance to international business are evolving.

The International Level

As of the late 1980s, an institutional gap still existed for dealing with issues related to international direct investment and multinational enterprises. Pressures to fill this gap are most likely to continue, with the outcome quite uncertain. At the same time, many existing international institutions are extending their programs to handle problems that impact on international business.

A few examples can be cited of actions by existing international institutions that affect international business. In the health field, the World Health Organization has proved to be an effective forum for establishing a worldwide code to restrict the marketing of infant formula in Third World nations. In the area of international transfers of technology, UNCTAD continues its efforts to obtain agreement on a comprehensive code of conduct directed mainly to the activities of multinational enterprises. Although created to deal with international trade issues, GATT has been forced to move cautiously into the area of international direct investment because of complaints by member countries that other parties to the agreement have established restrictions on investment through the so-called performance requirements. These requirements, such as requiring certain degrees of local content in products manufactured by foreign firms, are alleged to be a trade restriction.

The issues exist. So, too, does the need for an international institutional mechanism for handling the problems related to international business. In the absence of an appropriate forum for dealing comprehensively with international business issues, other institutions will be called upon to resolve conflicts. The difficulties inherent in reaching international agreement on a new institution, however, are dramatized by the complex and extended negotiations that have taken place in the area of the ocean's resources.

The importance for international business of the development gap between the North and the South cannot be overstressed. Almost 80 percent of the world's population by the year 2000 will be located in the developing countries. Business performance in these countries will depend upon the success achieved in raising the incomes (and purchasing power) of this vast population. Whatever contribution international business firms can make directly, or through their influence on the development assistance programs of their home countries, toward improving economic levels in these areas can be both good international citizenship and good international business.

Another issue at the international level that should not be overlooked is the possibility of accelerated moves toward military disarmament. As of the late 1980s, global pressures for disarmament have become extremely strong. To the extent that the "peace movement" is successful, patterns of international trade and production will change. International trade in arms, as noted in an earlier chapter, has been large and growing. As arms producers, many multinationals will be affected. Military goods have become high-technology products; and many multinationals in aircraft, electronics, communications, chemicals, and so on have a significant share of their production in military goods.

The National Level

At the national level, the environment for multinational firms is certain to be one of more sophisticated national controls. The developing countries in particular have become better informed on international business and more experienced in developing controls to increase national benefits. The LDCs will give great emphasis to employment benefits and the transfer of technology. There will be continued pressure for joint ventures that share ownership with nationals and for licensing and turnkey projects in lieu of foreign-owned production facilities. There will be increased attention to environmental issues.[26]

---

[26] See Charles S. Pearson, ed., *Multinational Corporations, Environment, and the Third World* (Durham, N. C.: Duke University Press, 1987).

The concern for location of R&D facilities in host countries will continue unabated. Given the future importance of the developing countries, more multinationals are likely to respond to these pressures and will benefit accordingly. New products or adaptations of present products that can serve the vast markets of the Third World could open up valuable business opportunities.

A good possibility exists that the control environments in many countries may shift from a regulatory to an incentive approach—to use of a carrot rather than a stick. In this respect, the trend may follow the example of several developing countries that have been successful in attracting foreign direct investment and in influencing foreign firms to make major contributions toward national development goals. Such efforts have often succeeded because the host countries recognize that business firms can only undertake in the longer term what is profitable, and have accordingly offered profit incentives to influence business patterns.

A new feature of many national environments is the emerging opportunities for foreign enterprise resulting from a growing *privatization* trend, formerly called *denationalization*. Previously, numerous countries reserved certain key business sectors for government enterprises, thereby precluding foreign and domestic private firms from these business areas. But growing dissatisfaction with the performance of many government enterprises caused a surprising number of countries to initiate programs to sell selected government enterprises to private investors. The United Kingdom began such a privatization program in the early 1980s, and the trend spread to such advanced countries as France, Germany, Sweden, Italy, and Canada, as well as such developing countries as Mexico, Argentina, and Thailand. In some cases, ownership participation by foreign firms has been limited. But in other situations, significant new business possibilities for foreign firms have resulted.

INTERNATIONAL MANAGEMENT IN THE FUTURE

What does the future hold for the multinational enterprise and the international manager? The general consensus is that some form of the multinational enterprise will successfully survive for several more decades. The ideological debate as to whether multinationals are good or evil continues in intellectual and academic circles, but is greatly muted as compared to recent years. At the operational level, government officials and political leaders have evolved toward a pragmatic and receptive attitude, as they have become increasingly aware that host countries have great potential power for shaping the conditions under which foreign firms operate.

But countervailing forces from governments, unions, and the wider public may cause major transformations in the forms of multinational enterprises. The organizational structures of the multinationals are increasingly having to respond to a more active role by governments and labor unions. Perlmutter foresees more enterprises becoming geocentric and less ethnocentric or polycentric. He also sees an increasing number of organizational forms other than the wholly owned and two party joint-venture types. Evolving forms in which a larger number of parties participate are referred to as "industrial systems constellations" that can have multinational ownership participation, including that of governments.[27] A related forecast of changing organization forms is that of Peter Drucker, who foresees the multinational enterprise becoming a "transnational federation."[28] And the growth of strategic alliances between multinational competitors is likely to continue.

How will the role of the international manager change? With more complex organization forms and more constituencies within and outside of the enterprise involved, new and greater demands will be made on the managers who are heading foreign affiliates and the parent companies. One of the most apparent demands will be in the area of external relations. As one writer suggests, "The major challenge to the continued success of the multinational corporation is not lack of technical skills, but rather, the need to establish and develop procedures and practices which enable the corporation to operate effectively in an uncertain, challenging and concerned host country environment."[29] The same might be said about the need for managing external affairs in the home-country environment.

The growing external affairs responsibility is related to the almost universal pressures on business firms for greater social responsibility—except that in the international field the concerns and reactions of many groups in many national environments must be recognized. The management of external affairs requires that the firm should be measuring its social and economic impact on the country and make such information available. The firm should also take advantage of, and assume responsibility for, legitimately shaping the environment. External affairs will place demands on the manager for developing skills for political, diplomatic, and technical negotiations. They will also require great expertise in adapting to many varied cultures and understanding diverse national aspirations.

Although the advanced industrial countries will continue over the near future to be the main arena for multinational business operations, the developing countries and the centrally planned economies are the frontier areas with the most dramatic long-run potential for increased multinational business activity. And it is in these countries that the new demands on the international manager will be heaviest. In contrast to operations in the advanced countries, the manager will have to be more skilled for negotiations with governments, more patient in waiting for things to happen, more flexible in accepting business arrangements such as countertrade and barter, more imaginative in dealing with subsidiaries that are likely to be joint ventures with the multinational in a minority ownership position, and more

[27] See Howard V. Perlmutter, "A View of the Future," in *The New Sovereigns: Multinational Corporations as World Powers,* eds., Abdul Said and Luiz Simmons (Englewood Cliffs, N.J.: Prentice-Hall, 1975), pp. 167–86; see also G. Hedlund and L. Otterbeck, *The Multinational Corporation, The Nation State and the Trade Unions: An European Perspective* (Kent, Ohio: Kent State University, 1977).

[28] Peter Drucker, *Managing in Turbulent Times* (New York: Harper & Row, 1980).

[29] David H. Blake, *Managing the External Relations of Multinational Corporations* (New York: Fund for Multinational Management Education, 1977), p. 2.

BOX 25–3
The Future According to Philips

Unless Philips NV, the giant Dutch electronics group, develops new markets and products by 1991, nearly a quarter of its 87,500 jobs in Holland will disappear. This startling piece of information is contained in a survey prepared by the group on likely social developments up to the year 1991.

How do companies like Philips, which has 391,500 employees worldwide and is the largest private sector employer outside the United States, go about looking into the future? And why the need to add its own crystal gazing to that carried out by many private and government forecasting institutes?

The aim is to see "if the forecasting was sufficiently tangible to make a real contribution to decisions on the company's social policies," the forecast group says. Philips, like many other companies, usually restricts itself to a four-year review. This survey was completed in May 1978 and looks 13 years ahead to 1991—not too close and not too far into the future.

The survey begins with a list of assumptions about the future, drawn from the written sources and based on Philips' own experience in social matters. These assumptions are then worked out in more detail in several areas, including income, personnel, and company structures. In the final section of the 65-page report, a number of points raised are checked to see if they could form the basis for policy decisions.

SOURCE: Adapted from *World Business Weekly*, February 12, 1979, p. 25.

---

responsive in meeting national performance requirements such as adding local content and training local employees. In addition, working with the centrally planned economies requires the manager from the West to become familiar with, and probably even tolerant of, a radically different economic system and ideology.

For future operations in all areas, the international manager will need to digest greatly increased flows of information, particularly about the environment, and participate in forecasting possible future trends. The futures planning of one major multinational is described briefly in Box 25–3.

The internal management issues for the future are many. Some of these have been identified in a joint project undertaken by American and European business schools to examine the changing expectations of society as they relate to management training for the 21st century.[30] Some of the trends identified have special relevance for international business. Among these is the growing influence of worker participation in the decision-making function of management. With continued pressure for the hiring of nationals in overseas subsidiaries, interna-

---

[30] See *Management in the XXI Century* (Washington, D.C.: American Assembly of Collegiate Schools of Business, 1980).

tional managers will have to deal with potential conflicts in cultural and moral systems.

To some degree, the "new" demands on the international manager are already present, and to some extent they are being anticipated in management education programs. But as a former dean of a leading business school once observed, "Changing a university curriculum is like moving a graveyard." Business schools in the United States have made some progress in internationalizing the training of future managers by offering courses such as the one for which this textbook is being used. Nevertheless, business education has lagged seriously behind the needs of international business operations, and the lag is almost certain to continue. Consequently, international business firms will be required to sponsor a great deal of in-house training in the future.

SUMMARY

The changing economic, social, and political environment around the world has had a profound impact on international business and will continue to do so. The future of multinational enterprises depends heavily on their ability to anticipate rather than react to significant future events, analyze their impact on the enterprise, and incorporate that analysis directly into corporate planning and decision making.

The field of forecasting "alternative futures" has become a growth industry and international firms are increasingly making use of such internal and external forecasting to guide their operations. These forecasts indicate that international managers and multinational enterprises will need new frames of reference, changing values, and revised skills. International managers can rely on present practices and hope to get by. Or they can treat the new trends and pressures as challenges and devise ways to harness them.

EXERCISES AND DISCUSSION QUESTIONS

1. What are the advantages and limitations of alternative futures methodologies? Give examples of international business issues that might most appropriately be analyzed by each of the principal methodologies.
2. What future developments are likely to cause a major growth in the expansion of multinational enterprises into the Third World with its vast population and market potential?
3. How do you evaluate the forecast that multinational enterprises are likely to involve more ownership participants and become "industrial systems constellations"?
4. What are the principal new demands on international managers for the 21st century that may be most difficult to meet?

PART SEVEN

Cases and Problems in International Business

The Nature and Scope of
International Business

Which Company Is Truly Multinational?

Four senior executives of the world's largest firms with extensive holdings outside the home country speak:

Company A. "We are a multinational firm. We distribute our products in about 100 countries. We manufacture in over 17 countries and do research and development in three countries. We look at all new investment projects—both domestic and overseas—using exactly the same criteria."

The executive from Company A continues, "Of course most of the key posts in our subsidiaries are held by home-country nationals. Whenever replacements for these men are sought, it is the practice, if not the policy, to look next to you at the head office and pick someone (usually a home-country national) you know and trust."

Company B. "We are a multinational firm. Only 1 percent of the personnel in our affiliate companies are nonnationals. Most of these are U.S. executives on temporary assignments. In all major markets, the affiliate's managing director is of the local nationality."

He continues, "Of course there are very few non-Americans in the key posts at headquarters. The few we have are so Americanized that we usually don't notice their nationality. Unfortunately, you can't find good foreigners who are willing to live in the United States, where our headquarters is located. American executives are more mobile. In addition, Americans have the drive and initiative we like. In fact, the European nationals would prefer to report to an American rather than to some other European."

Company C. "We are a multinational firm. Our product division executives have worldwide profit responsibility. As our organizational chart shows, the United States is just one region on a par with Europe, Latin America, Africa, etc., in each division."

The executive from Company C goes on to explain, "The worldwide product division concept is rather difficult to implement. The senior executives in charge of these divisions have little overseas experience. They have been promoted from domestic posts and tend to view foreign consumer needs as really basically the same as ours. Also, product division executives tend to focus on the domestic market because the domestic market is larger and generates more revenue than the fragmented foreign markets. The rewards are for global performance, but the strategy is to focus on domestic. Most of our senior executives simply do not understand what happens overseas and really do not trust foreign executives, even those in key positions.

Company D (non-American).   "We are a multinational firm. We have at least 18 nationalities represented at our headquarters. Most senior executives speak at least two languages. About 30 percent of our staff at headquarters are foreigners."

He continues by explaining that "since the voting shareholders must by law come from the home country, the home country's interest must be given careful consideration. But we are proud of our nationality: we shouldn't be ashamed of it. In fact, many times we have been reluctant to use home-country ideas overseas, to our detriment, especially in our U.S. subsidiary. Our country produces good executives, who tend to stay with us a long time. It is harder to keep executives from the United States.

1. Which company is truly multinational?
2. What are the attitudes of a truly multinational company?
3. Why quibble about how multinational a firm is?

Igloos versus Fastbacks

1. Assume that in each of two economies, the United States and Greenland, there are a total of five productive units. A productive unit can be used in the production of either Fastback cars or Igloos. The "cost" to an economy of producing a Fastback or an Igloo is measured in terms of opportunity cost, that is, the number of one good that must be given up in order to produce the other.

2. The table below summarizes the production possibilities in each of the two countries. *Assume that the countries decided on the respective production functions indicated by the asterisks.*

Productive Units Utilized		Goods Produced United States		Goods Produced Greenland	
For Igloos	For Fastbacks	Fastbacks	Igloos	Fastbacks	Igloos
5	0	0	30	0	10
4	1	4	24	.5	8
3	2	8	18	1.0	6
2	3	12	12	1.5	4
1	4	16*	6	2.0*	2
0	5	20	0	2.5	0

3. Analyze the data and work through the following questions:

   a. What country is best able to produce Fastbacks? Igloos?
   b. In which good is the United States advantage greatest? Why?
   c. Will it pay for either country to trade with the other? Why?
   d. If yes, which way should the goods flow? Why?
   e. In order for there to be an exchange of goods, a *price* is required. What is the minimum acceptable price to each country?

Anglo-American Seeds

Before leaving to visit his firm's U.S. subsidiaries, Alan Normanby spent the first weekend in May 1981 preparing the summer flower beds around his home in London's stockbroker belt. A Saturday visit to the garden center provided him with seedlings and seed packets that he carefully planted in the spring rain on Sunday morning. Now, two days later, he stood in a Boston discount store facing a large container of reduced-price seed packets. He picked up a packet of Giant African Marigold seeds selling at 67 cents, reduced from 89 cents, that seemed much larger than the packet he had just paid 25p for in England. Instead of holding 50 or so loose seeds, Alan saw it contained 150 prespaced seeds affixed to 15 feet of decomposable seed planting tape. The package bore the name of the Fredonia Seed Co. of Fredonia, New York, and a note, "Seed of U.S. origin. Assembled into strip in England."

At £1 = $2.30, which must have been about the exchange rate when the seeds were processed in the United Kingdom, the U.S. seeds were costing under one half what Alan had paid in London. Of course, the dollar had risen to £1 = $1.80 over the past few months, because oil prices had fallen while the United States had retained its tight monetary policy and high interest rates; but even at this exchange rate the U.S. seeds were still far cheaper. Furthermore, to bring prices back to purchasing power parity, the rate would have to fall again before too long.

One up for comparative advantage, thought Alan. If British manufacturing could fix U.S. seeds onto strips for the U.S. market more cheaply than similar seeds could be supplied loose for the U.K. market, then British firms could do the same in textiles, too. Alan's international production director in London had, for the past six months, been pressing to shift more production to the United States, where productivity was higher in their household cotton textile mill. The marigold seeds would provide Alan with a good illustration for arguing that the best way might simply be to make sure that his U.K. factory increased its productivity ahead of the United States.

1. What could cause such a disparity in prices?
2. Does comparative advantage have any relevance for this example?
3. Is there any validity in the comparison between seeds and textiles?
4. What do you think of the productivity argument?
5. How does the change in exchange rate affect the textile situation?
6. What is the relationship between exchange rate, interest rate, and future rate?
7. If exchange rates are affected by different interest rates, is it reasonable to expect purchasing power parity?

The Framework for International Transactions

Freelandia

Freelandia's main exports came from its primary industries and included wool, meat, butter, timber, fruit, and a variety of less advanced manufactures. For 1987 the total exported was US$3,360 million.

Imports totaled US$3,309 million, made up mainly of heavy manufactured goods, such as machinery and transport equipment, while an additional US$36 million was spent on foreign transport and travel and US$15 million on other services.

The country had recently begun to encourage foreign industry to invest in new factories and plants, provided that the output either substituted for imports or had export potential and included at least 40 percent of Freelandian content. This campaign had proven quite successful and during 1987 a total of US$348 million was remitted for direct investment in Freelandia. The policy was beginning to meet resistance from the opposition political parties, however, because the considerable income these companies were earning was payable to them in overseas funds and placed a strain on the balance of payments. In 1987 a total of US$198 million was repatriated by overseas companies, out of their net earnings of US$294 million.

The Freelandian government had also been encouraging its major domestic producers to establish processing plants overseas to increase the country's income from primary exports. A total of US$126 million was invested in this way in 1987 and was expected to add significantly to the future inflow from overseas business investments, which totaled only US$54 million in 1987.

There was an additional reinvested income of US$66 million from these direct investments overseas during 1987, but it was still true, as the opposition argued, that foreign firms' ownership in Freelandia far outweighed Freelandia's overseas business activities—in cumulative figures at the end of 1986, a comparison of US$2,889 million to US$726 million. This comparison, moreover, was similar for holdings of investment securities. Foreign investment in Freelandian securities totaled US$1,080 million at the end of 1986 and increased in value by US$132 million during 1987, while Freelandian holdings of overseas stocks and bonds were valued at only US$366 million in 1986, increasing in value by US$39 million over the year. Heavy restrictions permitted only US$15 million to be remitted by Freelandia for further purchases during 1987, but foreigners purchased a further US$126 million in Freelandia.

The government's policies had also led them to borrow US$84 million from overseas investors during the year in order to finance new container facilities at the major ports, but their indebtedness to the IMF was reduced to US$963 million with a repayment of US$75 million. Interest payments of US$168 million were made to service government debentures floated overseas that totaled US$1,209 million at the end of 1986. The central bank's holdings of convertible currencies overseas increased during the year by US$57 million to US$378 million.

Shorter-term commercial finances were less important to the Freelandian situation but local holdings of foreigners again more than offset Freelandian holdings overseas. Short-term overseas holdings by Freelandian companies were US$240 million at the end of 1986 and liquid holdings US$18 million, while overseas companies held US$168 million short-term claims and US$144 million in liquid funds within Freelandia. By the end of 1987, the net change on short-term nonliquid funds was US$42 million. Overseas companies had increased their claims by US$18 million, and Freelandian companies had increased their claims by US$60 million. There was no change over the year in Freelandian liquid claims, but foreign banks increased their holdings by US$54 million.

1. From the above particulars, prepare balance-of-payments accounts for Freelandia for 1987 and show the country's international investment position at the end of 1986 and 1987.
2. What do you think might happen if Freelandia's currency were to be devalued against other currencies by 20 percent? Do you think this devaluation is likely?

The Korean Won (A): A Swap Proposal

In mid-December 1979, John Bergsma, general manager of the Seoul branch of a large U.S. multinational bank, was trying to decide whether or not his bank should contract a $5 million "swap transaction" with the Bank of Korea, the central bank of that troubled but dynamic country. If he wanted to contract the transaction he had to submit an application to the Bank of Korea before the end of the week. But Bergsma was pensive and reluctant to make his decision because of widespread rumors of an imminent devaluation of the Korean won.

Banking in Korea is attractive and very profitable for large multinational banks. Although there are some restrictions on foreign bank operations in Korea, almost unlimited domestic demand for credit and limited capability of local banks to meet domestic demand provide excellent opportunities for large multinational banks. But the key to the attractiveness of the Korean market is the very high interest rates at which banks can lend funds. Foreign banks have a special advantage because they can acquire lendable funds relatively cheaply from their home-country headquarters or from sister branches in various countries around the world and lend these less expensive funds at very high rates in Korea.

However, this foreign lending in Korea has attracted the attention and regulation of the Bank of Korea for two reasons: (1) the unfair advantage which foreign banks enjoy may lead to a long-term weakening of domestic Korean banks, and (2) the inflow of credit from abroad via foreign banks might undermine the effectiveness of the central bank's monetary policies. For these reasons, the Bank of Korea regulates the supply of foreign banks' loanable funds on a quarterly basis with swap transactions.

These swap transactions work as follows. Under the Korean Banking Law and the conditions of banking operation permits, loans denominated in foreign currencies are not allowed: that is, if an American bank wants to lend to a Korean client, that loan must be denominated in local currency, the Korean won. Foreign banks wishing to lend in Korea must sell foreign currencies to the Bank of Korea (i.e., buy won with dollars or yen or francs, etc.) and contract a swap transaction with the central bank in order to acquire won to make loans to local customers. In a swap transaction, foreign banks agree to repurchase the foreign currency at the end of the transaction period at the market (official exchange rate) price prevailing then.

Although the last devaluation of the won had occurred in 1974, concern

Prepared by J. Frederick Truitt, Associate Professor of International Business, Kang-Rae Cho, and Chong-S. Lee, research assistants, Graduate School of Business Administration, University of Washington, as a basis for classroom discussion. Copyright 1980 by the authors.

over the possibility of another devaluation has existed for years. This concern intensified after the assassination of President Park on October 26, 1979, but most observers had not expected a devaluation until at least after the election of the new government under the new constitution sometime late 1980. They thought the current "caretaker" interim government would not make such a tough and sensitive decision. But some observers expressed the possibility of devaluation by the interim government, pointing out the appointment of Mr. Shim and Mr. Lee as prime minister and head of the Economic Planning Board, respectively. The new prime minister was a career businessman and the head of EPB was a former professor of business and public administration. Both were believed to have no political background or ambitions, hence no reluctance to take a painful course of action if such action were necessary and correct for the health and prosperity of the Korean economy.

Bergsma had just returned from a meeting with several good longstanding customers who urgently needed credits before year end. But if Bergsma's bank was to provide credit to these customers he would have to make his decision by tomorrow morning so paper work on the swap application could begin.

EXHIBIT 1

Outlook for Korea's Won: Devaluation Hinges on Other Policies' Success

Despite Korea's current export slowdown and evidence of chronic inflation, discount rumors that a devaluation of the won is imminent. Devaluation will not come before year-end and then only if other measures which the government has been vigorously promoting fail. These measures include:

Acceleration of industrial restructuring, with the emphasis on promotion of heavy and chemical industries and the development of higher value-added products more appropriate to Korea's increasingly expensive workforce.

Expansion of export credits and reduction of tariffs on key raw materials used by export industries in an attempt to ease cash flow traumas and boost exports.

Imposition of severe fiscal and monetary restraints aimed at reducing inflation but selectively relaxing these in order to promote high-priority industries.

Whether this combination of traditional belt tightening and industrial restructuring succeeds, remains to be seen. But devaluation for the moment clearly is viewed as a cure worse than the disease. Inflation is already running at 21–22 percent, and the Bank of Korea estimates that a 10 percent devaluation against the U.S. dollar would add 4.34 percentage points.

Three yardsticks will be used to measure the success or failure of this attempt to stave off devaluation and should be closely monitored by firms concerned: balance of payments, company profits, and unemployment.

EXHIBIT 1 *(continued)*

Balance of Payments

Although officials expect a trade deficit of nearly US$4 billion in 1979, this poses no immediate problems. Invisibles—especially earnings from overseas construction services—will lower the current account deficit to about US$3 billion. Seoul will borrow US$3.9 billion to cover the balance and boost foreign exchange holdings to US$5.9 billion by year-end. Korea has succeeded in lowering its debt service ratio in recent years, and its excellent credit rating ensures that it will have no difficulty borrowing on favorable terms.

Pressure to devalue will intensify, however, if exports begin to fall appreciably. So far the government's remedial measures—expanding export credits and reducing tariffs—have succeeded in averting a serious downturn. Exports were poor in July but rebounded in August, posting a 26.8 percent increase over the same month last year. In the first eight months, exports totaled US$9.2 billion, nearly 60 percent of the US$15.5 billion goal. But if exports drop in the final quarter, it will have important repercussions—not only on balance of payments but also on the solvency of Korean companies and unemployment.

Corporate Profits

Pressure to devalue has come primarily from exporters that have succeeded in increasing sales in recent years only by cutting profits. The central bank's analysis of the combined income statements of some 1,437 enterprises shows that exporters operated at a net loss in 1978. Even the large general trading companies (GTCs) have registered dangerously low profitability (*BA* '79, p. 286).

The difficulties Korean exporters face are clear from a comparison of inflation rates and foreign exchange fluctuations since 1975. The table shows that Korea's inflation rate since end 1975 has been 74.3 percent—much higher than that of major competitors like Taiwan, 26.1 percent; Hong Kong, 29.2 percent; or Singapore, 8.4 percent. At the same time, the won has depreciated only marginally against these currencies. The final column indicates the cost disadvantages based on inflation and currency fluctuations that Korean exporters have in each market. The cost disadvantages have been particularly serious in the U.S., which accounted for 31.9 percent of Korea's exports in 1978 and where the exchange rate has been fixed. In Korea's second largest market, Japan, which accounted for 20.7 percent of its exports in 1978, Korea's high rate of inflation has been offset by a 27 percent effective depreciation since 1975. But Korea's success in increasing exports to Japan this year is more a credit to Japan's expanding economy, since Korea's major competitors have enjoyed both depreciation of their currencies against the yen and lower rates of inflation than Korea.

The figures tend to support the exporters' contention that the won is overvalued. The government hopes that declining profitability will force exporters into more competitive product lines. But unless government efforts to restrain inflation begin to take effect, companies will be forced to cut back exports and sustain greater losses than they will be able to bear.

EXHIBIT 1 *(concluded)*

Unemployment

Given the labor shortage that has existed in Korea in recent years, the slight increase forecast in unemployment will not pose serious problems and, in fact, should help relieve inflation. But recent labor incidents, increased pressure from opposition groups (*BA* '79, p. 266), and the general threat of disorder ensure that the government will not let unemployment pass the 6 percent mark—the level at which it chose to devalue in 1974. Presently, the government is seeking to reduce the impact of layoffs by stepping up vocational education and retraining efforts, consistent with its goal of restructuring the economy.

The government will approach the triple threat of a widening trade gap, declining profits, and rising unemployment with selective measures. By year-end it will be clear whether selective action will have to be replaced by devaluation. At the moment, *BA* believes chances are good that the selective policies will head off an exchange-rate adjustment.

Long-Term Threat

The longer-term issue affecting the won's future is inflation. Boosting the value added of Korean exports, reducing the labor content, and increasing productivity will, in the long term, overcome the competitive disadvantages inflation has imposed on firms since the 1974 devaluation. Continued chronic cost spirals, however, would threaten Korea's industrialization plans and hence the value of the currency.

The crunch will not come this year or next. The sharp jump in inflation this year has been largely induced by the government, and *BA* believes prices will come under control by year-end. The government's decision to release many products from price control early this year and the decision to pass on immediately the full effect of oil price hikes—plus a comfortable margin to allow for future increases—forced up inflation rates in July, but should in the long run stabilize prices. Similarly, the sharp increase in imports has been caused largely by the liberalization of import restrictions. Together with the decontrol of domestic prices, however, this step should increase domestic supply and dampen inflation. Finally, the total money supply (M2) will be held to a 25–28 percent rate of increase this year, down from the 34.7 percent increase of last year.

Unless the government can maintain monetary and fiscal discipline and prevent both national and corporate expansion plans from overheating the economy, however, the won may again come under pressure.

SOURCE: *Business Asia,* September 21, 1979, pp. 298–300. Reprinted with permission of the publisher.

Profile of Korea's Won (relates to Exhibit 1)

	Inflation Rate (%) 1975–June 1979*	Price Parity Ratio†	Equivalent Exchange Rate (won per unit of foreign currency)	Won's Effective Depreciation since 1975 (%)	Actual Exchange Rate (Sept. 19, 1979)	Korea's Cost Disadvantage in Overseas Markets (%)
Korea	74.3	—	—	—	—	—
Taiwan	26.1	1.38	17.58	6	13.56	22.9
Hong Kong	29.2	1.35	129.64	0	95.60	26.3
Singapore	8.4	1.61	313.01	13	224.59	28.2
United States	34.4	1.30	629.20	—	484	23.1
Japan	27.1	1.37	2.17	27	2.17	0.0
West Germany	16.3	1.50	276.86	31	268.59	3.0

* Measured by consumer price indexes reported by IMF; for Hong Kong based on *Hong Kong Monthly Digest of Statistics*.
† Korea's price index divided by the price index of the country to which it is compared yields the price parity ratio—the factor by which the won would have to be devalued to make the price of its exports competitive with those of the country to which it is compared.

EXHIBIT 2

Prospects for Profits; South Korea
The Next Five Years—political liberalization,
continued fast expansion, shift to heavy industry

Social dynamics.   South Korea's reaction to the sudden death last month of its long-standing strong man, President Park Chung-hee, exemplifies the social cohesiveness that helps see the country through rapid growth that could otherwise cause major upheaval. Despite a succession problem still largely unresolved, normalcy has returned. Several factors account for the relative calm.

One is a single-mindedness concerning economic development. Koreans are willing to accept virtually anything for the sake of this goal, which helps explain the acceptance of the Park regime for 18 years. The removal of Park from the scene has provoked a call for a political liberalization with initial support from the government and the military. However, the national consensus is to keep political confusion to a minimum so as not to endanger the economic development drive.

The other key factor is the presence of a common enemy—North Korea. A strong anticommunist sentiment in South Korean society results in moderation and mutual cooperation among the different interest groups.

Labor and the middle class will emerge as the new power groups in the next five years. Labor, tightly controlled under Park's regime, will strongly assert its rights in a more liberal environment. Restrictions that have virtually prohibited strikes are likely to be lifted and labor unrest will intensify during difficult economic periods. Unionization will grow. The government will retain an important role in labor-management mediation, but officials will pay greater attention to labor's needs.

The growing middle class will become an important political force. Rising personal income has sparked an explosive demand for consumer goods, and has already prompted the government to reverse its previous policy of suppressing the consumer market.

Politics.   Constitutional reforms that will allow for a more democratic election framework and a bigger role for the opposition parties have been pledged by the interim government. However, elections are not expected before 1981. Moreover, the ruling Democratic Republican Party (DRP) holds a clear advantage over the opposition in terms of party organization, financing, and control over the government's censorship apparatus. It can also use the transitional period to boost its candidate's image.

Ultimately, continued dominance by the DRP hinges on its ability to nominate a popular successor to Park. At present, the strongest contender from the DRP is new party boss Kim Jong-pil (a former prime minister and nephew-in-law of Park), who has both popular appeal and army support. By installing the politically weak Choi Kyu-hah as president of the interim government, the DRP may be able to allay opposition fears that the constitutional reform will be postponed indefinitely. It also allows Kim to further disassociate himself from Park's authoritarian system.

Major opposition candidates are Kim Young-sam, current leader of the New Democratic Party (NDP), and Kim Daejung, a formidable contestant in the last

EXHIBIT *(continued)*

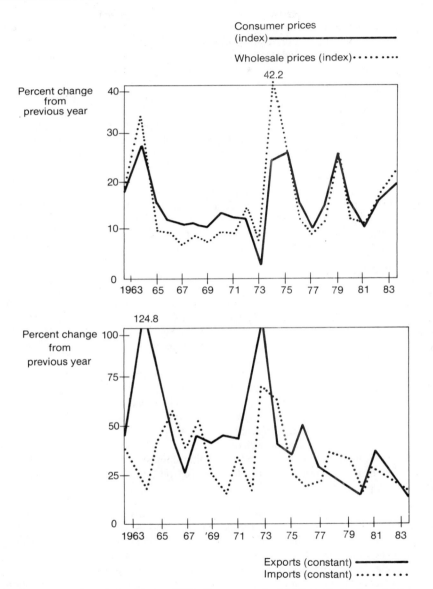

Consumer prices
(index)———————

Wholesale prices (index)··· ···· ···

Percent change from previous year

Percent change from previous year

Exports (constant) ——————
Imports (constant) ·· ···· ···

general presidential election in 1972. However, the NDP, with its long history of factional disputes, may find it difficult to agree on a candidate or formulate a platform.

No matter who will lead South Korea in the 1980s, no significant change in economic policy is expected. Several adjustments will be made, however, to channel

EXHIBIT 2 *(continued)*

resources to the domestic consumer market and improve social welfare through better housing, infrastructure, and transportation. Close cooperation between the government and the private sector will continue to assure that growth, industrialization, and export targets are met; but government intervention is expected to be reduced.

The external political threat may assume less importance. The U.S. decision to delay troop withdrawal plans allows time for South Korea's economic growth to fund buildup of its own defensive forces. Meanwhile, North Korea is likely to be influenced by China's modernization and concentrate in the future on economic development and expanding trade relations rather than on armed conquest of the South.

Economy.   South Korea is undergoing an anti-inflationary stabilization program that will slow the economy to 8.5 percent real annual growth for 1979 and 1980. However, over the following five years, a 10 percent yearly growth can be expected as the world economy picks up again and with it, the demand for the kinds of goods and services South Korea offers. Companies should watch out for a shift to heavy and high-technology industries as major growth sectors.

Exports will remain the lifeblood of the economy. Merchandise exports will exceed $17.5 billion in 1980 and reach nearly $40 billion by 1983. Imports will increase steadily as the government lifts restrictions and lowers tariffs to head off protectionism abroad, meet local demand, and fight inflation. Nevertheless, the $4 billion trade deficit anticipated in 1979 and 1980 will be significantly reduced in subsequent years, as exports increase and Korea becomes less dependent on imported machinery equipment and intermediate goods.

In the face of an increasingly costly labor force, the government will try to maintain the country's competitiveness by promoting high-technology, capital-intensive industries such as machinery, electronics, electrical power, and chemicals. MNCs that can provide technology and know-how that will improve the quality and reduce the price of light industrial or consumer products for either the domestic or overseas markets will also be welcome.

Given Korea's rapid growth and expanding domestic market, the profitability of foreign firms will remain high. However, despite efforts to contain inflation, the upward price spiral will remain a problem.

Investment.   Foreign investment will be pursued, especially in advanced technological fields. While most foreign participation will be limited to a minority joint-venture position, projects involving a high level of technology that local companies cannot match may be able to bypass local equity requirement rules.

Recent foreign investments in Korea include: a $3.5 million investment by Continental Group Inc. of the United States for a 49 percent interest in the production of cans with Hanyang Food; a 50–50 joint venture between ITT and Daewoo Industrial Co. for the production of prefabricated pipes for nuclear plants; and a $4.2 million 50–50 undertaking by CPC International (United States) in food processing. Also, IBM is investing $4 million in an expansion of its electronic leasing/servicing operations. Foreign investment approvals will exceed $100 million in 1979.

While Korea will increase its national savings and significantly reduce its savings-

EXHIBIT 2 *(continued)*

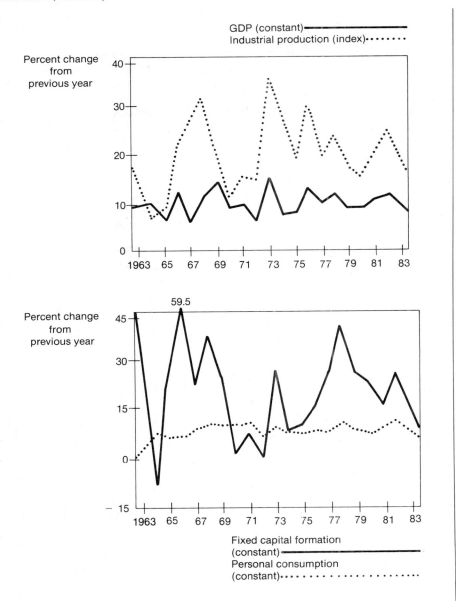

GDP (constant)——————
Industrial production (index)·······

Percent change from previous year

Percent change from previous year

59.5

Fixed capital formation
(constant)——————
Personal consumption
(constant)·················

investment gap, heavy dependence on foreign borrowing will continue, because of the large investment required to build up heavy industry.

Currency. In spite of a large current-account deficit—expected to reach $3 billion in 1979 and 1980—and high inflation, devaluation will be resisted. Instead, the

EXHIBIT 2 *(concluded)*

government will employ tight monetary policy and channel resources to meet supply shortages in the domestic consumer market.

In the latter half of 1980, recovery of export demand and a possible weakening of the U.S. dollar [to which the Korean won is pegged] will head off pressure for devaluation. In the long run, rapid industrial restructuring, with emphasis on heavy and chemical industries and higher value-added products, will improve the trade picture, and will eventually eliminate the current-account deficit, possibly forcing a revaluation.

SOURCE: *Business International,* November 23, 1979, pp. 374–75. Reprinted with permission of the publisher.

EXHIBIT 3   Exchange Rates of Won to U.S. Dollar

Date	Official Rate (won/$)
May 1, 1951	2.5
November 10, 1951	6.0
December 15, 1953	18.0
January 20, 1960	50.0
August 15, 1960	65.0
January 1, 1961	100.0
February 2, 1961	130.0
May 3, 1964	255.0
December 31, 1965	272.0
December 31, 1967	274.6
December 31, 1968	281.5
November 3, 1969	304.35
June 28, 1971	370.80
December 30, 1972	398.90
December 31, 1973	397.50
December 7, 1974	484.00

SOURCE: Bank of Korea, *Monthly Economic Statistics.*

EXHIBIT 4a Korea's Balance of Payments (US$ millions, 1960–1972)

	1960	1961	1962	1963	1964	1965	1966	1967	1968	1969	1970	1971	1972
Goods and services (70)	-262	-198	-292	-403	-221	-194	-323	-417	-665	-793	-801	-1017	-540
Trade balance FOB (70a)	-273	-242	-336	-410	-245	-240	-429	-574	-836	-992	-922	-1046	-574
Central government, n.i.e. (70b)	48	67	80	55	62	75	123	190	235	276	248	212	202
Other (70c)	-37	-23	-36	-48	-38	-29	-17	-33	-64	-77	-127	-183	-167
Transfers:													
Private (71a)	19	25	37	52	54	69	98	91	105	142	95	106	119
Central government (71b)	256	207	200	208	141	134	122	134	119	102	83	63	50
Capital, n.i.e.:													
Private (72a)	3	-2	-4	61	7	17	184	279	396	428	414	429	248
Central government (72b)	-13	17	11	34	16	-19	33	13	26	203	174	231	228
Net errors and omissions (76)	-2	-2	-2	-1	—	-2	4	10	5	-6	-15	12	39

Note: Minus sign indicates debit.
n.i.e.: Not included elsewhere.

SOURCE: *International Financial Statistics.*

EXHIBIT 4b Korea's Balance of Payments (US$ millions, 1973–1979 III)

	1973	1974	1975	1976	1977	1978	1979 I	1979 II	1979 III
Merchandise: Exports FOB (77aad)	3,284	4,516	5,003	7,814	10,046	12,712	3,025	3,590	3,991
Merchandise: Imports FOB (77abd)	−3,849	−6,454	−6,674	−8,404	−10,526	−14,496	−4,054	−5,087	−4,942
Other goods, serv., & income; Cred. (77acd)	852	837	877	1,646	3,063	4,456	1,065	1,273	1,177
Other goods, serv., & income: Deb. (77add)	−783	−1,147	−1,322	−1,712	−2,754	−4,228	−1,093	−1,209	−1,168
Private unrequited transfers (77aed)	155	154	158	194	172	433	92	102	104
Official unrequited transfers (77agd)	36	67	71	156	53	39	5	17	3
Direct investment (77bad)	93	105	53	75	73	61	24	27	−52
Portfolio investment, n.i.e. (77bdd)	—	—	—	74	70	42	43	—	−10
Other long-term capital, n.i.e. (77bed)	520	939	1,291	1,176	1,256	2,009	770	455	878
Other short-term capital, n.i.e. (77ccd)	3	696	1,123	534	−9	19	222	1,153	492
Net errors & omissions (77d.d)	41	116	−213	−240	−71	−318	−240	47	−138
Counterpart to mon/demon of gold (78c.d)	—	—	—	—	—	—	—	—	—
Counterpart to SDR allocation (78b.d)	—	—	—	—	—	—	21	—	—
Counterpart to valuation change (78d.d)	4	−1	9	986	330	−1,350	2	1	−1
Liab. const. fgn. author reserves (79x.d)	—	—	—	—	—	—	—	—	—
Total change in reserves (79k.d)	−354	172	−374	−2,299	−1,703	622	119	−367	−334

Note: Minus sign indicates debit.
n.i.e.: Not included elsewhere.

EXHIBIT 5 Korea's International Reserves, 1973–1979 III (US$ millions, except line D)

	1973	1974	1975	1976	1977	1978	1979 I	1979 II	1979 III
A. SDRs	31.5	1.7	3.9	7.9	12.2	14.9	42.8	29.7	27.5
B. Reserve position in the fund	24.1	—	—	—	—	13.6	13.4	25.1	25.6
C. Foreign exchange (held by Bank of Korea)	829.2	275.5	777.4	1,962.1	2,954.9	2,735.5	2,675.1	2,459.1	2,741.6
D. Gold (million fine troy ounces)	.110	.110	.111	.112	.147	.275	.276	.276	.277
E. Gold (national valuation)	4.6	4.7	4.7	4.7	6.2	29.7	29.7	29.8	29.8
F. Total (including all Korean banks' holdings of foreign exchange and gold at national valuation)	1,094.3	1,055.8	1,550.1	2,960.5	4,306.8	4,920.2	2,726.1	5,041.4	5,377.9

SOURCE: IMF, *International Financial Statistics.*

EXHIBIT 6   Selected Economic Indicators

Year	Money Supply M_2 Billion Won	Industrial Production Index (1975 = 100)		Economic Growth Rate	Unemployed as Percent Economically Active Population
		All items	Manufacturing		
1962	51.6	10.5	9.2	2.2%	—
1965	97.1	13.7	11.9	5.8	—
1970	897.8	37.4	35.3	7.6	—
1971	1,084.9	43.1	41.1	9.4	—
1972	1,451.8	49.4	47.8	5.8	4.5
1973	1,980.5	65.9	64.8	14.9	4.0
1974	2,456.5	84.0	83.7	8.0	4.1
1975	3,150.0	100.0	100.0	7.1	4.1
1976	4,204.8	129.8	131.8	15.1	4.0
1977	5,874.8	155.6	158.7	10.3	3.8
1978	7,928.7	191.2	196.4	11.6	3.2
1979:					
1	8,092.2	197.9	203.5	} 13.2	—
2	8,197.3	200.2	206.6		—
3	8,190.3	223.0	229.8		4.0
4	8,211.0	218.3	225.2	} 9.5	—
5	8,084.7	229.9	237.5		—
6	8,311.0	220.5	227.9		3.5
7	8,466.8	213.4	219.9	} 4.8	—
8	8,641.3	207.8	214.0		—
9	8,992.4	217.1	223.9		*
10	9,061.1	206.0	212.2	—	—

* In late 1979 the Korean newspaper, *Hankuk-ilbo,* reported that unemployment was 4.1 percent and increasing.

SOURCE: Bank of Korea, *Monthly Economic Statistics.*

EXHIBIT 7a Commercial Bank Deposit Rates (at or near end of month)

	1976	1977	1978	1979						
				June	July	August	September	October	November	December (projected)
United States	4.70	6.80	10.90	9.90	10.30	11.35	12.10	14.50	13.20	13.55
Canada	8.00	7.25	10.45	11.05	11.55	11.80	11.90	14.50	13.40	14.05
Japan	4.50	3.25	2.50	3.25	3.25	4.00	4.00	4.00	4.00	4.00
Switzerland	1.50	1.12	0.12	0.75	0.75	1.25	1.00	2.25	3.75	4.75
Brazil	45.60	39.60	46.80	41.04	40.92	40.80	40.68	42.12	43.20	45.00
Hong Kong	3.25	1.75	4.50	7.75	7.75	9.25	9.25	9.25	9.25	9.25
Korea	15.00	13.20	15.00	15.00	15.00	15.00	15.00	15.00	15.00	15.00
Mexico	9.50	9.50	12.00	12.00	12.00	12.34	13.68	15.13	16.80	16.75
Philippines	8.50	8.50	8.50	8.50	8.50	8.50	8.50	8.50	8.50	10.50
Singapore	3.75	5.31	7.31	7.00	7.44	8.12	8.44	8.31	8.12	10.31
Eurodollars	5.00	7.19	11.69	10.50	11.31	12.12	12.75	15.69	14.00	14.44

SOURCE: Morgan Guaranty Trust Company, *World Financial Markets.*

EXHIBIT 7b Commercial Bank Lending Rates to Prime Borrowers (at or near end of month)

	1976	1977	1978	1979						
				June	July	August	September	October	November	December (projected)
United States	6.00	7.75	11.75	11.50	11.75	12.75	13.50	15.00	15.50	15.25
Canada	9.25	8.25	11.50	12.00	12.50	12.50	13.00	14.75	15.00	15.00
Japan	7.42	5.47	4.50	4.87	5.06	5.38	5.68	5.68	6.16	6.40
Switzerland	7.50	6.45	5.00	5.00	5.00	5.00	5.00	5.00	5.00	5.00
Brazil	30.00	52.05	61.70	61.82	63.00	63.00	57.00	57.00	57.00	57.00
Hong Kong	6.00	4.75	8.75	13.00	13.00	14.50	14.50	14.50	14.50	14.50
Korea	17.00	15.00	18.50	18.50	18.50	18.50	18.50	18.50	18.50	18.50
Mexico	15.50	17.00	17.50	17.50	17.50	17.50	17.50	19.00	19.00	19.00
Philippines	14.00	14.00	14.00	14.00	14.00	14.00	14.00	14.00	14.00	14.00
Singapore	6.78	7.02	7.65	8.12	8.35	8.78	8.92	9.10	9.18	9.50
Eurodollars	5.50	7.56	12.06	10.87	11.68	12.49	13.12	16.06	14.37	14.81

SOURCE: Morgan Guaranty Trust Company, *World Financial Markets.*

EXHIBIT 8 Price Index: Korea and Selected Countries

Wholesale Price Indexes during:	Korea	China, Rep.	Japan	Philip- pines	Thailand	United States
1974	79.0	105.3	97.1	94.9	96.4	91.5
1975	100.0	100.0	100.0	100.0	100.0	100.0
1976	112.1	102.8	105.1	109.2	103.9	104.6
1977	122.2	105.6	107.0	120.0	109.5	111.0
1978	136.5	109.3	104.3	128.2	114.7	119.7
1979:						
1	143.4	114.8	103.9	137.5	117.6	126.2
2	145.6	115.8	104.8	136.3	121.1	133.8
3	149.0	118.2	105.7	140.6	123.1	129.6
4	153.1	121.3	107.5	145.3	124.8	131.5
5	157.4	122.7	109.2	147.1	126.0	132.6
6	158.3	123.6	110.6	149.1	127.3	133.3
7	166.4	127.3	112.7	151.0	131.1	135.4
8	171.5	128.6	114.5	160.2	132.6	136.2
9	173.8	128.9	116.1	162.3	135.3	138.4
10	175.0	129.4	117.4	163.0	137.3	144.2
11	174.7	129.5	119.2	163.7	138.1	141.2
Consumer Price Indexes during:						
1974	79.8	95.0	84.4	92.4	96.1	91.6
1975	100.0	100.0	100.0	100.0	100.0	100.0
1976	115.3	102.5	109.3	106.1	105.0	105.8
1977	127.0	109.7	118.1	114.5	112.1	112.7
1978	145.3	116.0	122.6	123.2	121.0	121.2
1979:						
1	154.6	119.2	123.4	130.8	124.1	127.0
2	160.0	119.8	123.0	130.3	125.0	128.5
3	162.8	121.4	124.0	133.2	126.1	129.7
4	166.9	123.8	125.7	139.8	127.4	131.2
5	172.1	124.8	127.0	144.1	129.2	132.8
6	173.7	126.1	127.1	145.8	130.2	134.4
7	174.5	127.2	128.2	148.8	133.8	135.8
8	175.1	130.6	126.9	153.9	135.8	137.2
9	177.5	134.8	128.5	155.7	138.7	138.6
10	178.7	134.4	130.1	157.1	141.3	139.8
11	181.4	132.6	129.6	157.7	141.6	141.1
12	181.4	132.6	129.6	157.7	141.6	141.1
1980	192.1	138.8	131.6	—	—	144.7

SOURCE: Bank of Korea, *Monthly Economic Statistics.*

EXHIBIT 9 Repayments of Foreign Debt
(U.S. $ millions)

1974	338.4
1975	284.1
1976	406.6
1977	536.0
1978	825.1
1979	
I	209.3
II	290.8
III	349.0

SOURCE: Bank of Korea, *Monthly Economic Statistics.*

The Korean Won (B): Devaluation

JAL flight 007 from Tokyo to Chicago leveled out at cruising speed after an uneventful takeoff on a crisp, unusually clear Tokyo morning. Kimono-clad hostesses were already scurrying about the first-class cabin bearing the first round of that endless flow of *saké, sushi,* and *sashimi* which made JAL first class so enjoyable.

David Louis didn't usually travel first class, but the tourist section was full when he made his reservation and he had just finished 10 rough days in Seoul negotiating with Korean government officials. Ten days in Korea in early January can be hard on even an experienced businessman, and Louis was still a bit under the weather from a bad case of the flu he came down with over Christmas and New Year's, which he had spent in Bangkok.

Louis enjoyed his new job as manager of the International Division at Willingford Electronics. He was home based in Chicago but spent one month out of three traveling in the Far East and Latin America. He had been with Willingford since leaving his position as assistant international treasurer at Fibrex Corporation in 1977. Recently most of his time was taken up with Willingford's plans to establish a subsidiary in Korea. Willingford had proposed a 2,000 million won semiconductor manufacturing operation, KOAM Electronics Company, in Korea. Negotiations with Korean government officials had been proceeding well, and Louis was looking forward to a meeting with Willingford's board of directors at 9:00 A.M. the day after he arrived home.

Louis settled back in the snug luxury of his wide first-class seat and opened his January 13, 1980, *Japan Times* to the front page. He could hardly believe what he saw. The headline, KOREAN WON DEVALUED 17 PERCENT (from 484 to 580), rudely blasted away his anticipation of first-class creature comforts. He must have let out an audible gasp because when he looked up an attractive young woman seated next to him was staring intently at him.

"Anything wrong?" she inquired.

"Only this," he replied as he held up the headline, completely unprepared for the long low whistle the headline elicited from the young woman.

"Will this have some impact on you too?" Louis asked.

"You'd better believe it! I'm the buyer for Midwest Sportswear, Inc., and it will certainly impact my operation and plans for this year's purchases. How is it going to affect you?"

Prepared by J. Frederick Truitt, Associate Professor of International Business, and Chong S. Lee, research assistant, Graduate School of Business Administration, University of Washington, as a basis for classroom discussion. Copyright 1981 by the authors.

EXHIBIT 1 Memo to Willingford Board

CONFIDENTIAL: Circulation Restricted

To: Willingford Board of Directors
From: Management Committee
Re: KOAM Electronics Company, *Prospectus*

I. After evaluating several potential sites in the Far East and Latin America, we have decided that Korea is the most promising location for our new semiconductor manufacturing operation.

   A. Under current Foreign Investment Promotion Regulations of Korea, our proposed investment is classified as a "recommendable investment project."

   B. As a recommendable investment project, it is entitled to favorable treatment including:
       1. Favorable tax treatment.
       2. Government financial assistance.
       3. Duty-free import of raw materials.
       4. Protection in the domestic (Korean) market.

   C. But the quid pro quo for this favorable treatment means that Willingford must:
       1. Train workers and managers.
       2. Surrender all equity in our project to the Korean government after five years at full compensation in won at value of initial equity contribution.

II. Willingford's proposed equity contribution to KOAM is 1,000 million won. Another 1,000 million won provide the other half of the investment and will be borrowed locally in Korea at favorable rates.

III. Pro forma income statement for KOAM for each of five years of Willingford ownership is given below:

Pro Forma Income Statement

		Won (millions)
Sales (1,000,000 @ 5,000 won/set)[a]		5,000
Costs		(4,000)
Labor—skilled[b]	(1,700)	
Raw materials:		
Imported (duty-free)	(1,000)	
Local	(500)	
Overhead	(300)	
Interest[c]	(500)	
Profit (before tax)[d][e]		1,000

[a] The present market price of imported semiconductors is 4,500 won/set. This price includes 500 won/set of import duties.
[b] The prevailing market price of skilled labor is about the same as the price used in KOAM's income statement. The location where KOAM plans to build its plant is a booming region with very little unemployment.
[c] KOAM has access to a special low interest loan from local banks. It plans to borrow necessary capital at the interest rate of 10 percent per year, while the average lending rate in Korea is 20 percent for this kind of project.
[d] Tax incentives offered by the Korean government to encourage foreign investment will lower the profit tax rate on KOAM from the normal 30 percent to the "full incentive" rate of only 10 percent.
[e] KOAM plans to repatriate all net profits to Willingford, Chicago. These profits will play a crucial role in Willingford's modernization and expansion program.

"Well . . . ," said Louis, as he opened his briefcase, and pulled out his Texas Instruments MBA calculator, "that's what I'm going to have to figure out before this plane lands in Chicago. What say we pool resources and compare notes. I think we both have some work to do. By the way, maybe I could buy you a drink?" inquired Louis.

"The drinks are free and I'm having Perrier," she replied as she unzipped her programmable HP. "By the way, I'm Annika-Karin Vilms. I didn't catch your name."

The material that Louis and Vilms had in their briefcases, is summarized in Exhibits 1 to 9 of the Korean won (A) case. Exhibits 1 and 2 of the Korean won (B) case show the reports that Louis and Vilms had recently composed concerning operations of their respective firms in Korea.

EXHIBIT 2   Summary of Midwest Sportswear Position in Korea (December 31, 1979)

CONFIDENTIAL

To: Mr. F. X. O'Malley, President

From: Annika-Karin Vilms, Buyer

Korea continues to be one of our principal offshore sources of high-quality merchandise. Along with Hong Kong and Taiwan, Korea provides more than half of the total value of our merchandise.

We are currently buying from four major producers and expect to do $20 million (FOB Korea) worth of purchases in Korea in 1980. The peak shipping period this year will be in May and June.

We continue to finance our Korean imports with 90- or 120-day U.S. $ FOB* letters of credit. The value of the letters of credit we have drawn will vary over the year, but at this time we project the following:

1980, 1st quarter	$4 million
1980, 2nd quarter	$8 million
1980, 3rd quarter	$6 million
1980, 4th quarter	$2 million

* The letter of credit authorizes the beneficiary (Korean exporter) to draw payment from a bank once the conditions stipulated (putting a specified shipment on a vessel in Korea) are met. The letter of credit is denominated in U.S. $ and is open for a period of from 90 to 120 days, i.e., the Korean exporter has from 90 to 120 days from the date the L/C is opened to do what is specified in the document.

Global Business Strategy

Alfa-Laval Thermal

In November 1975, senior members of Alfa-Laval's Thermal Subdivision, based in Lund, Sweden, had come together to review the subdivision's strategy. The subdivision was a major international force in the manufacturing and marketing of thermal products. It still held—as it had done over the last two decades—the position of dominant market leader in its chosen product area; but small cracks appearing in its structure and strategy were causing some managerial concern.

ALFA-LAVAL'S INTERNATIONAL ORGANIZATION

Alfa-Laval was in 1975 one of the largest Swedish companies. The original establishment had been founded in 1883, and over the years the company had diversified into a wide range of businesses. A fundamental Alfa-Laval philosophy, however, was its intention to remain in the manufacture and marketing of industrial products.

The company's activities could by 1975 be divided into three broad categories:

Industrial Equipment—centrifuges, pumps, thermal equipment and installations for the food industry, power production, mechanical engineering industries, shipbuilding, the chemical, pulp and paper industries, as well as for environmental control.

Dairy Processing Equipment—special processes and complete plants for dairies and certain beverage industries.

Farm Equipment—equipment and systems for milking, feeding, manure removal, hygiene, and cooling.

In 1975 there were four major company divisions: Farm, Separation, Thermal and Dairy, and Rosenblads. Activities which could not be easily incorporated into one of the four divisions were referred to as "Other Companies and Units." The divisions were profit centers, each responsible for a defined range of products and applications, producing for sale to the Group's worldwide marketing network and monitoring and influencing worldwide performance within the scope of their business mission.

Alfa-Laval market companies, as listed in Exhibit 1, provided outlets for

This case was prepared by Professor Kenneth Simmonds and Mr. Shiv Mathur, Senior Research Officer, of the London Business School. It was written with the cooperation of Alfa-Laval management. Facts and figures have been disguised to preserve corporate confidentiality. Copyright © 1980 Professor Kenneth Simmonds.

EXHIBIT 1   Geographical Distribution of Market Companies

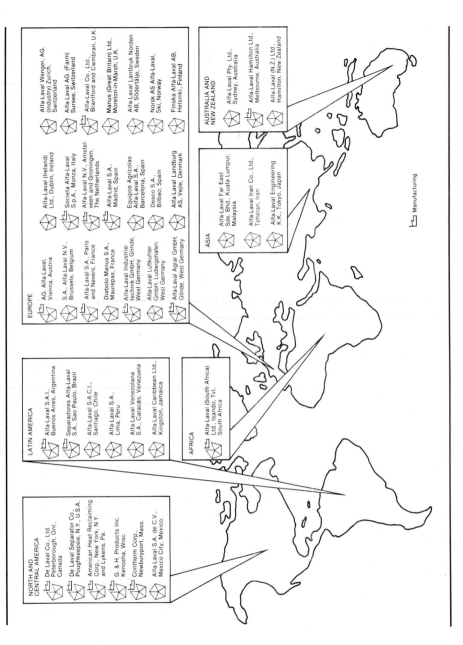

NORTH AND CENTRAL AMERICA

De Laval Co., Ltd., Peterborough, Ont., Canada

De Laval Separator Co., Poughkeepsie, N.Y., U.S.A.

American Heat Reclaiming Corp., New York, N.Y. and Lykens, Pa.

G. & H. Products Inc. Kenosha, Wisc.

Contherm Corp., Newburyport, Mass.

Alfa-Laval S.A. de C.V., Mexico City, Mexico.

LATIN AMERICA

Alfa-Laval S.A.I., Buenos Aires, Argentina

Separadores Alfa-Laval S.A., Sao Paulo, Brazil

Alfa-Laval S.A.C.I., Santiago, Chile

Alfa-Laval S.A., Lima, Peru

Alfa-Laval Venezolana S.A., Caracas, Venezuela

Alfa-Laval Caribbean Ltd., Kingston, Jamaica

AFRICA

Alfa-Laval (South Africa) Ltd., Isando, Tvl, South Africa

EUROPE

AG. Alfa-Laval, Vienna, Austria

S.A. Alfa-Laval N.V., Brussels, Belgium

Alfa-Laval S.A., Paris and Nevers, France

Diabolo Manus S.A., Maurepas, France

Alfa-Laval Industrie-technik GmbH, Glinde, West Germany

Alfa-Laval Luftkuhler GmbH, Ludwigshafen, West Germany

Alfa-Laval Agrar GmbH, Glinde, West Germany

Alfa-Laval (Ireland) Ltd., Dublin, Ireland

Societa Alfa-Laval S.p.A., Monza, Italy

Alfa-Laval N.V., Amstel-veen and Groningen, The Netherlands

Alfa-Laval S.A., Madrid, Spain

Equipos Agricolas Alfa-Laval S.A., Barcelona, Spain

Desco S.A., Bilbao, Spain

Alfa-Laval Landburg AS, Velje, Denmark

Alfa-Laval Wenger, AG. (Industry) Zurich, Switzerland

Alfa-Laval AG. (Farm) Sursee, Switzerland

Alfa-Laval Co., Ltd., Brantford and Cwmbran, U.K.

Manus (Great Britain) Ltd., Moreton-in-Marsh, U.K.

Alfa-Laval Lantbruk Norden AB, Södertälje, Sweden

Norsk AS Alfa-Laval, Ski, Norway

Finska Alfa-Laval AB, Helsinki, Finland

ASIA

Alfa-Laval Far East Sde. Bhd., Kuala Lumpur, Malaysia

Alfa-Laval Iran Co., Ltd., Teheran, Iran

Alfa-Laval Engineering K.K., Tokyo, Japan

AUSTRALIA AND NEW ZEALAND

Alfa-Laval Pty. Ltd., Sydney, Australia

Alfa-Laval Hamilton Ltd., Melbourne, Australia

Alfa-Laval (N.Z.) Ltd., Hamilton, New Zealand

Manufacturing

the Groups' products in many countries of the world. In countries with less demand, Alfa-Laval had distributors and commission agents. Senior management felt the coverage more than adequate for the Group's current needs.

Over the years, many market companies had drifted away from their original role as outlets for Alfa-Laval products. Some had set up manufacturing operations, enabling them to cut down freight costs and reap the advantage of a better local presence. It was, however, neither technologically nor economically justified to move all stages of production to local sites, and the more highly capital-intensive production tasks remained in Sweden for almost all products. As a consequence, the overseas manufacturing establishment needed for any one product was not large, and the local market companies had generally combined local manufacturing for various products and divisions under one roof. These manufacturing activities had often expanded to such an extent that the term "market company" had become a misnomer.

In a few instances, the manufacturing activities of market companies had expanded to include production for export to other group companies. For items that were manufactured by market companies for export within the Group, "Product Centers" at Divisional Headquarters in Sweden attempted to coordinate the manufacturing activities of the various units. Production for local markets, however, was considered the sole responsibility of the domestic market company. Exhibit 2 shows the breakdown of manufacturing activities for the Group.

Though some market companies manufactured both for the local market and the Group, there was a significant difference between the manufacturing activities of market companies and divisions. Production within divisions was in higher volumes, involved larger capital investments and greater R&D, and produced a much more comprehensive range of products. For example, the basic plates for heat exchangers were pressed only in Lund, Sweden, while frames and other components were made in Germany, Spain, the United States, and some other countries.

LIAISON BETWEEN CUSTOMER, MARKET COMPANY, AND DIVISIONS

The primary contact for either a Scandinavian or overseas customer was the local market company. In some instances, the customer could have a choice of two or more market companies; but such instances were rare, and Alfa-Laval attempted to ensure that in any one market there was only one representative for a particular product or service. In many instances, the local market company was competent to deal with all aspects of customers' requirements. In others, especially in cases of small market companies and complicated inquiries, there was a need to refer the inquiry to the concerned division.

Just as Product Centers within divisions coordinated manufacturing, so "Application Centers" coordinated and assisted market companies with marketing. A market company requiring assistance would get in touch with the appropriate

EXHIBIT 2 Geographical Distribution of Manufacturing Units

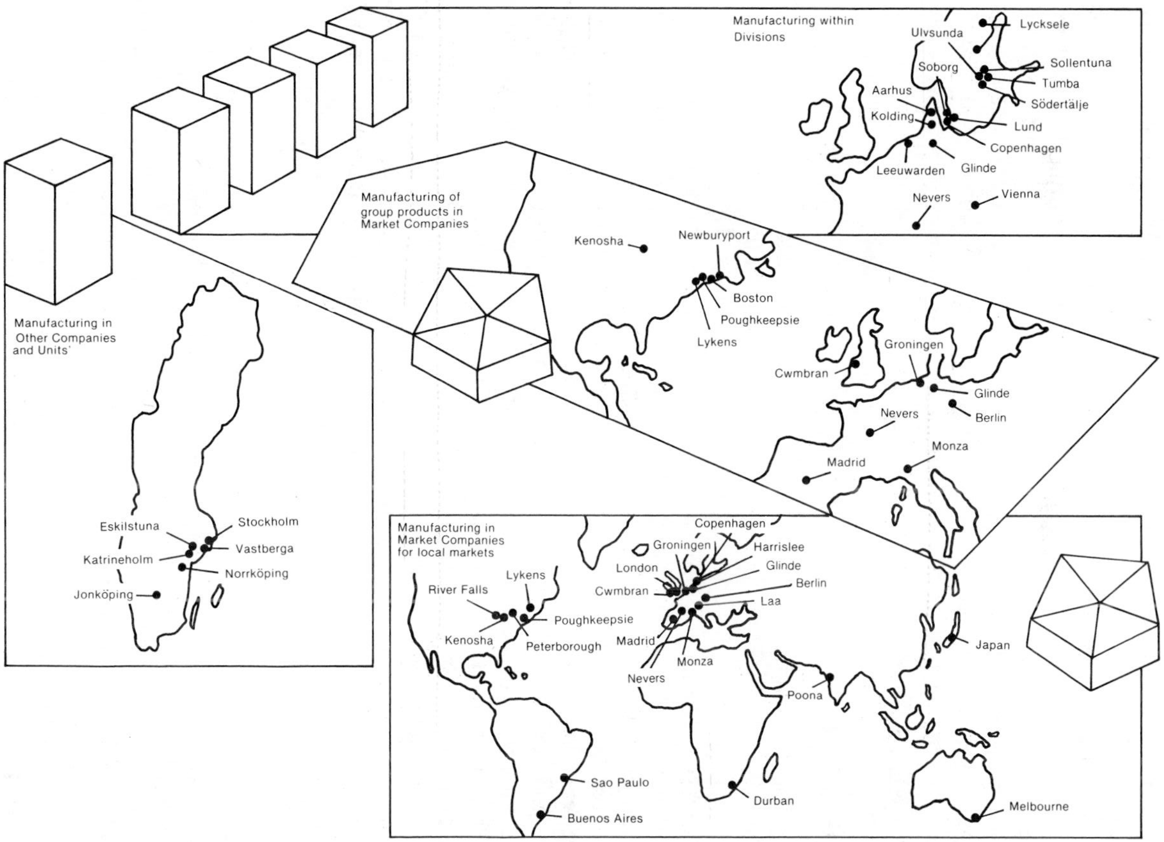

Manufacturing within Divisions

Lycksele, Sollentuna, Tumba, Södertälje, Lund, Copenhagen, Vienna, Ulvsunda, Soborg, Aarhus, Kolding, Leeuwarden, Glinde, Nevers

Groningen, Glinde, Berlin, Monza, Nevers, Cwmbran, Madrid, Japan, Melbourne

Newburyport, Boston, Poughkeepsie, Lykens, Kenosha

Manufacturing of group products in Market Companies

Manufacturing in Market Companies for local markets

Copenhagen, Harrislee, Glinde, Berlin, Laa, Groningen, London, Cwmbran, Monza, Poona, Nevers, Durban, Poughkeepsie, Peterborough, Madrid, Lykens, River Falls, Kenosha, Sao Paulo, Buenos Aires

Manufacturing in Other Companies and Units

Stockholm, Vastberga, Norrköping, Eskilstuna, Katrineholm, Jonköping

651

Application Center and the Application Center would answer the query or arrange for further assistance.

For the less sophisticated products, the local market company was usually competent to deal with the customers. For products like Farm and Dairy Equipment, where a complete system had often to be designed and tendered for, the liaison between the market companies and the concerned division had been developed through frequent contact. Over the last few years, the company had consciously promoted the sale of complete systems and often tendered bids on a turnkey basis, even to the extent of taking on the civil engineering work.

THE THERMAL SUBDIVISION

The Thermal and Dairy Division of Alfa-Laval had a total 1974 sales figure of Swedish kronor 312 million,[1] representing a tenth of the Group's total turnover. The division was in turn divided into four subdivisions. The Thermal Subdivision was responsible for the worldwide sale of thermal products and prided itself on being able to sell anything in its product area from small individual components to complete processes required for large and complex operations.

The key product in the thermal engineering field was the "heat exchanger." Heat exchangers were used whenever it was necessary to heat or cool any fluid. The conventional tubular heat exchanger, still used most frequently, consisted of a tube pack inside an outer casing with one fluid flowing through the tubes and the other fluid flowing around them at a different temperature and thus exchanging heat. The Alfa-Laval product strategy had been to concentrate on specially compact heat exchangers, based on more sophisticated engineering designs. There were four basic types of heat exchangers in the Alfa-Laval range, of which the plate heat exchanger (PHE) was the most versatile and represented the bulk of the sales. The others were spiral, lamella, and closed tube heat exchangers.

The principle of the plate heat exchanger is fairly simple. As shown in Exhibit 3, it consists essentially of a pile of metallic plates clamped together. Each adjacent pair of plates forms a "flow channel" with the two fluids at different temperatures flowing in alternate channels. Gaskets separate each plate from the others, thus preventing the mixing of the two fluids. Though the basic concept is comparatively straightforward, it is essential that the material used for the plates, the corrugations on them, and the material for the gaskets be chosen to fit the particular task in hand. Thus a corrosive fluid of high viscosity at a high temperature and pressure necessitates an entirely different solution from another at different operating conditions.

Alfa-Laval prided itself on its lead in the design of the most efficient engineering solutions for various operating conditions. The choices of plates, material, size, corrugations, and gaskets were carefully examined to provide a tailor-made match for a customer's thermal requirements. Often it would be necessary to

---

[1] In December 1975, 1 Swedish krona = £0.12 Stg. or US$0.22.

include other types of heat exchangers and ancillary equipment such as cooling towers and air coolers to meet the complete requirements of a client. The Thermal Subdivision had gradually expanded and diversified its activities in these fields to meet the market. In fact, this emphasis on technical competence and coverage had been explicitly recognized by the Subdivision in 1968 in its "Business Mission and Policy" statements:

> We are in the "heat transfer market" and should act and become known as "thermal engineering specialists." Our goal is to develop, produce, and market on a worldwide level, thermal engineering equipment and processes of a high technical standard and to get a growing share of the world market.
>
> It is our aim to obtain a reputation among engineering customers as the most reliable supplier in our range and also to maintain our reputation as the biggest and most advanced supplier of heat exchangers including software services.

With the growing software needs, the Application Centers at Lund expanded to take on a number of qualified thermal engineers capable of designing complicated systems and of consultation on a wide variety of design problems. There was

---

EXHIBIT 3   Alfa-Laval Plate Heat Exchangers

Alfa-Laval Plate heat exchangers are assembled on the construction kit principle from individual standard channel plates that can be arranged according to the needs of the specific duty.

The plates are assembled in packs and clamped in a frame, each adjacent pair of plates forming a flow channel with the two media flowing in alternate channels. Different channel groupings can be chosen to give the desired pressure-drop characteristics and flow pattern. Two or more independent sections, separated by special connection plates, can be housed in the same frame. The gaskets separating the plates—which may be made of different materials according to the nature of the medium—prevent any mixing of the two media in the unit.

Flexible Construction System

The construction system used for Alfa-Laval plate heat exchangers makes it possible to tailor them exactly to the requirements of varying working conditions throughout their wide range of applications. A plate unit is easily opened for inspection and cleaning of the plates and gaskets, but it can also be cleaned in place by detergent circulation, in which case it need not be dismantled at all.

The special corrugations of the channel plates generate an intensely turbulent thin-layer flow. They also stiffen the plates so that extremely thin-gauge material can be used. This improves the heat transfer coefficient and at the same time makes it economically feasible to use such expensive materials as titanium.

Typical Applications

Plate heat exchangers are maids of all work. Their handiness, high thermal efficiency, and flexibility make them far and away the most economical choice in a host of applications, subject only to the pressure and temperature limits of the type.

This is true above all in the food industry with special reference to pasteurization and sterilization of cheap food and beverage products, where heating costs must be kept to a minimum, and regular cleaning of the equipment is an essential feature of the high standard of hygiene demanded today.

Other suitable fields are general heating and cooling duties. Dissipating the heat from engine and machinery coolants—for example, on shipboard and in stationary power plants—is a field in which plate heat exchangers have proved their worth many times over. Another natural application for the plate type of unit is heat recovery in cases where a small difference in temperature between the media means that only a really efficient heat exchanger can do the job economically.

EXHIBIT 3 *(concluded)*

Flow Pattern in a Plate Heat Exchanger

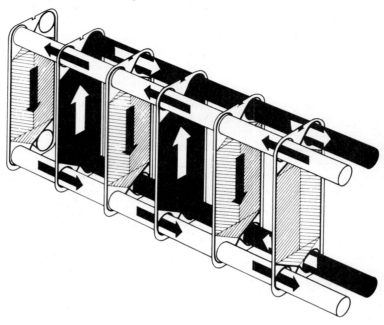

Plate Heat Exchanger Type A 20

also a gradual shift in the development section at Lund toward the development of large PHEs and those made of special materials for difficult operating conditions. Emphasis on the manufacture of large units and complete systems gave Alfa-Laval a competitive edge in the more advanced uses. Quality of Alfa-Laval products had always been good; but with steady attention to quality, it had become difficult by 1975 for company officials and customers to recall an example of outright failure of an Alfa-Laval component. After-sale service was mainly limited to replacing plates and gaskets which had succumbed to wear and tear.

By 1975, the Thermal Subdivision had five Application Centers in its Marketing Department at Lund (Exhibit 4). Market companies requiring assistance on an inquiry were free to get in touch with the relevant Application Center but were under no compulsion to do so. Market companies were given direct access to the comprehensive computer programs that had been written to calculate specific heat exchanger requirements, and a backup service assisted with technical drawings and after-sale service. The Marketing Department also offered training for marketing personnel in the technical aspects of the heat exchanger business. For all these services there was little or no direct charge, as Lund believed that these services more than paid for themselves through increased sales and better customer liaison and gave the company the very advantage that it was eager to retain in a market that was becoming increasingly competitive.

Thermal know-how was particularly important in the chemical, steel, power, and mining industries. These market segments were distinguished by large orders and large HE units often involving international contracting. Thermal management saw a great opportunity here for expansion in sales. While few products from other Alfa-Laval divisions were sold along with HEs to these industries, Thermal could draw on its strength of a complete thermal line and use its extensive application know-how to effect. In 1975, the subdivision's "Business Mission" was amended to read:

> We shall also promote marketing of complete functions for the large and fast growing central cooling market. That can be done by selling complete installations for seawater or cooling towers or by selling installation software with our heat exchangers.
>
> We shall have the largest resources, the best know-how with superior products and a reliable delivery capacity.

On large bids, or on business that might involve international contracting or that might be of continuing importance to the Group, market companies could if they wished approach the Application Center for an advantageous transfer price on centrally produced components to enable them to make a more competitive quote. Frequently, a market company would ask for assistance to get Alfa-Laval products specified at the design stage for a major contract; but in keeping with the company's policy of autonomy for its market units, the rule was quite clear—assistance was given by invitation rather than any Head Office imposition.

EXHIBIT 4 Subdivision U.2—Organization 1975

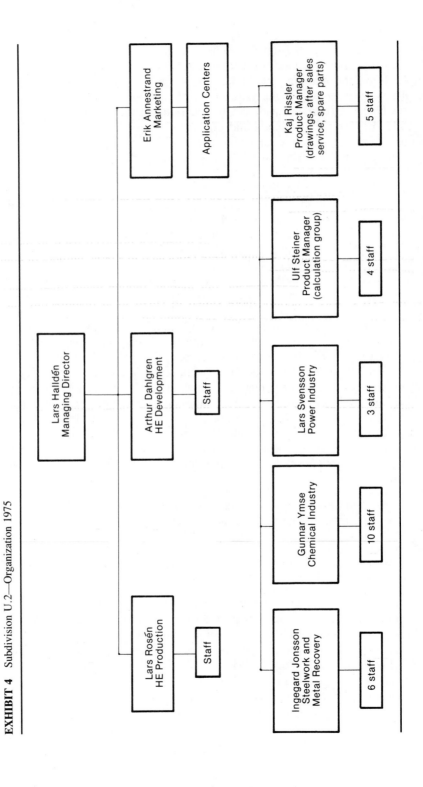

COMPETITIVE POSITION

The greater part of Alfa-Laval's heat exchanger orders—about 75 percent—was accounted for by plate heat exchangers, which competed with conventional tubular heat exchangers and PHEs of other makes. The tubular HE was, by far, the most widely used HE for industrial application and had a surprisingly strong hold on the American market. Acceptance of the PHE as a suitable replacement, however, was growing. For application in the marine, dairy, and other fields, where compactness, hygienic, or environmental effects of heat exchangers were major considerations, the competition was all between different makes of PHEs. In marine and dairy industries, moreover, Alfa-Laval's other subdivisions had strong process know-how. Exhibit 5 shows a breakdown of Thermal PHE sales by industry of application.

Through conscious choice, Alfa-Laval had not involved itself in the market for conventional tubular HEs, which were fabricated in a large number of countries by many small, highly competitive but technically less advanced companies. In the view of Alfa-Laval management, this market, though many times larger than that for PHEs, was generally more suited to small local manufacture and was not one where a company like Alfa-Laval could compete effectively.

The mix of small, medium, and large PHEs sold from Lund had altered over the years, as shown in Exhibit 6. Exhibit 7 also indicates the increase in size of orders serviced from Lund. Thermal Subdivision sales were shifting toward larger units and larger customers. This shift was not altogether an unwelcome change. The percentage of profit contribution from small PHEs for 1974 was not very significant, and the segment was coming under increasing fire from small national competitors. They had cut prices in order to break into a stronghold where Alfa-Laval earlier had great market and technical superiority.

EXHIBIT 5 Plate Heat Exchangers: Sales by Industry of Application

	1970 Percent	1972 Percent	1974 Percent
Power	2	3	2
Factory	5	4	4
Mining	1	1	1
Steel	12	15	18
Chemical, organic	14	13	12
Chemical, inorganic	18	15	15
Marine	18	20	21
Brewing, fermentation	7	7	7
Dairy plant	12	12	10
Other	11	10	10
Total	100	100	100
Index of invoice value adjusted to 1974 prices	83	78	100

EXHIBIT 6   Plate Heat Exchangers: Sales and Profitability by Size

	Percent of Total Thermal Subdivision Sales		Percent of Total Thermal Profit Contribution
	1974	(1975 est.)	1974
Small PHE	13	(10)	4
Medium PHE	51	(48)	40
Large PHE	12	(19)	35

In 1975, there were about 20 PHE manufacturers in the world. Of these, about seven were of any significance. The more important competitors were:

1. APV—United Kingdom.
2. Schmidt—West Germany.
3. Hisaka—Japan.
4. Vicarb—France.
5. Ahlborn—West Germany.
6. DDMM—Denmark.

There were very significant variations in the market share of these main competitors. Alfa-Laval now held perhaps 50 percent of the world market for PHEs as against

EXHIBIT 7   Plate Heat Exchangers: Alfa-Laval Thermal Sales by Size of Order and Model

Size of order in Sw. Kr.	Percent of Total Number of Orders	
	1972	1975
Below 50,000	92	80
50,000–500,000	7	18
Above 500,000	1	2
Total	100	100

	Percent of Total Unit Sales	
	1972	1975
Small	48	34
Medium	52	56
Large	—	10
Total	100	100

60 percent in 1970. APV was the leading contender, with Schmidt and Hisaka following to take much of the remaining volume. Even more noticeable, however, was the different level of technical services provided. Competition was largely confined to small and medium PHE segments. The bigger specialized products and systems that Lund was putting on the market faced little or no competition. Alfa-Laval's advanced designs, protected by patents, had given the company substantial cost advantages which the smaller companies found difficult to match. For applications in which the competition for plant construction was international, then, Alfa-Laval held a very high percentage of the market share.

The international distribution outlets for the leading competitors as estimated by Alfa-Laval staff are listed in Exhibit 8. Not all could be thought of as competitors in the international PHE market. Some could more adequately be described as national companies with export activities.

Of the really international competitors, APV of the United Kingdom was the closest with a broad range of activities in thermal engineering and a wide distribution and marketing system. APV had fifteen affiliated companies in the principal industrialized countries and numerous agents across the globe. In a manner similar to Alfa-Laval, APV had developed a wide variety of technical information and computer programs to promote its products. APV was particularly strong in the chemical, food, and dairy industries.

Competition from the remaining companies had been largely confined to domestic markets and, even then, often in specialized segments of the market. But the competition when faced could be very real indeed; and there were increasing instances of prices and quotations undercutting Alfa-Laval by as much as 15 percent or 20 percent, and these companies seemed to be gradually looking further afield for business.

In spite of its great strength and momentum, Alfa-Laval was receiving small

EXHIBIT 8   Alfa-Laval and Competitors' Distribution Systems

	Affiliated or Associated Companies	*Licensees*	*Agents*
APV	15 in principal industrialized countries	—	Numerous globally
Schmidt	Austria	—	10–15
Hisaka	—	1—United Kingdom 1—United States	Australia, India, Korea, Taiwan, Netherlands
Vicarb	—	—	10
Ahlborn	—	—	10–15; several agents in same country
DDMM	—	—	5–10

EXHIBIT 9 Penetration of Market Segments

	Industrial Sector									
	Dairy		Brewery		Food		Marine		Industrial	
Company	1973	1975	1973	1975	1973	1975	1973	1975	1973	1975
APV	Good	Strong	Strong	Strong	Strong	Strong	—	Weak	Good	Strong
Schmidt	Fair	Good	Good	Good	Strong	Strong	—	Good	Good	Good
Hisaka	Weak	Fair	?	?	Weak	Fair	—	Good	Good	Good
Vicarb	—	—	?	?	—	Weak	—	?	Fair	Good
Ahlborn	Good	Strong	?	?	Good	Good	—	Weak	Weak	Weak
DDMM	Good	Strong	?	?	Good	Good	—	Strong	Weak	Fair

EXHIBIT 10   Plate Heat Exchangers: New Models Introduced 1965–1975

Company	Number of PHEs Introduced 1965–73	Number of PHEs Introduced 1973–75	Expected Introduction
Alfa-Laval	8	1	—
APV	3	—	1
Schmidt	12	—	1
Hisaka	—	3	1
Vicarb	4	—	1
Ahlborn	3 (2 withdrawn)	1	—
DDMM	—	4	—

bits of information from various market companies that were causing concern. The Japanese company, Hisaka, for instance, had captured about 85 percent of the Japanese market and was looking enviously at the European and North American markets. There were rumors that Hisaka, DDMM, and the French company Vicarb were about to expand plate pressing capacity and might extend the size range of PHEs they manufactured. DDMM and the French had been having some success in getting into the coveted marine market. Exhibits 9 and 10 summarize Alfa-Laval's information about competition in various industrial sectors and indicate the changes taking place.

PRODUCT DEVELOPMENT PHILOSOPHY

Product Development in the Alfa-Laval group of companies continued to build on the very impressive technological lead that the company had established. There had been a steady expansion of the range of thermal equipment offered, and the company had most recently ventured into central cooling systems. Instead of providing individual HEs for the many local requirements in various parts of a factory, these developments made it possible to provide a single central cooling system. Such systems meant a substantial change in not only the hardware sold by the company but also in the software service provided. Some Thermal managers believed that the emphasis should be to educate the market on the economic and technical benefits of single large PHEs and associated complete systems, and to explain that these benefits far outweighed the disadvantages. Smaller but parallel systems could provide a built-in backup facility in the event of technical failure of single large units. Alfa-Laval management pointed to the absence of technical failure to emphasize the very low probability of such an event.

The philosophy of the Development Department at Lund, as shown in the following extract, was to retain Alfa-Laval leadership through creative new products:

A brief historical sketch of the 50s and 60s shows clearly that the key concepts for successful companies have been production and marketing. The company that realized the importance of building up an efficient, rational production apparatus in the 50s and learned to do so, was able to compete most successfully. In the 60s, which can be characterized as the decade of marketing, it was the companies who concentrated on developing their marketing capability that laid the best foundation for favorable development.

In the future, production engineering and marketing are unlikely to have the same decisive importance as in the past. They are, of course, still two important components of a company's operations, but their importance from the point of view of competition is declining. Most companies know how to run their production and marketing operations, so standards in these respects have now become more uniform.

It is research and development that will be the big thing in the future. Although product development has always played an important part in corporate strategic planning, the constantly changing external demands on both our company and our products means that in the future it will not be enough to concentrate only on the traditional engineering aspects. We shall have to broaden the base of product development in the future and integrate it into the corporate strategic planning process in a more concrete manner.

An ambition to lead the market, demands products of a very high standard and by the same token, product development of a very high standard. It is not enough for our products to satisfy the demand of the market, they must also be technically superior to those of our competitors.

The Thermal marketing group, however, believed that the development of new products and systems should follow an increase in the application of know-how within the company, including:

1. The search, within known and established processes, for areas of application:
   a. Where heat exchangers have not previously been used.
   b. Where compact heat exchangers have not previously been used but where other types such as tubular heat exchangers are already used.
   c. Where it is possible to deliver a high degree of process know-how.

2. The search for applications of the company's product mix in new processes.

Only a small part of the company's application resources had been directed in the past toward these objectives. The division's application centers had been more occupied in providing technical and commercial support to the field organization within established markets. This past orientation was partly an outcome of the technical superiority of Alfa-Laval's products, which had created their own markets in areas where the competition was not troublesome. There had been, however, a gradual change in the attitude of Lund's marketing personnel, who now felt that with the increase in competitive activity and pressure on Alfa-Laval's profits and margins, the application departments should adopt a more aggressive stance. Marketing personnel felt that they should be informed as a matter of course of all important activity and specially large projects in their respective industrial sectors and not have to sit and hope that the marketing companies would have the goodness to get in touch with them. To face the growing competition, the Marketing Department saw the remedy in aggressive central marketing activity.

There was another school of thought, however, that argued for decentralization of product development rather than centralization of marketing. Frequent discussions had taken place as to whether it would be preferable to retain the relatively large development group working internationally with the national market companies or build small engineering groups in each of the major national companies. Until now the primary responsibility for product development had rested with the division, but it had been found practical to keep some development activities close to production and sales in market companies. Thus most of the development work for cooling towers had been done in Spain where the relevant production unit was located.

PRICING POLICY

The Thermal Subdivision administered a complicated pricing policy. Despite a general acceptance that this policy was unsatisfactory, it had not been changed because the various alternative suggestions were either too cumbersome to implement or did not accomplish what the subdivision considered to be the central purpose of its pricing strategy—that is, to maintain divisional autonomy and, at the same time, provide the required incentive to maximize total company performance. Management's attitude had been to accept the "devil you know."

A company catalog laid down the Internal Sales Prices for products calculated as follows; note that these are disguised percentages but should be taken as actual for the purpose of this case:

Standard variable production costs, stock holding charges, etc.		**Production cost**
Work's overheads, specially installed equipment.		**Manufacturing price (MP)**
Product Division's charge for development and coordination.	Approximately 30% on MP	
Product Division's profit charge.	Approximately 20% on MP	**Internal sales price**
Market company cost charge.	Av. 40% on MP	
Market company profit.	Av. 10% on MP	**Customer sales price (CSP)**

Interdivision sales took place at the manufacturing price, and in about 80 percent of the cases the market companies paid the catalog price less a discount varying according to the country of destination. The size of the discount was determined through negotiation between the management of the Thermal Subdivision and the respective market company, though occasionally Group Management was involved. The discount for a particular market company, however, remained constant unless there were very special reasons. The aim of this market discount was to allow for the different competition, and hence price levels, that had grown up in the different country markets. In Germany, for example, Alfa-Laval held a leading market share, but Germany was a large, price-conscious market and under continual competitive pressure.

Where it was felt that a particular order was of such importance to the Group that a particularly low price be quoted, it was possible to request a special discount. This happened for under 10 percent of the business, but the assessment of whether an order justified a specially preferential price had become one of the major concerns of the application centers at Lund.

A number of dysfunctions of the pricing system had been recognized. These statements are taken from internal subdivision papers:

- It appears that the subsidiary is treated as an external customer. Since the easiest way for a subsidiary to improve its profitability is to obtain extra discounts from the product division, attention is drawn to the wrong quarter. But, on the other hand, the price system does not guarantee that the subsidiary gets enough freedom of action, e.g., in external pricing. The information transferred to the subsidiaries via the price system does not correspond to the actual position for the current decision.

- A subsidiary company can show good profits at the expense of a product division in Sweden.

- Each fixed internal pricing system has effects on resource allocation. To use a price system with a resource allocating purpose without either inform-ing the units involved or drawing out the consequences must be condemned. The relation between different product divisions (e.g., competition for the favors of the subsidiary) or between different subsidiaries (e.g., competi-tion for the same internal buyer) can be serious.

- The structure of the internal pricing system provides the subsidiary with little incentive to increase its volume. There is a tendency to "skim" the market.

- The Internal Sales Price is determined by a precalculated standard catalog price. A preliminary calculation such as this is always based on a number of assumptions about volume, distribution of joint costs, depreciation, and interest on fixed assets. Each estimation of these costs is more or less arbitrary and, in turn, is based on a number of more or less unspoken assumptions. With the present system for internal sales price calculation, it is hard to relate the cost calculation to the actual decisions.

As the Thermal Subdivision found itself dealing more and more with large international customers, problems were becoming evident on large bids with regard to division of profits, differences of price levels, and differences in technical solutions suggested by various market companies. For the Thermal Conference of 1975, a partially fictitious case had been written to open the discussion as to how the marketing approach, particularly pricing, should be amended.

THE CASE OF A MAJOR OPPORTUNITY

Alfa-Laval has market companies (MkA, MkB, etc.) in six countries: A, B, C, D, E, and F. There are three contractors competing to obtain the main contract:

> Contractor 1B has its head office in Country B and subsidiaries in Countries C and D.
>
> Contractor 2E has its head office in E.
>
> Contractor 3F has its head office in F and a subsidiary in B.

The ultimate customer, an end user, is located in Country A, and local regulations require 20 percent of the equipment to be manufactured in A. Alfa-Laval's MkA in A has local assembly facilities for some types in the product range, but not the types specified in the quotations.

Step 1. MkA informs Thermal about the project, stating which contractors are bidding.

Step 2. Thermal forwards information to MkB, MkE, and MkF, where the three contractors have their head offices. Since the project is at a very early state, none can obtain material for a quotation but must wait.

Step 3. Contractors start work in project design, and MkC, which has previously collaborated with Contractor 1B's subsidiary in C on other projects, receives an inquiry without knowing which project it refers to.

Step 4. MkB, MkD, MkE, and MkF now also receive inquiries from Contractor 3F's subsidiary in B. All inquiries except the one to MkF are forwarded to Thermal for coordination. MkA receives an inquiry direct from the end user.

Step 5. MkC, which has its own manufacturing facilities for some products, makes its own technical solution and its own price quote to Contractor 1B's subsidiary in C, still unaware of which project is involved.

Step 6. Thermal makes its calculations and prepares quotations with a recommended technical solution and bid price, which are then forwarded to our MkA, MkB, MkD, MkE, and MkF.

Step 7. The reactions to Thermal's proposal from the various Mks are:

> MkA.   Our MkA accepts and quotes the price proposed by Thermal direct to the end user and persuades him to specify plate heat exchangers.
>
> MkB.   Relations with Contractor 1B have previously been good, and MkB has virtually a fixed price level for this customer. Contractor 1B is committed to a particular technical solution for this kind of application and MkB will, therefore, not accept the Thermal proposal.

MkD.   MkD has generally been able to maintain a very high price level and, therefore, does not approve the level recommended by Thermal. The technical solution is acceptable.

MkE.   The quotation is accepted and passed on to Contractor 2E.

MkF.   It is discovered that MkF has already submitted its own quotation to Contractor 3F with almost the same technical solution but at a higher price than the one recommended by Thermal.

Step 8.   Thermal advises that its technical solution and price level should be used regardless.

Step 9.   Contractor 1B gets the order.

Step 10.   What happens now to relations between Alfa-Laval and the contractors?

Contractors 1B is irritated because Alfa-Laval has also quoted direct to the end user and takes the line that Alfa-Laval is competing with its own customer. Discovers that Alfa-Laval has different price levels in different countries and will in future ask for quotations from several Alfa-Laval offices.

Contractor 1B is annoyed that we argue for different technical solutions for the same application depending on the country in which the discussion takes place. We can, however, counter this by pointing to a different operational experience in different countries.

Contractor 2E has no problem.

Contractor 3F has also discovered that Alfa-Laval has different price levels in different countries, and having previously done business with MkF on other projects, now suspects that he has been overcharged on previous occasions. Will not give Alfa-Laval another chance.

Step 11.   Contractor 1B places the order with MkB.

Step 12.   What efforts have the Alfa-Laval market companies made and what permanent changes have resulted?

MkA.   Has persuaded the end user to specify PHEs.
Has passed on Thermal's quotation.
Gets the after-sales service.

MkB.   Has passed on Thermal's quotation.
Has carried on technical and economic discussions with the customer to explain away the differences in price and technical solution.
Has secured the order.
Has lost some of its goodwill in its relations with Contractor 1B.
Has lost a customer: Contractor 3F's subsidiary in B.

MkC.   Has worked out its own technical solution.
Has written its own quotation.

MkD. Has passed on Thermal's quotation.
      Has had its price level cut.
MkE. Has passed on Thermal's quotation.
MkF. Has lost a customer: Contractor 3F.

Subjects for Discussion

How should we modify our organization and methods to ensure:

- Closer contacts and coordination with main contractors?
- Involvement at an earlier stage?
- A correct price policy?
- Optimum technical solutions?

How can we keep the question of division of profits out of the quotation work and ensure that a fair division is made *after* the order has been secured?

- Who should be responsible for the technical solution?
- The price level?
- Who should make the quotation?

THE WAY AHEAD

Though "The Case of a Major Opportunity" was fictitious, it was sufficiently accurate to characterize the sort of problems that the Thermal Subdivision was facing in the international marketplace. The discussion brought home to all participants that fairly fundamental changes were called for, both in terms of distribution strategy and cross-country sales. Management was keen to decide what a future Thermal Subdivision should be like, what it should do, how it should control, and how such an organization should be reached, given the constraints of a hundred years of organizational tradition. Some managers felt that the well-established organizational culture was going to be a major stumbling block, that changes should be moderate and gradual. Others disagreed.

Blue Ribbon Sports

Blue Ribbon Sports, BRS, was the developer, manufacturer, and distributor of Nike athletic shoes. Based in Oregon, BRS management was currently considering the strategic impact of expanding manufacturing via a company-owned factory in Malaysia.

THE BRS STORY

Jogging first gained widespread attention in the United States in 1964 through the efforts of Bill Bowerman, who was the University of Oregon track and field coach. Recently returned from New Zealand, where recreational jogging was being made popular by the famous New Zealand coach, Arthur Lydiard, Bowerman published a book titled *Jogging,* which sold over 2 million copies. Then in the summer Olympic Games (1972) in Munich, Frank Shorter, an American, won the marathon. At the same time, a series of articles published by American doctors endorsed the physical benefits of jogging. What followed was a surge of interest in road races covering a range of distances from 10,000 meters to the 26-mile 385-yard marathon. Until 1972, a marathon was considered a quirk event, which kept many good athletes from competing.

These events and the resultant public interest highlighted the need for better designed, more comfortable racing flats. With insight, Phillip Knight formed BRS, Inc., and launched a new line of shoes designed by and for American athletes. This new line was named "Nike" after the Greek goddess of Victory. The first Nikes were manufactured in Japan based on designs developed by Bill Bowerman, who was by now the head track and field coach for the 1972 U.S. Olympic team. The famous Nike "wing" design made its debut across the cover of sporting magazines as John Anderson, wearing a pair of Nikes, won the prestigious Boston Marathon in 1973.

During 1973, BRS established four "Athletic Department" retail stores in key areas across the nation to bring Nike shoes to the public. Three more stores were added later, with a goal of bringing product information to consumers as well as feedback to the expanding research and development team. Contract assembly for new shoes was expanded into Taiwan and later into Korea. Up until the 1980s, all foreign manufacturing of Nike shoes was based on supply agreements with non-company-owned factories.

These factories produced shoes to the exact specifications and requirements

This case was prepared by L. N. Goslin. It is based on research by J. E. Isbell. The case provides a basis for class discussion and does not illustrate either effective or ineffective handling of administrative situations. Names and data are disguised. Copyright © 1981 by Lewis N. Goslin.

EXHIBIT 1 BRS, Inc., Annual Production (by country)

	Calendar Year 1978			Calendar Year 1979			Calendar Year 1980		
	Number of Factories	Pairs (000)	Percent of Total	Number of Factories	Pairs (000)	Percent of Total	Number of Factories	Pairs (000)	Percent of Total
United States	2	1,208	11	2	1,915	11	2	2,750	11
Republic of Korea	2	3,804	34	3	9,172	52	4	13,700	53
Taiwan	4	4,377	40	5	6,159	35	5	8,000	31
Japan	1	1,705	15	1	332	2	1	180	1
Malaysia	—	—	—	—	—	—	1	540	2
Thailand	—	—	—	—	—	—	1	400	1
Philippines	—	—	—	—	—	—	1	230	1
Total production	9	11,094	100	11	17,578	100	15	25,800	100

EXHIBIT 2   Nike Sales History*

Fiscal Year-End Sales ($ millions)		Percent Increase
1972	2.0	—
1973	3.2	60
1974	4.8	50
1975	8.3	73
1976	14.1	70
1977	28.7	104
1978	72.4	152
1979	149.8	107
1980	270.0	80
1981	430.0 (est.)	59

* Data estimated.

of BRS. To ensure a superior product quality standard, BRS maintained branch offices in Taiwan and Korea, which were staffed by American BRS employees. Branch staff visited each factory on a weekly basis, spot-checking the manufacturing process and finished goods inventory. Exhibit 1 shows BRS production totals by country.

Also in 1973, Nike shoes were distributed to non-company-owned retail stores by independent salesmen. In 1973, the Nike court shoe and wrestling shoe were introduced to the marketplace.

In 1974 BRS brought its innovative shoe-making technology to the United States with the opening of the first BRS factory in Exeter, New Hampshire. Before the year was out, 250 employees were cranking out 50,000 pairs of shoes a month. Research and development operations were transferred from Eugene, Oregon, to the Exeter facility.

The patented waffle sole, which was introduced in 1975, moved the Nike shoe line to the forefront of popularity in a nation suddenly obsessed with a need to revitalize itself through physical fitness.

To meet growing sales demand (see Exhibit 2) BRS expanded domestic

EXHIBIT 3   Nike Sales by Sport (percent of total sales)

	FY 1977	FY 1978	FY 1979	FY 1980
Running	45	49	52	43
Basketball	25	23	19	24
Tennis/Racquet	16	15	17	18
Children's	—	2	4	9
Other	14	11	8	6
Total	100	100	100	100

EXHIBIT 4   Estimated Market Share (percent)

	Running Flats		Basketball		Tennis/Racquet	
	10/77	10/79	10/77	10/79	10/77	10/79
Nike	42	50	11	36	6	30
Adidas	33	18	9	18	35	26
Brooks	1	12	—	—	—	—
Converse	2	—	61	37	3	1
Etonic	—	5	—	—	—	—
New Balance	3	5	—	—	—	—
Tiger	10	2	—	—	—	—
Puma	6	—	13	4	5	3
Pro Keds	—	—	—	3	—	—
Tretorn	—	—	—	—	15	7
All other	3	8	6	2	36	33
Total	100	100	100	100	100	100

production by acquiring a bankrupt shoe factory in Saco, Maine, during 1978.

BRS currently produced over 100 different style shoes for the athletic and recreational market. The running market continued to dominate Nike sales (see Exhibit 3). Nike shoes had a dominant market share position in the United States for running flats and tennis/racquet sports (see Exhibit 4). The company expected soon to become the number one seller of premium basketball shoes. Premium athletic shoes excluded those brands sold in discount stores or under a private brand label for Sears, Penney's, or Kinney's.

By 1981, BRS distributed Nike athletic shoes throughout the United States and in 25 foreign countries. For all practical purposes, the sales shown in Exhibit 2 consisted entirely of shoes. Approximately 89 percent of all Nike shoes were manufactured in contract assembly factories in the Orient, with the remaining 11 percent manufactured in its two company-owned domestic factories. Contract assembly factories refer to non-company-owned factories that contracted with BRS to produce Nike shoes for a specified FOB price.

MARKETING STRATEGY

The goal of Nike's marketing strategy was to achieve a generic brand identification, thereby making the name Nike synonymous with high-quality athletic shoes. Initial marketing was based on the idea that if you could develop a shoe to satisfy the serious athlete, then the market would follow. Excluding its leisure, children's, and "athletic look" shoes, this philosophy continued to be the focus of Nike's development efforts.

Nike achieved its dominant market position in sales of running, basketball, and tennis shoes sold in the United States by: (1) being an innovator in new shoe design, (2) demonstrating commitment to stand behind its product, (3) establishing a strong sales and distribution network throughout the United States, and (4) instituting a program which guaranteed price and delivery for up to six months from date of order. These points continued to guide the marketing efforts as the company developed its foreign market sales.

The concept of guaranteed price and delivery was first introduced to the shoe industry by Nike. The "futures" program was available to qualifying accounts (based on a minimum number of pairs ordered per year) under one of two programs. Futures I was available to large accounts, which placed their orders five months in advance of delivery. Smaller specialty stores could order under the Futures II program. These accounts placed their orders six months in advance of delivery. Accounts accepting 90 percent of its futures order qualified for a discount of 6 percent under Futures I and 3 percent under Futures II.

The futures programs accounted for approximately 60 percent of Nike unit sales. Besides bringing some stability to production scheduling, valuable market feedback for ordering the balance of the inventory was obtained from the futures programs.

Advertising was based on a soft-sell approach, relying mainly on word-of-mouth and through the wearing of Nike shoes by top professional and amateur athletes, although printed advertisements appeared regularly in selected running and specialty sports magazines. Financial support was also available to retailers who placed Nike advertisements in local newspapers. Top professional athletes in basketball, tennis, and, more recently, football, baseball, and soccer were on financial contracts to wear Nike shoes. The company also worked with amateur athletes and schools in promoting the use of Nike shoes. Regarding the latter, Nike offered athletic teams shoes which were often color coordinated to match the individual school's colors.

Nike's attitude toward marketing was best summed up by a phrase appearing in one of its more popular jogging posters: "Beating the competition is easy, but beating yourself is a never ending commitment."

COMPETITION

Converse and Keds were the predominant manufacturers of branded athletic footwear in the United States during the fifties and sixties. Their product was primarily canvas upper court shoes. Adidas and Puma were the two major foreign manufacturers. From the late 1970s, however, the athletic shoe market in the United States had become extremely competitive, reflecting a continuing high-growth demand and apparent ease of entry for new competition. Many shoe companies throughout the United States and the world had excess manufacturing capability and were willing to manufacture shoes under someone else's brand. Distribution and quality control, however, were crucial barriers for new shoe companies to surmount. Quality control was especially difficult where foreign manufacturing was involved. In some cases quality inspection at the factory by American personnel was done by U.S. firms.

Company	Market Area Penetration	Type of Shoes Representing Majority of Product Line
Nike	Nationwide	Running/basketball/tennis
Adidas	Nationwide	Running/basketball/cleated*/soccer
Converse	Nationwide	Basketball
Keds	East Coast	Basketball/children's shoes
Puma	East Coast	Basketball/cleated/soccer
Brooks	Nationwide	Running/baseball
Pony	East Coast	Basketball/cleated
New Balance	Nationwide	Running

* Cleated shoes refer to both football and baseball shoes.

The future demand for Nike shoes appeared strong. Current projections showed Nike's domestic shoe sales growing at an annual rate of 40 percent to 60 percent. These projections took account of the current state of the United States and world economy, production capacity, and BRS's ability to warehouse and distribute shoes.

PRODUCTION

BRS was currently focusing their attention on high-quality athletic shoes, either running or court shoes, sold within the United States. Characteristics of construction and material used for each of these two shoe categories are shown:

	Running Shoes	Court Shoes
Construction method*	Heat activated cement	Autoclave
Material used in upper	Nylon, suede, canvas, leather, PVC	Canvas, leather, PVC
Tongue material	Polyester, polyether, foam	Polyether, foam
Midsole	Sponge, EVA	——
Outsole	Natural and synthetic rubber combination	Natural and synthetic rubber combination
Foxing tape/toe cap	——	Natural and synthetic rubber combination

* See Exhibits 5 and 6 for definitions of terms.

MALAYSIAN ALTERNATIVES

Investigation of possible Malaysian manufacturing sources was begun in late 1978. A supply agreement was signed with a Malaysian shoe company, Malay Shoe Company, in 1980. Monthly production, 20,000 pair of autoclave-style shoes, commenced in April 1980, to reach 130,000 pairs by December 1980.

EXHIBIT 5   Heat-Activated Cement Shoe[*]

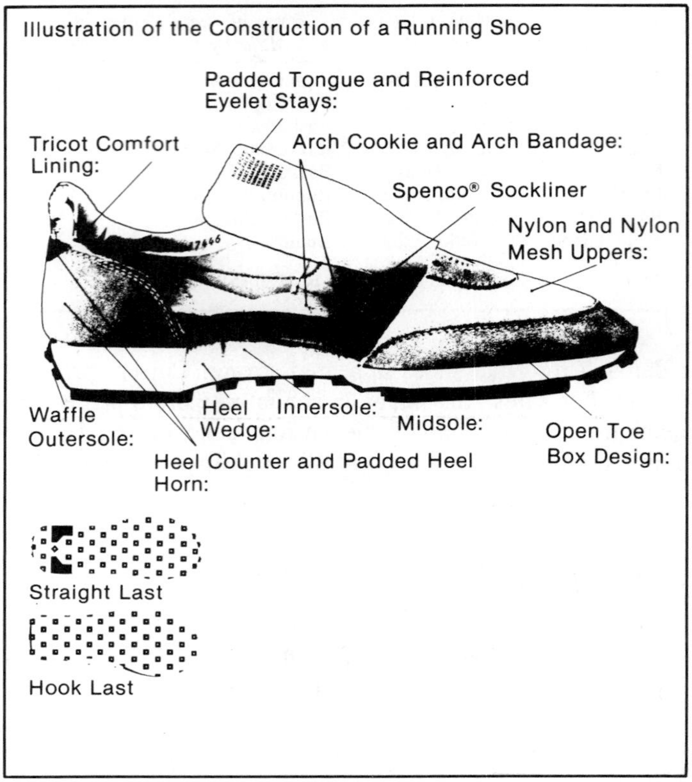

Illustration of the Construction of a Running Shoe

Padded Tongue and Reinforced Eyelet Stays:

Tricot Comfort Lining:

Arch Cookie and Arch Bandage:

Spenco® Sockliner

Nylon and Nylon Mesh Uppers:

Waffle Outersole:

Heel Wedge:

Innersole:

Midsole:

Open Toe Box Design:

Heel Counter and Padded Heel Horn:

Straight Last

Hook Last

[*] For shoe construction, cement is defined as chemical fasteners to make objects adhere to each other. Athletic shoes use a latex cement, which is applied to the surfaces to be combined, air dried, and then heat activated prior to assembly. It is this process in which the sole (midsole and outsole unit) is attached to the upper.

Two additional shoe companies—one ceased operations in August 1979— had also been evaluated. Both companies had the potential to manufacture Nike court shoes. Since each company manufactured very inexpensive canvas court shoes, a major capital investment would be required. The one factory still operating faced continuing financial losses (US$1.9 million current accumulated losses). These losses were attributable to poor management and a product with too low a gross margin.

In order to utilize either factory to manufacture Nike shoes, BRS felt it would need to make an acquisition and insert its own American personnel to manage the operations. Since this would be the first company-owned, foreign manufacturing operation, BRS was giving this decision careful consideration.

EXHIBIT 6   Autoclave Shoe*

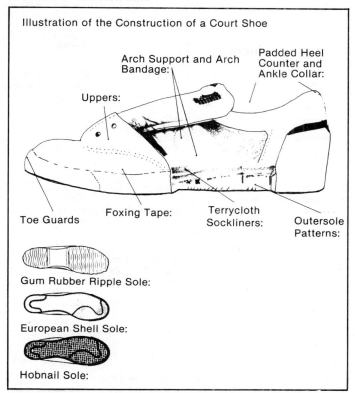

Illustration of the Construction of a Court Shoe

Arch Support and Arch Bandage:

Padded Heel Counter and Ankle Collar:

Uppers:

Toe Guards

Foxing Tape:

Terrycloth Sockliners:

Outersole Patterns:

Gum Rubber Ripple Sole:

European Shell Sole:

Hobnail Sole:

* Autoclave is a steam-filled chamber used for curing or vulcanizing rubber-soled canvas upper footwear. Vulcanization involves cross-linking the linear chain molecules of rubber to produce a stronger, less plastic material more resistant to temperature changes. The shoes are "cooked" within the oven at a temperature around 230°F. for 70 minutes. The oven is a pressurized chamber to prevent the rubber from sagging during vulcanization.

EXHIBIT 7   Nike Production by Style of Construction

Style of Construction	Percent of Total	
	FY 1979	FY 1980
Cement	53	51
Autoclave	46	48
Other	1	1
Total	100	100

EXHIBIT 8   Malaysia Investment Incentives

Pioneer Status:
1. BRS would receive six-year grant (five years for investment and one year for local content).
2. No taxes paid during pioneer period.

Postpioneer Period:
1. Capital investments during pioneer period are redepreciated at their original cost.
2. Cumulative net losses during pioneer period can offset profits earned in postpioneer period.
3. Dividends withheld during pioneer period can be paid without being taxed.

Basic Tax Structure:
1. 40 percent basic corporate income tax.
2. 5 percent development tax.
3. 5 percent excess profits tax levied on chargeable income in excess of 25 percent of shareholders' funds or M$200,000, whichever is higher.

Tax Incentives:
1. Export allowance: 2 percent of total export sales plus 10 percent applied to export sales in excess of previous period's export sales.
2. Foreign content: 5 percent if foreign investment is less than 30 percent of total paid-in capital and Bumiputra participation is 30 percent or more. If BRS were to manage the operation, MIDA requested an investment above 30 percent.

Financing Available:
1. Short-term loans at 1 percent over prime, which was 7½ percent.
2. Malaysia Industrial Development Financing (MIDF) would finance 50 percent of total fixed assets for a period of six years with a 12-month grace period during which only interest would be payable.
3. Preshipment financing was available up to a maximum of 90 days at 4½ percent. Amount was based on export sales.

Malaysia offered several attributes for an equity position.

Malaysia was the largest producer of natural rubber. BRS's chemist, in working with Malay Shoe Co., had developed a natural rubber compound which when compared to the regular synthetic rubber outsole, demonstrated a higher wear resistance.

Malaysia's political stability was excellent.

English, besides being the business language, was spoken by the majority of Malaysians.

Malaysia had a good source of labor with a prevailing daily wage rate for semiskilled workers ranging between $2.38 and $4.76.

Malaysia offered substantial financial and tax incentives to investors, especially to investments generating 100 percent export sales (see Exhibit 8).

Two firms were available for acquisition, NoMal and SoMal.

NOMAL SHOE COMPANY

NoMal was located in the city of Ipoh (E-poe), which is in the inland, central portion of peninsular Malaysia. NoMal commenced shoe production in

EXHIBIT 9 NoMal Shoe Company Capital Investment

Timing of Investment	Description	Amount (U.S. $000)
Initial	Land, building, equipment	$1,400
Initial	New equipment	950
2nd year	Replacement of worn equipment	50
	New rubber mixer	200
3rd year	Equipment to extend capacity	670
4th year	Replacement of worn equipment	50
5th year	Replacement of worn equipment	50
6th year	Replacement of worn equipment	50
Total capital investment		$3,420

1976. Due to poor management and an insufficient market for its product, the company ceased operations in August 1979. The asking price for the land, building, and equipment was $1.4 million. The total six-year capital investment would be $3,420,000 (see Exhibit 9).

A pro forma cash-flow statement for the NoMal investment is available in Exhibit 10. The calculations assume that one half of the capital investment, excluding replacement of worn equipment, would be financed by a Malaysian governmental agency (MIDF) at 9 percent with equal semiannual payments over six years. Principal payments would not commence until 15 months after project start-up. Short-term financing would be obtained at 4½ percent under the government's preexport shipment scheme. (These assumptions regarding financing would also apply to the other investment opportunity, SoMal.)

The major uncertainty surrounding NoMal was how much of the previous labor force would be rehired. The former personnel manager felt he could recall approximately 200 of the previous 400 employees. Employment needs would reach 750 employees by the third year after plant startup.

Two major problems existed with NoMal's location which could negatively impact the proposal. One problem concerned transporting the completed shoes to the nearest seaport at Penang. The shoes would be loaded into containers at the factory for ocean vessel shipping. Normally, BRS would use 40-foot containers on inland highways. This meant NoMal's freight costs would be almost double SoMal's annual freight costs.

The second problem involved living conditions in Ipoh for BRS's three American employees. Ipoh was largely a Chinese community, population about 500,000. The nearest international airport in Penang was a three-hour drive away. Although the international community was small, a British school was available. These aspects, together with Ipoh's inland, isolated location, could have a negative impact on the wives and families who would live there. See Exhibit 11 for other pros and cons associated with NoMal Shoe Company.

EXHIBIT 10

NOMAL SHOE COMPANY
Cash-Flow Statement
($000)

	Initial Investment	First Year	Second Year	Third Year	Fourth Year	Fifth Year	Sixth Year
Raw material purchases	$ 325	$3,418	$7,290	$ 9,880	$10,859	$10,849	$10,849
L/C and exchange costs		39	71	98	112	112	112
Nonmaterial portion of cost of sales		600	1,436	1,912	2,174	2,190	2,190
Operating expenses:							
Administration payroll		230	230	213	191	191	191
Administration expenses		180	180	166	152	152	152
Freight expenses		81	198	265	302	307	307
Interest on MIDF loan		99	79	119	115	93	69
Startup expenses		100					
Training expense		335	110				
Total operating expense		1,025	797	763	760	743	719
Capital investment	2,350		250	670	50	50	50
Portion financed by MIDF	(1,175)		(100)	(335)			
Principal payments			76	198	239	261	285
Total expenditures	1,500	5,082	9,820	13,186	14,184	14,205	14,205
Revenue received		4,084	9,926	13,318	15,179	15,400	15,400
Positive/(negative) cash flow		(998)	106	132	995	1,195	1,195
Accumulated S.T. borrowing		1,804	1,877	835	0		
S.T. interest expense		32	43	41	17		
Pairs shipped (000s)		952	2,206	2,760	3,373	3,422	3,422

EXHIBIT 11   Evaluation of NoMal

Location: North Central Malaysia

Pros:
1. Purchase would include fixed assets only, assume no liabilities of previous company.
2. Labor market appears strong, located in Malaysia's third largest city (500,000).

Cons:
1. Transportation limited to 20-foot containers from factory to ocean ports. Round trip cost to nearest port plus port fees is $336 per container.
2. The two autoclave ovens need to be modified to minimize labor involved in opening and closing door. Changing pressurized vessels in Malyasia involves a lot of red tape and time (five to eight months).
3. Labor force unknown quality.
4. Future expansion of the stitching operation will have to be off-site.

SOMAL SHOE COMPANY

SoMal was located in Johore Bahru (Joe-hoe Ba-rue), which is situated across from the island of Singapore in the southernmost tip of peninsular Malaysia.

SoMal currently produced a low-quality canvas court shoe for a Japanese company. Although their contract expired six months earlier, they still had four months of production to process. Because of the shoe company involved, BRS could not begin manufacturing Nike shoes until SoMal discontinued manufacturing for the Japanese company. See Exhibit 12 for SoMal's most recent balance sheet.

The present owners were willing to sell SoMal for $2,187,000 or $.63 per share. For conservative purposes, the cash-flow projections, Exhibit 13, incorporate this price.

Comparing NoMal's and SoMal's individual cash-flow statements, there were the following differences:

1. SoMal had an existing loan with MIDF and the Bank of Bumiputra (Malaysian State Bank), which would be restructured and paid off over a term of six years and four years, respectively.

2. Assuming you could retain most of SoMal labor force, the training time would be less and output would be higher in the first 18 months.

3. A private loan to the Japanese shoe company would be paid off immediately.

4. Less future capital investment, Exhibit 14, would be required at SoMal due to the existing equipment configuration.

Although SoMal's labor force would have to be completely retrained to manufacture the Nike athletic shoe, BRS felt the training would be less extensive because of the employees' present knowledge and understanding of shoe construction. Retraining was required because Nike shoes were machine-lasted as opposed to hand-lasted. BRS quality control demands were much higher due to major changes in the assembly process. One problem regarding labor involved the availability of additional labor in the area to staff future growth. The Johore Bahru

EXHIBIT 12

SOMAL SHOE COMPANY
Balance Sheet
9/30/79
(U.S. $000)

Assets

Current assets:

Accounts receivable: Trade	$ 37	
L/C	80	
Inventory: Raw material	253	
Fuel and parts	80	
Work in process	82	
Finish goods—first quality	197	
Finish goods—second quality	132	
Prepayments and deposits	44	
Total current assets		$ 905

Fixed assets:

Land (current market value with building $1,500)	319	
Building	680	
Equipment	1,270	
Total fixed assets		2,269
Intangible assets		101
Total assets		$3,275

Liabilities and Stockholders' Equity

Current liabilities:

Current portion L/T debt	$ 176	
Accounts payable	501	
Interest payable	253	
Other	36	
Total current liabilities		$ 966

Long-term debt:

MIDF loan*	633	
Bank of Bumiputra†	234	
Private loan‡	100	
Total liabilities		967

Stockholders' equity§

Initial paid-in capital	$1,248	
Additional paid-in capital	1,465	
Premium on stock	2	
Asset revaluation reserve (current market value $1,017)	516	
Retained earnings	(1,889)	
Total equity		1,342
Total liabilities and equity		$3,275

* MIDF loan:	Outstanding loan as of October 31, 1979	$663
	Interest payments in arrears	253
	Total balance due	$916

This would be restructured over six-year term at 9.5 percent with 12- to 15-month grace period during which only interest would be paid.

† Bank of Bumiputra restructured at 8 percent over four years with semiannual payments.

‡ This loan has to be paid off immediately.

§ Equity:
Number shares outstanding: 3,471,000
Goodwill estimated by current owners: $.10/share:

	Without Goodwill	With Goodwill
Without revaluation	$.39	$.49
With revaluation	$.53	$.63

Owner's proposed purchase price: 3,471,000 × $.63 = $2,187,000

EXHIBIT 13 SoMal Shoe Company Cash-Flow Statement (U.S. $000)

	Investment	First Year	Second Year	Third Year	Fourth Year	Fifth Year	Sixth Year
Raw material purchases	$ 325	$ 4,519	$7,332	$ 9,880	$10,849	$10,849	$10,849
L/C and exchange costs		47	73	98	112	112	112
Nonmaterial portion of cost of sales		801	1,512	1,912	2,174	2,190	2,190
Operating expenses:							
Administration payroll		230	230	213	191	191	191
Administration expenses		180	180	166	152	152	152
Freight expenses		50	99	123	151	153	153
Interest on MIDF loan		100	200	190	168	134	98
Interest on Bumiputra loan		11	17	13	7	2	
Startup expenses		100					
Training expense		297					
Total operating expense		$ 968	$ 726	$ 705	$ 669	$ 632	$ 594
Private loan payment	2,600	100					
Capital investment	(1,300)		50	400	50	50	50
Portion financed by MIDF	1,625			(200)			
Principal payments		25	196	376	426	430	432
Total expenditures		$ 6,460	$9,889	$13,171	$14,280	$14,263	$14,227
Revenue received		5,108	9,936	12,420	15,179	15,400	15,400
Positive/(negative) cash flow		$(1,352)	$ 47	$ (751)	$ 889	$ 1,137	$ 1,173
Accumulated S.T. borrowing		2,490	2,696	2,157	1,337	279	
S.T. interest expense		41	60	79	79	36	
Pairs shipped (000s)		1,135	2,208	2,760	3,373	3,422	3,422

EXHIBIT 14   SoMal Shoe Company Capital Investment

Timing of Investment	Description	Amount (U.S. $000)
Initial	Land, building, equipment	2,600
2nd year	Replacement of worn equipment	50
3rd year	Equipment to expand capacity	400
4th year	Replacement of worn equipment	50
5th year	Replacement of worn equipment	50
6th year	Replacement of worn equipment	50
Total capital investment		3,200

EXHIBIT 15   Evaluation of SoMal

Location: Southern tip of Malaysia, across the channel from Singapore

Pros:
1. Acquiring an existing labor force, although requiring extensive retraining, should result in faster achievement of desired product goals.
2. Location to Singapore will facilitate shipping. Forty-foot containers can be shipped directly from factory to ocean port. Round trip cost plus port fees is $357.
3. Autoclave ovens employ hydraulic-lift door mechanisms allowing fast loading and unloading.
4. Includes purchase of five acres adjacent to the plant for future expansion.

Cons:
1. Acquiring working capital and debts of an existing company.
2. Competition with electronic firms and Singapore regarding future labor source. At one time, plant employed 700 people; although current employment is 400 people.
3. Currently committed to manufacturing shoes for Japanese company through April 1980, based on a contract which expired in September 1979.

area competed with Singapore (higher pay) and electronic firms, which offered higher pay and better working conditions. Since SoMal's employment reached a high of 700 people one year ago, the present management felt BRS could attract an additional 350 people to reach the necessary 750 people required for the third year expansion plans. See Exhibit 15 for a further assessment of SoMal.

OBSERVATIONS

If BRS decided to acquire either NoMal or SoMal, they would relocate three of their U.S. employees to run the operation. A personal sketch of each individual is shown below:

Art Evans—Selected for general manager position
Age: 50
Years of employment with BRS: 2 years
Years of shoe mfg. experience: 20 years
Current position: Assistant general manager at Saco factory (Maine)

EXHIBIT 16 Nike, Inc., Organization Chart

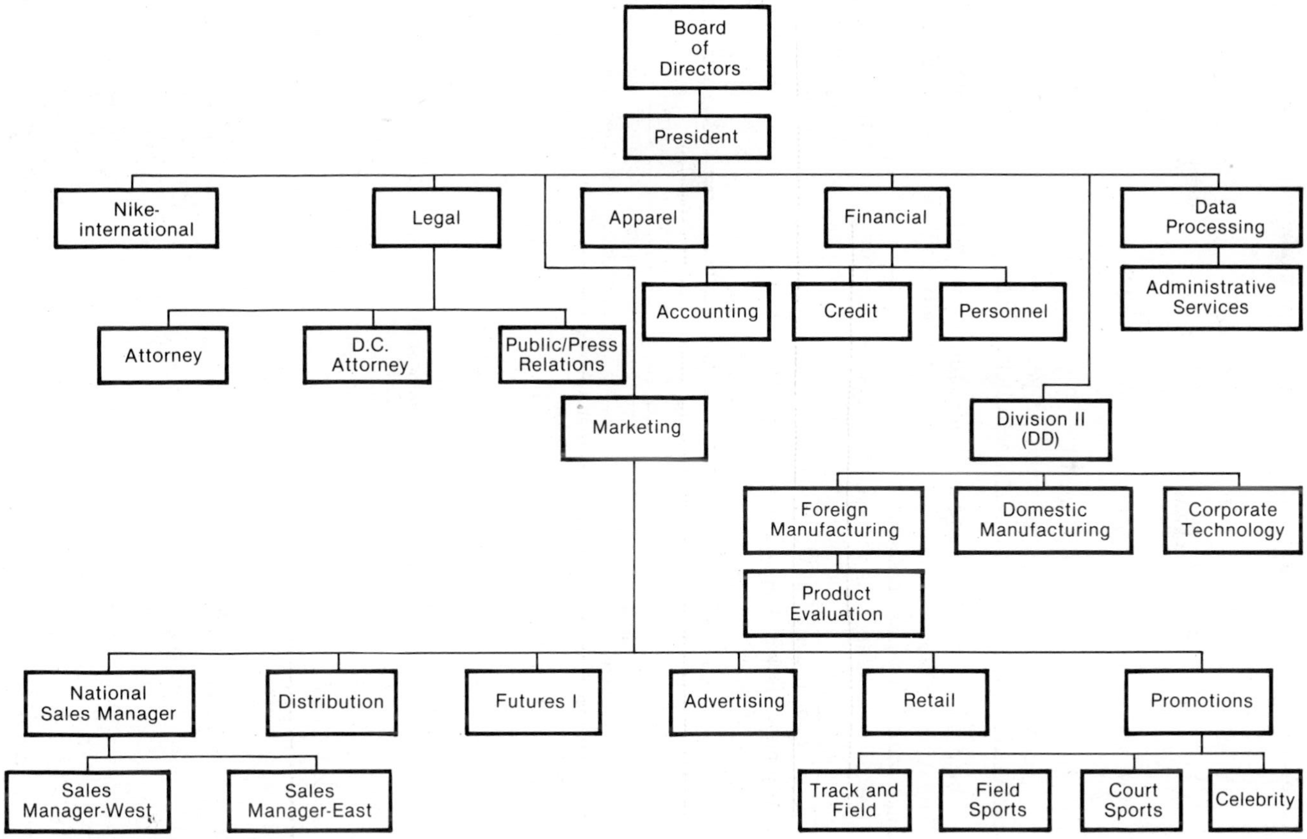

Sam Pickett—Selected for production control manager position
  Age: 30
  Years of employment with BRS: 5 years
  Years of shoe mfg. experience: 2 years
  Current position: Production control manager at Saco factory

Jim Anderson—Selected for controller position
  Age: 29
  Years of employment with BRS: 2 years
  Years of shoe mfg. experience: 2 years
  Current position: Assistant controller at Saco plant

The production control and controller functions would be handled eventually by Malaysian nationals. Sam and Jim would probably be reassigned after the second and third years, respectively.

BRS, in conjunction with the Malaysian government's desire, would keep their foreign equity in the new corporation at 49 percent. The remaining equity would be contributed by Malaysian partner(s), whom BRS had already invited to participate. Depending on which company, if any, was acquired, the equity picture would be:

	NoMal	SoMal
BRS, Inc.	49%	49%
Malaysian partners in rubber	51	30
SoMal's president and largest shareholder	—	21

EXHIBIT 17a

NIKE, INC.
Consolidated Statement of Income
Nine Months Ended February 28
($000)

	1981	1980
Revenues	$322,958	$177,149
Costs and expenses:		
Cost of sales	231,279	130,074
Selling and administrative	43,673	26,365
Interest expense	11,569	5,610
Other (income) expense	(57)	(94)
	286,464	161,955
Income before taxes	36,494	15,194
Income taxes	17,874	7,444
Net income	$ 18,620	$ 7,750
Net income per common share	$ 1.11	$ .48
Average number of common and common equivalent shares outstanding	16,740	16,140

EXHIBIT 17b

NIKE, INC.
Consolidated Balance Sheet
February 28
($000)

	1981	1980
Assets		
Current assets:		
Cash	$ 2,261	$ 18
Accounts receivable	90,845	53,629
Inventories	126,556	53,659
Deferred income taxes	1,150	—
Prepaid expenses	3,030	1,405
	223,842	108,711
Property, plant, and equipment	21,476	12,513
Less: Accumulated depreciation	6,507	3,069
	14,969	9,444
Other assets	672	432
Total assets	$239,483	$118,587
Liabilities and Shareholders' Equity		
Current liabilities:		
Current portion of long-term debt	$ 6,411	$ 467
Notes payable to bank	64,065	36,000
Accounts payable	61,111	31,586
Accrued liabilities	13,332	17,378
Income taxes payable	8,874	3,696
Deferred income taxes	—	531
	153,793	89,658
Long-term debt	9,697	4,621
Redeemable preferred stock	300	300
Shareholders' equity	75,693	24,008
Total liabilities and shareholders' equity	$239,483	$118,587

BRS felt Malaysia could become a valuable production source country. A supply agreement had been signed with the Malay Shoe Company (MSC), which would be producing 130,000 pairs of Nike athletic shoes per month by December 1980. MSC, however, wanted to limit Nike shoe capacity to 175,000 per month.

If BRS decided to purchase either NoMal or SoMal, this would be the first equity position in a foreign factory. BRS was estimating that an additional monthly production of 285,000 pairs could come from Malaysia.

STRONG TRENDS IN THE 80s

Nike would surpass Adidas in domestic shoe sales.

Converse would remain a solid number three, having stabilized their previous years of sales decline. They should continue to lose market share to Nike in basketball sales.

Keds, having been purchased from Uniroyal by Stride-Rite, should have renewed momentum; although not significant, it should keep them at number four.

Brooks would continue its fast growth if they had another good year of ratings in the Runners World survey. Nike had publicly withdrawn from the shoe survey which could have a negative impact on its sales of running shoes. Brooks was also introducing a line of court shoes in 1980.

New Balance also showed strong growth in running shoes.

Dexion Overseas Ltd.

In November 1975, Mr. John Foster, recently appointed Managing Director, and Mr. Keith Galpin, Marketing Manager, of Dexion Overseas Limited (DOS), were attempting to give new direction to Dexion's overseas activities. Dexion had, over the years, grown substantially but somewhat haphazardly in its export markets; and it seemed to the two managers that it was time for a full review of the company's present position and future overseas activities. They were particularly concerned with DOS's operations in Africa and the Middle East as these regions characterized the changing political and economic conditions in most of Dexion's overseas markets.

DEXION-COMINO INTERNATIONAL LTD.

Dexion-Comino International Ltd. was founded before World War II to manufacture slotted angles invented by Demetrius Comino as a solution to the recurring need for easily erectable and demountable industrial structures. What was initially jokingly referred to as "industrial meccano" soon acquired wide acceptance. Mr. Comino's initial investment of £14,000 in a 4,000-square-foot factory in north London had by 1968 grown into a 200,000 square-foot site at Hemel Hempstead producing well over 50 million feet of slotted angles. By 1973 Dexion was well established as a worldwide name with wholly owned subsidiaries in North America, Europe, and Australia, and exports accounting for over 60 percent of the U.K. factory's total turnover.

Product Range

As the group's turnover and geographic coverage had increased, so had the company's range of products. What had started as ordinary slotted angles (known as DCP—Dexion Catalogue Products) that could be erected by almost anybody, had gradually grown in sophistication. By 1975 Dexion was a world leader in manufacturing and installing complete materials handling systems.

In the developed countries the continuing search for more efficient techniques of storage and materials handling resulted in a rapid growth of the "unit load concept" (various small parts being containerized for efficient storage)—and in

This case was prepared by Shiv Mathur, of the London Business School. It was written with the cooperation of Dexion management. Facts and figures have been disguised to preserve confidentiality. Financial support was provided by The British Overseas Trade Board. © London Business School, 1976. Revised 1981.

particular the use of pallets. Dexion systems like "Speedlock" adjustable pallet racking were developed to meet this need. The Speedlock range permitted vertical storage to a height limited only by the height of the building itself. When fitted with wheels the racks, then known as "Powerpacks," could be mounted on steel rails permitting the closing down of an aisle and opening up of a new one at the touch of a switch.

By 1975 Dexion manufactured a whole family of products that served particular applications. "Apton" square tube framing had been designed for the smarter display of goods; "Clearspan" and "Impex" shelving for better storage of hand-loaded goods; and "Maxi" for storing small items. The basic DCP range was also modified and extended to meet entirely new applications. For example, DCP products that were usually used for storage had been modified to facilitate the construction of prefabricated housing units in developing countries. The growth of new products in many instances had also produced growth for DCP products as they constituted basic ingredients of the more advanced designs.

Overseas Activities

Until 1970 overseas growth of Dexion's activities had been largely organic. As Dexion products had gained popularity, the company had set up subsidiaries in North America, Europe, and Australia. In other countries of the world Dexion had appointed distributors to stock and retail the products. Where local demand was fairly substantial but import restrictions prevented direct export and circumstances did not justify a subsidiary, local manufacturers had been licensed to produce and sell some products in the Dexion range. By the early 1970s Dexion had licensing arrangements with manufacturers in various parts of the world (Exhibit 1), although few were in Africa and the Middle East.

The actual agreement varied from licensee to licensee and reflected the company's attitude at the time the agreement was actually signed. Agreements usually specified a royalty income based on a percentage of turnover, often with a minimum annual payment. Dexion had little control over the pricing and marketing policies of its licensees, though sometimes restrictions were placed on their export activities. As the majority of licensees were mainly concerned with building up strong positions in their home markets, pressure to export to third countries in competition with Dexion's own direct export activities was not a major factor. The problems as seen at Dexion headquarters were not so much of licensee exports to third-country markets, but of ensuring that they developed their home markets and that licensee income due was in fact repatriated. Since many of the licensee markets had recurring balance-of-payment problems, the actual collection of royalties was of continuing concern.

Competition with Dexion products, both in the United Kingdom and overseas, had multiplied. Dexion, however, had maintained its market leadership in the United Kingdom. Overseas, in addition to budding indigenous manufacturers, Dexion was facing growing competition from Italian and continental exporters and lately the Japanese and Indians. But Dexion products were well established

EXHIBIT 1   Licensed Product Sales, Royalty Income, and Products Licensed

Country (year of agreement)	Licensee (1974) Sales (£)	Royalty Rates*	Products Licensed
Spain (1957)	650,000	£13,000 per annum (fixed sum)	DCP, pallet racking
Portugal (1957)	620,000	2%	DCP, Apton, Speedlock
New Zealand (1959)	210,000	2%	DCP
India (1960)	420,000	Profit participation agreement	DCP, Apton
El Salvador (1961)	50,000	4%	DCP
Canada (1964)	1,950,000	£25,000 per annum (fixed sum)	DCP and accessories
Mexico (1964)	1,170,000	2%	DCP, Apton, Speedlock
Brazil (1966)	490,000	4%	DCP, Apton, Speedlock
Argentina (1966)	160,000	4%	DCP, Speedlock
Peru (1967)	230,000	£4,000 per annum (fixed sum)	DCP
Jamaica (1968)	87,000	4%	DCP
Nigeria (1970)	490,000	4%	DCP and accessories
S. Africa (1971)	325,000	4%	DCP, Apton, Speedlock
Hungary (1971)	650,000	£65,000 (lump sum royalty)	DCP

* Expressed as percentage of turnover unless otherwise indicated.

and the company prided itself on having a much more comprehensive product range and better design and other backup services than the non-European competition. Cheaper British steel gave Dexion exports a very real advantage, but it seemed that the position was gradually changing. Mr. Foster was getting increasingly concerned about Japanese and subsidized Indian competition in the Middle East and the gradual erosion of the cost advantage of using steel made in Britain.

DEXION OVERSEAS LIMITED

In 1970 Dexion-Comino International Ltd. had set up Dexion Overseas Limited (DOS) as a separate company within the organization to look after and coordinate its entire overseas export and licensing activities. Markets where Dexion had established subsidiaries or associates were excluded. In order to supervise distribution closely, DOS had divided the overseas market into five regions and appointed regional sales managers (RSMs) located in London to oversee Dexion's interests in each of these areas. The five regions were: (1) the Middle East and North Africa, (2) Europe, (3) the rest of Africa, (4) the Far East and Southeast Asia, (5) the Caribbean and South America. Exhibit 2 gives DOS results for 1973 to 1975 and Exhibit 3 gives a breakdown of 1975 results by region.

Direct exports and involvement in the Far East and Central and South Europe were comparatively small. Dexion's operations in Europe were mature in nature; and the increasing similarity between the United Kingdom and continental Europe

EXHIBIT 2   DOS Operating Results (£000s)

	1973	1974	1975
Invoiced sales	5,672	6,444	6,914
Gross profits*	1,076	1,770	2,088
Variable distribution costs	156	221	290
Gross profit (after distribution costs)	920	1,549	1,798
Home office and regional expenditure	565	560	703
Operating profit	355	989	1,095
Miscellaneous income (including royalties)	94	122	136
Interest	(13)	(75)	(75)
Profit before tax	436	1,036	1,156

* After deducting transfer prices payable to Dexion-Comino International Ltd.

in terms of competition, products, and customers had gradually resulted in most of Western Europe being treated as an extension of the home market, at least so far as the existing product range was concerned. With U.K. entry into the EEC in 1973, this similarity between the home market and continental Europe was becoming even more obvious, although differences in channels of distribution remained. .

Keith Galpin had carried out a detailed analysis of the various international markets that could provide it with substantial business in the future. This analysis had incorporated not only informed views within the company but also interpreted

EXHIBIT 3   Allocation of 1975 DOS Results by Region (£000s)

	Invoiced Sales	Gross Profit	Regional Expenses
Middle East and North Africa	3,016	1,006	96
Europe	1,829	378	33
Africa	1,090	408	42
Far East	257	61	26
Caribbean and South America	426	142	49
Miscellaneous	296	93	13
Total	6,914	2,088	259
Variable distribution expenses		290	
Gross profit (after distribution)		1,798	
Less:			
Regional expenses	259		
Central expenses	133		
Marketing and promotion	104		
Administration and rent	130		
Technical	77		
		703	
Operating profit		1,095	

demographic and economic data. The attempt was to highlight not only those markets which would continue to grow, but also select those which could become major profit generators in future. This exercise had brought to light some Southeast Asian and Middle Eastern countries which could be the target for more concentrated attacks.

DOS was of the opinion that during the next five years the company's business in the oil-rich countries of the Middle East and North Africa would expand much more rapidly than elsewhere. This called for a strategy that took into account the prominent position of the region. But the company felt that such a strategy would be applicable in principle to most overseas activities of the company, and Africa generally might follow the developments in the north.

DOS'S INTERNATIONAL POLICY

Markets and Organization

Galpin divided the Dexion market in Africa and the Middle East roughly into three kinds of buyers. *Bazaar buyers* were customers who bought mostly DCP-type products to erect small and fairly crude storage and other structural units. Though DOS had no hard data on the buying behavior of these customers, it was generally believed that they designed their requirements themselves or with some help from local Dexion dealers. Their main criteria for buying Dexion products in preference to those of other suppliers were price and availability. The demand was more for the less sophisticated Dexion products and an important characteristic of the buyer was his lack of awareness and perhaps need for more sophisticated storage and material handling systems.

The second group were *installation buyers*. Installations could vary from small simple racking units (similar to those put up by the bazaar buyer himself) to complete warehouse units made up of products such as Speedlock pallet racking and Impex hand-loaded shelving. This type of business was invariably handled by local distributors, sometimes with the help of Dexion staff, and often required detailed designs and site construction. This design and construction service was increasingly being provided by the local distributor, although Dexion's U.K.-based units assisted with jobs which were outside the resources and capability of a particular distributor.

There was occasional demand for relatively large and sophisticated systems requiring special resources such as system analysis, structural design, subcontracting, contract negotiation, financing, project management, and so on, outside the scope of any distributor. DOS referred to this third type of business as *project business,* and it invariably involved sales and implementation resources not available locally from a distributor (even when supported by a local Dexion salesman). Support of the local distributor for this type of work was by the payment of a negotiated commission.

In order to serve the growth in both installation and project business, DOS had established in London a technical services cell (see Exhibit 4 for organization

EXHIBIT 4 DOS Organization Chart

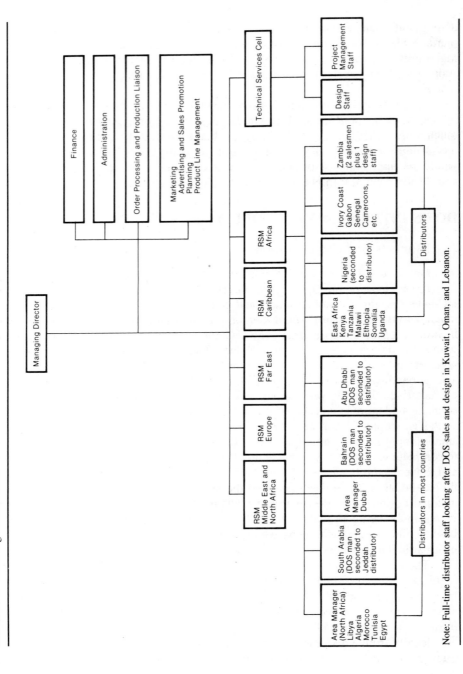

Note: Full-time distributor staff looking after DOS sales and design in Kuwait, Oman, and Lebanon.

chart). The regional sales managers could refer their design problems to this unit and the cell itself undertook some marketing activities. It stayed in touch with U.K.-based architects, specifiers, and designers to influence them to use Dexion equipment in projects they were associated with. The cell had developed over the years the expertise to quote for and supervise a wide variety of overseas projects. Its links with the regional sales managers were close.

As part of its central marketing function the DOS staff at headquarters attempted to coordinate the advertising and sales promotion campaign for Dexion products in national markets. Films, pamphlets, and information material in various languages had been prepared. The marketing department together with regional staff undertook to arrange seminars in various overseas capitals aimed at specific audiences. The marketing department also looked after the promotion of individual products and retained staff product managers who coordinated the activities for a particular product in the regions.

Pricing

DOS was supplied by the plant at Hemel Hempstead at a transfer price that reflected the direct costs of production and an allocation of works and general overheads. DOS, in turn, set prices for its distributors by adding a percentage markup to cover the cost of its own operations and provide a satisfactory profit.

In Mr. Foster's view, the essence of DOS's policy on distributor pricing was

> A question of competitive activity—we should evaluate what price competitive products are selling at and adjust our margins to account for the comparative advantages and disadvantages of Dexion goods.

Distributors in national markets were quoted different prices to take into account expected local distributor markup, the prices of competitive products, and the local customers' ability to pay. For example, during 1974, when transfer prices charged to DOS rose by 15 percent (Exhibit 5a), there was no corresponding across-the-board increase in prices charged to customers. European customers were charged only an extra 5 percent, while Middle East prices went up the full 15 percent in sterling prices. When the devaluation of sterling had been accounted for, however, the local prices ended up lower.

EXHIBIT 5a   Increase in Transfer Price to DOS, 1974

	Cost Increase		Percentage Costs	Increase
Steel	− 5%	on	40%	− 2.0%
Auxiliary material	20	on	35	7.0
Accessories	10	on	10	1.0
Other costs	0	on	15	0
Volume down 30 percent on budget				9.0
Total increase in transfer price				15.0%

EXHIBIT 5b   DOS Product Margins (excluding project sales) (£000s)

	1973			1974		
	Sales	Gross Profits	Percent	Sales	Gross Profits	Percent
DCP	2,079	610	29.3	2,530	874	34.5
Apton	305	120	39.3	481	164	34.1
Speedlock	1,120	238	21.3	1,347	393	29.2
Others	590	108	18.3	570	107	18.8
Total	4,094	1,076	26.3	4,928	1,538	31.2

As a result of the value pricing policy, the markups charged to distributors on various Dexion products differed considerably. Exhibit 5b gives an indication of gross margins by product category. Though DOS informally indicated to its distributors in various national markets the price at which they should retail their products, it did not, and in management's view could not, lay down firm directives. This policy had both its advantages and disadvantages. The company did not retain any firm control on its prices and occasionally found distributors in well-protected or prosperous markets charging exorbitant markups. But with its flexible pricing policy, DOS had built for itself an extensive distributor network. Distributors, it was hoped, would in turn set retail prices to maximize their own and consequently DOS's profits. That this did not always happen was seen as a largely unavoidable consequence of using independent companies as part of the distributor system.

AFRICA

The regional sales manager (Africa) had for administrative convenience divided the countries south of the area of Arab influence into four areas: East Africa, Zambia, Nigeria, and the erstwhile French West Africa. The four areas were roughly equal in terms of market potential and four area managers were based in convenient local capitals. Though Dexion had a distributor in virtually every African capital, choice had been limited and determined more by the distributor's general business standing and connections with the local government than by previous experience of selling products related to storage and materials handling.

Apart from South Africa and Nigeria, the region was comprised largely of developing countries with foreign exchange problems and complicated systems of tariff and exchange controls. Often there was no dearth of demand for Dexion products but a noticeable lack of buying power for foreign products. This was in the regional sales manager's view the single most important impediment in exporting to the African market. There were few areas where concentrated marketing effort could be justified. Not only was the entire region plagued by controls, but it was also in a state of constant economic and political flux.

Many suppliers besides those in the developed countries had found it possible to meet the less sophisticated level of African demand. Continental, Japanese, and Indian exports abounded, but Dexion with its wide and well-established network of distribution had a firm grip and in some countries like Tanzania had almost wiped out the use of competitive products. In virtually all markets, small local manufacturers making a restricted range of generally low-quality products were a continuing threat. In the regional sales manager's opinion, what Dexion had and the competition did not, were the local contacts and a name for quality and service that was well established.

It was not the overseas exporters who provided the major threat in African markets but the growing desire in most developing countries to set up their own production units. As the outlay for such a project would be about £500,000 it was well within the reach of most governments, if not individual entrepreneurs. It was possible that the small African markets would not support economic production units. But there was always the possibility of some countries getting together to come to tariff arrangements to form a quasi-common market or to look actively for regional exports. Some countries in East Africa and French West Africa had shown just this sort of inclination and this was seen as the thin end of the wedge at DOS headquarters.

The richer countries of Africa—Nigeria, Zambia, and South Africa—were different in their purchasing behavior. Areas of industrial concentration had resulted in a demand for a host of Dexion products and services. To South Africa and especially Nigeria, in spite of the presence of local licensees, Dexion directly exported the more modern systems, which were not manufactured locally. In

EXHIBIT 6   Africa: Orders Received (£000s)

	1973			1974			1975		
	DCP	Other	Total	DCP	Other	Total	DCP	Other	Total
Ethiopia	32	—	32	25	2	27	16	—	16
Ivory Coast	12	—	12	5	3	8	38	7	45
Kenya	26	—	26	18	5	23	55	8	63
Nigeria	44	61	105	60	79	139	103	109	212
South Africa	3	8	11	11	9	20	16	56	72
Sudan	44*	—	44	—	—	—	—	—	—
Tanzania	—	—	—	5	—	5	18	—	18
Zambia	74*	35*	109	61*	71*	132	140*	279*	419
Zaire	5	13	18	1	2	3	—	—	—
Others: Cameroons Gabon Ghana Gibraltar Senegal Niger Etc.	85	26	111	72	29	101	49	8	57
Total	325	143	468	258	200	458	435	467	902

* Project activity.

Zambia, the company had obtained a large contract to design, supply, and erect a complete materials handling and storage system. The Zambian case characterized an obvious trend in buying behavior. Developing country governments keen to put up large industrial complexes, often with the help of overseas funds, increasingly contracted for the complete supply, design, and erection of turnkey projects.

MIDDLE EAST AND NORTH AFRICA

The regional sales manager (Middle East) described his region:

> In spite of popular beliefs it's not all gold. For us there are three to four countries that contribute most of the sales. And it would be fair to say that in most countries the results are directly proportional to the effort we put in. When I say "we," I mean "we"—the local distributors have far too much on their plates and are often so badly organized that they need all the assistance we can give. The real selling force is frequent visits and resident expatriate staff—people who are willing to live in Arab countries and promote the Dexion name. And they are harder to find than you would imagine.

In spite of the massive oil revenues there was a growing inclination in some Arab countries to ban foreigners from setting up purely trading companies. The United Arab Emirates (UAE), Iraq, Iran, and Algeria had formulated, or were in the process of formulating, controls for limiting the activities of foreigners. Others like Libya, who were at that moment big customers of DCP products, had already outlined their intention to set up their own slotted angle plants to reduce the economy's dependence on imports.

Everywhere there was an explosive industrialization underway. All over the Middle East new plants were being constructed and the host countries, while embarrassingly rich financially, lacked human skills and infrastructure to cope with the growth. Even Iraq and Algeria, while attempting to lower their reliance on foreign companies, recognized the necessity to permit foreigners to bid for and undertake large projects. In fact, almost all Dexion's business in Iraq, Algeria, Iran, and a substantial portion of that in Saudi Arabia had been obtained by negotiating large contracts (see Exhibit 7).

Though the growth in project activity was generally welcomed by Dexion management, it had created some organizational problems. Contract negotiation took a comparatively long time and resulted more often than not in "next year's sales and this year's expenses." The regional sales managers were always under considerable pressure to maintain expenditure within agreed budgets and treated project activity with mixed emotions. However, when the organizational problems, both within DOS and with the local distributors, had been overcome, the profits were very welcome. Gross profits on successful tenders in the Middle East were broadly similar to those obtained on the sale of hardware alone.

Competition in the Middle East was strongest from the Japanese, Italians, and Indians in the supply of DCP-type hardware and from Japan and Germany in the project market. The Japanese and Germans often had a slight edge on

EXHIBIT 7   Middle East and North Africa—Orders Received (£000s)

	1973			1974			1975		
	DCP	Other	Total	DCP	Other	Total	DCP	Other	Total
Abu Dhabi	73	7	80	155	25	180	285	33	318
Dubai	32	11	43	78	3	81	85	27	112
Iraq	147*	—	147	478*	2	480	209*	4*	213
Libya	377*	21*	398	356*	17*	373	252*	60*	312
Oman	18	15	33	58	80	138	130	104*	234
Saudi Arabia	65	48	113	134	247	381	257	369†	626
Bahrain	18	9	27	35	34	69	25	21	46
Qatar	9	—	9	17	3	20	25	—	25
Algeria	—	1,235†	1,235		47*	47	—	—	—
Others: Cyprus Egypt Iran Jordan Kuwait Lebanon Malta Pakistan Syria Tunisia Yemen	94	14	108	294	29	323	91	9	100
Total	833	1,360	2,193	1,605	487	2,092	1,359	627	1,986

* Project activity.
† Projects not broken up by product groups.

Dexion, as they had been able to quote for complete turnkey projects. In Libya, DOS's distributor had established very good links with the local government, and Dexion products had reached a large market share; but only by pricing below DOS's normal markup to offset the price advantage of Italian products. In Saudi Arabia and the UAE, which still constituted the bulk of the hardware business, DOS's response to competition had been first to pare margins and second to promote slightly more advanced systems like Speedlock. In spite of overseas and local manufacturers crowding these markets, there was still ample opportunity for all. Saudi Arabia and the UAE had five-year plans that budgeted a threefold increase in public expenditure—justification enough for the most forceful of selling efforts.

Alternative Possibilities

With its target of achieving a 15 percent annual increase in sales and profits, DOS management was aware that a series of long-term strategic decisions had to be made. These decisions would have to encompass almost all the activities of the company and would have to bear in mind that 100 percent owned subsidiaries would be difficult to establish overseas. They included:

1. Should the company continue to license overseas manufacturers to produce the DCP range in areas of high tariffs and foreign exchange problems, or should the licensing policy be extended to cover more products and markets? In particular, should DOS agree to permit the manufacture of the Speedlock and Apton range in Nigeria?

2. If licensing was not a viable option, in view of local government hostility to royalties, should DOS look to joint ventures?

3. Another possibility could be to discontinue all overseas manufacture and cancel where possible the existing licensing arrangements and manufacture and export from the United Kingdom, or another suitable European base.

4. Which markets should be focused on and with what products?

5. Should the existing policy be changed?

6. Was there any need to restructure the distribution strategy?

The list of issues which needed to be questioned and sorted out seemed endless. DOS management was also aware of the fact that it would be impossible to put hard figures on many of these options but Mr. John Foster felt that the data he had were reliable, in the sense that they were indicative of the situation. He was particularly aware that the issues were interrelated (e.g., the company could not have a production policy that required licensing arrangements and a marketing strategy that required distributors) and the direction that DOS's total strategy took should at least be compatible within itself.

Bancil Corporation (A)

Struggling to clear his mind, Remy Gentile, marketing manager in France for the toiletry division of Bancil, stumbled to answer the ringing telephone.

"Allo?"

"Remy, Tom Wilson here. Sorry to bother you at this hour. Can you hear me?"

"Sacrebleu! Do you know what time it is?"

"About 5:20 in Sunnyvale. I've been looking over the past quarter's results for our Peau Doux . . ."

"Tom, it's after 2:00 A.M. in Paris; hold the phone for a moment."

Remy was vexed with Tom Wilson, marketing vice president for the toiletry division and acting division marketing director for Europe, since they had discussed the Peau Doux situation via telex no more than a month ago. When he returned to the phone, Remy spoke in a more controlled manner.

"You mentioned the Peau Doux line, Tom."

"Yes, Remy, the last quarter's results were very disappointing. Though we've increased advertising by 30 percent, sales were less than 1 percent higher. What is even more distressing, Remy, is that our competitors' sales have been growing at nearly 20 percent per year. Furthermore, our percent cost of goods sold has not decreased. Has Pierre Chevalier bought the new equipment to streamline the factory's operation?"

"No, Pierre has not yet authorized the purchase of the machines, and there is little that can be done to rationalize operations in the antiquated Peau Doux plant. Also, we have not yet succeeded in securing another distributor for the line."

"What! But that was part of the strategy with our increased advertising. I thought we agreed to . . ."

Tom Wilson hesitated for a moment. His mind was racing as he attempted to recall the specifics of the proposed toiletry division strategy for France. That strategy had guided his earlier recommendations to Gentile and Pierre Chevalier, the Bancil general manager in France, to increase advertising and to obtain a new distributor. Tom wanted to be forceful but tactful to ensure Gentile's commitment to the strategy.

"Remy, let's think about what we discussed on my last trip to Paris. Do

This case was prepared by Lawrence D. Chrzanowski under the supervision of Ram Charan, Associate Professor of Policy and Environment, as a basis for class discussion rather than to illustrate effective or ineffective handling of an administrative situation. The case was made possible by a corporation which prefers to remain anonymous. All names, figures, and locations have been disguised.

699

you recall we agreed to propose to Chevalier a plan to revitalize Peau Doux's growth? If my memory serves me well, it was to increase advertising by 25 percent, groom a new national distributor, reduce manufacturing costs with new equipment, increase prices, and purchase the 'L'aube' product line to spread our marketing overhead.''

"Oui, oui. We explored some ideas and I thought they needed more study.''

"Remy, as you recall, Peau Doux has a low margin. Cutting costs is imperative. We expected to decrease costs by 5 percent by investing $45,000 in new equipment. Our test for the new strategy next year was to increase advertising this quarter and next quarter while contracting for a new distributor. The advertising was for naught. What happened?''

"I really don't know. I guess Pierre has some second thoughts.''

Tom spoke faster as he grew more impatient. Gentile's asking Tom to repeat what he had said made him angrier. Tom realized that he must visit Paris to salvage what he could from the current test program on Peau Doux. He knew that the recent results would not support the proposed toiletry division strategy.

"Remy, I need to see what's going on and then decide how I can best assist you and Chevalier. I should visit Paris soon. How about early next week, say Monday and Tuesday?''

"Oui, that is fine.''

"I'll fly in on Sunday morning. Do you think you can join me for dinner that evening at the Vietnamese restaurant we dined at last time?''

"Oui.''

"Please make reservations only for two. I'm coming alone. Good night, Remy.''

"Oui. Bon soir.''

COMPANY BACKGROUND

Bancil Corporation of Sunnyvale, California, was founded in 1908 by pharmacist Dominic Bancil. During its first half century, its products consisted primarily of analgesics (branded pain relievers like aspirin), an antiseptic mouthwash, and a first-aid cream. By 1974, some of the top-management positions were still held by members of the Bancil family, who typically had backgrounds as pharmacists or physicians. This tradition notwithstanding, John Stoopes, the present chief executive officer, was committed to developing a broad-based professional management team.

Bancil sales, amounting to $61 million in 1955, had grown to $380 million in 1970 and to $600 million in 1974. This sales growth had been aided by diversification and acquisition of allied businesses as well as by international expansion. Bancil's product line by 1970 included four major groups:

	Sales ($ millions)	
	1970	1974
Agricultural and animal health products (weedkillers, fertilizers, feed additives)	52	141
Consumer products (Bancil original line plus hand creams, shampoos, and baby accessories)	205	276
Pharmaceutical products (tranquilizers, oral contraceptives, hormonal drugs)	62	107
Professional products (diagnostic reagents, automated chemical analyzers, and surgical gloves and instruments)	60	76

In 1974, Bancil's corporate organization was structured around these four product groups which, in turn, were divided into two or three divisions. Thus, in 1973 the consumer products group had been divided into the Dominic division, which handled Bancil's original product line, and the toiletry division, which was in charge of the newer product acquisitions. The objective of this separation was to direct greater attention to the toiletry products.

INTERNATIONAL OPERATIONS

International expansion had begun in the mid-1950s when Bancil exported through agents and distributors. Subsequently, marketing subsidiaries, called National Units (NUs), were created in Europe, Africa, Latin America, and Japan. All manufacturing took place in the United States. Virtually the entire export activity consisted of Bancil's analgesic Domicil. An innovative packaging concept, large amounts of creative advertising, and considerable sales push made Domicil a common word in most of the free world, reaching even the most remote areas of Africa, Asia, and South America. A vice president of international operations exercised control at this time through letters and occasional overseas trips. By the mid-1960s, overseas marketing of pharmaceutical and professional products began, frequently through a joint venture with a local company. Increasing sales led to the construction of production facilities for many of Bancil's products in England, Kenya, Mexico, Brazil, and Japan.

Bancil's international expansion received a strong commitment from top management. John Stoopes was not only a successful business executive but also a widely read intellectual with an avid interest in South American and African cultures. This interest generated an extraordinary sense of responsibility to the developing nations and a conviction that the mature industrial societies had an obligation to help in their development. He did not want Bancil to be viewed as a firm that drained resources and money from the developing world; rather, he desired to apply Bancil's resources to worldwide health and malnutrition problems. His personal commitment as an ardent humanist was a guideline for Bancil's international operations.

While Bancil had been successful during the 1960s in terms of both domestic diversification and international expansion, its efforts to achieve worldwide diversification had given rise to frustration. Even though the international division's specific purpose was to promote all Bancil products most advantageously throughout the world, the NUs had concentrated mainly on analgesics. As a result, the growth of the remaining products had been generally confined to the United States and thus these products were not realizing their fullest worldwide potential.

According to Bancil executives, these problems had their roots in the fact that the various product lines, though generically related, required different management strategies. For consumer products, advertising consumed 28 percent to 35 percent of sales; since production facilities did not require a large capital investment, considerable spare capacity was available to absorb impulses in demand created by advertising campaigns. For agricultural and animal health products, promotion was less than 1 percent of sales, but the capital-intensive production (a facility of minimum economic scale cost \$18 million) required a marketing effort to stimulate demand consistently near full production capacity. Furthermore, the nature of the marketing activity for the professional and pharmaceutical products placed the burden on personal selling rather than on a mass-promotion effort.

In response to this situation, a reorganization in 1969 gave each product division worldwide responsibility for marketing its products. Regional marketing managers, reporting to the division's vice president of marketing, were given direct authority for most marketing decisions (e.g., advertising, pricing, distribution channels) of their division's products in their area. The manufacturing division, with headquarters in Sunnyvale, had worldwide responsibility for production and quality control. (See Exhibit 1 for the 1969 organization chart.)

Corporate management also identified a need in key countries for a single local executive to represent Bancil Corporation's interests in local banking and political circles. There was no single criterion for selecting, from the divisions' representatives in each country, the Bancil delegate, the title given to this position. A corporate officer remarked: "We chose whom we thought was the best business executive in each country. There was no emphasis on functional specialty or on selecting an individual from the division with the greatest volume. In one country, the major candidates were opinionated and strong-willed, and we therefore chose the individual who was the least controversial. The Bancil delegate generally had a marketing background if marketing was the primary Bancil activity in the country or a production background if Bancil had several manufacturing facilities in the country."

While international sales had grown from \$99 million in 1970 to \$147 million in 1972, profit performance from 1971 to 1972 had been disappointing. A consultant's report stated:

> There are excessive communications between the NUs and Sunnyvale. The marketing managers and all the agents are calling for product-line information from the divisional

EXHIBIT 1 Bancil Corporation 1969 Organization Chart

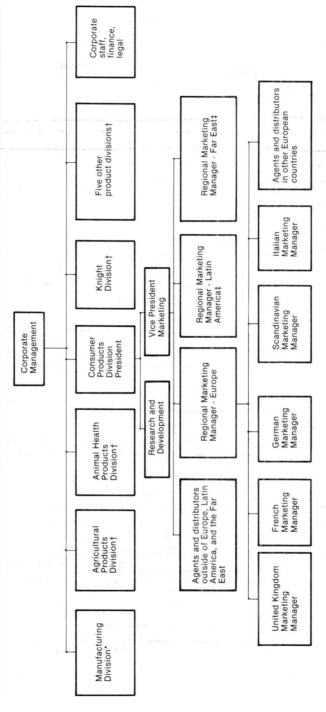

* The manufacturing division manufactured products for all the product divisions. Overseas manufacturing (not shown) reported to the manufacturing division in Sunnyvale.
† Organization similar to that of the consumer products division.
‡ Organization similar to that for Europe.

SOURCE: Company records.

headquarters. Five individuals are calling three times per week on an average, and many more are calling only slightly less often.

It appeared that a great deal of management time was spent on telex, long-distance communications, and travel. In response to these concerns, the divisions' staffs increased in each country. Overhead nearly tripled, affecting the growth rate of profits from international operations.

With the exception of financial decisions which were dictated by corporate headquarters, most decisions on inventories, pricing, new product offerings, and facility development were made by corporate headquarters in conjunction with the local people. Local people, however, felt that the key decisions were being postponed. Conflicting demands were a problem as every division drew on the local resources for manpower inventories, receivables, and capital investment. These demands had been manageable, however, because even though profits were below target no cash shortages had developed.

Current Organization of International Operations

To improve the performance of its international operations, Bancil instituted a reorganization in mid-1973. The new organization was a matrix of NU general managers and area vice presidents, who were responsible for total resource allocation in their geographic area, and division presidents, who were responsible for their product lines worldwide. (See Exhibit 2 for a description of the matrix in 1975.)

The general manager was the chief executive in his country in charge of all Bancil products. He was also Bancil's representative on the board and executive committee of local joint ventures. The Bancil delegate usually had been chosen as the general manager. He was responsible for making the best use of financial, material, and personnel resources; pursuing approved strategies; searching for and identifying new business opportunities for Bancil in his NU; and developing Bancil's reputation as a responsible corporate citizen. The general manager was assisted by a financial manager, one or more plant managers, product-line marketing managers, and other functional managers as required.

The divisions were responsible for operations in the United States and Canada and for worldwide expertise on their product lines. Divisions discharged the latter responsibility through local product-line marketing managers who reported on a line basis to the NU general manager and on a functional basis to a division area marketing director. The latter, in turn, reported to the divisional marketing vice president. Where divisions were involved in other functional activities, the organizational structure was similar to that for marketing. The flow of product-line expertise from the divisions to the NUs consisted of (1) operational inputs such as hiring/termination policies and the structure of merit programs, and (2) technical/professional inputs to the NU marketing, production, and other staff functions on the conduct of the division's business within the NU.

Only the Dominic division was represented in every NU. Some divisions lacked representation in several NUs, and in some cases a division did not have

EXHIBIT 2 Bancil Corporation Shared Responsibility Matrix

Vice president
international operations
Clark B. Tucker

		Europe Andre Dufour			Latin America Juan Vilas			Far East	Area vice presidents
Product group vice presidents	Division presidents	France P. Chevalier	Germany D. Rogge	Four other national units	Argentina and Uruguay S. Portillo	Brazil E. Covelli	Two other national units	Four national units	General managers
Agricultural and animal health (3 divisions)	Rodgers division								
	Division B								
	Division C								
Consumer products (2 divisions)	Dominic division								
	Toiletry division (Robert Vincent)								
Pharmaceuticals (2 divisions)	Division A								
	Division B								
Professional (3 divisions)	Knight division								
	Division B								
	Division C								

SOURCE: Company records.

a marketing director in an area. For example, the Rodgers division had area marketing directors in Europe, the Far East, and Latin America, all reporting to the divisional vice president of marketing to whom the division's U.S. marketing personnel also reported. However, the Knight division, which had a structure similar to that of the Rodgers division, could justify area marketing directors only in Europe and Latin America.

The new matrix organization established for each country a National Unit Review Committee (NURC) with its membership consisting of the general manager (chairman), a financial manager, and a representative from each division with activities in the NU. Corporate executives viewed the NURC as the major mechanism for exercising shared profit responsibility. NURC met quarterly, or more frequently at the general manager's direction, to (1) review and approve divisional profit commitments generated by the general manager's staff; (2) ensure that these profit commitments, viewed as a whole, were compatible with and representative of the best use of the NU's resources; (3) monitor the NU's progress against the agreed plans; and (4) review and approve salary ranges for key NU personnel. When the division's representatives acted as members of the NURC, they were expected to view themselves as responsible executives of the NU.

Strategic Planning and Control

NURC was also the framework within which general managers and division representatives established the NU's annual strategic plan and profit commitment. Strategy meetings commenced in May, at which time the general manager presented a forecast of Bancil's business in his NU for the next five years and the strategies he would pursue to exploit environmental opportunities. The general manager and the divisional representatives worked together between May and September to develop a mutually acceptable strategy and profit commitment. If genuine disagreement on principle arose during these deliberations, the issue could be resolved at the next level of responsiblity. The profit commitment was reviewed at higher levels, both within the area and within the product divisions, with the final approval coming from the Corporate Executive Committee (CEC), which required compatible figures from the vice president of international operations and the product group executives. CEC, the major policy-making forum at Bancil, consisting of the chief executive officer, the group vice presidents, the vice president of international operations, and the corporate secretary, met monthly to resolve policy issues and to review operating performance.

For each country, results were reported separately for the various divisions represented, which, in turn, were consolidated into a combined NU statement. The NU as well as the divisions were held accountable, though at different levels, according to their responsibilities. The division profit flow (DPF) and NU net income are shown in the following example for the Argentine National Unit in 1974:

	Rodgers Division	Dominic Division	Toiletry Division	National Unit
Division sales	$250,000	$800,000	$1,250,000	$2,300,000
Division expenses	160,000	650,000	970,000	1,780,000
Division profit flow (DPF)	$ 90,000	$150,000	$ 280,000	$ 520,000
NU other expenses (general administrative, interest on loans, etc.)				350,000
NU income before taxes				170,000
Less: Taxes				80,000
NU net income				$ 90,000
Working capital	$100,000	$300,000	$ 700,000	

The product divisions were responsible for worldwide division profit flow (DPF), defined as net sales less all direct expenses related to divisional activity, including marketing managers' salaries, sales force, and sales office expenses. The NU was responsible for net income after charging all local divisional expenses and all NU operating expenses such as general administration, taxes, and interest on borrowed funds. Because both the general managers and the divisions shared responsibility for profit in the international operations, the new structure was called a shared responsibility matrix (SRM). The vice president of international operations and the division presidents continually monitored various performance ratios and figures (see Exhibit 3). In 1975 international operations emphasized return on resources, cash generation, and cash remittance, while the division presidents emphasized product-line return on resources, competitive market share, share of advertising, and dates of new product introductions.

The impact of the 1973 organizational shift to the SRM had been greatest for the general managers. Previously, as Bancil delegates, they had not been measured on the basis of the NU's total performance for which they were now held responsible. Also, they now determined salary adjustments, hiring, dismissals, and appointments after consultations with the divisions. In addition, general managers continued to keep abreast of important political developments in their areas, such as the appointment of a new finance minister, a general work strike, imposition of punitive taxes, and the outbreak of political strife, a not-infrequent occurrence in some countries.

Under the new organizational structure, the area marketing directors felt that their influence was waning. While they were responsible for DPF, they were not sure that they had "enough muscle" to effect appropriate allocation of resources for their products in each of the countries they served. This view was shared by Nicholas Rosati, Knight division marketing manager in Italy, who commented on his job:

> The European marketing director for the Knight division keeps telling me to make more calls on hospitals and laboratories. But it is useless to make calls to solicit more orders. The general manager for Italy came from the consumer products division.

EXHIBIT 3   Bancil Corporation Control Figures and Ratios

Vice President of International Operations for National Unit		Division President for Product Line
X*	Sales	X
X	Operating income: percent sales	X
X	General manager expense: percent sales	
X	Selling expense: percent sales	X
X	Nonproduction expense: percent operating income	
X	Operating income per staff employee	
X	Percent staff turnover	
X	Accounts receivable (days)	X
X	Inventories (days)	X
X	Fixed assets	X
X	Resources employed	X
X	Return on resources	X
X	Cash generation	
X	Cash remittances	
X	Share of market and share of advertising	X
X	Rate of new product introduction	X

* X indicates figure or ratio on organization's (national unit or division) performance of interest to the vice president of international operations and the division presidents.

SOURCE: Company records.

He will neither allocate additional manpower to service new accounts for the Knight division nor will he purchase sufficient inventory of our products so I can promise reasonable delivery times for new accounts.

Divisions, nevertheless, were anxious to increase their market penetration outside the United States and Canada, seeing such a strategy as their best avenue of growth. The recent increase in international sales and profits, which had by far exceeded that of domestic operations (see Exhibit 4), seemed to confirm the soundness of this view. Not all NU general managers shared this approach, as exemplified by a statement from Edmundo Covelli, the general manager of Brazil:

The divisions are continually seeking to boost their sales and increase their DPF. They are not concerned with the working capital requirements to support the sales. With the inflation rate in Brazil, my interest rate of 40 percent on short-term loans has a significant effect on my profits.

The Peau Doux Issue

The telephone conversation described at the beginning of the case involved a disagreement between Tom Wilson, who was both marketing vice president for the toiletry division and acting division marketing director for Europe, and Pierre Chevalier, Bancil's general manager for France. It also involved Remy

EXHIBIT 4   Sales and Profits for Bancil Corporation, Domestic and
International ($ millions)

Year	Domestic		International		Total	
	Sales	Profit	Sales	Profit	Sales	Profit
1955	61	5.5	—	—	61	5.5
1960	83	8.3	6	0.2	89	8.5
1965	121	13.5	23	1.3	144	14.8
1969	269	26.7	76	9.2	345	35.9
1970	280	27.1	99	12.3	379	39.4
1971	288	28.7	110	14.2	398	42.9
1972	313	32.5	147	15.8	460	48.3
1973	333	35.3	188	21.4	521	56.7
1974	358	36.7	242	30.9	600	67.6

SOURCE: Company records.

Gentile, who reported on a line basis to Chevalier and on a functional basis to Wilson.

Pierre Chevalier had been a general manager of France for 18 months after having been hired from a competitor in the consumer products business. Upon assuming the position, he identified several organizational and operational problems in France:

> When I took this job, I had five marketing managers, a financial manager, a production manager, and a medical specialist reporting to me. After the consumer products division split, the new toiletry division wanted its own marketing manager. Nine people reporting to me was too many. I hired Remy for his administrative talents and had him assume responsibility for the toiletry division in addition to having the other marketing managers report to him. That gave me more time to work with our production people to get the cost of goods down.

In less than two years as general manager. Chevalier had reduced the cost of goods sold by more than 3 percent by investing in new equipment and had improved the net income for the French NU by discontinuing products which had little profit potential.

Remy Gentile had been the marketing manager for the toiletry division in France for the past year. In addition, five other marketing managers (one for each Bancil Corporation division operating in France) reported to him. During the previous six years Gentile had progressed from salesman to sales supervisor to marketing manager within the Knight division in France. Although he had received mixed reviews from the toiletry division, particularly on his lack of mass-marketing experience, Chevalier had hired him because of his track record, his ability to learn fast, and his outstanding judgment.

The disagreement involved the Peau Doux line of hand creams which Bancil Corporation had purchased five years earlier to spread the general manager's overhead, especially in terms of marketing, over a broader product offering.

Wilson's frustration resulted from Chevalier's ambivalence toward the division's strategy of increasing the marketing effort and cutting manufacturing costs on the Peau Doux line.

The total market in France for the Peau Doux product line was growing at an annual rate of 15–20 percent, according to both Wilson and Gentile. However, Peau Doux, an old, highly regarded hand cream, had been traditionally distributed through pharmacies, whereas recently introduced hand creams had been success- fully sold through supermarkets. The original Peau Doux sales force was not equipped to distribute the product through other outlets. To support a second sales force for supermarket distribution, the toiletry division sought to acquire the L'aube shampoo and face cream line. When Gentile had informed Chevalier of this strategy, the latter had questioned the wisdom of the move. The current volume of the Peau Doux line was $800,000. Though less than 10 percent of Chevalier's total volume, it comprised the entire toiletry division volume in France.

Tom Wilson viewed the Peau Doux problems primarily in terms of an inade- quate marketing effort. On three occasions within the past year, he or his media experts from Sunnyvale had gone to Paris to trouble-shoot the Peau Doux problems. On the last trip, Robert Vincent, the toiletry division president, had joined them. On the return flight to Sunnyvale, Wilson remarked to Vincent:

> I have the suspicion that Chevalier, in disregarding our expertise, is challenging our authority. It is apparent from his indifference to our concerns and his neglect in allocating capital for new machinery that he doesn't care about the Peau Doux line. Maybe he should be told what to do directly.

Vincent responded:

> Those are very strong words, Tom. I suggest we hold tight and do a very thorough job of preparing for the budget session on our strategy in France. If Chevalier does not accept or fundamentally revises our budget, we may take appropriate measures to make corporate management aware of the existing insensitivity to the toiletry division in France. This seems to be a critical issue. If we lose now, we may never get back in the French market in the future.

After Wilson and Vincent had departed for Sunnyvale, Chevalier commented to Dufour, his area vice president:

> I have the feeling that nothing we say will alter the thinking of Wilson and Vincent. They seem to be impervious to our arguments that mass advertising and merchandising in France do not fit the Peau Doux product concept.

Andre Dufour had been a practicing pharmacist for six years prior to joining Bancil Corporation as a sales supervisor in Paris in 1962. He had progressed to sales manager and marketing manager of the consumer products division in France. After the untimely death of the existing Bancil delegate for France in 1970, he had been selected to fill that position. With the advent of SRM he had become the general manager and had been promoted to vice president for Europe a year later. Dufour had a talent for identifying market needs and for thoroughly planning and deliberately executing strategies. He was also admired for his perseverance and dedication to established objectives. Clark B. Tucker, vice president of international operations and Dufour's immediate supervisor, commented:

> When he was a pharmacist he developed an avocational interest in chess and desired to become proficient at the game. Within five years he successfully competed in several international tournaments and achieved the rank of International Grand Master.

In the fall of 1974, Dufour had become the acting vice president of international operations while his superior, Clark Tucker, was attending the 13-week Advanced Management Program at the Harvard Business School. Though Dufour had considerable difficulty with the English language, he favorably impressed the corporate management at Sunnyvale with his ability of getting to the heart of business problems.

The toiletry division had only limited international activities. In addition to the Peau Doux line in France, it marketed Cascada shampoos and Tempestad fragrances in Argentina. The Cascada and Tempestad lines had been acquired in 1971.

Tom Wilson and Manual Ramirez, toiletry division marketing director for Latin America, were ecstatic over the consumer acceptance and division performance of Cascada and Tempestad in Argentina. Revenue and DPF had quintupled since the acquisition. In his dealings with Gentile, Wilson frequently referred to the toiletry division's clearly stated responsibility for worldwide marketing of toiletry products, Wilson felt that his position in proposing the new strategy for France was strong.

On the other hand, Sergio Portillo, general manager of Argentina and Uruguay, and Juan Vilas, vice president for Latin American operations, had become alarmed by the cash drain from marketing the toiletry divison products in Argentina. The high interest charges on funds for inventories and receivables seemed to negate the margins touted by the division executives. In describing the Cascada and Tempestad operation to Vilas, Portillo commented:

> I have roughly calculated our inventory turnover for the toiletry division products marketed in Argentina. Though my calculations are crude, the ratio based on gross sales is about four, which is less than one half the inventory turnover of the remainder of our products.

Neither Portillor nor Vilas shared the toiletry division's enthusiasm and they suspected that Cascada and Tempestad were only slightly above breakeven profitability. Chevalier and Dufour were aware of this concern with the toiletry products in Argentina.

As Chevalier contemplated the toiletry division strategy, he became convinced that more substantive arguments rather than just economic ones would support his position. In discussing his concerns with Dufour, Chevalier asked:

> Are the toiletry division product lines really part of what John Stoopes and we want to be Bancil's business? Hand creams, shampoos, and fragrances belong to firms like Colgate-Palmolive, Procter & Gamble, and Revlon. What is Bancil contributing to the local people's welfare by producing and marketing toiletries? We

have several potentially lucrative alternatives for our resources. The Rodgers division's revenues have been increasing at 18 percent. We recently completed construction of a processing plant for Rodgers and we must get sales up to our new capacity. The Knight division is introducing an electronic blood analyzer that represents a technological breakthrough. We must expand and educate our sales force to take advantage of this opportunity.

Chevalier sensed that Gentile was becoming increasingly uneasy on this issue, and the feeling was contagious. They had never faced such a situation before. Under the previous organization, NUs had been required to comply, although sometimes reluctantly, with the decisions from Sunnyvale. However, SRM was not supposed to work this way. Chevalier and Gentile stood firmly behind their position, though they recognized the pressure on Tom Wilson and to a lesser degree on Vincent. They wondered what should be the next step and who should take it. Due to the strained relationship with Wilson, they did not rule out the possibility of Wilson and Vincent's taking the Peau Doux issue to the consumer products group vice president and having it resolved within the corporate executive committee.

Case of the Reluctant Multinational

It's 1978. Until recently, Henry ("Harry") Brooks, a tall, imposing man, has excelled at growing the business and putting out the various organizational fires that threatened the international division of Midvale Corporation. But the effects of growth and change are finally catching up with Midvale, as with most American multinationals. And Brooks has problems.

During the past ten years, overseas sales, as a percentage of total revenues, have more than doubled. Expansion abroad had been easy at first, but now the sheer number and size of foreign subsidiaries are bewildering and have become virtually impossible to control. Far more than their domestic counterparts, international managers at Midvale seem to have a mind and life of their own.

The Midvale board thinks everything has gone haywire. The major issue facing the company is how best to make the international operation a fully integrated member of the corporate family and yet allow it to grow as well as it had in the past. Brooks waits for a meeting with top Midvale executives to review the organizational changes he made the year before, changes that are not working out as planned. In defense, he plans to strengthen those initial moves with a new program. As he looks out over the rolling hills surrounding corporate headquarters south of Cleveland, Brooks wonders if he will get a chance to execute the program.

THE FIRST MEETING

The meeting includes Jerry Bradford, Midvale's chairman; John Hines, vice chairman and Harry Brooks's immediate boss; Antonio Giordano, the European area manager and former head of the Italian subsidiary; and Alexandra Watts, the company's top marketer, just named president of domestic operations. Each has been studying a management memo outlining the company's international history up to this point (see Exhibit 1). The memo details the organizational changes Brooks implemented during the past year.

Bradford jumps right into the problem. "I don't want to waste any time," he says. "We've got quite a mess here. You've read the memo—but you probably didn't have to.

"For a year now, Harry has struggled to get international to behave as if it were a part of Midvale instead of a separate kingdom. In return, he's been trying to give international managers the same status as their domestic counterparts. They've always complained about that. The idea was that everyone would be governed by the same administrative systems, and international managers would be on the same level as domestic.''

His color rises. ''No luck, though. No one likes the system. They're giving Harry and his people all kinds of hell. Now, I want to know what's wrong and how we can fix it. Let's not pull any punches. We're all senior managers here; we should be able to be honest with each other. I want everyone to be as open as possible. Tony, you go first.''

EXHIBIT 1   Management Memo

To:
Members of the executive committee

From:
Harry Brooks   *HB*

Date:
November 3, 1978

Subject:
International organization

Until recently, our international organization has evolved according to market demands, mirroring the development of domestic operations. Technology is our key; we pursue no conscious product line diversification but let technological development point out our markets.

We started exporting to countries like Germany and the United Kingdom where the markets were very similar to those in the United States. European companies began to manufacture under our license in the 1940s and 1950s; gradually we took minority positions in their equity. Control was local; each operation maximized its own return.

By the end of the 1960s, we had grown too large. To be able to profit from our future as an international operation, we expanded control and bought majority interests. We also moved quickly into Eastern Europe, Japan, Australia, and South America.

We organized the international division along area lines with individual area managers for Europe, Asia, and Latin America. Each area had its own headquarters and was served by individual administrative teams. Country subsidiary managers continued to run their local sales and manufacturing operations autonomously. The area managers exercised little strategic control over the subsidiaries. All they did was install reporting systems and consolidate accounts. Contacts between domestic and overseas managers were informal, but effective. Technical managers at the country level maintained contacts with counterparts at headquarters to exchange ideas about new opportunities or to gain assistance on problems.

This organizational history clearly says several things about Midvale Corporation. Having acquired majority control in many of our international interests, we need to provide overall strategic direction from the highest levels of management if we are to continue our growth. This requires control of all operations from headquarters.

EXHIBIT 1   *(concluded)*

But we also need to remember that our strength has been in our flexibility and responsiveness to separate and diversified markets. We can't undermine the strength that we have at the subsidiary level.

In 1977, we decided to acknowledge the importance of international growth. The international division became Midvale International, a separate legal entity, a subsidiary of Midvale Corporation. We upgraded the status of our area managers to make them equivalent to domestic product vice presidents, and charged them with the responsibilities of coordinating activities among subsidiaries in their area. Requests for capital are approved by the area VP (now stationed at headquarters in Ohio), the president of Midvale International, and the corporate level financial and technical VPs.

Taken together, the changes subordinate the individual concerns of domestic and international divisions to those of the parent, while allowing manufacturing operations room for their own development.

"Thanks." Giordano pauses and then starts softly. "I know that Harry worked hard on these organizational changes, and they sure looked good on paper. But we're having trouble in the field. Essentially, we have been trying to bring foreign managers into an American corporate system without paying enough attention to the problems involved."

"Tony, I know how those under you feel, but you are overstating the case," Brooks says. "I gave presentations to almost all of the middle managers affected and sent out detailed memos."

Giordano tries to remain calm. "I know. But many of those people were with Midvale subsidiaries when they were independent companies. They've had the same systems in place for years.

"Take the basic accounting concepts. My financial officer in Belgium nearly keeled over last week when he received a telex from the accounting people here wanting to know what happened to the report on the level of receivables. It seems they're supposed to be at a certain number of days' sales by a certain time. He said he couldn't do it."

Alexandra Watts agrees. "Generally, I support more centralized control. But these systems may kill innovation. About six months ago, a product developer, Jim Hunt—I think some of you know him—well, he came up with something he thought would go over in Germany. When he contacted the head of the German sub, he didn't understand what it was all about. So Jim used R&D to get the whole thing moving. The German R&D experts got the information and even came over to review preliminary specs.

"Then, last month, I asked how things were going, Jim didn't know and checked again with the German sub. They said we hadn't approved their capital allocation request yet, Jim found out that a corporate controller was deliberately holding up the approval documents in order to make them get expenses under control.''

John Hines intervenes. ''Listen, all of this is too bad. But you can't expect us to let things go on as they've been going. Sure, for ten years international sailed along—but it's different now. When most economies are falling apart, you have to have some kind of system to coordinate policies. Have you looked at it hard? You've got the parent exporting products to Europe where they compete with products of its local subs—who are themselves exporting to Africa and competing there with licensees of the parent.

''When you try to point out that we can't let this go on, all you get is flak—more justification for the good old days, the 1960s. You know, fixed exchange rates, friendly governments, no interference from us. Well, I'm here to say it's too darn bad, but those days are dead and gone.''

Giordano picks up. ''Sure, that's the reality, but every time we try coordinating with domestic, it doesn't work, I flew a top technical guy from consumer products over to talk to my people in the field about new product ideas. He was real gung ho: wanted to see Rome, wanted to see Paris, wanted to go look for his roots in Scotland. But could he help me? Not on your life. He couldn't judge which products would be best for *us* down the line. He just told us what worked in Cleveland!''

Bradford speaks up. ''I think that's enough. I didn't call you in here to argue again. Actually, it's because Brooks has a new idea, Harry?''

Brooks looks around the room. ''The heart of our problem is that we've had no luck integrating the technical and administrative ends of the business with local product requirements. I've worked out the beginning of a response—a kind of super-organization to supplement the one we've got.

''Now, I'm not going to pretend there isn't more than one reason for this. The board has decided we should make the move to portfolio planning—at least in some respects. Since we'll have to restructure for planning purposes anyway, we might as well use the opportunity to solve these other problems.

''We're going to provide overall strategic direction for international without integrating it completely into any worldwide product division structure. I'm appointing three international business managers, each with the status of vice president and each responsible for developing one or two product lines. They'll bring some of the product expertise that we have in domestic into the international field without threatening the autonomy of international. They'll hold equal status with the area people and staff.

''Here's a copy of the new organizational chart. (See Exhibit 2.) There's not going to be any job description at first. Rather than make international subordinate to the heads of the domestic product divisions, I'm going to put the accent on flexibility and responsiveness to opportunity. Cleveland will continue to provide staff services. Area managers will oversee day-to-day doings.''

Giordano looks glum. ''Don't you think that's a bit vague?''

''I've done that on purpose,'' says Brooks. ''While the function of these international managers is vague, our corporate systems are going to be tighter.

EXHIBIT 2   Organization Chart

Midvale Corporation

Midvale U.S. President			Midvale International President		
Vice President	**Vice President**	**Vice President**	**Staff**	**Area Managers**	**Business Managers**
Consumer products	Industrial products	Financial services	Controller	Europe	Consumer products
			Legal	Latin America and Canada	Industrial products
			Manpower	Asia-Pacific	Financial services
			Manufacturing		
			Treasury		

Something has to give. Portfolio planning requires us to set up strategic business units. We're going to try to make ours correspond somewhat to operational units. That should help the overseas operations fit with planning.''

Brooks looks at them each in turn. "I think the problem here is that we're all trying to rush evolution. If we simply let the system function for a while, it will eventually achieve its own rationale. When I began in domestic manufacturing 30 years ago, Midvale was a simple, medium-size company. And we let the organization evolve slowly. Everyone seemed to cope. Why can't international?''

A SUPER SUPER-ORGANIZATION?

It's 1979. Things are, if anything, worse. Almost from the first day, people in the field rebelled against Brooks's new round of changes. They didn't like portfolio planning, or they didn't understand it. They saw the presence of international business managers simply as an extension of the "organizational blitz" that had been going on for about three years.

Worse still, foreign executives didn't think the business managers really wanted to help them out. So they stonewalled the whole system. They resisted the attempt at portfolio planning by taking weeks to "define" their businesses, and when they handed in definitions, they used the wrong terms. When reprimanded by top management, they replied that they didn't like a planning process that was so "numbers oriented." Planning used to be "more natural."

For their part, the international business managers, who came from the domestic side of operations, seemed to be more interested in controlling overseas country operations than in forging a worldwide strategy.

This time Brooks and Bradford are alone. Brooks is more than a little exasperated. He inquires, "Why can't anyone give these ideas a chance?"

Bradford says, "Brooks, you've been traveling 75% of your time, trying to make the thing work. But all that energy hasn't even begun to mediate the conflict between domestic and international—it's worse than it's ever been. You can't ignore it. Look at your business manager for consumer products. He had over 25 years of experience in domestic sales and wanted to get more consumer-oriented thinking into international. But he came down too hard on the subsidiary managers, sometimes even accusing them of ignorance about the product line."

Brooks agrees. "No one seems to be able to rise to his new level of responsibilities. The guy who used to be in marketing ignores production. The guy who was a planner spends his time talking to everyone shuttling back and forth across the Atlantic, spilling his information but not getting anything accomplished."

Bradford replies, "I called you here because *I'm* going to try this time. I'm giving a speech next week in Geneva that will outline the formation of worldwide product boards. The idea is to provide a forum in which the two sides can come closer together. Rather than simply relying on one product manager to oversee a product line, we're going to bring together managers to sit on a board for each product line. This way we'll get the U.S. product division manager, members of the division's technical and marketing staff, country subsidiary general managers, and their appropriate product managers together. The international business manager will chair. We'll give everyone the same title. I'm going to emphasize that the idea isn't to plan or control but to *communicate*. We want to make it clear that we don't want to favor domestic product division managers or country subsidiary managers."

"It might work. Especially if you introduce it as *your* idea. I'll even put Tony in charge of one board. If nothing else, he might become sympathetic to our concerns," Brooks says with a laugh.

"THIS VERY RATIONAL SYSTEM"

Now, in late 1982, the original group meets again. The atmosphere is gloomy. Simply put, the boards haven't worked any better than the international business managers. Bradford gave the speech. Brooks set up the boards. But, after a brief fanfare, they fell apart. Domestic product managers thought the company was making the structure for them. They listened politely but didn't want to tolerate too much "international garbage." The overseas managers agreed. They saw the system not as a conciliatory effort but as the final attempt to subordinate geographic and area expertise to the whims of domestic product managers, another extension of Cleveland's power over their operations. Discussions turned into shouting matches about who was stepping on whose territory.

Supposedly rational businessmen balked at this very rational system. One of the boards hadn't met for nine months. Another completely collapsed. Only the one headed by Giordano was still functioning.

Giordano is expansive. "I think my board works because it was set up last. We learned from the mistakes of others. And, anyway, my product lines are pretty global. Sid, the domestic product manager on my board, is an old friend. We go over the agenda before each meeting and kill any item that might explode on the battlefield.''

Brooks is defeated. ''This whole experiment tells me there are no solutions to any of these problems. Perfect systems need perfect people to make them work. And perfection is one item that we don't seem to have much of. The boards are clumsy, there are just too many parochial views, special interests, local problems. No one wants to think about the larger Midvale concerns.''

Alexandra Watts scowls, ''Maybe if I had been consulted at the outset, none of this would have happened.'' She suggests, ''Our company's strength lies with its technology. And these systems are a barrier to the free flow of resources.''

Bradford looks at Brooks. ''Okay, Alix. We know. But too much freedom can be dangerous too. Harry, I want you to think about this again. Whatever we decide this time, it's got to work. Otherwise, we may never fully control our own company.''

WHERE TO GO FROM HERE

Put yourself in Brooks's shoes. What were the most important problems he had to deal with during the 1970s? What was wrong with the way he handled them? What would you have done differently? Could his ideas have worked if they had been implemented in a different way?

What would you do next to solve Midvale's organizational problem? If you decide to return to the old way of doing things (reliance on an international division and area specialization), how would you control the subsidiaries to give the company a unified strategic direction? What kind of administrative systems would you employ?

If you decide the company has to make its worldwide product system work, what about geographic expertise? If domestic product managers must control overseas subsidiaries, how would you make them sympathetic to international concerns? Left to themselves, would they allow local entrepreneurs to do what is necessary to succeed?

Should you try to get help from someone with more international expertise? Are there other alternatives?

The Nation-State and International Business

Technology Transfer: The Cyber 76

Across the country, defenders of America rushed to their mail boxes and television stations in June 1977 to demand that the government deny Control Data Corporation a license to export a Cyber 76 computer to Russia. Jack Anderson wielded his mighty pen, congressmen petitioned the President, and Jimmy Carter and Zbigniew Brzezinski requested Juanita Kreps, Commerce Secretary, to deny the license even before the Commerce Department had completed examination of the proposed sale. Opposing the shipment one congressman commented, "I don't know what it is called today, but in earlier times it would have been called treason."

The Cyber 76 was intended for Hydromet (the Soviet Hydrometeorological Research Center in Moscow). Both the United States and the USSR were members of the World Meteorological Organization, a UN agency, and members had agreed to share information, analyses, forecasts, and research on weather. The U.S. National Oceanographic and Atmospheric Agency (NOAA) claimed that there were major gaps in the data available to the Worldwide Weather Watch (WWW) because inadequate Soviet computer capability prevented important weather data from Siberia being processed on time. With a third-generation computer such as Cyber 76, data would flow from the Soviets as well as to them. At the time, U.S. weather agencies had three such machines and Britain, Canada, West Germany, and Union of South Africa each had one. Furthermore, the United States and USSR had signed a series of agreements in 1972–73 to expand mutual technological cooperation and trade.

Representative Robert Dornan, a Republican congressman from California serving on the House Science and Technology Committee, argued, however, that the Cyber 76 could be used for "navigation and weapons guidance in modern missile, aircraft, tanks, high performance satellite-based surveillance systems, ABM [antiballistic missile] defense systems, and submarines. Soviet assurances that this computer will be used for peaceful purposes are unreliable at best and there is no practical method of monitoring the uses to which the computer is put."

At a press luncheon hastily pulled together by the American Security Council, Dornan called the sale "the top strategic issue in the country today—and selling to the country that wants to do us in.

This case was prepared by Professor Kenneth Simmonds, London Business School, from published data. Copyright © 1981 Professor Kenneth Simmonds.

"We've bailed out their agriculture; bailed out their aerospace industry.

"We risk making Lenin's prophecy come true" [i.e., capitalism will sell us the rope to hang them].

Dornan claimed that Control Data was pushing the sale because they had saturated the market for Cyber 76 and it was a survival instinct to keep on selling more—rationalizing that it was not a military threat.

Control Data grosses $2 billion in annual sales and had sold a total of 54 Cyber 76s, 30 within the United States. Depending on what the customer required in software, the selling price varied from $5 to $10 million per computer and about half a dozen were shipped per year. The Cyber 76 contained about 3 million transistors, with some so difficult to make and with so small a market that Control Data had had to make them itself and was the world's only supplier.

It would be possible, of course, to reprogram the Cyber 76. For a weapon systems tracking analysis something over 1,000 man-years of software development would be needed. Moreover, as the meteorological needs would use all of its capacity, it would be immediately obvious if the machine were not in use for meteorological purposes. It could not do both tasks at the same time—and supply of spare parts could be easily stopped. Some estimates of Cyber life without replacement parts placed it as low as 30 days but three months was more likely. To produce replacement transistors through "reverse engineering" would take the Soviets many years. Yet it was true that the Pentagon used Cyber 76s for a wide range of military purposes.

A strong Control Data argument for supplying the computer was that failure to supply could speed up USSR development of their own large main frames. This would totally remove an estimated annual $1 billion communist-bloc market from U.S. firms over the following eight years and build a further competitor for third-world sales of about the same amount. If the Soviets did not make their own main frame, they would anyway get something similar from Germany or Japan and strengthen these foreign competitors. Every $20,000 sales lost would represent one U.S. job lost.

Control Data claimed that the USSR had the basic technology to become completely self-sufficient in computers by 1980. Largely due to U.S. export restriction in the past, the Soviets had already developed a Ryad series of small and medium computers, several times faster than the IBM 360-145 for scientific calculations. For some time, the Soviets had been making the largest investments in basic research of any nation in the world and computer technology formed a large part of these amounts.

The Department of Defense policy on the Export Control of U.S. technology was being developed following the "Bucy Report" of the Defense Science Board Task Force the previous year. The following extracts are taken from the DOD Interim Policy Statement:

Background

U.S. policy on international trade consists of two elements that are not always reconcilable: (1) to promote trade and commerce with other nations and (2) to control exports of goods and technology which could make a significant contribution to the military potential of any other nation or nations when this would prove detrimental to the national security of the United States. While the Defense Department's chief concern is with the second of these goals, it must discharge its concern without restricting U.S. trade and exports any more than necessary.

Defense's primary objective in the control of exports of U.S. technology is to protect the United States' lead time relative to its principal adversaries in the application of technology to military capabilities. This lead time is to be protected and maintained as long as is practical, in order to provide time for the replenishment of technology through new research and development. In addition, it is in the national interest not to make it easy for any country to advance its technology in ways that could be detrimental to U.S. interests. These controls, however, are to be applied so as to result in the minimum interference in the normal conduct of commercial trade. This policy statement provides interim internal guidance to the Defense Department to maximize the above objectives to the maximum practical extent.

Definitions

The term *critical technology* as used herein refers to the classified and unclassified nuclear and non-nuclear unpublished technical data, whose acquisition by a potential adversary could make a significant contribution, which would prove detrimental to the national security of the United States, to the military potential of such country— irrespective of whether such technology is acquired directly from the United States or indirectly through another recipient, or whether the declared intended end-use by the recipient is a military or nonmilitary use.

"Technical data" means information of any kind that can be used, or adapted for use, in the design, production, manufacture, utilization, testing, maintenance, or reconstruction of articles or materials. The data may take a tangible form, such as a model, prototype, blueprint, or an operating manual, or they may take an intangible form such as technical service.

Control of such critical technology also requires the control of certain associated critical end products defined as "keystone" that can contribute significantly in and of themselves to the transfer of critical technology because they (1) embody extractable critical technology and/or (2) are equipment that completes a process line and allows it to be fully utilized.

Defense Department policy in export control of U.S. technology

In assessing and making recommendations upon those export applications referred to it by the State and Commerce departments, Defense will place primary emphasis on controlling exports to any country of arrays of design and manufacturing know-how; of keystone manufacturing, inspection, and test equipment; and of sophisticated operation, application, or maintenance know-how.

In order to protect key strategic U.S. lead times, export control of defense-related critical technology to all foreign countries is required. To this end, Defense will:

1. Request the Department of Commerce to alter existing regulations so as to require a validated license for proposed exports of critical technology to all destinations.

* * * * *

Defense will support the transfer of critical technology to countries with which the United States has a major security interest where such transfers can (1) strengthen collective security, (2) contribute to the goals of weapons standardization and interoperability, and (3) maximize the effective return on the collective NATO Alliance or other Allied investment in R&D.

* * * * *

Defense will normally recommend approval of sales of end products to potential adversaries in those instances where (1) the product's technology content is either difficult, impractical, or economically unfeasible to extract, (2) the end product in question will not of itself significantly enhance the recipient's military or warmaking capability, either by virtue of its technology content or because of the quantity to be sold, and (3) the product cannot be so analyzed as to reveal U.S. system characteristics and thereby contribute to the development of countermeasures to equivalent U.S. equipment.

There shall be a presumption for recommending disapproval of any transaction involving a revolutionary advance in defense-related technology to the proposed recipient country (if the resultant military capability threatens U.S. interests). Defense will assess a proposed export of technology not on the basis of whether the item is obsolete by U.S. standards, but on whether the proposed export would significantly advance the receiving country's potential and prove detrimental to the national security of the United States.

End-use statements and safeguards are not to be considered a factor in approving exports to potential adversaries of critical technologies and products except as may be otherwise provided in presidential directives. . . .

Defense recommendations to approve the export of end products to potential adversaries are to be made primarily on the basis of an assessment that the products' inherent performance capabilities, or the quantity sold, do not constitute a significant addition to the recipients' military capability which would prove detrimental to the national security of the United States.

Russell Karagosian

Winging south to Latin America aboard Pan American, Russell Karagosian had five hours flying time and an evening in his hotel room to prepare a presentation to the Minister for Industry outlining the basic characteristics of a scheme for evaluating new foreign investments.

Russell was a principal consultant for a Boston firm of business consultants. He had worked with this firm since completing his degree at a leading business school and had been mainly engaged in international market surveys and feasibility studies for multinational corporations.

The current assignment stemmed from a Christmas party at which Russell was introduced to Senor da Silva, a prominent lawyer from one of the smaller Latin American countries. On learning that Russell was an international business consultant, this gentleman had inferred that perhaps Russell's specialty was inventing ways to get higher profits out of Latin America and referred to the topical editorial shown in Appendix 1. Defending himself, Russell argued that any problems stemmed from the countries themselves. They had not made up their minds precisely what was in their best interests and then given a clear indication of what they wanted and how they would measure it. It was not too difficult, Russell asserted, to develop a standard set of questionnaire forms that would require potential investors to show clearly the benefits and disadvantages of any proposal from the viewpoint of the recipient country.

Three months later, after a change of government, Senor da Silva was appointed Minister for Industry of his country. Shortly thereafter, Russell Karagosian received a telephone call inviting him to meet the minister the following day to discuss his ideas further with a view to a more formal assignment to develop them into operative plans. There was no time to build a careful presentation but Russell was able to put his hands on a set of measurements introduced in the Philippines some years previously as a guide for profit remittance, shown as Appendix 2.

APPENDIX 1: THE LATIN AMERICAN REPATRIATION GAME[1]

"If I were a Minister of Finance in South America, I'd get me a good tough audit staff of young guys trained in Uncle Sugar Able. Then I'd comb the books of the bigger *Yanqui* subs in my country . . . and I'd sock it to 'em, sock it to 'em, sock it to 'em."

With this malediction my international controller buddy, Chuck McGregor, slid into

---

[1] *Worldwide P & I Planning,* November–December 1969.

place next to me at Charlie Brown's in the Pan Am Building. He certainly was more than slightly steamed (and oiled) as he flipped open a copy of *Fortune* to the article "Threatening Weather in Latin America."

"Here's someone who says U.S. subsidiaries in Latin America contribute 20 percent of that area's tax revenues. If I had the job, I could get that up to at least 35 to 40 percent, without half trying. Hell, in some subs, my company is taking out its original investment every year or more and there are others like us."

I chastised him for being un-American, unpatriotic, and warned him, with loose talk like that he could be drummed out of the National Foreign Trade Council as well as the Council for Latin America and the International Executives Association. And, if he kept on blithering that he wanted to repatriate less money from South of the Border, he would soon talk his way out of the cushiest controller job in mid-Manhattan.

Didn't he know, I emphasized, that U.S. subs "down there" accounted for 12 percent of all Latin production? And 20 percent of that area's exports? Or didn't he care?

"Sure I know these things and I care," he sniffed. "But I'm running scared. What with the anti-*norteamericano* climate in Peru and Bolivia—and rumblings elsewhere—I don't want our five Latin plants to be expropriated. So we damn well better come up with some more loot for the locals—and fast. I hate to say it, but as *Fortune* hinted, they're beginning to wise up."

But hadn't his firm done a lot for local Latin economies? I mentioned a double-page ad spread in *Time,* which dramatically showed what his company's sub had done for a small Latin town "before" and "after." Money was pumped in with no promise of return. And look what happened. New schools, new roads, with illiteracy down, disease down, and employment up.

"I remember that ad," he chuckled. "Our local guys had a helluva time rounding up enough good-looking Indians for the photo. Sure we did something for them. But we're doing a lot more for us. Do you remember what the copy said? 'We are again proving our faith in ____ by reinvesting profits for our workers' future.'

"But," Chuck went on, "do you want to know the real score? After our 'allowable' repatriation and after we took our several hundred thou' more in pre-tax 'expenses,' then we're glad to invest the little that's left. Because in weak-currency countries, we've been taking out 50 to 100 percent ROI every year."

Was he intimating U.S. subsidiaries in Latin America kept two sets of books?

"Well, it isn't two sets of books in the classic Tuscan sense. We only have one, but we make it do the work of two. Any local tax man can see we carry 'expenses' on the books. But they're just a neat device to siphon off as much pretax income as we can."

I cautioned him not to give away company secrets as I looked around to see if any of his competitors or Latin tax authorities were tuning in. Chuck tends to get boisterous after his third Tanqueray.

"The only trouble is," he said, ignoring my blunt warning, "that we're weakening, not shoring up, the economies of these countries by scarfing off all the foreign exchange the traffic will bear. Let's take a hypothetical case. I'll exaggerate somewhat but I'll show you how to play the Latin American repatriation game.

"Let's say our investment is $500,000 . . . and local authorities fix our repatriation ratio at 10 percent of investment. Then we quick pump in a $2 million loan from our Mexican sub at 20 percent interest for fixed asset expansion. We 'convince' Exchange Control that our fixed assets are now $2.5 million—and 10 percent of *that* begins to look pretty good. With our true return of $1 million on $6 million sales, then I can 'legitimately' get out $250,000—50 percent of our original investment—as our allowable dollar repatriation.

"But," Chuck grinned slyly, "I'm still way ahead of the game because I'm getting 400 thou' as interest on our $2 million Mexican loan. Then I work up some nifty Home Office charges such as technical management advice, special research, packaging design, etc. We figure these at 4 percent of sales, so this is a cool $240,000."

Are the charges real, I wanted to know.

"Of course not," he said spiritedly. "You sure are green. But who's to prove me wrong? And aren't our trademark and name worth something? Of course, they are," he said, answering his own question. "And I value these at 3 percent of sales, which is another $180,000.

"When I have loaded on all the hard currency pretax expenses, I have one final fillip left. I make the local sub pay $500 a month toward the salary of our regional Latin vice president in Coral Gables. It's a real check, but he never sees it.

"Let's total up," Chuck said briskly, writing on the bar with his Cross ballpoint.

Home office charges	$ 240,000
Trademark value	180,000
Share of "salary"	6,000
Interest on loan	400,000
Repatriation	250,000
Total	$1,076,000

"So here I am repatriating just over twice our original $500,000 investment! Not bad for a country boy from Indiana. By the way, we never go through with expansion. We'll cancel the loan quietly, but it's served its real purpose—to really jump our investment base. The authorities won't catch on for some time—if ever—as we'll finance expansion out of local accounts."

As I reached for the check, he made one final point. "But we just have to cut back. Most Latin countries are training some sharp MBA types up here. And, remember, they have a legitimate bitch. A lot of us haven't left *that* much behind in the local economy—and I'm afraid we'll have to pay the piper and dance to the Finance Minister's tune."

How much would he pay and how fast would he dance, I asked.

"A lot more. On our Baton Rouge tank farm, we went for 10 percent ROI over 10 years. I'd settle for 20 percent in five in Latin America. This should keep the wolves at bay for awhile. It's less for us, but it's better than losing everything. The good old carpetbagging days are done."

APPENDIX 2: CENTRAL BANK OF THE PHILIPPINES, MANILA—MEMORANDUM TO ALL AUTHORIZED AGENTS

As a result of continuing analytical studies, the system of measurements has been amended to improve the method of implementing the Central Bank's policy on investment remittance. Under this policy, which applies equally to precontrol investments as well as to approved post-control investment, Philippine companies and branches of foreign companies are allowed to remit profits and dividends due to their nonresident stockholders or head offices on the basis of the net contributions of the companies to *(a)* national income and employment or "the national income effect," *(b)* strengthening the balance-of-payments position of the country or "the balance-of-payments effect," and *(c)* supply of goods and services to serve the basic needs of the economy or "the product essentiality." The system of measurements, as amended, is indicated below.

I. NATIONAL INCOME EFFECT
   A. The national income effect is the ratio of the net domestic value added by the firm to the amount of scarce resources utilized in production and is expressed by the equation:

   $$Y = (V_g/I_t) \times 100\%$$

   where

   Y = national income effect, percent
   V_g = net domestic value added by the firm, pesos
   I_t = amount of scarce resources utilized in production, pesos

   B. Net domestic value added consists of the sum of the shares of the four factors of production in the income of the firm. This is obtained by adding the shares of:
      1. Labor—consisting of salaries and wages, bonuses, and commissions received by the employees and wage earners of the firm.
      2. Land—rent of land and buildings used by the firm in production.
      3. Entrepreneur—profits before income tax.
      4. Capital—interest payments on loans.
   C. Scarce resources consist of:
      1. Replacement of fixed assets—current amortization (depreciation) of fixed assets of both domestic and imported origin.
      2. Maintenance of fixed assets—cost of spare parts, labor, supplies, and other costs incurred in maintenance. (If maintenance is done by an outside firm, the total charges of the outside firm plus the cost of spare parts and supplies provided by the firm will be deducted.)
      3. Foreign exchange utilized—the foreign exchange cost of raw materials and supplies (including fuel) directly imported and indirectly (domestically purchased) imported, salaries of foreign personnel remitted abroad, and all other foreign exchange costs (royalties, service charges, expenses of business trips abroad, and so forth.)
   D. Automatic rating for firms producing intermediate products. Firms producing intermediate products necessary for the production processes of other essential industries are credited a minimum 3-point rating in the national income effect. Necessity is established if the intermediate product possesses either or both of the following characteristics:
      1. It forms an integral part, physically or chemically, of the product of the other essential industry.
      2. It is a necessary accessory for handling or merchandising, that is, containers, of the final product.

E. The rating accruing from contribution to national income effect is obtained by the following schedule:

SCHEDULE 1

National Income Effect (percent)	Accrued Rating* (points)
Above 300	5
251–300	4
201–250	3
151–200	2
101–150	1
100 and below	0

* Except for firms producing intermediate products which are credited a minimum 3-point rating.

II. BALANCE-OF-PAYMENT EFFECT

A. The balance-of-payments effect is measured by the ratio of the net foreign exchange earned and saved to the amount of scarce resources utilized during the period and is expressed by the following equation:

$$B = (F_n/I_t) \times 100\%$$

where

B = balance-of-payments effect, percent

F_n = net foreign exchange earned and saved, pesos

I_t = amount of scarce resources utilized in production, pesos

B. The net foreign exchange earned and saved is determined by subtracting the foreign exchange costs of production from the foreign exchange value of the product.

C. The foreign exchange costs consist of the foreign exchange utilized in production (IC3 above) plus the current amortization of imported fixed assets. Generally, land, furniture, and building are considered domestic fixed assets; and all the rest, imported fixed assets.

D. The foreign exchange value is determined by:
1. Earnings—foreign exchange received for payment of exports.
2. Savings—in the case of import substitutes, the foreign exchange cost of the product if it were imported (c.i.f. value of the product shall be used). A product shall be considered as an import substitute if it is an essential commodity or its manufacture began subsequent to the imposition of exchange control (December 9, 1949) and it displaces products imported prior to the import control.

E. The rating accruing from the strengthening of the balance-of-payments position of the country is given by the following schedule:

SCHEDULE 2

Balance-of-Payments Effect (percent)	Accrued Rating (points)
Above 200	5
166–200	4
131–165	3
96–130	2
61–95	1
60 and below	0

III. PRODUCT ESSENTIALITY
A. Products are first classified according to (1) export products and (2) products for domestic consumption.
B. Export products are further classified according to the degree of processing they have undergone as:
1. Manufactured products.
2. Semimanufactured products.
3. Raw materials.
C. Products for domestic consumption are further classified into:
1. Highly essential products.
2. Essential producer products.
3. Essential consumer products.
4. Nonessential producer products.
5. Nonessential consumer products.
The Central Bank Commodity Classification shall be used as the primary basis of classifying products for domestic consumption. For this purpose, the unclassified items in the Central Bank Commodity Classification shall be reclassified. The criteria to be used in the reclassification shall be "utility" of the product.
D. The corresponding rating accruing from the essentiality of the product is determined by the following schedule:

SCHEDULE 3

Products for Domestic Use	Export Products	Category	Accrued Rating (points)
Highly essential	Manufactured	I	5
Essential producer		II	4
Essential consumer	Semimanufactured	III	3
Nonessential producer		IV	2
Nonessential consumer	Raw materials	V	1

IV. SCHEDULE OF ALLOWABLE REMITTANCES
   A. A straight 40 percent of the nonresident's share in the net profits shall be allowed to be remitted by the following firms:
      1. Firms operating under a government franchise wherein the output is of the character of a public service.
      2. Banks and insurance companies.
   B. Beginning with profits realized for financial years ending in 1958, all other companies are allowed to remit dividends or profits to their nonresident stockholders or head offices abroad according to the following schedule of allowable annual remittances:

SCHEDULE 4

Social Productivity Rating (SPR)	Allowable Remittances (whichever is lower)	
	Percent of the Nonresident's Share in Current Net Profit	Percent of Foreign Capital Invested*
13–15	100	60
10–12	80	50
7–9	60	40
4–6	40	30
1–3	25	20

* As of the beginning of the period for which the profit is realized.

The Social Productivity Rating of a firm is the sum of the ratings accruing from the national income effect, balance-of-payments effect, and product essentiality. For non-Philippine companies, the depreciated or net book value of capital assets as at the beginning of the fiscal year for which the profit is realized will be used instead of capital invested.
   C. Withholding taxes on dividends are to be deducted from the remittable amounts as determined.

Flexoid Carribia

The Flexoid Corporation wished to invest in a new plant in Carribia to manufacture Myoprene, a speciality chemical. The company held the patents for the process and had several plants on stream in Europe. Myoprene imports had been prohibited from Carribia for some years as they were not included within the local government's category of "essential imports," but Flexoid management had come to the conclusion that a plant solely to serve the Carribian market could be justified.

The company analysts had worked out a pro forma income statement for a typical year of expected operations as shown in Exhibit 1, and were preparing a note for management as a basis for negotiations with the Carribian government's Foreign Investment Review Board. Management had asked for an evaluation of the advantages of alternative financing plans and an outline of the arguments that might be used to justify the project to the Review Board.

Carribia was still basically an agricultural country, reliant for foreign exchange earnings on the export of agricultural commodities. Mechanization in agriculture and a high birth rate, however, had combined to produce widespread underemployment, and the creation of new jobs in manufacturing had been given high priority on the government's list of objectives.

To spur the development of import-replacing investments, many "infant-industry" tariffs had been introduced. Normally only one investor was permitted to manufacture a given product, and the tariffs were set sufficiently high to give the manufacturer at least a temporary monopoly. Myoprene from a Carribian plant would be priced at 20 percent above the prevailing world supply price, but preliminary discussions with Carribian trade officials had indicated that a tariff at 30 percent ad valorem would be imposed on Myoprene and substitutes in the event of the plant being authorized.

As yet there was no important chemical investment in Carribia. The recent government five-year development plan, however, called for such investment. The establishment of a Myoprene facility would provide local demand for several base chemicals and would certainly add to the interest of major international chemical companies in further Carribian investment.

Carribia had numerous development options, and it was known that the government planners had been using a rate of 20 percent per annum as a gauge of the "opportunity cost" of capital in determining priorities among competing projects.

The total capital cost for the new Myoprene operation was estimated at

This case was prepared by Professor John Stopford and Professor Kenneth Simmonds of the London Graduate School of Business Studies. Copyright © 1976 John Stopford.

900,000 pesos and would be financed by 400,000 pesos of equity from Flexoid and 500,000 pesos of long-term debt. Flexoid's founder, just recently retired as president, had viewed minority partners as "getting a free ride on profits" and had shaped Flexoid's financial policy to retain full ownership of all subsidiaries with maximum use of fixed interest debt. If Flexoid raised the debt finance outside Carribia and secured it against its home-base assets the interest rate would be 10 percent per annum. Money raised in Carribia solely against the security of the proposed plant, however, would cost 15 percent per annum. The peso was valued on a par with the U.S. dollar and the Carribian government had followed a policy, which seemed unlikely to change, of maintaining this parity.

EXHIBIT 1   Pro Forma Income Statement for a Typical Year's Operations in Carribia

		Pesos (000s)
Sales		1,000
Cost of goods sold		
Labor—local	200	
Raw materials—imported	400	
local	100	700
Gross margin		300
Indirect expenses—maintenance, depreciation, selling, administration, etc.		100
Profit before interest and 50 percent local taxation		200

The Unitary Tax Campaign

Peter Wates, chairman of Gordon Industries PLC of the United Kingdom, was approached in March 1984 to join a unitary tax lobby group of the largest European companies with subsidiaries in the United States. The aim of the group was to put pressure on the U.S. government to legislate against the unitary tax method, which had been adopted by 12 of the 50 American states. The group would not only adopt direct lobbying techniques but would also endeavour to persuade their own national governments to threaten Washington with retaliation if unitary tax laws were not abolished, and threaten retaliatory actions by the firms themselves.

Peter was not sure whether it would be a good thing for Gordon Industries to become identified with such a campaign. It might rebound to affect Gordon in any of the 60 countries in which it had local branches or subsidiaries. Furthermore, the company had for years been striving to develop a purely local image within the United States. Action to pressure the U.S. government would emphasise its foreign identity. He therefore asked John Morley, the assistant corporate treasurer, to prepare a recommendation as to what actions Gordon Industries would hope to influence the lobby group to take and whether they should join.

THE NATURE AND IMPACT OF UNITARY TAX

The unitary system was introduced in the 1920s within the United States to apportion profits of railways that crossed state boundaries. By the 1980s, the system had evolved so that states using it simply levied tax on a specified proportion of a corporation's worldwide income. In California, the proportion of worldwide income on which its state income tax of 9.6 percent was levied was defined by the arithmetic average of three ratios:

- California turnover to world turnover.
- California assets to worldwide assets.
- California payroll to worldwide payroll.

Each state, however, adopted its own rules, and when the system was combined with those of countries taxing only locally recorded profits, more than 100 percent of income might be taxed.

The dangers of overtaxation had been illustrated years earlier by the experience of Canada's aluminium producer, Alcan, which bought a loss-making plant in

This case was prepared by Professor Kenneth Simmonds of London Business School. Copyright © Professor Kenneth Simmonds, 1988.

the Los Angeles area in the 1960s. The plant, which employed around 1,500, continued to lose money; and as Alcan could not find a buyer, it eventually dismantled the plant. Yet California assessed Alcan $1.7 million in taxes for the period 1965 to 1971, by treating Alcan's worldwide operations as a single unit for assessment purposes. Oil companies that had paid a huge percentage of turnover as taxation to the OPEC states had also ended up paying high U.S. state tax on "unitary" profits that came largely from investment in merchandising in other countries.

The motives of the U.S. states in switching to unitary tax, however, were not to tax when losses had in fact been recorded, but rather to overcome the undertaxation they believed existed because of multinationals' ability to arrange for profits to be recorded in units operating in low-tax regimes. The unitary system was easy for states to operate, and its protagonists argued that a state with, say, 10 percent of a corporation's property, payroll, and sales had a right to tax 10 percent of its worldwide income. In October of the previous year, the Controller of the State of California had written to the Editor of the *Financial Times* in London, presenting the state's case strongly. This letter is reproduced in Exhibit 1.

Corporations, on the other hand, complained that the unitary method failed to take into account lower costs, greater risks, and higher profit rates outside the United States. Furthermore, states had picked formuli that were biased in their favor—particularly those that heavily weighted the percentage of local turnover. On top of this, the system was not as simple as it was made out to be. Compliance costs were extremely high because each state required data on total worldwide operations broken down in different ways. And the complications introduced by the need to record multiple exchange rates were major.

While 12 U.S. states had adopted the unitary system, only 3 had used it before 1978. Multinationals were particularly worried that its recent popularity would result in other countries adopting it; there were current rumors, for example, that both Nigeria and India were considering doing so. Competition between countries to gain a larger proportion of the taxable base would only serve to lower both reinvestment and further investment from the capital markets. After all, few multinationals paid out much of their profits in dividends. They were largely reinvested.

MOUNTING PRESSURE AGAINST UNITARY TAXATION

Initially, multinationals tried to exert pressure by making well-publicized statements of their refusal to contemplate further investment in a unitary tax state. Some even claimed to have closed operations for the same reason. As the use of the system expanded, however, the pressure was directed more towards the Federal level. In summer 1983, Mr. Akio Morita, Sony's chairman, wrote to George Shultz, the U.S. Secretary of State, saying that he regarded unitary tax as "grossly inequitable," adding that unless the Administration acted to prohibit it, investment and trade relationships would be seriously and adversely affected.

EXHIBIT 1

Tax Avoidance by the Multinationals

From the Controller of the State of California

Sir,—As Controller of the State of California and chairman of the State Franchise Tax Board which administers California's unitary tax, I read with great interest your editorial of September 19, 1983 and the correspondence it generated.

You are absolutely correct that the multinational corporations try to minimise their taxes by shifting income from one country to another. This gives them a great advantage over their smaller competitors who cannot minimise their taxes in this fashion and who have to bear the tax burden shifted on to them by these multinationals. The states and other taxing jurisdictions have neither the manpower nor the knowledge to catch these increasingly sophisticated tax avoidance schemes.

After all, who can really say what the arm's-length price ought to be in each of thousands of complicated transactions in a vertically integrated company? The Marc Rich situation leaps to mind as a rather glaring example of this problem.

Thus, as you point out, some states decided, rather than chase the will-o'-the-wisp of arm's-length pricing, they would allocate profits on the basis of a formula that reflects the economic reality of multinational corporations. It is a much simpler and far more effective means of insuring that these multinationals do not escape taxation.

While I agree that there are possibilities of abuse, we have sought from the companies for many years, so far unsuccessfully, concrete examples of unfairness. The reason they have not been able to present concrete examples is that the system provides ample administrative means of dealing with exceptional situations that might cause unfair results.

While I for one would be willing to support efforts to negotiate treaties that would establish the acceptable bounds for a unitary tax formula, I doubt the companies would be willing. For, if the effort were successful, these multinational companies would be unable to use tax havens to such advantage and would be forced to pay their fair share of taxes.

Kenneth Cory,
Sacramento, California

SOURCE: *The Financial Times,* October 31, 1983.

He also declared that Sony had been obliged to halt investment in its San Diego television plant, had ruled out California as a site for a videotape factory, and had put its magnetic tape factory in Alabama because Alabama was not a unitary tax state.

Later in the year, U.K. Prime Minister Margaret Thatcher also urged President Reagan and Treasury Secretary Regan in private discussions to take action to limit states' powers to tax income arising outside U.S. jurisdiction. At the annual conference of the Confederation of British Industry in November, delegates voted unanimously for a resolution urging the government to bring the "strongest pressure" on the U.S. administration to outlaw unitary taxation. The proposer of the motion described the taxes as "disruptive, fickle, and downright mean." A pressure group of British multinationals had earlier put forward a clause for the 1983 Finance Act that would have denied credits on advance corporation tax to U.S. companies operating in Britain whose headquarters were in unitary-tax states. Action to do so, however, might have breached the U.K.-U.S. double tax treaty and ended up harming British corporations even more. Still, such a clause might yet galvanize the U.S. federal authorities into action.

The Australian Chamber of Commerce had also joined the attack. The Chamber claimed that unitary tax laws were in breach of the Australian double tax accord with the United States. In a note delivered to the U.S. Ambassador in Canberra, it claimed it had asked the Australian government to consider retaliatory taxes on the large number of U.S. multinationals in Australia if something were not done.

U.S. ATTITUDES TOWARDS UNITARY TAX

In June 1983, the Supreme Court reviewed a California unitary tax case, *Container Corporation v. Franchise Tax Board,* and upheld the constitutional right of a state to apply the unitary approach to worldwide income. In its judgment, the Supreme Court rejected the "formal geographical or transactional accounting" practices of international accountants:

> The problem with this method is that formal accounting is subject to manipulation and imprecision, and often ignores or captures inadequately the many subtle and largely unquantifiable transfers of value that take place among the components of a single enterprise.

* * * * *

> Separate (geographical) accounting while it purports to isolate portions of income received in various states, may fail to account for contributions to income resulting from functional integration, centralisation of management, and economies of scale.

* * * * *

> We have seen no evidence demonstrating that the margin of error (systematic or not) inherent in the three-factor formula is greater than the margin of error (systematic or not) inherent in the sort of separate accounting urged upon us. Indeed, it would be difficult to come to such a conclusion.

Under the interstate income and foreign commerce clause of the U.S. constitution, however, the federal government was responsible for tax policy toward foreign trading partners. Largely because the U.S. Solicitor did not file a brief supporting Container Corporation, the Supreme Court also reached the conclusion that the unitary tax method applied to worldwide income was not a threat to U.S. foreign policy. But the court was careful to state that it reserved judgment on whether foreign parents of U.S. subsidiaries should be excluded. This left open the possibility that a foreign company would have a very good chance of winning a lawsuit arguing for such an exclusion.

Following the Container Corporation ruling, the Cabinet Council on Economic Affairs recommended that President Reagan support legislation restricting the states' reach to the confines of the United States—known as a "water's edge" restriction. The President instead established a Treasury Working Group, which decided against federal legislation. As John Morley set out to write his report, members of the Working Group were seeking to find a consensus on reporting requirements that would remove the basis of multinationals' complaints against the unitary method.

The U.S. administration had on several occasions asked U.S. corporations whether they would support federal legislation giving relief from worldwide combination to companies with foreign parents. The corporations had consistently answered that they would actively oppose any legislation that discriminated in favor of foreign competitors. Some foreign governments had also argued that to retain the method even for U.S. companies would discourage investment abroad by those companies and would inhibit international trade.

Several U.S. states remained insistent, on the other hand, that they should retain their right to tax U.S. companies on their dividends from overseas subsidiaries and their income accruing in tax havens. California's deputy director of finance said that while U.S. multinationals might regard foreign dividends as after-tax income already assessed abroad, California regarded excess foreign taxes as a federal issue. Furthermore, an exemption for foreign dividends from taxed income would lose state revenue of some $300 million annually.

But there were signs that some of the unitary tax states were weakening in their resolve. Florida had adopted a worldwide combination and unitary tax soon after the *Container* decision. But during a trip to Japan in March by Florida governor Robert Graham, the Japanese had made it very clear that they would not consider further investment in the state unless he reversed his position and supported repeal. For the single city of Tampa, at least 12 companies said to employ between 100 and 1,000 workers each had already decided against moving there as a result of unitary taxation. The governor of Indiana was also arguing that multinationals viewed Indiana as a unitary tax state even though it had never used the concept. He proposed that a resolution to rule out the possibility of using the unitary approach would enhance the economic growth of the state by making it easier to attract foreign investment. Its neighbor, Illinois, had repealed the unitary tax in 1982 for precisely this reason. The governor of Georgia had gone even further, giving a firm assurance to businessmen in London during a trade promotion visit that his state would not introduce unitary taxation during the course of his administration. In Massachusetts, which was considered the toughest taxing authority, subsidiaries of foreign corporations had already been excluded from taxation on the worldwide unitary basis. U.S. multinationals, predictably, had been considerably upset by the move and were bringing major pressure to bear for equal treatment. The high technology multinationals based in Massachusetts, such as Polaroid, Digital Equipment Corporation, Prime Computer, and Wang Laboratories, were especially active.

GORDON INDUSTRIES' U.S. INVOLVEMENT

Gordon Industries had a 1983 turnover of approximately $5 billion (£ 3.6 billion) of which $1.1 billion represented sales recorded through its U.S. subsidiary. These were largely electronics and electrical items purchased by the building and construction industries, and many were manufactured in the Far East. The firm, however, did own a builders' merchant chain in California with a substantial labor force and was also active in Florida and Massachusetts. All three states were recording high building growth.

On a worldwide unitary tax basis, Gordon Industries was currently assessed on its turnover of $600 million in these three states at its average worldwide profit to turnover of 11 percent. Under traditional geographical accounting, however, Gordon's U.S. subsidiary was a very low profit earner, recording only 4 percent profit to sales after allowing for interest on the loan raised to cover the purchase of the merchant chain, and rental of the properties involved. Actual ownership of all Gordon's U.S. real estate had been transferred to a Curacao subsidiary of Gordon Industries PLC to take advantage of the taxation convention between the United States and the Netherlands Antilles. Although provision had been made annually for state tax assessed on the unitary tax basis, Gordon had not paid state taxes to any one of the three unitary tax states since 1978. The tax files were still open, for there was a considerable backlog in assessment, partly resulting from the litigation concerning the unitary basis and partly resulting from the complexity of the calculations involved. Furthermore, Gordon's U.S. tax attorneys were claiming that Gordon Industries PLC had no legal obligation to supply state authorities with certain details of its foreign operations outside the United States that in no way impinged on the performance of the U.S. subsidiary.

Nitrofix Ghana

Craig Michael Lee, the project advisor to the vice-president of Nitrofix Inc.'s international division, had a long meeting in mid-1982 with Bawol Cabiri, the commercial consul at the Ghana Trade and Investment Office in New York City. Lee hoped that the talk would enable him to decide whether it might be worthwhile to pursue an investment opportunity in Ghana.

A Ghanaian government representative had first approached Nitrofix about establishing a fertilizer plant in 1981, two years after Dr. Hilla Limann became the country's first democratically elected president in over a decade. The Limann government was actively seeking foreign investment, reversing previous governments' socialist practices and antipathy to private investment. However, Nitrofix was hesitant to enter an agreement because of Ghana's past political instability and economic chaos, and negotiations had proceeded fitfully. Then the Limann government was overthrown in a military coup on December 31, 1981. Lee had assumed that was the end of the matter until the Ghana Trade and Investment Office contacted him again in mid-1982 and mentioned that some very favorable terms might now be possible for the investment. His recent meeting with Cabiri focused on the possibility that Nitrofix might invest in a plant in Ghana to be operated as a joint venture with either private Ghanaian entrepreneurs or with the government. A tentative name was agreed upon: Nitrofix (Ghana) Ltd. Lee had been impressed by Cabiri's knowledge and understanding and by the potential profitability of the project. However, he knew that he had to evaluate a number of issues of vital importance including:

- The condition of the Ghanaian economy.
- The political climate in Ghana and West Africa.
- The existence of a Ghanaian and/or African market for fertilizer.
- Ghana's policies toward foreign investment.
- The financial arrangements.

He also knew that if his company decided to follow up on the possibility, it would have to prepare for negotiations on a wide range of matters.

NITROFIX INC.

Nitrofix was a medium-sized U.S. manufacturer of nitrogenous fertilizers that had made a specialization of setting up plants to serve the local markets in

Prepared by William A. Stoever, Keating-Crawford Professor of Business Administration, Seton Hall University, South Orange, N.J. Copyright © 1982 by William A. Stoever.

smaller countries overseas. In the 1960's their first international ventures had gone into the smaller countries of Western Europe, but in the 1970's they had expanded into friendly Third World countries such as the Philippines, Indonesia, Thailand, and Venezuela. The company thoroughly analyzed its overseas investments, and they had generally panned out well, contributing most of Nitrofix's growth in sales and profits for two decades. In the 1960's Nitrofix had usually insisted on 100 percent ownership of each overseas subsidiary, but in the 1970's they had come to recognize both the necessity and the desirability of entering into joint ventures with local partners when terms and conditions were suitable.

THE POLITICAL ECONOMY OF GHANA

After a day of library research, Lee pieced together the following information about Ghana's political and economic situation. The country had received independence from Great Britain in 1957, the first black colony in Africa to become independent. Its first Prime Minister (later President) was Dr. Kwame Nkrumah, an eloquent spokesman and leader for the emerging aspirations of Africa. Thanks largely to its position as the world's largest cocoa exporter, Ghana was the richest country in Africa at the time of independence. Continuing a British colonial tradition, the new government invested a substantial part of its revenues in education at all levels from primary school through university. As a result Ghana had a high level of literacy and more college graduates than the country could absorb. But economic policy moved from one disaster to the next. The Nkrumah government embarked on a series of expensive projects such as grandiose industrialization schemes and public buildings that drained the country's coffers while contributing little to its growth. The government's policies toward private enterprise (both Ghanaian and foreign) reflected a basic ambiguity that has persisted for two decades. On one hand, the Ghanaians recognized their need for the capital, entrepreneurial initiative, managerial know-how, and technology that domestic and foreign companies could supply, but on the other hand, they were impressed with the socialist, state-directed model of development and were concerned that private capitalists, if left unchecked, would accumulate most of the country's wealth and benefits of development for themselves. Nkrumah's solution was to attempt to channel and control private investment by establishing four categories of enterprises:

1. State Enterprises: wholly government-owned, supposed to include most large businesses.

2. Private Enterprises: owned by Ghanaians or foreign investors or joint Ghanaian-foreign ventures.

3. Joint State/Private Enterprises: partnerships, generally between the government and foreign investors.

4. Cooperatives.

A government agency was to supervise domestic and foreign investments to ensure that they complied with the requirements of their assigned categories.

A Capital Investments Act was passed in 1963. It set up a scheme of priorities and incentives to attract foreign investment, provided such investment conformed to the conditions set down by the government. Initially a fair amount of investment was attracted, but a lot of it went into capital-intensive, high-technology plants that were inefficient and expensive producers for the small Ghanaian market. Meanwhile agricultural development was neglected.

Nkrumah was overthrown by a military coup in 1966. The military regime attempted to liberalize the economy, reduce import and currency controls, increase the role of the market in allocating resources, and create a more attractive climate for foreign investment. In spite of their efforts, however, the economy remained largely stagnant.

The military stepped aside as promised in 1969, and a former university professor, Dr. Kofi Busia, was elected president. Buoyed by a boom in cocoa prices during his first year in office, Busia initiated an expansionary program intended to increase the rates of domestic savings and investment. But imports of consumer items swelled, world cocoa prices fell, inflation heated up, and the balance-of-payments deficit worsened.

Another military coup was staged in January 1972, bringing to power a group calling itself the National Reconciliation Council (NRC). This group set out to undo the liberalizations of the previous five-and-a-half years. They clamped on wage, price, and rent controls; vastly increased import and currency controls; reasserted the program of state enterprises; nationalized 55 percent of most of the larger domestic- and foreign-owned businesses; and held down prices paid to cocoa farmers in an attempt to increase the state share of agricultural revenues. The consequences were disastrous. Cocoa production fell off, and farmers began smuggling their crops to neighboring Ivory Coast and Togo, where they could obtain much higher prices. Once one of the most abundant food-producers in Africa, the country now had to import canned goods and staples from Europe and the U.S., and it was caught in the vise of spiralling oil prices. Inflation, the government deficit, the money supply, and the balance-of-payments deficit ballooned. Corruption and mismanagement in the government machinery and the state enterprises were rampant. Skilled and educated people fled to jobs in Nigeria, England, and the U.S. The cumbersome administrative procedures prevented the government from utilizing even the foreign aid that was given to it. Some factories were operating at less than 25 percent of capacity because the shortage of foreign exchange made it impossible to import necessary raw materials and spare parts. Foreign companies faced a proliferation of controls and hindrances; for example, one company applied in 1972 for permission to repatriate a dividend and was still waiting in 1979 for the foreign-exchange allocation to come through. Some foreign companies pulled out, and virtually no new investment came into the country. Meanwhile, the military rulers divided into factions and struggled among themselves for control of the government, with the result of paralysis and continuous crisis in the country's political leadership.

In June 1979 a group of junior air force officers overthrew the NRC regime and installed as President flight lieutenant Jerry Rawlings, the son of a British father and a Ghanaian mother. Rawlings stepped aside three months later, after the election of Hilla Limann, a former diplomat and economist, as President. In spite of his lack of political experience, Limann proved to be an adept politician. He neutralized some potential coup-makers in the military and lined up enough support in the newly reconstituted Parliament to institute a program of economic reforms. His government imposed severe austerity measures, enabling the country to meet its obligations on its foreign debts for the first time in five years and to regain a measure of international creditworthiness. Prices paid to cocoa farmers were trebled, reversing the declining production figures and reducing the amount of smuggling. Many problems remained, however. The inflation rate was still above 50 percent a year, shortages of food and spare parts continued, and the country's best managers continued deserting the inefficient state industries in favor of higher-paying jobs abroad. The government hesitated to take one of the most necessary but politically risky steps, devaluation of the Ghanaian currency, the cedi. The I.M.F. tried to impose devaluation as a condition for the granting of further credits, but Limann feared that such a move might trigger another coup, and the I.M.F. relented somewhat. In spite of an increase in cocoa production, the country's export revenues declined because of a steep fall in the world price.

President Limann made clear his intention to seek new foreign investment for Ghana. His government enacted a new Investment Code designed to

> encourage foreign investments in Ghana by the provision of incentives, to promote the development of Ghanaian entrepreneurs, to indicate enterprises in which the State and Ghanaians are required to participate in any investment and the extent of such participation, to make provision for the registration of technology transfer contracts.

The Code assured foreign investors of "protection" and a fair return on their investment. It specifically eliminated any restrictions on transfers out of Ghana of fees, charges, capital and profits to the investor's country of origin. It established a Ghana Investing Centre chaired by the Vice-President of Ghana to dismantle regulatory and administrative barriers to investment and to review investment projects; the Centre could decide which projects should qualify for special incentives. All approved enterprises were to receive five-year exemptions from customs duties for machinery and equipment imported for use in the enterprises, three years' customs exemption for spare parts, guaranteed manufacturing or establishment licenses, guaranteed immigration of necessary expatriate personnel, and certain tax exemptions and remittance guarantees for such personnel. In the manufacturing sector the government sought industries in which the country had a raw material advantage, underutilized existing plant capacity, or the capacity to conserve and/or earn foreign exchange. Projects qualifying for investment included agro-based industries, those processing raw materials originating in Ghana, animal feed, and fertilizer, among others. Companies in the export sector could be exempted from company income tax during an initial period provided they declared no dividends during that period.

Evidently the new Investment Code made a favorable impression on at least a few potential investors, because Lee recalled seeing a couple of items in the newspapers during 1981 mentioning that a few American and European companies were exploring possibilities for new investments in Ghana. Lee himself was attracted by the country's advantages—rich soil, adequate rainfall, an educated and energetic population, potential mineral wealth, and the beginnings of a national development program. Lee thought it would be very desirable for Nitrofix to be the first fertilizer producer in Ghana and thus secure an entrenched position in what could become a very prosperous market. But he knew that many problems remained. The country was still deeply in debt, its currency vastly overvalued, its foreign exchange reserves close to zero, its economy dependent on the vagaries of the world cocoa market, its borrowing power from the I.M.F. and private lenders essentially exhausted, and its record of economic mismanagement still needing much improvement. If only they could get their act together.

On New Year's Day 1982, Lee was shocked to learn that the Limann government had been overthrown in yet another military coup, Ghana's fifth in fifteen years. This one too was led by Jerry Rawlings, then 34 years old. In radio broadcasts Rawlings claimed that Limann had been incapable of solving Ghana's economic problems, and he announced his intention to retain the presidency "as long as necessary." It soon became apparent, however, that he did not enjoy much popular support and did not have many ideas on how to improve the country's economic situation. Ghana appeared to have suffered another political and economic setback, at least temporarily.

Table 1 gives the most recent statistics Lee could find on the Ghanaian economy. Tables 2, 3, and 4 give some statistics on the world production, consumption and price of cocoa. Table 5 shows the consumption of fertilizer in Ghana and other countries.

MARKET FOR FERTILIZER

Agriculture is a way of life for the people of Ghana, employing 60 percent of the labor force and producing 42 percent of the gross domestic product in 1980. However, out of the 23 million hectares suitable for farming, only 3 million hectares, or 13 percent, were under cultivation. Methods of cultivation were divided into two general categories: traditional (or subsistence) and new improved practices. Traditional methods were characterized by the use of simple tools; they relied almost entirely on human labor, resulting in inefficient processing and storage methods and low crop yields. The new methods stressed the use of chemicals (fertilizers and pesticides) as well as farm machinery and implements.

Over 90 percent of farming was undertaken by subsistence-level private farmers cultivating small plots of land, generally between 3 and 4 hectares. Soil fertility on these farms was generally maintained by crop rotation and burning of vegetation cover; the latter practice returned potash and some minerals to the soil, but it caused the loss of important organic matter and other minerals. Burning was especially damaging if done too frequently or at the wrong season, conditions likely to result as land use intensifies.

While the cultivation of tree crops (cocoa, coffee, rubber, and palm oil) was labor-intensive, mechanization had been introduced in the cultivation of field crops such as maize and rice. Mechanical cultivation leads to rapid deterioration of the organic matter in the soil and the depletion of soil nutrients. Therefore fertilizers must be used to replenish lost minerals, or else crop yields decline.

The Limann government declared that agriculture would be the number one priority for development and investment. The government encouraged the development of large-scale commercial farming, which required the use of modern techniques. In order to boost overall productivity and expand agricultural output, the government supplied many inputs including hoes, seed rice, and groundnuts (peanuts). It also distributed over one million bags of fertilizer to small producers, commercial farms, and para-state organizations.

These steps alone would not be sufficient to improve productivity or increase the usage of fertilizers, however; raising the educational level of the farm population was a fundamental necessity to boost the understanding and acceptance of fertilizers. Such an educational program would require a massive effort by the government. But the more energetic and literate younger generation who might be more amenable to adopting new practices had been leaving the countryside for the cities. Furthermore, the archaic land tenure system was based on traditions and customs that discouraged innovation and thus constituted a formidable obstacle to the acceptance of fertilizer by small farmers.

Cocoa was raised both by small farmers who converted a portion of their subsistence holdings to production of the cash crop and by larger plantations and state farms. The cocoa industry was the main source of Ghana's foreign exchange earnings, accounting for approximately 65 percent in an average year. It employed 11 percent of the nation's labor force and was believed to account for a large part of its fertilizer usage. However, cocoa production had declined steadily since the early 1960's, and by 1980 Ghana had fallen from first to third place among the world's major exporters. The factors responsible for the decline in output included low producer prices, poor maintenance of cocoa farms, aging of cocoa trees and cocoa farmers, scarcity of farm labor in the major producing areas, and ineffective control of pests and diseases. Poor transportation and a lack of infrastructure were problems, as well as smuggling to neighboring countries where better prices were obtainable. Storage facilities had also deteriorated.

After reviewing the preceding information, Lee concluded that there would be many imponderables in any effort to estimate the growth potential of the Ghanaian fertilizer market. So much would depend on non-economic factors such as the effort and expense the government might decide to put into promoting the use of fertilizer and the pace at which Ghanaian farmers would accept it. Lee did find some tables apparently indicating that the use of fertilizers was growing in Ghana and enabling comparisons with other countries. (See Tables 5 and 5a.) However, he also found another source that said that Ghanaian consumption of nitrogenous fertilizers had peaked at 11.0 thousand metric tons in 1975–76 and had declined somewhat for several years thereafter. Consumption of potash and phosphate fertilizers had also decreased since 1975–76.

Lee also wondered whether some Ghanaian fertilizer production might be exportable to other West African countries. Ghana had joined the Economic Community of West African States (ECOWAS) at its inception in 1975. This community had a total of sixteen member states, many of which were even smaller and poorer than Ghana.* It was supposed to become a common market with the elimination of trade barriers among its members and a common external tariff. Its members were supposed to work cooperatively for agricultural development, the construction of infrastructure to improve regional transportation and communications, and industrial growth. However, most of the members could not afford to lower their own tariff barriers or to take any concrete steps to implement the regional integration plans. Furthermore, Nigeria, with its oil wealth and naptha feedstocks, would be likely to grab the lead as the dominant nitrogenous fertilizer exporter in the region.

PLANT TYPE AND SIZE

Lee knew that the technical and economic factors involved in the choice of plant size and production methods for nitrogenous fertilizers were very complex and were subject to change depending on the price of the primary input, naptha, a petroleum derivative. Nonetheless, he knew that Nitrofix had three basic choices of technology and that significant economies of scale could be achieved in both construction and per-unit production costs as plants were made larger and more advanced. He obtained some ballpark figures from one of the company engineers:

Annual Production Capacity (tons)	Production Technology	Factor Proportions	Construction Cost (U.S.)	Production Cost per Ton of Ammonia
20,000	Steam-reforming	Relatively labor-intensive	$20 million	$130
80,000	Reciprocating compressor	Relatively capital-intensive	$60 million	$120
160,000	Centrifugal compressor	Capital-intensive	$90 million	$100

The ammonia (from whatever source) would then be converted into ammonium nitrate—the actual fertilizer—in a technologically simple process. This diluted the value of the ammonia by about 50 percent: one ton of ammonia made two tons of ammonium nitrate. Lee was aware that construction and production costs had a way of soaring when plants were put into developing countries because of shortages of materials and the added costs and inefficiencies of trying to train and use unskilled manpower. The steam-reforming production technique was

---

*Benin, Cape Verde, Gambia, Ghana, Guinea, Guinea-Bissau, Ivory Coast, Liberia, Mali, Mauritania, Niger, Nigeria, Senegal, Sierra Leone, Togo, Upper Volta.

outdated and inefficient, but it had the advantages of being easier to learn and using equipment that could be obtained already used from other LDCs.

Another alternative was for the Ghanaians to import U.S. or European ammonium nitrate. The world price was rather volatile, fluctuating between $50 and $90 per ton during the previous five years. Lee estimated a good average would be $65 per ton (the equivalent of paying $130 per ton of ammonia). In all likelihood importing fertilizer would be cheaper than trying to produce it in Ghana because of the added expenses and hassles of operating in a faraway LDC. (Lee figured that transportation costs would approximately even out regardless whether unprocessed naptha or processed ammonium nitrate were shipped to Ghana.) By producing it themselves, however, the Ghanaians *might* save some foreign exchange, raise the skills and industrial experience of some workers, and add to the foundation for the country's industrial development. A shiny new plant would also make the government leaders look good.

THE FINANCIAL AND OWNERSHIP ARRANGEMENTS

The Investment Code required that any foreign investment in fertilizer be a joint venture, 55 percent Ghanaian and 45 percent foreign. All other things being equal, Nitrofix might have prefered 100 percent ownership and control, but they also knew that there were some advantages to having a local partner. Lee noted that in spite of the apparent rigidity of the Code, the 1979 Constitution allowed some room for further negotiations. If the enterprise was cast as a joint venture, he assumed that each partner would put in equity capital proportional to its percentage ownership. This was not a rule cast in stone, however, and considerable flexibility might be achieved by negotiating the valuation of whatever machinery Nitrofix contributed, the rate at which contributions in cedis were valued, and the mixture of equity and debt contributed by each partner.

If the partners agreed to go with the 20,000-ton plant employing steam-reforming technology, it would be ideal from Nitrofix's point of view to make its entire contribution in the form of used equipment. The valuation of such equipment would be quite arbitrary: its value as scrap might be $100,000, but it might produce several million dollars worth of output per year for somebody who could keep it running. Lee suspected the Ghanaians were too sophisticated to accept such outdated technology or at least to give it a very high valuation, however.

As to choice of partner, Nitrofix would probably have preferred a private businessman or group, but Lee doubted that private citizens would be capable of raising that kind of money in Ghana, and Nitrofix was most reluctant to take on a partner who didn't contribute a fair share of the risk capital. Realistically, therefore, they would probably have to go with the government.

Another question was the matter of debt versus equity. In order to minimize their exposure in a country like Ghana, Nitrofix would have preferred to put in a relatively small amount of its own capital as equity and to obtain most of the financing in the form of loans. On a $20 million project, for example, Lee wondered whether Nitrofix could put in as little as $4.5 million, the Ghanaian partner $5.5 million, and the remaining $10 million come from outside lenders. However, it was questionable whether outside lenders would put up this large a percentage on such a risky venture, and Nitrofix might end up having to pay for a much higher percentage of a much larger project. What's more, interest rates in the Eurodollar market were then running about 15 percent, which would make them think carefully about taking on a hard-currency debt. And there wasn't a lot of money available for soft loans at this time, either.

Cabiri said the government would help arrange local financing for plant construction and local supplies and would try to help obtain hard-currency financing for necessary imports. It might offer to guarantee any borrowings from international banks, for example. But in view of the country's desperate financial straits, Lee seriously doubted whether the banks would give much weight to such guarantees. Furthermore, he was most reluctant to have Nitrofix bear the entire foreign-exchange risk of the project; the Ghanaians were going to have to come up with a decent share of the dollars.

Overhead expenses and taxes were other imponderables. Lee made the optimistic assumption that overhead expenses might run only 10 percent of gross sales, although he was aware that red tape, delays, and corruption often ate up a much larger percent of the profits in LDCs. Ghana imposed a 50 percent tax on corporate income, but Lee assumed Nitrofix could get a holiday from all taxes for at least the first 5 years of production, and maybe for 10. However, he knew the Bank of Ghana and the Ministry of Finance would object if the tax abatement was too generous.

It was obvious from all these considerations that the problems of financing and risk might be enough to discourage Nitrofix from the venture. However, Lee's preliminary calculations suggested the possibility of some very handsome returns if everything went right. Nitrofix would of course seek tariff protection against fertilizer imports. If they got a 100-percent tariff, they might be able to sell their Ghanaian production for as much as $260 per ton. He recognized that the higher the tariff, the less the net economic benefit to the host country would be. But he calculated that if they went ahead with the 160,000-ton plan *and* obtained 50 percent financing at 15 percent *and* were able to sell their entire output at $260 per ton *and* were able to hold their overhead costs to 10 percent of sales *and* could get a complete tax holiday, Nitrofix Inc. might earn $6.6 million per year on a $20 million investment—a handsome return. And the returns could be even higher if they could get subsidized loans, a subsidized plant site, payments for training workers, etc. Perhaps if they waited a year or two they could get a lower rate on their hard-currency borrowings. On the other hand, the returns would be lower as soon as the tax holiday ran out or was cancelled, or if they decided to go with the 80,000-ton plant, or if Lee's assumptions regarding the size of the market or the low amount of overhead did not pan out. (Lee also calculated that they would need at least 22 percent tariff protection in order for the plant to break even if all his optimistic assumptions held true.)

In some ways the 20,000-ton plant seemed the most attractive for both

Nitrofix and Ghana, despite its badly outdated technology. Lee wondered if Nitrofix Inc. could get a 45 percent stake in exchange for some obsolescent steam-reforming equipment from their Greek or Philippine subsidiaries plus a promise to provide technical assistance and train Ghanaians to run the plant. The Ghanaian partner would get 55 percent in exchange for supplying 15 million cedis ($5.5 million at the official exchange rate); this money would pay local expenses for setting up the plant. They would seek a $10 million Eurodollar loan to cover the hard-currency expenses. With a 100 percent tariff, this plant should produce a pre-tax profit of $580,000 if everything went right. Nitrofix Inc.'s share would be $261,000—not bad considering that it would be an essentially costless investment for them.

Another factor that could help make the investment more attractive would be if Nitrofix could find a way of reducing some of the risks. Lee wondered whether they could bargain the Ghanaians into giving Nitrofix's shares a priority claim to dividends, for example. Maybe Nitrofix could cast part of its compensation in the form of a management fee or licensing payment off the top—say 1 or 2 percent of gross revenues. They might be able to obtain insurance from the Overseas Private Investment Corporation (OPIC) against the risks of expropriation, war, and currency inconvertibility; the premiums on such insurance could run up to 1.5 percent of the amount of coverage (0.6% for expropriation, 0.6% for war, revolution or insurrection, and 0.3% for currency inconvertibility, if Nitrofix elected to take the full coverage).

Reviewing all of the above information, Lee realized that he faced a daunting task in trying to evaluate it and formulate a decision. But he also looked forward to it as an interesting challenge.

TABLE 1 Statistics on Ghanaian Economy

	1974	1975	1976	1977	1978	1979	1980	1981
Total exports	840	929	952	1,106	1,645	1,201	—	—
Exports of cacao	866	551	516	680	1,033	—	—	—
Imports	944	909	969	1,176	1,653	1,299	—	—
Foreign debt								
(claims on government)	574	881	1,513	2,527	4,287	4,413	5,724	9,494
Official reserves	92	149	203	162	288	300	216	196

Note: Above figures in millions of cedis at official exchange rate.

	1974	1975	1976	1977	1978	1979	1980	1981
Official exchange rate	.8696	.8696	.8696	.8696	.3636	.3636	.3636	.3636
*Black market exchange rate	.65	.52	.23	.13	.10	.07	.04	.02

Note: Above figures in U.S. dollars per cedi.

	1974	1975	1976	1977	1978	1979	1980	1981
Consumer price index: 1975 = 100	77.0	100.0	156.1	337.8	584.8	903.0	1355.4	2934

SOURCE: *International Financial Statistics*, except where noted otherwise.
* SOURCE: *Pick's Currency Yearbook*, 1977–79; 1980 and 1981 rates from current news articles.

TABLE 2 World Production of Cocoa Beans in Principal Exporting Countries (in thousands of metric tons)

Crop Year	Brazil	Ghana	Ivory Coast	Nigeria	World Total
1967–68	145	422	147	239	1,352
1968–69	165	339	145	192	1,242
1969–70	201	416	181	223	1,435
1970–71	182	392	180	308	1,499
1971–72	167	464	226	255	1,583
1972–73	162	418	181	241	1,398
1973–74	246	350	209	215	1,448
1974–75	273	377	242	214	1,549
1975–76	258	397	231	216	1,509
1976–77	234	320	230	165	1,340
1977–78	283	268	304	205	1,502
1978–79	314	250	312	137	1,480
1979–80	294	290	373	169	1,617
1980–81	350	255	352	165	1,584

SOURCE: *1981 Commodity Yearbook*, p. 85.

TABLE 3 Consumption of Cocoa (thousands of metric tons)

Year	World Total
1967	1,366
1968	1,410
1969	1,353
1970	1,355
1971	1,438
1972	1,565
1973	1,556
1974	1,478
1975	1,462
1976	1,525
1977	1,367
1978	1,391
1979	1,437
1980	1,468

SOURCE: 1967–80 figures from *Commodity Yearbook*.

TABLE 4 Spot Cocoa Bean Prices (yearly/monthly average, New York)

Year		In U.S. Cents per Pound
1975		75.9
1976		109.2
1977		214.4
1978		174.2
1979		160.4
1980		135.4
1981		108.5
1982	Jan.	116.0
	Feb.	107.0
	Mar.	102.0
	Apr.	99.0
	May	94.0

SOURCE: Figures for 1967–1980 from *Commodity Yearbook*, 1981. Figures for 1981–1982 from *Survey of Current Business*.

TABLE 5   World Fertilizer Usage—Kilograms of Inorganic Fertilizers[*] per Hectare of Land under Arable Cultivation and Permanent Crops

	1961–1965 (yearly average)	1967	1972	1977
World	27.9	39.9	54.3	68.0
Africa	4.7	6.3	10.0	12.4
North and Central America	41.2	61.3	69.7	83.2
South America	8.4	11.2	24.7	38.8
Asia	11.8	18.5	31.0	45.4
Europe	103.9	139.6	188.7	210.3
Oceania	34.0	34.1	37.4	36.2
USSR	18.0	33.7	53.2	77.6
Selected Countries				
Africa				
Egypt	109.9	100.2	146.7	187.5
Ghana	0.6	0.5	1.7	10.9
Kenya	9.6	17.2	24.9	22.7
Nigeria	0.1	0.3	0.8	3.1
South Africa	23.4	32.9	47.6	59.6
Sudan	3.7	6.3	8.0	4.3
Uganda	0.7	0.8	1.5	0.5
Zaire	0.2	0.5	0.7	1.4
North and Central America				
Canada	12.4	20.4	23.2	34.3
Cuba	94.0	169.3	76.2	132.7
Mexico	11.3	18.5	29.3	46.0
USA	52.2	77.4	86.2	99.5
South America				
Argentina	0.9	2.2	2.5	2.2
Brazil	9.1	13.8	45.2	77.4
Asia				
Bangladesh	4.4	10.6	20.0	37.1
China	13.2	24.1	45.5	74.3
India	3.7	7.1	16.7	25.3
Indonesia	8.4	8.6	28.9	35.0
Japan	305.2	387.4	389.5	428.1
Thailand	2.2	7.7	10.8	15.6
Turkey	3.9	10.6	22.4	46.5
Europe				
France	133.9	191.6	284.5	277.6
Netherlands	534.9	626.2	719.5	737.3
Hungary	52.9	91.3	182.7	278.7
Italy	60.2	73.8	125.3	140.9
Poland	65.2	117.9	201.1	241.0
Romania	7.8	27.4	40.1	54.2
UK	198.9	254.2	240.0	287.6
Oceania				
Australia	24.5	26.6	26.1	24.5
New Zealand	737.6	720.3	1,319.5	1,296.3

[*] Inorganic nitrogenous, phosphatic, and potash fertilizers.

SOURCE: *The World Food Book* (1981) pp. 214–15.

TABLE 5a Kilograms of Inorganic Fertilizers per Hectare of Land under Arable Cultivation and Permanent Crops, 1977 (log scale)

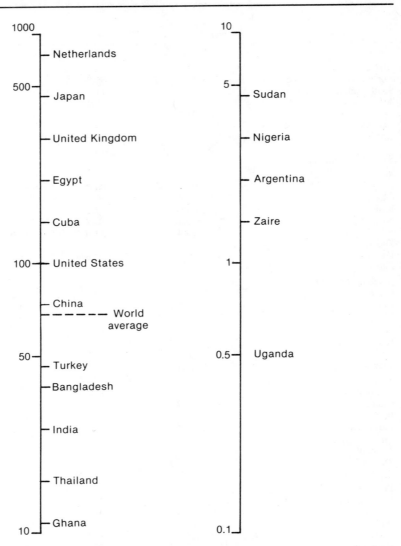

Multinational Operations Management

British Airborne

Dr. Amar Singh, an Indian national who had been in Canada for four weeks at the invitation of the government to lecture on some obscure aspects of neurosurgery—a subject on which he was a leading expert—was going back to Delhi. He had, in fact, been on his way to Montreal's airport at Dorval, when he decided that he would like to stop in London for a day or two on his way home to meet his old friend and teacher, Sir Michael Shannon.

On arrival at Dorval Airport, the 5'4" disheveled and untidy doctor made his way to the counter of British Airborne. There was a well-groomed and charming lady in attendance with "Jane Smith" boldly splashed on her name tag.

"Yes, sir?"

"I want a booking on your evening flight—to London and on to Delhi," said Dr. Singh.

Miss Smith punched a few keys. "Yes, we can manage that, sir."

Dr. Singh handed over his ticket. "I would like to stop in London for about 12 hours."

Miss Smith looked at the ticket, her brows furrowed, and she consulted a manual on her desk. "You have an excursion ticket, sir, and there's no way we can permit you to break your journey in London."

"But when I came to Montreal, Trans Am permitted me to stop over in London. Perhaps I can speak to someone in your organization who could assist me."

"I can't speak for Trans Am, sir. It may have been an oversight on their part, but we don't do it. The airline's rules are very specific and the answer is no. There's nobody else who could help you," said Miss Smith firmly but suavely, adding with a smile, "Should I make a reservation straight to Delhi?"

Dr. Singh was slightly taken aback. "Perhaps I could pay the difference."

"We can't accept that ticket in part exchange. You will have to buy an entirely new ticket and perhaps you wouldn't want to do that, sir."

Dr. Singh looked at her.

"I am afraid the answer remains definitely no." With these words Miss Smith looked over Dr. Singh's head at the tall American hippie next in the queue.

This case was prepared by Mr. Shiv Mathur, Research Fellow, and Professor Kenneth Simmonds of the London Graduate School of Business Studies. It is not intended to illustrate the policies or practice of any particular firm. Financial support was provided by the British Overseas Trade Board. Copyright 1976 by London Business School.

Dr. Singh looked around, seemed upset, then picked up his bags and walked over to the Mediterranean Airways counter.

Later that evening when Miss Smith was having a cup of tea with John Parry-Green, British Airborne's marketing manager for eastern Canada, she recounted the incident with Dr. Singh.

"Quite right, too," agreed Mr. Parry-Green when he heard the stand she had taken. But when Miss Smith had returned to her counter, Mr. Parry-Green continued to think about the matter.

Since his appointment to the region six months previously, Mr. Parry-Green had been trying to drum up business for British Airborne in the eastern provinces of Canada. He had had talks with travel agents and some of the larger business houses in the province of Quebec and he felt that negotiations had, by and large, been satisfactory. However, he had been unable to come to terms with the two Indian travel agents who made the majority of bookings for the large population of Indians and other Asians resident in eastern Canada. Mr. Parry-Green had invited them to his office and quite specifically laid down his attractive terms on discounts and commission, but they had, in his opinion, taken an extreme bargaining position and it all seemed of little use. The two travel agents had telephoned him on several occasions to ask him if he would contact British Airborne's London office to explain their position, but Mr. Parry-Green had assured them that though he could not alter his terms he quite understood the nature of their demands and would advise them if his airline was ever in a position to change its policy. As he felt quite competent to deal with the situation, he did not think it necessary to refer the question to London and negotiations had now been deadlocked for a few weeks.

Asians and Arabs with their extended families were frequent travelers and British Airborne could certainly do with their business. But Mr. Parry-Green felt that they wanted him to bend not only British Airborne, but also IATA (International Air Transport Association) rules. He suspected other airlines, and especially Mediterranean Airways, of making illegal concessions to passengers. These concessions could take many forms, such as overlooking excess baggage and giving unallowed stopovers and large discounts.

Of course, local managers of other airlines denied this, and Jean Cohen of Mediterranean Airways was most vociferous in his denials. But could one trust that lot? Mr. Parry-Green had, on his own initiative, once or twice tried to check on Mediterranean Airways' activities, but had been unable to document any irregularity. However, such concessions were almost impossible to detect on a cursory check and would require a much more thorough investigation. Mr. Parry-Green had himself been tempted to make some concessions to his passengers that would technically infringe IATA rules and had, in fact, noted this as a point of serious discussion at the forthcoming marketing managers' conference in London. If London did not permit him to try some concessions, he had almost decided that he would register a complaint anonymously with the IATA authorities regarding Mediterranean Airways' activities. IATA would surely uncover many irregularities and although the substantial fines that would be imposed following the detection of such offenses might not worry an airline of Mediterranean Airways' standing, it would at least give Jean Cohen something to account for to his head office and customers. The International Air Transport Association had not been lenient in recent years about infringement of rules.

Over the last three months, British Airborne's comparative load factor from Dorval had fallen at an increasing rate, in spite of the additional facilities and staff that Mr. Parry-Green had employed to serve customers. Mr. Parry-Green felt that this was partly due to the growing recession and consequent excess capacity on flights and competition for customers. Still, it did not look good in the first year of his appointment, and the incident with Dr. Singh made him wonder again whether he should not suggest that counter staff fail to notice excursion rates when passengers held British Airborne's own tickets and wanted to stop over.

Rediplant N.V.

Early in 1981 John Bryant, owner of an English timber products firm, was asked by his close friend Martin Nievelt whether he would consider becoming a commisar[1] of Rediplant N.V.—a company being formed to exploit the new Rediplant method for packaging bulbs. Martin also wanted John's opinion on the number of sealing machines that should be purchased in advance of the first full season of Rediplant sales. This was a particularly difficult decision for him, as there was little guide as to how much they would sell and most of the packaging would have to be carried out during the month of August.

Martin Nievelt and Walter Praag were owners and joint Managing Directors of Hans Praag & Co., an old established Dutch bulb exporter based in Hillegom, Holland. Before the Rediplant development, Praag had concentrated on bulb sales to France, the United Kingdom, Switzerland and Germany. They sold to nurserymen, wholesalers and large retailers as well as directly to the public through mail order catalogues. There were two seasons each year. The larger was for spring bulbs which were lifted from the bulb fields and distributed in the autumn for planting up to mid-winter. This season represented 70 percent of the bulb market and covered tulips, crocuses, narcissi and hyacinths.

Recent performance of firms in the bulb business had been poor and there had been numerous failures over the previous two years. The 600 exporting houses all belonged to an industry association and argued the need to hold price levels, but competition amongst them resulted in continual margin cutting. Praag had recorded losses both years, mainly because of low response to their mail order catalogues, attributed by Martin Nievelt to cold, wet weekends that discouraged customers from thinking about gardening. While substantial profits could still be made in a good mail order season, the response rates had been dropping at an average rate of 8 percent per year. The development of the Rediplant system therefore came at a particularly opportune time and gave Praag an opportunity to differentiate its product and increase its margins. Praag decided to withdraw from the direct mail order side of the business and concentrate on building the broadest possible sales of Rediplant packed bulbs. Sales of the mail order list, moreover, would provide finance for the new effort and avoid surrender of ownership interest which was usually required in order to obtain long-term bank lending for small private companies.

The French, German and Swiss mailing lists were sold to Beinum & Co.

---

[1] Commissars of Dutch corporations are outside directors appointed by the shareholders to oversee the employee directors. They have a number of specific powers and their consent must be obtained for all borrowing by the company.

late in 1980. Beinum was the largest Dutch bulb merchant with a turnover around 100 million guilders (Fl. 100m) and a mailing list of 5 million catalogues.[2] Praag's United Kingdom mail order list and the U.K. wholesale business were sold to Sutcliffe Seeds Ltd. of Norwich. Sutcliffe was moving into the bulb market as an extension to their traditional seed activities and the agreement provided for Praag to supply all Sutcliffe's requirements for Dutch bulbs, whilst retaining the right to go directly to a selected list of retail chains and large stores in the United Kingdom.

DEVELOPMENT OF THE REDIPLANT SYSTEM

The idea for Rediplant was first conceived in November 1979 by Walter Praag, who concentrated on the engineering and production side of the business, leaving the commercial side to Martin Nievelt. (See the appendix at the end of the case for a chronology of Rediplant development.) Rediplant was basically a transparent plastic strip moulded to hold bulbs in equally-spaced blisters open at the top and bottom. It was designed as a usage container that could be planted directly in the soil without removing the bulbs, giving them protection from frost, birds, rodents and slugs, and enabling the bulbs to be easily retrieved for planting in subsequent seasons.

Walter Praag explained the development in this way:

> I got the idea at the end of 1979 and aimed only to make our competitive position easier and to solve planting problems for the buyer. We ran trials and found that it made not only for easier planting but also gave protection and a better flower, though it was not invented for that purpose. We tested a great quantity with a sensitive control test and the packaged bulbs showed up better than bulbs planted by hand. We limited our tests to hyacinths, tulips, narcissi, crocuses and gladioli, because the others have extra difficulties for packaging and these are the main selling items. With gladioli we had some trouble and I had to redesign the pack as the sprouts came out of the side of the bulb rather than the top. When we told people the name of our new pack was Rediplant many remarked that it was not a very good name—but minutes later they would all use the name without any prompting. We decided it must be a very good name.

The bulbs were packed automatically into previously formed plastic strips which were then sealed and fitted into a cardboard sleeve printed with details of the bulbs and planting instructions. After considerable experimentation the new pack was ready for launching and in May 1980 a vacuum forming machine was purchased to make quantities of the strips. At this stage the pack was comparatively crude, with a single coloured cardboard sleeve which totally enclosed the plastic strip which was in turn stapled together to hold the bulbs.

Mr. Nievelt did his own market research by asking friends, acquaintances and the general public what they thought of the packs and if they would buy

---

[2] The standard abbreviation for a Dutch guilder or florin is "Fl." Exchange rates were £1.00 (U.K.) = Fl. 4.30, $1.00 (U.S.) = Fl. 3.00.

them. On his frequent sales trips to England, for example, he asked customers in garden centres and large stores he visited whether they would buy the packs and they all said they would. The packs contained six tulips with a suggested retail price of £1.30 as against a price of £1.00 for similar loose bulbs. Martin also asked retailers in England what they thought of the packaging. He recalled:

> Large retail chains, Woolworths, Boots, Debenhams and John Lewis liked it and after a while the larger garden centres would say that they would buy it. Small centres and garden stores, however, generally said they did not like Rediplant. They gave few reasons but they seemed worried that it would mean other types of stores would find it easier to sell bulbs.

Martin also persuaded three different outlets to test market the strips—a store on a U.S. air force base at Woodbridge, a seedshop in Ipswich and a garden centre at Ramsey, Essex. Each received one hundred strips, without charge, and each quickly sold the entire assignment at £1.30 each.

Rediplant packaging was next featured in Praag mail order catalogues for spring bulbs sent out in autumn 1980. These were mailed to some 300,000 customers in Britain, France and Germany at a cost including postage of £0.20 (or equivalent) each. Prices for a Rediplant package of six bulbs were set about 30 percent below the catalogue prices for a standard quantity of 10 loose bulbs, making the price for a Rediplant bulb 15 percent higher than an equivalent loose bulb. Rediplant packaging appeared on the cover, and the catalogue started with a two-page spread outlining the Rediplant system and offering a 200 percent guarantee to replace every non-flowering Rediplant bulb with two new bulbs. The spread also showed how Rediplant strips could be planted in evenly spaced rows or in cartwheel or zigzag patterns. Walter Praag commented that this sort of thing seemed to appeal particularly to the German market, which was also much more concerned with rodent and insect damage than other nationalities. He thought the British tended to be keener gardeners and more knowledgeable about bulbs, while many more potential customers in France and Germany would avoid buying loose bulbs that they did not understand, or else buy some and plant them upside down. With Rediplant packages these customers would find planting much easier. Praag's experience had been, too, that the British tended to be much more price conscious than the others, while the French tended to identify value with the price charged.

As orders began to come in during the early winter months, Praag was very encouraged by the high proportion of Rediplant sales. Final figures were as follows:

Country	Catalogues Posted	Number of Orders Received	Average Order Size	% of Total Bulbs Ordered in Rediplant Packs		
				Tulips	Hyacinths	Narcissi
U.K.	150,000	8,056	£14.00	18	20	10
France	101,000	5,581	£20.80	27	32	13
W. Germany	50,000	2,091	£21.80	44	39	39

Examination of 160 U.K. orders at random showed the average order for Rediplant to be £8.00, representing on average 50 percent of the customer's total order.

Walter Praag continued work on the Rediplant design. The cardboard sleeve was redesigned with full colour pictures of the blooms and better instructions, and the strips were made narrower and extended to include seven bulbs rather than six in a new pack measuring 40 centimeters. Martin Nievelt thought this might discourage price comparison with loose bulbs sold in dozens. Exhibit 1 shows these new strips on the display stand.

For sales through retail outlets, special units were designed containing 180 strips with wire pegs for each six strips. These pegs could be fitted onto pegboards

EXHIBIT 1   Rediplant Display Stand

Assortment 180 s

REDIPLANT

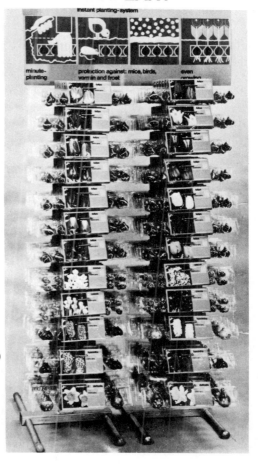

An exclusive new pre-assembled Assortment for You!

- 112 packs of tulips in 14 varieties 7 bulbs per pack
- 24 packs of hyacinths in 4 varieties 5 bulbs per pack
- 12 packs of narcissi in 2 varieties 5 bulbs per pack
- 32 packs of crocus in 4 varieties 14 bulbs per pack
- ___
- 180 packs in 24 well-chosen varieties

Floor space: 15" x 33"
Height display: 63"
Size display poster: 31½" x 18½"
Weight case: 59 lbs.

This display offers an easy and fast set-up with a minimum of floor space

Advantages:
REDIPLANT is unique (patent pending)
Honest presentation in see-through packs
Optimal ventilation preserves the quality of the bulbs
Packs are delivered on pegs, saving labour in setting up display (except assortment 180 and 90)
REDIPLANT has been successfully tested
Over a century of successful bulb-growing experience guarantees a high quality product
Your Department as well as the Dutch Dept. of Agriculture inspects all bulbs before they are exported

or specially designed Rediplant display stands for floor or counter displays. The mix of varieties for the units was based on a statistical analysis of the historical proportions of bulb sales and would not be varied for individual orders. The unit contained 112 strips of tulips in 14 varieties, 24 strips of hyacinths in 4 varieties, 12 strips of narcissi in 2 varieties and 32 strips of crocuses in 4 varieties. Large display posters illustrating the planting of Rediplant strips were designed to accompany each unit, which would be boxed with or without a display stand as required.

Patents for the Rediplant system of packaging were applied for and obtained in the Benelux countries, the United Kingdom, France, Germany, Canada and the U.S.A. This patent was granted for a 'usage' package and competitors would find it difficult to break through simply by altering the design. Moreover, anyone wishing to compete would find it essential on a cost basis to package in Holland, rather than to ship, pack and then redirect the bulbs—and Praag was sure that they would be advised by the Dutch Customs if their patent was infringed.

PARTNERSHIP WITH VAN DIEMEN BROS.

In late 1980 Praag was approached by Van Diemen Bros., who had seen the packages and wanted to explore ways by which they, too, could use the new packaging method. Discussions led to the idea of a partnership for developing the system. Van Diemen had the largest sales force in the Dutch bulb industry, owned their own bulb fields and research laboratories, and were suppliers by appointment to the Netherlands Royal Family. "The idea went against the mentality of the industry that it is not right to work together," said Martin Nievelt. "We had the idea but the other firm had forty sales people against Praag's two, as well as contacts with wholesalers all around the world. A partnership would provide resources and backing at the same time as it removed one of the major sources of potential competition."

Nievelt believed that the fragmented nature of the industry and the lack of product differentiation were the prime causes of low prices and small or non-existent profits. He hoped that the combined strength of the two firms would enable them to make a much larger impact on the bulb market and eventually claim a significant proportion of Dutch bulb sales at higher margins.

The arrangement worked out on a friendly basis with Van Diemen was that Rediplant NV would be formed as a limited company, with Hans Praag & Co. and Van Diemen Bros. each owning 50 percent of the equity. Rediplant would lease Praag's storage and packing facilities in Hillegom and manufacture for the two sales companies, invoicing them at cost after payment of a royalty to Praag of Fl. 0.04 per strip. Praag would retain the right to all sales anywhere in the world destined for customers via mail order and also to wholesale sales in the United Kingdom, Holland and Switzerland. Van Diemen would cover wholesale sales in all remaining countries. This arrangement meant that there would be little change from past concentration because Praag had had very little wholesale revenue from France or Germany. The direct mail market, moreover, accounted for some 20 percent of Dutch bulb exports for dry sales. Martin Nievelt and the senior Van Diemen agreed to act as commissars for the new firm and to ask John Bryant to act as a third neutral commissar. Solicitors were asked to draw up formal agreements. As of the end of February 1981 the drafts had not yet been received.

Meanwhile, Walter Praag and Dik Van Diemen, son of the Van Diemen president, had agreed to become joint managing directors of Rediplant and had become immersed in detailed planning of the production requirements for the 1981 spring bulb season. The elder Van Diemen had also applied to the Dutch government for a grant to develop the invention and Rediplant had received a non-returnable grant of Fl. 130,000.

MEETING THE DEMAND

The period for selling spring bulbs to intermediate outlets ran from January through August, but delivery requirements would be very tight. Excluding mail order business, 55 percent of all sales had to be packed by mid-August, the next 30 percent by the end of August, and the last 15 percent by the end of September. All United States sales were included in the initial 55 percent because of the need to meet shipping dates, but another week could be saved by air freight although it would increase the freight cost for a standard shipment from Fl. 43.00 per '180' unit to Fl. 129.00. After September, mail order business could then be supplied fairly evenly until early December. Delivery commitments were regarded as very important by all the Rediplant executives. The retail buying season was concentrated and a supplier who failed to meet his commitments would ruin his chance of repeat business. Martin Nievelt considered it would be better to take a limited amount of Rediplant orders in the first season rather than run the risk of not being able to meet orders on time and ruining the Rediplant name.

The supply of bulbs themselves presented few problems. Most bulbs were bought from the growers on a contract basis in the spring while still in the ground. A buyer would contract to buy all the production of a given acreage at a fixed price per bulb. As he sold to his customers before he knew how many bulbs he would receive from this acreage, he had to buy any additional requirements or sell any excess on the free market where the price could fluctuate wildly depending on whether there was a glut or a poor season. Although the average price of bulbs could usually be predicted within 10 percent, a given tulip had fluctuated in price between Fl. 28.00 and Fl. 44.00 per hundred over the previous few years. By industry agreement, payment to growers was required promptly on 1st November. For a merchant to retain a good name amongst suppliers payment could not be delayed.

The real problems in supply stemmed from the short packaging season after the bulbs were taken from the fields. Crocuses might not be ready to be packed until 25th July, narcissi and hyacinths a week later, and tulips between the 25th July and 10th August depending on the variety. Packaging, therefore, had to be very carefully planned.

When the bulbs arrived for packaging they would be inspected and sorted before being placed in the PVC strips by semi-automatic filling machines. The strips would then pass along conveyors to an automatic radio frequency sealing machine and from there to a station where they would be fitted with the cardboard sleeve and packed into cartons. While the vacuum-forming machine making the PVC strips could produce only 900 strips per hour, stocks could be built up before packaging began. The sorting machines worked rapidly and could take large quantities of bulbs so they did not limit the output in any way. The speed of the filling machines could also be increased if needed. Four filling machines, moreover, had been built and these could keep at least four sealing machines busy. The limiting factor, then, seemed to be the number of sealing machines. These operated with an output of 900 strips per hour and at Fl. 33,000 were the most expensive items. One machine had been specially designed for Rediplant. Orders for further units would have to be placed immediately as there was a three month delivery time and orders placed after the beginning of March might not be received in time for the packaging season. The machines were believed

EXHIBIT 2   Rediplant Costings

Equipment		
Vacuum forming plant	Fl.	84,000
Transformer and electrical installation		20,000
Moulds		40,000
Sorting machines 10,000 × 4		40,000
Filling machines 7,500 × 4		30,000
Transport lines		20,000
Sealing machines 33,000 × 2		66,000
		300,000

Packaging Cost		
Electricity and maintenance	Fl.	10,000
Rent		40,000
Labour (25,000 hours @ Fl. 12)		300,000
Other overheads		100,000
Depreciation @ 20%		60,000
Interest: on equipment		30,000
on materials and working capital		20,000
		560,000

Packaged Cost (excluding display stands)

	Per Strip	Per Unit (180 strips)
Bulbs	Fl. 1.24	Fl. 223.2
PVC	0.08	14.4
Sleeve	0.12	21.6
Royalties (all sales)	0.04	7.2
Packaging (@ 1 m strips)	0.56	100.8
Carton packaging including labour	0.08	14.4
Point of sale advertising		
(display posters and pegs)	0.06	10.8
Packaged cost	2.18	392.4

to be reliable, but if an electronic component should break down an engineer from the manufacturer would be required.

Praag and Van Diemen were annoyed that the manufacturer of the sealing machine was insisting on payment before delivery, had raised the price to Fl. 33,000 from a verbally agreed figure of Fl. 25,000, and would not make any effort to schedule shorter delivery. They had, therefore, investigated other methods of sealing that did not require expensive equipment. All had major disadvantages. Adhesives and stapling were much slower and stapling spoilt the look of the package, while adhesives attracted the dust from the bulbs and were not 100 percent effective.

Martin Nievelt argued that only one further sealing machine should be ordered. He pointed out that there was no guarantee that huge volumes of Rediplant could be sold in the first season when the buyers knew it to be experimental; moreover, financial difficulties could limit the opportunity to expand in later years. Hans Praag & Co., had little finance available and this had been a further reason for the partnership with Van Diemen. The total requirement for subscribed capital had to be kept to Fl. 400,000 (see Exhibit 2) if Praag's share in the partnership was not to fall below 50 percent. There was no chance of credit from the machinery supplier and the bank had said previously that it would advance funds only in exchange for some of the ownership equity.

During the busy season it was usual to work two shifts, seven days a week, using mainly student labour. For the peak period from 27th July until 17th August, Martin calculated that two sealing machines would enable a production of 605,000 strips (21 days × 16 hours × 900 strips × 2 machines). As this period would represent 55 percent of the season's activity this would mean a total production limit of 1.1 million strips. To be on the safe side he set a first tentative limit of 4,750 units (855,000 strips) for the season's selling activity.

REDIPLANT SALES

While Walter Praag and Dik Van Diemen concentrated on the production planning, Martin Nievelt took on the task of coordinating the Rediplant sale commitments. With Van Diemen's agreement, he had in January allocated the tentative target limit of 4,750 units on the following basis:

1,500	United Kingdom
1,000	United States
1,000	Germany
500	Sweden
250	France
250	Holland
250	Switzerland

Martin was quick to admit that these were little more than rough guesses but he felt that the overall demand figures offered even less help. These are shown in Exhibit 3.

EXHIBIT 3   Dutch Bulb Exports, 1979

	Total Exports (Fl. millions)	Exported for Dry Sales* (%)
Germany	236	31
United States	96	70
United Kingdom	70	35
France	68	64
Italy	62	59
Switzerland	42	42
Canada	16	68
Austria	12	64
All other markets	10	55

* Dry sales refer to the proportion of the sales going to the general public either directly or through outlets. Wet sales refer to sales to nurserymen for forcing cut flowers.

By the end of February the sales force was just commencing its main effort and there was still very little sales feedback to go on. One large order of 1,000 units without stands, however, had just been confirmed by the largest garden supply wholesaler in Germany who had placed this initial order against a request that he be the sole German distributor next year. This firm employed a sizeable sales force calling on both garden supply outlets and major retail chains. The price negotiated by the Van Diemen sales force was Fl. 2.66 per strip net ex Praag warehouse. The German retail mark-up was usually 35 percent on sales and the Van Diemen sales representative had been told that the wholesaler himself would take a 20 percent mark-up on retail price. Transport costs to be met by the wholesaler would be small and there was no duty into Germany.

There had also been other enquiries for large volume supplies but Martin Nievelt had argued against pursuing these for 1981. For example, Beinum, the mail order house who had purchased Praag's mailing lists, had enquired about Rediplant. They would supply their own bulbs and purchase only the packing and packaging but the volumes required could be very large indeed. After initial discussions that ranged around a figure of Fl. 1.20 per strip it was decided not to do anything until the following season. A very large U.S. mail order firm, Henry Field Seed Nursery Co. of Iowa, also showed interest, but would have required delivery for September when their mail order packing commenced. Several of the large U.S. retail chains had expressed interest. Other than arrangements for a modified test by A&P, the supermarket chain, however, these were not followed up because the A&P firm alone could absorb all Rediplant output in just one of its regions. This supermarket chain planned to test sales of the product at US $2.69 per strip. Van Diemen's United States salesmen were instead concentrating on the suburban garden centres which mainly purchased loose bulbs. One of them had reported that, by chaining the size of the Rediplant order he would

EXHIBIT 4   Van Diemen Bros.—Geographical Performance

	% of 1979 Turnover	No. of Agents
Sweden	20.1	4
W. Germany	19.7	4
Finland	16.7	1 + 1 agent
France	10.7	6 + 3 agents
Italy	8.2	1
Norway	7.0	1 + 6 agents
United States	4.5	5
Denmark	3.8	1
Switzerland	3.0	1
Canada	1.4	—
Austria	1.2	1
Iran	1.1	—
United Kingdom	0.9	1
Greece	0.4	—
South Africa	0.4	—
Belgium	0.4	—
Japan	0.1	—
Portugal	0.1	—
Hong Kong	0.1	—
Rest of world	0.1	—

accept to the amount of loose bulbs ordered, he had been able to gain a substantial increase in his sales of loose bulbs.

Martin Nievelt felt that he could safely leave the Van Diemen sales effort to Van Diemen management. They were well organized, with a worldwide sales director and four area managers. He had, however, provided sets of Rediplant brochures and price sheets drawn up in five languages. The prices Van Diemen chose were set to allow them around 20 percent on sales and to meet the usual trade margins in the particular country. In the United States, for example, the standard price for a strip at port of entry had been set at the equivalent of Fl. 3.30 to cover such a margin, 12½ percent duty, and delivery costs.

Van Diemen salesmen were paid a basic salary of Fl. 35,000 plus a commission of 2 percent for the first Fl. 800,000 increasing by ½ percent for each additional Fl. 200,000. Detailed technical training was given and maintained on all aspects of bulb culture, although there was no special sales training. A geographical breakdown of Van Diemen's sales is shown in Exhibit 4, together with the numbers of salesmen concentrating on each country. Scandinavia, with a 5 percent growth rate, was the fastest growing market as well as bringing Van Diemen its largest sales.

UNITED KINGDOM MARKET

Having reserved 1,500 units for the United Kingdom market, Martin Nievelt was anxious to meet this figure. He was awaiting news from Jan Straten, Praag's only other salesman, who was currently on a sales trip to Britain. Martin expected him to come back with some good orders for Rediplant, some of which would be test orders from the major chains.

Praag's United Kingdom bulb turnover in 1980 had been £360,000, of which £160,000 was direct mail. At this level of activity Praag was 6th or 7th in the ranking of about 300 Dutch bulb exporters to the United Kingdom. It was this entire turnover that Praag had sold to Sutcliffe Seeds Ltd. at the end of 1980. As part of the agreement Sutcliffe undertook to purchase all their Dutch bulbs from Praag at an agreed formula, whether sold by direct mail or through outlets. Prices were to be set to cover packing and shipping costs and give Praag a 20 percent mark-up on the packaged cost. The suggested retail price would then be set at 100 percent mark-up on the price to Sutcliffe (50 percent on sales). Sutcliffe would give its outlets a discount of 33.3 percent off this suggested retail price plus an additional 5 percent for payment within 30 days.

Sutcliffe had been actively looking for ways of expanding their sales of bulbs. They had recently taken over the garden seed division of Charles Gibb & Sons and now held over 30 percent of the retail seed market in the United Kingdom. With a total U.K. seed market of only £24 million, however, further growth would be difficult. Against this, the U.K. bulb market of around £40 million offered more opportunity and Paul Duke, managing director of Sutcliffe, had set his sights on 10 percent of this market by 1985. Although Sutcliffe had bulb sales of only £160,000 at this time and there were a great number of competitors, Duke planned to develop into the quality end of the market using Sutcliffe's name and selling only the best Dutch bulbs. Local bulb growing had expanded considerably in recent years and Dutch mail order firms had been undercut by local suppliers, but there were still many bulb varieties better provided from Holland and direct container shipment in bulk could offset almost all the location advantage.

Paul Duke had also asked if Sutcliffe could have an exclusive distributorship for Rediplant in the United Kingdom. Martin Nievelt knew that Praag would not have the resources to set up a significant sales force and had agreed to Duke's proposal, subject to Praag retaining the right to visit a number of their existing outlets and 20 of the largest chain stores and department stores in the United Kingdom. Nievelt undertook not to sell to these outlets at a price lower than Sutcliffe's net price to its outlets less 2 percent cash discount, on the under-standing that Sutcliffe would use the same mark-ups as for loose bulbs.

Nievelt was very pleased with the agreement made with Sutcliffe. He thought that in the first year Sutcliffe's sales force of 60, which called on all the garden centres and hardware and garden stores in the U.K., would take orders for some-where in the vicinity of 600 units. The top salesmen sold between £200,000 and £240,000 of merchandise each year. Sutcliffe planned, moreover, to spend £80,000 on advertising their bulbs in the ensuing year and was planning to hold a cocktail and dinner party to announce their venture, which would be widely covered in the trade papers.

With the major demands of the Rediplant development, Martin had been unable to manage a selling visit to the major outlets he had retained for Praag, and had sent Jan Straten in his place. Jan Straten had started with Praag eight years ago at the age of eighteen and with the exception of a two-year spell in the Dutch army had worked with them ever since. He was paid a fixed salary of Fl. 35,000 and received £30 a day to cover his expenses while in the U.K. He retained his home in Hillegom, seldom being away from home for more than a month at a time, and had sold £100,000 last year, which Martin Nievelt thought was fairly good for a younger man.

The price at which Jan was seeking Rediplant sales in the United Kingdom was £0.88 per strip delivered to the customer, less 2 percent discount for payment within 10 days. This price was based on a suggested retail selling price of £1.32 per strip, which Martin had decided would be necessary to give Sutcliffe the same mark-up as for loose bulbs and still leave a reasonable profit for Praag. Costs of packing, freight, insurance, duty (10 percent), delivery, etc., would amount to about 20 percent of the packaged cost although this percentage might be reduced for full container deliveries. Martin would have preferred the retail price to be £1.16, which would have about equalled the price for similar loose bulbs in garden stores, but was convinced that at £1.32 Straten should be able to persuade several of the chains to place orders.

APPENDIX: CHRONOLOGY OF CASE EVENTS

Late 1979	— Idea for Rediplant conceived by Walter Praag.
May 1980	— Lab testing of Rediplant complete. Relatively crude pack of six bulbs ready for market launch. Vacuum forming machine for strip manufacture purchased.
Summer 1980	— Test sale in three U.K. outlets. All sell 100 strips quickly at £1.30.
Autumn 1980	— Rediplant in "6-pack" featured on cover and 2-page spread of Praag mail order catalogue.
	— Continued improvements to Rediplant—redesigned sleeve and instructions, switch to 7 bulbs instead of 6.
	— Patent applied for.
	— Hans Praag & Co. goes out of mail order business.
	— Praag enters marketing agreement with Sutcliffe for U.K. market covering all Praag products.
Late 1980	— Praag approached by Van Diemen Bros. regarding partnership in Rediplant. Friendly agreement reached, but not yet formally signed.
February 1981	— Preliminary production and marketing plans for Spring 1981 season.
	— Preliminary selling efforts for Rediplant by Van Diemen salesmen in Germany and U.S. Negotiations for mail order with Beinum.
	— Jan Straten of Praag in U.K. selling to U.K. customers not covered by Sutcliffe.

Aigle Engineering

Aigle Engineering Ltd. was a precision engineering shop of 35 employees in south Manchester managed by the 51 year old owner Alan Mohr. Mohr had started the business ten years previously, taking on jobbing work that other firms priced to avoid. He had, however, kept a continual lookout for specialised products that would give him a stable work load. Three years ago, after manufacturing several batches of hand presses for pressing simple metal pin badges, Alan had acquired the rights to the press from its designer. The firms selling the blanks, rings and pins for the badges were happy for Aigle to take over the direct supply and warranty for the presses. They referred all enquiries to him, often stimulated by their own advertising, and a steady volume of orders came in from all around the world. A press cost about £500, and the typical order came from a novelty store owner, a small entrepreneur who sold badges at fairs and shows or someone who circulated clubs or political parties offering to produce an appropriate badge for them.

Before he set up Aigle Engineering, Alan Mohr had been works engineer for a sewing machine manufacturer and for many years he had pursued a hobby of adapting sewing machines to new or extended uses. Eight months ago, he had finally perfected an electronically guided, multiheaded machine for high-speed sewing of shirt collars. Thinking he would get many enquiries from shirt manufacturers, Alan had shown the machine, on which he had applied for a patent, on a small stand at this year's Textile Machinery Exhibition in Munich. A reporter from a machinery journal was attending the show and had included a piece on Aigle's machine in the journal's "What's New" section.

As a result of this exposure, Alan had received two letters from firms wishing to distribute his machine—one from New Jersey and the other from Korea. The Korean firm, Soon Lee & Co., was an importer in Seoul and was asking for permission to import and sell within the Korean market. The New Jersey firm, Moreno Equipment Inc., on the other hand, manufactured a range of machinery and was interested in manufacturing rights. One of their executives had visited Aigle's stand in Munich and spent a lot of time examining the prototype. Their letter is reproduced in Exhibit 1.

Alan was tempted to give Moreno the world manufacturing rights because his existing staff were not really experienced in electronic work. The additional working capital required would also be high for a firm that had strained to capitalise itself out of the profits he had not withdrawn. Of the three prototypes, each so

This case was prepared by Professor Kenneth Simmonds of the London Business School. Copyright © 1986 Professor Kenneth Simmonds.

far had cost about £20,000 in materials and manufacturing time. Mohr wondered what terms he should offer Moreno and whether he should air-freight one of the prototypes to New Jersey.

EXHIBIT 1

Moreno Equipment Inc.
Manufacturers of Textile Machinery & Equipment

Aigle Engineering Ltd.
64 Penine Drive
Sale
Cheshire
United Kingdom

Attention: Mr. Alan Mohr

Dear Mr. Mohr,

On his return from Munich, Mr. William Shergold commented favourably on your Aigle Multi-Collar machine. Mr. Shergold was unable to see the machine in other than a short test operation but we understand that you have several prototypes that are being tested by local manufacturers. We are wondering, therefore, if you would consider freighting us one of these when current tests are completed so that we might assess its potential in various applications.

In the meantime, we would be very pleased to know what you would propose regarding a license for manufacturing by ourselves. As we believe that the market for the machine would be limited, we suggest that you might be prepared to consider granting us world manufacturing rights. Alternatively, we would consider world rights excluding the European Community.

We await your reply with interest.

Sincerely yours,

Klaus Graham
Manager, Licensor Relations

Tony Sheehan

"I have four alternatives but I really don't know which is best. I could look for a job in another company, I could confront George Baker, I could ask Alastair Thomson for clarification of my responsibilities, or I could sit tight and wait for developments." Tony Sheehan, marketing director of British Continental Brands (BCB) of London, was mulling over the frustrations of his new position as he sat over dinner with his wife.

Sheehan, aged 40, had been headhunted three months previously by an executive search firm working for the BCB chairman Alastair Thomson. Thomson had wanted to get the best, most up-to-date practitioner of the marketing of packaged consumables that the headhunters could find. He had felt for some time that the BCB organization tended to slip away from attention to its consumer markets and to pursue its brand marketing as though it was an age-old ritual. He wanted someone who would pull the organization up to the frontiers of marketing practice.

A substantial increase in salary had succeeded in enticing Tony Sheehan from his position as U.K. marketing director for an international beverage firm. Moreover, BCB offered him a real challenge with its worldwide turnover approaching £2 billion and high and consistent profits—although with very little growth. At the same time, there was almost no central marketing input. Management of BCB's national sales subsidiaries was controlled from the small holding company headquarters largely through budget planning and review sessions run by the triarchy of BCB's chairman, managing director, and finance director. Although subsidiary performance in terms of volume growth and market share achieved was considered at the budget meetings, marketing details were not required. The same was true for the brand-owning subsidiaries. These companies produced and sold their products largely through the national sales subsidiaries; although in some cases they sold direct to outside distributors, and in other cases they licensed a larger sales subsidiary to manufacture on their behalf. Some of these brand-owning subsidiaries employed international brand managers. They operated at arms' length from the sales subsidiaries, and any influence they exercised over the sales activities was based on the weight of the particular case they presented, not on any organizational power.

Alongside Tony and also reporting directly to Thomson, was George Baker, the international brand coordinator. Baker, aged 53, had been with BCB for many years. He worked primarily with the management of the brand-owning

This case was prepared by Professor Kenneth Simmonds of the London Business School. Copyright © 1986 Professor Kenneth Simmonds.

companies to stimulate development and testing of new brands and their worldwide release. He was also involved with issues concerning the management and rejuvenation of existing brands. While George had been warm and welcoming to Tony, he had not provided him with any details of his current activities and concerns. George never volunteered to talk to Tony about brands, and all brand correspondence came directly to George.

Only yesterday, Tony had learned from a group circular that George had organized and run a Worldwide Brand Managers' Conference in Rome two weeks previously. When Tony had asked for a summary of the proceedings, George had stated blandly that they had not kept minutes in that sense. Tony had begun to feel that George had expropriated the job of the marketing director, leaving him with nothing but some central public relations budget.

Amtexco Venture in Asiana (Case A)

Amtexco has just received the preliminary approval of its plans to set up a textile mill in Asiana from the Foreign Investment Board of that country. The company is now proceeding with the detailed planning of the investment. At this stage the Asiana Project Committee, which is responsible for this planning work, is choosing the equipment to be installed in the new mill. Since the choice of equipment will be the main determinant of the size of the investment to be made in Asiana and of the size of the labor force to be hired and trained there, this issue promises to be a very controversial one. The Project Committee has, therefore, decided to give it a lot of attention and to be ready for a full justification of the choices made.

As a member of the staff of the Project Committee, you have been put in charge of writing a short issues paper proposing a methodology to compare alternative types of equipment and making recommendations about the guidelines that should be followed in choosing equipment for the Asiana Project. You have been instructed to make these as simple and precise as possible since, after consideration by the Project Committee, your method of analysis and guidelines will be used for the actual choice of equipment. Furthermore, you are to apply your proposed methodology and make specific recommendations as to the choice of looms for the Asiana project.

COMPANY BACKGROUND

Amtexco is one of the largest textile producers in the United States. Its textile sales were nearly half a billion dollars in 1975. Twenty plants manufacture a wide range of products including sheets, pillow cases, towels, draperies, quilted bedspreads, and various woven, nonwoven, and knitted fabrics for apparel, decorative furnishings, and home sewing.

Amtexco has gained recognition in the American textile industry for its capacity for technical innovation. A pioneer of the one level flow-through design of textile plants, it found low-cost, efficient ways to modernize its old multilevel plants rather than write them off. In the same fashion, old modernized machinery and equipment of the latest technology are often combined in its plants in such a way as to minimize both investment and production costs.

However, like most of the textile industry in the United States, Amtexco has been suffering for several years from depressed sales resulting from a general

---

This case was prepared by Professor Michel Amsalem of the Graduate School of Business, Columbia University. Copyright © 1982 Professor Michel Amsalem.

recession as well as increased competition from low-cost textile producers in Asia and Latin America. In fact, Amtexco net sales have been stagnant in real terms and its net income has been declining for several years.

THE DECISION TO GO ABROAD

As a part of a strategy aimed at restoring the company's market position and profitability, Amtexco's management has decided to start textile manufacturing ventures abroad, particularly in the low-wage countries which are the source of the competition. Amtexco's international exposure has been very limited up to now. Its International Division's main activity is the export of high-quality items, mostly to other developed countries, and its foreign investment is limited to marketing ventures for the distribution of export products in a few European countries.

As a first step in the expansion of its international activities, it was decided that Amtexco should make an investment in a developing country from which it would learn more of the problems and opportunities of this kind of venture. The first choice to be made was whether this facility should produce for export and sale on the American market or whether it should produce for the local market of the country in which it was to be established. Given Amtexco's general level of inexperience with overseas manufacturing ventures, it was decided that a safer strategy would be to produce for the local market first. Production for the American market would only be considered at a later stage, in the framework of either an extension of this facility or of a new one to be set up specifically for this purpose.

To minimize financial exposure and to have a facility of a relatively easy size to manage, it was decided that the project would be of the minimum size compatible with economies of scale in the industry. In the words of one of the managers responsible for planning the project, although the plant should be profitable and self-sufficient, "this investment is not made for profit as the volume is too small to pay for the effort and staff time involved. This investment is made as a learning experience in going abroad. This is why we are ready to spend so much time on each of its details."

CHARACTERISTICS OF ASIANA

Following the screening of a number of possible host countries and preliminary contact with their foreign investment authorities, it was decided that Asiana offered the best prospects. An investment proposal describing the main features of Amtexco's proposed venture was presented to and approved by Asiana's Foreign Investment Board. Amtexco is now proceeding with the detailed definition of the proposed production facilities prior to final negotiations with the government of Asiana as to investment incentives.

Asiana is one of the largest countries of Asia, both in terms of area and in terms of population. Although its level of per capita income is extremely low, it offers a very large market for a basic product such as woven polyester/cotton cloth. Its textile sector is mostly composed of artisan spinning and weaving firms, and the modern sector is extremely small for a country of its size, owing to the economic and political difficulties the country went through during the last decade. Although it is estimated that about 100,000 handlooms are in operation in the artisan sector, the textile sector of Asiana cannot satisfy local demand, and large quantities of cloth and yarn are imported. The quality of cloth available on Asiana's market is relatively inferior. However, the low income levels of the population put a definite limit on the price premium that better quality cloth can command.

As can be expected, the availability and cost of the factors of production in Asiana are very different from the United States. Due to large unemployment, unskilled workers can be hired at a cost to the firm, including social charges, of about $1.50 a day, a twentieth of their salary plus social benefits in the United States. However, these workers generally come from the agricultural sector and have never been employed in an industrial firm. They have to receive some basic training even to perform simple production tasks. Semiskilled, skilled, and supervisory workers, on the other hand, are in extremely short supply in Asiana.

This means that all semiskilled workers have to be hired as unskilled and trained on the job by skilled and supervisory workers who themselves have been hired at the semiskilled level and trained at headquarters during the firm's construction and startup. Through discussions with other firms operating in Asiana, it has been estimated that at the beginning, Asiana workers' efficiency can be expected to be 50 percent of the U.S. workers' efficiency and to climb to about two thirds of U.S. workers' efficiency after two years on the job.

Electric power in the quantity needed to operate a textile plant is unavailable outside of Asiana's main cities. Even in the main cities power supply is unreliable. All modern industrial ventures therefore have to generate their own power, and this at a cost per kilowatt hour generated of roughly two and a half times the U.S. cost. Building costs, including air conditioning and humidity control equipment, are comparable to U.S. costs although their breakdown is very different. Construction costs are low in Asiana due to the low cost of labor, while air conditioning, humidifying, and even some metallic structures have to be imported and the installation of such equipment requires expatriate labor.

On the raw materials side, cotton and polyester fiber as well as the chemicals required for finishing are not produced in Asiana and will be imported. Amtexco has received assurances that no import duties will be levied on them.

MAIN CHARACTERISTICS OF THE PROJECT

In light of a study of Asiana's market, the following main features of the project have been decided upon and approved by the Foreign Investment Board:

1. The production facility would be an integrated, balanced facility composed of a spinning department, a weaving department, and finishing facilities.

2. The output of the mill would be a 65 percent polyester/35 percent cotton suiting fabric of medium weight. The production of such fabric requires a higher degree of expertise than the production of shirting material, for example, but the production process is still simple enough not to require the use of any specialized equipment. In selecting this product, Amtexco hoped to emphasize its technical expertise without becoming heavily dependent upon the skills of untrained manpower or sacrificing flexibility in its manufacturing facilities.

3. The production facilities should be able to produce, at full capacity, 12 million linear yards of dyed and finished 58-inch-width suiting fabric.

4. The facility would be operating 8,400 hours per year, which means 350 days a year, 7 days a week, 24 hours a day. Given that the legal number of working hours per week per worker in Asiana is 42, the factory would function on a three-shift basis with four gangs, the fourth gang filling in on a rotation basis for weekly rest days and holidays.

5. The investment would be made in the form of a joint venture in which Amtexco would hold a majority position and a local partner a minority position. Following contacts with development banks and businessmen in Asiana, a capital structure where Amtexco would hold about 60 percent of the equity, a local partner between 15 and 20 percent, and development banks 20 to 25 percent was thought to be feasible. A potential local partner was found in a leading local businessman who up to now had been involved in the import-export business and the wholesale distribution of textiles. Such an association was thought to bring better relations with the government, which favors joint ventures rather than wholly owned subsidiaries by foreign investors and extends better investment conditions to them. It should also facilitate relations with local authorities, marketing channels, and workers of which the local partner will be in charge. Furthermore, it should help Amtexco in its learning process of how to manage ventures in developing countries.

THE CHOICE OF EQUIPMENT

The next major issue to be dealt with was the choice of equipment for the Asiana production facility. In preliminary discussions held by the Project Committee on this issue, a large amount of controversy emerged, most of which had centered around two points.

The first was the extent to which alternative technologies were available. Most members of the committee were of the opinion that equipment embodying alternative technologies or different levels of automation of the same technology were available in most steps of the textile production process. Some, however, argued that a number of these alternatives were outdated and inefficient, not leaving much scope for a real choice. The second controversial issue was the criteria to be used to make choices if and when alternatives were available.

Nevertheless it was agreed that:

1. The magnitude of the differences in availability and cost of the factors of production between the United States and Asiana justified a reexamination of the alternative equipment available and of the criteria used by Amtexco to proceed to a choice.
2. The Project Committee should reach an agreement on this question and issue guidelines to be used by the staff in selecting equipment for the Asiana venture.

The Asiana Project staff was therefore asked to prepare an issues paper dealing with these questions. In a first meeting on this assignment, the Asiana Project staff discussed the format and content of the paper, and reached several conclusions. First, it was agreed that the textile manufacturing process is composed of a number of discrete processing steps and that the choice of technology and equipment in each of these processing steps can be made independently from the choices in the other steps. The study could therefore concentrate on the evaluation of alternatives at the processing step level without having to replace this step in the framework of the whole plant. Second, it was decided that, rather than try to prepare an all-encompassing general document, it would be more effective to concentrate on one step in the production process for which a choice of equipment had to be made. General principles that could be used as guidelines for other cases would then be derived from the analysis of this particular step.

Weaving was selected as the processing step on which to base this document. Looms traditionally represent a large percentage of the total investment in equipment in a textile mill. Weaving is also considered by engineers to offer a wide range of alternative production technologies of varying degrees of sophistication and cost.

In further discussions about the way in which this issue should be tackled it was agreed that the analysis should proceed in three steps. First, engineers should study equipment available and determine which could be considered as alternatives for the production of the output desired. Second, a financial analysis should be performed on each of the alternatives identified in the first step in order to estimate the processing cost of each alternative. The third step should be a qualitative evaluation of the factors not quantified in the financial analysis but to be taken into account in the choice of technology decision.

The engineering unit was asked to perform the first step. They came up with a list of eleven technologies (see Exhibit 1) that "technically" could produce the type of suiting material contemplated for the Asiana venture. However, they voiced such strong reservations about the use of hand looms and multiphase looms that these two alternatives were dropped. They also provided the project staff with a list of the main equipment manufacturers producing looms embodying these different technologies (see Exhibit 2). They insisted that, from their point of view, the choice of a manufacturer was as important as the choice of a technology. Following discussions between the project staff and the engineering unit, the range of shuttleless loom technologies was further reduced in order to simplify the analysis. Only projectile looms were kept to represent this group of technologies.

EXHIBIT 1   Classification of the Different Looms Available (by type of technology)

Technology Level		Characteristics			
1	Hand				
2	Power	Shuttle	Nonautomatic		
3	Power	Shuttle	Shuttle change		
4	Power	Shuttle	Cop change	Side picking	Mechanical control
5	Power	Shuttle	Cop change	Parallel picking	Mechanical control
6	Power	Shuttle	Cop change	Parallel picking	Electronic control
7	Power	Rigid rapier			
8	Power	Flexible rapier			
9	Power	Projectile			
10	Power	Air jet			
11	Power	Multiphase			

To evaluate the processing cost using each alternative technology, project staff requested from the engineering unit an estimate of the factor requirements of each technology. The engineering unit chose, in each of the six technologies retained, the models of looms it considered most suited to the task, computed the number of such looms necessary to obtain the volume of production desired, and listed the factor usage of these models (see Exhibit 3). The business economist assigned to the project staff then prepared a document showing the cost of the different factors of production in Asiana (see Exhibit 4) as well as a description of a few modern textile mills in Asiana and of the weaving technology they chose (see Exhibit 5).

As the coordinator of the project staff on this issue, you must now prepare a draft report to the Asiana Project Committee. In your report you want to provide management with a complete analysis of and recommendation on the choice of looms. You want this analysis to provide a methodology to be applied to other steps in the production process and you want to propose guidelines as to what these other choices should be.

Upon inquiring about the choice of looms made for the U.S. production facilities of Amtexco, you have found that the main criterion has been savings in manpower even when, in some cases, it did not seem to minimize production cost at today's wage rates. The oldest looms to be found in Amtexco U.S. plants are Draper automatic cop change looms, dating from the 1950s. At one time electronic features were added to a number of these looms. During the last few years, Draper flexible rapier looms were purchased. Recently, however, several Sulzer projectile looms were purchased and following satisfactory testing of these looms, it has been decided that these will be adopted in further replacements or expansions.

EXHIBIT 2   Manufacturers of Looms and Types Produced by Them

Company*	Country	Loom Types	Technology Level
Draper Division, Rockwell	United States	Automatic cop change	4, 5, and 6
		Shuttleless flexible rapier	8
		Shuttleless projectile	9
Machinenfabrick Rüti A. G.	Switzerland	Automatic cop change	5 and 6
		Shuttleless flexible rapier	8
		Shuttleless air jet	10
		Shuttleless multiphase	11
Adolph Saurer, Ltd.	Switzerland	Automatic cop change	5 and 6
		Shuttleless rigid rapier	7
Sulzer Brothers, Ltd.	Switzerland	Shuttleless projectile	9
N. V. Weefautomaten Picanol	Belgium	Automatic cop change	4, 5, and 6
		Shuttleless flexible rapier	8
SACM	France	Shuttleless rigid rapier	7
Howa Machinery, Ltd.	Japan	Automatic cop change	4, 5, and 6
Toyoda Automatic Loom Works, Ltd.	Japan	Automatic cop change	5 and 6
Enshu, Ltd.	Japan	Automatic cop change	4, 5, and 6
		Shuttleless projectile	9
	India[†]	Nonautomatic	2
		Automatic shuttle change	3
		Automatic cop change[‡]	4 and 5
	Korea[†]	Nonautomatic	2
		Automatic shuttle change	3
		Automatic cop change	4

Note: Manual looms—technology level 1—are not included in this list.
* Named companies are major manufacturers of looms, accounting for 80 percent of loom sales worldwide.
[†] Various manufacturers.
[‡] Manufactured under license form Ruti A. G.

EXHIBIT 3   Characteristics of Looms by Type of Technology Used[a]

Technology Level	Shuttle Looms[b]					Shuttleless Looms
	Power Non-automatic (2)	Shuttle Change (3)	Cop Change Simple (4)	Cop Change (5)	Cop Change Electronic (6)	Projectile (9)
Number of looms needed[c]	380	303	260	228	190	88
Cost of a loom[d] (U.S. $)	1,200	1,700	4,000	7,000	12,000	33,000
Power consumption (kwh per loom)	0.49	0.74	0.74	1.10	1.10	2.58
Floor space requirement[e] (m² per loom)	9.00	9.50	10.36	10.36	10.36	35.00
Spare parts requirement per loom[f]	0.02	0.025	0.025	0.02	0.02	0.01
Labor requirements:[g]						
Supervisory	6	6	3.5	3.5	3.5	3.5
Skilled	19	14.5	12	12	9.5	7
Semiskilled	344	99	51	48	46	22
Unskilled	21	21	16	15	14	10

Notes:

[a] The loom types in this table correspond to the different technologies described in Exhibit 1.

[b] In shuttle looms the weft (filling) yarn is supplied from small bobbins (cops or pirns) which are placed in the shuttle while in shuttleless looms it is supplied from large bobbins attached to the side of the loom. For this reason, shuttle looms require one processing step more than shuttleless looms before weaving. In the pirn winding step the large spools produced by the winding machines are rewound on pirns before being supplied to shuttle looms while these large spools are directly supplied to shuttleless looms. Therefore the cost of pirn winding has to be added to the shuttle looms alternatives (technologies 1 to 6) to make them comparable. The capital cost of pirn winding would be $60,000, the power consumption would be 31.35 kw per hour of operation, the floor space required for this processing step would be 103 square meters, and the spare parts requirement .02 of the capital cost of the equipment. Pirn winding labor requirements have been included into the shuttle looms labor requirements.

[c] Number of looms of a given technology required to obtain a plant output of the level sought for the factory in Asiana (12 million linear yards per year on the basis of 8,400 working hours per year).

[d] The estimated cost of a loom is a total cost, "ready to operate." It includes the loom itself, its driving motor, its auxiliary parts (harness, belts, etc.), as well as packing for sea shipment and transport. Equipment will be depreciated over 10 years on a straight-line basis. Looms of good construction, if well maintained, normally operate more than 10 years. Because of hard working conditions expected to result from the low skill level of the workers it should be considered that looms have no salvage value at the end of the 10 years.

[e] The "floor space requirement per loom" figures include not only the area covered by the loom but also the working space needed around it for service. The total area of the weaving shed required can be obtained by multiplying this figure by the number of looms to be installed. Buildings should be depreciated over 20 years and be considered to have a zero residual value at the end of that time.

[f] The "spare parts requirement per loom" is expressed in terms of the proportion of the price of the loom to be spent in spare parts each year. It includes all "consumables," parts that wear out during normal operation and have to be regularly replaced. It does not include spare parts necessary for exceptional breakdown and assumes that the loom is operated and maintained properly.

[g] The "labor requirement" figures are for a weaving shed with the number of looms of that technology recommended for this plant. These estimates have been made on the manufacturers' manning specifications and should therefore be adjusted to reflect the expected productivity of Asiana's workers in comparison with the hypothetical workers' productivity used by equipment manufacturers.

EXHIBIT 4   Cost of the Factors of Production in Asiana versus in the United States

	Unit	United States	Asiana
Labor:[a]			
Supervisory	U.S. $ per 8-hour day	63.08	4.50
Skilled	U.S. $ per 8-hour day	43.24	2.79
Semiskilled	U.S. $ per 8-hour day	32.75	2.00
Unskilled	U.S. $ per 8-hour day	27.92	1.55
Power[b]	U.S. $ per kw/h	0.013	0.03
Capital[c]		9%	12%
Construction cost[d]	U.S. $ per sq. meter	210	207
Labor efficiency[e]		0.9	0.6

Notes:

[a] Labor costs include all fringe benefits, whether paid to the worker directly (transportation allowance), given in kind (work clothes), or paid by the firm to a fund (accident insurance) or to the government on the basis of salaries paid; they, therefore, represent the total cost to the firm of employing a worker of a given category. Furthermore, the eight-hour day cost has been adjusted to reflect payments for sick leave, weekly holidays, and annual leave as well as premiums paid for night work to reach a 24-hours-a-day, 7-day-a-week operation. These costs have been estimated on the basis of the salaries paid by similar foreign-owned companies; they are some 15 percent above the ones paid by modern local firms of a comparable size.

[b] In the locations being considered for the plant, power will have to be self-generated. These cost estimates have been based on the cost of diesel fuel in Asiana and include depreciation cost of the generating equipment as well as direct and indirect costs.

[c] This cost of capital is to be used in constant terms computations. It takes into account business and political risks but does not reflect inflation. It reflects the debt equity ratio of the company and the cost of equity capital and borrowed funds.

[d] The estimated cost of construction is an all-inclusive cost in the sense that it includes building cost, electrical wiring, air conditioning, and humidity control installations. It does not include the cost of the land. However, as constructed area only represents a small portion of the land to be acquired for this project, the latter should not be influenced by the choice of technology decisions.

[e] Factor by which manning requirements proposed by equipment suppliers should be divided to obtain a likely figure for manning needs in a country, given the worker's productivity in this country.

EXHIBIT 5   Choice of Loom Technology by Some Other Textile Producers in Asiana

Characteristics	Companies			
	A	B	C	D
Volume of production (million yards)	10.2	24.0	4.1	9.5
Number looms	400	912	200	520
Technology level[*]	4	4	5	4
Ownership	Japanese— weak local partner	Japanese— strong local partner	Local cooperative— government	Government
Start of operations[†]	September 1972	July 1972	February 1972	1973

[*] Technology level of most recent looms acquired: levels as defined in Exhibit 1.
[†] Date at which the plant started commercial production.

Peters Brass Company

Peters Brass Company, a rapidly growing Pittsburgh casting company, invested $2,350,000 in 1966 to establish a local unit in Argentina. The investment represented a 65 percent share in a new Argentinian company established in partnership with Sr. Pedro Gomez y Silvo of Buenos Aires. At the time of the initial investment, the Argentinian peso was worth 1.2 U.S. cents, but periodic devaluations of the Argentinian currency brought the exchange rate to a point in mid-April 1971 when it fell from 180 pesos to 205 pesos to the U.S. dollar.

For four years the parent company had shown the Argentinian operation in

EXHIBIT 1a

PETERS BRASS COMPANY OF ARGENTINA
Cuadro Demostrativo de Ganancias y Perdidas al 31 de marzo de 1971
(Profit and Loss—Year Ending March 31, 1971)

	Pesos	
Entrada (Revenues):		
Ventas menos costo de la mercaderia vendida		
(Sales less cost of goods sold)	220,500,000	
Comision		
(Commissions)	40,000,000	
Renta		
(Rental income)	50,000,000	
Varias entrada		
(Miscellaneous income)	30,000,000	
Total entrada (total revenue)		340,500,000
Gastos (Expenses):		
Remuneraciones al personal		
(Wages and salaries)	130,500,000	
Gastos de operacion		
(Fuel, heat, and light)	40,000,000	
Amortizaciones		
(Depreciation)	15,500,000	
Gastos de comision y regalias		
(Commission expenses and royalties)	35,000,000	
Impuestos		
(Taxes)	50,500,000	
Total gastos (Total expenses)		271,500,000
Utilidad del Ejercicio (Net profit)		69,000,000

Adapted from a case written by Professor Richard N. Farmer. Graduate School of Business, Indiana University.

its books at the original investment cost, recording the profits (which were all paid out as dividends) as investment income. At the time of the April 1971 devaluation, the new president had been thinking about consolidating the subsidiary accounts for 1971 (see Exhibit 1). He asked Bill Adams, the controller, to calculate for him what the effect of consolidation would be and what the recent devaluation would mean.

EXHIBIT 1b

PETERS BRASS COMPANY OF ARGENTINA
Balance General al 31 marzo de 1971
(Balance Sheet, March 31, 1971)

	Pesos
Activos (Assets)	
Caja y bancos (Cash on hand)	8,100,000
Deudores en cuenta (Accounts receivable)	32,700,000
Bienes de cambio (Inventories)	90,700,000
Maquinarias y accesorios (Machinery and equipment)	142,400,000
Immuebles (menos amortizacion) (Buildings, less depreciation)	253,400,000
Terreno (Land)	129,800,000
Total	657,100,000
Pasivos (Liabilities)	
Deudas (Debts):	
Comerciales (Accounts payable)	40,000,000
Bancarias (Bank overdraft)	25,000,000
Equipo hipotecarios (Equipment notes payable)	55,000,000
Capital, reserves y resultados (Shareholders' equity):	
Suscripto (Common stock)	300,000,000
Reservas y utilidades (Capital surplus)	237,100,000
Total	657,100,000

Stability, Inc.

Stability, Inc. was founded in the mythical republic of Bellerivia on January 1, 1984. On December 31, 1987, its condensed balance sheet was as shown in Exhibit 1. All figures are stated in Bellerivian doubloons, a decimal currency represented by the dollar symbol ($).

Stability, Inc. does only wholesale business, with no manufacturing operations. All wages and salaries are charged to expense as earned. Inventory is valued on the first in, first out (FIFO) basis.

Prices were stable during the first four years of the company's life. The general price index on December 31, 1987 was 100—the same as it had been on January 1, 1984. Early in 1988, however, the government of Bellerivia launched large-scale rearmament and social-welfare programs. These activities were financed mainly by government borrowing from the Bellerivian central bank, which was allowed to treat the government's promissory note as part of its required legal

EXHIBIT 1

STABILITY, INC.
Condensed Balance Sheet
December 31, 1987
($000)

Assets

Current assets:
Cash	$ 400	
Accounts and notes receivable	1,500	
Inventories	2,500	
Total current assets		$4,400

Fixed assets:
Plant and equipment	$2,000	
Deduct accumulated depreciation	400	
Total fixed assets		1,600
Total assets		$6,000

Liabilities

Current liabilities:
Accounts and notes payable	$1,300	
Total current liabilities		$1,300

Stockholders' Equity

Capital stock	$2,000	
Retained earnings	2,700	
Total stockholders' equity		4,700
Total liabilities		$6,000

reserves. Taking prices at January 1, 1984, as 100, the general price index changed as follows during the year:

Date	General Price Index
January 1, 1988	100
First quarter average	110
Second quarter average	130
June 30	140
Third quarter average	150
Fourth quarter average	170
December 31, 1988	180
1988 average	140

The company's trial balance, on an original cost basis, was as follows on December 31, 1988 (in thousands of doubloons):

	Debits	Credits
Cash	190	
Accounts and notes receivable	1,400	
Inventories	4,250	
Plant and equipment	2,210	
Accumulated depreciation		521
Accounts and notes payable		1,550
Capital stock		2,000
Retained earnings, December 31, 1987		2,700
Sales		15,400
Cost of goods sold	12,250	
Salaries and other current expenses	1,750	
Depreciation expense	121	
Total	22,171	22,171

Purchases during 1988 were as follows (in thousands of doubloons):

Quarter	Historical Cost
1	2,750
2	3,250
3	3,750
4	4,250
Total	14,000

Under the FIFO inventory method, the goods in the December 31, 1988, inventory were those purchased at various times during the final quarter of 1988. The ending inventory represented the same physical quantity as the January 1, 1988, figure. During the year, purchases and sales of physical units of goods were the same in each quarter.

The major part of the plant and equipment, costing $2 million, was acquired on January 1, 1984, when the business was founded. Depreciation had been recorded on this part of the asset account at the rate of 5 percent per year. On June 30, 1988, additional equipment costing $210,000 was acquired. It was expected to have a useful life of five years, but depreciation was recorded for only one-half year in 1988.

At a meeting early in 1989, the board of directors was considering the question of how large a cash dividend to pay.

1. Prepare an income statement, balance sheet, and a source and application of funds statement for 1988 on the basis of historical cost.
2. Prepare the same statements for 1988 on a price-level adjustment basis.
3. Compute the gain or loss from holding monetary assets in 1988.
4. Compute the gain or loss from holding inventories and fixed assets during 1988. What is the meaning of your answer?
5. How do the procedures used for adjusting account balances for general price-level changes resemble the procedures for translating the accounts of a foreign business subdivision into the domestic currency? In what major ways do the two types of procedures differ?
6. What policy should Stability, Inc. follow if it wishes to minimize the gain or loss on monetary accounts?
7. How can the management of Stability, Inc. use the adjusted financial information? What are its shortcomings?

Global Enterprises, Incorporated

INTRODUCTION

A meeting has been scheduled for the first week in March, 1986, to reconsider several of the group's current policies which affect its international operations. Pat Kilpatrick, Senior Vice President and Chief Financial Officer of Global Enterprises [GLE] summarized the current issues in a memo in January, 1986, which was sent to the General Managers and Financial Officers of each of the subsidiaries.

> The volatility of the U.S. dollar in 1985 and the continuing uncertainty of its future path has made it imperative for us to reconsider many of our current planning and control policies. Subsidiaries which were expected to incur heavy losses are suddenly highly profitable and vice versa. Furthermore, the budgets which were prepared between September and the end of the year now look ridiculous. Our U.S. production and marketing personnel are demanding an increase in the transfer price of the materials they send to the foreign subsidiaries. These issues will be discussed in depth at a meeting at our retreat in Harriman, New York in March once the fiscal year-end results are finalized. Please ensure that you have evaluated all alternatives and how these will affect your operating results.

THE GROUP

GLE is a medium-sized U.S. company which produces high-grade synthetic fibers that are woven into fabrics used in a variety of mining and industrial processes. The primary production of the fibers is undertaken at a large plant near Clifton, New Jersey. The fibers are transferred to three plants where the fabrics are made. The plants are situated in Clifton, N.J.; just outside The Hague in The Netherlands; and in Sao Paulo, Brazil. The finished goods are marketed through companies operating in several countries. Figure 1 gives an outline of the basic corporate structure.

MANAGEMENT STRUCTURE

Each of the manufacturing companies has a General Manager, Financial and Personnel Officers, as well as relevant Production Line Officers. In addition, a retail division operating out of the U.S. headquarters supplies the staff functions for the sales companies, although each sales company has a general manager. The U.S. headquarters in Stamford, Connecticut, has a full set of staff activities including a quality control division which is an independent unit reporting directly

This case was prepared by Trevor S. Harris, Graduate School of Business, Columbia University. Copyright © 1986 American Accounting Association. Reproduced with permission.

to the Chief Executive Officer. Each of the subsidiary staff officers reports to a group officer in Stamford. Finally, all research and development is undertaken at GLE FIBERS in Clifton by the R&D division.

DISTRIBUTION OF AUTHORITY

Each group has autonomy over its operating activities, subject to the technical specifications set up by R&D. Strategic decisions and non-operating financing decisions are centralized at the headquarters in Stamford.

THE OPERATING CYCLE

GLE FIBERS purchases its raw materials and other factors of production all in the U.S. The process is heavily capital intensive, so that approximately 40 percent of the total cost of a ton of fiber is attributed to fixed costs. The total cost is $800 per ton in 1985/6.

GLE FIBERS transfers the fiber to the *fabric* manufacturers at $1,000 per ton. The current world market price for similar fibers has recently dropped to $910 per ton from an average price of $1,050 which held through 1985. Tables 1, 2, and 3 give summarized financial statements for the trading companies for the 1985/6 fiscal year.

The *fabric* manufacturing companies sell the finished product to the *sales* companies at a price of *cost* plus 25 percent. The price is denominated in the local currency of each fabric company. Most *sales* companies sell in their local currency to their customers except for GLE SALES (COMECON) which sells in German marks.

THE COMPETITIVE ENVIRONMENT

In each market GLE has at least one major competitor and in the U.S. and Europe there are several competing companies. Approximately half the sales in the U.S. and Europe are special orders which are based on specifically developed technology.

THE BUDGETING SYSTEM

The budget cycle begins towards the end of August each year once the half year results are completed. The group companies all have January 31 year ends. The cycle is as follows:

1. In mid-August, the sales representatives are asked to project their sales for the next fiscal period with a clear separation between special orders and standard product lines. The sales are specified in terms of physical volumes only.

2. By August 31, the head of marketing and the general manager in each region must submit their regions' projected sales to the Senior Vice President for Marketing who may ask for certain clarifications and/or revisions. By September

7, the basic projections must be completed so that they can be sent to the production officers at each of the three fabric plants.

3. By September 21, the production officers must have scheduled their production based on the sales projections and any conflicts with the marketing division should have been resolved. The fabric companies send their purchasing estimates to the production manager of GLE FIBERS who must develop his own company's production plan and have all bottlenecks resolved with the three fabric producers by September 30.

4. On October 1, GLEFBR's production forecast is given to the company's financial officer who develops a full budget. This is discussed with the General Manager and together they arrive at a transfer price equal to full cost price plus 20 percent. This is based on the estimated cost of oil which is the primary material input. By October 15, the transfer price is given to the fabric companies, and their financial officers prepare budgets using the transfer price and (where appropriate) the budgeted exchange rates sent to them by Pat Kilpatrick, the chief financial officer (CFO).

5. The financial officers prepare their budgets and again derive a transfer price which they send to the sales division financial officer in Stamford by October 31. The budgets for the sales division are completed by November 15 and sent to the respective companies.

6. The budgets are reviewed, and then in the week following Thanksgiving all the general managers, sales managers, production managers, financial officers and the respective vice presidents meet in Stamford. Any problems within the group have to be resolved in the first 3 days of the week. The group budget is finalized on the 4th day and submitted to the CEO who discusses it with the general managers and vice presidents. If there are any major problems the meeting continues until these are resolved.

7. By mid-December the final approved budgets are sent out to the relevant companies.

PERFORMANCE EVALUATION

There are several criteria which are important in assessing each company's performance. However, the primary criterion is considered to be return on investment (ROI). The detailed evaluation measures used include:

1. **Adjusted ROI.** This is the reported net income adjusted for income in the transfer prices, royalties and technical fees and for penalties incurred if intercompany purchase projections are not met. This measure is used primarily to evaluate the company and general manager's performance, but cannot be used explicitly by the general manager for "within-company" evaluations as the adjusted returns are not allowed to become public knowledge.

2. **Standard ROI.** This is an ROI measure based on reported income. It is used partially in evaluating the general managers but has to be used for evaluating

lower level managers. It is also used for staff officers operating out of Stamford. The general managers can choose the currency they use to measure ROI for their subordinates, but they themselves are judged on a U.S. dollar basis.

3. **Budget to Actual.** Comparisons are made on sales, variable costs, and net profit. Assessments of companies and general managers are based on comparisons of U.S. dollar based measures.

4. **Market Share.** This measure is based on volume and value.

5. **Standard Efficiency Measures.** Managers in different functional areas are evaluated on efficiency ratios which are relevant to the area, e.g., productivity per man hour, asset turnover, inventory turnover, etc.

6. **An Annual Review.** This is performed by each person's direct superior.

There are quarterly reports prepared which match budget to actual performance and require a basic variance analysis to separate out price, usage and efficiency variances. These are discussed by management in a comments sheet which accompanies each report.

Points for Discussion

1. The 1985/6 budgeted sales and income are shown for several group companies in Table 4. Compare these to the 1985/6 actuals in Tables 1–3 and consider to what extent the differences should be used in the evaluation of performance.
2. Managers in the manufacturing companies have argued that they are unfairly prejudiced because they are evaluated on a "false" price. At the same time, managers in the fabric and retail companies have been complaining for several years that their costs of raw materials are inflated because they have to buy from group companies. The non-U.S. company managers have been particularly concerned as they say it is difficult to remain competitive when their costs are so high and, in addition, they have exchange losses on their intercompany payables and loans. How can this conflict be resolved? Should the subsidiaries be responsible for the exchange losses/gains? [Some of the foreign subsidiary managers seem to have dropped their concern in the last quarter of the year.]
3. Using the basic financial statements of some of the subsidiaries outlined in Tables 1–3, consider the relevance of the two ROI measures, particularly from the perspective of the non-U.S. companies. Which currency is the more useful/relevant for evaluating performance?
4. How meaningful will the efficiency ratios be? Does it matter which currency we use?
5. Table 5A contains exchange rates for four relevant currencies. How do you feel about the budgeted exchange rate for 1986/7? If you had to decide on an alternative rate what would you choose for the Dutch Guilder? Should the budget be revised?
6. What recommendations would you make if you were:
   (a) Pat Kilpatrick, CFO;
   (b) The General Manager of GLE Fibers;
   (c) The General Manager of GLE Fabrics (Neth);
   (d) The General Manager of GLE Sales (WG);
   (e) The General Manager of GLE Fabrics (Brazil)?

FIGURE 1 Global Enterprises, Incorporated, Critical Structure and Intercompany Flow of Goods

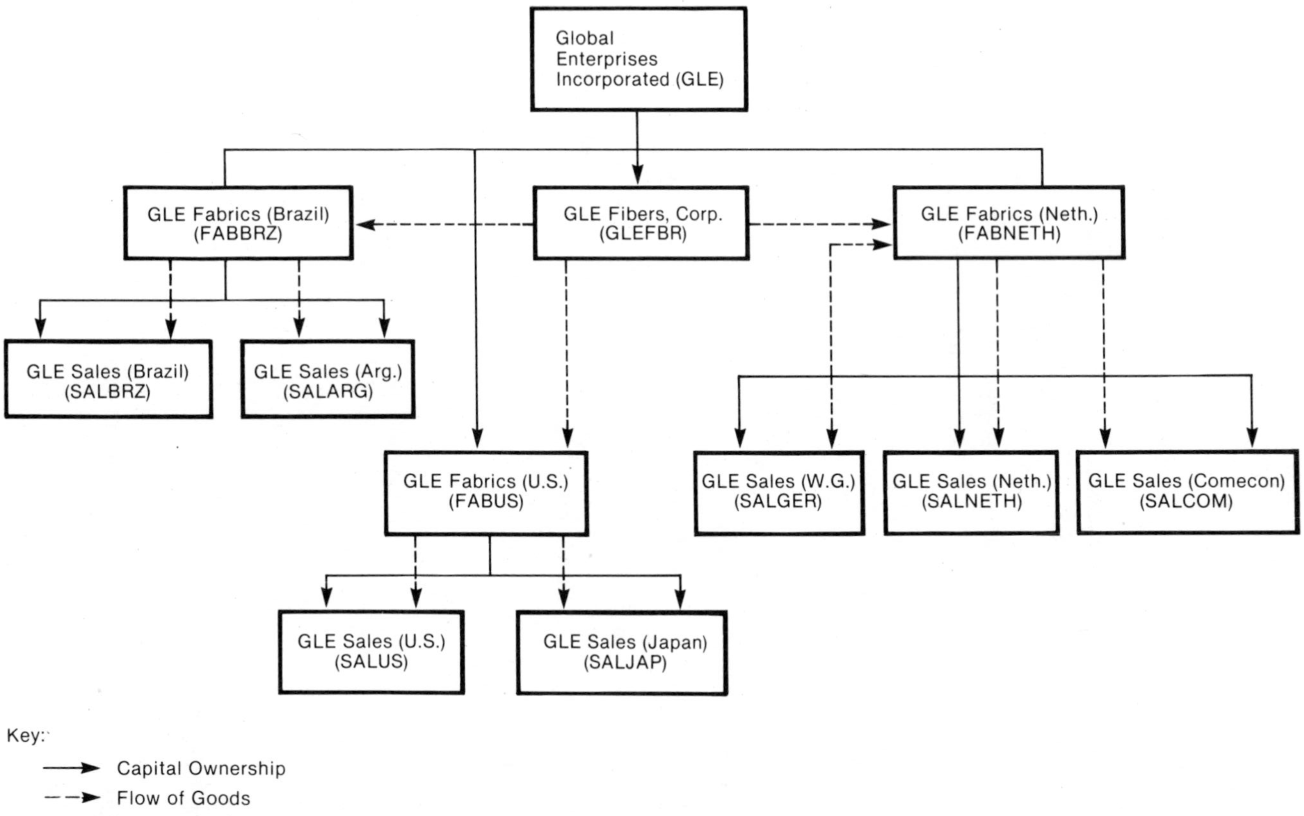

Global Enterprises Incorporated (GLE)

GLE Fibers, Corp. (GLEFBR)

GLE Fabrics (Neth.) (FABNETH)

GLE Fabrics (Brazil) (FABBRZ)

GLE Fabrics (U.S.) (FABUS)

GLE Sales (Comecon) (SALCOM)

GLE Sales (Neth.) (SALNETH)

GLE Sales (W.G.) (SALGER)

GLE Sales (Japan) (SALJAP)

GLE Sales (U.S.) (SALUS)

GLE Sales (Arg.) (SALARG)

GLE Sales (Brazil) (SALBRZ)

Key:

⟶ Capital Ownership

⟶ (dashed) Flow of Goods

790

TABLE 1A   1985/6 Income Statements for U.S. Manufacturing Companies and
Their Subsidiaries

	GLEFBR ($000s)	FABUS* ($000s)	SALUS ($000s)		SALJAP (¥mills)
Sales: Intercompany	11,500	15,000	17,800		2,900
Foreign exchange gain	—				50
Cost of raw materials	(3,000)	(4,800)	(10,000)		(1,150)
Labor	(1,500)	(1,800)	(2,500)		(600)
Royalty/technical fee	—	(1,500)	—		—
Other variables	(1,000)	(900)	(500)		(200)
Fixed	(3,700)	(3,200)	(800)		(200)
Interest	(1,000)	(800)	—		—
Net income before tax	1,300	2,000	4,000		800
Tax (45%)	(585)	(900)	(1,800)	(50%)	(400)
Net income after tax	$ 715	$ 1,100	$ 2,200		¥400
Net income in $(000s)					
(I) Average rate					$ 1,740
(II) Year end rate					$ 2,075

* Excludes dividends received.

TABLE 1B   Balance Sheets at January 31, 1986, for U.S. Manufacturing Companies and Their
Subsidiaries

		GLEFBR ($000s)	FABUS ($000s)	SALUS ($000s)	SALJAP (¥mills)
Cash		560	900	400	163
Accounts receivable:	Intercompany	2,340	2,400	—	—
	Third party	—	—	1,400	240
Inventory		600	700	700	100
Prop. plt. & eqpt.:	Net	20,000	18,000	500	40
Investment in subs			1,000	—	—
Total assets		$23,500	$23,000	$3,000	¥543
Accounts payable:	Intercompany	—	1,000	1,400	193
	Third party	500	—	—	—
Long term loans:	Intercompany (2½%)	9,000	8,000	—	—
	Third party	10,000	8,500	—	—
Share capital		1,000	2,000	500	100
Retained earnings		3,000	3,500	1,100	250
Total liabilities		$23,500	$23,000	$3,000	¥543

TABLE 2A 1985/6 Income Statements for GLE Fabrics (Netherlands) and Its Subsidiaries

	FABNETH* (HFL 000s)	SALNETH (HFL 000s)	SALGER (DM 000s)	SALCOM (DM 000s)	
Sales: Third party	—	30,000	35,600	12,000	
Intercompany	43,750	—	—	—	
Exchange gains (losses)	1050				
Cost of raw materials	(15,500)	(17,250)	(18,200)	(5,350)	
Labor/commissions	(5,800)	(4,750)	(6,000)	(1,400)	
Royalty/technical fee	(3,800)	—	—	—	
Other variable	(2,400)	(600)	(800)	(650)	
Fixed	(7,500)	(1,000)	(1,200)	(400)	
Interest	(1,650)	—	—	—	
Net income before tax	8,150	6,400	9,400	4,200	
Tax (47.5%)	(3,870)	(3,040) (50%)	(4,700) (55%)	(2,300)	
Net income after tax	HFL 4,280	HFL 3,360	DM 4,700	DM 1,900	
Net income in $(000s)					Total
(I) Average rate	$1,343	$1,055	$1,665	$675	$4,738
(II) Year end rate	$1,586	$1,245	$1,970	$795	$5,596

* Excludes dividends received.

TABLE 2B Balance Sheets at January 31, 1986, for GLE Fabrics (Netherlands) and Its Subsidiaries

		FABNETH (HFL 000s)	SALNETH (HFL 000s)	SALGER (DM 000s)	SALCOM (DM 000s)
Cash		800	1,520	1,100	100
Accounts receivable	Intercompany	7,200	—	—	—
	Third party	—	2,400	3,000	1,000
Inventory		2,000	1,000	1,500	400
Prop. plt. & eqpt:	net	47,000	5,000	6,000	1,500
Investment in subs.		1,000	—	—	—
Total assets		HFL 58,000	HFL 9,920	DM 11,600	DM 3,000
Accounts payable:	Intercompany	3,500	2,520	3,200	960
Long terms loans:	Intercompany (2½%)	27,000	—	—	—
	Third party	14,500	—	—	250
Share capital		2,500	400	400	80
Retained earnings		7,500	7,000	8,000	1,710
Translation adj.		3,000	—	—	—
Total liabilities		HFL 58,000	HFL 9,920	DM 11,600	DM 3,000

TABLE 3A   1985/6 Income Statements for GLE Fabrics Brazil and Its Argentinian Subsidiaries

	FABBRZ (CRZ Mills)	SALBRZ (CRZ Mills)	SALARG (AUS 000s)
Sales (Intercompany)	40,000	38,000	2,000
Exchange gains (losses)	(26,000)	—	—
Cost of raw materials	(11,900)	(27,000)	(1,250)
Labor/commissions	(4,700)	(5,500)	(300)
Royalty/technical fee	(3,000)	—	—
Other variable costs	(2,600)	(900)	(80)
Fixed	(3,000)	(600)	(70)
Interest: Intercompany	(465)	—	—
Third party	(10,000)	—	—
Net income before tax	(21,665)	4,000	300
Tax (46%)	—	(1,840) (48%)	(144)
Net income after tax	CRZ (21,665)	CRZ 2,160	AUS 156
Net gain (loss) in $ (000s)			
(I) Average rate	$(2,795)	$299	$232
(II) Year-end rate	$(1,664)	$178	$195

TABLE 3B   Balance Sheets at January 31, 1986, for GLE Fabrics Brazil and Its Subsidiaries

	FABBRZ (CRZ Mills)	SALBRZ (CRZ Mills)	SALARG (AUS 000s)
Cash	600	200	30
Accounts receivable: Intercompany	9,000	—	—
Third party	—	4,100	180
Inventory	2,500	1,500	60
Prop. plt. & eqpt: Net	12,000	4,200	130
Investment in subs.	900	—	—
Total assets	CRZ 25,000	CRZ 10,000	AUS 400
Accounts payable Intercompany	6,350	6,000	200
Long term loans: Intercompany (2½%)	21,000	—	—
Third party	10,000	—	—
Share capital	8,000	500	20
Retained earnings	(20,350)	3,500	180
Total liabilities	CRZ 25,000	CRZ 10,000	AUS 400

TABLE 4   1985/6 Budget Summaries for Certain Companies

	Sales Units (000s)	Sales Values (mills)	Cost of Raw Materials (mills)	Net Income after Tax (mills)
GLEFBR	11.0 tons	$11.00	$3.3	$0.45
FABUS	2600 yds	$13.00	$4.6	$1.00
SALUS	1750 yds	$17.00	$8.75	$2.25
FABNETH	2300 yds	HFL 39.75	HFL 16.0	HFL 2.6/$0.73
SALNETH	780 yds	HFL 25.75	HFL 13.5	HFL 3.5/$1.00
SALWG	1000 yds	DM 34.2	DM 17.2	DM 4.44/$1.40
FABBRZ	1000 yds	CRZ 30,000	CRZ 9000	CRZ 1000/$0.15

TABLE 5A

	End of	Exchange Rates HFL:$	DM:$	DM:HFL	¥:$	CRZ:$
1984	August	3.259	2.887	0.886	241.3	2,107
	November	3.492	3.100	0.888	246.3	2,881
	December	3.550	3.148	0.887	251.1	3,184
1985	January	3.581	3.168	0.884	254.7	3,585
	February	3.768	3.323	0.881	259.5	3,951
	March	3.482	3.093	0.888	252.5	4,450
	April	3.527	3.090	0.876	252.3	4,980
	May	3.482	3.089	0.887	251.9	5,480
	June	3.447	3.061	0.888	249.0	5,980
	July	3.133	2.788	0.889	236.7	6,440
	August	3.132	2.782	0.888	237.3	6,970
	September	3.017	2.670	0.884	217.0	7,825
	October	2.952	2.617	0.886	211.5	8,560
	November	2.826	2.512	0.888	202.0	9,350
	December	2.772	2.461	0.887	200.5	10,490
1986	January	2.698	2.389	0.888	192.7	12,120
1985/6	Fiscal average	3.186	2.822	0.886	230.0	7,215
1986	February	2.509	2.219	0.885	179.7	13,840
1986/7	Budgeted rate (Set during Sept. 85)	3.000	2.664		210.0	18,000

SOURCE: *International Financial Statistics.*

TABLE 5B Summary of Macroeconomic Data

	Netherlands		West Germany		Japan		Brazil		United States	
	Interest Rate (%)	CPI*	Interest Rate (%)	CPI*	Interest Rate (%)	CPI*	Interest Rate	CPI*	Interest Rate	CPI*
August 1984	8.8	119.9	9.5	118.2	6.4	111.0	Var.	3185	14.5	126.8
January 1985	8.8	121.1	8.7	120.0	6.3	113.8	Var.	5286	12.75	128.1
August 1985	8.8	122.6	9.4	120.7	6.5	113.6	Var.	10528	10.0	131.1
January 1986	7.5	122.8	6.4	121.6	6.4	115.4	Var.	18813	9.5	133.1

* (CPI) Consumer Price Index.

American Level Corporation

On graduation from business school, James Bennett joined American Level Corporation in June 1981 as assistant to the corporate treasurer in the New Jersey headquarters.

American Level had two wholly owned manufacturing subsidiaries, one in Australia and a second in Brazil, but apart from a quarterly review of the foreign exchange situation by the corporate finance committee, there had been no regular procedure for avoiding the foreign exchange risks arising from the international operations. The treasurer was aware of the gaps in the American Level procedures and asked Bennett as his first major assignment to outline a methodology for forecasting exchange-rate changes as well as a set of decision rules to be followed for minimizing foreign exchange costs. The treasurer thought it would be wise to prepare the way for the procedure recommendations with a clear statement of the foreign exchange exposure of the two subsidiaries, based on their accounts to May 31. This was to be ready for the finance committee meeting on July 25, along with the usual estimate of the previous month's foreign exchange gains or losses.

The spot rate on May 31 for the Australian dollar was .878 = U.S. $1, and for the Brazilian cruzeiro 84.5 = U.S. $1. During June, however, the high levels of foreign investment into Australia were maintained, pushing the Australian dollar to .871 = U.S. $1. The Federal Reserve authorities continued their tight money policies and the rate of inflation decreased. With the conventionally higher inflation levels in Brazil, the exchange rate for the cruzeiro moved to 91.0 = U.S. $1.

The balance sheets of the two subsidiaries on May 31, 1981, are shown in Exhibit 1. In the case of Armel S.A. about 50 percent of the raw material and packaging material was imported from the United States, mainly from the parent company.

EXHIBIT 1

AMERICAN LEVEL CORPORATION
Subsidiary Balance Sheets
As of May 31, 1981

	Amel Ltd. (Aust. $000)	Amel S.A. (cruzeiro millions)
Assets		
Current assets:		
Cash	4,419	8.3
Accounts receivable, trade, other	25,134	261.6
Inventories:		
Raw materials	9,807	319.4
Packaging material	744	64.4
Work in process	10,323	106.4
Finished goods	3,525	39.4
Total current assets	53,952	799.5
Fixed assets	11,246	62.1
Less: Depreciation	1,479	18.3
Net fixed assets	9,767	43.8
Deferred expenses	—	22.4
Total assets	63,719	865.7
Liabilities		
Current liabilities:		
Notes payable	3,418	177.5
Accounts payable: trade and intercompany	18,259	276.1
Accrued expenses	1,369	9.5
Accrued taxes, miscellaneous	7,803	87.3
Total current liabilities	30,849	550.4
Reserve for patent infringement	186	—
Capital	16,508	130.5
Retained earnings	11,075	163.8
Current profit	5,101	21.0
Total net worth	32,684	315.3
Total liabilities	63,719	865.7

Standard Electronics International

On December 29, 1978, Charles Duvalier, the Treasurer of Standard Electronics International (SEI), began to review a loan request just received from the firm's German affiliate (Exhibit 1). The loan was for DM 2,500,000 and intended to be used for financing working capital needs.

SEI was a medium-sized manufacturer of computer peripheral equipment based in Sunnyvale, California (40 miles south of San Francisco). It had grown rapidly during the past 10 years and sales were forecasted to reach $250 million in 1979. About 40 percent of its revenues were earned outside of the United States, mostly in Europe. Manufacturing affiliates were located in Sunnyvale, Munich, and Singapore. Eleven sales affiliates were located throughout Europe, Japan, and the United States.

SEI maintained excellent relations with its banks and had been able to obtain financing on favorable terms in the countries where it operated as well as on the Eurocurrency markets. The affiliates commonly borrowed or temporarily placed on deposit funds in a number of major currencies including U.S. dollars, U.K. sterling, Swiss francs, deutsche marks, French francs, and yen. It had been SEI practice, until recently, to allow the foreign affiliate management considerable discretion to negotiate the terms and currency of these arrangements providing that the overall amounts had been included in the budget and approved at corporate headquarters.

However, the continuing volatility of the foreign exchange markets had convinced Duvalier that the effective cost (return) of many loans (time deposits) was turning out to be substantially different from that originally thought when the terms were agreed upon and the decision taken. He strongly believed that the cost of borrowing (or return from a time deposit) had to be measured in terms of the effect on after-tax parent consolidated profits; he was concerned that these could be seriously affected by movements in the exchange rates, by the tax treatment of certain costs and earnings at both the level of the affiliate and the parent company, and by the accounting rules used to translate the financial statements of foreign affiliates in preparing the consolidated accounts of the corporation (see Exhibit 2).

For these various reasons, Duvalier had instructed the affiliates to begin to submit to his office for approval all requests to borrow or place funds on deposit. He realized, however, that to make a detailed analysis of each request would add considerably to the administrative burden of his office as well as perhaps create some resentment in the affiliates by reducing their autonomy.

Therefore, in reviewing the request just submitted by the German affiliate, he hoped also to be able to come up with a simple approach that would allow such decisions to be taken from the point of view of maximizing parent consolidated after-tax earnings, and yet be easily delegated to the affiliate management. To be effective, Duvalier believed that any such approach would have to be simple and easily understood, and require a minimum amount of data and computation.

EXHIBIT 1   Working Capital Loan Request

To: Charles Duvalier, Corporate Treasurer, SEI, Sunnyvale
From: Fritz Schmidt, Director of Finance, SEI, Munich
Subject: Request for approval of working capital loan

As you have instructed, we have set out below the required information concerning our request for a loan to finance working capital needs over the next three months.

1. *Amount of Loan:* DM 2,500,000 (or foreign currency equivalent)
2. *Period for which loan is required:* 3 months

3. *Loan Options:*

	Nominal Interest Rate 12-Month Basis
a. Deutsche marks	6.200%
b. Eurodollar	11.75
c. EuroSterling	14.125
d. EuroSwiss francs	0.8125
e. Intracompany (as indicated in your telex of 22/12/78)	12.00

4. *Exchange Rates*
   Please note that foreign currency loans can be covered for the period of the loan by a forward contract to buy the foreign currency forward in the amount of the loan principal and interest.

	DM per $	*SFR per $*	*$ per £*
Spot rate (28/12/78)	1.90500	1.69175	1.97160
Forward rate (contract maturity 28/3/79)	1.87055	1.64625	1.96325

5. *Tax Rates*
   We assume that the present policy of remitting all earnings after tax will continue. On this basis, corporation and municipal taxes will be 43.70 percent. To this, another 15 percent withholding tax on dividends should be added. Total taxes will therefore be 52.145 percent on these assumptions. We also expect that foreign exchange gains will be added to, and losses can be deducted from, taxable income. This applies equally to gains and losses on interest, principal, and forward contracts. All interest expense, including that on intracompany loans, can be deducted from taxable income.

6. *Earnings*
   Earnings *before* interest on the above loan and before taxes are expected to be DM 4,000,000 during the next three months.

7. We would be grateful if you would telex your reply as soon as possible.

EXHIBIT 2   Standard Electronics International Selected Financial Date

SEI GERMANY
Pro Forma Balance Sheet
December 31, 1978

	Deutschemarks (000)	Dollars[†] (000)
Assets		
1.		
Plant and equipment	8,500	4,461.94
Inventories	5,000	2,624.67
Accounts receivable	4,000	2,099.74
Cash	3,000	1,574.80
	20,500	10,761.15
Capital and Liabilities		
Owners equity	12,000	6,299.21
Loans[*]	6,000	3,149.61
Accounts payable	2,500	1,312.34
	20,500	10,761.15

2. As one of the loan options, SEI Sunnyvale would lend dollars to SEI Germany at a 12 percent rate of interest. This would be financed by borrowing dollars in the U.S. domestic money market at 11.25 percent.
3. Earnings of SEI as a whole before taxes and exclusive of any foreign income received from SEI Germany or expenses connected with financing the DM 2,500,000 loan were expected to be $6 million during the first three months of 1979.
4. The tax rate applicable to U.S. domestic earnings is 48 percent. A maximum of 48 percent on foreign source income (dividends, interest, royalties, etc.) could be charged, but this may be changed if excess foreign tax credits are available.

[*] Includes the DM 2,500,000 loan requested.
[†] DM amounts translated into dollars at DM 1.905 per $.

Imperial Power Corporation

In 1971, Imperial Power Corporation (IPC), a U.S.-based multinational firm, completed a new plant in Spain to manufacture fractional horsepower electric motors. These motors were sold to IPC subsidiaries in France and Germany, who assembled them into various end products that were then sold throughout Europe. Penetration of the Spanish market was, however, negligible. The plant site near Madrid had been chosen because of inducements from the Spanish government, the availability of a stable, suitably skilled labor force, and the expectation that presence in Spain would aid the marketing effort. To provide the required capital for the new subsidiary, Imperial Power of Spain, or IPS, IPC provided US$800,000 as a long-term loan in addition to equity capital. Chase Manhattan Bank in New York provided US$300,000 as an equipment mortgage guaranteed by IPC. In early 1982, the Madrid plant was operating at 70 percent of design capacity. The French and German subsidiaries were operating near full design capacity.

In late 1981, top management at IPC was concerned about the possibility of a devaluation of the Spanish peseta. Strong political unrest and an economy weakened by strikes led management to conclude that a devaluation of up to 20 percent was likely by the end of September 1982. Although the peseta/dollar exchange rate was technically floating, it was known that the Spanish monetary authorities often intervened to keep the exchange rate within a narrow band. Therefore, the devaluation, if it happened, would be sudden rather than gradual. The current exchange rates (local currency per US$1) were:

DM	2.4127	SPta.	106.67
FF	6.27	£	0.5602

In addition to the debt incurred at the time of start-up, IPS had borrowed Pts. 7.5 million each from Banco Espanol de Credito and Chase Manhattan Bank (Madrid). The equipment mortgage, however, had been 50 percent repaid. Monthly reports received by IPC indicated that IPS had an average gross margin of 50 percent. Direct and indirect imported material accounted for 25 percent of the variable manufacturing cost, Spanish domestic material 15 percent, and the remainder was labor and overhead.

In an effort to reduce cash balances in anticipation of the devaluation, Imperial Power-Spain had purchased a $250,000 CD from Credit Lyonnais and bought

EXHIBIT 1   Imperial Power of Spain, Balance
Sheet as of March 31, 1982 (in
thousands of pesetas)*

Assets		
Cash	Pts.	6,300
Receivables and securities		53,763
Inventories		41,000
New plant and equipment		75,100
Total	Pts.	176,163
Liabilities		
Accounts payable	Pts.	32,620
Accrued wages and taxes		2,300
Long-term debt		116,336
	Pts.	151,256
Equity		24,907
	Pts.	176,163

* Foreign currency assets and liabilities translated at current exchange rates.

Spanish treasury notes for Pts. 14 million. Payments due from the French and German subsidiaries totaled FF 250,000 and DM 200,000, respectively. IPS owed £32,000 to Essex Wire (UK), Ltd., and DM 125,000 to Ruhr Steel. The remainder of accounts payable was owed to local suppliers.

Exhibit 1 is the balance sheet for IPS as of March 31, 1982. Budgeted sales for the year ending March 31, 1983, were Pts. 280 million.

Questions

1. As Assistant Treasurer (International) for IPC in the United States, prepare an analysis of the exposure of the Spanish subsidiary:
   (a) using the current rate method,
   (b) using the monetary-nonmonetary method.
2. Then prepare an analysis of the economic (cash flow) effects on IPC of a possible devaluation of the peseta.
3. Finally, recommend a plan to prevent or minimize any losses.
4. Consider the company's transfer prices for sales between affiliates. What effect might alternative transfer pricing policies have on the gains or losses from exchange rate changes?

Dahl Systems Incorporated

"Salary policy has got to be the main item on the board agenda. What I want the board to agree on is the principle of local salary levels for all those on the payroll of any subsidiary, and a shift of the international headquarters staff in London out of the United Kingdom division and into a separate company for pay purposes." Ronald Cunningham was speaking by telephone in October 1976 to Brent Wojciekowski, Vice President International of Dahl Systems Incorporated. As managing director of Dahl's German subsidiary, Ronald Cunningham sat on the international board which met bimonthly in London at Brent's headquarters for all of Dahl's operations outside the Americas. Cunningham went on, "We have lost two English team heads to our competitors in the last month. With the deutsche mark revaluation of 6 percent this week and more to come, and the fall in sterling with more to come too, we will probably need a 30 percent increase in salary level to keep any non-Germans. An increase in housing subsidies and education allowances may be needed as well."

Himself an Englishman, Ronald Cunningham had nearly 20 expatriate Englishmen and Americans in his managerial team in Frankfurt. This had come about because Dahl had expanded to London from its Chicago base very early in the development of the specialist computer and systems services industry. It was only four years ago, however, that the company had moved into Germany in any strength. To establish the unit Dahl had moved a senior team to Frankfurt, including many who had already been handling some German business from the London office. While the proportion of expatriates in Germany was especially large, the international movement of management and systems specialists would remain at a high rate throughout Dahl. Dahl was in a fast-moving business and the transfer of state-of-the-art knowledge of systems and applications was best achieved through transferring individuals who had built up the appropriate expertise and proved they could sell it.

Dahl's salary policy for those transferred internationally was to set the salary in the currency of the executive's home country at a level that would be appropriate in the home country and to translate this base salary at the current exchange rate. With fluctuating exchange rates, the sum received could change dramatically from month to month. On top of this base salary, though, a local sum was established yearly for each executive to cover increased cost of living. This sum covered actual increases in the cost of housing, including local taxes, heating, telephones, and so on, plus costs of children's schooling and a further percentage

This case was prepared by Professor Kenneth Simmonds of the London Graduate School of Business Studies. Copyright 1976 by Kenneth Simmonds.

of base salary set annually for the country of residence. The percentages allowed for each country were reviewed at the main board each year and tended to reflect both differences in relative price levels and subjective assessments of the costs felt by the various executives who were affected. Currently the percentage allowed for expatriates in Germany was 30 percent and for expatriates in the United Kingdom it was 20 percent.

Differential movement in price levels and exchange rates during 1976, as shown in Exhibit 1, indicated that some trenchant memoranda would be arriving at the head office over the next few months arguing for increases in these rates. To date, no foreign executives had been transferred to the U.S. parent company for other than short visiting periods, so there was as yet no U.S. residence percentage.

Dahl's policy was quite new. It had been reshaped under considerable pressure from expatriate U.S. executives in London barely three years previously. The U.S. executives had also pressed for taxation equalization to reduce the impact of U.K. taxes down to the U.S. levels, and Brent Wojciekowski had himself been a prime mover in making these demands. The taxation equalization privilege had not been extended beyond U.S. expatriates, however, as others had not presented a specific case for it. Moreover, Dahl's treasurer in Chicago said that he was not prepared to have corporate staff diverted from their main function into a morass of calculations concerning taxation differences between third countries.

Following his telephone conversation with Cunningham, Brent Wojciekowski had a long luncheon discussion with John Jones, the managing director of the United Kingdom division. "I think Ronnie is really thinking about himself," said John. "He already receives 50 percent more than I do, for instance. And

EXHIBIT 1

	United Kingdom	West Germany	United States
Consumer price index (1970 = 100):			
1973	127	119	114
1974	147	127	127
1975	182	135	138
1976 (second quarter)	208	141	145
Exchange rate:	£1 =	1DM =	
March 1973	$2.48	$0.354	
March 1974	2.39	0.387	
March 1975	2.41	0.426	
March 1976	1.91	0.392	
October 1976	1.57	0.415	
Representative local salary of a Dahl senior systems specialist in 1976	£9,500	DM 130,000	$36,000
Marginal tax rate (on last $1,000 of an income of $40,000 after deductions)	83%[*]	45%	58%

[*] Ninety-eight percent on interest and dividends over $1,600.

that's before tax. If we followed Ronnie's suggestion we would have an even greater outflow of U.K. staff to cope with. Before we do anything on salaries we should first change the policy of internal advertisement of all job openings internationally. We really promote transfers by selecting the best-qualified applicants and paying relocation costs. It is a ridiculous situation when overqualified Englishmen apply in large numbers for any continental job opening at all. Our bread and butter still comes from the U.K. division and if we are going to continue to perform against our competition here, we just have to hang on to the key people we still have. What's more, we should bring some back on salaries that bear some relationship to British levels. We really need David Symes back here. But I can never forgive him bragging to everyone before he went off to join Ronnie last year that his children would now get a good English public school education.''

McTain (China) 1997

It was March 1988, and Robert Morrison was presented by his Hong Kong manager with a detailed and carefully developed proposal to build apartments in Lisbon, Portugal, for sale to management of McTain's Hong Kong subsidiary. Robert was a U.K. citizen and managing director of the international civil engineering division of McTain International Corporation. McTain's Hong Kong manager, Kim Chok Lim, reported directly to Robert in London, as did all civil division managers operating outside the United States.

McTain, itself, was one of the largest U.S. civil, construction, and building contractors. Its world headquarters were in New York, although in 1984 the firm had switched incorporation from Delaware to Panama by an exchange of shares in its Panama subsidiary for the Delaware shares. The new shares, however, continued to be traded on Wall Street, and the prime benefit of the exchange had been to make it possible for profits from McTain's numerous subsidiaries outside the U.S. to be switched within the group without becoming subject to U.S. taxation.

McTain had carried on business in Hong Kong for 30 years and Lim had joined the firm as a clerk for its first major contract. Kim presented the proposal as a way of retaining and rewarding the local middle management in the period before the reversion of Hong Kong from British to Chinese sovereignty. Many skilled Chinese residents of Hong Kong were already seeking out opportunities of emigrating before 1997 as their own nationality would otherwise revert to Chinese in 1997. Exchange control and restrictions on ownership investment and travel were widely forecast to follow 1997. Not only that—many felt that they would find it very painful to adjust to a communist regime from the freewheeling environment of Hong Kong.

Knowing that McTain had a European subsidiary developing homes in Portugal's Algarve, primarily for United Kingdom retirees, Lim had seen this as an opportunity to do something for the managers who had served McTain so well and so profitably in the past. Moreover, they would be in a better position to continue to do so in the future if they could stay on in Hong Kong with a foreign nationality.

The scheme was a development of one of the approaches to obtaining a non-Hong Kong passport that had been actively marketed in Hong Kong by a growing band of emigration experts. Under Portuguese law, someone who had owned a property in Portugal for five years and had been registered as a resident

---

This case was prepared by Professor Kenneth Simmonds of the London Business School. Copyright © 1988 Professor Kenneth Simmonds.

throughout that period gained an inalienable right to take a Portuguese passport. As Portugal was now a member of the European Community, a Portuguese passport would mean that a holder could live and work anywhere within the European Community, including the United Kingdom. While it was necessary to register as a resident formally with the Lisbon authorities after purchasing a Portuguese 'home,' it was not necessary to live there permanently. Moreover, the home could be rented to others. Registration needed to be renewed each year for five years before it became permanent, but again this could be carried out by a Portuguese lawyer on behalf of an absent 'resident.' Finally, as Portuguese law had developed from the Roman law, it would be legally impossible to backdate any new law to remove residence. Once granted, residence could not be withdrawn.

The scheme that Lim had sent to Morrison involved modest apartment accommodation on the outskirts of Lisbon that could be rented without any trouble to city workers. Purchasers would be expected to find the equivalent of $2,000 U.S. The remainder would be provided by 20-year mortgages from McTain's Lisbon banker. There would be 30 apartments, and rentals would be arranged and managed by the Lisbon estate agents McTain currently used in selling to Portuguese developments. Legal costs would be kept to a minimum. One firm of lawyers would cover the entire deal, and their costs would be paid by McTain Hong Kong. The initial construction would be carried out at a negotiated price by McTain Portugal contracting to McTain Hong Kong, whose overdraft was guaranteed by McTain International.

As far as Morrison could see, there was no particular problem on the financial side. Construction was straightforward, costs included reasonable contingencies, and net rentals at reasonable rates would easily cover the mortgage repayments. He was, however, worried about the principle of the firm engaging in nationality change for its employees. Furthermore, the idea was based on a loophole in the Portuguese emigration rules. The United Kingdom had declined to accept British Hong Kong passports as a basis for U.K. residence. The only provision officially made in acknowledgment of the 1997 handover to date had been formal acceptance that members of the administrative class of the Hong Kong civil service and their families could emigrate to Britain. What Lim was proposing seemed to ask McTain to go against the basic interests and wishes of a country under whose laws it operated—Britain now, China after 1997. At the same time, if McTain did not participate in the scheme, it was unlikely that most of its Hong Kong managers would be able to emigrate on their own. Wealthy entrepreneurs were quite easily able to enter Canada and Australia and even the United States— but McTain's managers had little capital and were dependent on their jobs with McTain in Hong Kong.

Morrison knew that if he approved the project, he could avoid mentioning the nationality change objective when asking the main board—which was made up of 100 percent U.S. nationals—for formal approval. The apartments could be presold to the Hong Kong management and the project described simply as arranged as an in-company scheme on this basis.

Author Index

Subject Index

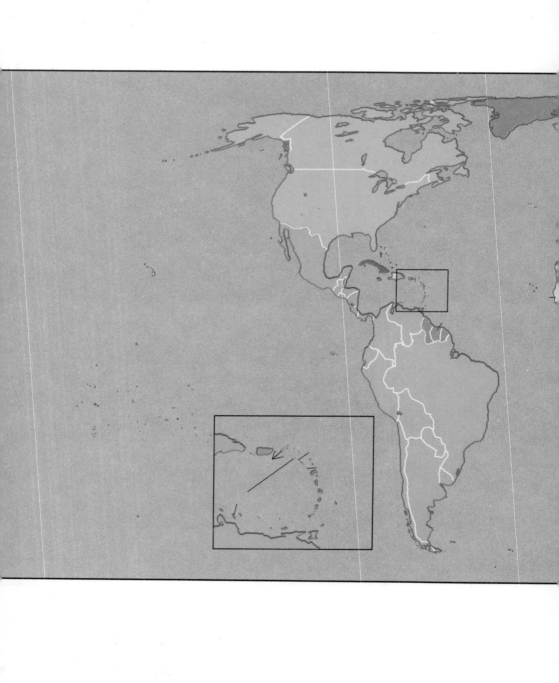